LEGACY
of NEBRASKA

1874 – 2015

Joan Fink, AT, Tecumseh
Past State President, Lead Editor

Cindy Biehl, GZ, Hastings
Past State President

Jan Loftin, ES, Lincoln
Past State President

Mary Schwaner, AI, Lincoln
Publisher

Prairie Muse Publishing

P.E.O. is a philanthropic organization where women CELEBRATE the advancement of women; EDUCATE women through scholarships, grants, awards, loans, and stewardship of Cottey College and MOTIVATE women to achieve their highest aspirations.

Legacy of Nebraska P.E.O.
© Nebraska State Chapter - P.E.O. Sisterhood
All Rights Reserved.
The material in this volume is historically accurate insofar as the contributors deemed possible. Every effort was made to ensure the preservation of historical data.

ISBN 978-1-937216-61-0
[First Print Edition - Hardcover June 2015]
Second Print Edition - Hardcover September 2023
Prairie Muse Publishing
www.nebraskapeo.org

Cover design by Mary Schwaner utilizing hand-painted china image by artist Darlene Jansen
© 2004

Dedication

W. Joyce Goff

CHAPTER HJ, GRAND ISLAND

PRESIDENT OF INTERNATIONAL CHAPTER
OF THE P.E.O. SISTERHOOD
2003-2005

MEMBER OF THE
INTERNATIONAL EXECUTIVE BOARD
1995-2005

INTERNATIONAL
STUDY AND RESEARCH COMMITTEE
1990-1995

PRESIDENT
NEBRASKA STATE CHAPTER
1987-1988

P.E.O. ...Small as a daisy, great as a star

LEGACY Tribute

WILLA JOYCE GOFF WITH HER HUSBAND, WAYNE

W. Joyce Goff

Eighty-five years ago, in the land of corn, cattle and cranes, a star was born. That star, Nebraska's Joyce Goff, was destined to forever shine as one of the brightest in P.E.O.

Joyce started her Nebraska P.E.O. journey in Alliance in 1965. Chapter GC benefitted from her many talents as she thrived in P.E.O. in countless creative ways.

Joyce is a diminutive woman. Little but mighty, she is a powerful dynamo in personality. She is tough and strong, but always acts with compassion and sensitivity. Joyce possesses a keen wit and an uncanny ability to connect on a personal level with everyone. She is a writer; she is an orator. She makes us laugh. She tells stories everyone identifies with. She dazzles an audience.

Ever the teacher, she thrives on preparation, organization and attention to detail. Those of us who served on the Nebraska P.E.O. executive board with her lovingly remember her constant admonishment: "Be Neat!" We were!

Joyce Goff's P.E.O. star became grander, as the sphere in which she shone grew to include the entire state of Nebraska. At the 1981 state convention in Chadron, Joyce was elected to the Nebraska State Chapter Executive Board. She served in all the offices and presided at the Convention of Nebraska State Chapter in Kimball in 1988.

During Joyce's tenure on the Nebraska P.E.O. Executive Board, she visited dozens of chapters and presented many workshops. She is truly beloved by all with whom she has worked. Nebraska P.E.O.s adore her.

Her outstanding abilities allowed Joyce to be recognized beyond the Nebraska horizons. She was destined to bring the message of our sparkling P.E.O. star to the U.S. and Canada when she accepted a five-year appointment to the P.E.O. International Study and Research Committee in 1990. She continued to impress and inspire all those with whom she worked. Her P.E.O. star shone more intensely as her sphere of influence broadened.

Joyce's P.E.O. star reached its zenith when she was elected to the Executive Board of International Chapter in Denver in 1995. After serving in all executive board offices, Joyce was elected President of International Chapter at its convention in Oklahoma City in 2003. She logged hundreds of thousands of miles visiting most of the states and provinces, meeting thousands of P.E.O.s along the way.

It was in September of 2005 that Joyce presided over the Convention of International Chapter in Vancouver, British Columbia.

To each and every person she meets, she impresses with her humility, kindness, wit, brilliance and strength.

Joyce chose for her state convention theme *"P.E.O....Small as a Daisy, Great as a Star!"* She feels the "smallness" of P.E.O. is embodied in the personal caring exhibited within the local chapters…a loving hand on the shoulder of a sister in need, a cup of coffee with a sister who is sharing joys. The greatness of P.E.O. is demonstrated through the vast reach of its projects, making differences in the lives of countless women who are able to further their educations.

Nebraska State Chapter lovingly dedicates this book to its inspirational leader Joyce Goff. She is "small as a daisy and great as a star." Once in a lifetime, a star shines so brilliantly.

By Robley Garrigan, Past State President
Nebraska State Chapter 1990-1991

Joyce Goff in the Des Moines office
she occupied during her tenure as International President

...is...

"Women who care helping women who dare."

~ a quote Joyce often shared,
attributing it to Ann Conway, Past President
New Jersey State Chapter

International First Vice President Joyce Goff with International President Nancy Hoium (Minnesota) share the podium at International, upper left; are introduced to Nebraska longhorns in North Platte, center; and greet convention delegates at the 2007 convention in North Platte, upper right.

At right, Joyce makes her debut as Rhett Butler alongside members of Nebraska Chapter AX during the 1995 Period of Instruction in Scottsbluff.

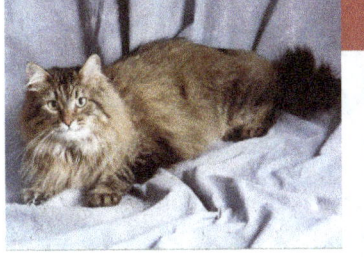

Joyce's cat Mister Fisher

Joyce with Nebraska Past State Presidents Alice Fisher (left photo) and Phyllis Blanke and Mary Owens (right photo)

Joyce with the Nebraska Delegation in the convention hall, 1995 Denver

International President Joyce Goff presides at the 2005 International Convention in Vancouver

Photo at left: Nebraska Past State President Mary Olsen celebrates with Joyce Goff, newly elected to the International Executive Board at Colorado in 1995. At right, Joyce (seated left) joins other Past International Presidents to take care of business at the 2011 Convention of International Chapter in St. Louis.

2005 Nebraska delegation to Vancouver joins International President Joyce Goff in making history for Nebraska P.E.O.

Contents

TRIBUTE TO JOYCE GOFF...5-6
FOREWORD BY PAST STATE PRESIDENT JOAN FINK.....13
SECTION ONE .... THE SEEDS ARE PLANTED.....15
SECTION TWO .... NEBRASKA—P.E.O.'s FIRST STATE CHAPTER.....17
SECTION THREE..................... CHAPTER LEGACIES (HISTORIES)......21
SECTION FOUR .... PIONEERS AND VISIONARIES...381
GALLERY OF STATE PRESIDENTS...381
GONE TO PAINT THE STARS...493
NEBRASKA PAST STATE PRESIDENTS' GROUP...495
GALLERY OF NEBRASKA STATE EXECUTIVE BOARDS...497
P.E.O. JEWELRY...510
ARTICLES BY INTERNATIONAL PRESIDENT W. JOYCE GOFF...512
OTHERS WHO SERVED NEBRASKA STATE CHAPTER...516
ASSISTANT SECRETARIES AND PAID ASSISTANTS...518
SECTION FIVE .... NEBRASKA P.E.O.s WHO HAVE LED THE SISTERHOOD...521
and GALLERY OF NEBRASKA'S INTERNATIONAL PRESIDENTS
OTHERS WHO HAVE SERVED INTERNATIONAL CHAPTER...523
MEMBERS OF INTERNATIONAL BOARDS OF TRUSTEES...524
COMMITTEES AND OTHER SERVICES...524
SECTION SIX ....NEBRASKANS WHO HAVE INFLUENCED P.E.O...527
NEBRASKA P.E.O.s WHO SERVED AS PRESIDENT OF OTHER STATE CHAPTERS...528
GIFTS OF LOVE...529
SECTION SEVEN.................... CHANGES GRACE THE SISTERHOOD...533
"IT'S NOT YOUR MOTHER'S P.E.O."...533
HISTORY OF THE OPENING ODE...538
SECTION EIGHT.................... GALLERY OF OUR SEVEN FOUNDERS...540
SECTION NINE ....THE LEGACY PRESERVED...551
ARTICLES OF HISTORICAL VALUE BY JULIA MCDOUGAL...551
REMINISCENCES FROM BERTHA CLARK HUGHES...557
A LEGACY OF HISTORIAN REPORTS BY JULIA MCDOUGAL AND SUSAN HARR...559
1991 OMAHA INTERNATIONAL CONVENTION REMEMBERED...577
SECTION TEN .... NEBRASKA STATE CHAPTER CENTENNIAL...587
"CENTENNIAL MELODY" SHEET MUSIC...592
SECTION ELEVEN .... THE BIG PICTURE OF P.E.O...597
STATE CONVENTION HIGHLIGHTS 1995-2015...597
CONVENTIONS OF NEBRASKA GRAND AND NEBRASKA STATE CHAPTER...606
CONVENTIONS OF INTERNATIONAL CHAPTER...615
SECTION TWELVE .... P.E.O. PROJECTS IN NEBRASKA...639
LOVE IN ACTION...639
SECTION THIRTEEN............. RECIPROCITY AND COLLEGIATE GROUPS...659
SECTION FOURTEEN ...."THE HOME THAT LOVE BUILT"...665
NEBRASKA P.E.O. HOME...665
ALPHABETICAL LISTING OF CHAPTERS .... NSC...686
ALPHABETICAL LISTING OF TOWNS WITH CHAPTERS................. NSC...687
AFTERWORD ...."IT'S OK TO TALK ABOUT P.E.O."...689

"P.E.O. Marguerites"
by Darlene Jansen, GQ

About the Cover

In the spring of 2004, with Joyce Goff presiding as International President of P.E.O., the International Executive Board met in Lincoln for a working session. Gathering with Joyce at the Cornhusker Hotel were Ann Fields, Barbara Andes, Elizabeth Garrels, and Susan Sellers, all representing the mind, the heart, and the mission of P.E.O.

They would slip quietly into town, burn the lamp oil well past midnight for the better part of a week, then quietly depart. No fanfare. No brass band proclaiming their presence. Just five women, settling into yet another hotel to accomplish the work of the Sisterhood.

How could we let them go home without seizing the opportunity to let them know how very much we appreciated them? How very much we valued the work they were doing in our behalf? How very much we loved them, these sisters of ours from across the land?

The answer was simple. We couldn't.

And so Lincoln Reciprocity Roundtable conceived the idea to place in their hands a unique memento, a hand-painted china plate exemplifying our beautiful stars and marguerites. Five plates of a kind, and no more, created in the studio of our very gifted sister, Darlene Jansen of Chapter GQ, and gifted to these special women in behalf of Nebraska P.E.O.

Seven daisies, each uniquely lovely, and seven stars, each with timeless symmetry denoting the Sisterhood's seven Founders, grace each plate. Every small bud nestled amongst the daisies represents a P.E.O. sister yet to come. Each lovely plate—bearing the symbols of our Sisterhood—carried with it the love and gratitude of more than ten thousand Nebraska P.E.O.s.

> MARY SCHWANER, AI, INCORPORATED DARLENE JANSEN'S
> CHINA PLATE ART IN THE COVER DESIGN OF *LEGACY*.

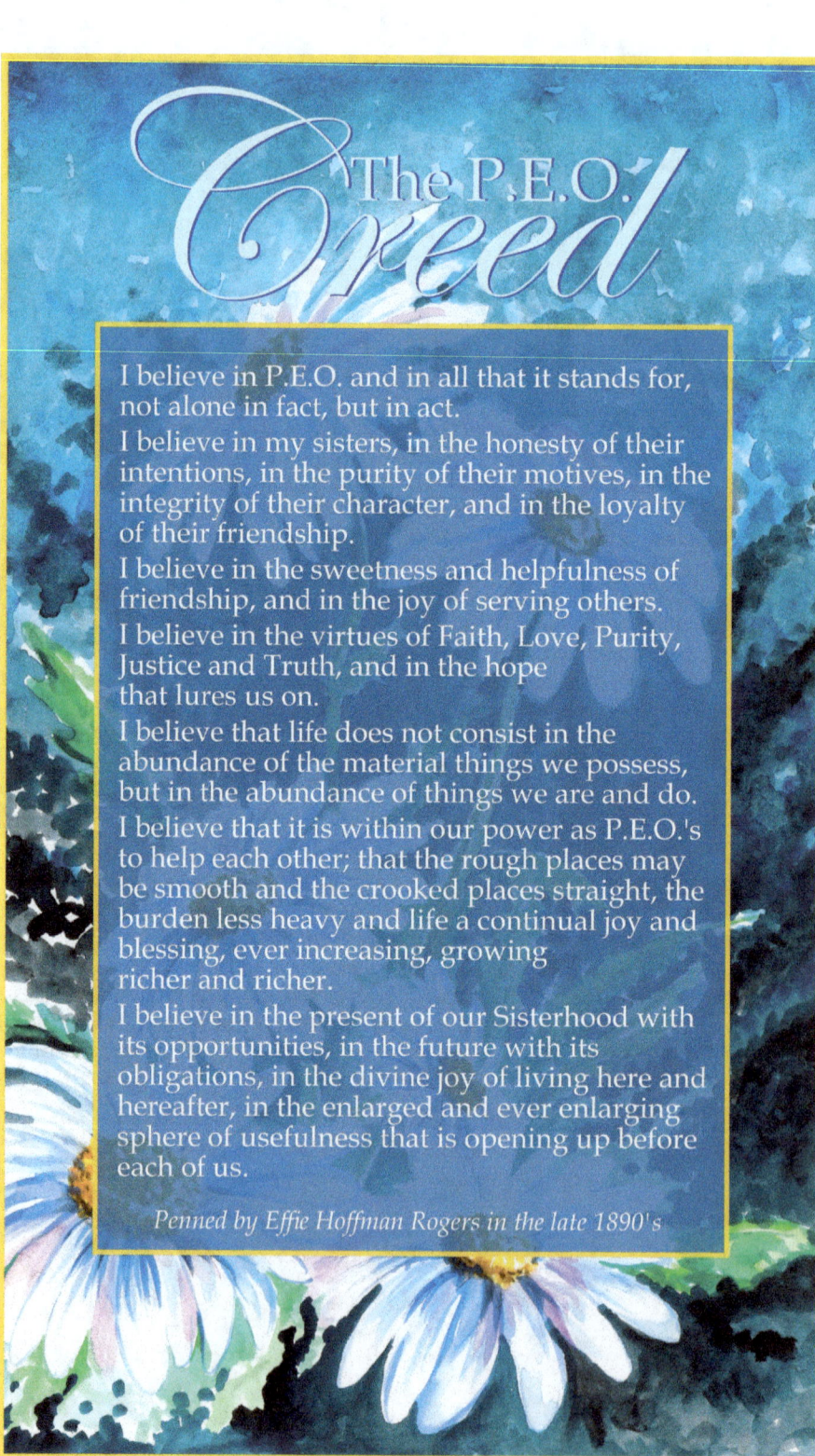

Foreword

Legacy of Nebraska P.E.O. is a gift from the past and a gift that we leave for those in the future who follow our footsteps in the proud tradition of Nebraska P.E.O. It is your story. It is the story that chronicles the long and illustrious history of P.E.O. in Nebraska. We repeat this story every twenty years so that each generation will not lose this legacy of Nebraska P.E.O.

Our legacy of Nebraska P.E.O. began in the late 1800's in Omaha with a group so secretive that to this day little is known about it. But the seeds of P.E.O. were planted and continued to grow. On April 2, 1890, the first state chapter was organized in Omaha. Today 235 chapters are scattered across the state, and Nebraska P.E.O. is a premier women's organization.

Legacy is a tribute to Nebraska P.E.O.s who shared a vision of helping other women and who continued to work together to promote our Sisterhood. *Legacy* is more than a chronicle of what happened in the past. It is a celebration of our vision for the future. Our chapter histories illustrate the best meaning of P.E.O. We discover that P.E.O. is about women working and growing together. It is about women building close relationships with each other. It is about women helping other women, and women having a good time together. *Legacy* recognizes these amazing women and their challenges and accomplishments. It is their history, and it is our responsibility to share it with each generation of P.E.Os.

Each chapter history is unique and reflects the unique personality of its membership. Common threads weave through each history. Pride in what their chapter has accomplished both in their community and in the state. Support for the Sisterhood's philanthropies which improve the lives of women. Loving concern for each sister shines out above all others.

In a world of technology that promotes the individual, our Sisterhood promotes the benefits and strengths of a group or a unit. Nebraska P.E.O.s welcome change, but we appreciate history and tradition. P.E.O. is a success story, and *Legacy* is your success story. Read it and pass it around to each sister. Use it as a reference for programs and as an inspiration. Don't let *Legacy* languish in the president's box.

In Nebraska we are fortunate to have been guided by women with a vision of preserving our P.E.O. heritage. Dorothy Smithberger began this preservation when she served as the editor of Nebraska's first P.E.O. history, *The Saga of Nebraska P.E.O.*, which was published in 1975. Dorothy's daughter, Past State President Susan Harr, is historian for our state chapter and entertains each state convention with vignettes from our past history. Susan shares her mother's passion for history and is a contributor to *Legacy*.

Spirit of the Prairie, published in 1995 and edited by Past State President Robley Garrigan, is the benchmark for Nebraska P.E.O. history. What a marvelous resource for P.E.O.s in our state, and an inspiration for all of us. *Spirit* has been the guiding light for the current history committee. From the beginning, the History Committee agreed that we needed to incorporate parts of *Spirit* into *Legacy* so that future P.E.O.s would always have access to this information. The result is a hybrid: past, present, and future combined. You will be the judge whether we succeeded.

It has been said that committees rarely accomplish anything. I am proud to say that this was not the case with the History Committee. As lead editor, I have only been the organizer of this book. The real work has been done by my committee. Past State Presidents Cindy Biehl and Jan Loftin, and publisher Mary Schwaner carried most of the load. These talented P.E.O. sisters spent countless hours researching, writing, editing and providing valuable advice. We all agree that this endeavor was a learning experience, and that we were the ones who benefited the most. We are especially thankful for the counsel and direction that Mary has provided. Her experience in the publishing field has been invaluable. We could not have done it without her.

The true stars in this project are the 235 local chapter editors who wrote the story of their chapters. Their stories reflect their achievements, their goals, but most of all, the love they share for each other. This is their gift to their chapters, and we are the beneficiaries.

This is your story. Read it, enjoy it, and utilize this book. Our hope is that by reading about the success stories of Nebraska P.E.O. chapters you will be inspired to continue to work and strengthen not only your own life, but the lives of all those around you.

JOAN FINK, AT, TECUMSEH, PAST STATE PRESIDENT
LEAD EDITOR FOR "LEGACY OF NEBRASKA P.E.O."

*Tomorrow hopes we have learned
something from yesterday.*
-*John Wayne*

Section One

The Seeds Are Planted

Nebraska, the unpredictable, had long beckoned to the pioneers, as bonneted wagons made of her a pathway to the West. But men's minds had been intent on a secluded Mormon haven, or upon gold and other treasures to the west and northwest. There had been numerous towns developing along the Missouri River and missionaries had followed fur traders, establishing churches and schools. Each arrival precipitated needs for others to supply necessary goods and services. Julius Sterling Morton had arrived in 1855 and was planting trees. In 1872 he was to begin promotion of Arbor Day—to beautify the land, to provide protection, shade and fruit.

The Homestead Act in 1862, the end of the Civil War, Nebraska statehood in 1867, arrival and extension of the railroads accompanied by glowing descriptions of the land—all these soon enticed many new arrivals, eager to make a new home in the heartland. Nebraska smiled her warmth and welcome through the fertility of her prairies. Seeds and high hopes were planted together.

Of many river towns seeking to become the gateway to the west, "Omaha City" —promoted vigorously as a rail center by Council Bluffs across the river—leaped ahead in growth and activity. "Century Flashbacks" in the Omaha World Herald in 1973 depicted the city's many needs in 1873—water and sewer systems, good sidewalks, paving for central streets when money should become available.

About this time, sometime in 1874, Etta Hurford (or Hereford), a P.E.O. initiate at Belden's Seminary in Mount Pleasant, Iowa, must have returned for a time to her Omaha home. With her, she carried the desire to promote the P.E.O. standards of character and culture by organizing a group in Omaha. Apparently she succeeded— but only for a few years. So secretive were the members that the chapter vanished from sight and memory, and later no one in Nebraska knew that it really existed. Perhaps disbanding of the chapter followed because of marriage, moving and scattered interests. No one knows for sure. Or perhaps the nationwide economic depression, which was followed by the Midwest drought and grasshopper scourge in 1874-76, reflected on the members' families in Omaha. Or perhaps the new state was not yet ready for the growth of P.E.O. But Mrs. Hurford had sown the seeds for the future blooming of the Sisterhood in Nebraska.

Nebraska remained a difficult place to settle, often with stormy, tempestuous weather which was capable of blistering heat, drought and bitter cold. In many places, only the stout-hearted remained. Many who expected free land for minimum effort left for easier living elsewhere. Several years followed which presented a gentler climate—sunny, warm and moist weather which proved ideal for crops and man. Enticed by the period of "calm between the storms," people surged into Nebraska again. The years following 1880 saw a period of considerable population growth—first along rivers and streams, and then fanning out across the windswept, treeless prairies. The newcomers came from everywhere. People came for economic purposes from all over the country and many came from Europe fleeing political upheaval and avoiding military involvement. It became a fad for wealthy young men from eastern states or England to invest in Nebraska ranches to raise purebred cattle and other blooded stock.

The feminist movement and desire for women's organizations were felt keenly in eastern Nebraska, perhaps because women were often lonely and longed for the more advanced culture of their former homes. Their hearts and minds hungered for education, female companionship and spiritual growth. The appealing ideals of the P.E.O. Sisterhood gave a lift to their groping spirits. Although several of the early chapters ultimately disbanded (Fairfield and Norfolk, organized immediately after York, disbanded in the early 1890s), P.E.O. had found willing and strong homes in several communities.

While the disastrous drought and financial trauma of 1890 took its toll on many disillusioned settlers who ultimately trundled their wagons out of Nebraska, others moved to urban areas and helped the cities become established as centers of commerce and education. Omaha grew as a meatpacking and rail center. Lincoln became the home of government and education as the University of Nebraska prospered to educate its native sons and daughters.

P.E.O. began to thrive as five more P.E.O. societies began in 1889 and another in 1890. The existing groups courageously sought and obtained a charter for the first state chapter in P.E.O. This was a milestone in the history of the Sisterhood. The climate was right. The "seed" of P.E.O., planted in Nebraska's infancy by Etta Hurford, had germinated. The time had come for P.E.O. to flourish and grow in Nebraska.

> The credit for much of this chapter goes to Dorothy Smithberger, the editor of Nebraska's first P.E.O. history, entitled *The Saga of Nebraska P.E.O.* The source of Chapter 1 is from "*A Wilful Maiden - Nebraska.*"

Section Two

Nebraska–P.E.O.'s First State Chapter

The Grand Design

The source for this chapter is ***The Saga of Nebraska P.E.O.***, Chapter Three entitled "Nebraska–First State Chapter." The editor wishes to thank and acknowledge the contribution of past historian of Nebraska State Chapter Dorothy Smithberger and her committee, who spent countless hours researching Nebraska P.E.O.'s early history. Other P.E.O. historical publications which were quoted and researched are ***Out of the Heart*** and ***The White History***.

Precious by virtue of both its content and origin, we could not fail to preserve this important history in our ***Legacy of Nebraska P.E.O.***

Early P.E.O. historical documents occasionally refer to Nebraska as the "revolutionary" state since its chapters were the first to petition for a state charter and since, in 1892, it called a conference of all P.E.O. chapters to form a National Chapter. Some confusion reigned for a time, but through sisterly understanding and good will, it dissipated and eventually led to the present system of administration of P.E.O. through international, state, provincial, district and local chapters.

The first idea of such a plan came from one of the seven Founders of P.E.O., Ella Stewart, at the 1887 Convention of Grand Chapter. At the time, Grand Chapter was the highest level of organization of all P.E.O. chapters which had been organized from 1883 to 1893. The Iowa chapters dominated this organization, since P.E.O. was founded there at Iowa Wesleyan College in Mount Pleasant, Iowa. There were many more of them than P.E.O. chapters from other states.

In the 1889 Convention of Grand Chapter, four delegates represented the seven Nebraska chapters. Delegates were Alice C. Briggs of Superior; Mary M. Houseworth of Plattsmouth; Jenny Bryant of Omaha; and Florence Wightman of York. Convention voted to require eight chapters in a state before a state grand chapter could be organized. Delegate Alice Briggs moved that Nebraska be granted permission to organize a state chapter of its own as soon as it had eight chapters. Grand Chapter voted to allow Nebraska to organize its own state chapter.

After the organization of the Holdrege and Wahoo chapters later that year, Nebraska had met the eight-chapter requirement for organization of its own state chapter. Nebraska Grand Chapter was organized on April 2, 1890, at the home of Jennie Bryant in Omaha. The organizer was Grand Chapter President

Nannie Torrence (Stockman). Elected delegates present were Daisy Sanford, Wahoo; Lida Patterson and Mary M. Houseworth, Plattsmouth; Dora Budenz, Norfolk; Lulu B. Patrick, Holdrege; Alice Briggs, Superior; Carrie Smith and Lena Knott, York; Lillie Chamberlain and Jennie Bryant, Omaha; and Minnie Dutton, Hastings.

Elaborate plans were made by Omaha Chapter AN (now E). Mrs. Bryant was to entertain the organizer, Miss Torrence, and seven other members were to entertain two delegates each. Mrs. Bryant had her house shining in every nook and cranny. Her four young boys dutifully carried chairs from a church four blocks away.

Disaster struck the first convention in the forms of an influenza epidemic and two other personal emergencies. As Mrs. Bryant retold the story many times in later conventions, the members of the Omaha chapter one by one "fell by the wayside." Each asked Mrs. Bryant to keep her delegates. Mrs. Bryant herself was stricken a few days before the convention and carried to her bed. Only the maid was left to provide and cook for the thirty guests on Thursday. Only two young ladies of the chapter remained to handle the entire convention! And one of those, Miss Hutchinson, came with one eye bandaged because of an injury. The ill Mrs. Bryant, so enthusiastic about the organization, insisted on being carried downstairs to the couch to watch the event.

Convention was called to order with the remaining well delegates in spite of the many disasters which had befallen the event. After devotions, roll call, a welcome, musical numbers and a scholarly paper reading, another mishap occurred. One of the only two well hostesses (and the only one who could see out of both eyes!) was called away due to the illness of her fiancé. Poor one-eyed Miss Hutchinson—the sole survivor of the Omaha hostess chapter—was left to carry out the duties of running the convention.

The *formal organization* took place in the afternoon with the following being installed as the first officers of Nebraska State Chapter: Alice C. Briggs, president; Dora Budenz, first vice president; Minnie Dutton, second vice president; Jennie Bryant, recording secretary; Lulu B. Patrick, corresponding secretary; Carrie Smith, treasurer. The determined Nebraska P.E.O.s persevered and Nebraska Grand Chapter (as it was first called before becoming Nebraska State Chapter) became a reality on that fateful April day.

As authorized by the previous convention of Grand Chapter, the chapters were relettered in Nebraska. The new officers were eager to progress as a state chapter but no rules existed under which to function. An error in wording on the charter issued to Nebraska brought matters to a head. The charter stated that it was granted by "The Grand Chapter of the State of Iowa"! During the 1890 Grand Chapter convention in Burlington, Nebraskans asked for a higher governing body, to which Iowa, Nebraska and all other state chapters would be subordinate. An attempt was made to organize a National Grand Chapter. A set of competent officers was elected but they really had no organization to serve, no laws defining authority. It was a valiant attempt with good intentions. The original Grand Chapter still had its own active officers and the question of authority remained unclear.

At the Grand Chapter convention the following year in 1891, Nebraska again created a problem which led to its nickname, "the revolutionary state." The delegate presented herself as a delegate from Nebraska Grand Chapter but she came as the elected delegate to "National" Grand Chapter and not elected to the original Grand Chapter. Without credentials to the body assembled, it took a vote of the convention to offer her a seat with the delegates. The matter of Nebraska's charter, privileges and obligations were discussed at great length at that convention but without settling the question. As one of P.E.O.s historical publications, *The White History*, stated, it was fortunate for Nebraska P.E.O.s that their delegate, Mrs. Winnie Durland, was "a woman of quick wit, ready speech, patient and persistent and, most fortuitously, a parliamentarian of skill and resource." Mrs. Durland obviously knew the proper steps to be taken to allow her a seat with the delegation. Pointed articles concerning the problem appeared in The P.E.O. Record during the following year.

A year later, before the Grand Chapter convention in 1892, Nebraska P.E.O. proved revolutionary again. After consulting with the Grand Chapter officers, the executive board of Nebraska Grand Chapter issued a call through The P.E.O. Record to all P.E.O. chapters to attend a conference to be held in Des Moines two days before Grand Chapter convened there. The purpose of the call was to establish a National Grand Chapter to act as a supreme power for the Sisterhood. At that time, there were 70 chapters representing eight states and the District of Columbia. Only 22 chapters sent representatives to the meeting, hardly enough representation to legalize any action. However, those in attendance had given considerable thought to the problems. Lengthy discussion ensued and from the meeting that Nebraska Grand Chapter executive board had called, two important steps were taken.

Mrs. Alice Spilman, N, Ottumwa, Iowa, moved that the delegates assembled there, representing chapters outside of Nebraska, pledge themselves to use their influence to grant a seat for Nebraska in the delegation in the Grand Chapter of P.E.O., provided that a state charter be issued in exchange for the one granted to Nebraska as the Nebraska Grand Chapter, and provided that Nebraska recognizes the Grand Chapter of P.E.O. as the supreme power of the order. Mrs. Spilman also moved that, correspondingly, all of the delegates there agree to recognize the Grand Chapter of P.E.O. as the supreme power of the order.

When Grand Chapter convention opened two days later, Nebraska delegates indeed were given seats with the delegation. The two motions made by Mrs. Spilman at the conference were explained. The spirit of cooperation was evident and from that moment on, the convention was one. The Nebraska delegates were welcomed and freely participated in deliberations and assisted in devising plans. All selfishness and prejudice had been banished by the wisdom and kindness of the 22 chapter delegates who had attended the pre-convention meeting.

During lengthy legislation, the highest body of P.E.O. was named Supreme Grand Chapter. Seeing the necessity for revision of its bylaws, the convention of the Sisterhood appointed a committee to draft a constitution and bylaws by the next convention. A year later, at the 1893 convention, the convention voted on dividing the constitution into three parts—Supreme, state and local chapters, as well as the laws governing each part. Nebraska P.E.O. goals at last were realized in the new constitution and bylaws. Alice Briggs of Superior, Nebraska, was elected president of Supreme Grand Chapter.

Charter Members of Chapter A, York (Originally Chapter R)

1. Lena Knott (left on floor)
2. Clem Wilde (left first row)
3. Carrie Gandy (left back row)
4. Lily Smith, Organizer (middle back row)
5. Emma Davis (Middle first row)
6. Ella Davis (Right first row)
7. Rose Dobbs (Right back row)
8. Carrie Zoe Smith (right on floor)

Section Three

Chapter Legacies

At the time this book was organized, there were 235 active P.E.O. chapters in Nebraska. While Chapters B, C, D, L, M, R, U, AD, AF, AY, BA, CR-DZ, DB, DD, DH, DO, DR, ER, GD, GY, and IF had already disbanded, their histories of love and service to P.E.O. are preserved in this book.

In the beginning, with the Mount Pleasant chapter having been lettered Chapter A, Nebraska chapters and chapters in other states were given successive letter names. For example, Chapter A in Mount Pleasant was followed by Chapter B, which materialized at the Seminary. A chapter designated 2nd B was organized in Fairfield, Iowa, in 1881, followed by 1st C in Jacksonville, Illinois, 2nd C in Leon, Iowa, and D in Oskaloosa, Iowa. As P.E.O. grew, that naming method became quite complex.

By 1890, with the development of Grand Chapters (later called State Chapters) the chapters within each state were re-lettered, each state now having its own Chapter A, Chapter B, Chapter C, and so on. The Mount Pleasant chapter is known as Chapter Original A.

The first Nebraska chapter, very quietly begun in Omaha in 1873 or 1874, was designated Chapter 1st H. It disappeared as quietly as it began in 1879 or 1880. The second Nebraska chapter was Chapter 2nd K formed in Norfolk in 1887. It became Nebraska Chapter C and disbanded in 1892.

Next came Nebraska's oldest surviving chapter organized in York as 1st R, and then designated Nebraska Chapter A in 1890. Fairfield's Chapter 1st V in 1886 became Nebraska Chapter B in 1890 and disbanded in 1893; Superior's Chapter AL became Nebraska Chapter D in 1890 and disbanded in 1909. Omaha organized Chapter 1st AN in 1889 which became Nebraska Chapter E in 1890, and Plattsmouth's Chapter 1st AP organized the same year became Nebraska Chapter F in 1890.

Also organized in 1889 were Hastings, designated 1st AQ and then becoming Nebraska Chapter G in 1890; and Holdrege designated 1st AR, becoming Nebraska Chapter H. A chapter was organized that same year in Wahoo and was designated AS, then became Nebraska Chapter I; and Nelson's Chapter J was organized in 1891, the first Nebraska chapter to receive Nebraska lettering upon its organization.

And so began the legacy of Nebraska P.E.O.

Chapter A York
(Originally R) Organized February 14, 1885
by Lily Smith

Valentine's Day, February 14, 1885, was a red-letter day in York, Nebraska. In a small Victorian house (still standing on East 7th Street), Chapter A, originally known as Chapter R, was formed.

A petite, blonde girl named Lily Smith had spent the summer in Mount Pleasant, Iowa, where she had been initiated into the Mother Chapter of P.E.O. Upon her return to York, she received permission to organize a new chapter and chose seven friends to join her in wearing the gold star.

The privileged members were Lena Knott, Carrie Gandy, Carrie Smith, Rose Dobbs, Clem Wilde, Ella Davis and Emma Davis. Each candidate slipped into the house on 7th Street, one by one, so as not to attract attention from outsiders. All were students at York Methodist College and were of an average age of seventeen (later changed to eighteen). The initiation fee was $3 and the yearly dues were 50 cents. Meetings were held once a week and eleven members were added during the first year.

These lively girls were bound by love, friendship and dedication as are the sisters in Chapter A today.

In 1935 Chapter A celebrated its 50th birthday. Adelia Mead wrote in The P.E.O. Record the following: "Chapter A celebrated the 50th birthday at a dinner also attended by the state president, Mrs. Ruth C. Kennedy. Tables were arranged in the form of a star. Each was centered with a large gold star outlined with lights."

In 1977 a charter was granted to fourteen members to form a new chapter, HH. Nebraska State Chapter Organizer Bobbie Koefoot conducted the meeting and was assisted by other state officers.

On Valentine's Day 1985, Chapter A celebrated 100 wonderful years of P.E.O. The occasion and the memories were shared with sisters in Chapter HH and six state officers.

1912 Valentine party at Chapter A York

This was written on a note accompanying the picture: "On Feb. 14, 1912, Chapter A held a valentine party at the home of Bertha Copsey at 8PM. All came in costume and exchanged valentines. Van Decar, Mansfield, Parks, Neill, Smith, Reader, Hass, Harrison, Stephens, Kirkpatrick, Purington, Detrick, Spurlock, Diffenbacker, Price, Moore, Haner, Hanna, Copsey, Gilbert, Haggard, Snyder" (Note the two "bathing costumes" with striped stockings in the front row.)

Two of Chapter A's members have served as president of Nebraska State Chapter. Maud Harrison was president in 1908 and Helen Copsey Riddell in 1949. Helen was also on the Boards of Trustees of both The P.E.O. Record and the Nebraska P.E.O. Home.

In 1980, Elaine Bonham painted a still life of marguerites as a tribute to Helen Riddell. It hangs in the Nebraska P.E.O. Home in Beatrice in a room furnished in her honor.

During its 127 years, Chapter A has hosted Nebraska State Chapter Convention in York three times—in 1891-92, 1941-42, and 1970-71. It also has had the privilege to sponsor several loan and grant recipients.

In this, the second century of Chapter A's existence, the members share, as did our Founders so long ago, the love for their sisters and the true meaning of the star.

Celebrating its 127th year Chapter A has been taking a look at the history of not only the chapter, but the city of York. It has been fun taking a stroll down memory lane…looking back at old minutes and scrapbooks.

Chapter A's philanthropic committees have used unique ways of collecting monies for the educational funds and other P.E.O. projects. Sisters who share special moments in their lives contribute to the "brag box." The committee organizes a Cookie Walk each year in order to raise funds for the P.E.O. projects. Sisters are asked to bake ten dozen festive holiday cookies which are sold on the first Saturday morning in December each year. We are thrilled with the success of this project which is our largest fundraiser.

Recent programs have included a historical Walking Tour of York Theatres, a visit to Wessel's Living History Farm, High Tea with everyone bringing their favorite teacup, and socials with and without the BILs.

CHAPTER A'S ACTIVE MEMBERSHIP IS 76; TOTAL ENROLLMENT 469

★

CHAPTER B FAIRFIELD
(ORIGINALLY V) ORGANIZED MARCH 31, 1886
BY ROSA DOBBS, YORK
DISBANDED, 1893

Records vary as to the exact organization date of the chapter at Fairfield. The 1903 *White History* of the P.E.O. Sisterhood and *The Story of P.E.O.*, Volume I, give the date as March 31, 1885. Rosa Dobbs, who promoted its organization, was a member of Chapter A, York. A story in the *White History* submitted by the York chapter states, "During the first year after our organization, members of this chapter organized the chapter at Fairfield, Nebraska." This gives the impression that it was March 31, 1885. However, the organization of Chapter A was only a few weeks earlier. Nebraska State Chapter records the date as May 1886, and *Out of the Heart* gives the organization date of Chapter B (Originally V) as March 31, 1886. Since Chapter U, Thorntown, Indiana, was organized March 26, 1886 and Chapter W, Unionville, Missouri, was organized May 8, 1886, it is likely that V would have been organized between those dates—probably March 31, 1886. Early records were hand written and erasures frequent, making them often difficult to read.

The town of Fairfield was small, and by February or March 1893, books, papers and charter were sent to Lulu B. Patrick, president of Nebraska Grand Chapter. Some members later dimitted elsewhere.

Charter members as shown in Nebraska State Chapter records were: May Randall (McKee), Fannie Mason (McClure), Bessie McDonald (Anawalt), Mary Mitchell, Kittie Pierman, Ella Spencer, and Jessie Ferguson. Seven more members were initiated later. Names given in *The Story of P.E.O.*, Volume I, were taken from Effie Hoffman Rogers' Catalogue of P.E.O.s, 1887. Spelling varies somewhat.

CHAPTER B'S TOTAL ENROLLMENT 14

The past is a guidepost...not a hitching post
-L. Thomas Holdcroft

Chapter C Norfolk
(Originally K) Organized September 27, 1887
Disbanded May 1892

The *White History* of 1903 listed the charter members as Margaret Burrows, Dora Budenz, Mrs. J.S. McClary, Mrs. J.M. Collamer, Winnie Durland, Josie Durland, Etta Durland and Mrs. H.J. Mason. However, Nebraska State Chapter and International Chapter records do not list all these names among the first eight. Total enrollment includes Lettie McCleary, Winnie R. Durland, Dora Budenz, Margaret B. Meninger, Mary Rainbolt, Emma Durland, Ida Mast, Josie Durland, Flora Callamer, Eva Hayes, Mary Richards, Inez Kail, Phemie Mason, Lillian Durland, Clara Mapes, Adela Gericke, Millie Bridge, Mrs. A.E. Birchard, Etta L. Durland, Sallie M. Powers, Mary Leggett Huse Kennedy, Sadie B. Iles, Rose Chilson, Kate L. Burrows, Imogene Holmes, Susan M. Hasson, Ella Holbert, Mary Cole, Flora S. Johnson.

In 1890 Dora Budenz was a delegate to Omaha for organization of Nebraska Grand Chapter and became first vice president. Josie Durland was Nebraska Grand Chapter treasurer, 1891-92. Winifred Durland served as Supreme Grand Chapter second vice president, 1891-92, first vice president, 1892-93, and organizer, 1893-97, first to hold that office after it was created in 1893. She dimitted to J, Iowa, November 11, 1892, the year Chapter C, Nebraska, was disbanded. An account of the 1892 convention from the *White History* lauds Mrs. Durland's service, her knowledge of parliamentary rules and P.E.O. law, and her ability as a speaker.

Chapter C's Total Enrollment 29

Chapter D Superior
(Originally AL) Organized April 10, 1889
by Miss Randall of Mount Pleasant, Iowa
Disbanded April 1909

The charter members of Chapter D, Superior, were Alice Cary Briggs, Mary C. Bloom, May Belle Ebert, Ophelia S. Johnston, Kate Meek Scoular, Carrie McGrew, Valeria Ann Padden and Dora Speer.

P.E.O. in Superior was promoted by Alice Cary Briggs, sister-in-law of Hattie Briggs, Founder. It was a very active chapter in its twenty years of existence. A letter to The P.E.O. Record in February 1890, states that their "'lodge' of twenty-six members received calls on New Year's Day in the Odd Fellows' Hall, which was beautifully decorated for the occasion. The affair was pronounced a grand success by everyone and quite as brilliant a reception as was ever given in Superior. The universal verdict was that the lodge should be proud of itself and it is—modestly so, of course, as becomes the P.E.O.s. The society is busy rehearsing a drama entitled *Anita's Trial*. The cast is composed of eleven female characters."

At the 1889 Grand Chapter convention in Mount Pleasant, Mrs. Briggs, delegate, was soloist, served on the Resolutions Committee, and was appointed to solicit advertisements and subscriptions to The P.E.O. Record. She organized Chapter

AR, Holdrege, that year. Winifred Connet was appointed assistant editor of The P.E.O. Record. In 1890 Mrs. Briggs became the first president of Nebraska Grand Chapter, and in 1893, president of Supreme Chapter.

In 1894, Chapter D produced a local talent operetta, "Pauline, the Belle." The local paper gave Alice Briggs credit. "Weeks ago she chose her orchestra, selected her voices, trained and drilled them, piece by piece, until they were able to present such a perfect whole as the public saw last night."

Carrie McNaughton, journalist, told about parties with the M.M.'s, the first BILs in P.E.O. Mrs. McNaughton was president of Nebraska Grand Chapter, 1895-96.

CHAPTER D's TOTAL ENROLLMENT 68

★

CHAPTER E OMAHA
(ORIGINALLY AN) ORGANIZED JUNE 1, 1889
BY CLARA MASON, P, IOWA

The seven charter members of Chapter AN (later E) were Clara B. Mason, president; Maggie Truland Burns, vice president; Mary A. Fitch, treasurer; Jenny H. Bryant, recording secretary and chaplain; Reginia S. Atwater De Sales, corresponding secretary; Lilly Chamberlin Andrews, guard; Sadie Pittman, organist.

Quoting Mrs. Bryant, "I had always lived in Mount Pleasant, knew the original seven and was familiar with P.E.O. Miss Mason came from Burlington, Iowa, to Omaha to teach school and boarded next door to me. We often talked of P.E.O. and finally thought of a chapter. We each invited our friends and had to explain the principles of the Society. We met at my home for organization. Miss Mason gave a beautiful talk and fully explained the ideals and objects of the Sisterhood; then in a dignified manner she initiated us into P.E.O. We adjourned, feeling the responsibility before us and that more ideals had come into our lives."

Through Miss Mason, Chapter F, Plattsmouth, and I, Wahoo, were soon organized. The nine Nebraska chapters met at the home of Mrs. Bryant, April 2, 1890, and Nannie Torrence Stockman, president of Supreme Grand Chapter, organized Nebraska Grand Chapter, the first to receive a separate charter. Chapter E helped P.E.O. to grow in Omaha by organizing Chapters M, BK, BN, BX, DH, and sponsored GU.

Mrs. Bryant was president of Nebraska State Chapter for two terms, 1893-95, and first vice president of Supreme Grand Chapter 1895-97. Clara Wilson served as president of Nebraska State Chapter 1910-11, and Dorothy Yeager, 1963-64; Eva Wagner served as state organizer; Ella Allen as state corresponding secretary; and Grace Funkhouser as state treasurer. Metta Updike, Carrie Tribble, Mary Peckham, Ruth Lucke and Dorothy Johnson were presidents of Omaha P.E.O. Association. Janet Benton and Joan Green served as treasurer.

Chapter E hosted Supreme Convention in October 1895, and secured P.E.O. rooms at the Omaha 1898-99 Trans-Mississippi Exposition, where P.E.O.s from almost every state registered. Chapter E assisted at Supreme Convention in Omaha in 1917. Members were earlier urged to plant marguerites and cosmos to provide for convention.

Fine arts abound in Chapter E. Reginia Atwater DeSales, concert singer, became Madam Reginia De Sales of New York and Paris, was awarded the Palmes d'Officer d'Academie in 1913 and decorated by Anatole de Mouzie, minister of Public Instruction, with the Palmes d'Officer d'Instruction in 1933.

Mary Peckham served on the Omaha Playhouse board for twenty years, received the Fonda-Maguire award for best actress twice, wrote monologues, was a noted reviewer, and provided excellent programs for any audience. Pianist Anna Christensen, listed in 1972 Marquis "Who's Who in American Women," had many elementary piano solos published. Marnie Ellison has published several fictional books.

Minutes reveal constant chapter generosity and philanthropy. When the Nebraska P.E.O. Home opened in 1938, Chapter E's Jessie Zachary was the first to enter. Chapter E had furnished a room as a memorial to Jenny Bryant. Dorothy Yeager served as president of the Nebraska P.E.O. Home Board of Directors and served as president of Nebraska State Chapter in 1963-64. Activities during World Wars I and II were outstanding.

In the early days a room was furnished in the Salvation Army hospital. For about 20 years Christmas packages for the Nebraska University Hospital were given under the guidance of Dorothy Haber. In 1959, through Luree Douglas, Chapter E became exclusive agent for the sale of P.E.O. recognition pins in Nebraska for many years.

Chapter E continues the tradition of initiating daughters who, when they leave Omaha, find P.E.O. homes all over the United States. It has continued to grow in love. As each of our sisters passes to Chapter Eternal there is somehow always a new sister ready to step up into our organization. Taken together, we represent hundreds of years of hard won experience in life and its problems. We joyfully share our hopes and disappointments. We support each other both through the darker parts of living and also cheerfully encourage the celebrations and accomplishments of our sisters.

We utilize our creative energies and our fully embraced drollness as a group to find ways of raising money that are fun. Apart from the usual bake sales, our Ways and Means Committee has organized P.E.O. T-shirts, fees for the number of pairs of shoes owned by each sister and a new, or gently used, purse sale with notes in the purses giving their history. Our sales table at the Omaha Reciprocity meeting is very successful and the handmade cards and confetti filled eggs are beginning to be sought out by the delegates. Because of our work, we have cheerfully been able to fulfill our obligations to support the seven projects of P.E.O. through the years.

Since 1997 we have successfully sponsored one ELF applicant, two STAR applicants and six PCE applicants. The last two PCE applicants were a mother and daughter in the same year.

Our sisters in Chapter E have served on the Omaha Reciprocity Association board as president and twice as corresponding secretary.

Our meetings are always fun and well attended. In 2001 we established an annual "Winter Picnic" to blow away the winter blues and in 2002 we started a "Friend's Coffee" meeting where we take the opportunity to introduce new friends to the P.E.O. Sisterhood. In 2008 we held a "Fall Garden Party" where everyone wore hats and gloves. Our BILs have been entertained by a wine tasting given by another BIL, and an evening at a lakeside cabin where sunset boat rides were the order of the day (or evening).

In 2010 the sisters of Chapter E together sewed a Comfort Quilt. This is lent to any sister who needs comfort to remind her that we all embrace her with our love.

In 2010 we had our original charter from 1889 professionally preserved so that we can keep the unique record of our founding for many more years to come.

Finally, we wish to acknowledge and remember the loss of our dear sister Mary Brumback, whose abrupt and tragic death shocked us all. As her sisters, we reached out to her family and were able to offer comfort and support to them during this time of great sadness.

CHAPTER E'S ACTIVE MEMBERSHIP IS 44; TOTAL ENROLLMENT IS 388

★

CHAPTER F PLATTSMOUTH
(ORIGINALLY AP) ORGANIZED SEPTEMBER 7, 1889
BY CLARA MASON

In 1889 the Grand Chapter, the governing body of P.E.O., asked Clara Mason, a P.E.O. from Chapter AN, Omaha, to form a P.E.O. Society in Plattsmouth. With the assistance of her sister, Mary Houseworth, a list of seven to ten women from the community was compiled. The charter list was comprised of women who were favorably known in the community, who would enjoy each other's company and who could work and study together harmoniously.

Eight women accepted the invitation to meet at Mary Houseworth's home and listen to Clara Mason explain the history, principles and aims of P.E.O. All of the women accepted the invitation to become sisters and were initiated into Chapter AP, Nebraska (later changed to Chapter F, Nebraska). The charter members, each an officer, were: Mary Houseworth, president; Jennie Windham, vice president; Ola Campbell, recording secretary; Edna Young, corresponding secretary; Ellen Patterson, treasurer; Margaret Dovey, chaplain; Minnie Houseworth, guard; and Dora Herold, pianist.

In October 1889, just a month after its formation, the chapter sent a delegate to the P.E.O. convention in Mount Pleasant, Iowa. Mary Houseworth was chosen as delegate because the new chapter was short on funds and Mary's husband worked for the railroad and could obtain a pass for her.

Some notables during the early years of Chapter F were Eda Herold, Lillian Parmele and Ona Baird. Eda Herold was the first initiate into Chapter F and was an active and beloved sister for 78 of her 103 years. Besides being Chapter F president three times, Lillian Parmele was president of Nebraska Grand Chapter in 1903-1904 and served as recording secretary of Supreme Grand Chapter. Mrs. Parmele originated the idea of using the Supreme Grand Chapter Memorial Fund for education. It became the P.E.O. Educational Loan Fund. She served as its first chairman. Another sister, Ona Baird, was a talented writer who published many articles in The P.E.O. Record and also served as president of Nebraska State Chapter in 1922-1923.

Chapter F remembers special times: the felt floor star; the large metal star hung outside the door to ensure privacy during the meetings; the fire in the home where all Chapter F history and memorabilia was kept, when sodden early minutes books and records were tossed out the third floor window and hung on clotheslines to dry, (most of them were saved). In 1989, Chapter F celebrated our 100th anniversary with a large gala celebration at a historic home in Omaha. A style show of historic costumes, a luncheon, and a presentation on the history of Chapter F entertained the Chapter F sisters and state officers in commemoration of our previous 100 years. Our 125th anniversary in 2014 was celebrated with enthusiastic reverence.

For 125 years Chapter F has been enriched by youth and age, loving, learning and sharing together the special bonds of the P.E.O. Sisterhood. Chapter F has presently or has had sisters who have been members for more than 50 years. There are also families that have had five generations of P.E.O.s. Chapter F has sponsored many candidates for P.E.O. scholarships and have had a few who were awarded scholarships.

Chapter F enjoys a variety of programs arranged by the Yearbook Committee. The programs are given by members and occasionally by community resources. Three socials—summer, fall and Christmas—are planned for the year, some involving the BILs. The chapter is also involved in community projects (adopting and maintaining an area of Rhylander Park, assisting the Plattsmouth Conservancy, providing cookies on a monthly basis for the Senior Center, and providing supplies for Heartland Family Services). Fundraisers have included a garage sale, making and selling travel jewelry bags, and the brag box.

CHAPTER F'S ACTIVE MEMBERSHIP IS 48; TOTAL ENROLLMENT IS 330

★

CHAPTER G HASTINGS
(ORIGINALLY AQ) ORGANIZED OCTOBER 2, 1889
BY HELEN OFFICER AND KITTIE DUTTON

It was a beautiful day on October 2, 1889, when Chapter G (originally AQ) was organized at the home of Grace Kipp. Helen Officer, A, Iowa, and Kittie Dutton, I, Iowa, were the organizers. The charter members were Mollie Campbell, May Dilley Graham, Elizabeth D. Jones, Mary L. Jones, Grace B. Kipp, Florence Lowman, Lillie C. Main, Carrie Brown McLaughlin, Flora Lyman Pearl, Minnie Dutton Pickens, Minnie Ryan, Ada Nolan, and Laura Dilley Wahlquist. Though the minutes of the organization do not list Kittie Dutton as a charter member, she was the first chapter president.

Our fourteen charter members were young women just beginning their adult lives in a relatively new city, ranging in age from twenty to twenty-nine. Many of them eventually left Hastings, but we honor them for gathering on that October afternoon so long ago.

At the Convention of Grand Chapter in 1889, Chapter G was introduced as one of four new chapters organized in Nebraska. It was also at this convention that Nebraska was given the go ahead to organize a state grand chapter. In 1890, when the state chapter became official, Chapter AQ became Chapter G, Nebraska.

In 1894 Chapter G was hostess for the state convention, the first of seven conventions in which Chapter G has been involved. A favorite Chapter G story relates that the cost was $99.11 for the convention, but chapter funds were $25 short. However, the gallant BILs of the day came to the rescue. They defrayed the expenses and then treated the ladies to ice cream and cake.

Chapter G has had four Nebraska State Chapter presidents: Ruth Gellatly, 1954-55; Sheila Shreck, 1969-70; Lois Ann Hansen, 1978-79; and Mary Lainson Olsen, 1995-96.

In 1972 Marjorie Fuller designed and made our lovely white initiation robes and donated them to our chapter. They are still used today.

For many years Chapter G's programs were in-depth, serious studies based on an annual theme. For example, Greek Art was the subject chosen for 1890-91 — "Life and Works of Raphael" highlighted the last meeting before Christmas 1890. The 1915-16 year was devoted to Studies in Opera. In 1934, the theme was Philosophy and the Sciences, with lectures given by Hastings College faculty.

Finally, Nina King wrote in her 1936 president's letter, "For several years we had had rather heavy programs, so this year it was the consensus of the members that a miscellaneous program would be a good thing for the chapter." Miscellaneous programs with themes chosen by the chapter president continue to today.

In 1890 Chapter G began its local philanthropic work. As P.E.O. projects were created, the chapter took them on.

Chapter G's support of several charities lasted for decades: (1) beginning 1916, furnishing and maintaining a P.E.O. Room at Sunnyside (the "Old Peoples' Home"); (2) contributing to the local Milk Fund (later the Infant Welfare Fund), which fed undernourished children (1927); (3) providing support to two orphanages— Christian Home at Council Bluffs (1906) and the Child Saving Institute at Omaha (1927); (4) contributions to Goodfellows (1919).

During World War I the chapter met with other women of the city weekly at the Presbyterian Church to make bandages. Members made garments for refugees, surgical dressings for the Red Cross, kits for servicemen, and assisted with the local USO during the World War II and Korean War years.

Since 1965 the bulk of fundraising has gone to the P.E.O. Sisterhood projects, which have been very important to Chapter G. It has continued to be financially generous to both the International and the Nebraska P.E.O. projects. Chapter G has sponsored thirty-two women for loans and scholarships over the years.

In 2006, past presidents of Chapter G presented an historical program of their presidential years. Those present were: (Front row) Mary Olsen, 1984-85, 1985-86, 1997-98; Charlotte Welch, 1973-74, 1974-75; Pat Kingsley, 2002-03; Janet Hunter, 1990-91, 2001-02, 2003-04; Evadne Vaughn, 1999-2000; Gretchen Lainson, 1951-52, 1952-53, and Joan Swan, 1967-68. (Back Row) Jerri Haussler, 2000-01; Colleen Adam, 1991-92; Sally Smith, 1977-78; and Josie Anderson, 1983-84.

For many years the P.E.O. projects were supported by individual gifts. Chapter G reported 100 percent participation for most years, even during the 1930's depression era. To generate more interest, the chapter began an annual silent auction to raise funds. In 1996, this was changed to a raffle, culminating in a big drawing of surprise items at the December meeting. The chapter members look forward to this enjoyable holiday event which proves more successful every year.

Social events have fluctuated with the times. The first noted was an hour of taffy pulling in 1889. A wide variety of happy gatherings has followed, such as costume parties, picnics, mother-daughter Valentine teas, musicales, and luncheons.

In 1942 the BILs entertained the chapter with a dinner at the Clarke Hotel and their own humorous play, "Model P.E.O. Meeting." Another memorable BIL party was held at the Hastings Motorsports Park in 2009. Several BILs brought their specialized cars and took people of all ages around the twisty, freeform track at speeds over 90 mph.

Celebrating the 50th anniversary of Chapter G in October 1939, members boarded a hayrack in their Victorian costumes. Front row (l to r): Gwen Beck, Clair Anderson, Mabel Hamil, Roberta Brandes, Bettie Kissinger, Stella Coffeen, Besse Foote, and Irma Uerling. Back row: Beth Marvel Marti, Maurine Stiner, Gretchen Lainson, Marie Foote, Celia Lainson, Nettie Simms, Myrtle Kipp, Floy Matthiesen, and Belle Cotton.

Chapter G celebrated its fiftieth anniversary in 1939 with a luncheon at the home of Mrs. Adah Pratt. Members came dressed in old-fashioned costumes, some of them arriving in a hayrack (because there were no automobiles in 1889).

On October 2, 1989, Chapter G celebrated its 100th birthday. A Victorian Tea was held at the home of Gretchen Lainson, and many members were dressed in Victorian style clothes. The music for the afternoon was from the 1880s and 1890s and the program was on the life and times of women in the 1800s and the history of Chapter G. All attending received a hand-painted ceramic pin box commemorating the special event. The centennial celebration concluded with a BIL party.

Chapter G has deep roots in the past, particularly as we celebrated our 125th year in 2014. With many recent young initiates, we also look forward to the future, aspiring to the principles that P.E.O. membership has always set. As Gretchen Lainson, our member of longest standing (initiated April 1939), said in an interview, "Through the years I have gradually come to regard the words of the Initiation Ceremony and the Objects and Aims of P.E.O. as some of the greatest words I know. They set such high and worthwhile standards for all women."

CHAPTER G'S ACTIVE MEMBERSHIP IS 84; TOTAL ENROLLMENT IS 528

★

CHAPTER H HOLDREGE
(ORIGINALLY AR) ORGANIZED DECEMBER 14, 1889
BY ALICE CARY BRIGGS

Nine enthusiastic women became the charter members of Chapter H: Ada Breech, guard; Alice Sheldon Young, chaplain; Ida M. Scott, vice president; Jettaline Warnick, treasurer; Carrie A. McGrew, recording secretary; Dora C. McNaul, corresponding secretary; Lulu B. Patrick, president; Jennie Moore; and Carrie Norberg. In 1895, Chapter H was the first chapter in Nebraska to organize a new chapter (N, Minden).

Lulu B. Patrick, H, an outstanding pioneer in Nebraska P.E.O., was instrumental in organizing the Nebraska Grand Chapter for which she served as president in 1891-1893, and a National Grand Chapter, which later was renamed Supreme Chapter and finally International Chapter. Holdrege has hosted the Nebraska State Chapter three times—in 1896, 1936 and 1965. Chapter H has had two other members serve as president of Nebraska State Chapter—Florence Davis in 1942-43 and Helen Magill in 1971-72.

In 1939, Gladys Titus was appointed to the Nebraska P.E.O. Home Board of Directors. Mildred Nelson also served as a board member. Visiting the Home and participating in activities are special projects of present day sisters.

Through the years the chapter has given generous donations of time and money to local and state charities and projects. It has become a tradition to give the public library classical recordings and books as memorials to deceased members of Chapter H. Now, all philanthropies are directed toward all P.E.O. projects, especially the privilege of sponsoring PCE, ELF and STAR recipients. Also, the chapter is proud of the many sisters who give of their time as volunteers in so many ways in the community.

Chapter H was especially pleased to sponsor a new evening chapter in Holdrege. Chapter HM was organized September 8, 1979. The charter head was Helen Magill, Chapter H. Since the beginning, the two sister chapters have shared Founders' Day luncheons and an annual Christmas program and other special times. There is a true feeling of sisterhood between the two chapters.

A particularly impressive date for Chapter H was on December 14, 1989–the 100th anniversary of the organization of the chapter. Chapter H was honored during a special "Centennial" program at the 100th Convention of Nebraska State Chapter on June 2-4 at the Hastings College campus. This celebration was the first of its kind in the nation as Nebraska was the first state chapter organized and the first to celebrate its centennial. Twenty Holdrege members were present for the celebration and were given special recognition. Memorabilia from the past 100 years of Chapter H was displayed at the convention. Chapter H has several three, four and five generation P.E.O.s and one 75-year active member.

A lovely tradition anticipated each year is the Christmas Tea. Each year, the committee spends much thought and time on making it a memorable occasion. Plates of decorative cookies and candies are shared with shut-in sisters. A "fun" tradition is the initiation of our newest BILs by the older BILs every few years.

Many talented members enhance chapter programs through drama, music inspiration, education, literature, humor and beautiful entertaining skills. Each sister has a talent. Sometimes she, herself, is surprised to learn what it is. All are enriched by each other's growth.

Though changes may occur, Chapter H's 125-year love for P.E. O. and its ideals will continue undiminished.

CHAPTER H'S ACTIVE MEMBERSHIP IS 72; TOTAL ENROLLMENT IS 489

★

CHAPTER I WAHOO
(ORIGINALLY AS) ORGANIZED JANUARY 24, 1890
BY CLARA MASON

Chapter I, Wahoo, is 125 years old. The charter members were: Nan Katherine Alexander, Leila Henderson Bass, Ella Jamison Collins, May Evans Frush, Jennie Jessen Good, Augusta F. Moore, Etta Andrus Michner, Eutha McClennon Rupp, and Daisy Reese Sanford. Miss Clara B. Mason, Chapter E, Omaha, was the organizer. Mrs. Jennie H. Bryant, also of Chapter E, Omaha, was a friend of charter member Ella Collins and it was through Mrs. Bryant's influence that the Wahoo chapter was organized.

Chapter I's founder and first president, Ella Jamison Collins, was only sixteen when she enrolled at Iowa Wesleyan in Mount Pleasant, Iowa. At that time, P.E.O. was only two years old and Ella knew and remembered all of the seven Founders well. She also remembered when Franc Roads Elliot taught art at the University of Nebraska.

The early P.E.O.s gave a number of plays at the Opera House to raise money. In 1897 Chapter I entertained Grand Chapter—quite an undertaking considering the chapter had so few members! It was at this time that the Star Ceremony was first used outside of Chapter K, Lincoln.

Chapter I has always been very interested in philanthropic work. During World War I, Chapter I adopted two French orphans and contributed to their support for five years. All members assisted in the war effort during World War II, buying war bonds and stamps, providing food and entertainment to the USO in Lincoln and helping to support the Red Cross. For many years the chapter sent out baskets of provisions at Christmas to needy families in the community and donated to several children's organizations.

Chapter I has generously supported the P.E.O projects over the years. In 1996, a pledge of $1,000 was given to the Nebraska P.E.O. Home to help rebuild the Home's endowment. Begun in 1998, Daisy Dollars were given by members who share highlights from their lives. Our Birthday Barrel, courtesy fund, and Daisy Dollars are sent to the projects in addition to annual project giving.

To further support P.E.O. projects, Chapter I has held a variety of fundraisers. Several years of bake sales, silent auctions, Christmas greenery sales, and garage sales are a few of Chapter I's fundraisers. One fundraiser was named "Tables, Tea and Temptation." Members displayed special china, linens and prized possessions followed by delicious desserts.

Chapter I has sponsored several project recipients in the last twenty years. Kelcie Lindahl Keeling, Stephanie Stukenholtz Bellamy, Amy Norris Reis, Larianne Polk, Amber Watton and Krystal Johnson received ELF loans. Diane Tillman, Larianne Polk, Kathy Becker, Kristi Klemme, and Amber Watton received PCE grants. Malinda DuBois and Beth Johnson Divis received Cottey Scholarships.

Charlotte Kolterman, Milrae Anderson, Marjorie Harris, Eunice Brodahl and Janet Lindley have received 60-year membership recognition in the last ten years. A sizable monetary donation was given to the chapter from Milrae Anderson's estate; the money provides scholarships for women. Our first recipient, Megan Griffin, received $2,500 from this scholarship for the fall 2013 semester.

Social gatherings have become a popular addition to our regular meetings. Chapter I has had a fondue party, deli night, barbecues with BILs and a "Drive-in Movie Night" complete with pajamas. Many sisters have gathered to attend various activities in Lincoln or Omaha. In 1998 and 2003, Chapter I members enjoyed a special outing to Lincoln for lunch and a tour of the Governor's Mansion.

Chapter I is honored to have had several initiates who later held state offices. June Ayers Brunmeier served as president of Nebraska State Chapter in 1989-90. Several sisters have served within our state P.E.O. in a variety of positions. Helen Hansen (1998) and Lorraine Urban (2012) were delegates to Convention of International Chapter from Reciprocity Group VII. Vicki Simons was appointed head guard for the 1999 state convention. Linda Little served as Reciprocity Group VII president in 2011. Chapter I members, young and experienced, hosted the hospitality room for the 2013 state convention. It is this spirit of dedication and giving and a special spirit of both young and mature sisters working together that will ensure a good future for Chapter I, Wahoo.

CHAPTER I'S ACTIVE MEMBERSHIP IS 57; TOTAL ENROLLMENT IS 289

Our deeds still travel with us from afar,
and what we have been makes us what we are.
-George Eliot

Chapter J Nelson
Organized September 1, 1891
by Dora Baumbach

At the home of Mary Lyon on September 1, 1891, seven charter members met with Dora Baumbach, who was authorized by the state president to serve as organizer. Charter members were Alberta C. Fox, Celia A. Gorby, Mary J. Lyon, Lena Moon Jones, Lillie Smith, Jennie M. Voigt, and Clara Crawford.

The *White History* states: "Chapter J under Mrs. Crawford's able executive skill soon attained prominence among the other chapters in the state. From its membership five Grand Chapter officers have been selected."

Three months after its organization, Chapter J voted to start a P.E.O. library. It was the nucleus for the present Nelson City Library.

In April 1899, Chapter J entertained the Grand Chapter Convention on its ninth anniversary. Twenty-nine delegates were present. The horse-drawn dray carrying the delegates' luggage was gaily decorated.

Around 1910 Chapter J's big project was raising the money and having a 1200-foot walkway built to the Nelson Cemetery. The sidewalk spanned a deep ravine and was a tremendous undertaking. Another early project involved the erection of a windmill at the cemetery in 1894.

Early meetings included elaborate musical and literary programs. Superior's Chapter D often was invited, and sometimes a special train was chartered for the guests. On June 10, 1928, Chapter J assisted in organizing Chapter DS, Superior.

In September 1966, in honor of Chapter J's diamond anniversary tea, guests were Helen Noble, state chapter president, and Sheila Shreck, organizer. Sheila was an initiate of Chapter J. For a historical skit written by Charlotte Clabaugh, a handmade item originally from Chapter J was borrowed from Nebraska State Chapter's collection of historical articles.

The P.E.O. Cemetery Walk is still maintained by efforts of the chapter. A grant and fundraisers held by Chapter J for several years enabled the restoration of the walkway in 2005. The Cemetery Walkway was placed on the National Register of Historic Places on December 5, 2002.

Reciprocity meetings with Chapter DS, Superior, have become an annual tradition. Chapter Eternal graves are decorated with marguerites by the courtesy committee each Memorial Day.

Sandra Sterkel is a 50-year member and three women have over forty years of membership.

Minutes of Chapter J are complete from the date of organization to the present and there is a nearly complete file of yearbooks—one or two are handwritten.

CHAPTER J'S ACTIVE MEMBERSHIP IS 25 AND ITS TOTAL ENROLLMENT IS 206

*The present is an edifice
which God cannot rebuild.*
-Ralph Waldo Emerson

Chapter K Lincoln
Organized March 28, 1893
by Clara A. Crawford West

The first chapter in Lincoln, Chapter K was organized on March 28, 1893, by nine women who were P.E.O. members from chapters in Nebraska and Iowa. They were: Mary Johnson Axtell, Estelle DeVore, Ida Gilkerson, Ida B. Johnson, Mary McKinnon, Anna Risser, Mary Shepherd, Johanna Van Boskirk, and Clara Crawford West. Six Chapter K members have served as president of Nebraska State Chapter: Clara C. West, 1896-98; Mary J. Axtell, 1901-1902; Flora W. Jones, 1908-1909; Ida B. Johnson, 1912-1913; Minnie M. Stuff, 1918-1919; and Dee Anne Weyeneth, 2003-2004. Mary J. Axtell also was recording secretary of Supreme Chapter from 1903-1907. In June 1895, Chapter K, although only two years of age, entertained the Nebraska Grand Chapter, and in October 1903, entertained the Supreme Convention. Both meetings were held in the Nebraska State Capitol Senate Chamber.

The star initiation ceremony used by all chapters was conceived and planned by Miss Ida B. Johnson, a charter member of Chapter K. The first star, constructed of yellow and white satin, was made over a wire frame by another chapter member, Joanna Van Boskirk. The ceremony was exemplified for the first time at the Nebraska Grand Chapter Convention in Wahoo in 1897 and adopted at the following Supreme Convention in Chicago in 1899.

In its first century, Chapter K was instrumental in the development of the P.E.O. Educational Loan Fund, the Nebraska P.E.O. Home in Beatrice, the P.E.O. Roundtable of Lincoln, and the College Chapters. It has helped organize and has granted dimits to its members for charter lists of ten other Nebraska chapters and has sponsored fourteen P.E.O. Educational Loan Fund women. Interesting first century fundraising activities included a candy and popcorn booth at the Nebraska Epworth Assembly in Epworth Park in Lincoln. Auctions, raffles, garage sales, luncheons, sales of pecans and knives were other fun sources of income. Special events have been the annual Christmas Cookie Tea, in which members bring their special Christmas cookies for our enjoyment and for cookie plates which are made up and taken to our shut-in members and the Spring Luncheon honoring the 50-year members.

Chapter K's second century brought a more modern demand on both fundraising efforts and goals for the chapter. When Dee Weyeneth was elected to the Executive Board of Nebraska State Chapter in 1997, Chapter K proudly went to work to support her efforts and ultimately sponsor her installation and convention. Dee continued her leadership skills by serving as Lincoln Reciprocity Roundtable president in 2006-2007.

In 2001 Willie Shafer, Chapter K member and retired Lincoln Public School teacher, founded Willie's Underwear Project, where Lincoln Public School nurses are supplied with spare clothing for school children of all ages. Whether a primary student experiences an accident at school, or a needy child appears on a bitterly cold day without warm clothing, the nurses have a ready supply thanks to Willie and the generosity she inspires. WUP provides the necessary clothes through contributions both from Lincoln P.E.O. chapters and outside donations.

Special events changed dramatically in the second century. Member social interaction was most important and was readily accomplished at the annual Halloween supper with costumes required. Brunch at the Country Club of Lincoln always ushers in the holiday season. The traditional spring event is lunch at the Governor's Mansion where our 50-year members are recognized.

Fundraising efforts also "stepped up" to the times as Chapter K members assembled a hearty soup mix and sold the results in festive fabric bags. Sales soared to include many P.E.O. chapters and lots of Lincolnites. One fundraiser that began as a reason to raise money for Dee's convention has remained a viable winner—our lovely star notecards, that have been sold and used by P.E.O.s all over the state for sympathy cards, thank you's, birthday wishes, and invitations. Other projects included the sale of pecans and Rada knives.

In 1900, Chapter K was recognized as the largest chapter in the state (then with 48 members), an honor which it maintained for many years. Membership reached a peak in 1925 with a total of 173, and remained above 130 through 1965, including many 50-year members.

CHAPTER K'S ACTIVE MEMBERSHIP IS 69; TOTAL ENROLLMENT IS 661

WUP (Willie's Underwear Project) is a free "store" where Lincoln Public School nurses can shop for emergency clothing to keep on hand at each school. When a child has an accident, the child can't be sent home, because the parents may not be there. So emergency clothing is necessary. The photo above shows the "store" where local chapter donations of children's undergarments, pants, shirts and more are kept. (Willie is in orange, right of center.)

Chapter L Harvard
Organized April 28, 1893
by Lulu Patrick
Disbanded June 2, 2007

*The great clock that never stops, Nor speaks to human ears,
Has pushed its hands round and round, And marked one hundred years.*

Yes, one hundred years have passed since Mrs. Olga Jorgenson Iddols, a member of Chapter G, Hastings, suggested to her Harvard friend, Mrs. Nella Weil, that a P.E.O. chapter be organized in Harvard. Six other Harvard ladies who had the qualities of a P.E.O. member, along with Mrs. Weil, organized Chapter L on April 28, 1893. Charter initiates were Nellie Weil, Ida White, Mary Hurd, Alice McBride, Lena Campbell, Alice Blanchard and Carrie Budlong.

In its first month, twenty-two invitations to membership were extended and thirteen ladies accepted. For many of its first meetings, members met in the homes of two of its members. Later, the Masonic Hall was rented as the size increased. Then, local dues were one dollar and Grand Chapter dues were one dollar.

On June 5, 6, and 7, 1900, the eleventh Nebraska Grand Chapter Convention was held in Harvard with Chapter L serving as hostess. Fifty delegates attended and the total convention cost was $50.

During the early years, programs were long and of a truly educational nature. A sample of the programs: "Paper on the Architecture of Egypt," "Paper on Egyptian Mythology," and the 13th and 14th chapters of "Nebraska Romance." Often special meetings were called to complete the programs.

Founders' Day programs have been varied and special. One memorable one was called "The Golden Gate" where seven members in Founders' era costumes (complete with apron and large gold star) entered through a flower-covered gate while a narrator told of their life histories.

Parties have been a source of pleasant entertainment. On April 28, 1899, a "Masquerade Carnival" was held with eighty participants. BIL parties often were held. A popular one of many years ago was a "taffy pull and popcorn party." One memorable BIL party was a huge production which included: a paper on the effect of women's clubs in the home, two discussion sessions on that topic, a vocal solo, a discussion of current events, an instrumental solo and another paper on "what constitutes a woman's culture." The local newspaper article reported that "the men were reticent about discussing the subjects of the two papers" but remarks were all complimentary to P.E.O.

For many years, Chapter L entertained junior and senior girls at coke and chip and dip parties to acquaint them with Cottey College. Also, Chapter L was very active during the war years, with a "war activity committee" to remember the military men assigned to the Harvard Air Field.

Chapter L's 75th Anniversary was observed in 1968. Charter members were portrayed and the first meeting was re-enacted with material copied from the first minutes. The 100th Anniversary was celebrated with a lovely birthday party, complete with a birthday cake and a display of P.E.O. treasures gathered through the years. Due to low membership, Chapter L disbanded in 2007.

Chapter L's active membership is 4; total enrollment 193

CHAPTER M OMAHA
ORGANIZED JUNE 17, 1893
BY CHAPTER E, OMAHA
DISBANDED JUNE 7, 2003

On June 17, 1893, Chapter M was formed, known then as "The P.E.O. Society of South Omaha." Chapter M was an outgrowth of Chapter E and, in turn, has sponsored formation of Chapters CR, ED, FK and HY. The seven charter members and first officers were: May Corbett Smith, president; Mollie Sipe, vice president; Margaret Young, recording secretary; Anna Cressey, corresponding secretary; Lou Householder, treasurer; Alma Frances Foote, chaplain; and Emma McCreary, guard. Dues were 50 cents a year; a minutes book cost 75 cents; and a $1 tin box was used for "keeping papers of importance."

The Grand Chapter was entertained for two days in 1897. Chapter M members always have been charitable. Books have been donated to libraries; monetary gifts made to YWCA, hospitals, 1913 tornado victims, American Red Cross and the Salvation Army. Many Christmas baskets have been filled and distributed through the years, and in 1933, 37 dozen garments were stitched by members for donation to the unemployed in the depths of the Great Depression.

During World War II, members volunteered as Air-Raid Wardens, Gray Ladies and hostesses at Union Station to serve coffee and cookies to the soldiers. Chapter M was honored for the most hours served, most money donated and the most War Bonds sold of any P.E.O. chapter. Again in 1948, Chapter M was honored for the best volunteer record in assisting during the polio epidemic.

In 1913, Chapter M's beloved Bertha Clark Hughes was elected president of Nebraska State Chapter and later became president of Supreme Chapter. For twenty years she was parliamentarian of Chapter M and served as parliamentarian for national republican conventions and also for the National Association of Parliamentarians.

One of Chapter M's most successful fundraisers was the sale of quizzes prepared by Mrs. Hughes. One was a quiz on parliamentary law, the other a quiz on the P.E.O. Constitution. These were advertised in The P.E.O. Record. Profits went into the Chapter Welfare and Trust Fund for the needy, which later became the Bertha Clark Hughes Foundation. From member Helen Houseman's estate, Chapter M received funds for the Foundation. When the Foundation was dissolved, approximately $30,000 each was distributed to Cottey College and the Nebraska Cottey Scholarships Fund.

In June 1943, Chapter M celebrated its 50th anniversary with an elaborate banquet attended by eighty members and guests. Miss Gertrude Reynolds was president and mistress of ceremonies. The oldest living member in attendance was Maude Watkins who was the first initiate in 1893.

Over the years several young women have been assisted by the P.E.O. Educational Loan Fund and the P.E.O. Program for Continuing Education through Chapter M's sponsorship. The most recent graduated in 1992 and is an aeronautical engineer.

The spirit of P.E.O. and sisterly love brought Chapter M to its 100th birthday in 1993 in fine style. A year-long celebration of history programs by members, parties, and monetary gifts to our P.E.O. projects resulted in a renewed effort to meet the challenge of the next century.

Chapter M disbanded June 7, 2003.

TOTAL ENROLLMENT 245

Chapter N Minden
Organized March 29, 1895
by Lulu Patrick

Officers from Holdrege, Chapter H, came twenty-two miles to organize Chapter N, Minden. Chapter H was the first chapter in Nebraska with a sufficient number of officers to organize a new chapter. A luncheon at the home of Lura Chapin preceded initiation. Chapter N, Minden, was organized March 29, 1895, by Lulu B. Patrick.

Charter members and first officers were: Mary C. Palmer, president; Harriette Rogers, vice president; Clara Hague, recording secretary; Lura Chapin, corresponding secretary; Carrie R. Hapeman, treasurer; Julia Klinck, guard; Eldora Pharr, assistant guard; Carrie McPheeley, journalist; and Hattie Klinck.

At first there were no dues, but later the members were assessed 25 cents. Five members were added the first year. Three years later, there were twenty-two members and printed yearbooks were used for the first time.

The winter of 1897, a committee of members McPheeley, Slater and Hapeman was appointed to make a floor star. For this, a bill was presented for $1.40 for 10 yards of muslin at 70 cents, 12 yards of calico at 60 cents and 10 yards of tape at 10 cents.

During meetings in homes, a wooden star was placed outside the door. This informed would-be callers that P.E.O. was in session. Later, members decided to rent the lodge above the W.H. Craig store to hold meetings.

Carrie Hapeman was president of Chapter N in 1897 and 1898. After being state organizer and vice president, she served as president of Nebraska Grand Chapter (1899-1901) and served as president of Supreme Grand Chapter (1901-1903).

At the Chicago convention in 1899, Carrie presented the installation ceremony suited for local, state and supreme chapters. She also was a member of the committee that wrote the form of proposal blanks used by chapters and the committee that adopted the star ceremony and assisted in the revision of the Constitution. She was a chairman of the committee that wrote the printed invitations to members. She served as the president of Supreme Grand Chapter during its convention in Lincoln in 1903. During her term, P.E.O. grew rapidly in membership and the state Grand Chapters in Colorado, Illinois and Kansas were organized. She accomplished much before her death at age 55.

Two members of Chapter N were Carrie's nieces—Ruth Russell Taylor, a 52-year member, and Veva Russell, chapter historian who joined Chapter Eternal in 1993 at the age of 108. She was a 68-year member.

Chapter N's Harriett M. Clearman served as treasurer of Nebraska Grand Chapter from 1907-1909 and as second vice president from 1909-1910.

On permanent loan from Chapter N to the Nebraska State Chapter Historical collection are the wooden star, the floor star and a picture of Carrie Hapeman. Items sent to the Memorial Library at Mount Pleasant include an enlarged picture of Carrie mounted in a leather portfolio and a plate which she painted. Chapter N received the plate at a convention for having the best treasurer's report for the year.

When Chapter N celebrated its fiftieth anniversary on March 10, 1945, Clara Hague was the only remaining charter member. Chapter N's Diamond Jubilee was celebrated March 17, 1970, with Sheila Shreck, the Nebraska State Chapter president, as honored guest. In March 1995 Chapter N celebrated 100 years.

Philanthropic projects have been important in the history of Chapter N. In 1903 members were eager to assist in the P.E.O. Educational Loan Fund and assessed fines of five cents for tardiness, ten cents for being absent, and encouraged a freewill contribution to the "mite box" at each meeting. Recently, to raise money for P.E.O. projects, Chapter N has held a garage sale and sold pecans to members and the public. Currently Chapter N holds an annual auction of boutique items and baked goods before Christmas. Also at each meeting members can contribute to a brag box when they have significant events in their lives to share. In addition to supporting various P.E.O. projects, Chapter N annually donates to a local philanthropic project. Donations are collected from our members and a community project is selected to receive these funds.

In 1996 Chapter N embarked on an ambitious project to sell afghans featuring historical sites in our county. This successful project resulted in donations to the Nebraska P.E.O. Home and many other P.E.O. projects. This was also the impetus to start an annual college scholarship given to a local high school senior girl. This enables Chapter N to be an educational influence in our community.

CHAPTER N'S ACTIVE MEMBERSHIP IS 54; TOTAL ENROLLMENT IS 314

★

CHAPTER O GENEVA
ORGANIZED MAY 2, 1895
BY KATHARINE HARTIGAN

P.E.O. Chapter O was organized with the help of Miss Katharine Hartigan (Gobel) on May 2, 1895. The seven charter members were Hattie Edgecombe, Fanny Elmore, Luella McKelvey, Addie Sexton, Mary Brereton, Blanche Stewart, and Mattie Cox.

In June 1902, fifty delegates attended the 13th convention of the Nebraska Grand Chapter, hosted by Chapter O in Geneva. Hattie Little served the Nebraska Grand Chapter as treasurer and recording secretary and later as president of the Nebraska delegation to Supreme Chapter Convention in Brookfield, Missouri. She also served as recording secretary for Supreme Chapter from 1911 to 1913.

Chapter O is excited to have initiated ten fourth-generation members from three local families. We are very proud of our six Golden Girls: Jean Ashby, Kathryn Ashby, Suzanne Brinkman, Dorothy Brooke, Maria Waring, and Beth Wilkins.

On May 2, 1995, Chapter O celebrated its 100th birthday! Members dressed in formal period attire for a dinner and meeting that were held at Janice Ashby's turn-of-the-century home.

A highlight in 1997 was to have Suzanne Shaw serve as Nebraska State Chapter's ELF chairman. Chapter O's Deb Bennet served as president of Reciprocity Group XI in 2012.

Chapter O continues to financially support all of the P.E.O. projects. We have also adopted Cottey College students and Nebraska P.E.O. Home residents by sending care packages and cards. Three daughters of our members have attended Cottey College. We have supported our community by contributing to the renovation of the Geneva Library, helping with the library secret garden, the elementary playground, and other local projects.

Through the years, Chapter O has provided financial assistance to several young women through ELF loans and PCE grants. In 1994 Stacy Nichols received the P.E.O. Scholar Award. In 2012, we sponsored Abby Adkisson as an ELF recipient. Most recently, our nominee Sally Moore became a recipient of the P.E.O. STAR Scholarship. We also nominated Cathi Biba for a P.E.O. Scholar Award, and Erica Yound for the STAR Scholarship.

Since 1978, Chapter O has awarded scholarships to a graduating senior woman from Fillmore County. This scholarship was established through a bequest from the estate of Louise Gibbons, who was a 65-year member.

Our chapter members enjoy getting together for our meetings and for social events. Social activities have included dining at area restaurants, soup suppers, bunco parties, cookie exchanges, Christmas caroling, volunteering at the local Rialto Movie Theater, a basement Husker tailgate party, and wine tasting events.

Throughout the years, Chapter O has held several fundraisers. Those that have been most successful are sales of coffee cakes, frozen cookies, and Fillmore County afghans. The proceeds from our local fundraisers have gone to P.E.O. projects and our local communities. We are a diverse, talented and lively group who are proud to be sisters of P.E.O Chapter O!

Chapter O's active membership is 56; total enrollment is 287

★

Chapter P Bloomington
Organized November 30, 1895
by Carrie McNaughton.

Chapter P, Bloomington was organized on November 30, 1895, with eight members when Bloomington and the surrounding area was a thriving community.

Chapter P honors its founding sisters—Clara Hart, Candace Black, Dr. Ella Sumner, Hanna McGrew, Mary Patterson, Rose Owens, Fanny Tucker and Margaret McGrew. Three of these women held office in Nebraska Grand Chapter: Mary Patterson, second vice president in 1898-1899 and first vice president in 1899-1900; Candace Black, treasurer in 1900-1902; and Rose Owens, corresponding secretary in 1912 and president in 1915. Rose later dimitted to Chapter BN, Omaha, and was treasurer for Supreme Chapter from 1935 to 1947.

Today our Chapter P survives in a much smaller town and despite that factor we are able to function quite well, bringing in new members from the surrounding countryside. There is a loving connection in our twenty-eight resident member base as we meet monthly. We have an average of fourteen members in attendance at our meetings at 6:30PM on Tuesday evening.

We are proud to say we have sponsored many grants consisting of a grand total of $11,950. Also our loan awards add up to total of $36,000. Chapter P also gives a yearly $200 scholarship to a qualifying Franklin High School student. We also are honored to say we have sponsored a member to attend Cottey College. With our support and help and with a two-year $5,000 Nebraska Cottey Scholarship she was able to graduate from the two-year college.

Our membership gives of body and mind to work hard at fundraisers so we can give generously to the projects. Along with the fundraisers we gather socially many times a year to promote goodwill. We serve soup to the elderly, we have Christmas dinners with our BILs, we help serve funerals, and we attend our local Opera House. We also join the Parade of Lights in November, flying our P.E.O. flag to say "come join us." It's common for Chapter P to take part in bake sales that help our funds. Sometimes those are bakeless sales. We have worked together to provide brunches at a Victorian home in our adjoining town. For Founders' Day we invite three other chapters for a luncheon. We have cookie and ice cream socials for our fundraising project. Our P.E.O. sisters' talents help all these gatherings to be fun and profitable.

Virginia Goedeken, Chapter P's most senior member, was initiated March 5, 1946 in Bloomington, Nebraska

Our qualified officers guide and direct our members to provide one of the most highly respected organizations in our county. Chapter P will soon begin its 118th year. In our rural communities with declining population we have a challenge before us. We must find ways to stay on course and continue to grow through the years. Our members consider it an honor to be one of the most promising chapters in our state.

Chapter P's active membership is 32; total enrollment is 194

You cannot step twice into the same waters,
for other waters are continually flowing.
-Heraclitus

Chapter Q Wymore
Organized May 28, 1898
by Clara West

The charter members of Chapter Q were: Laurie M.L. Vance, president; Ada C. Hargrave, vice president; Elizabeth H. Rogers, recording secretary; Sara D. Reuling, corresponding secretary, Lillian E. Sage, treasurer; Harriette C.L. Vance, guard; and Etta Whitmer, chaplain. Chapter Q was organized May 28, 1898, by Clara A. West. During the summer months, meetings were held on Saturday afternoons. In September, meetings were set for alternate Mondays and Monday still is traditionally P.E.O. day with Chapter Q. By 1901 Chapter Q boasted a total membership of thirty-two. The program committee outlined the topics to be divided equally between ancient history and the study of Shakespeare.

As early as 1899, preparation for the initiatory star began and was completed in April of the following year. It has been carefully preserved through the years as a treasured item of our history. It since has been placed with the Nebraska historical items at the P.E.O. International headquarters in Des Moines, Iowa.

During the first year after organization, a book circle was formed. This evolved into a city project. Members canvassed the town for donations of books to form a nucleus for a city reading room; thus, the beginning of the Wymore City Library was helped by Chapter Q.

In 1902 Chapter Q assisted in the organization of Chapter Z, Beatrice. In June of 1903, Chapter Q hosted the Nebraska Grand Chapter convention. It was recorded that there was a "galaxy" of prominent P.E.O. women present, even after the postponing of convention for a week due to high flood waters.

Chapter Q has been honored to furnish one state president, Mrs. Sarah Reuling (1917-1918). Others serving on the state board include Mrs. Laurie Vance and Mrs. Cora McMullen.

Monetary donations to all P.E.O. projects have been given yearly. Five daughters from Chapter Q have attended Cottey College and two women have been sponsored as P.E.O. Educational Loan Fund recipients.

Philanthropic projects have varied throughout the years according to needs. Food and clothing have been donated to the needy and garments have been made for the Child Saving Institute in York.

During the 1940's, the chapter supported war activities by purchase of bonds and contributions to the United Victory Fund and the Red Cross. Food baskets and Christmas cookies are more recent donations during the holidays.

In May 1938, Chapter Q celebrated its 40th anniversary with a luncheon and program. The three living charter members were honored.

Chapter Q's 50th anniversary was celebrated on May 28, 1948, with a tea at the home of Florence Patton. A 50-year pin was presented to Mrs. Eva Lang, Chapter Q's first initiate. Since then numerous sisters have been honored for 50-year membership: Lenore Fritz, Ruth Windle, Edith Neumann, Lena Pirie and Vena Rist. The most recent 50-year members are Clarice Jones and Lucille Irwin.

Some of Chapter Q's successful money-making projects consist of silent auctions, bake sales, galloping teas, 1988 cookbook and "25 cents a dip" salad suppers.

Chapter Q tries to schedule a yearly meeting at the Nebraska P.E.O. Home, with guests of the Home participating and enjoying the meeting and visit. It is a special time to visit residents who might be Chapter Q members and also to tour the Home. In recent years, Chapter Q sisters have chosen a secret sister from the Home and kept in touch with her by correspondence or by sending little specialties of surprise. The members receive special joy in being able to do something for the Home residents. Chapter Q also has held meetings at the Good Samaritan Home for the benefit of a member now residing there.

The lives of Chapter Q members have been enriched by their association with Reciprocity Group VIII and the chapter has been strengthened through this tie. The creation of the centerpieces for the 1991 International Convention was only a small part of a huge project, but there was a feeling of harmony and love as Chapter Q sisters worked together. The feeling was symbolic of the P.E.O. Sisterhood.

CHAPTER Q'S ACTIVE MEMBERSHIP IS 28; TOTAL ENROLLMENT IS 259

★

CHAPTER R CRETE
ORGANIZED SEPTEMBER 9, 1898
BY CLARA WEST
SURRENDERED CHARTER, JUNE 1899

Charter members of Chapter R, Crete were Emma E. Morriss, Maude Hollingshead, Grace B. Vance Funkhouser, Leona W. Hopkins, Maud Hank (or Hauk, or Hawk) Campbell, Mae G. Stelle, Fannie B. Stelle, Hattie Johnson, Josephine Speier, and May Anderson. Later, five other members were taken in.

The chapter existed less than a year. Perhaps too much responsibility came to them too soon. The 1903 *White History* relates that when Alberta Fox, Chapter J, Nelson, was Nebraska Grand Chapter president, it was Chapter J's turn to entertain convention. It seemed difficult for them at this time, and L, Harvard, readily accepted the honor. Later it was changed to Chapter R, Crete, by mutual consent. A few weeks before convention, problems arose in Chapter R, and the convention entertaining once more reverted to Chapter J, Nelson, which rose to the occasion.

Having received a request from Chapter R to disband, Mrs. Fox appointed Lillian Parmele, Maud Cornell and Carrie Hapeman to visit Crete after convention. After careful examination, "it was the unanimous opinion the Nebraska Grand Chapter should accept the return of the charter." (*White History*) Nine members later dimitted to other chapters in Nebraska and elsewhere.

TOTAL ENROLLMENT 15

★

CHAPTER S BROKEN BOW
ORGANIZED APRIL 5, 1899
BY KATE BARBOUR

Chapter S, Broken Bow, was organized on April 5, 1899, through the efforts of Nannie Alexander, a teacher from Chapter I in Wahoo. Charter members were Nellie Humphrey, president; Carrie Willing, vice president; Julie Wilson, recording secretary; Nannie E. Robertson, corresponding secretary; Della Adamson, treasurer; Martha Hunter, chaplain; Mary Beal, guard; Carolyn Salisbury, organist;

and Nannie Alexander. Dues were 25 cents and in 1900, Chapter S had seventeen members.

Chapter S celebrated their 100th anniversary with a luncheon to which all of the state officers were invited.

Five of our sisters have been members for 50 years or more. Chard Hirsch and Ann Keller, 66 years; Sherrill Jones, 61 years; Penny Ashenfelter and Judy Talbot, 50 years.

In June 1904, Chapter S was hostess to convention, at which time Martha Hunter was elected first vice president of Nebraska Grand Chapter. Delegates were guests in the homes of members. In 1950 Edith Melville was elected treasurer of Nebraska State Chapter. At the 1965 state convention, Chapter S presented the model meeting. Chapter S has sent four delegates to Supreme Chapter: Pearl Schneringer in 1939, Marvel Johnson in 1950, and Clarine Dickinson in 1962. In 1971 Jean Wenquist was named delegate to Supreme Chapter, but was unable to attend. Vera Koefoot, member of Chapter GP, Grand Island, served as the delegate. Vera became very active in the years to follow. She was first vice president of International Chapter at the time of her death in 1990. June Steggs is an outstanding member of Chapter S. She was elected state convention chairman in 1978 and served on the executive board through her presidency of Nebraska State Chapter in 1985. From 1987 to 1992, June was a member of the Nebraska P.E.O. Home Board of Trustees and she served four of those years as president. Chapter S is very proud of June's accomplishments and of her service to P.E.O.

Others who have served the state chapter include Kay Norden, Nebraska P.E.O. Home Board of Directors; Diane Whitesel, state chairman of the Nebraska Cottey Scholarship Committee and Marcia Simmons, State Finance and Budget Committee.

Our project recipient was Carol D'Josey, P.E.O. Educational Loan Fund and P.E.O. Program for Continuing Education.

Social meetings of interest have included playing bells at the Methodist Church, visiting Elyria Gardens and lunch, visiting Fox Farms and hayride, visiting Secret Garden and lunch, a visit to the Nebraska P.E.O. Home, a lunch and tour of Runza, Christmas soup social, and winetasting and lunch at Mac's Creek Winery near Lexington.

Some of our fundraisers included a luncheon and style show, a May basket auction, Junk Jaunt (serving rolls and coffee),a bake-less bake sale, our Brag Bag, a Halloween auction, and failure to wear our pin to meeting costs us 50 cents.

Our Chapter has had many projects: cookies for the Bloodmobile, meals for sisters in need, sponsorship of a Cottey College student, gifts for newborns, markers and flowers at the cemetery, cookies for shut-ins and nursing homes and gifts for the Nebraska P.E.O. Home.

The things that make our chapter special are, first and foremost, our sisters. Also, a generous increase in our giving to projects, very good participation in the Green Hornet House Race. We are a welcoming chapter, who share and care and are pleased to have younger sisters.

CHAPTER S'S ACTIVE MEMBERSHIP IS 43; TOTAL ENROLLMENT IS 318

The greatest of these is Love. -1 Corinthians 13

CHAPTER T CLAY CENTER
Organized March 19, 1900
by Kate Barbour

Chapter T was organized on March 19, 1900, by the state organizer, Kate Barbour, assisted by Mrs. L.C. Hurd, both of Chapter L in Harvard. Charter members were Gertrude Spanogle, president, Elizabeth Thompson, vice president, Harriett Moulton, recording secretary, Nettie Gardiner, corresponding secretary, Jennie Harris, treasurer, Elizabeth Clark, guard, Eva Barnett, organist, Lillian Campbell, journalist, Josephine Noble and Hattie Churchill. One of the first meetings was held at the country home of Lillian Campbell, one mile from town. From the minutes: "Those were the good old days when it rained. Such a downpour, all members were forced to stay all night."

Chapter T entertained Nebraska Grand Chapter convention on June 21-22, 1905. Sixty delegates were entertained in P.E.O. homes. Expenses were $27.25 for entertainment, $1.50 for livery, and $44.92 for refreshments served throughout the convention.

Chapter T has celebrated its 50th, 70th and 100th anniversaries. Celebration of the 100th anniversary included three special events. On March 13, 2000, we met in the United Church of Christ Fellowship Hall and honored Wilma Nowka, Lois Swanson, Helen Schroder and Louise Hertel for being P.E.O. members for over 50 years. In Beatrice, at the 2000 Nebraska State P.E.O. Convention, members represented Chapter T as it was honored as one of the state's 100-year chapters. While in Beatrice members toured the Nebraska P.E.O. Home. Then on August 12, 2000, a final celebration was held at Zion Lutheran Church. State President Trish Robertson and State Treasurer Joan Fink, many former members, sisters from neighboring chapters and several BILs all enjoyed an afternoon trip down memory lane.

For many years Chapter T met on two evenings each month, but in 1999 after a two month trial period, members voted to hold our second meeting each month at noon. This has worked out well for us since some members cannot attend noon meetings while others often cannot attend evening meetings and now most are able to participate in at least one meeting each month. The first meeting in January is always our Founders' Day program. It is interesting how different the programs are each year. Silk marguerite bouquets are placed on the graves of Chapter Eternal members each Memorial Day.

State convention reports are given in June. We have reports of our projects at each meeting. Early programs were literary book reviews, articles from magazines and from The P.E.O. Record. Records of World War I years recount activities in Red Cross bandage rolling, sewing and knitting. Today we follow our yearly themes and members are very creative in delivering a great variety of programs. In 2004 Chapter T had a float in Clay Center's 125th birthday parade.

Chapter T takes pride in three initiates who became presidents of state chapters — Helen Swanson Gale, past president of Idaho State Chapter, Emma Sanderson (1957-58) and Terri Ridgway (2012-2013) of Nebraska State Chapter. The chapter hosted the annual meeting of Reciprocity Group XI in 1977 and 2012 when a Chapter T member served as president of that group. Official delegates to Convention of

International Chapter were Laura Cundiff (1997) and Jeanne Briggs (2012).

We continue to support all of the P.E.O. projects as well as several local projects. Chapter T has sponsored applicants for the STAR scholarship each year and encouraged a participant in the 2004 Cottey College Sciencescape. Three ELF loans given to applicants sponsored by Chapter T were well used and repaid over the years. Chapter T has had two graduates and two one-year students of Cottey College. We have donated to the Clay Center Scholarship fund, the Clay County Giving Tree at Christmas and to a family with a parent in Iraq. Some of our fundraisers include selling pecans and wild rice; cookie and cupcake sales; silent auctions; loose change bank; a basket of goodies to a member who enjoyed the goodies, then put $5 into the fund and refilled the basket to pass it on to another sister; and recently added the selling of Miracle Cloths.

We have three social meetings a year with various themes. Family picnics in summer, Mystery Dinner Theater, fun nights with the BILs, annual Christmas Party, etc. Chapter T sends a box of goodies each spring to a Cottey College student and often takes cookies, etc. to the Nebraska P.E.O. Home in Beatrice. In December 2010 several members went to the Home to celebrate resident Helen Schroder's 70 years in P.E.O. Through the years Chapter T has also celebrated with Wilma Nowka (70-year member), Louise Hertel (60 years), and 50-year members Clarice Tice, Gladys Kinyoun, Roberta Kissinger, Deanna Buescher, Linda Redline and Genevieve Northrop. One 70-year member and four 50-year members are still in Chapter T.

CHAPTER T'S ACTIVE MEMBERSHIP IS 34; TOTAL ENROLLMENT IS 227

★

CHAPTER U BUTTE
ORGANIZED JUNE 30, 1900
BY JENNIE BURCH
DISBANDED MAY 31, 1997

In the summer of 1899, Emma A. Warner traveled to Iowa to visit her sister, who happened to be a P.E.O. Emma learned something of the objects of the organization and was impressed. She also learned that future chapters might be limited to towns of a population of at least 1000, so upon her return home she immediately made plans for realizing her hopes for a P.E.O. chapter in Butte. She interested seven close friends and with the help of the organizer, Jennie Burch, Chapter U was born. The charter was signed by Carrie M. Chapman, Grand Chapter president and Mary Johnson Axtell, Grand Chapter recording secretary, on June 13, 1901.

Charter members were Emma A. Warner, president; Emma Meholin, vice president; Fannie Goble, recording secretary; Rose Sinclair, corresponding secretary; Clara Spores, treasurer; Hattie L. Maxam, guard; Minnie Burson, chaplain.

In the early years of the century, much less entertainment was available, so a great deal of thought and energy went into planning for P.E.O. There was never any lack of activity, and the early minutes abound with accounts of social as well as business affairs. There were musicals, original skits, innovative parties, literary gatherings, fundraisers, dinners, bazaars and many activities which also included the BILs.

Chapter U supported all P.E.O. interests and projects throughout the years. Seventeen girls have benefited from the P.E.O. Educational Loan Fund, and these loans have been repaid promptly. For many years, the chapter sponsored a spring tea or coke party for junior and senior high school girls and their teachers to acquaint them with the Cottey College material.

In addition to its faithful support of P.E.O. projects, the chapter has contributed to many local needs and community charities, such as getting a water supply into an early schoolhouse and starting the first city library in 1930.

In the early years the chapter sponsored an annual party for all P.E.O. mothers and all mothers over 60. The tradition continued with the annual candlelight tea and entertainment for all the mothers and older ladies at the Butte Nursing Home.

Chapter U brought many treasured memories and friendships to Butte, and gave not only loyal support to P.E.O. itself but also generous service to the community. Chapter U was disbanded May 31, 1997.

TOTAL ENROLLMENT 113

★

CHAPTER V LINCOLN
ORIGINALLY UNIVERSITY PLACE ORGANIZED NOVEMBER 16, 1900
BY JENNIE BURCH

Chapter V was organized November 16, 1900, in University Place, (now Lincoln) Nebraska. Charter members were: Julia Green, Alice Shepherd, Etta Brooks, Marie Fordyce, Alma LeHew, Ina LeHew, Iva Howard Kirk, Abbie C. Burns, Blanche Alabaster, Sara Hall Warfield, Ella M. Hursey, Ruby Lovejoy, and Stella O'Neill. The original group included women who were homemakers and women who were employed outside their homes. The initiation fee was $3 and dues were 50 cents. Dues were raised to $2.50 in 1913.

The meetings were held on the first and third Tuesdays at 7:30 pm. The first program was on American composers and the total refreshment cost was $1.80. Other early programs were devoted to talks about literary figures; many were musical including vocal and violin solos and even a whistling solo.

In 1902 each member was assessed ten cents for yearbooks, and later a fine of ten cents was imposed if one was absent from a meeting, (excuses included being ill, traveling out of town or doing charity work.)

Chapter V received an award recognizing their help during war years.

Members bought sugar lumps for meetings to help with rationing. Refreshments were eliminated temporarily and the hostess put $1 into the Soldiers' Fund. The opening ode was dispensed with in favor of singing patriotic songs. Hundreds of cookies were donated to the USO. P.E.O. sisters located temporarily in Lincoln during the war were accepted as "permanent guests" who desired to assume responsibility while living here. In 1942 a Defense Committee was formed. The members purchased bonds, did Red Cross sewing and acted as civil defense volunteers. Some meetings were devoted to rolling bandages.

Philanthropy and volunteerism played an important role in the early history of Chapter V. Members gave gowns, dresses and shoes to a family of children to prepare them for the orthopedic hospital. They gave a boy clothes and paid tuition for him to attend night school at the YMCA. One member donated $4 so that a family could have a fifty-cent roast each week for eight weeks. Members made many visits to the detention home, juvenile court and the orthopedic hospital. In 1914 the chapter passed a resolution to limit refreshments to three solids and a liquid and if the hostess did not abide by this rule, she would be fined fifty cents!

In the early years Chapter V members have done many things to add interest to their meetings. Roll call has been answered by members reciting quotes from Shakespeare, women of the hour, Nebraska birds and flowers, naming a recent book read (with summary) and the meaning of P.E.O. to each sister.

Unlike our charter members, today's members live in all parts of the city of Lincoln. We continue the tradition started 100 years ago by continuing to volunteer in our churches, schools, museums and many other organizations vital to the community. We support our P.E.O. projects. Chapter V has sponsored women for various P.E.O. scholarships and we continue to "adopt "a Cottey student.

Chapter V has continued to have programs that show a varied interest in our community and our world and each other. We have had programs that share our individual histories, and programs that help keep us safe in our world today.

Chapter V continues to grow because its membership is still made up of interesting women from a variety of backgrounds, careers and ages. Our members include homemakers, an ordained minister, teachers, university professors and administrators, a librarian, a missionary, women working in different branches of government and many in the field of business. In deference to our changing society, Chapter V has recently dispensed with our annual BIL party in favor of our annual "Picnic at the Farm." Each member is encouraged to bring a guest which allows for an evening of fun and inclusivity.

At the start of our second century Chapter V continues to strive to be as current today as it was for our founding mothers.

To keep us connected to each other and our past we have implemented some fun new changes. We now have a technology committee to keep us current on the latest ways of keeping in touch with each other. The Daisy Chain is published and emailed or hard copies mailed insuring that all our sisters know all the latest news from Chapter V. Topics developed by our fellowship committee that require short answers have provided us with some fun surprises about each other. A memorial from our earliest chapter members is read at each meeting and keeps us in touch with our history. We continue to support the Nebraska P.E.O. Home with bingo prizes and having occasional meetings and tours at the

Home. Basket parties, participation in the Lincoln Roundtable Cake Ball, and letters requesting gifts have helped us fundraise for our P.E.O. projects.

Two gifts in honor and memory of Chapter V sisters totaling more than $60,000 have been given to the P.E.O. Foundation.

As we continue into our second century we continue to follow the star and ideals of P.E.O. to ensure that Chapter V will continue to be a vital part of our community.

CHAPTER V'S ACTIVE MEMBERSHIP IS 48; TOTAL ENROLLMENT IS 442

★

CHAPTER W BLUE HILL
ORGANIZED APRIL 18, 1901
BY JENNIE BURCH

Chapter W of Blue Hill was organized on April 18, 1901, by Jennie Burch, state organizer from South Omaha. Charter members were Maude Beever, Josie Draper, Letha Frahm, Mame Garrison, Stephanie Martin, Maude Pope, Lena Walters and Hattie Whitten.

Chapter W still has the chapter's first secretary's book.

In June of 1906, Chapter W hosted Nebraska P.E.O. Grand Chapter for a total cost of $131.28 for 90 women. Preliminary suggestions for the establishment of the P.E.O. Educational Loan Fund were mentioned during the 1906 state convention in Blue Hill.

Chapter W is proud of its achievements. Local projects have included assisting women to obtain loans from the P.E.O. Educational Loan Fund, obtain grants from the P.E.O. Program for Continuing Education, and furnishing equipment for the Home Economics Department at Blue Hill Community School.

A local scholarship is given annually for a graduating senior girl. This scholarship was established in 1992 and continues today. Fundraisers such as bake sales and a garage sale helped to begin the fund for the scholarship.

Chapter anniversaries are celebrated each year by a salad supper, which includes the traditional birthday cake. For the 50th anniversary in 1951, nearby chapters were invited to the celebration which was held in the United Methodist Church. The 75th anniversary celebration was at Ash Hollow Country Club and the 90th anniversary celebration took place at the new Blue Hill Community/ Senior Center with a catered dinner. During the June 2000 state P.E.O. Convention at Beatrice, Chapter W was honored for their 100th anniversary. Our sister and member Ellen Jones was honored as a Chapter W P.E.O. member for 65 years.

Although all members are special, one of Chapter W's guiding stars was Letha Frahm, a charter member. She faithfully kept a record of chapter anecdotes and activities. A play written by Letha was presented at the 50th anniversary celebration. The play recalled the days previous to and the day of one's initiation into P.E.O. Another shining star was Ellen Jones, a Chapter W P.E.O. member for over 78 years, who became a member in 1934. She passed away May 2013 at the age of 100.

CHAPTER W'S ACTIVE MEMBERSHIP IS 21; TOTAL ENROLLMENT IS 229

Chapter X McCook
Organized November 20, 1901
by Jennie Burch

Chapter X, McCook, was organized November 20, 1901, by Jennie Burch. Five P.E.O.s from different towns became charter members by dimit: Anna Schobel, Nell Ebert, Ida White, Elizabeth Thompson and Cecelia Gorby. There were three initiates: Harriet Willetts, Mabel Wilcox and Ellie Leonard. Anna Schobel served as the first president. In 1904, Ellie Leonard (later Mrs. George Norris) served as president and has the distinction of becoming the oldest charter member before her death in 1972 at age ninety-eight.

P.E.O. has special emphasis on philanthropy and education and Chapter X is proud to have sponsored between 20 and 25 women for the P.E.O. Educational Loan Fund. Early philanthropies included such things as sewing layettes for needy infants, filling and distributing food baskets, giving money to provide milk in the schools and donating jams and jellies to the school lunch program.

During World War II, members gave much of their time and talent working for the Red Cross, rolling surgical bandages and working in the servicemen's canteen. While these tasks sometimes interfered with P.E.O. duties, the chapter carried on with meetings, initiations and the presentation of interesting programs. Mrs. Norris gave one on the atomic bomb.

In April of 1946, Chapter X assisted in the organization of a second chapter, FA, in McCook. Five Chapter X sisters dimitted to Chapter FA. Again in 1974, Chapter X assisted in the organization of another chapter in McCook, Chapter GY. Seven members dimitted to the new chapter. Chapter X enjoys great fellowship with their sister chapters. They enjoy meeting together on Founders' Day for dinner and a program.

Contributing to P.E.O. projects has been important to Chapter X. Their favorite fundraiser, which began in 1950, is the annual harvest sale—an auction of baked goods, crafts, garden produce, etc. When Chapter X wants to honor or memorialize a member, or raise money for a special Nebraska P.E.O. Home benefit, garage sales have been popular and successful. We have also raised money by filling baskets with special items and passing them between sisters for their enjoyment, monetary donation and refilling for the next sister.

Chapter X first entertained Grand Chapter in 1907. Subsequently, Chapter X has hosted two other state conventions as members of Reciprocity Group I. Chapter X boasts two presidents of Nebraska State Chapter—Flora Stevens in 1956-57 and Marion Larmon in 1985-86.

While some traditions have faded, others remain year after year. Favorites are decorating sisters' graves on Memorial Day, honoring long time members and taking meals to bereaved members and members who have new babies. Annually we enjoy getting together for a chapter Christmas social and sharing in a cookie exchange. We usually have enough to share with each sister in attendance and then create plates for those sisters who are not able to get out as often. The past few years we have enjoyed taking an evening to prepare and serve a community supper at a local church to those in our area who are less fortunate. We have enjoyed adopting a Cottey College girl each year and sending her a small gift after Christmas.

Chapter X is proud of each of its sisters. Together they have grieved, celebrated and strengthened the bonds begun for them by their eight charter members 114 years ago.

CHAPTER X'S ACTIVE MEMBERSHIP IS 44; TOTAL ENROLLMENT IS 382

★

CHAPTER Y RED CLOUD
ORGANIZED JANUARY 10, 1902
BY JENNIE BURCH

When Jessie Kellogg of Red Cloud attended the University of Nebraska at Lincoln, she met several girls who were P.E.O.s. She was so impressed with their idealism that she wanted her friends in Red Cloud to have this same inspiration. After a long chain of influence and circumstances, Jessie Kellogg selected seven other young women about twenty years of age to be charter members of a P.E.O. chapter in Red Cloud. The task was easier because they had been intrigued by the mystery of P.E.O. and by the pin worn by a popular high school teacher, Miss Mitalda McClelland, a P.E.O. from Bloomington.

Mrs. Jennie Burch, organizer, met with eight girls at the home of Mrs. LeRoy Tait to organize Chapter Y. Officers elected were Jessie Kellogg, president; Florence Cotting, vice president; Jessie Ducker, corresponding secretary; Grace Stonebreaker, recording secretary; Jessica Cather, treasurer. The president appointed Grace Tait as chaplain and assistant guard and Lois Pope as journalist. Gertrude Coon was appointed guard.

Dues of ten cents a month were levied to pay all expenses. Members presented programs of literature and music. The boys often played Whist with them after meetings and attended various parties. In 1907, the girls initiated seventeen BILs. As an early custom, Chapter Y gave P.E.O. spoons to members when they married and to new babies of members.

Red Cloud entertained the nineteenth annual state convention in 1908. Miss Ella Cook was president of Chapter Y. Delegates from 45 of the 50 chapters came by train. They required a baggage car to hold the trunks and luggage accompanying the 75 ladies of the "petticoat, parasol and plume" period! The members made money for this convention by having a recital, a bazaar in Mr. Bomford's store, an ice cream social, a pastry sale at Chautauqua, and a cake sale.

The 25th anniversary of Chapter Y was celebrated with an outstanding party at the home of Mabel Morhart. Three charter members attended.

Forty members celebrated the 50th anniversary banquet dinner. Charter members attending were Jessie Kellogg and Gertrude Coon of Red Cloud, Florence Cotting Mitchell of Denver, Colorado, and Jessica Cather Auld of Palo Alto, California.

A progressive dinner with BILs marked the 75th anniversary celebration. Chapter Y continues to observe the birthday of its organization every January.

In January of 2002 our Chapter's 100th anniversary was noted during our meeting. After the meeting, birthday cake and ice cream was served and the members sang Happy Birthday. At a later date, we took a trip to the local nursing home and had a group picture taken of chapter members. In October of that year, we had an anniversary banquet at the Catholic Church Parish Hall, with our BILs and we also had a BIL initiation with some of our new members' husbands. A good time was had by all.

Chapter Y annually serves a meal at the Willa Cather Spring Conference. This productive money making project allows the chapter to be very generous in its contributions to the various P.E.O. projects.

Through the years, Chapter Y has been able to sponsor women through the P.E.O. Educational Loan Fund and recruit young women from the area to attend Cottey College. Recently, the chapter initiated a scholarship to be given annually to a graduate of area schools to begin her educational opportunities beyond high school.

Each member is allowed to choose her own topic, with the exception of the Founders' Day program, which reveals the depth of unique talents and interests of Chapter Y.

CHAPTER Y'S ACTIVE MEMBERSHIP IS 48; TOTAL ENROLLMENT IS 245

★

Chapter Z Beatrice
Organized March 7, 1902
by Jennie Burch

Chapter Z was organized at the home of Helen M. Drake in Beatrice. Flora Bradley, Chapter F, Iowa, took the initiative in organizing the new chapter of six dimitted members and six initiates. Chapter Q, Wymore, assisted in the organization of Chapter Z. Charter members were Flora Bradley, president; Laura Wemple, vice president; Martha Quien, recording secretary; Mattie Cox, chaplain; Lula Beeler and Lillian Sage. Initiates were Helen Drake, corresponding secretary; Minnie Davis Ladd, treasurer; Elizabeth Kidd, guard; Josephine Gilliland, Carrie Harden, and Floretta Beeson.

Chapter Z celebrated its 100th anniversary on March 15, 2002, with a festive birthday party and program, attended by twenty-two members and five guests.

Annie Kyd was the first member of Chapter Z to serve on the Nebraska Grand Chapter board. She served as corresponding secretary, 1906-1908. Chapter Z has had four state presidents: Helen Drake, 1911-1912; Elizabeth Robertson, 1921-1922; Josephine G. Waddell, 1933-34; and Helen Noble, 1966-67. Helen Drake served as president of Supreme Chapter 1915-1917.

Chapter Z member Margaret Waddell Peters was instrumental in organizing Georgia State Chapter of P.E.O. Margaret received the Georgia state charter at Supreme Convention in Vancouver, British Columbia, in 1953. She entered Chapter Eternal in 1995.

In June 1909, Chapter Z hosted its first convention of Nebraska Grand Chapter. Again in the years 1928, 1961, and 2000, the state convention was held in Beatrice.

In March 1962, Elizabeth C. Robertson Hall was dedicated at Cottey College. Mrs. Robertson's daughter, Jane Robertson Layman, of Chapter Z, shared generously in its construction as a beautiful memorial to her mother.

A very important event in Chapter Z's history was the gift of the beautiful Nebraska P.E.O. Home in 1937 by Chapter Z member Martha Elliott and her husband, Mr. J. Stewart Elliott. All Nebraska P.E.O.s are indebted to them for their generosity. Elizabeth Robertson was chairman of the remodeling committee and represented Chapter Z in the presentation of the home to the state organization. The dedication ceremony took place May 25, 1938, and was attended by many P.E.O. dignitaries and a crowd of nearly 1,500. Chapter Z has continued to cherish and support the Home through gifts, through its "adopt-a-resident" program, and by visiting its residents and helping with activities such as bingo. Chapter Z holds a meeting in the Home at least once a year, which is always eagerly attended by our members.

Thirteen members of Chapter Z became the nucleus of Chapter FM, which was organized in 1951. Chapter Z enjoys a close relationship with FM, and traditionally celebrates Founders' Day with them at a luncheon and program. In 2008, we established a joint scholarship with FM which is now given annually to a local graduating high school senior girl.

Chapter Z is proud to have sponsored twelve women who received the P.E.O. Educational Loan Fund, four women who received P.E.O. Program for Continuing Education grants, and two women who were given Chapter Z Cottey Scholarships. We have also sponsored two young women who were selected for the STAR Scholarship. We recently initiated a P.E.O. International Peace Scholarship recipient into our chapter.

Chapter Z has always given generously to the P.E.O. projects. Our main fundraiser for many years has been a lively craft and bake auction, which our members look forward to each fall. In 2013, we raised over $2,000 at this auction, which was split among the projects and the Nebraska P.E.O. Home. Additional fundraising activities over the years have included the sale of fruitcakes, brooms, and packaged pecans.

Our membership is comprised of women across several generations, who enjoy a close bond of friendship and a common goal of supporting women in their educational needs. Our meetings are blessed with interesting and original programs (and delicious desserts!), and the room is always filled with laughter, chatter, and the enjoyment of our sisters' company.

CHAPTER Z'S ACTIVE MEMBERSHIP IS 62; TOTAL ENROLLMENT IS 393

Before me, even as behind, God is, and all is well.
-John Greenleaf Whittier

Chapter AA Edgar
Organized March 5, 1902
by Jennie Burch

On the evening of March 5, 1902, a group of ladies met at the home of Mrs. Jessie R. Coons for the purpose of organizing a P.E.O. chapter. Mrs. Jennie Allen Burch, state organizer and member of Chapter M, South Omaha, presided, and Chapter AA, Edgar, was formed with seven charter members. They were: Jessie R. Coons, Lucy Lenfest, Lottie McNally, Pearl Christy Hill, Amelia Asby Hazlett, Emma Donahue Taylor and Viola Kirk. Meetings were held on the first and third Monday evenings of the month.

In 1910 Chapter AA entertained the convention of Nebraska Grand Chapter. Plans were made years ahead for raising money. All of the members of Chapter AA made marguerites in streamers to decorate the Presbyterian Church where the convention was held. Every member's spare moments were given to making flowers all winter. The double doors at the entrance, the whole ceiling, the front of the church, windows, etc. were draped with marguerites. Chapter AA put on a model meeting and each member had a house full of guests. There were about one hundred in attendance and the local hotel served the meals.

On March 5, 1952, Chapter AA celebrated its 50th year. The Woman's Club building was beautifully decorated and a large birthday cake had a prominent place in the center of the room. The one o'clock luncheon was enjoyed by twenty-three members and out-of-town guests. Honored were charter members Pearl Christy Hill, Jessie R. Coons and Lucy Lenfest Livingston, vice president of Nebraska State Chapter.

May 22, 1961. Mothers and daughters of Chapter AA who were officers at the same time. Mothers: Alta Swanson, Stella Organ, Mildred Kollman. Daughters: Bettie Swanson Merrill, Lela Organ Hansen and Betty Kollman Koontz.

Chapter AA celebrated their 80th anniversary at the Church of the Plains on March 5, 1982. Special guests were State President Bernice Zajicek and Second Vice President Julia McDougal. Other guests were sisters from Chapter J, Nelson; Chapter L, Harvard; Chapter T, Clay Center; and Chapter BH, Sutton.

Chapter AA became the 55th chapter in Nebraska to become a Golden Anniversary Chapter supporting Cottey College in January 1984. In 1989 the chapter gave its first scholarship to a graduating senior girl in the area. In 1991 the amount of the scholarship was increased.

The 90th year of Chapter AA was observed on a regular meeting day with a luncheon at the Christian Church on March 5, 1992. During that summer a friendship basket was circulated and the contributions were used to purchase trees for the cemetery in honor of Chapter AA's sisters in Chapter Eternal.

Chapter AA celebrated 100 years of sisterhood in 2002 with the production of a commemorative porcelain plate painted by a local china painter, Ione Lipovsky. It was available for all Chapter AA sisters to grace their homes and china cabinets. The chapter sisters also arranged for a special luncheon celebration at the Italian restaurant, *Mama Mia's*, in Hastings to celebrate this significant anniversary.

The 110th year of Chapter AA sisterhood was celebrated to the day on March 5th, 2012, at the home of Mary Crumbliss with a birthday cake and ice cream. This was our annual March chapter dinner with election and installation—a very fitting anniversary setting.

Chapter AA is extremely proud of the strong connection to Cottey College that we have developed over the years. Sister Pam Shuck has very ably served on the state Cottey College Committee and the Nebraska Cottey College Scholarship Committee. Sisters from our chapter who have graduated from Cottey College include Celia Merrill Hunter (class of 1934 and now deceased); LuluBelle Wilson Loehr (class of 1954); Nancy Graham Hunt (class of 1964) and Breanna Shuck Elting (class of 2010).

Although the world is an ever-changing one, Chapter AA remains united in the ideals of P.E.O., as the Founders dreamed, with a strong commitment to our state and International philanthropies.

CHAPTER AA'S ACTIVE MEMBERSHIP IS 32; TOTAL ENROLLMENT IS 192

★

CHAPTER AB CENTRAL CITY
ORGANIZED MARCH 20, 1902
BY JENNIE BURCH

Chapter AB, Central City, Nebraska, celebrated its 100th anniversary March 23, 2002, with a brunch at the Lincoln Manor restaurant, original site of the organizing charter. We were honored to have in attendance Joyce Goff, past president of Nebraska State Chapter. Joyce later went on to serve as president of International Chapter in 2003-2005. Chapter AB was organized March 20, 1902, with the initiation of fourteen members at a meeting in the Schiller Hotel. On that day, the infamous Carrie Nation was in town on one of her tours and burst into the room thinking this gathering was to honor her. Much to her dismay she was told otherwise and this remains a source of amusement to the group to this day.

Chapter AB's charter members were: Florence Thompson, president;

Minnie Muirhead, vice president; Ada Tyndale, recording secretary; Margaret Anderson, corresponding secretary; Addie Schiller, treasurer; Bettie Webster, Marion Edna Hord, Grace Yungblut, Alice King, Olive Ayers, Mary Bissell, Daisy Nettleton, Frank Kelley, and Helen Burgess. The organizer was Jennie Burch of Omaha. All charter members were initiated on the date of organization except Mrs. Muirhead, who dimitted from Iowa, Chapter F.

In 1911 Central City hosted the convention of Nebraska Grand Chapter. Eva McEndree was serving as treasurer of Nebraska Grand Chapter when she moved from the state and Addie Schiller of Chapter AB was appointed to fill her vacancy, serving from September 1911 until 1913. Chapter AB's Kathryn Kerr White served Nebraska State Chapter through all the offices from 1964 to her presidency in 1970-71.

Chapter AB has supported P.E.O. projects generously through the years. In addition to the STAR Scholarship we also offer a local scholarship for a deserving young woman from our community. For fundraising Chapter AB has sponsored an annual bridge luncheon as well as the selling of pecans, silent auctions, bake sales, and selling afghans featuring local landmarks. Chapter AB has sponsored women for the P.E.O. Educational Loan Fund and the P.E.O. Program for Continuing Education grant. Four women have attended Cottey College. Dr. Sara Brandes Crook, who was initiated into Chapter AB, was a P.E.O. Scholar Award recipient the first year of that new project in 1991.

Our chapter is rich in tradition. In 2013 our membership included one 60-year member and four 50-year members. Humorous episodes have dotted Chapter AB's history, beginning with that first meeting when Carrie Nation crashed the party. Another from early days was the horse and buggy tip-over with Central City sisters on their way to a meeting in Archer, ten miles away. When a member or spouse of a member is deceased, our chapter president contacts the family to see how we can be of practical help in a loving way. A meal is usually brought in to serve that purpose. On occasion the P.E.O. memorial service has been given at a funeral of a sister if a family wishes it.

Our meeting programs are varied and given by members or guest speakers. We include social activities as well as informational programs to bring a balance to our chapter life. Special times have included BIL parties, our annual Christmas tea and other outings.

Chapter AB continues the legacy of Nebraska P.E.O.

Chapter AB's active membership is 79; total enrollment is 300

★

Chapter AC Aurora
Organized April 16, 1902
by Jennie Burch

Chapter AC was organized in 1902. Charter members were: Carrie Peterson, president; Margaret Bell, vice president; Eleanor Rodgers, recording secretary; Alice Green, treasurer; Sarah Hart, corresponding secretary; Jean Shuman, chaplain; Julia Hainer, journalist; Maude Beamer, guard; Nelle Moore and Eloise Alden. They voted to limit their membership to sixteen members. These early sisters were a talented group. They sang arias and duets, played sonatas and concertos, and gave poetry readings and original dramas. They gave lessons on a variety of topics and also gave five-course dinners. Is it any wonder their bylaws stated "business to be conducted only every other meeting"?

In just five years this fledgling chapter sent its first president, Carrie M. Peterson, off to be the 15th president of Supreme Chapter after she had served as president of Nebraska Grand Chapter, 1904-06.

Soon came the war years. Culture and social events turned to patriotism and Red Cross sewing. About this time a spirit of conservatism seemed to grip our sisters. They voted to endorse movements against tight skirts and in support of movie censorship.

Chapter AC has always been strongly philanthropic. In the post war years our chapter undertook charitable and educational projects. During the depression, our sisters, in spite of their own financial hardships, sponsored many other people in Aurora with their generosity.

In addition to yearly contributions to the P.E.O. projects, the Nebraska P.E.O. Home, the Nebraska Suite at Cottey, the local Ministerial Association, and to the local elementary school, the chapter was a Cottey Anniversary Chapter, donating $50 per member to the Cottey College Endowment Fund and $100 to the Nebraska P.E.O. Home during renovations and other improvement projects. A $500 donation was made to the Cottey College music department in memory of a member.

The Mae Gunnerson Scholarship, the result of a bequest from a past member, has been awarded each year to a local student. Chapter AC has sponsored several PCE and ELF recipients.

Through the years Chapter AC has participated in hosting several convention functions. The 23rd annual convention of the Nebraska State Chapter enjoyed the hospitality of Chapter AC. We have also joined other chapters in hosting Convention of International Chapter, other state conventions, and our own reciprocity group meetings. These opportunities have strengthened personal ties to our P.E.O. sisters.

We have enjoyed membership longevity in Chapter AC. Chapter AC can cite 50, 60, and even 70-year members. In 2002 Chapter AC celebrated its 100th year anniversary. As a special recognition on Memorial Day each year members decorate over fifty graves of Chapter Eternal members in the Aurora cemetery. We have been impacted by the national trend of many members working outside the home. This trend has brought about scheduling changes to suit member needs.

CHAPTER AC'S ACTIVE MEMBERSHIP IS 75; TOTAL ENROLLMENT IS 276

★

CHAPTER AD SEWARD
ORGANIZED APRIL 15, 1902
BY JENNIE BURCH
DISBANDED JUNE 17, 1912

Charter members of Chapter AD in Seward were Edith Stonicker (or Slonecker), Addie Walker, Anna Clark, Della Smith, Edythe Williams, Edna Ruby, Grace Stewart, Alice White-Morton, Grace Barrett-Oaks, Nelle Davis, Gabrielle Palmer, Mayme Anderson, Gertrude Kerrihard-Thomas, Minnie Atkins. All were initiates except Mrs. Atkins who dimitted from Chapter H, Albia, Iowa.

The chapter disbanded in June 1912. Many members later dimitted to other chapters. Nine of Chapter AD's members dimitted to Chapter CC in Seward which was organized in May 1919.

TOTAL ENROLLMENT 29

Chapter AE Hebron
Organized April 23, 1903
by Grace Thomas

Seven women, with faith in God and in each other and hope in the future of P.E.O., organized Chapter AE April 23, 1903, under the guidance of Grace Thomas. The charter members were Mary Shepherd, Belle Hill, Maude Hayes, Estella Bothwell, Laura Mitchell, Edith Rafter and Lana Bozarth.

In 1913 when only ten years old, Chapter AE hosted Nebraska Grand Chapter Convention with 91 delegates present from Nebraska's 54 chapters. This was quite an undertaking for a small town.

The members have answered the growing needs of the community over the years. They organized and ran the Public Library from 1916-1921, then turned it over to the city. During WWII, Chapter AE members made surgical dressings for the Red Cross and worked at the USO.

The P.E.O. projects have been regularly supported and AE has been an achiever chapter. By having "dessert-less" meetings and a gigantic garage sale, the chapter was able to contribute $2,000 to the Cottey Endowment Fund. The chapter has also searched out some deserving recipients for the P.E.O. Educational Loan Funds. We also sponsored a college girl with a scholarship, notes, stamps, "goody baskets" and other small gifts. The most recent support was saving change in a sock. "Sock it to the Projects" was a successful way to increase our giving to all the projects and to give an additional amount to both the Nebraska Cottey Scholarship and the Cottey Bus Trip funds. All projects need money and through the years we have had different methods of getting the funds. At one meeting the members were asked to weigh their purses and pay per pound. Another time they were charged 10 cents for each pair of shoes they had in their closets. We sponsored a Scrapbooking Day and friends were charged to attend. There was a "non-event" wherein sisters gave a $20 donation and enjoyed wine tasting with cheese trays and fellowship. We also made cookie mix jars and sold them at the annual Hebron Christmas Fair. There were monthly gift baskets where everyone would buy chances for 50 cents and then a name would be drawn. We continue to charge $1 for each sister's brag.

The Cottey Chairman represented Cottey College during Career College Night at the local high school. The format for Cottey night always attracts interest. Sandra Hoins has served as the state Cottey College chairman.

At chapter meetings the members learn of many program subjects including writing poetry, discovering the towns in Nebraska with P.E.O. chapters and Nebraska authors.

Chapter AE celebrated its 90th birthday in April 1993. The relationships of our sisters have deepened with time. As the members share with each other, bonds develop and grow stronger. The entire Sisterhood benefits from these bonds.

On April 25th, 1998, Chapter AE played the role of "Big Sister" by participating in the organization of Chapter IQ.

In April 2003, we celebrated our 100th birthday. Members dressed in vintage clothing and enjoyed an "old fashioned meal" using recipes of former members.

For our social meetings we enjoy an annual birthday dinner with Chapter IQ.

We have had a Pinterest Party where we shared appetizers and craft ideas found on Pinterest, as well as a "Fitness Social" where breakfast was served early in the morning and members were invited to walk on the town's new walking trail.

Chapter AE BILs have been anxious to join the sisters at picnics, boating at the lake, or at sit down dinners. Back in the infancy of AE the gentlemen served an eight course dinner complete with a footman, a butler, and even an orchestra!

Although we have many commitments to the International and state levels of P.E.O., we also actively participate in community projects. For example, we decorate the graves of our departed sisters for Memorial Day. We have supported the "Backpack" program at our local school which supplies food to be sent home to needy families for each weekend. The "Relay for Life" is supported by donating gift baskets to be auctioned off for funds to be used in the fight against cancer. Movie theaters are vanishing from our small towns, so our chapter made a generous donation to the "Arts Council of Thayer County" who had adopted the project of "Saving the Majestic," our local theater. The theater has been refurbished and has new digital equipment. This is just another example of P.E.O.s declaring their interest in the arts.

A highlight of the P.E.O. year has been a trip to the Nebraska P.E.O. Home in Beatrice. Sometimes it is to share a meeting or just to take the ladies jams, napkins, stamps or just some good fellowship. Our chapter recently adopted a resident, and she is remembered each month with a card, note, or other small gesture. Some of our members were able to meet with our adopted resident and even got to enjoy a meal with her at the home.

Chapter AE is special because of the leaders we have and the volunteering and love of our members. A perfect example happened in 2013 as the bus en route to Convention of International Chapter in Dallas made a stop in southern Nebraska. Some of our members joined with two other chapters and prepared the sack lunches for the busload of sisters headed to Dallas. This was a nice bonding time for our three chapters.

CHAPTER AE'S ACTIVE MEMBERSHIP IS 33; TOTAL ENROLLMENT IS 285

CHAPTER AF OXFORD
ORGANIZED APRIL 27, 1903
BY GRACE THOMAS
DISBANDED MAY 7, 1980

Chapter AF was organized in an afternoon meeting in the home of Florence Hamilton, sponsor of the chapter. Linna Cone, who served as corresponding secretary, signed first on the charter list, with Florence Hamilton, president, next. Then followed Harriett Humphrey, vice president; Kate Hooper, recording secretary; Ella Lee, journalist; Emma Tomlinson, chaplain; Meta Mackprang, treasurer; and Addie Young, guard. Fannie Ayer was the first initiate.

In the early days, the chapter president carried every book and paper that belonged to the chapter to every meeting in a big tin locked box. Two of the members who were little girls in Oxford in 1903 told of the curiosity with which they looked at that "Pandora's Box."

Chapter AF was mentioned in the 1924 State Proceedings as the first chapter in Nebraska to have memorized the Objects and Aims. Chapter AF sponsored five women for the P.E.O. Educational Loan Fund.

Fifty-year members were honored on their special days. They included (with their year of initiation): Bertha Pettygrove, 1909; Grace Banta, 1909; Mary Hindenach, 1910; Maude Sawyer, 1912; Margaret Sherwood, 1916; Madge Cadwallader, 1918; Jennie Ballard, 1921; and Harriet Heaton, 1923.

Chapter AF showed special interest in the sisters in the Nebraska P.E.O. Home and remembered each of them on their birthdays and other special occasions.

Chapter AF was disbanded on May 7, 1980.

TOTAL ENROLLMENT 112

CHAPTER AG FULLERTON
ORGANIZED JUNE 26, 1903
BY GRACE THOMAS

Chapter AG was organized June 26, 1903, by Grace Thomas. Seven initiates and one dimitted member formed the charter list. Officers were: Ella Patton, president; Ellinor Kemp, vice president; Anna Barber, recording secretary; Cora Harris corresponding secretary; Catherine Koch, treasurer; Lillian Spear, chaplain, Olive Mangels, guard. Dimitted member was Ella Prentice from Chapter T. Chapter AG's charter was presented June 8, 1904, during Nebraska Grand Chapter Convention in Broken Bow.

Chapter AG has had many members on state boards and committees, but only one state officer. Ellinor Kemp was treasurer of Nebraska Grand Chapter 1915-1917, and organizer, 1917-1919. She organized six chapters. Concerning her experiences as organizer, she wrote, "I have traveled 5,645 miles in temperatures varying from 25 degrees below zero to 104 degrees above, trains often late, but no matter what the weather or hour, always a smiling P.E.O. sister waiting to welcome me. I visited every chapter in Nebraska and no finer women can be found anywhere." Our current president, Karen Delaney, is presently the P.E.O. STAR Scholarship committee chairman for Nebraska State Chapter.

In June 1915, Nebraska Grand Chapter met in Fullerton, with Rose Owens presiding. Honored guest was Edith Prouty, president of Supreme Chapter; honored members were Helen Drake, organizer of Supreme Chapter, Carrie Peterson, past president of Supreme Chapter; and Ida Johnson and Bertha Clark Hughes, past presidents of Nebraska Grand Chapter. Bernice Tillett was a convention delegate. Convention was held in the then new Presbyterian Church and delegates were housed in private homes.

Rain fell continuously during convention, breaking a Nebraska drought. Humorous stories were told of long skirts trailing in muddy, unpaved streets, and BIL drivers with their cars bogged down while transporting P.E.O.s to and from the train depot. In spite of the rain and mud, a fine convention was reported by delegates and guests.

In 2003, Chapter AG proudly celebrated 100 years of P.E.O. A luncheon and program was held at the Presbyterian Church in Fullerton with many present and past members of the chapter in attendance.

One hundred and twelve years of treasured friendships, loyal and financial support of all P.E.O. projects, involvement, service and financial support of community projects show an earnest desire of members to exemplify P.E.O. ideals. Churches, schools, library, youth groups, senior-citizen organizations, historical societies, arts and music all find P.E.O.s active and loyal. A scholarship is presented to up to two deserving girl graduates of Fullerton High School each May. In 2010 Chapter AG was proud to have nominated a recipient of the P.E.O. STAR Scholarship from Fullerton, a daughter of one of our members. On Memorial Day, each P.E.O. grave in the Fullerton cemetery is decorated with yellow and white flowers, an act of sisterly love. Through the years Chapter AG has sponsored women for the P.E.O. Educational Loan Fund, had a student attend Cottey College and had two members who became residents at the Nebraska P.E.O. Home.

Chapter AG has worked hard to change with the times and busy schedules by varying meeting times so that more members are able to attend. Programs are interesting, educational, fun and interspersed with pleasant social events. BIL parties and fun holiday events are enjoyable. Each year is interesting and challenging with capable dedicated officers. Chapter AG boasts of one 60-year plus member, and six 50-year plus members and 44 Chapter AG stars in Chapter Eternal's sky.

CHAPTER AG'S ACTIVE MEMBERSHIP IS 42; TOTAL ENROLLMENT IS 181

★

Chapter AH Alliance
Organized July 1, 1903
by Grace Thomas

A train whistle blasted throughout the intersection of First and Box Butte in 1888 when the Burlington Railroad began transporting from Alliance. The Iron Horse brought employees and families to Alliance and subsequently the organization of P.E.O. Chapter AH. Lyde S. Kridelbaugh and Belle Coutant, who had been initiated into Chapter H in Holdrege, with an interested friend, Jean Raymond, decided to inquire. Lyde Kridelbaugh wrote to the Nebraska state organizer who gave them approval to proceed slowly and cautiously to draw up a charter list in Alliance.

On July 1, 1903, at 9:30 AM at the Kridelbaugh home located at 614 Laramie, organizer Grace Thomas and eleven charter members held the organizational meeting. Charter members were Lyde S. Kridelbaugh, Belle Coutant, Catherine Hampton, Jean Raymond, Ottie Simonson, Olive Fletcher, Minnie Hall, Kate Harris, Bernice Kridelbaugh (who became Mrs. Bernice Tillett), Corrine McCracken, and Marie Emery. Over time all eleven members became officers and AH has been progressive for over one hundred years.

Chapter AH is immersed in rich history with a myriad of sisters contributing to the longevity of the chapter. Estimable women like Bernice Kridelbaugh Tillett served at local, state, and International levels. She stated, "We belong to our yesterdays, for they make us what we are today, hold the promise of what we will be tomorrow..." Many sisters have held the promise and have contributed time and dedication to our chapter. Jacqueline Irwin, president of Nebraska State Chapter in 2002, reflected, "Serving on the convention committee and the state board were both wonderful experiences. I could not have done it without the love and support of my wonderful sisters in Chapter AH who made it all possible." In 2013, AH sister and state organizer Patti Cowher stated, "The more I become involved in P.E.O., the more I love it. And the more P.E.O.s I meet, the more I grow in love."

Chapter AH - Past State President Jacqueline Irwin with her sister, Cheryl Spurrier (left) and her mother, Dorothy Stull (right)

Chapter AH consistently contributes to P.E.O. philanthropies financially as well as by sponsoring and nurturing young women. We have had recipients for the P.E.O. STAR Scholarship as well as for PCE and ELF. AH has often sponsored IPS recipients, has been a Designated Award Chapter several times, and has achieved status as a Laureate Chapter for the P.E.O. Scholar Award. In 2013 Chapter AH was recognized for making the largest financial contributions per person to our P.E.O. philanthropies.

We have raised funds in many ways to accomplish our goals of contributing to P.E.O. philanthropies. Fundraisers have included silent auctions at Christmas time and selling Kaywos cloths. A long-standing way to increase the coffers and stay informed about sisters' lives outside of P.E.O. is for a sister to "cluck" to the chapter about events in her life, then place a monetary gift into a basket.

We balance fundraising and care of each other through enjoyable socials such as attending Fort Robinson Post Playhouse performances and surprise secret sister dinners. We take food to the family of departed sisters, send cards to the ill and make calls. On Memorial Day departed sisters' graves are decorated with a P.E.O. marker and marguerites.

Chapter AH has supported philanthropic needs such as the backpack food program, assisted our local DOVE chapter, contributed to Jane's Closet, the local program benefiting cancer patients, and Jaycees Christmas toy drive.

Chapter AH celebrates its past and present. Each year in late January we rotate with local chapters to host a Founders' Day celebration. In 2013 Chapter AH hosted with lunch and a skit, "Sisters in Harmony." A recent enjoyable way to interact with local chapters has been an annual bridge marathon.

Chapter AH on the occasion of their 100th Anniversary June 29, 2003

Marie Nelson, a nearly 80-year member of P.E.O., and International President-elect Joyce Goff chatted at the one hundredth anniversary celebration in 2003.

We have celebrated our milestones throughout the years. For our 50th anniversary Grace Grantham, 1953 recording secretary, wrote, "A group of P.E.O.s dressed in old-fashioned clothes gave a very enlightening program on an old-fashioned meeting." On our 75th anniversary Eda Hempel hosted a morning coffee in her home. Ruth Knight, historian, gave a history of Chapter AH. Alice McCall reported on the 80th celebration, "An open house was held at Jacci Irwin's where all Alliance P.E.O.s were invited to the celebration and to view a quilt display collected from AH members." For the 90th year, Maryetta Lyman hosted a celebration at her home and noted, "Chapter AH was 90 years old this year, so a birthday tea was held. Chapters GC and HS also attended. Since this was AH's 90th year, the chapter donated $90 to each of the projects."

The theme for our centennial celebration was "*A Star in the Window, Time for Tea–One Hundred Years Since 1903.*" The tea table was arranged with the lovely silver service presented to our chapter by Bernice Tillett. Guests from local, state and International levels were greeted, early history was read, and each AH member was presented an ornament-sized china teacup and saucer.

Many amazing women have entered Chapter AH through initiations and dimits. We've been privileged to have ten 50-year members, six 60-year members, one 70-year member and another who was three months short of being a 70-year member and one sister who was four months short of being an 80-year member.

In 2013, six new sisters were initiated bringing our total enrollment to 318 members.

CHAPTER AH'S ACTIVE MEMBERSHIP IS 64; TOTAL ENROLLMENT IS 318

★

CHAPTER AI LINCOLN
ORGANIZED DECEMBER 30, 1903
BY LILLIAN PARMELE

On December 30, 1903, Chapter AI was born in the village of Havelock, located in the northern part of Lincoln. Charter members were Blanche Frantz, president; Gertrude Fulton, vice president; Sylvia Holmstrom, recording secretary; Alta Corey, corresponding secretary; Irma Berlet, treasurer; Clara Kier, chaplain; Mary Hewitt, Clara Ballard, Josephine Barber, Mary Cahill, Lora Ballard and Bessie Rawson. The first initiate was Laura Blume in 1905.

Members often took the trolley to join Chapters K and V for entertainment—including box suppers, bobsled rides, picnics and dominoes. In 1913, Chapter AI records show that a "vote" on the issue of women's suffrage resulted in three yes's and seven no's.

Early records also show that philanthropic activities of Chapter AI included providing food for needy families and aiding World War II efforts through the Red Cross and USO. For over twenty years, Chapter AI entertained several dozen older boys from the Whitehall State Children's Home at a Christmas party.

AI members have traditionally been ready to serve wherever needed. Ethelyn Hermanson Voltz was secretary-treasurer of the Nebraska P.E.O. Home Board for two terms. Sylvia Holmstrom, charter member, designed the cover of The P.E.O. Record which was used beginning in 1919 (see more page 529). She and AI member Elva McFie started Chapter AI's beautiful history book. Irene Johnson is remembered for her leadership as chairman of the P.E.O. Program for Continuing Education for fourteen years (1974-1988) which resulted in Chapter AI's sponsorship of eleven women. These four sisters, now in Chapter Eternal, are remembered for their contributions to P.E.O. Another treasured star, Betty Anderson, whose husband Vic served Nebraska as governor from 1955 to 1959, graced the chapter for nearly five decades.

The first gathering in September is our general fundraiser, which is held in a member's home with a light dinner served. One year each member brought a special pair of shoes and shared the story about why this pair mattered. An ongoing activity is updating a book of members' autobiographies. This book, *Starlight and Marguerites*, is distributed to chapter members and provides us all a chance to know each other a little better.

Chapter AI has historically been active beyond the local chapter. Seven members have served as Lincoln Reciprocity Roundtable president: Mabel Fordyce, 1927, Beryl Black, 1932, Nelle Hickam, 1943, Ethelyn Volz, 1956, Lovell Moser, 1989, Mary Schwaner, 2003, and Donna Marvin, 2012. In 1990, Mary Schwaner wrote and directed the musical program *Avenue of P.E.O. Dreams* for project night at state convention in Lincoln. It was later presented at the 1991 convention of International Chapter in Omaha. (see more on page 579). Gretchen Treadway appeared in *A Star in the Window* at Convention of International Chapter in Seattle, 1997. (see photo "Convention of International Chapter" on page 618).

Chapter AI - 1990 (above); 2012 (below and next page)

Chapter AI - 2012 (above) and 1978 (below)

Our membership has given generously to all of the International P.E.O. projects and we have had much fun creatively raising funds for our donations. Members made beautiful pearl bookmarks, pot scrubbers and dish cloths; a cookbook was started and continues to expand each time we hold a food event.

Over the past twenty years several of our candidates have been awarded P.E.O. loans and scholarships and we take pride in their achievements. Through fundraising we have also been able to contribute to Cottey College and to sponsor a student attending there by providing gift cards and care packages. The Nebraska P.E.O. Home in Beatrice, which we love to visit, also benefits from our donations and care packages.

Each incoming chapter president has chosen a theme, and we strive to meet these new and continuing goals. "Ever Onward," "Live, Love, Laugh and be Happy," and "The Daisy-Chain of Sisterhood - Our Circle of Love," exemplify our activities and meetings. We have had programs with informative speakers, social evenings with BILs, as well as tours of interesting places in Lincoln.

Our chapter has a number of mother-daughter pairs, and is grateful for the influence of our longstanding members. Our Alice Dittman has served Nebraska P.E.O. for more than 66 years, and Pat Beams for 63 years. Serving P.E.O. for 50+ years are Susan Stanley Eno, Betsy Johnson, Portia Reed, and Mary Schwaner. Four active members, Phyllis Beck, Ann Brase, Shirley Larsen, and Helen Moors, have served P.E.O. for over 45 years.

Chapter AI celebrated its centennial in 2003, and in 2013 celebrated its 110th birthday by taking a road trip to the P.E.O. International Headquarters in Des Moines, Iowa. Our anniversary celebration continued with a special luncheon in December at the Country Club of Lincoln. It was a time of remembrance and a chance to look forward to many more successful years of P.E.O. in Chapter AI.

CHAPTER AI'S ACTIVE MEMBERSHIP IS 69; TOTAL ENROLLMENT IS 299

★

CHAPTER AJ FREMONT
ORGANIZED JANUARY 19, 1904
BY GRACE THOMAS

Chapter AJ was organized at the home of Emma Snow on January 19, 1904, by Grace Thomas. Emma Snow, Nellie Theresa Pascoe, Mary Edgerton, Hannah Stephens, Dell Blakeslee, Stella Laird, Daisy Spickard, Ada Hicks and Mary Golden complete the charter list. State Organizer Grace Thomas Nelson was assisted by the state vice president, Mrs. Dillenbacker of York. A few months later, Emma Snow, Nellie Pascoe and Mary Edgerton initiated the first six new members into Chapter AJ.

Emma Snow and Nellie Pascoe had been P.E.O. members in York and Mary Edgerton was a P.E.O. from Iowa. Many of the charter members were teachers. At the first meeting, the first and third Friday were set as the regular times for meetings. We still meet on those days. At an early meeting, the men were initiated as BILs. To show their appreciation, they gave the chapter $20 to pay expenses for a delegate to attend convention in Broken Bow. The P.E.O. dinners were held in the homes of members and were described in the minutes as being "bountiful," "disposing of the dainties," and "serving dinner faultlessly in three courses."

The first dues were $1. There were no official P.E.O. projects then, but assessments of 25 or 50 cents were made to support local projects. In early bylaws, this announcement was made: "The entire order of business shall be passed over before members can enter in friendly conversation." In the spirit of friendly conversation, the Brag Box, later the Good News Box, was proposed in 1996. Members could share their good news by contributing $1. We have continued this for 17 years, but it is now the Brag Bag and is a highlight of our times together. Other fundraisers have been a lunch fee, silent auctions, and P.E.O. T-shirts. One member, a children's book author, has donated a percentage from her books sold to chapter members.

When the P.E.O. Educational Loan Fund started, AJ contributed $17. Years later, 100 percent of our members contributed a dollar each to this project. Our PE.O. Program for Continuing Education committee has been active in recruiting at least ten women since 1995 who were accepted as recipients of the PCE grant. We support the P.E.O. STAR Scholarship by working with the other three chapters in

Fremont. Each chapter recommends a student after considering the applications.

Two AJ members have served Nebraska P.E.O. as state president—Clara Waterhouse in 1920 and Rebecca Lee in 1942. State conventions were held in Fremont in 1917, 1941 and 1955. We co-hosted in Sioux City in 1970 and in 1984 in Blair. Our four Fremont chapters—along with Reciprocity Group VI—hosted the convention in Fremont in 2012.

Chapter AJ helped with establishing three new chapters—CT, North Bend, in 1922; EX, Fremont, in 1943; and GH, Fremont, in 1963 in cooperation with Chapter EX.

A special time at each meeting is devoted to reading from our old minutes of the early 1900s. This is our history.

TLC is an important part of our chapter. We serve dinners at the time of death in a sister's family. We visit, bring flowers, and remember special occasions. We offer rides to meetings. Our membership is diverse—including nine members who have been part of P.E.O. for periods from 53 to 70 years. We have a wide variety of ages, working women, daughters, and a dozen nonresident members. We were honored at the 2012 Nebraska State Convention as the chapter with eight initiates—the most in the state.

CHAPTER AJ'S ACTIVE MEMBERSHIP IS 90; TOTAL ENROLLMENT IS 406

★

CHAPTER AK NORTH PLATTE
ORGANIZED MARCH 25, 1904
BY GRACE THOMAS

In 1904, Teddy Roosevelt was president; and in North Platte, eight women gathered to charter Chapter AK of the P.E.O. Sisterhood. Since that time more than 370 women have shared in Chapter AK. Each of the eight women who signed the 1904 charter was elected to office at the founding meeting. They included Susie Frazier Lucas, president; Clara E. Davis, vice president; Minnie Wilcox, recording secretary; Hestor Bronson Copper, corresponding secretary; Annie Adams, treasurer; Jennie Miltonburger, chaplain; Daisy Hinman, guard and Eunice Babbitt, journalist. At that same meeting Emma Buchanan was initiated.

Lue R. Spencer, a dimit to Chapter AK, was president of Nebraska Grand Chapter in 1916-1917. Convention was held in North Platte in 1918 and Hattie Rincker served as vice president of Grand Chapter. Maude Hendy, president of Nebraska State Chapter in 1925, had served seven years as a state officer and was later on the Board of Trustees of the P.E.O. Educational Loan Fund. Bessie Buchanan was president of Nebraska State Chapter in 1950, and Leann Drullinger presided at the state convention in 2009. Leann served on the International Study and Research Committee (2009-2015) and as its chairman for 2013-2015. Other members with state and International recognition include: Hattie Rincker, Winnie Scott, Florence Antonides, Cora May Crosby, Mildred States, Mattie Rumery and Nada Ellyson.

Chapter AK assisted with the organization of Chapter CL, Ogallala, in 1921; Chapter EB, North Platte, in 1932 and Chapter GO, North Platte, in 1966.

Chapter AK celebrated our 100th Anniversary in March 2004 with a chapter luncheon followed by a reception attended by members of the other North

Platte chapters. Our chapter can boast several 50 plus year members. Those still active in our chapter are Kay Bodeen (1961), Helen Raetz (1959) Mary Pendleton (1957) Janet Miller (1956) and Myra Satterfield (1950).

Charter members of Chapter AK - Back row: Annie Adams, Jennie Miltonberger, Daisy Hinman. Front Row: Hester Cupper, Clare Davis, Susie Frazier Lucas, Minnie Wilcox and Eunice Bobbitt

Our philanthropies have always included contributions to the P.E.O. projects along with the Cottey Bus Trip, Nebraska Cottey Scholarship, the Nebraska Suite at Cottey College and support of local organizations such as the Goodfellow Shoe Fund and the Salvation Army. We have been proud to nominate women for the projects and are excited when those nominees have received an award. The addition of the P.E.O. STAR Scholarship has given us the opportunity to create our own scholarship so that our chapter can contribute to the education of a high school student whom we have nominated, but was not fortunate enough to receive the STAR Scholarship.

Members of Chapter AK at the celebration of the chapter's 100th anniversary in March of 2004

Over the years our fundraisers have consisted of auctions, plant sales, silent auctions, a brag bag and Community Day Coupons.

In over a century since that first gathering, many women have shared in the sisterhood of Chapter AK. Currently, we have an average attendance of twenty-eight members. We miss our ninety-two dear and wonderful sisters that have joined Chapter Eternal.

CHAPTER AK'S ACTIVE MEMBERSHIP IS 62; TOTAL ENROLLMENT IS 401

★

CHAPTER AL MADISON
ORGANIZED AUGUST 25, 1904
BY GRACE THOMAS

Well over 100 years ago, on August 25, 1904, Nebraska State Chapter Organizer Grace Thomas met with eight ladies of Madison, Nebraska, to form Chapter AL. Those eight charter members were: Kate Robinson Phillips, Cora Bancroft, Florence Dawson, Belle Mossman, Sarah Robinson, Margaret Memminger, Phoebe Foster and Emma Hume Field. Thus began the history of Chapter AL.

Theodore Roosevelt was in the White House, and Queen Victoria had just died in 1901. The standards and morés of the "Victorian Age" insisted that one was to cross the street rather than walk in front of a billiards parlor or saloon. Henry Ford's assembly-line Model T was still four years in the future. But the ladies of Chapter AL were undeterred, as their attendance was nearly perfect. They walked or were driven in carriages to the meetings.

Throughout its history, Chapter AL members have been involved in community affairs. Chapter AL charter members were instrumental in establishing the Madison Public Library. To continue this connection, and to celebrate their Centenary, Chapter AL selected a bronze art piece for the library, "Checking Out," sculpted by artist Jerry Boyle of Longmont, Colorado. The statue of a young girl taking home an unwieldy pile of books was donated to the library through funding from Madison's Chapter AL of the P.E.O. Sisterhood, the Eunice Moyer Foundation, the Alice Jones-Della Remender Foundations, and the Madison Public Library Foundation. The chapter continues to donate memorial books in honor of sisters who have passed into Chapter Eternal.

Chapter AL's members include teachers, medical professionals, paraprofessionals, administrative assistants, a pastor, bankers and retired people who are busier now than they ever were. We are proud to have two sisters who have served as Nebraska State Chapter president: Mildred Robertson, 1960-61, and Jeanne Reigle, 2002-2003. Mary Davis Garvin also served as president of California State Chapter in 1958. Our sister Gretchen Wells did much of the art work in Nebraska State Chapter's first history book, *The Saga of Nebraska P.E.O.*

For many years, Chapter AL's main source of income was its biennial rummage sale. Within the last twenty-five years, the most successful fundraiser has been the sale of Christmas greenery. Each year, members collect pinecones, paint them and wire them together, then decorate our beautiful wreaths and centerpieces. One of our BILs builds lovely pin boxes which hold the pin backs crocheted by another sister's mother-in-law. These are advertised in The P.E.O. Record and provide a steady income through the year. We have increased our giving to P.E.O. philanthropies, and also give scholarships to graduating young women in several surrounding towns that no longer have P.E.O. chapters.

In the past, Chapter AL sponsored women for the P.E.O. Educational Loan Fund and the P.E.O. Program for Continuing Education. A Chapter AL member and her high school exchange student sister from Japan both graduated from Cottey College. Currently, we are sponsoring a candidate for a PCE grant.

Chapter AL is very proud of the accomplishments of each member and of the achievements of the chapter as a group. But the best part of all is the love we have for our sisters, "the permanency of a friendship that we loved too strongly to have it perish." Those words from founder Mary Allen Stafford hold true for all of our sisters–those who have joined Chapter Eternal, those who are currently attending meetings, and those who have yet to be discovered.

Chapter AL's active membership is 44; total enrollment is 248

★

Chapter AM Fairmont
Organized January 31, 1905
by Eva Wagner

A group of women met weekly in the home of a blind woman who wanted so desperately to read. They brought items of interest which they shared at their gatherings. Louisa B. Hill was one of these ladies and following a visit to western Iowa, she returned to form a P.E.O. chapter in Fairmont. Sophia Cubbison had attended college with the original seven Founders, so she had heard of P.E.O.

It was a cold winter day January 31, 1905, when the furnace in Almira Wheeler's home refused to work, but a roaring fire in the fireplace and the determination of the ten new members kept them warm. Charter members were Louisa Bailey Hill, president; Nellie C. Ashby, vice president; Vinnie Cubbison, recording secretary; Anne L. Jackson, corresponding secretary; Hattie Horan, treasurer; Emily Dumond, chaplain; Charlotte Jenkins, guard; Sophia Cubbison, Hannah Swartz and Almira Wheeler.

Supporting the school was important to Chapter AM as they formed a committee to raise interest toward building a badly needed new school. The cornerstone was laid for the new school in 1909. Other philanthropies of the chapter included donations to the Child Saving Institutes, the I.O.O.F. Home in York, the Orthopedic Hospital, the library and scholarships. Many hours were contributed to Red Cross work during World War II.

Chapter AM hosted the state convention in Fairmont in 1920, where 142 delegates attended and were entitled to vote. Our chapter found sleeping accommodations for 101 delegates and the total bill was only $470 for the three day convention which was a huge success.

Five of Chapter AM's earlier members wrote a story, *The Transplanted Rose*, which is read every ten years. Authors were Nellie Ashby, Mary Goodrich, Beulah Brown, Elizabeth Wright and Ema Smith.

For the 2003 state convention held in Hastings, Chapter AM made decorations and delegate gift boxes and enjoyed hosting the hospitality room.

A special highlight of Chapter AM was our 100th Anniversary celebration in 2005. Following a delicious meal, an entertaining skit was given by our "charter members" as they peeked down from heaven and realized our chapter was still functioning well after 100 years.

The chapter members find they are busy with their projects. We adopt a Cottey College student and send her goodies throughout the year. Our annual silent auction proceeds contribute to alternating projects.

In May, Chapter AM assembles plates of goodies and delivers them to shut-ins and people in need of loving concern. On Memorial Day, we remember our sisters in Chapter Eternal by placing daisies on their graves. Our philanthropic and courtesy committees remember special events as well as the sad and trying times of our sisters. In September we look forward to our annual salad supper and in December we enjoy our Christmas gathering ending with an ornament exchange. Our BIL party is well attended with good food and fellowship.

Our Founders' Day Program consists of lighting candles in remembrance of our seven Founders and we place daisies in a vase in memory of our dear sisters in Chapter Eternal.

We sponsored two ELF recipients, Stephanie (West) Bryson and Heidi (Lightwine) Farmer, and P.E.O. STAR Scholarship recipient Kelsey Moore.

Even though we represent several small communities, Chapter AM has initiated thirteen new P.E.O.s since the history book was last printed in 1995. We are of diverse ages and occupations and have many outstanding talents among our members who not only enrich the Sisterhood, but also contribute to their community.

CHAPTER AM'S ACTIVE MEMBERSHIP IS 30; TOTAL ENROLLMENT IS 154

★

CHAPTER AN LEXINGTON
ORGANIZED MARCH 27, 1905
BY EVA WAGNER

Chapter AN was organized on the cold, dark, dreary afternoon of March 27, 1905, with Eva Wagner as organizer. Nine charter members were: Jennie Temple, Lou Spencer, Josephine Temple, Myrtle Roberts, Belle Shankland, Libby Branson, Kate Darr, Edith Roberts, and Mae Thornton. Their first official meeting was that same evening at Kate's house and the weather was even drearier. Jennie and Libby drove a horse and buggy down streets of almost inky blackness and hitched the horse in the mud in front of the Darr home. They said they needed "all the enthusiasm generated at the afternoon meeting to nerve them for the evening session, but the house was warm and bright, and all discomforts were soon forgotten." Chapter AN members have been hosting "warm and bright" meetings for 110 years in Lexington.

Charter member Lou Spencer served the chapter as president for five years. She later dimitted to Chapter AK, North Platte, and served Nebraska State Chapter as president in 1916-1917.

Chapter AN has been instrumental in helping form three additional P.E.O. chapters in Lexington. Chapter AN members have organized and dimitted to the following chapters: Chapter FS in 1954; Chapter GR in 1968; Chapter HV in 1983. Those sisters are missed in Chapter AN, but the chapter is grateful to see the Sisterhood grow in Lexington.

Chapter AN members always have been leaders within the community and have a tradition of giving interesting educational programs. Some of these topics, as well as other historical events include: 1908—an evening with Mother Goose featuring an operetta presented by members; 1921—hosting the Convention of Nebraska State Chapter in Lexington (breakfast was 40 cents, lunch was 45 cents, and dinner was 75 cents!); 1926—Chapter AN member Nellie Grantham was Nebraska State Chapter president; 1939—a program about socialized medicine; 1944—members helped with the war effort at the nationally famous canteen in North Platte; 1955—Chapter AN's Golden Anniversary celebration; 1979—providing banquet table decorations for Convention of Nebraska State Chapter in North Platte; 1991—AN members Dottie Anderson and Connie Talbott with their employees constructed all the uniforms for International Convention in Nebraska; 2005—Chapter AN's 100-year celebration. The chapter also participates with other Lexington chapters to decorate P.E.O. graves on Memorial Day.

Chapter AN has supported P.E.O. projects throughout the years. Fifteen women have received support through the P.E.O. Educational Loan Fund. Four women have received a P.E.O. Program for Continuing Education grant. One member received a Nebraska Cottey Scholarship. Funding for the projects has come from the sales of candy, magazine subscriptions, bean soup mix, homemade vanilla, and craft and bake holiday auctions. Our most successful fundraiser has been geranium sales begun in 2005 with 400 plants and recently 1,242 geraniums were sold!

From the days of attending meetings by horse and buggy, approaching houses on wooden sidewalks and lighting the homes of meetings with kerosene lamps, Lexington's Chapter AN continues its rich history of sisterly love.

Chapter AN has honored twelve 50-year members, ten 60-year members, and three 70-year members.

CHAPTER AN'S ACTIVE MEMBERSHIP IS 47; TOTAL ENROLLMENT IS 333

Chapter AO Fairbury
Organized November 20, 1905
by Eva Wagner

Chapter AO was organized through the vision of Althera Letton and friends who desired to be involved in self-improvement, philanthropy, and culture. The following officers were elected: president, Carrie Jenkins; vice president, Elizabeth Whitmore; recording secretary, Nina Hansen; treasurer, Anna Steele; chaplain, Lula Perry; and guard, Mary Hansen. Althera Letton and Emily Jenkins, as members, brought the total to the necessary eight ladies for a chapter, which was organized in the home of Mrs. Letton by State Organizer Eva Wagner of Omaha.

During WWI, WWII and the Korean conflict the chapter took an active role in supporting our country through Red Cross and YWCA. projects, sewing at meetings, adopting nine residents living in Great Britain and serving as hostesses at the local USO. Currently our meetings are geared more toward projects supported by P.E.O. Chapter AO has supported all of the International projects. Six of our P.E.O. daughters have attended Cottey College. We also contributed to the Golden Anniversary Fund, purchased a brick for the Academic Center Walkway, and contributed to the Defining Moment Campaign. We made provisions for the Nebraska suite and supported Nebraska students by sending survival baskets during finals week.

Helen Harring was one of the first P.E.O. Program for Continuing Education grant recipients in Nebraska. Denise Pahl and Linda Moore were also sponsored by AO and received grants. Kelly Reams Louk and Stephanie Epp received loans from the P.E.O. Educational Loan Fund. Pamela Epp was a Vera Koefoot Scholar in 1995-96 and spoke at the Convention of Nebraska State Chapter in 1996. We recommended students for the P.E.O. STAR Awards.

Fairbury was the site of the Nebraska State Convention in 1922 and 1946. Two sisters served on the state board. Mae Bond served as president in 1927-28 and Lucy Livingston served as president in 1952-53. Alta Stark was superintendent of the Nebraska P.E.O. Home in 1960-62 and Lucy Livingston was chairman of the P.E.O. Home Board for five years. Other sisters that served the state chapter were Mary Denney, chairman of the building committee for the addition to the Home; Loneta Luce, Cottey representative; Margaret Livingston, Welfare and Trust Fund; and Pauline Nuckolls, committee for publication of Nebraska history.

We continue to support the Nebraska P.E.O. Home with practical gifts, monetary donations, and participation in the adopt-a-resident program. We often hold chapter meetings at the Home. Eight chapter members were residents at the Home including Virgina Gallamore whose mother was a charter member of our chapter.

In 1995-96 Chapter AO granted consent for Kris Jenkins to select a charter list for another Fairbury chapter. In 1997-98 six dimits from AO were granted to the new Chapter, IP. A monetary gift was given to bolster their treasury. Our two Fairbury chapters share Founders' Day and social meetings.

In 1995 a committee designed and developed a local afghan depicting historical sites in Fairbury. Over 600 of these were sold over several years to support P.E.O. projects, the Goff's Goal fund honoring Joyce Goff as International president, our local library, and the refurbishing of statues on our historic courthouse. The family of Ruth Hansmire made a generous memorial gift of $1,000, which was divided among the five International projects and the Nebraska P.E.O. Home. We continue to fund projects through our annual chapter paddle auction and yearly community yard sale. A local scholarship is given annually to a graduating senior.

Chapter AO celebrated its 100th anniversary during the entire year of 2005 with the yearbook theme "A Century of Memories." At a luncheon during October of that year Maxine Ward shared an original poem she had written, and C. J. Freese compiled and read the AO history to International, state and local guests. In celebration of our anniversary, a $500 donation was presented to the Home. We honored Heral Phelps as a 75-year member and two years later in 2007, Pauline Patrick as a 50-year member.

We no longer follow the rule of serving "two dries and a wet" at our meetings but the long established tradition of placing daisies on the graves of sisters buried in the Fairbury Cemetery continues each Memorial Day.

Our Chapter has a rich history that can be explored further through president's letters and past minutes. In reviewing these documents it was comforting to know some things have been repeated year after year, but as new sisters emerge, new ideas are explored and many times implemented to make AO the same as when it first started: friends who desire to be involved in self-improvement, philanthropy, and culture.

CHAPTER AO'S ACTIVE MEMBERSHIP IS 61; TOTAL ENROLLMENT IS 318

Chapter AP St. Paul
Organized January 8, 1906
by Eva Wagner

Chapter AP in St. Paul was the 37th chapter to be organized in Nebraska. It was organized on January 8, 1906, by State Organizer Eva Wagner. The records show that annual dues were set at 25 cents.

There were eight St. Paul ladies who were charter members of Chapter AP. The offices that they assumed are included, along with a little information about each member. Minerva Agor, first president of the chapter, was a music teacher here for many years. She was also an organist in the Presbyterian Church. Georgina Grothan, vice president, practiced medicine for many years. Pearl Andrews, recording secretary, was on the Board of Directors of the Methodist Church. Davise Parker, corresponding secretary, was a teacher in our public school. Mary Van Cott, treasurer, was originally from Scotland and was active in the Presbyterian Church. Frances Fleming, chaplain, was an artist and taught china painting, water color and oil. Lizzie Leftwich, guard, was active in the Methodist Church. Byrdie Taylor, pianist/journalist, was active in the Presbyterian Church and played the organ for many years. She was a member of the City Library Board for twenty-three years and was the first historian of Chapter AP.

The thirty-fifth annual convention of P.E.O. in the State of Nebraska was held in St. Paul and hosted by Chapter AP in May of 1924. The members took great pride in planning and participating in that convention. One of the highlights of this convention occurred during a "model meeting" when twin daughters of Mrs. Vera Taylor, Cathryn and Harriett, were initiated into the P.E.O. Sisterhood. Their grandmother, Mrs. Harriet Force, also a member of Chapter AP, was present for their initiation.

On January 9, 1956, members of Chapter AP celebrated their 50th anniversary as an organized chapter. Twenty-seven members and six guests were in attendance. They honored Byrdie Taylor, the only remaining charter member, at that celebration. Special guests included Mrs. Bernice Bell Field, first vice president, Kansas State Chapter, Mrs. Harriett Taylor Lumbard, recording secretary, Nebraska State Chapter.

Former St. Paul residents whose mothers were active in Chapter AP, who served as officers of the Nebraska State Chapter, included: Harriet Taylor Lumbard, recording secretary of Nebraska State Chapter in 1956, and Ellen Ann Armstrong Qualsett, Nebraska State Chapter president in 1974.

On January 12, 1981, members of Chapter AP celebrated their 75th anniversary with thirty-one members and three guests present. Three members and one former member of Chapter AP were honored for over 50 years of membership in P.E.O. They were Beulah Haggart, Grace Krueger, Harriet Lumbard and Edna Nelsen.

On January 8, 1996, Chapter AP members celebrated their 90th anniversary. Four members were honored at this celebration. Adnelle Oakeson, who has been a member for 60 years, and Hilma Welsh, Alyce Paul and Lillian Anderson who have each been members for 50 years. Special guests included Mary Olsen, president, Nebraska State Chapter, Phyllis Blanke, first vice president, Nebraska State Chapter, Alice Fisher, second vice president, Nebraska State Chapter and

Joyce Goff, recording secretary, International Chapter.

On January 8, 2006, we enjoyed the celebration of our 100th anniversary. We planned for over a year to make this celebration very memorable for present members, former members and our guests. Thirty members and thirteen guests were in attendance. Special guests included immediate Past President of International Chapter Joyce Goff; President of Nebraska State Chapter Cyndi Jarecke; Corresponding Secretary of Nebraska State Chapter Cindy Biehl, and several former members of Chapter AP.

One of the traditions in Chapter AP is to offer a hot meal to a member who has lost a loved one, served before or after the funeral, to show our love and support for our sister in her time of need.

Annually, Chapter AP makes monetary gifts to the various P.E.O. projects, usually doing so at Christmas time. Each spring for the last several years we have provided a scholarship to a local graduating senior girl. We also support local needs, like the Food Pantry as well as the local Christmas Cheer project. In the past few years, we have donated towels and toiletry items to Hope Harbor in Grand Island.

In 2013 we started a Secret Sister Project and those involved will remember their sister in various anonymous ways throughout the year. Our hope is to become more involved with our sisters, whether they are newer members or long time members of P.E.O., and show our love and concern for each other with small remembrances throughout the upcoming year.

We enjoy our social time before the business meeting, so our members are able to get home to their family earlier in the evening. Many of our members are working, so they aren't always able to attend each meeting. We send regular emails and make phone calls to pass along necessary information. Each year we enjoy a social meeting for our Christmas party, and in the fall we have been having a social meeting where we each bring our BIL.

CHAPTER AP'S ACTIVE MEMBERSHIP IS 37; TOTAL ENROLLMENT IS 219

★

CHAPTER AQ LOUP CITY
ORGANIZED JANUARY 9, 1906
BY EVA WAGNER

Marian Mellor and Blanche Starr brought the idea of P.E.O. to Loup City. Charter members were Marian Mellor, president; Frances Outhouse, corresponding secretary; Blanche Starr, recording secretary; Zella Long, journalist; Emily Nightingale, chaplain; Ada Mason, treasurer; Eugenie Hale, vice president; Della Johnson, guard; and Alice Sleeth and Rena Miller.

In 1925, Chapter AQ hosted the thirty-sixth annual convention of Nebraska State Chapter, presenting the model meeting. Chapter AQ also gave the model meeting at state conventions in Ord in 1935 and in Grand Island in 1950.

Chapter AQ sister Elizabeth Stephens served as Nebraska state president, presiding at the convention in Peru in 1929. Originally initiated into Chapter AQ, Mary Owens served as president of Nebraska State Chapter in 1992-93.

Etta Swanson of Chapter AQ had eight P.E.O. daughters, seven of whom were members of Chapter AQ. Over the years, Chapter AQ has had one four-generation and seven three-generation P.E.O. families. In 2000, a very special sister, Harriet

Conger, celebrated her 100th birthday in the Nebraska P.E.O. Home.

Chapter AQ loyally supports all the P.E.O. educational programs, the Nebraska P.E.O. Home and the Nebraska Cottey Scholarship. For years, a silent auction has been a very successful means of raising donation funds. Recently, a holiday cookie and candy sale was added to our annual fundraising activities. In the chapter's past history, AQ reached out to the needs of the community. Today, Chapter AQ has savings funds to help defray the cost of the Cottey Bus Trip and to provide a Chapter AQ scholarship for a local high school graduate.

Social activities were many and varied for early P.E.O.s. It is recorded that Chapter AQ hosted a picnic for P.E.O.s and their BILs from ten neighboring towns, and sisters donned their favorite hats to attend English tea parties. Presently, the Founders' Day Dinner, Summer Celebration and Christmas Dinner are the annual social events.

In 1931, the BILs joined in the 25th anniversary celebration of Chapter AQ with an evening dinner followed by playing bridge.

In 1956, Chapter AQ celebrated its 50th anniversary with many wearing beautiful dresses from the 1906 era, a dinner featuring menu items which carried out a yellow and white color scheme and a program from the chapter historian. In 1981, Chapter AQ observed its 75th anniversary serving a dinner that featured a menu patterned after the recipes of the seven Founders.

In January 2006 the chapter began its 100th anniversary celebration at a house built in1906 that was the home of Frances Outhouse, an AQ charter member. A wonderful picture album depicting Chapter AQ's 100-year history was presented.

Chapter AQ has successfully sponsored recipients for the P.E.O. Educational Loan Fund, the P.E.O. Program for Continuing Education, the P.E.O. STAR Scholarship and a Nebraska Cottey Scholarship. Two AQ daughters, Tyra Damratowski and Teresa Hostetler, are Cottey College graduates.

In the recent past, Chapter AQ has focused on increasing membership and project giving. In 2010, Chapter AQ increased membership by ten members. In 2013, the chapter donated $2,800 to the Cottey College Challenge and was recognized at the 2013 Nebraska State Convention for exceptional per member contributions.

CHAPTER AQ'S ACTIVE MEMBERSHIP IS 46; TOTAL ENROLLMENT IS 192

★

CHAPTER AR STROMSBURG
ORGANIZED MAY 22, 1906
BY EVA WAGNER

Like the first chapter in Mount Pleasant, Chapter AR was founded by seven close friends. Carrie Peterson, president of Nebraska Grand Chapter, installed the following charter members as officers: president, Minnie Clark; vice president, Hannah Skelton; recording secretary, Nellie Barnard; corresponding secretary, Cora Headstrom; treasurer, Ada Sharp; chaplain, Matilda Netsell; guard, Tillie Buckley. The first minutes recorded, "After some very good instructions by the state organizer, all members and visitors repaired to the dining room, where a very dainty three course luncheon was served."

Carrie Hapeman, past president of Supreme Chapter, presented the charter to Chapter AR at the convention in Blue Hill on June 20, 1906.

Early members purchased hand painted china, featuring a wide gold band with marguerite decor, table linens to match and sterling silver flatware. These were used for special dinners, often including BILs. Several place settings of the hand painted china have been given as gifts to surviving chapter members. Special gifts to the chapter include a brass candelabrum from a charter member, and a beautiful cloth, handmade by Jennie Stanton, an early member.

Social activities centered on birthdays, Mothers' Day, and holidays, with the merriment of skits, family picnics, music, recitations, and poetry. A beautiful black lace and crepe dress worn by charter member Cora Headstrom has been treasured and modeled at various Founders' Day programs and anniversary events.

Special celebrations for 50th, 75th, 80th, and 90th anniversaries included dinners, programs, and reminiscences. In 2006, we celebrated our 100th anniversary in several ways. When Chapter CN, Osceola, hosted us at the annual Founders' Day program, they surprised us with a birthday cake. We also had a musical program which spanned the 100 years, a program centered around decorated tables representing each decade in the century and, for the community, we planted an oak tree in the city square.

Chapter AR 100th Anniversary

In 2002, Chapter AR committed itself to placing P.E.O. star markers on the graves of its Chapter Eternal members. We continue this project and have placed about 35 markers so far. Chapter AR members show a loving concern for each sister by providing a family meal at the time of death in the family.

Chapter finances have changed since the early days. From the minutes in 1907, "the expense of the first anniversary dinner was settled by assessing each member 89 cents" and "a fine of 25 cents was fixed for any member serving more than two eatables at any regular meeting." In 1913, delegate's railroad fare of $2.85 to the state convention was allowed.

During the two World Wars, members sent butter, jelly and cookies to the soldier boys, collected bandage material, bought War Bonds, sewed kits, donated to the Red Cross, and honored mothers of service men. Chapter AR continues in its philanthropic tradition by supporting the P.E.O. projects and various local charities. Some of the successful fundraisers have been: selling fresh Christmas holly, pecans, cleaning cloths, hosting bake sales, silent auctions, "passing the hat," "paying taxes" assessed by various arbitrary criteria.

We have been fortunate to have sponsored many girls through the P.E.O. Educational Loan Fund and the P.E.O. Program for Continuing Education, in addition to providing a scholarship to a local high school graduate each year.

Chapter AR's historian has a scrapbook of all chapter yearbooks and a book of snapshots and memorabilia of special occasions. We are proud of the many treasured items of historical value to our chapter.

Chapter AR's active membership is 43; total enrollment is 176

★

Chapter AS Kearney
Organized March 8, 1907
by Myra Grimes

Chapter AS was organized March 8, 1907, under the supervision of organizer Myra Grimes at the home of Ellamay Thomas, wife of Kearney Normal President A.O. Thomas. Her home is now Alumni House at the University of Nebraska at Kearney. There were twelve charter members, most of them teachers or librarians at Kearney Normal or the high school and one was city librarian. Ethel Masters was the first president; Mary Ray, vice president; Marie Reasoner, recording secretary; Helen Adair, corresponding secretary; Bessie Brown, treasurer; Marion Smith (whose paintings are often displayed at MONA and in Lincoln) guard; and Alma Hosic, chaplain. Other charter members were Gertrude Gardner, Anna Jennings, Mary Bailey, Anna Ray, and Alice Venters. A dinner was held at noon at Mrs. Pratt's "as the members from Minden would be in need of substantial food after jogging behind a team of horses across country over rutted dirt roads." Afterward, those attending walked around the corner to the Thomas home for the meeting.

Chapter AS members serving as Nebraska State Chapter president were Nora Killian, 1920; Nelle Grantham, 1926; and Dora Wenner, 1933. Kathy Gosch had been a member of AS before helping to charter Chapter HB, subsequently becoming state president in 1998.

Chapter AS could be described as mother and grandmother to the other Kearney chapters. In March 1935, the chapter divided to form Chapter EG; in 1951 both Chapters AS and EG cooperated in forming Chapter FN. Five members dimitted in 1963 to help organize Chapter GG, and in 1974, several young mothers chartered a morning chapter, HR.

Chapter AS celebrated its Golden Anniversary on March 3, 1957, with a banquet in the Crystal Room of the Fort Kearney Hotel and a program by Margaret Nielsen, "A Golden Treasure Chest." Margaret traced AS history again in 1982 for the 75th anniversary with "A Diamond Prism," this time at the old First Presbyterian Church. Both the hotel and the church have since been demolished to make way for banks.

We celebrated our 90th anniversary at Alumni House with an afternoon tea in 1997. Two members of Chapter N, Minden, drove over for the event. Several sisters from other chapters in Kearney also attended. It was a beautiful spring day, just as it had been in 1907 and would be again in 2007 for our 100th. Again, we had an afternoon tea attended by sisters from other chapters and state officers at Alumni House, but also a banquet at the Holiday Inn. We have pictures in the scrapbook commemorating that event with dainty tea sandwiches and cookies at the tea and grapefruit and potatoes au gratin at the dinner, just as in 1907.

Above: Chapter AS Vice President Mary Jo Morrow; Treasurer JoAnn Hoffman; Corresponding Secretary Nancy Williams; Guard Pat Smith; Recording Secretary Carolyn Menke; President Carol Dart; Chaplain Lanna Bishop;

Below: Chapter AS 100th Anniversary celebration December 2006

The P.E.O. projects continue to have our support. In 1994 and 1996 we sponsored Cynthia Evers and Karol Bankson-Recknor for PCE grants to continue their education in nursing and in speech/language pathology at UNK. Since then we have unsuccessfully submitted applicants for the P.E.O. Scholar Award, PCE grants, P.E.O. STAR Scholarships, and IPS. Otherwise, Chapter AS substantially increased our giving to the projects. To raise funds for this, we held our first annual auction in 2002, collecting enough to double our contribution. The last four auctions were joint social meetings with Chapter FN.

In addition to the P.E.O. projects, Chapter AS is active in both national and local causes. After September 11, 2001, we sent a donation to Chapter AS in Rockville Center, NY, for a fund to help victims of the terrorist attacks. We renewed our contact with that chapter in 2012 by sending a donation to help those hurt by Hurricane Sandy. The annual "tea plates" between Thanksgiving and Christmas are still used as a source of funds for a local needy family or organization. It was started in the 1920's to prepare for state convention when Nelle Grantham was state president. Also, a Happy Bag is available at each meeting for members to make a contribution in honor of a happy event. Sometimes we have garage sales or sell cutlery or cream whips. Under Marian Brown's direction we made a P.E.O. star quilt and raffled it off.

Chapter AS member Mim Worlock was 1965 Nebraska Mother of the Year, and Miriam Drake was the first woman honored with the Kearney State College Distinguished Service Award and for whom the theater at UNK is named. In 1996 Maribeth Lynn received the Kearney Hub Freedom Award in Arts and Entertainment for promoting Nebraska Public Radio in the area, and Marian and George Brown received it in education for their work with senior citizens and Elderhostel. In 2001 Carol Cope was named Nebraska Philanthropist of the Year and in 2006 she received the Governor's Arts Award. Most pertinent to Chapter AS is her bequest of $25,000 which provides for the Carol Cope Chapter AS Scholarship Endowment at UNK. She entered Chapter Eternal on her 103rd birthday in 2012 and was celebrated in 2013 with the "Walk in the Copes' Shoes" campaign urging people to perform acts of kindness in honor of Ron and Carol Cope. Dr. Helen Stauffer is the author of several works on Mari Sandoz. She served in the WAVES during World War II. Mary Sommers, Director of Financial Aid at UNK, has received several honors, most recently the 2012 Meritorious Achievement Award from the National Association of Student Financial Aid Administrators. Kathy Morrow was awarded the Hub's Freedom Award in 2013 for signing for the hearing impaired. Carolyn Menke received the Freedom Award in 2010 for her work in business and industry.

Chapter AS keeps in touch with sisters through email, our "Daisy" newsletter, cards from the courtesy committee, and monthly Lunch Bunch meetings in addition to regular meetings.

CHAPTER AS'S ACTIVE MEMBERSHIP IS 64; TOTAL ENROLLMENT IS 414

★

Chapter AT Tecumseh
Organized May 31, 1907
by Myra Grimes

Chapter AT was the outgrowth of a girlhood friendship of two Tecumseh girls, Jessie Stover and Jessie Dillon. Jessie Stover Knowlton, then a member of Chapter Q, Wymore, sponsored the group, recommended it to the state chapter, and came with Myra L. Grimes to the home of Jessie Dillon Thurber to organize the chapter May 31, 1907. The charter members were Belle H. Hassett, guard; Mittie H. Hedrick, recording secretary; Jennie H. Haworth, treasurer; Willa D. Shaw, vice president; Jessie D. Thurber, president; Jessie Seaver, chaplain; Blanche D. Chittenden, Ethel H. Cowan and Margretta S. Smith.

In 1927, only twenty years after the chapter's founding, Tecumseh was the site of the Nebraska State P.E.O. convention.

Highlights of the last twenty years include hosting Reciprocity VIII "Under the Big Top" in 1996 and taking "Hats Off to P.E.O." in 2013. Chapter AT also served as the registration committee at the Convention of Nebraska State Chapter in Beatrice in 2000 which was chaired by new state board member, Joan Fink of Chapter AT.

However, hands down, the two most important recent events for this chapter both occurred in 2007. The first was the honor of Joan Fink serving as state president. Joan was elected to the executive board in 2000 with her service culminating at her convention—*Reaching for a Hand, Touching a Heart*—at North Platte. Chapter AT enjoyed hosting the President's Tea and board meeting that September.

The second main event was 100 years in the making as Chapter AT celebrated its centennial year. All former and current members were invited to a luncheon and entertaining program. A highlight of the day was a style show featuring fashions of the previous decades.

As a 100-year chapter, many 50-year members have been recognized. Chapter AT has regularly initiated new P.E.O. members and has maintained a stable number over the years. *"Getting to Know Your Sister"* was a program which extended over one year. It included each sister's biography and was especially valuable and enlightening.

Chapter AT anniversary style show - 2007

Since 1994, Chapter AT has been active in seeking candidates for philanthropic projects. In the history of the chapter, a total of five girls have attended Cottey College. Two applications for P.E.O. STAR Scholarships and one candidate for the P.E.O. Scholar Award have also been submitted. Chapter AT sponsored four successful ELF students, one PCE recipient, and two successful P.E.O. STAR Scholarship recipients.

Chapter AT hosts Reciprocity Group VIII

The chapter is also proud to have a number of members with state appointments including LaVonne Rowe on the P.E.O. Home Board for nine years, and Pat Poppe, who served on the Nebraska Cottey Scholarship Committee for three years.

Gifts to all P.E.O. projects have been generous, as have contributions to local needs. The Tecumseh library and Community Action Center are favored recipients. Chapter AT has also regularly supported the Area Arts Council, the high school scholarship fund, the local ministerial association, and food and clothing drives as they occur. A popular cookbook was produced in 2005, and became a staple in many kitchens, and proved to be a major money-maker.

The experience of Chapter AT during the past two decades can be summed up in a quote from Past State President Joan Fink: "P.E.O. has been a wonderful support system in our lives. It has given us so many opportunities for personal growth and warm relationships with wonderful women."

Chapter AT's active membership is 47; total enrollment is 225

Chapter AU Peru
Organized June 10, 1907
by Myra Grimes

Chapter AU, Peru, Nebraska, was organized on June 10, 1907, with Nebraska State Chapter Organizer Myra Grimes. She was assisted by Mrs. Nettleton and Mrs. Searson in the home of Grace Culbertson White with other AU Charter members Carrie Gregg, Ida Estella Fairchild, Maybelle Cushman Weldon, Nelia C. Bedell, Mesa M. Bedell, and Mary E. Hart. Our list of sisters is a history of our town and Peru State College, with many professors, wives of professors and ancestors of the founding fathers of the city of Peru, Nebraska. Our first initiate, Elizabeth Crawford, was welcomed on June 17, 1907, and in 1924 Chapter AU assisted in organizing Chapter DB, Auburn. Each year we celebrate our founding AU sisters and our other Chapter Eternal sisters by decorating their graves on Memorial Day with a seven-daisy spray. The Peru Cemetery sits on a hill overlooking Peru and is full of the P.E.O. star markers and we feel our sisters watching over us and the heritage of Chapter AU.

AU has hosted four state conventions, 1929, 1974, 1986 and 2014 on the Peru State College campus. Our history has stories of the 1929 convention which was a rainy one, with leaky roofs causing clothing and sleeping distractions and muddy roads making transportation to and from a big problem. Some of our decorations for this convention were purchased from the preceding convention held in Tecumseh for a whopping $10. The 1986 convention is remembered by many of our current membership as we recall the number of beds we made in the campus dorms and the extra work of providing the amenities that are taken for granted now in the use of motels and hotels. Peru Chapter AU and Reciprocity Group VIII again hosted the 2014 Nebraska State Convention at Peru State College.

Our chapter has the distinction of having had two Nebraska state presidents—Ruth Kennedy in 1934-35 and Mary Ruth Wilson 1980-81. Ruth Kennedy has a living legacy of a daughter, two granddaughters and a great granddaughter having been initiated into our chapter. One of her major accomplishments in 1932 was organizing a reciprocity group in Southeast Nebraska to meet every fall. Many other chapters followed the example. Mary Ruth Wilson chose her theme as "Walk in Beauty" and many of her AU sisters followed her all the way to the other end of the state, (not walking thank goodness) to Chadron, to support her convention. Current members remember Mary Ruth as a tough act to follow, especially if she was the officer before you, as she was our local expert of P.E.O. procedures and protocol. She was our ultimate P.E.O. sister, and our motto is still "What would Mary Ruth have done."

Through the years Chapter AU has maintained a membership of up to 50 members but is now down to an average of 26 members holding consistently 15 to 16 meetings yearly including our social functions. Each year our programs follow a theme, many of them being the interests of the sisters or the special events of the time. The talents of the sisters of AU are displayed in the array of programs and presentations, from poetry writing, exploration of occupations, hobbies and of course our children and their accomplishments. We have an annual silent auction of our talents and our baking expertise bringing in good proceeds to be used on the philanthropies. At the end of every meeting we get out our "Grateful Pig"—a piggy bank introduced in 1979—so we can each share our blessings since the last meeting and "feed" him to fatten our coffers.

We are a membership of support for each and every sister in their celebrations, daily problems and tragedies, by hugs, laughter, shoulders to cry on, hands to hold and of course the ever present food offerings. Once a year we gather with our BILs for a Christmas wine party which is one of the most anticipated events of the year. Our BILs really like this and each year it gets higher attendance as we use this to invite prospective members also.

In 1981 Chapter AU celebrated its diamond anniversary with a luncheon at Peru State College. A lot of research was done on our history at that time by Louella Adams and passed on to us to preserve. In 2007 we celebrated our 100th anniversary with a tea at the Peru Museum inviting friends, other chapter sisters and state officers. We did a commemorative handkerchief for each member which was worn for the event under our star pins.

We have always supported all areas of P.E.O philanthropies. We have had two Cottey College students, Linda Kennedy and Stephanie Wheeler and a member of the past, Ruth Van Zant, lived in the Nebraska P.E.O. Home in Beatrice for many years. Our ever productive members have been on different P.E.O boards of the state and committees. In 2005 AU introduced the Mary Ruth Wilson/P.E.O. Chapter AU scholarship for a high school girl entering Peru State College or Cottey College. We say we beat International in helping high school girls achieve a dream of education long before the P.E.O. STAR Scholarship was started. Every year we support all P.E.O. Philanthropies with monetary gifts and through our history we have supported many recipients of the different grants, scholarships and loans of the philanthropies. We are very proud of our inheritance of a wonderful chapter from our Peru founders and we honor them by working to keep AU strong and ongoing.

CHAPTER AU'S ACTIVE MEMBERSHIP IS 27; TOTAL ENROLLMENT IS 279

Use what talent you possess; the woods would be very silent if no birds sang except those that sang best. -Henry David Thoreau

Chapter AV Pawnee City
Organized August 28, 1907
by Myra Grimes.

The idea of forming a P.E.O. chapter in Pawnee City was brought by Julia A. Lowry, Chapter A, and Mary Shephard, Chapter AE. Charter members and first officers were: Julia Lowry, president; Fanny Stebbins, vice president; Jessie Harding, recording secretary; Pearl Johnson, corresponding secretary; Alice Meeker Mahaffy, treasurer; Mary Shepherd, chaplain, Flossie Hassler, guard. Also, Edith Shepherd Reynolds dimitted to Chapter AV.

Chapter AV lost minutes in a house fire at one time. Fortunately the formative years were saved. It has brought joy to our chapter to share these early AV times. Those ladies had lots of dinner parties and the BILs were often guests.

Chapter AV has had active members in P.E.O. Lulu S. Wolford served as president of Nebraska State Chapter in 1923-24, and Julia Lowry as treasurer of Nebraska State Chapter in 1930-31 and as corresponding secretary, 1931-32.

A highlight in Chapter AV's history was entertaining the forty-first Nebraska State Chapter convention on May 14, 1930. Lula T. Andrews presided. There were many guests of honor including Edith Markham Wallace, president of Supreme Chapter; Helen Drake and Bertha Clark Hughes, past presidents of Supreme Chapter. Musical numbers were provided by Pawnee City's P.E.O.s and the men's community chorus. Townspeople opened their homes and the businessmen furnished transportation—with rain and mud!

Chapter AV

Bernadine Wherry served on the Nebraska P.E.O. Home Board for ten years. Rosanne Schilling served on the Nebraska Cottey Scholarship Committee.

Chapter AV presented a Memorial Hour entitled "Green Pastures" to the 1974 state convention in Peru and the Convention of International Chapter in Omaha in 1991. Bernadine Wherry also served as Music Chairman at the Omaha Convention.

Several AV members assisted in the Nebraska Centennial pageant written by Mary Ruth Wilson and given at a Convention of Nebraska State Chapter in Crete.

AV assisted in the organization of two P.E.O. chapters, Chapter CY, Falls City, and Chapter DI, Humboldt. We hosted a Reciprocity fall meeting with the "Big Red" theme in 1997. Chapter AV is looking forward to hosting in 2015.

In 2007, AV celebrated its 100th anniversary. We took a celebratory cake to the P.E.O. Home for a social time. We decided to wait until 2008 to attend the state convention in Omaha for our recognition. Chapter AV was well represented by twenty-two smiling members, all wearing black and white scarves decorated with daisies made by our member/seamstress, Irene Faesser.

AV enjoys social times and BIL parties. We have dodged pucks at a hockey game, attended plays in historic Brownville, escaped on summer picnics and most recently attended a Salt Dogs game in Lincoln. Our chapter yearly supports the P.E.O. projects and enjoys our time together at meetings.

CHAPTER AV'S ACTIVE MEMBERSHIP IS 51; TOTAL ENROLLMENT IS 205

★

Chapter AW Gothenburg
Organized September 25, 1907
by Myra Grimes

It was Clara Vroman who first brought the idea of P.E.O. to Gothenburg. Upon the arrival of a very late train, nine young ladies met and escorted the state organizer Myra Grimes and other guests to the home of Martha Spaulding for dinner and then to Clara Vroman's for their meeting. That evening, on September 25, 1907, with the assistance of Chapter AN, Lexington, these nine ladies became charter members of Chapter AW. The nine charter members were: Mattie Spaulding, Florence Bartholomew, Jessie Jennings, Maude Beghtol, Marian Williams, Beryl Cornell, Annie May, Anna Stevenson, and Clara Vroman. Maude Beghtol served as AW's first president and Beryl Cornell as corresponding secretary.

In 1931 Chapter AW hosted the Nebraska State Convention. Anna Loutzenheiser was president of Chapter AW. In 1935 she became president of Nebraska State Chapter.

Chapter AW has worked diligently to raise money for the P.E.O. projects. The chapter has sponsored women for the P.E.O. Program for Continuing Education and P.E.O. Scholar Awards. Chapter AW presents scholarships to local high school seniors. Each year we administer the memorial scholarship in honor of Chapter AW sister Jo Reichstein.

"A Tisket a Tasket P.E.O. Basket" has been a major source of revenue during the past few years. White elephant auctions, garage sales and various other projects have helped with our projects.

During the past twenty years, Chapter AW has initiated 54 new members, but sadly has lost 16 members to Chapter Eternal. Our chapter is blessed with having members ranging in age from 20 to 90. We are proud to have three 50 plus year members, Trudy Greene, Kay Linsaday and Jan Gill; one 60-year member, Janet Kranua, and one 70-year member, Elaine Tollefson.

Chapter AW celebrated our 100th anniversary on September 25, 2007, with dining and fun at Mac's Creek Vineyard in Lexington.

In remembering our sisters of Chapter Eternal, memorial markers are placed on their graves each Memorial Day.

Chapter AW is a remarkable chapter and upholds the ideals of our Sisterhood.

CHAPTER AW'S ACTIVE MEMBERSHIP IS 69; TOTAL ENROLLMENT IS 306

Chapter AX Crawford
Organized May 16, 1908
by Myra Grimes

With much excitement and no small amount of mystery, a group of nine friends met at the home of Effie Ayer on May 16, 1908, and pioneered more than a century of P.E.O. in the little western Nebraska town of Crawford.

As Myra Grimes initiated the charter members and instructed them in the virtues of P.E.O., Ida D. Forbes, a member of Original A, must have been pleased, for it was she who brought the Sisterhood to town. Besides Ida, Emma W. Minick, Effie M. Ayer, V. Genevieve Porter, Effie G. Roberts, Anna M. Sheldon, Georgiana G. Masters, Bessie E. Chapman, and Mayme L. McAndrews established the foundations of Chapter AX.

This first meeting included election of officers, a practice meeting, exemplification of initiation and appointment of a delegate to convention and was adjourned leaving the new initiates "feeling very happy to be members of the P.E.O. Sisterhood."

During World War I, Chapter AX became involved in wartime activities. Soldiers stationed at nearby Fort Robinson were the recipients of many dozens of cookies and other gifts. Political issues were often discussed and one program topic was "Weapons of Modern Warfare." In 1918 the corresponding secretary was instructed to write to their congressman regarding the "prohibition question"; a later program was titled "The Right Use of Liquor."

In 1938 Hattie Engelman of Chapter AX served as president of Nebraska State Chapter. It was during the thirties that the chapter discussed "Thrift," having had their assets in a local bank frozen and their hopes of hosting state convention shattered. The 1940's brought more wartime activities and members pledged to write at least one letter each month to a serviceman. A post-war project sent packages of food and clothing to German children and was coordinated by chapter member Marion Elliott, who was stationed in Germany with the Foreign Service. A prayer for peace throughout the world was given before the closing of each meeting during the "Cold War."

In 1961 chapter members were asked to compose a song for state convention and a "used hat" auction netted ten dollars.

Ruth Forbes, daughter of charter member Ida Forbes, was recognized at the 1973 state convention as Nebraska's only sixty-year member. Ruth died in 1991 having been an active member of Chapter AX for 78 years.

Chapter AX initiate Alice Fisher served as president of Nebraska State Chapter in 1998.

A 100th birthday celebration featured the P.E.O. poetry of Zula Hall and the chapter received special recognition at state convention in 2009.

Chapter AX has donated gift baskets to local needy families for more than one hundred years. For eighty some years an outstanding local high school senior girl has been the recipient of a monetary award and she and her classmates informed of the P.E.O. projects that could help them to further their educations. Graves of deceased members are decorated each Memorial Day.

Charter member Effie Ayer reflected in her minutes of 1910: "We felt that P.E.O. was brighter in all Faith, Love, Purity, Justice and Truth for the star we added that day." Chapter AX has added 248 stars to the brightness of P.E.O., and the P.E.O. star has added brightness to the lives of each of these members.

CHAPTER AX'S ACTIVE MEMBERSHIP IS 32; TOTAL ENROLLMENT IS 266

CHAPTER AY AUBURN
ORGANIZED JANUARY 4, 1909
BY CLARA WILSON
DISBANDED JUNE 20, 1918

Chapter AY charter members were Jessie Lynch from Chapter BP, Iowa; Grace Gilman from Chapter F, Plattsmouth; Anna A. Wilkinson from D, Superior; Emma Berlet-Taylor; Katherine Dailey; Olive Holmes and Jessie Gerlaw. Initiated the first year were Ethel Reed Hare and Pearl Matthews, and in December, Cora Salsbury dimitted from Chapter F.

During the first two years, Chapter AY met all obligations, gave to the P.E.O. Educational Loan Fund and to local charities. Then two members moved away and two died. The remaining six were handicapped in many ways. Perhaps it was the lack of growth which eventually led to the disbanding for total enrollment never exceeded the ten members of the first year. No meetings were held for a year and the chapter was disbanded by action of the Nebraska Grand Chapter at the 1918 convention in North Platte. Jessie Gerlaw and Emma Taylor became charter members of the new Chapter DB in Auburn in 1924. Others dimitted to other chapters. Grace Gilman, who lived in California, was the only active member of a disbanded chapter for some time, paying her dues to the treasurer of Nebraska State Chapter. In 1951, she dimitted to Chapter K, Lincoln.

TOTAL ENROLLMENT 10

CHAPTER AZ WAYNE
ORGANIZED MARCH 3, 1909
BY CLARA WILSON

Chapter AZ, the first chapter in northeast Nebraska, was organized on March 3, 1909, at the home of Elizabeth Heckert. Charter members were Edith Hufford, president; Gertrude Morris Ley, vice president; Minnie Wightman, Irma B. Kate, guard; Clara Ellis, corresponding secretary; Alice Philleo Horner, Elizabeth Heckert, chaplain; Clara Jones, treasurer; and Eva Davies, recording secretary.

The first initiate of Chapter AZ was Reba Jones in September 1909, whose great niece, Joan Lage, is a current active member of the chapter. Ironically, the first president's letter we can find is that of Reba Jones, president of Chapter AZ in 1925-1927. We treasure each of those letters. Thanks to one of our members, the presidents' letters have been placed in archival sleeves.

A 100th anniversary picture of Chapter AZ was taken in the College Willow Bowl. It appeared in an edition of The P.E.O. Record and resulted in many comments—and in one case a financial response from a former member who had seen the picture.

Chapter AZ is committed to the P.E.O. projects. Each year a Christmas auction is held, the proceeds of which help to support those projects and Cottey College. Several Chapter AZ members have been recipients of the P.E.O. Educational Loan Fund and one local resident received the P.E.O. Program for Continuing Education grant. Currently we have submitted an applicant for the P.E.O. STAR Scholarship.

Recent projects for Cottey have included "A Brick for Cottey" along with Wayne's Chapter ID; "Bucks for Beds"; and "Defining Moments."

During World War I the chapter established a silver drill and daisy dollars where members may contribute dollars to share a happy event. Some of the monies go for the operation of the chapter. The December contributions go to the Nebraska P.E.O. Home in Beatrice.

We have worked with the community on several projects of local interest: Mittens for the local "coat closet," the Wayne Community Schools, building of a local hospital, construction of a Senior Center-Library, renovation of the local theatre, and just recently, the city as it coped with an E4 tornado that demolished many businesses. These have provided an opportunity to "give back" and promote the image of P.E.O. in Wayne.

Themes for recent years have included "Reflections on the 20th Century," "Sharing the Gifts of P.E.O.," "A Network of Love," and "Make Time for P.E.O."

Helen Bressler was an active member of Chapter AZ and was a 76-year member of P.E.O. when she passed into Chapter Eternal. Starting in 2008 members of her family have given a $5,000 annual scholarship to honor her and the ideals she and P.E.O. represent. The scholarship is for one junior or senior girl to attend Wayne State College.

In 1998 the chapter initiated a biennial scholarship to a junior or senior girl attending Wayne State College, in the amount of $500, raised to $750 in 2006. Fundraisers to support these scholarships have been a table decorating competition and dinner, and several quality garage sales.

A Technology Committee has been appointed and as money permits we are archiving materials from past records to a digital format.

In 2013 our vice president started a new program. After each meeting she sends a Smilebox via email to every chapter member. It reviews the actions and discussions of the previous meeting. It is hoped that it will keep those who are less active involved in the activities of the chapter. Everyone gets the news and a personal invitation from the vice president to attend the next meeting.

CHAPTER AZ'S ACTIVE MEMBERSHIP IS 53; TOTAL ENROLLMENT IS 339

★

Chapter BA Sidney
Organized March 31, 1909
by Clara Wilson
Disbanded March 1, 1911

Charter members of Chapter BA were Adeline Hall, Jennie Harper, Tyrone E. Simon, Dorothea Campbell, Mary Mayme McIntosh, Valeska Neubauer, Elvira Jack, Marie Neubauer and Josephine Jones.

Four years after Chapter BA was disbanded, seven of the same group became the charter members of Chapter BO, Sidney, on June 11, 1915. Marie Neubauer had died July 6, 1911. Adeline Hall, co-sponsor of BO, was received by dimit into Chapter BO on July 27, 1915.

TOTAL ENROLLMENT 9

Chapter BB Ord
Organized November 19, 1910
by Bertha Clark Hughes

Chapter BB was organized by Bertha Clark Hughes on November 19, 1910. The first president was Minnie L. Daniels, who dimitted from Original A, Mount Pleasant, Iowa. She had been a member of that chapter for fifteen years. Other charter members were Rose Williams, vice president; Winifred Haskell Mattely, recording secretary; Blanche T. Cornell; corresponding secretary, Nellie W. Mount Chinn, treasurer; Bessie F. Davis, chaplain; Emma Robbins, guard; Ruth Williams Blakeslee and Mildred Daniels Davis.

The 46th Convention of Nebraska State Chapter was held in Ord in 1935. Ruth Kennedy, state president, presided. Supreme Chapter President Mabel D. Doud also attended. Two hundred sixty-five delegates attended. This was the final convention to be entertained by an individual chapter before the group hostess system was adopted.

In 1939 at the Golden Anniversary Convention held in Norfolk, Chapter BB exemplified a model meeting with Clara McClatchey presiding. Mary Koupal became president of Nebraska State Chapter in 1941 and presided at the state convention in York in 1942.

In the year Joyce Goff was president of Nebraska State Chapter and during the year Vera Koefoot was recording secretary of International Chapter, they honored Chapter BB with visits. Special occasions since then include Chapter BB's 100th anniversary, which was November 19, 2010. Members celebrated with a birthday party at the Ord First United Methodist Church Fellowship Hall. A group picture of thirty-five sisters was taken. We enjoyed a historical skit written by chapter member Claudia Cecetka and a letter written by charter member Bessie Davis in 1936. Chapter BB was honored as a 100-year chapter at the 2010 state convention in Norfolk. An anonymous member's donation and chapter funds allowed us to donate a framed township map to the Ord Township Library in honor of our 100th birthday on October 4, 2010.

Jan Goodsell, who was originally initiated into Chapter BB, served as president of the Tennessee State Convention in 2009. Four Chapter BB members attended her convention to honor and celebrate with her.

Joyce Goff, also a former member of Chapter BB, served as president of International Chapter in 2005. We contributed to Nebraska's Goff's Goals project.

Chapter BB was honored to have Linda Hruza, a woman we had sponsored for a P.E.O. Program for Continuing Education grant, named the Outstanding LPN of Nebraska in 2010. Also, our sister Linda Studnicka received a national award in the "Keep America Beautiful" project.

Since 1995, we have celebrated four 50-year members and one 70-year member, Lucile Tolen, in 1999, who is now deceased. Fifty-year members were Shirley Majors, 2008, Deloris Christensen, 2008, Jo Anne Willis, 2011 and Marie Mason, 2013.

Our chapter hosted reciprocity meetings in 1997 with Phyllis Garnick as president, and in 2012 with Tenille Rogers as president.

Chapter BB gives annually to all P.E.O. projects. We also contribute to special projects such as the 125th Anniversary Challenge in 1995, the Bucks for Beds campaign for the Nebraska Cottey College Suite bedroom furniture in 2010, scholarships for our P.E.O. daughters and an annual scholarship for an Ord High School senior girl. We also gave to the Defining Moment Campaign for Cottey College in 2013.

Chapter BB 100th anniversary celebration November 1st 2010
Below, Claudia Cecetka and Carol Keyser sell Ord chant flags
for a chapter fundraiser

We participate in the community selling lemonade and cookies at the airport for Evelyn Sharp Days, meetings at the nursing home where we provided coffee and cookies, and in city-wide garage sales.

Social activities include wine, cheese and chocolate parties, movie nights in a member's home, sweetheart dinners, tailgate parties before a home football game, touring a hunting lodge and a pottery business, going to theater productions, progressive dinner parties and visiting the Nebraska P.E.O. Home, bringing dessert to the residents there.

Fundraising projects have included silent auctions, Tour of Homes, birthday raffles, and the brag bag, where we put loose change in the bag and share news about our families at our meetings. In addition to garage sales we have sold Ord Chanticleer garden flags.

Chapter BB has had many interesting programs including evaluations of our antique treasures, our annual salad and potato hugger dinners, Christmas parties where we exchange gifts and bring hats and mittens to give to needy children, and daughters and granddaughters entertaining us with their talents. We also enjoy having our Founders' Day Program and dinner meeting every year with Chapter CJ, Burwell, at a favorite restaurant.

Our chapter is special because we have members of all ages with a variety of backgrounds and careers.

Since 1995 we have sponsored three women for the P.E.O. Educational Loan Fund and five women for the P.E.O. Program for Continuing Education grant.

CHAPTER BB'S ACTIVE MEMBERSHIP IS 47; TOTAL ENROLLMENT IS 289

★

CHAPTER BC CAMBRIDGE
ORGANIZED MAY 20, 1911
BY BERTHA CLARK HUGHES

P.E.O. Chapter BC, Cambridge, was organized May 20, 1911. Grace McClelland, kindergarten teacher, interested eight young Cambridge women in the P.E.O. Sisterhood and instigated the organization of Chapter BC. Dimitting from Chapter G, Hastings, she became the first president and served with Ruth Babcock, vice president; Alice M. Porter, recording secretary; Stella Enlow, corresponding secretary; Hazel T. Rankin, treasurer, and charter members Edna C. Perry, Caroline Thuman, Bessie R. Daly and Ina Johnston.

Concert violinist Genevieve Trenchard and her trio from Chapter BC in Cambridge entertain at the 1950 P.E.O. convention banquet in Grand Island. Genevieve represents the beginning of a four-generation P.E.O. family.

In 2011 we celebrated our 100th birthday and held a special dinner meeting to recognize and remember all our chapter has accomplished since its beginning. In the last one hundred years, Chapter BC has studied many topics of interest such as: Our State of Nebraska; Prohibition; Inventions; the President and the White House. Debates have been held by members with topics including "Shall Women Have the Ballot" and "Is College Education meeting the Demands of the Day." Chapter BC presented a one act comedy in 1912, made bandages during World War II, made annual donations of books to the local Christmas drive for needy families, contributing to both the local community and beyond at its beginning and still today.

Chapter BC is blessed by the contributions of sisters of varied ages and occupations, professional and career women, homemakers and retired sisters. Through cooperation and sisterly love, Chapter BC has been fortunate to sponsor women who have received grants from the P.E.O. Program for Continuing Education, helped students attend Cottey College, sponsored numerous women for the P.E.O. Educational Loan Fund, and nominated several lovely women for both the P.E.O. Scholar Award and the P.E.O. STAR Scholarship.

Chapter BC contributes to the P.E.O. projects each year with the funds raised through various means. These include silent auctions, bakeless bake sales, the sale of a basket filled with a sister's special treats, the sale of hand-painted marguerite pins and boxes, and proceeds from a "happiness box," which contains monetary gifts from a sister who shared her special joy with the chapter. One year, Chapter BC sent handmade ornaments to the Nebraska P.E.O. Home.

Members of Chapter BC have served on Nebraska State Chapter committees and on Convention of International Chapter committees. We have been proud to have our sisters of Chapter BC serve as Convention of International Chapter teller, state convention vice chairman, Cottey Area Chairman, and most recently state convention chairperson.

Chapter BC holds three social meetings each year. During those meetings we've enjoyed visiting area nurseries in the spring, having holiday dinners, conducting fundraisers, going out for dessert and coffee, and just generally taking a few hours out of our busy lives to relax. Chapter BC has been blessed to recognize many special anniversaries including several sisters as 50-year members and one 75-year member.

Chapter BC looks forward to helping women reach for the stars for the next 100 years!

Chapter BC's active membership is 22; total enrollment is 173

★

Chapter BD Ashland
Organized May 27, 1911
by Bertha Clark Hughes

Bertha Clark Hughes organized Chapter BD on May 27, 1911, with nine charter members: Vera Railsback, Violette Fuller, Clara Meredith, Lena Cowan, Lillian Bell, May Wiggenhorn, Florence Hovey, Alexandra Cowan and Sue Railsback. She returned for our 20th and 50th birthday celebrations and was a special guest when Chapter BD members presented the model meeting at the 1941 state convention on the eve of the chapter's 30th anniversary. The 75th diamond anniversary was celebrated with former members and state officers present and on May 21, 2011, we celebrated 100 years with a gala attended by 41 members, 11 former members and 3 guests. A memory book of personal histories was published for the occasion.

Chapter BD was recognized at the 2012 state convention as a centennial chapter by our own Joyce Victor, an initiate of Chapter BD and then president of Nebraska State Chapter. Lisa Gatzemeyer Helmick, new state chapter secretary, is a former member of Chapter BD.

Through the years, Chapter BD has been supportive of all P.E.O. projects. A woman was sponsored for the P.E.O. Educational Loan Fund during the early years. More recently, representatives have journeyed to Cottey College seminars and one P.E.O. daughter/member attended this fine school. Visits to the Nebraska P.E.O. Home have been frequent and a dear sister was a part of the Home family. Chapter BD is a Golden Anniversary Chapter for the Cottey Endowment Fund. Founder May Wiggenhorn was memorialized in a gift to the Centennial Center.

Chapter BD Centennial Gala May 11, 2011

Chapter BD has always donated monetarily to the P.E.O. projects. We also fund a scholarship for a local graduating high school senior. We have raised sums for our philanthropies with high-bidding auctions and white elephant sales. The highly-qualified granddaughter of a member was presented for the P.E.O. Scholar Award in 2013.

In the early years of Chapter BD, there were many social events for BILs and families: elegant luncheons, bridal or stork showers, housewarmings, summer picnics and BIL model meetings. In March of 1966 a sudden blizzard trapped the sisters in a farm home overnight creating material for many stories, poems and memories. Children of members often presented holiday musical programs and the school faculty were always entertained at a tea. We have gone from afternoon meetings to several night meetings, to only night meetings with a Founders' Day luncheon. Everyone has enjoyed the three yearly social meetings. We have traveled out of town to try a new café, have made a farm visit with wiener roast and hayrack rides, and have toured a local vineyard.

At each Christmas brunch a picture is taken and sent to non-resident members with a greeting. A video tape was made of 50-year members replying to questions of younger members which will prove interesting for future historians. At Memorial Day, daisies are placed on the graves of departed sisters.

Chapter BD has always taken its responsibilities seriously. Members have accepted offices, raised funds, participated on committees, and have laughed together, rejoiced in successes and supported in times of trouble.

CHAPTER BD'S ACTIVE MEMBERSHIP IS 61; TOTAL ENROLLMENT IS 242

★

CHAPTER BE PIERCE
ORGANIZED MARCH 1, 1912
BY BERTHA CLARK HUGHES

The seed for Chapter BE was planted in the heart of a young woman, Anna Fowler Magdanz. In 1906, at a time when few women went to college, Anna Fowler, daughter of an Omaha judge, graduated from the University of Nebraska. In about that year this University of Nebraska graduate became a teacher of mathematics and Latin at Omaha South High School. Next door to her at South High was an English teacher named Bertha Clark Hughes who became Anna's friend and coworker, not only at school, but at the Presbyterian Church they both attended. Anna knew Bertha and some other women who were P.E.O.s and was impressed by their character.

A few years later Anna was living in Pierce, Nebraska, having married Albert Magdanz, a Pierce native. When a Pierce Women's Culture Club and study group of which she was a part decided to disband, Anna suggested they form a P.E.O. chapter. This suggestion came even though she and the others really had, for all practical purposes, no idea what P.E.O. actually was. Anna was asked, "What kind of club is that?" To help answer this question Anna approached her friend, Bertha Clark Hughes. Upon contacting Bertha to learn more about the nature of P.E.O. and to propose the idea of forming a new P.E.O. chapter, Anna Magdanz discovered that her friend, Bertha Clark Hughes, was currently serving as the Nebraska State organizer for this organization! It was she who vouched for the ten women in Pierce who would be Chapter BE's charter members and selected the organizing date of Friday, March 1, 1912.The charter members for Chapter BE were Emma Berg, Ida Brande, Ida Henzler, Anna Magdanz, Suza Mohr, Ethel Pheasant, Ada Pohlman, Emma Pohlman, Ida Pohlman and Jennie Riley.

Bertha Clark Hughes came by train from Omaha, a six-hour trip, and brought with her a "most delicious chocolate cake." A locked president's box had been shipped earlier in the week with everything needed to organize a new chapter. All was business for the next two days as the ten women learned everything about P.E.O., held initiation and elected officers. In April 1912, three new chapters in Nebraska were welcomed into the P.E.O. Sisterhood. In her welcoming address to these three chapters Bertha Clark Hughes admonished Chapter BE to "Be Earnest."

Two members of Chapter BE served as state presidents. Ethel Desparias became California's State President in 1939. Harriet Salter was president of Nebraska State Chapter in 1926. In 1927 Dr. Salter placed a fountain in the

Memorial Library at Mount Pleasant, Iowa, in memory of his wife, Harriet.

From the years 1925-2013 we have sponsored many women with their higher education goals through ELF, PCE and our own local scholarships. Since 1997—seventeen years—Chapter BE, Pierce/Osmond has contributed generously $24,000-plus to the advancement of education for individual women. This figure does not include our regular yearly contributions to the six P.E.O. projects.

CHAPTER BE'S ACTIVE MEMBERSHIP IS 30; TOTAL ENROLLMENT IS 157

★

CHAPTER BF WILBER
ORGANIZED MARCH 12, 1912
BY BERTHA CLARK HUGHES

Nebraska's 51st chapter, Chapter BF, Wilber, Nebraska, was organized on a bitterly cold day, March 12, 1912, by Bertha Clark Hughes, assisted by Chapter Z, Beatrice. Our first president was Julia Mahoney Elder (Mrs. Charles Adrian). A history of Chapter BF was compiled for the 100th birthday celebration in 2013 by Mary Garrison, PP. We need to compliment our early diligent record keepers for their foresight in maintaining our histories.

Our current president Terese Francis's theme centers around Tea ("Life is like a Tea Cup, to be filled to the brim and enjoyed with friends") and our active membership is 33. We are fortunate that most of the new members we initiate are young adults, which will ensure a solid future of our chapter. We work together nicely and enjoy each others' company. We are truly sisters!

Most of us are just ordinary ladies. The Quakers call it "divine ordinariness." It is a quality that comes from the heart and touches all ordinary things with loveliness. Our members range from many with professional occupations to homemakers, but always seeking growth in knowledge and in culture. In the words of one of our Founders, Mary Allen Stafford, "It should be our purpose to not only make P.E.O. greater and better all the time, but womanhood and humanity greater and better, because of P.E.O."

It has been our honor to have a state president of Nebraska P.E.O. in 1981-82, Bernice Zajicek, now in Chapter Eternal.

We have had a variety of fundraisers and are currently selling Rada knives, Kaywos cleaning cloths, handmade jewelry, packaged dry soup mix, and we have a Sister Sharing Jar. This money goes to support our P.E.O. philanthropies and state convention expenses. In years past we've had dimes for lunch, silent auction, rummage and bake sales, candle sales, raffles, cookbooks, etc.

Members of Chapter BF are active in area communities growing in charity toward all with whom we associate. Wilber is the Czech Capitol and many sisters are busy with this celebration held annually now for over 50 years. We have had members featured in The P.E.O. Record for various honors. BF has made an impact in our area and community.

The first president's letter from our records was to Mrs. Nellie Grantham of Kearney, by Chapter BF President Anna F. Jelinek. The programs that year were devoted to book reviews, musicales, and short stories. By 1928, meetings were held alternately afternoons and evenings so that the business women would be able to attend at least once a month. Guests and husbands attend at least one event a year.

By 1930 several members had 100 percent attendance at meetings. Chapter BF members acted as librarians for the new city library.

We hold Saline County meetings with our three chapters, exchanging with Chapters CM, Crete, and DQ, Friend.

During WWII our members did several patriotic projects as well as served on community committees in support of the war effort. Many family members served and continue to serve in the military. Flowers are placed on graves of deceased sisters for Memorial Day.

Scholarships are important to BF and we have given generously to the Wilber Clatonia and Tri County High Schools as well as sponsoring ladies for the P.E.O. philanthropy grants, loans and scholarships. Bus trips to Cottey have included girls from our area. Giving to community and outreach programs are regular projects. We have an annual meeting at the Nebraska P.E.O. Home in Beatrice, taking kolaches.

Our members have served in various capacities at Convention of Nebraska State Chapter as well as on state boards. We attend reciprocity, state convention and Convention of International Chapter events. We currently have three 50+ year members.

Celebrating our chapter birthdays in 5-year increments is enjoyable. Our Centennial was observed in 2012 with a lovely tea attended by some former active members.

Many of our members have mothers/aunts/daughters/sisters who are P.E.O.s. It certainly is a "Family Affair!" Membership is important to BF, but we are not just taking in members, we are building P.E.O!

We do share our spirit for education, of sisterhood, and our desire to help each other reach our own personal goals. Founder Franc Roads Elliott said, "P.E.O.s should always keep our eyes forward and look for possibilities of the future rather than to dwell on the achievements of the past." Chapter BF is proud of our past, but now look to the future of P.E.O. Our sisters have touched each others' lives and made them better, and are a precious gift! Our star and members are pure gold!

CHAPTER BF'S ACTIVE MEMBERSHIP IS 31; TOTAL ENROLLMENT IS 186

★

Chapter BG Franklin
Organized May 8, 1912
by Bertha Clark Hughes

The origins of Chapter BG, Franklin, started from the Athena's club. At first, the Athena ladies were a bit reluctant to change to a chapter of P.E.O. And then there was the matter of requirement that the P.E.O. chapters be organized in towns of 1,000 or more inhabitants, and that Franklin's 1,000 was a little doubtful. Rev. Alice Newell laid the matter before the Franklin Community Club; a count was taken which proved quite satisfactory, and was properly registered at Lincoln. Rev. Newell then wrote to Mrs. Bertha Hughes, Nebraska state organizer, and explained that Franklin would someday be the county seat and a prosperous little city, notwithstanding. Mrs. Bertha Hughes was present for a reception in her honor at the home of Mrs. C. V. Cross that Wednesday afternoon in May when Chapter BG was organized. Chapter P, Bloomington, gave the initiation that evening at the homes of Mrs. Wm. Humphreys and Mrs. Karl L. Spence with ten charter members: Alice Newell, president; Alfaretta Furry, vice president; Edna Feese, recording secretary; Hazel Wright, corresponding secretary; Ada Naden, treasurer; Sadie Spence, chaplain; Mamie Humphreys, guard; Bertha H. A. Ready, journalist; Ella Porter and Edna Cross. Among the guests at the ceremony were Myra Grimes, past state president, Rose Owens, state corresponding secretary and eleven members from Chapter Y, Red Cloud.

For over 100 years Chapter BG has celebrated the achievements of its members. In 1934, Anne Porter was asked to serve on a state committee to study the "geographical groupings of state conventions." She also later received the Ak-Sar-Ben "Good Neighbor" award. Another member, Peggy Bislow, also received that award in the 1980's. In 1934 Clara May Flood read a paper on the P.E.O. star at state convention. This essay was later published in The P.E.O. Record. In later years, Jill Houston was very active in the state chapter. Currently Sheri Rasmussen was selected as the paid assistant for Nebraska State Chapter.

In those early days, Chapter BG held many meetings, some with BILs and costume parties, Christmas parties, election year parties and their annual Twelfth Night meeting. Their members learned of the loyalty and love of P.E.O., of the philanthropic projects for their community and sisterhood, just as we have grown in heart and spirit with P.E.O. Our Christmas parties this century include collecting for the local food pantry. We have also contributed to a local family dealing with cancer and hardships.

To fund our P.E.O. contributions for all of the projects, the Defining Moment campaign, and our local Special Scholarship, we host an annual bake sale and homemade runza sale during the Bargains-on-Byways weekend. We have repeat customers that put their orders in early so they won't be disappointed if we have a sell-out before noon. We have added another successful PCE grant recipient to our list, as we continue to look for more women that can benefit from this grant. Our courtesy committee and local chapter brighten the day for our nursing home residents with cards and candy for special holidays. We continue our search for area girls who might be a good fit for Cottey College, with our local president serving as the Cottey Area Chairman.

We have enjoyed stable membership since our organization, with many having been members for over 50 years, and a few 60-year and 70-year members. Some of our members are fifth generation P.E.Os. Many have been added to our Chapter Eternal, but many will be added to our members in the next one hundred years. May we give thanks—for the star and its message, for purity, justice, faith, truth and love.

CHAPTER BG'S ACTIVE MEMBERSHIP IS 32; TOTAL ENROLLMENT IS 242.

How far that little candle throws 'her' beams!
So shines a good deed in a naughty world.

-William Shakespeare

Chapter BH Sutton
Organized June 6, 1913
by Lulah Andrews

Chapter BH was organized on June 6, 1913, by Lulah Andrews, exactly 100 years to the date prior to the 2013 convention. Charter members of Chapter BH were Mabel Easley, president; Ada Neumann, vice president; Elva Leubben, recording secretary; Clara Bender, corresponding secretary; Nellie Hoerger, treasurer; Ora Weber, guard; Viola Wheaton, chaplain; and Nellie Stevens, journalist. Three more members were initiated in 1913, and four in 1914. Two hundred and four members have been initiated into Chapter BH over the past 100 years.

Chapter BH members range in age from twenty to ninety-eight. As we are the only chapter in our community, we take great pride in our chapter. As with most chapters, ours is filled with active and generous ladies. Our members are not only active in our chapter, but also in their churches and community organizations. Chapter BH also contributes annually to all the P.E.O. projects and the Cottey Bus Fund. We have contributed to the Defining Moment Campaign. We also contribute to our local high school scholarship fund.

In addition to assessments through dues, money has been raised through special projects such as a chapter cookbook, silent auctions, raffles, and games. Chapter BH also has special meetings which include a Founders' Day salad or soup supper, our traditional Christmas cookie exchange, BIL parties, and an evening with nearby chapters.

Chapter BH has had the privilege of sponsoring recipients for ELF and PCE scholarships. Also, we have one member who graduated from Cottey College. One of our initiates became a member of Chapter IW, a newly organized chapter in Lincoln. Our seven 50-plus members were involved in celebrating our 50th anniversary in 1963, along with two charter members, Clara Bender and Nellie Hoerger. Chapter BH presented a model meeting at our 50th anniversary recognition at state convention. We celebrated our 75th anniversary on June 6, 1988.

A recent yearbook theme was, "The Best of P.E.O.—Past, Present, and Future…" One 50-plus member had a program sharing her invitation, letter of acceptance, and other memorabilia. We have many other programs planned about the present and future of our chapter.

In 2013, Chapter BH celebrated its 100th anniversary. In June, nine of our members attended the luncheon at Convention of Nebraska State Chapter in Columbus. We also had a special evening out in July at Chances R Restaurant in York. Linda Nuss and Pat Majors, two of our newer members, provided a great musical tribute to our chapter.

In 1985, Chapter BH's president's letter included the following comment: "You've come a long way, baby!" Our growth has paralleled the growth of women. From bloomers to bikinis, from gaining the right to vote to running for office, from riding in a Model T to co-piloting a spacecraft, from settling domestic quarrels to ruling on the Supreme Court, from seven young and idealistic women to sophisticated, educated and independent members of a complex society…the list could go on and on!!!

Chapter BH's active membership is 51; total enrollment is 230

Chapter BI Shelton
Organized February 28, 1914
by Lulah Andrews

The nine charter members of Chapter BI were Marie Johnson, president; Alice Emigh, vice president; Elizabeth Stedman, corresponding secretary; Blanche Smith, recording secretary; Blanche Robbins; Mary Hansen, treasurer; Lotta Barrett, Margaret Martin, chaplain; and Katherine Morris, guard. Marie Johnson of AS, Kearney and Alice Emigh of AL, Madison, were dimitted members. Chapter AS assisted with the organization. The charter was signed on June 18, 1914, by Bertha Clark Hughes, Grand Chapter president, and Abbie C. Burns, recording secretary.

In 1964, Chapter BI celebrated its 50th anniversary with a reenactment of the organizational meeting called "Golden Memories."

In August of 1980, Chapter BI was supportive in sponsoring the organization of Chapter HR in Gibbon. Gifts to Chapter HR included the complete furnishing of their tea table and an engraved white gavel.

Chapter BI has sponsored many women for the P.E.O. Educational Loan Fund throughout its history. Since 1995 we have sponsored Kelli Power, Tara Plautz, Jane Roseland, Stacy Fairbanks and Tess Bruner.

P.E.O. is an organization of amazing philanthropy. But, the magnitude of its accomplishments is a result of the integrity, generosity, faithfulness and talents of each member singularly. Besides faithfully supporting all P.E.O. projects, Chapter BI has contributed to several charities and community needs over the years. Chapter BI has had numerous fundraising activities. Some of these include the sale of Kaywos cloths, Christmas greenery, glass coasters, and staffing the concession stand at a local hockey game.

One of our treasured social events is our Progressive Dinner.

Chapter BI is proud of its Nebraska Cottey Scholarships Committee member and chairman, Marsha Fairbanks. She served as a member from 1997-1998 and chairman 1998-1999. Marsha honored Chapter BI with her commitment as Cottey College Area Chairman, Area XIV, from 2004-2006.

Listen to the music of the women's voices during the social part of any P.E.O. meeting. They are filled with laughter, with joy and with sisterly love that is actually audible. We may come tired, or frustrated, but we always leave refreshed and fulfilled.

In 2004 we were privileged to host Reciprocity Group XIV. "P.E.O. fits us to a Tea" was our theme. "Tilley Liverlilly and Friends" provided our program for the event.

Four current members with 50 years of sisterhood are: Janice Harris, Ruth Landell, Janie McBride and Joan Meyer. Their devotion and guidance have been inspirations for all Chapter BI members.

Our members were usually notified of an upcoming meeting by a personal phone call from our dear sister Joan Murr. Due to the wonders of technology, today sisters are notified via an email sent by the president.

Chapter BI has grown and changed in many ways since that day in February of 1914, but the ideals and traditions of the charter members remain as strong as ever. We celebrated our 100th anniversary in 2014.

The accomplishments of the members in Chapter BI are great both in number and diversity. In our kaleidoscopic world it is important to not lose focus of our goals and aspirations, both personally and as an organization. Helen Keller's words, "Alone we can do so little, together we can do so much" are fitting sentiments for the importance of what we, as a chapter, can do to enrich the lives of others.

CHAPTER BI'S ACTIVE MEMBERSHIP IS 33; TOTAL ENROLLMENT IS 202

CHAPTER BJ ALMA
ORGANIZED MARCH 31, 1914
BY LULAH ANDREWS

Leona McCleary's idea of a P.E.O. chapter in Alma was realized March 31st, 1914, when organizer Lula Andrews initiated ten members into Chapter BJ. Leona served as chapter president to Helene Patterson, Eliza Shallenberger, Helen Furse, Nora Carter, Fannie N. Whitney, Celestia Haag, Birdie Gould, Elizabeth G. Shaffer, and Fannie M. Porter. Chapter P of Bloomington assisted. Eager to grow, the new chapter initiated two new members just three months later, only to discover that it was "illegal" to do so at that time. Thereafter, new sisters Nora Keester and Estella Haskell were referred to as the chapter's premature babies!

In those early years, members volunteered all to the war effort—knitting, canvassing for war bond purchases, and sending cards, letters, and boxes of food to soldiers. During the war Jean Rogers served as Red Cross chairman for Harlan County. She was decorated by the United States and British governments for outstanding service during World War II in selling government bonds and giving service to soldiers.

1922 saw our most distinguished president installed. Eliza Shallenberger was a former Nebraska First Lady. 1920's programs included many on women in politics (remember we just won the right to vote!) and reports from members working and studying abroad. For fun, a "costume party" was held featuring styles of twenty years prior. Philanthropic activities targeted a nearby orphanage and local needy families. However, in 1933, $20 was donated to northeast Nebraska for "drought relief." Donations to P.E.O. were recorded as 100 percent.

The 1941 president's letter acknowledged that donations to P.E.O. projects were small—"due entirely to existing conditions and not to lack of interest." But funds were raised for Cottey College and the Nebraska P.E. O. Home.

Membership reached fifty members during the mid-fifties and stayed within that range for two decades. A 1959 program of note was "an interesting study of our juvenile situation!" In 1963 chapter president Lois Leach had the honor of initiating her daughter into our chapter, bringing a fourth generation into P.E.O.

A 1970's theme was "The Women," highlighting women of varied accomplishment. Not coincidentally, as members became more active in the work force, our meeting time was amended to nights only in the 1980's, and to flexible times later on. We are still challenged to accommodate the diverse lifestyles and ages of our members.

In 1989, Chapter BJ was recognized at the state convention in Hastings for its 75th anniversary, and in 2014 celebrated its 100th year.

Throughout the years Chapter BJ has supported all P.E.O. philanthropies, as well as local scholarships. Bake sales, style shows, cookie walks, and luncheons have been part of our experience. We have sponsored a number of PCE recipients. Together we have decorated downtown trees and yearly we honor the members of Chapter Eternal by decorating their graves for Memorial Day weekend. Whatever changes the past 100 years have wrought, sisterly love remains strong.

CHAPTER BJ'S ACTIVE MEMBERSHIP IS 26; TOTAL ENROLLMENT IS 185

★

Chapter BK Omaha
Organized April 2, 1914
by Lulah Andrews

Chapter BK (Be Kind) was organized by Lulah Andrews and ten members from Chapter E on April 2, 1914. These ten women were: Agnes Livesey, Grace Neale, Mary Phillips, Edna Pickering, Mattie Myer, Effie Weeth, Kate Darr, Elizabeth Craven, Gertrude Weeth and Clara M. Wilson.

A flag has flown at state convention ever since Effie Weeth gave one to the state chapter in 1917 after presenting a program on "P.E.O. and Patriotism" at the state convention. BK sister Viola J. Cameron was 1927 Nebraska State Chapter president.

While anticipating the celebration of Chapter BK's 100-year anniversary in 2014, chapter members happily recalled memories from the last twenty years. During these years chapter activities have included supporting philanthropic causes such as raising money to assist a college student suggested and selected by BK members. This was done annually from 2001 through 2012. One of our most delightful students attended Cottey College and then transferred to the University of South Dakota. She kept in close contact with the chapter and we enjoyed getting to know her. In 2002 another scholarship opportunity was presented via an invitation from Chapter BX to join them and other Omaha chapters to sponsor a P.E.O. International Peace Scholarship. Ultimately, ten chapters joined together to make this happen. Truly, women helping women—an important P.E.O. goal.

For many years, the chapter maintained an eight-bed ward at the Salvation Army Home, and endowed a crib and did mending for the Child Saving Institute. During World War II, members took gifts to the soldiers as they came through the Omaha airport. Chapter BK completely furnished and maintained a room at the Nebraska P.E.O. Home and they send gifts, money and birthday gifts there as well. A silver coffee urn was given to the Home in memory of BK's first president, and later two silver trays were added.

Chapter BK has sponsored five women for the P.E.O. Educational Loan Fund. One was initiated into the chapter. The 25th, 50th, 65th, and 75th anniversaries of Chapter BK's founding have been celebrated with lovely teas.

Garage sales, summer sewing projects, handmade dish cloths and scrubbies, "can do" bank cans, fundraiser calendars and socks to fill—these are some of the fun-filled ways we collected monies for the P.E.O. scholarship projects, community outreach and selected students. Admittedly, this is becoming a bit more difficult as our active attendance and involvement changes.

Chapter BK members are very active volunteers in the community and several have been recognized and received awards for the time and commitment they've given.

Fun and family events are recurring themes with BK members. One of BK's members appeared on the television show "Jeopardy" and then gave the chapter a "Behind the Camera" program on her adventure! Another chapter member and her BIL briefly appeared on the "Today" show. Newspaper articles and pictures often include BK members front and center. Several BK sisters shared their special wedding anniversaries of 40, 45, 50, 62 and 70 years. What a happy occasion each of these numbers celebrate.

Monthly chapter meetings have focused on reaching out—to the community, to sisters who don't attend often, to Cottey students and others. Programs often utilize the skills, experiences and abundant knowledge of our own members. This has allowed members to get to know each other better since much conversation occurs as work is being done on outreach projects (such as preparing and filling backpacks for grade and middle school students).

Many members of Chapter BK were effective leaders in the preparation for and the smooth running of the Convention of International Chapter in Omaha in 1991. Also, several members loaned quilts for the decorations.

Chapter BK, one of Omaha's older chapters, appreciates the significance of its 100th anniversary (2014) and would like to recognize that there have been eleven members (nine now deceased) in the last twenty years who achieved 50-year membership in P.E.O. Actually, most were 60+ year members; one was a 75-year-member! With the current membership at 31 resident and 1 nonresident member, it'll be difficult to echo this remarkable record. Times have changed and BK faces challenges in its future, but P.E.O. strengths will prevail, perhaps in new and interesting ways.

CHAPTER BK'S ACTIVE MEMBERSHIP IS 32; TOTAL ENROLLMENT IS 204

★

CHAPTER BL CHADRON
ORGANIZED APRIL 12, 1915
BY SARA REULING

On April 12, 1915, Chapter BL was organized by Sara D. Reuling. Three Chadron women, Genevra Renfro, Mettie Smith and Ethel Delzell, were instrumental in bringing P.E.O. to Chadron. Those three women dimitted from other Nebraska chapters and seven others were initiated into P.E.O.: Elizabeth O'Linn Smith; Lizzie S. Sparks, chaplain; Ida V. Stockdale, treasurer; Maude F. Slattery; Elizabeth J. Pollock, recording secretary; Elizabeth Coffee; and Edith E. Copeland. The three dimitting members served as officers also: Ethel Delzell, as president; Mettie Smith, as corresponding secretary; and Genevra Renfro, as vice president.

During the 49th Convention of Nebraska State Chapter held in Chadron, Chapter BL member Marion Crites was elected to the state board of P.E.O. In 1944-45 she served as president of Nebraska State Chapter.

Chapter BL 50-year members Jean Baker (right) and Meredith Graves (left). Meredith passed away February 15, 2014.

In 1952, ten members of Chapter BL dimitted to organize Chadron's new Chapter FP.

In 1995, Chapter BL started out with fifty-eight members and seven nonresident members. Several of our dear members who are long since gone contributed to our programs. Frances Chicoine, our author, read some of her poetry. Betty McCawley, a CSC professor, read her fascinating autobiography. Our dear Gladys Pegues and Lloy Chamberlin each had special birthdays. Gladys was ninety-five years old in April of 1995 and Lloy Chamberlin celebrated her 50th year as a P.E.O.

Chapter BL - P.E.O. sleep-over at Andrea Voss's ranch

Chapter BL has a special historic house, 113 years old, owned by past president Ermine Coffee and later her daughter, Jean Baker, who still resides in the house and has been a P.E.O. for 42 years. Many P.E.O. meetings were held in this lovely house.

Also, Chapter BL can be proud that the library at Chadron State College, built in 1967, was named for BL past president Reta King.

Education for our young women is a priority for Chapter BL and we can proudly say that we have sponsored three PCE scholarships, one Cottey College scholarship, and six ELF loans. Also, we started the Gladys Pegues Scholarship, now called the

BL Scholarship, in honor of a lady who was a longtime distinguished member of BL. This scholarship was given to Julie Lehman, who met with a tragic accident and later died. We also contributed over $600 to the Dollars for Scholars program at Cottey College in 2005-2006.

Our Heidi Wess, who served one year as Reciprocity president, has been responsible for helping many of the scholarship recipients. Sara Gamby received the first BL Scholarship and Beverly Chaney has been a recipient of the P.E.O. Scholar Award.

In the future, Chapter BL hopes to spend more time helping the Nebraska P.E.O. Home and honoring our longtime members. We will be having a celebration in the near future for Meredith Graves as a 50-year member of P.E.O. and Jean Baker as a 42-year member.

There is one event that was special and held during Andrea Voss's year as president. Andrea invited the entire chapter out to her ranch for a sleepover. At the time, it was a hunting ranch, so the ranch could sleep fifteen people at a time. The members held a birthday party and cookout. Each sister—even some that were over 80 years old—shot targets and rode an ATV. On Sunday morning they toured the ranch and held a church service on a bluff overlooking the Black Hills. Everyone had a magnificent time.

At each meeting a sister who has filled a gift basket brings it to the meeting and we have a drawing for $1. Someone wins the basket and in turn brings it to the next meeting filled with goodies. This has been a nice project.

CHAPTER BL'S ACTIVE MEMBERSHIP IS 42; TOTAL ENROLLMENT IS 267

★

CHAPTER BM AINSWORTH
ORGANIZED JUNE 5, 1915
BY SARA REULING

Chapter BM, Ainsworth, was organized June 5, 1915, by Sara Reuling. Mame McAndrew, a P.E.O. from Chapter AX, Crawford, and Bessie Lindeman, Chapter N, Grand Junction, Colorado, were anxious to organize a P.E.O. chapter in Ainsworth. New initiates were Lila McAndrew and Jessie McAndrew, sisters of Mame; a cousin, Cyla Moseley; Pearl Wilson and her mother, Clara Wilson, and her daughter-in-law Bettie Wilson; and Lena McLaren. Every member held an office that first year.

During World War II, social activities were cut to a minimum. Members supported the local USO with food, and men from the nearby Air Base were entertained at dinners in members' homes. One of Chapter BM's members served the country as a WAVE.

Chapter BM has supported the P.E.O educational projects and the Nebraska P.E.O. Home in Beatrice each year. Different sisters give a report of each of the projects throughout the year helping to better educate the members on the criteria and accomplishments of each project. Founders' Day reports given yearly helped us embrace the founding sisters' values and beliefs and how life was back in 1869.

In 2001, Chapter BM hosted Local Chapter Officers' Workshops and in 2011, we hosted Reciprocity Group IV with fifty-nine members in attendance. In 2011, we honored one 80-year sister, one 70-year sister and two 60-year sisters. Since

1995, fifteen sisters have gone to Chapter Eternal.

Social events occur yearly when families get together for picnics, tubing, and games; BILs join in for card games. Local coffee shops or restaurants are frequented for coffee or meals. The chapter also gets together for progressive meals and mystery suppers.

Fundraisers over the years have included auctions for "sister-made" wall quilts, rummage sales, white elephant sales, Daisy Drop Bag collections (passing the bag for loose change at each meeting), voluntary additional contributions at dues time, an open house with sisters selling their items and donating back part of the money to the chapter. Several Chapter Eternal sisters' families have given us donations in the sister's name. Memorial donations have gone for books purchased in their memory and given to the Ainsworth Public Library; and a $500 memorial donation went to the Nebraska P.E.O. Home.

The P.E.O projects have been supported each year as well as the Nebraska P.E.O. Home in Beatrice. The Home has also received care packages with gifts from the chapter each Christmas. We have yearly contributed to a Cottey College student living in the Nebraska Suite through 'Chellie Bucks', gift baskets or gift cards. The chapter is also supportive of area charities, needy families, care centers, schools and libraries during the years through the philanthropic giving of the sisters. Not to mention all the salads and desserts provided for funeral meals of P.E.O. sisters and their families.

Over the years, numerous nominations have been made for PCE grants and P.E.O. STAR Scholarships. Those awarded PCE grants include Charity Fay 2012, Lisa Schlueter 2011, Jodi Skibinski-Curlo 2007, Katie Weichman 2006, Shirley Wray 2004, Kara Welch 2000 and Lorinda Rice-Connley 1997.

CHAPTER BM'S ACTIVE MEMBERSHIP IS 51; TOTAL ENROLLMENT IS 243

★

CHAPTER BN OMAHA
ORGANIZED JUNE 10, 1915
BY SARA REULING

Chapter BN was organized at the home of Effie Woodward, president of Chapter E, Omaha. Nebraska State Chapter Organizer Sara Reuling was assisted by Past State President Bertha Clark Hughes. Seven of the nine charter members dimitted from Chapter E. Charter members and first officers were Vadie T. Cameron, chaplain; Luena Grout, recording secretary; Dawnie Dale Hascall (AJ, Kansas), journalist; Maurine L. Kilgore, corresponding secretary; Minnie Lehnhoff, vice president; Clara B. Mason, president; Mae W. Menold, treasurer; Louise A. Rix, guard; and Mae G. Buffington, initiate.

Perhaps the late 1930's might be called the Golden Years of Chapter BN. In 1937, members included Rose Owens, treasurer of Supreme Chapter; Alice H. Scott, past president of Supreme Chapter; Lulah T. Andrews, past president of Nebraska State Chapter and executive secretary of Supreme Chapter; and Ada Mead, president of Nebraska State Chapter. During these early years, Ada was also instrumental in promoting the acquisition and maintenance of the Nebraska P.E.O. Home. She served on its board continuously from 1939 to 1974. Also, she was secretary of the Centennial Committee and chairman of the Building and Furnishings

Committee for the beautiful P.E.O. Centennial Center in Mount Pleasant, Iowa. In Supreme Chapter Conventions, she served as head page and head guard and gave devotional and keynote messages.

Chapter BN has provided the Omaha P.E.O. Association with three presidents; Rose Owens, 1920; Florence Wilson, 1934; and Nadine Ristau, 1974. In 1935, Florence Wilson was instrumental in combining a group of locally unaffiliated P.E.O.s into a new chapter, EF, and became its first president. Officers of BN assisted in initiating three members for Chapter EF, which was organized by BN's Ada Mead.

The light of the P.E.O. star has shown through the years with the exceptional talents of Chapter BN sisters, especially in music, art and literature. The chapter's participation in local, state and International P.E.O. activities has strengthened the chapter. Many BN members and their BILs have enriched the community through their involvement and contributions to various civic organizations.

The 1980's were changing times for Chapter BN. In February 1984, due to low meeting attendance and difficulty in filling officer and committee appointments, chapter BN decided to reorganize from a daytime to an evening chapter. Under the loving guidance of Organizer Susan Harr, permission to reorganize was granted from International Chapter. A small group of chapter BN members joined with twelve unaffiliates to establish the evening chapter. With Bernice Smith accepting the office of president and the help of her six officers, Chapter BN began a new era and grew with pride. The few members who still preferred an afternoon meeting dimitted to other chapters who had meeting times better suited to them.

As an evening group, Chapter BN continues to thrive and grow. With an active membership of 33, Chapter BN attempts to initiate one new member per year and still seeks out unaffiliates looking for a new chapter home. Project involvement has become a major goal for Chapter BN. Through successful fundraisers, Chapter BN has increased giving to the projects and the sisters are thrilled to regularly be among the top chapters in giving to the projects in the state. Chapter BN is grateful for the legacy of the sisters who came before us and for those who were willing to change the chapter from a day to evening group. The chapter continues to work towards fulfilling the objects and aims.

CHAPTER BN'S ACTIVE MEMBERSHIP IS 33; TOTAL ENROLLMENT IS 265

★

CHAPTER BO SIDNEY
ORGANIZED JUNE 11, 1915
BY SARA REULING

Chapter BO, Sidney, was organized June 11, 1915, by Sara Reuling. Kate Williams, X, McCook, and Adeline Hall, S, Broken Bow, were sponsors. Charter members were Josephine B. Jones, president; Tyrone E. Simon, vice president; Mayme McIntosh, recording secretary; Valeska Neubauer, corresponding secretary; Elvira Jack, treasurer; Jennie Harper, chaplain, and Dorothea Campbell, guard. Seven members of this group had been charter members of Chapter BA, Sidney, that was organized on March 31, 1909, but disbanded two years later.

Programs in the early days often were on poetry, book reviews and plays. Christmas meetings featured programs by members' children. During the depression, the chapter lost its savings in bank failure. Money was raised by various means to help the needy. One winter tons of coal were given, as well as food and clothing to alleviate suffering. World War II found Chapter BO sisters busy helping with the Red Cross by knitting, and by collecting fat and tin cans. Instead of serving lunch and dinner at meetings the chapter purchased War Bonds. Later, the Post War Chairman for Nebraska State Chapter was an appointee from Chapter BO.

In 1953, P.E.O. grew in Sidney as eleven members of Chapter BO transfered to form a new Chapter FR. Both chapters continue to enjoy meetings together on Founders' Day. The Golden Anniversary of Chapter BO was celebrated in 1965. One remaining charter member, Dorothea Campbell, was honored and presented her 50-year pin. Chapter BO celebrated their 75th anniversary with a tea featuring chapter history and memories.

Nearly two hundred sisters from Reciprocity Groups III and X met in Sidney on September 8, 1979, as guests of Chapter BO. Shirley Flohr was elected to the Reciprocity board and served as president in 1982-83. Chapter BO entertained Groups III and X again in 2010, and Gayle Glover was elected to the Reciprocity board and served as president in 2011-2012.

The 1967 Convention of Nebraska State Chapter was hosted by the members of Chapter BO and Chapter FR in Sidney. Janet Atkins was elected to the Nebraska State Chapter executive board and served as president of Nebraska State Chapter in 1973-1974. In 1988, Chapter BO and their BILs created and constructed the "Projects Party" at the Nebraska State Convention in Kimball complete with booths for each project in a carnival atmosphere. Convention of International Chapter in Omaha in 1991, a special time for all Nebraska P.E.O.s, was remembered by the P.E.O. chapters in Sidney for the work in preparing more than 300 signs and shipping them to Omaha for the event.

Chapter BO's Julia Peetz served Nebraska State Chapter as assistant secretary/treasurer from 1990 through 2006.

Chapter BO has had a number of ladies who have participated in securing loans from the P.E.O. Educational Loan Fund and grants from the P.E.O. Program for Continuing Education. Applicants are found through co-workers, relatives and friends. The two Sidney chapters give financial support for a yearly scholarship to a local high school student who is an outstanding student and serves in community activities.

P.E.O. projects benefit from a special Chapter BO tradition—the "Christmas Auction." Hand-made goodies, art works, and crafts are auctioned to sisters in some highly spirited bidding—all in good fun. Another fundraising tradition that started in 1983 is the "Happy Bucks" box where one dollar is donated to the box for any happy occasion a member wishes to share with her sisters. Over the years, many of Chapter BO's talented sisters have been generous in sharing their talents at chapter functions by performing in singing groups and acting in skits.

Chapter BO—in conjunction with Chapter FR—has a special project of tending to the "The Angel of Hope" statue in Sidney's Legion Park. It remembers those who have lost a child. Chapter BO members keep busy with their "Special Interest Groups" that include a chapter book club, a chapter bridge group, and a chapter bell choir that meet regularly.

The chapter celebrates our 50-year members with a special recognition by chapter members honoring their life history, P.E.O. service, and community service. Chapter BO celebrated its 100th anniversary in June of 2015.

CHAPTER BO'S ACTIVE MEMBERSHIP IS 63; TOTAL ENROLLMENT IS 285

★

CHAPTER BP OMAHA
ORGANIZED FEBRUARY 12, 1916
BY NORA KILLIAN

Chapter BP was organized in 1916 to provide a home for unaffiliated P.E.O.s in Omaha. Charter members and the chapters from which they came were Mamie Patton, E, president; Anna L. Harrington, D, vice president; Blanche M. Parrot, Q, Iowa, recording secretary; Ida I. Haas, A, corresponding secretary; Amelia O. Hazlett, AA, treasurer; Ida J. Brown-Lennox, V, chaplain; Jennie B. Bovell, AJ, guard; Ella F. Griswold, X, Iowa, journalist; Bertha F. McVea, E; Mary L. Peacock, D; Ella C. Patrick, Y; Hanna D. Swartz, AM.

Involvement in P.E.O. activities beyond the scope of the chapters has always been one of Chapter BP's strong points. It was an early supporter of the P.E.O. Educational Loan Fund and during the 1920's BP gave $100 each year to this fund—at a time when $100 was an enormous amount! It has sponsored several women as recipients of the P.E.O. Educational Loan Fund, P.E.O.Program for Continuing Education and helped pay the way for several young women to go on the Cottey Bus Trip. Chapter BP has also sponsored two candidates for the newly established P.E.O. STAR Scholarship.

Chapter BP has done a creative job of fundraising. We sold bedding plants and poinsettias. We also made and sold homemade lotion as well as prepackaged wild rice. Our most recent success has been selling coupon packets for a local department store's Community Day sale. It has allowed us the luxury of contributing generously to the P.E.O. projects as well as the Nebraska P.E.O. Home and Nebraska Cottey Bus Trip.

Members have always been active and served as officers of both reciprocity and the Nebraska State Chapter Executive Board. Most recently in 2004, Mary Wright was president of the Omaha Reciprocity Group and in 2010 Karna Kudirka served as vice president. Almost all members were involved in some aspect of the Convention of International Chapter in 1991 when Susan Harr served as an assistant chairman of the Convention Executive Committee. Peggy Evert and Sharyl Baca were guards; Mary Clanton was a delegate. Rita Seiler was Opening Night chairman; Ivy Reifschneider and Marcia Hofstetter helped design worker costumes. Jackie McCartney and Pam Allen were hotel hostesses and Jackie also stored kit material in her basement—a stack "as big as a car." Donna Murphy wrote a docent script to be read on buses. Marge O'Keefe drove V.I.P.s. Other members were involved in meals, acting as hostesses, working with decorations, sewing, and baking cookies. In 2008, when Convention of Nebraska State Chapter was held in Omaha, Chapter BP put together the BIL Banquet with many members taking part in everything from decorations to entertainment. Marty VanEkeren headed up the decorations while Mary Wright arranged the entertainment.

Two members of Chapter BP have served for seven years each on the executive board of Nebraska State Chapter: Marthena P. Stevens, president in 1958-1959 and Susan Harr, president in 1986-1987. Susan continues to serve as Historian for Nebraska State Chapter.

The chapter has seen twenty-four sisters become 50-year members. Eleven of those are still active. Josephine Harrington Sage was a member 67 years; Mable Brown Hyland, 61 years; and Marthena Peacock Stevens, 60 years.

We celebrated milestones in the past decade with a 90th birthday celebration for Chapter BP in 2006. Susan Harr and her committee planned a wonderful lunch at the Regency Clubhouse and prepared detailed displays and memorabilia. It was a great celebration and a great opportunity to catch up with sisters we hadn't seen in a while. In 2009, we celebrated with 50+ year member Ivy Reifschneider as she reached her 100th birthday. Celebrating with her was very special since she entered Chapter Eternal the following year.

Beyond the scope of P.E.O., Chapter BP's interests have been noticed within the community. It began during World War I, when the chapter adopted a French War orphan, Lucian Maucoux of Boneal, France. It continued the next fifty years with emphasis on children's needs. Sewing, clothing and financial assistance has helped local organizations provide for disadvantaged children. Most recently, our community connections include chapter members: Margaret Clough, Jeanette Schlichtemeier, Dale and Pat TeKolste, Connie Park, Susan Harr and Rita Seiler who have all been recognized with awards for service within organizations of which they are members. In 2002, chapter member Leslie Andersen was elected to serve as president of the Nebraska Bankers Association. (She was the first woman to hold that title and a third generation president of the Bank of Bennington.)

In addition to our regularly scheduled chapter meetings, we get together socially. Chapter member Peggy Evert and her BIL Glen have been generous in holding many pool parties at their home which are great for families to get together. At least once a year chapter member Mirm Tredway hosts a social gathering in the evening during the summer, which allows us to catch up with our working sisters who can't always make it to meetings. We rotate between a Christmas luncheon at a local country club and a holiday open house at the wonderfully decorated home of Robbie and Doug Mang. We also have informal coffees at a local coffee house at which we can just talk and are able to bring friends. This has been a great tool to introduce prospective members.

Our 100th birthday will occur in 2016. As members of Chapter BP we are proud of our heritage, exemplifying sisterly love and friendship together, and we hope for continuing happiness in the future.

CHAPTER BP'S ACTIVE MEMBERSHIP IS 49; TOTAL ENROLLMENT IS 231

He who walks in another's tracks
leaves no footprints.
–Joan L. Brannon

Chapter BQ David City
Organized February 16, 1916
by Nora Killian

On February 16, 1916, state organizer Nora Killian of Kearney, assisted by officers of Chapter I, Wahoo, started Chapter BQ. The first officers were Alice Hughes, president; Phoebe Becker, vice president; Louise Fulmer, recording secretary; Nellie Hinds, treasurer; Georgia Rich, corresponding secretary; Carrie Roper, journalist; Sarah Ayres, chaplain; Bessie Jordan, guard; and Maud Krahl, pianist. Other charter members were Agnes Becker, Bessie Crosthwaite, Elsie Schweser, and Anna Skiles.

Service to others is a trait of P.E.O. In its early years Chapter BQ contributed to the Near East Relief, aided a young woman who was sacrificing to secure a medical education, sent gifts to those who were ill and in bed, and quilted a robe for the Veteran's hospital. In 1918 sisters assumed the responsibility for a six-year-old French War orphan. Although their treasury was empty, they pledged $36.50 semi-annually. They were literally saved by the bell when new member Rachel Bell paid the installments. During the World Wars, Chapter BQ members did Red Cross work, knitted, and wrote letters to servicemen.

Today many of those same qualities are exhibited by sisters. Donations are made to local projects such as the school's Backpack Program for hungry children, and Christmas gifts are purchased for needy families through the local Blue Valley Community Action office.

Chapter BQ has also supported P.E.O. projects to the best of its ability with each project today receiving an average of $40-$50 each year. In addition, the chapter supports the Nebraska P.E.O. Home by sending small gifts to its residents and remembers students at Cottey College during holidays and birthdays. BQ has sponsored two candidates for the P.E.O. Program for Continuing Education.

Educational, social, and fundraising projects keep sisters in contact and supporting each other. In recent years, trips to visit nonresident members, the Nebraska P.E.O Home in Beatrice, and the Lauritzen Gardens in Omaha, as well as hosting socials with BILs and families have been part of the fun shared by members. Fundraising projects have included style shows and brunches, a long-running bridge marathon, garage sales, and an antique sale in the 1990's in conjunction with the town's Vaudeville Days. For the last three years, the chapter has hosted a vendor fair that raises money to provide scholarships to local women. In 1998 support for the scholarships received major funding when a dear sister, Catherine Swanson, bequeathed Chapter BQ part of her estate to be used for scholarships.

As with most chapters, time has brought change. Since its beginning in 1916, 233 sisters have enrolled. The chapter currently has twenty-nine active members who balance busy lives. To accommodate these hectic lifestyles, twelve regular meetings each year are all held in the evenings now with three social meetings held at various times each year. Refreshments are no longer a sit down affair, but rather drinks and light snacks are offered informally before a meeting. A real effort is made to conclude meetings within an hour to an hour and a half.

Celebrations and commitment to P.E.O. have been and remain a part of

Chapter BQ. Three charter members attended Chapter BQ's 25th anniversary luncheon in 1941. In 1966, the chapter celebrated its 50th anniversary and were honored to have in attendance Nebraska's P.E.O. president and 2nd vice president, four members of Chapter I, Wahoo, and former members. On March 13, 1990, chapter officers had donned their robes to celebrate an initiatory ceremony when tornado sirens sounded. They ran to a neighbor's home for shelter. At sight of the women in white, the man of the house exclaimed, "Angels!"

BQ sister Eloine Gettys showed her commitment to P.E.O. by serving as organizer of Nebraska State Chapter 1924-1925 while a member of Chapter BY, Lincoln. More recently, sisters Kaye Larson (now of Chapter Eternal) and Barb Hedlund have filled officer positions in Reciprocity Group VII.

In 2016 Chapter BQ will be 100! Another celebration awaits the chapter.

CHAPTER BQ'S ACTIVE MEMBERSHIP IS 29; TOTAL ENROLLMENT IS 233

★

CHAPTER BR LINCOLN
ORGANIZED MARCH 17, 1916
BY NORA KILLIAN

The year 2016 marks the celebration of Chapter BR's 100th anniversary. What a history this chapter has enjoyed. Chapter BR was organized by Nora Killian on March 17, 1916. Charter members were: Cora A. Detweiler, president; Edith A. Lathrop, corresponding secretary; Jennie A. Hall, treasurer; Grace Tait, vice president; Genevieve Moritz, recording secretary; Myrta Tompkins, chaplain; Lulu S. Wolford, journalist; Alice Corrine Stanley, guard; Olive Ayers, Cassie Bixby, Margaret Brown, Grace E. Curley, Mamie Garrison, Elizabeth Hammond, Lottie B. Jenkins, Marion McGrew, Virginia McGrew, Jessie R. Raugh, Letha Troxel, Alma Williams, Rosalie Williams, Rose H. Williams, Nellie Youngson, and May Youngson-Long.

At one time Chapter BR was a large chapter, and while membership has declined considerably over the years, for a variety of very real and present-day reasons, the current members treasure their personal relationships and benefits of the chapter. They embrace the many opportunities to learn and serve the common good of the P.E.O. Sisterhood.

Our members range in age from early thirties to mid nineties. The wide age diversity and many interests are a major strength to our smaller chapter. Many active 50+-year members are still a vital part of the chapter. Meetings are scheduled both for day and evening to accommodate our working sisters. Many members are or have been active in the community through business, education, church, political or service organizations, music and the arts. These members bring their expertise to P.E.O. so we can all benefit from each other with mutual support.

In 1924, guest speaker Bess Streeter Aldrich entertained the chapter by "giving us an afternoon of her time." Still today, Chapter BR's programs have yearly themes that incorporate a versatile educational and entertaining line-up from community persons and equally from our very talented chapter members. Programs have included community needs of children and adults as well as the city and state issues. And, always realizing that women need to have fun, enjoyable programs in their lives, these needs are equally balanced with a serious program agenda.

BR's fundraisers are always a success as members use their creativity for Ways and Means events and the chapter contributes generously to support the P.E.O. projects. Our chapter has worked diligently in sponsoring a number of women for the many P.E.O. scholarship, loan and grant projects. It is important not only to contribute to these projects with money but with applicants for the projects.

Chapter officers and committee chairs have functioned with diligence, dedication, and commitment. They serve and leave behind a legacy of their efforts while gaining a deeper friendship with the board and membership they served. Chapter BR's Lulu S. Wolford served as president of Nebraska State Chapter in 1923-24; Cora Detweiler served as president of Lincoln Reciprocity Roundtable in 1923, as did Laura Hall in 1937, Edna Rosenlof in 1949, Grace Trott in 1953, and Jessie Mulder in 1967.

In great love, our sisters take loving care of our own members, perhaps sharing food or flowers, remembering those who need cheer and comfort while ailing or grieving, or even just celebrating personal happy occasions. BR sisters grow together, bonded in caring friendships and sharing the true meaning of P.E.O.

CHAPTER BR'S ACTIVE MEMBERSHIP IS 49; TOTAL ENROLLMENT IS 357

★

CHAPTER BS OMAHA
ORGANIZED MAY 31, 1916
BY NORA KILLIAN

Chapter BS was organized on May 31, 1916, by Nora Steen Killian in Benson, Nebraska, following a conversation between Marion T. McGlasson and Gertrude M. Welch. The nine members, all initiates, were Marion McGlasson (who was elected president), Gertrude Welch, Bessie H. Hodder, Frances R. Nerness, Mayme M. Person, Bertha H. Pickard, Elizabeth Y. Tracy, Isabel W. Tyson and Estelle Wilcox. The organizer was a school friend of Marion McGlasson's from Cornell College in Mount Vernon, Iowa. Another friend, Bertha Clark Hughes, set in motion the work necessary for the new chapter and acted as president until the new officers were installed. Originally known as the "Benson Chapter," we became an Omaha chapter when the city annexed the Benson community in 1917.

The first year of our existence members and BILs attended five lavish social events organized by the chapter. At present there is a BIL party each summer, with a highlight being the 1991 dinner during opening ceremonies of Convention of International Chapter held at Ak-Sar-Ben.

May of 1991 was our 75th birthday as a chapter. We were honored at Nebraska State Convention that year and also celebrated with a lovely tea at the home of Linda Budurek.

Chapter BS contributes annually to each project and has supported many local charitable institutions. During World Wars I and II members knitted, sewed and worked at Service Centers and the USO.

In the decade 1993-2003 membership numbers in Chapter BS ranged from 31-44 with several nonresidents each year. We initiated sixteen women, welcomed four dimits and mourned the loss of eleven sisters to Chapter Eternal. Of our members, one is a fourth generation P.E.O., one celebrated her 100th birthday and five were honored for fifty years of membership.

Program themes centered on growth and change within the life of the individual, leading to an increase of our influence in the community. "Growth in Culture," "Reaching for Renewal," "Seeking Knowledge" and "Living with Change" encompassed such diverse topics as pioneering women, hospice care, Christian components in family models and the history of aprons! We learned about old-fashioned porches, birds and Habitat for Humanity. One of our Founders' Day programs included not only a luncheon featuring recipes and food of that era but also information on clothing, women's education and living conditions. Innovative fundraising ideas included donating $1/pound for the weight of our purse, a stay-at-home tea party, BIL picnic-dinner on the lake, and the joy basket. In addition to the P.E.O. projects, Cottey College and the Nebraska P.E.O. Home, we have been long time supporters of the Omaha Food Bank and Open Door Mission.

Programs with a "P.E.O." theme included Founders' Day Jeopardy, a speaker from the Nebraska P.E.O. Home, a presentation by the Nebraska PCE Chair, and a visit from an IPS recipient from Zimbabwe. In addition, programs involved outside speakers from Girls Inc., Project Harmony, and Make-A-Wish Foundation. The program at one business meeting turned into a surprise baby shower for one of our newest members after the birth of her first child!

Innovative fundraising ideas included a "Fun-Raiser" wine and cheese event at one of our sisters' homes and filling wild and colorful socks with our loose change for several months. The chapter held a couple of garage sales which were very successful in raising funds for each of the P.E.O. projects. For one sale, our sisters collected things they didn't need for a couple of years. Then...while setting up before the sale, our sisters began trying on the garage sale clothes on top of their other clothes. There were smiles and giggles all around.

Social events included a couple of lakeside BIL parties as well as a family picnic. The Christmas social meetings are always a special way for us to spend time together during the holiday season. One Christmas social included a silent auction to raise additional funds and Christmas gifts for the Nebraska P.E.O. Home.

Chapter BS has been successful in nominating several scholarship recipients over the years; most recently with two PCE grant recipients in 2010, a P.E.O. STAR Scholarship recipient in 2011, and another PCE grant recipient in 2012. Chapter BS has adopted a Cottey student and donated our Joy Basket proceeds to Cottey Challenge.

We have continued to give back to the Omaha community by supporting several organizations that benefit women in Omaha and the surrounding areas including the Make-a-Wish and Project Harmony organizations. We collected underwear for the homeless on Undie Monday at one meeting and toys for children at another.

Chapter BS sisters show loving support as during the years we have helped each other cope with serious illnesses and the loss of our spouses and family members.

The decade ended with the 2013 theme of "Jump Out of Your Comfort Zone." We continue to challenge ourselves to be successful in supporting the various P.E.O. projects, community organizations and finding qualified scholarship candidates.

We look forward to celebrating our 100th chapter birthday in 2016.

CHAPTER BS'S ACTIVE MEMBERSHIP IS 35; TOTAL ENROLLMENT IS 227

Chapter BT Weeping Water
Organized June 3, 1926
by Nora Killian

As a recent arrival in the community of Weeping Water, Mrs. Sybil Wickersham recognized the talented women residing in the area and led the efforts to organize a P.E.O. chapter. Eight women were charter members: Sybil Wickersham, president; Fannie Truman, vice president; Henrietta Butler, recording secretary; Minerva Gorder, corresponding secretary; Ida Day, treasurer; Alice Davis, chaplain; Berenice Wickersham, guard; and Caroline Teft, pianist.

Through the years Chapter BT has regularly held meetings in members' homes as well as local churches. Some meetings have been held in retirement or nursing homes where members resided as well as at the Nebraska P.E.O. Home in Beatrice. Social gatherings have included BIL parties and family picnics. Several members recently enjoyed a visit to P.E.O. headquarters in Des Moines.

As for fundraising, Chapter BT has produced cookie and salad recipe booklets. One ongoing project involves the sale of "Pin Pals." The original pin pal, a small white marguerite, was designed by Kathy Koehler, daughter of Doris Duff, and is still used by many sisters to attach their P.E.O. emblem to their clothing. Members who forget their pins donate a quarter at the meeting. We also hold a "brag" session after our meeting concludes; each "brag" nets the chapter one dollar. Our not-so-silent auction, held at our December social meeting and luncheon, has become our most successful fundraiser. It also offers us the opportunity to invite many guests.

In addition to our support of P.E.O. projects and Cottey College, we have had a tradition of outreach. In WWII members worked 482 hours making garments and bandages, in addition to sending letters and packages to those in the armed services. More recently, we donate a book each year to each of three area libraries; we bought "bricks" in support of our new community building and our local community theatre, The Lofte. We've donated canned goods to the local food bank and treated the volunteer rescue squad and firemen to goodies in appreciation for their service.

Six local women have attended Cottey College: Kathryn Ellis, Ruth Shannon Wahlquist, Elizabeth Wolcott Houseman, Martha Wallick Morris Bender, Kathy Harmon Koehler, who received a Nebraska Cottey Scholarship, and Cathy Rhodes. Chapter BT has been pleased to sponsor sixteen young women who have benefited from the P.E.O. Educational Loan Fund and six who have been awarded grants from the P.E.O. Program for Continuing Education. Chapter BT also joined with a Plattsmouth chapter in sponsoring a P.E.O. International Peace Scholarship recipient.

Chapter BT celebrated its 25th anniversary at the home of Helen Clark; both the 40th and 50th were celebrated at the home of Marylouise Hobson; and the 75th at the home of Ellen Snell. In January of 2007, we celebrated our 90th anniversary with a special historical program. We are honored to have three 50-year members: Mary Owens, Doris Duff and Linda Rhodes. In May of 2008 we celebrated the 70th anniversary of Marylouise Hobson, who since then has become a member of Chapter Eternal.

Not only are we active in our own chapter but are pleased that many of the chapter sisters have served in support of P.E.O. outside the chapter. Several Chapter BT women have served as Reciprocity presidents: Esther Teft, Alberta Elliott, Doris Duff, Mary Owens, and Nancy Reissig. Delegates to conventions of Supreme and International Chapter have been Sybil Wickersham, Evelina Snipes, Lenore Day, Edna Shannon, Alberta Elliott, Esther Teft, Dagmar Lauritzen, Linda Rhodes, and Carol Wiles. At the 1991 Convention of International Chapter held in Omaha, Linda Rhodes served as teller.

In 1986 Mary Domingo Owens served as state convention chairman in Peru with Dorothy Groesser as convention treasurer. During 1992-93 Mary honored Chapter BT with her commitment as president of Nebraska State Chapter. A reception tea was also held as a tribute to her service. Since Mary's service on the executive board, she has also served on the following state committees: Finance and Budget, Amendments and Recommendations, Chapter Groupings, Nominating, and the *Spirit of the Prairie* history.

CHAPTER BT'S ACTIVE MEMBERSHIP IS 47; TOTAL ENROLLMENT IS 200

★

CHAPTER BU ATKINSON
ORGANIZED NOVEMBER 25, 1916
BY NORA KILLIAN

Chapter BU was organized November 25, 1916. So the "Objects & Aims" of our Sisterhood have been repeated for ninety-nine years by the members of Chapter BU, sisters who believe in capacity for growth and improvement in ourselves and others. We help form a chain with all the other P.E.O. sisters in the chapters making up the International chapter. This chain reaches back into the traditions and values of yesterday, stretches to the mind and spirit of today, and extends on into the future.

We are grateful that the charter members of Chapter BU were women of vision and could recognize the values attainable from the support of the Sisterhood. Our chapter was organized November 25, 1916, with ten members. Nora Killian, the organizer, came to Atkinson by train. Charter members were: May Hart, Clara Mack, Jessie Deck, Hester Sturdevant, Minnie Munger, Anna Hookstra, Flora Moore, Helen Rocke, Della Eby, and Lucretia Woods. Mrs. Hart served as the first president. In the early years, programs consisted mainly of studying the Constitution and making bylaws. Later, reading books and discussions were popular. In 1917 the yearbook was changed to dispense with the heavy literature part of their programs for the next year and to do miscellaneous Red Cross work. We are proud to have our framed Charter and bring it out for special occasions. Programs have progressed with the times. During World War I years programs were on knitting and again reading. In 2013 we were able to have programs shown on the laptops and with guest speakers in attendance.

Early in the history of Chapter BU, when members were unable to take their part in a P.E.O. meeting, a fine of twenty-five cents was assessed. A "light lunch" was served at a price of 10 cents per member. Money was given to the P.E.O. Educational Loan Fund and relief for the Armenian children. Minutes from February 1927 show that a "tea" was served, the price per member was 10 cents and the proceeds went to "philanthropic work." Also, in the early years,

Chapter BU sold "applets" and "truffles" as money-making projects.

Beginning in 1927, each member was charged five cents for failing to wear her pin. Starting in 1929, the chapter began donating to the Child Saving Institute. In 1932, instead of serving lunch, money was donated to the free milk fund. Our chapter was privileged to have celebrated with one 70-year member, Marie Wilbern; one 65-year member, Helen Snyder; one 60-year member, Bernice Kelly; and four 50-year members, Connie Ramsay, Ruth Krotter, Claudia Galyen and Vera McIntosh.

Some of the fond memories of our members originated in 1920, when delicious waffles and syrup were served at the home of Violet Schultz. This was repeated at a meeting in 1970—a fun tradition. In 1921 a vote was taken to hire a dishwasher for 75 cents for the BIL party. Our BILs have been treated to parties almost every year and it is always a fun social event everyone looks forward too. The latest social event was a movie night with private showing of a movie and pot luck supper.

Chapter BU has sponsored women for grants and scholarships. Grants from the P.E.O. Program for Continuing Education have helped deserving young women in our area enter careers in nursing, business, exercise physiology, and special education. In 1935 when the Nebraska P.E.O. Home committee was raising money, Chapter BU contributed. Chapter BU members Violet Schultz and Frances Weller were residents of the Home. In 1978 and again in 2013 a trip was made to visit the Home along with yearly contributions.

Chapter BU has celebrated all of its special anniversaries, starting with the 10th anniversary in 1926 to the 75th anniversary in 1991 and looking forward to our 100th in 2016. The Memorial committee visits the cemeteries in the area on Memorial Day to place daisies for our Chapter Eternal members.

Delegates from our chapter to Convention of International Chapter have been Helen Peterson to Boston, Jan Brayton to Canada, Cindy Gotschall to Baltimore, and Barb Shane to Dallas. The value of these experiences is immeasurable and has greatly improved our chapter.

In 1943, war bonds were purchased by members and some members served as air raid wardens. Many garments were knitted and sewing was done and donated to the Red Cross and Victory Fund. Work for the Red Cross was recorded many times in the early minutes. Chapter BU's first robes had detachable yellow collars, which we changed to all white later. In 2010 we started a project to make new robes and completed them just a year before it was changed to be allowed not to use robes, but we have decided to keep with tradition for a while yet.

Chapter BU today donates to all P.E.O. projects and the Nebraska P.E.O. Home. When sister Vera McIntosh entered Chapter Eternal in 1999, she left the chapter an endowment of $5,000 with the interest to be used for scholarships for local high school girls. With more family donations and good stewardship we are able to grant two scholarships in her name every year. A big change was made in 1995 when local dues were changed from two dollars and fifty cents to ten dollars so as to better distribute the costs of the chapter to all members. Fundraisers have included a "Goodie Basket" and a "Joy Box." In recent years a cake walk has been an annual event at our local Hay Days Celebration; with the funds raised we have been able to increase our giving. We have enjoyed taking our turn at hosting Reciprocity Group IV. We invited them to the "Heart of BU-ti-ful Hay County" in 2012.

During our ninety-nine years, the power for goodness, hope and excellence has been demonstrated, and speaks to the potential of P.E.O.s and to the potential within each one of us. Today Chapter BU enjoys a balance of younger and older members who live in the city and rural areas. The membership consists of teachers, college students, nurses, artists, business women, musicians, homemakers, farmers and ranchers. The members of Chapter BU are especially proud of their roles as mothers and grandmothers.

CHAPTER BU'S ACTIVE MEMBERSHIP IS 33; TOTAL ENROLLMENT IS 168

★

CHAPTER BV BEAVER CITY
ORGANIZED JUNE 13, 1917
BY NORA KILLIAN

A P.E.O. chapter for Beaver City was on the minds of several women as early as 1914, and a list of the names of everyone in town was drawn up to prove that there were over 1,000 residents. However, doubts were expressed by Nora Killian, organizer from Kearney, who asked in a letter, "Have you enough good (underlined several times) P.E.O. material in the town so the chapter would not die a natural death?" Over eighty years later, in a town of 750 people, Chapter BV is alive and well with twenty-three active members.

Charter member Glen Modlin describes Nora Killian's visit to Beaver City: "a momentous occasion and since she was to leave the train at Oxford, Nellie McMurran and I left to meet her about two o'clock on a lovely afternoon. We seldom drove twenty miles those days without a man along so when a terrific wind and dust storm struck us only five miles from home, we were much dismayed. But there could be no turning back so we kept on. We were in an open car and the dust was so thick it was difficult to see across the road. When we reached Oxford, we tried to phone back to our husbands to tell them we were all right but the wires were down. When Mrs. Killian arrived, she wanted food. By the time we were all fed it was dark and we felt far from home, and indeed it was almost nine o'clock when we were safely back in Beaver City. But we held our organizational meeting that night at Mrs. McMurran's home and got the promise of a charter." Glen later tells about that meeting in a poem she wrote for a 1933 chapter meeting program in which she says:

> "So Mrs. Killian came to see, she looked us through and through,
> Examined our teeth and our pedigree and said she guessed we'd do.
> Then we waited and waited some more—the waiting was rather trying
> And there were lots of moans and groans and a lot of sighing.
> After waiting many weeks at last we were rewarded
> Oxford ladies took our vows and we were P.E.O.s recorded.
> Since then we've always more or less had pleasure and some sadness,
> For P.E.O.s I must confess, sometimes are full of badness.
> But through sixteen years we've moved along
>   with much joy and some sorrow,
> We've conquered our vicissitudes and face a bright tomorrow."

Some important memories for Chapter BV included seeing Chapter BV's own

Flora Stevens installed president of Nebraska State Chapter in 1956-57; hosting Reciprocity meetings; becoming a Cottey College Golden Anniversary Chapter; donating the "Blackman" trunk filled with turn-of-the-century fashions to Stuhr Museum, having their own hand bell choir play for the Memorial Hour at the 1991 Convention of International Chapter in Omaha, and for the Convention of Nebraska State Chapter in Kearney; and sponsoring Jody Vanlaningham as a P.E.O. Scholar Award recipient.

Chapter BV hopes that charter members Glen Modlin, Nellie McMurran, Elizabeth Lambe, Verna Brewster, Emma McClelland, Ellen, Ruth and Elizabeth Smith, Myrta Blackman and Eve Kelley would feel their labors to organize Chapter BV on June 13, 1917, were worthwhile as the chapter follows their lead in continuing to support P.E.O. projects and community efforts and "face a bright tomorrow."

CHAPTER BV'S ACTIVE MEMBERSHIP IS 24; TOTAL ENROLLMENT IS 135

CHAPTER BW ORLEANS
ORGANIZED JUNE 14, 1917
BY NORA KILLIAN

Chapter BW was organized in Orleans on June 14, 1917, by the organizer of Nebraska State Chapter, Nora S. Killian of Kearney and members of Chapter BJ, Alma. Charter members were Sarah Kirtland, Selma Haggard, Maude Moench, Mabel Melick, Belle Simpson, Bessie Austin, Susan Smith, Della Rundle and Roseann Bodien. Chapter BJ gave the model meeting after which Sarah Kirtland was elected to be the first president.

Member Dorothy M. Mahn made a bequest of a 160-acre farm in Phillips County, Kansas, to the Nebraska P.E.O. Home. Proceeds from the sale of the farm crops contributed considerably to the support of the Home. Mrs. Mahn also gave a beautiful candelabrum to the chapter. It is used in initiatory services and Founders' Day programs. It was also used in remembrance of those of Chapter Eternal at the chapter's 50th birthday celebration.

On June 14, 1942, Chapter BW celebrated its 25th anniversary. Two daughters of officers were initiated. They were Patricia McGrew and Gloria Hansen. At this time Chapter BW had 25 active members.

On June 1, 1967, members of Chapter BW celebrated the 50th anniversary of the chapter with a luncheon in Oxford. Five surviving charter members were present: Sarah Kirtland Pierce, Roseann Bodien, Della Rundle, Susan Smith and Mabel Melick. They were presented with 50-year pins by chapter president Willa Ralston.

In 1996 the chapter had a unique money-making idea. Afghans were designed representing each town of the newly consolidated area school, Southern Valley. Over 200 were sold at $39.95. This was the beginning of two P.E.O. scholarships given annually to female graduates of Southern Valley High School.

In 1997 Chapter BW celebrated its 80th birthday with a luncheon. Many attended including the state president and first vice president. A program entitled, "A Tisket, A Tasket, Enjoy our Show of Baskets" was presented with many baskets decorating the tables and walls of the Harlan County Ag Center.

In 1998 our chapter was honored as longtime member Dorothy Burd gave the state convention report.

Grace Johnson celebrated her 104th birthday in 2004. She was an 80-year member of P.E.O. Sadly, she passed away later that same year.

June 6, 2007, Chapter BW celebrated its 90th birthday. All inactive and non-resident members were invited.

In March 2011 the chapter hosted a "Murder Mystery" evening. Women from area chapters were invited to attend and participate. Over sixty members from four other chapters were there including past state president of Nebraska State Chapter, Leann Drullinger.

In 2011 we began using emails to remind members of upcoming meetings and for posting the meeting notes for members who couldn't attend. President Gaynelle Blickenstaff also sent news releases.

Member Trudi George began a monthly fundraiser known as "Phillip the Pig." At every meeting a ceramic pig is passed and members are encouraged to "fill up the pig" with money. This provides the chapter with $10-$15 every meeting.

We choose a Secret Sister every year and remember her during the year with a small gift on her birthday. We also take a supper meal to the homes of our young working mothers each February. The graves of deceased members are decorated in May. Every year in June, we have a potluck family picnic at the home of a member P.E.O. Members and their children and grandchildren enjoy games and socializing. Every year in December we have a Christmas party which includes our BILs. In lieu of a Christmas gift exchange, members are encouraged to donate to the local "Caring Cupboard." Our yearly socials include going on outings to theatres or dining at area restaurants. We have bake sales as annual fundraisers at area celebrations including Applefest in Orleans and the Stamford Pork Days.

Along with the two scholarships given to Southern Valley seniors, we sponsor a student from Cottey College for a month each year. We continue to donate to the P.E.O. International Peace Scholarship Fund, the P.E.O. Program for Continuing Education, the Nebraska P.E.O. Home and Cottey College.

CHAPTER BW'S ACTIVE MEMBERSHIP IS 25; TOTAL ENROLLMENT IS 145

★

CHAPTER BX OMAHA
ORGANIZED OCTOBER 2, 1917
BY ELLINOR KEMP

In the spring of 1917, Anna Hogue and Retta Binder conceived the idea of organizing a neighborhood chapter in the Dundee area of Omaha. This would solve the problem of traveling across town when there were few automobiles and fewer women who drove them.

At the organization of Chapter BX, officers of Chapter BP performed the Ceremony of Initiation. Charter members were: Ione J. Cullison, Original A, Iowa, president; Ida B. Faulkner, P, Illinois, vice president; Grace Stanton, ED, Iowa, recording secretary; Leila Bingaman, corresponding secretary; Ellen Craven, treasurer; Helen R. Foster, chaplain; Elda M. Yates, guard; Retta Binder; Anna Hogue; Virginia M. Kearns, I, Minnesota; Lulu D. Rohrbaugh, M; Ruth H. Drake; Mabel E. Dimmery; and Lela B. Parker. The chapter's first president, Ione

Cullison, was the first girl born to any P.E.O. Her mother, Pauline Ambler Janes, was the 20th woman initiated into Original Chapter A, Iowa, in 1869.

On October 18, 1927, the restriction confining membership in Chapter BX to Dundee was removed. Membership now includes sisters from many parts of the metro Omaha area.

Philanthropies have been many and reflect the needs of the community as well as the P.E.O. projects. One of the most notable began in 1928 and continued for twenty years. The chapter provided shelter, food and clothing for a father and his six children until they were self-sufficient. Today, sisters continue to support all the P.E.O. projects and have been particularly generous with donations to Cottey College and the Nebraska P.E.O. Home. After programs featuring speakers from local nonprofit groups, a small donation is made in the speaker's honor.

One memorable meeting took place in 1984 when five women were initiated—all daughters or daughters-in-law of members. In 1990, the chapter was honored to have one of its members, Heather Simmons, crowned Queen of Ak-Sar-Ben. Under the leadership of Mary Kay Gustafson, Chapter BX sponsored the formation of Chapter IJ in the spring of 1991.

During the 1991 Convention of International Chapter in Omaha, Trish Robertson served as secretary of the Convention Committee and Teri Teutsch served as an usher. Trish later served as chairman of the 1994 state convention and was elected to the executive board of Nebraska State Chapter. She was installed as president at the 2000 state convention. Her years of service on the state board were a shining example of her continuing devotion to the Sisterhood. Ruby Pederson was a member of the Nebraska delegation at the 1998 Convention of International Chapter in Seattle and Polly Partsch was a delegate for the 2011 St. Louis Convention.

Chapter BX is proud of the sisters who have given and continue to give of their time, talent and resources to the chapter, their churches and the community. A number have been honored for their service. In 2004, Eleanor Swanson was recognized for her fifty years as a lawyer. She was one of the first one hundred female lawyers in Nebraska. In 2006, she was the third recipient of Nebraska's Outstanding Contribution of Women in Law Award. In 2012, Pat Berton received the first Honorary Lifetime Volunteer Award from the Nebraska Medical Center. Several sisters owe their volunteer experiences at the Medical Center to Pat's encouragement. Midge Vickery has entertained the chapter and many other groups as a member of The Dancing Grannies.

As the 100th anniversary of our chapter approaches, we are grateful for the many gifts that membership in the Sisterhood provides. We have embraced and adapted to changes with grace. We have mourned the loss of the love and friendship of our sisters to Chapter Eternal. We have welcomed new sisters through initiation and transfers and we continue to look forward to being together at our first and third Tuesday meetings.

CHAPTER BX'S ACTIVE MEMBERSHIP IS 25; TOTAL ENROLLMENT IS 230

Be like a postage stamp—
stick to one thing until you get there
-Josh Billings

Chapter BY Lincoln
Organized January 26, 1918
by Ellinor Kemp

Charter members of Chapter BY were Minnie Fried Watson, president; Winifred H. Mattley; Lillian Pugsley, vice president; Minnie Brackett, guard; Mabel D. Gramlich, corresponding secretary; Susan Chase, Mattie M. Fransden, Ethel Winship, chaplain; Endora Esterbrook, Sylvia Aldrich, treasurer; Elsie Matthews, and Jennie Bruce, recording secretary. One half of the members were connected in some way with the College of Agriculture at the University of Nebraska. This common tie marked chapter life for some time, but its influence lessened with the initiation of other city women and acceptance of dimits.

Organized in the middle of World War I, members were engaged in different phases of the war effort. Contributions in subsequent wars have largely been under the supervision of the International Chapter. Chapter BY supports all P.E.O. projects, especially the P.E.O. Educational Loan Fund. The chapter is fortunate to have enhanced chapter life through the growth and development of each member with her special talents and skills. The chapter is blessed with musicians, poets, writers, flower lovers and a variety of active hobbyists who have provided members with many interesting and varied programs. There is continuing participation in the reciprocity program, the Lincoln Reciprocity Roundtable.

Chapter BY will celebrate its 100th anniversary on February 6, 2018. Chapter BY membership includes many educators, including a clinical instructor for nurses, grade school and high school teachers and counselors, church youth group leaders, a librarian, and a YMCA youth program director. Other members have careers in finance, insurance, and law. Chapter members are CASA volunteers, a case manager for traumatic brain injury patients, officers on the Friends of the Lied Board of Directors, a United Way Steering Committee member, a Goodwill Industries Board member, a volunteer with the American Historical Society of Germans from Russia and members of a quilting group that volunteers for Mourning Hope projects.

Chapter BY has had two members on the executive board of Nebraska State Chapter. Eloine Gettys was the organizer during 1924-25. Lois Newell served Nebraska State Chapter as an officer for seven years, becoming president in 1961. Over the years, Chapter BY has had two members on the Nebraska P.E.O. Home Board of Directors and representatives of the P.E.O. International Peace Scholarship Fund and Cottey College.

Chapter BY has several fundraising projects. Contributions are made to the "brag box" by a member who wants to tell her sisters about an accomplishment of her own or that of a member of her family. Recent fundraising events include a wine and cheese tasting. Chapter BY members served on the Steering Committee for the first and second annual P.E.O. Cake Ball Galas, in which many Lincoln chapters participated. Chapter BY also sponsored bakers, donated silent auction items and supplied additional volunteers.

Chapter BY initiates new members every year, and attributes that growth to sincere concern for each other and enjoyable meetings. Recent meetings include musicals at the Lied Center, tours of art galleries and historical buildings, and presentations from social programs in our community. Chapter members enjoy picnics on the deck of past president Mary Lou Fredickson's home outside Bennet.

CHAPTER BY'S ACTIVE MEMBERSHIP IS 47; TOTAL ENROLLMENT IS 315

★

Chapter BZ Gordon
Organized April 30, 1918
by Ellinor O. Kemp

The idea to create Chapter BZ was conceived by Josephine Swigert, Worthy Matron of Eastern Star, at a Grand Chapter meeting of the Order of Eastern Star, in a conversation with Sara Reuling who, at the time, was the president of the Nebraska Grand Chapter of P.E.O. There were questions as to whether or not Gordon had a population of 1,000, as required to start a chapter, but on April 30, 1918, under the organizational skills of Ellinor O. Kemp and sponsoring Chapter BL, Chadron, Chapter BZ was born. Charter members were Josephine Swigert, Jessie Ross, Alma Olsson, Mary E. Magowan, Lillie Mills, Vera E. Griswold, Edna Hull, Lauretta Jordan, Ella Coates and Myrtle Mills.

Chapter BZ has a rich tradition of deep roots and dedication. We have a 5th generation member in Kimberly Turnbull-Campbell, who is the great-great granddaughter of charter member Lillie Mills, and 4th generation members Jessica Burleigh Metzger and Nicole Burleigh, who are great-granddaughters of charter member Edna Hull. One of our deceased 50-year members always told the story of riding her horse five miles, when the roads were impassable because of weather, so that she wouldn't miss a P.E.O. meeting. We are so very blessed to have Lois Hinton, a 64-year member, Ruth Gealy, Cleo Hull and Donna Mills, who are all 55-year members, as active members of our chapter. All were originally initiated into Chapter BZ. An interesting side note, the night that Ruth, Cleo and Donna were initiated into Chapter BZ there were also two others. All five were daughters-in-law of Chapter BZ members.

Since 1995, Chapter BZ has sponsored an additional nine ELF recipients: Bridget Sasse, Sarah Sasse, Andrea Levi Becker, Alicia Hunter, Lisa Eisenreich, Kody Benson Eisenreich, Amber Balius, Lauren Goranson and Whitney Larson. This makes a total of twenty ELF successful candidates since our conception.

Two deceased sisters, Selma Jones Barker and Correne Wilhite, left Chapter BZ with substantial funds and with them we have been able to establish two scholarships for young women through the P.E.O. Foundation. We have set these scholarships up so that we can award them to local girls. With Correne's monetary gift we will also be supporting the Fort Robinson Post Play House for the next twenty years. Our own Ruth Gealy has had several of her biblical story writings published and a couple turned into plays. Kris Ferguson has recently served as the chairperson of the Nebraska IPS Committee.

Each year we celebrate our anniversary with a social meeting and dinner. We have had some great social meetings with our BILs. They have come to our Christmas social dinner and participated in our auction to raise money for our projects. This past summer we had a progressive picnic supper with our BILs, with the main entrée being a cream can supper. It was a delightful evening, lots of fun and the weather was perfect for being outside at all the stops.

CHAPTER BZ'S ACTIVE MEMBERSHIP IS 45; TOTAL ENROLLMENT IS 163

★

CHAPTER CA VALENTINE
ORGANIZED MAY 2, 1918
BY ELLINOR KEMP

Chapter CA was organized May 2, 1918, by Ellinor Kemp. Charter members were: Margaret Kinkaid, Minnie Adamson, Adelia Hoenig, Edith Adamson, Jennie Wells, Virginia Broome, Bertha Helzer, Harriet Rossiter, Sarah Lamoureaux, Sylvia Quigley, Julia Broome, and Florence Morris.

Honored members at this writing are Margaret Fisher, 66 years, Maybelle Carr, 64 years, Sheila Carr, 50 years and many other members soon to hit that 50-year mark. They are: Karen Butler, Eldina Eickhoff, Mary Henderson, Venetta Arganbright, Anne Quigley, Mary Young, Jackie Ravenscroft, Ginny Lee and Mary Kay Gustafson. In 2018 Chapter CA will proudly celebrate 100 years as a P.E.O. chapter.

Chapter CA faithfully has supported all the P.E.O. projects with yearly monetary gifts. A number of local women have been sponsored through the P.E.O. Educational Loan Fund and the P.E.O. Program for Continuing Education. One of our faithful members, Pat Fischer, worked diligently in contacting the IPS board in 2003 to obtain a scholarship for a Chinese woman who was accepted at Michigan and Cornell Universities. However, the woman's visa was refused. We have attempted, unsuccessfully, in sponsoring women for the P.E.O. Scholar Award. Primarily, we give local grants and have referred a number of women to the P.E.O. Educational Loan Fund with some receiving it.

Our local scholarships started initially as $200 for receipted expenses, but we have increased that to $500 for receipted expenses toward their education. We attempt to offer three local scholarships a year—two for nontraditional students in the fall and one graduating high school senior in the spring.

Money for chapter operating expenses and project support was raised primarily by a yearly rummage sale for many years. In the year 2004 we gave up the rummage sale fundraiser for a Christmas Faire. One of our members, Kay Lee, contacted vendors and got the ball rolling. The vendors would buy a space at our faire and sell their crafts, products and/or art. In addition, we have the concession lunch stand and a bake sale. That same year, 2004, we completed our new cookbook (an earlier one had been produced in 1988) and have had that as an additional fundraiser.

"Winterfest" as we call it, nets usually around $2,000. That provides us the base for our project contributions, and our local grants to women.

Chapter CA established a public library in 1921 and handled it completely until 1936. Then it was turned over to the city of Valentine. In 1961 Chapter CA furnished the children's reading room at the library. In 1993 a quilt based on the 1992 convention theme "A Celebration of Love" was quilted and presented to the library. In the late 1990's we donated $1,000 to the library. We will always have a loving concern for the city library in Valentine.

Chapter CA is part of Reciprocity Group IV. We served in 2013 in Valentine as the host group. We enjoyed entertaining our sisters from Group IV with a lunch and our annual reciprocity meeting. There were about 50 in attendance. We also enjoyed having our treasurer of Nebraska State Chapter, Patty Cowher, AH, visit us in 2013. She gave us a few suggestions and primarily gave us a lot of support in our work. We were truly honored to have her come visit us.

Chapter traditions include sending "care" packages to CA's college students and chapter entertainment and programs during the year. We are proud to show love and support for each other and many in our community by donating to the Food Pantry and proudly assisting in women's education support. In February we send "Valentines from Valentine" to our state officers and our adopted Cottey student. In 1991 we began the June brunch to coincide with the State Convention report. Sherry Fischer and committee have graciously hosted this brunch for the past five or six years. We look forward to it.

"Over the rivers—Platte, Dismal, Loup, Niobrara
And through the woods—Halsey National Forest
    and McKelvie National Forest
To the Sandhills of Nebraska."

CHAPTER CA'S ACTIVE MEMBERSHIP IS 66; TOTAL ENROLLMENT IS 256

*Sow an act, reap a habit; sow a habit, reap a character;
sow a character, reap a destiny.*

-G.D. Boardman

Chapter CB Ravenna
Organized December 5, 1918
by Ellinor Kemp

Chapter CB was organized on December 5, 1918, by Ellinor Kemp. Charter Members were Blanche Starr, Lurline Bonson Hlava, Urilla B. Stimpfig, Grace B. Kinney, Vera R. Thomson, Ethel M. Howard, Margaret C. Moore, Minnie J. Skillman, Venla A. Dickinson, and Jean M. Clark. Blanche Starr, a member of Chapter AQ, Loup City, moved to Ravenna in 1918, and it was through her efforts that Chapter CB was organized.

Our chapter is proud of the fact that we currently have four sisters who are 50+ year members, including Margie Rohde (69 years), Carolyn Wolkensdorfer (60 years), Betty McMaster (57 years), and Delores Mingus (53 years). In 2010, Betty McMaster proudly informed us of the initiation of her granddaughter, Rachel Dinsdale into Chapter GJ, Lincoln, making her a 5th generation P.E.O., beginning with her great-great grandmother who was a charter member of Chapter EP, Wisner, in 1938.

Irene Mortensen Church was a Chapter CB initiate who later dimitted to Colorado. She served as president of Colorado State Chapter in 1980-81.

Traditions always strengthen ties and Chapter CB abounds with them. Foremost is the annual Christmas dinner and gift exchange. The party theme is always a well-kept secret. However, twinkling lights, festive table decorations and favors for all reveal the holiday theme. A catered turkey dinner with all the trimmings satisfies all hunger pains. Secret sisters are revealed and a silent auction completes the evening's festivities.

Chapter Eternal sisters are remembered on Memorial Day with flowers and markers placed on their graves.

Chapter CB has always proposed and initiated the daughters of our members, which makes the spirit of P.E.O. even more meaningful. Then, P.E.O. becomes part of their lives wherever duty or positions take them. We find that many become active in other chapters or states; presently, one such daughter is president of Chapter DB, Tucson, Arizona. Several daughters have returned to Ravenna and have served for many years as an officer of our chapter. Whatever the situation demands, they bring youth and enthusiasm to any chapter.

Chapter CB sisters enjoy celebrating together and always support each other in their time of need. Family picnics are held as a social event each summer with occasional light-hearted initiation of new BILs. In 2008, we visited the Nebraska P.E.O. Home in Beatrice. Our chapter pianist composed a musical program which included the characteristics of each Founder. Along with thoughts of the Founders, we took a "Sentimental Journey" down the musical lane of songs of the residents' times. The ladies thoroughly enjoyed singing tunes such as *Me and My Gal, School Days, I Love You Truly*, and many more. Chapter CB sisters have always responded to the needs of our sisters when adversity becomes present in their homes. We provided food and services for a family with a sick child, and have brought food and taken care of the family home when members require treatment for cancer or other illnesses.

To keep the spirit of sisterhood vibrant, two sisters started a newsletter in

2002, which was given or sent to all of the members. Included were all chapter updates of current activities, congratulations to specific members, a recipe and any future activities requiring our attention. Our chapter also purchased beautiful new initiation robes in 2009.

In 1997, Jeanne Ross-Muhlbach was appointed Cottey Area Chairman. In 1999, our chapter hosted the meeting of Reciprocity Group XIII with Jeanne serving as president. Another of our members, Teresa Mingus, was recently appointed vice president of Reciprocity Group XIII and served as president when Chapter CB hosted the meeting in 2014.

When requested, our chapter has called upon our creative talents to make decorations for Nebraska State Conventions. Dottie Vrbka served as guard to state convention in 1991 and Jeanne Ross-Muhlbach was a guard in 2005. Margie Rhode served as delegate to Convention of International Chapter in Vancouver, British Columbia in 2005. Our chapter also served as the Photography Committee at Nebraska State Convention in 2005 and produced a beautiful scrapbook for all to purchase.

In order for our chapter to continue the tradition of supporting our P.E.O. projects and other worthy causes, fundraising ideas are varied. Creativity is essential as we look for new ideas. We have published a cookbook, held a purse and jewelry auction, written letters from Santa to local children, to name a few. We also have our annual Christmas silent auction and in 2012 instituted two very profitable fundraisers: a raffle for an iPad Mini and a Valentine's Sweetheart's Dinner. Our treasury currently reflects our efforts and creativity.

Support of our projects has always been a priority. In addition to annual contributions to all P.E.O. philanthropies and the Nebraska P.E.O. Home, we award a scholarship to a graduating Ravenna High School girl. We have contributed to the cost of the bus trip for RHS girls to attend the Cottey College visitation. Chapter CB members send care packages to our assigned Cottey College student yearly, and frequently send goodie boxes to the Nebraska P.E.O. Home. We have contributed to the Academic Center Walkway at Cottey College, and also adopted a Nebraska P.E.O. Home resident to shower with love, prayers, and gifts. Locally, our chapter contributed to an RHS student to attend a High Abiliity Learners' Camp. Without our help, this girl would not have been able to attend. We have also sponsored several women who have received ELF loans, and have nominated others for the PCE and the P.E.O. Scholar Award.

Life is exceptionally busy for many of our members as they meet the needs of their families and our small community. However, many still find time to serve their respective churches as volunteers, Sunday school teachers and committee leaders. Our members are very active civic volunteers, also. Currently, we have two School Board officers, three Library Board members and many others who serve in other ways. In 2006, a member was the recipient of a Fulbright Scholarship to study in Japan and met her pen pal of thirty-one years. In 2009, Janelle Grabowski and her daughter, Lisa, both members of our chapter, went on a mission trip to China where they taught English to people of all ages. In 2012, Janelle then went to Russia on a mission trip, bringing the people medical supplies, food, and other supplies for the orphans. In 2011, Misti Fiddelke went on a medical mission trip to serve the people of Haiti.

Our yearbook themes always remind us to keep close to us the values we learned during childhood and expressed through our P.E.O. Sisterhood such as Faith, Love, Purity, Justice, and Truth. When a new P.E.O. year dawns, all members wait anxiously to learn what the new theme will be. We are always amazed at the creativity our sisters use when interpreting the theme for their particular program. Some themes have included "We Give Thanks For...," "Memories of Childhood" (as told through children's books), "Clichés," "Getting to Know our Projects," and "Pay it Forward."

CHAPTER CB'S ACTIVE MEMBERSHIP IS 36; TOTAL ENROLLMENT IS 189

★

CHAPTER CC SEWARD
ORGANIZED MAY 9, 1919
BY ELLINOR KEMP

Chapter CC was organized with nine charter members that included three dimits: Genevieve Moritz, president; Bessie Stoner, treasurer; Lela Emerich, recording secretary; Glen Babson, vice president; Vera Luhe, corresponding secretary; Marie Storey, chaplain; Abby Chain, guard; Victoria Hildebrand, pianist; and Lulu Woods, journalist. One of the first items of business was voting to issue invitations of membership to members of Chapter AD, Seward, a chapter which had been in existence from 1902-1912. All of the members who resided in Seward joined Chapter CC.

Original meetings of the chapter were held in the afternoon but were later changed to the evenings, twice a month from September through June. Another change found the chapter meeting monthly in the evening throughout most of the year with morning meetings in June and July. This tradition continues with monthly meetings held the second Tuesday evening of each month, with two evening meetings in March and October held on the 4th Tuesday. The months of August and February include BIL social events. Refreshments and conversation precede all meetings.

The Founders' Day Dinner in January is an extra special event. It is a bit more lavish than regular meetings. A catered meal is provided and the hostesses decorate more elaborately and always present a program honoring and remembering our Founders.

Our chapter is proud to have possession of an original copy of a front-page newspaper article (including photographs) about our Founders and P.E.O. They were featured in the Mount Pleasant, Iowa, Free Press on June 23, 1904.

Throughout its history, Chapter CC has participated in the state and International life of the Sisterhood. The first chapter president wrote the lyrics to the song, "Spirit of P.E.O." Members have served as musicians, guards, and tellers at conventions. In 1957, all of the woven bags given to the state convention delegates were designed and sewn by the chapter. In 1991 replicas of the original P.E.O. ballot bags were sewn by members for use at the Convention of International Chapter in Omaha. Chapter CC is proud of its executive board member of Nebraska State Chapter, Mary Ann Eberspacher, who served from 1985 to 1992, the last year serving as state president.

Our chapter is generous with giving to the P.E.O. projects. Community involvement continues with a Christmas tradition, "Adopt A Family." Funds are collected from members for a family designated by the Blue Valley Community Action Program. The chapter purchases clothing items for family members, toys for the children, and ingredients for a holiday meal. Our major fundraising project is the selling of RADA products (cutlery, candles, cookbooks, and food items).

Throughout its history, Chapter CC has participated in the state and International life of the Sisterhood.

Chapter CC expresses devotion to the Sisterhood and eagerness to share in its gifts by initiating new members, with a special desire to include eligible daughters of members. Transferring P.E.O.s are also welcomed into the chapter.

CHAPTER CC'S ACTIVE MEMBERSHIP IS 72; TOTAL ENROLLMENT IS 254

CHAPTER CD SCOTTSBLUFF
ORGANIZED OCTOBER 6, 1919
BY LULU WOLFORD

It was during the time of readjustment following the close of World War I that the unaffiliated members of P.E.O. felt the desire of P.E.O. companionship. Mrs. Cora Boggs of Chapter K, Lincoln, took the initiative in promoting the organization of a chapter in Scottsbluff. Illness, however, prevented her from becoming the sponsor and the responsibility was assumed by Nellie Barron of Chapter AK, North Platte.

Lulu S. Wolford of Lincoln, state organizer, assisted by Nora S. Killian of Kearney, state president, organized Chapter CD in Scottsbluff on October 6, 1919.

The organizational meeting was held in the home of Ada Carr for the purpose of organization and initiation. Chapter AH, Alliance, did the initiatory work with the assistance of Miss Wolford. Charter members numbered eleven. Five were dimits: Nellie Barron, AK, North Platte; Cora Boggs, K, Lincoln; Myrnie Schwaner, AQ, Loup City; Neva De Conley, T, Clay Center; and Estelle Campbell, U, Colorado. The six initiates were: Ada Carr, Jean Graves, Carrie Hunt, Lois Schrock, Minnie L. Toole and Elizabeth Wright. Twenty-five guests from surrounding towns arrived by train for the occasion. A banquet was held at the Lincoln Hotel with thirty-seven guests attending. The flowers were yellow and white.

Miss Wolford stayed a day to help the new officers: president, Nellie Barron; vice president, Cora Boggs; recording secretary, Lois Schrock; corresponding secretary, Estelle Campbell; treasurer, Elizabeth Wright; chaplain, Myrnie Schwaner; guard, Ada Carr; journalist, Jean Graves and pianist, Minnie Toole. The initiation fee was $3 and the dues were $6. Every member had to be active as officers, hostesses and committee chairmen. A short program followed each meeting. Attendance was excellent and the membership grew.

We continue to grow and evolve and remain proud of our heritage of being Scottsbluff's original chapter. In order to accommodate the busy and changing lifestyles of our newer and younger members, we have set a variety of meeting times providing working sisters with a chance to attend meetings. These include Saturday mornings and late afternoons in a more casual atmosphere. These have proved to be popular. We continue to provide a light lunch or brunch before the business meeting to allow members time to visit. Our meetings continue to be followed by a program planned by members and which cover a variety of topics of interest to our sisters.

Our chapter gives generously to the P.E.O. projects and to other worthy local causes. One of our most popular fundraisers has been the production and selling of vanilla extract to friends and members of other local chapters. We actively pursue candidates for the P.E.O. STAR Scholarship and continue to seek candidates for other P.E.O. scholarships. In addition, for several years we gave a scholarship to a nontraditional female student at the local community college and we now, at Christmas, gift a local woman who needs a financial boost. Reaching out to women has always been an important part of our chapter life.

Computer technology has given us the ability to communicate quickly and easily with our membership regarding notices and upcoming events. It also serves to inform us of any needs or joys our sisters may have. While we change with the times, we still strive to fulfill the precepts of P.E.O.

CHAPTER CD'S ACTIVE MEMBERSHIP IS 48; TOTAL ENROLLMENT IS 303

CHAPTER CE ARAPAHOE
ORGANIZED NOVEMBER 29, 1919
BY LULU WOLFORD

Starting with nine women on a cold November 29, 1919, evening in Arapahoe, Chapter CE started its walk down the path of P.E.O. sisterhood. Lulu S. Wolford was on hand to organize the Arapahoe chapter with the following charter members: Ethelyn M. Willis, president; Bessie Stout, vice president; Katherine Sweeney, journalist; Sara E. Sweeney, corresponding secretary; Esther Murray, chaplain; Bessie R. Cox, recording secretary; Nellie Boyd, guard; Grace C. Harbison, pianist; and Eva Kropf, treasurer. Although none of the charter members is still living, Chapter CE is privileged to have descendants of one: Cathleen Weber.

The present members have careers and challenges as diverse as each individual. No matter where our programs take us each meeting, love, faith, and hope are ever present. Our devotions are always inspiring and teach us of our responsibility to our sisters and our community—to always seek improvement and to exhibit the qualities of faith, love, purity, justice, and truth.

The sisters of Chapter CE have always been outstanding cooks and take pride in their baked goods sold at the annual July 4th Bake Sale held in conjunction with Arapahoe's Prairie Pioneer Days. The bake sale started in 1984 and usually nets around $1,000. The money is earmarked for P.E.O. projects and the local scholarship established in 1994 for an outstanding graduating senior girl. During Arapahoe's quasquicentennial in 1996, Chapter CE published a cookbook of *Favorite Recipes–Pure and Simple* that included the history of Arapahoe, the history of P.E.O. and wonderful recipes. From 2000 to 2003, Chapter CE operated the Ye Olde Candy Shoppe for Arapahoe's Olde-Fashioned Christmas Celebration. Candy and confections of all kinds were sold.

Special fundraisers are hard work but bring the sisters closer in friendship and loyalty. Many sisters remember two massive garage sales in the 1980's that raised money for the new Arapahoe Public Library and for the state P.E.O. Golden

Anniversary Project. A later garage sale provided funds to send an additional sister besides the president to the Convention of International Chapter in Vancouver, Canada. A special Fall Fling in 2007 served delicious salads to women of the community and helped publicize P.E.O. A February Friendship Tea, with all kinds of finger sandwiches and sweets, was enjoyed by P.E.O members and the community in 2010.

The legacy of P.E.O remains a precious gift. In Chapter CE, one family has been members of P.E.O. for six generations and many families have been members for three and four generations. Cathleen Weber's granddaughter, a fourth generation P.E.O., recently received a P.E.O Scholar Award and will be a surgeon. Ashley McCoy, a second generation P.E.O., received a P.E.O. STAR Scholarship in 2011 and is currently attending UNL in Lincoln. Ann Collins' daughter, Jennifer, received money from the P.E.O. Educational Loan Fund to become a nurse practitioner. Sylvia Morris, whose daughter Ingrid Tangeman and three granddaughters have been initiated into Chapter CE, and Helen Traupe composed the Nebraska State Chapter Song. Chapter CE has eight 50-year members: Cathleen Weber, Lila Adams, Lois Koller, Faye Loreen Lockenor, Grace Emmett, Shirley McCoy, Marguerite Longsine, and Sheryl Koller.

Over the years Chapter CE worked at projects big and small to help the community of Arapahoe and meet philanthropic needs that have changed with the times. In the 1920's Chapter CE supported the Holdrege Orphanage with gifts of food and clothing. For instance, on November 23, 1926, sixty-three dozen cookies, nineteen quarts of fruit and twenty glasses of jelly were delivered to the orphanage. For several decades the chapter donated money to the Child Saving Institute in Omaha. The chapter helped raise almost $1,800 towards a new library, conducted a citywide house-to-house survey in order to obtain block grant funds for a new sewer system and worked at the recycling center. Each December the members donate food to the Arapahoe Food Pantry. In recent years they have sent care packages to soldiers in Desert Storm and to students at Cottey College. They responded to the Nebraska P.E.O. Home with contributions to help with remodeling projects and adopted a resident. They collected household items and clothing for Haven House in Lexington and funded a Youth-in-Need project for Arapahoe Public School students. Since 2010 the chapter has planted flowers at the outdoor classroom for a Green Project called A Medley of Buds.

Chapter CE sisters take delight in traditions and special functions within the chapter. Sisters enjoy five special meals during the year. In June a brunch is served and then the president gives the state convention report. In August the BILs are celebrated with a themed dinner. In September sisters enjoy fellowship over a special meal. Then in December the chapter enjoys a semi-formal Christmas dinner and gift exchange. In February in honor of the Oscars and the presentation of the president's letter, more formal attire is worn as a delicious buffet is served. A special committee decorates the graves of P.E.O.s in nearby cemeteries on Memorial Day and sisters who are ill or recovering from illnesses are brought meals and marguerite flowers.

Over the last fifteen years, Chapter CE has used email to contact sisters about meetings. The use of computers has greatly helped the tasks of treasurer, recording secretary, and other officers. Reports can be filed electronically and with use of templates, the minutes of the meetings, the yearbooks, and other writings are more uniform and easier to produce.

Chapter CE is a diverse group of women with a common denominator—caring and concern, not only for the chapter and the Sisterhood, but also for their families, their community, their state and the great nation under God in which they live.

CHAPTER CE'S ACTIVE MEMBERSHIP IS 61; TOTAL ENROLLMENT IS 192

★

CHAPTER CF NEBRASKA CITY
ORGANIZED JUNE 12, 1920
BY LULU WOLFORD

Chapter F in Plattsmouth sponsored Chapter CF and gave the initiatory ceremony at the home of Helen Stocker on a blisteringly hot day. According to the local newspaper, even electric fans could not keep the flowers from wilting and the ice cream from melting. Despite the heat, the prospective P.E.O.s prepared and served a complete dinner at the Stocker home.

Charter members were: Helen Stocker, X, Iowa, president; Lillian Hrubesky, O, vice president; Etha Brooks, F, recording secretary; Enid Vance, Q, corresponding secretary; Elizabeth Steinhart, treasurer; Martha Payne Cresap, chaplain; Minnie White Thygeson, guard; Jessie Payne, Catherine Bosworth, Maude Stevenson, Minnie McAdams, Hallie Bruce Lathrop, Cornelia Petring Kimmel, and Cora Fastenau.

Charter member Cornelia Petring Kimmel had received the first high school diploma issued west of the Missouri River and was the only member of the class of 1880, Nebraska City Senior High School.

In 1956, Chapter CF granted dimits to eleven members in sponsoring the organization of Chapter FV in Nebraska City.

The 1960 Nebraska State Convention was held in Nebraska City. All sessions were held at the Bethel United Church of Christ on West Central Avenue. The presence of Bertha Clark Hughes was a real plus.

Chapter CF has observed its 93rd anniversary. In 2020, the chapter will become a 100-year chapter. We are looking forward to a very special celebration at that time.

Up to the present time there have been twenty-one 50-year members. Presently, five active members of Chapter CF claim fifty or more years of membership. They are: Nancy DeLong Hoch, Joyce Hofer, Adelene Vock, Gertrude Brown, and Helen James Lundak. All have served the chapter as officers and three hold the distinction of being a past president of the chapter.

Many chapter members shared in preparation for, helping with, and enjoying the 1991 Convention of International Chapter held in Omaha at the Ak-Sar-Ben Coliseum. Angie Madison from Chapter CF served as a guard for Convention. Chapter CF was especially pleased that Nebraska City was chosen as a pre-convention tour site. Chapter CF members conducted the all-day tour, beginning with meeting our tour guests at 7:00AM in Omaha. Many of the tour participants who represented urban chapters were fascinated with the "wide-open" rural area through which they were traveling.

Program themes over the years have varied. One early meeting report states that "members enjoyed a Kensington," defined as a period of needlework and visiting. Themes for the year have included: "Travel," "Open Portals," "It's a Small World," "The Right Exercise of Any Talent We Possess," "The Newspaper," and "Getting to Know Our Sisters." The last-mentioned program theme has been especially enjoyed by our newer members.

Over the years, activities that have been shared with our BILs have been most enjoyable. One party was in the Pennsylvania Dutch tradition, complete with sauerkraut and apple torte. A number of parties featured initiations of BILs. A potluck supper served a dual purpose—not only did we entertain our BILs, but two 50-year members were recognized and honored. Our most recent party was a wine and cheese patio party held at the home of our then-president, Betty Widoe, and her BIL, Dale. However, when the temperature outdoors was still at 90° Fahrenheit at 6:00PM, the party was moved into their spacious, air-conditioned home.

Each summer Chapter CF looks forward to getting together with the members of sister Chapter FV. Memorable parties have been held at a number of local museums, on the terrace of Arbor Lodge, in the Victorian Garden in Wildwood Park and at a local Bed and Breakfast.

At the present time, Chapter CF enjoys two social meetings each year. At our December meeting, we are treated to Christmas goodies. Each member is asked to bring a tree ornament or Christmas decoration. The committee in charge chooses the method by which the packages will be distributed and every sister goes home with a new ornament or decoration. One of our spring meetings features a bountiful dinner prepared by the members of the Social Committee. In conjunction with the dinner, we hold a silent auction of items brought by the members. The last several years this auction has featured many handmade items, such as purses, greeting cards, baked goods, jellies, garden produce, knitted and crocheted items, all of which have provided spirited bidding and produced a very sizeable addition to our treasury, from which we are able to support P.E.O. projects.

CHAPTER CF'S ACTIVE MEMBERSHIP IS 53; TOTAL ENROLLMENT IS 275

★

CHAPTER CG CURTIS
ORGANIZED MARCH 25, 1921
BY LULU WOLFORD

P.E.O Chapter CG in Curtis, Nebraska, was organized March 25, 1921. The twelve charter members were: Margaret C. Gilbert, Franc C. Boas, Vernette T. Ireland, Corrine M. Keith, Jean M. Morse, Nellie B. Patton, Alta L. Schroeder, Effie T. Schaeffer, Cora G. Kempton, Jennie A. Thorne, Una I. Adams, and Nina Latham. The first president of Chapter CG was Margaret Gilbert. It was through Lulah Andrews that P.E.O. was organized in Curtis. They met the 1st and 3rd Wednesday of each month. One of their early activities was a reception each year for the lady teachers of N.S.A. and the Curtis Public School.

After ten years there were 16 members, 7 nonresident members and 1 member in Chapter Eternal. In the 1930's CG sponsored girls for the P.E.O. Educational Loan Fund.

In February of 1942, Chapter CG celebrated twenty years in P.E.O. by five charter members giving the program.

During the World War II years CG gave clothing to Allied Relief, gave to the Victory Fund, made USO scrapbooks, knitted and sewed for the war effort, gave to the United War Fund, helped with Red Cross and United War Fund Drives, and members bought war bonds. In 1944 CG first sent money to the Nebraska P.E.O. Home in Beatrice. In 1946 members made eighteen scrapbooks and gave them to the North Platte Canteen.

Chapter CG

In 1971, fifty years since Chapter CG was organized, charter members Corrine Keith and Alta Schroeder were still active members. Chapter CG celebrated by having a 50th birthday party and highlights of the fifty years were given. There were 27 active members, 4 nonresident members and 7 in Chapter Eternal. Alta Schroeder also helped Chapter CG (now forty-five members) celebrate sixty years in P.E.O. in April of 1981.

The Nebraska State Chapter of the P.E.O. Sisterhood celebrated 100 years in 1990. CG members honored the event with a program at each meeting celebrating Nebraska and P.E.O. past and present. The 75th birthday of Chapter CG was celebrated all year with the program theme "75 years of Chapter CG... Heart Full of Treasures."

Chapter members have helped with the state conventions in Holdrege in 1965, North Platte in 1979, in McCook in 1993 and in North Platte in 2007.

Nadine Brown served as P.E.O. Scholar Award chairman at the state convention in Norfolk 2010. Several members were delegates to the Supreme and International Chapter Conventions including Bev Jurgens, 1966, Boni Hathaway, 1976, Paulyne Wilinson, 1988, and Marty Jergensen, a teller in 1991.

In 1963 CG hosted Reciprocity Group I with a Hawaiian theme. Jeanne Wilkinson was Group I president. Tables were decorated with palm trees and Hawaiian dressed dolls and sea shells. South Sea music and the hula dance were performed by members. On October 8, 1984, CG hosted another Reciprocity Group I meeting.

On October 11, 2003, Chapter CG hosted the Reciprocity Group I meeting in Curtis at the Methodist Church. Kim Krull was reciprocity president. The theme for the meeting was "Cherished Memories." The tables were decorated with fine china, crystal and antiques and collectibles. Members made crocheted doilies which were given to attendees.

Some of our fun social meetings have been visiting Dancing Leaf Lodge in Wellfleet, sampling wine at Three Brothers' Winery and vineyard in Farnam, visiting Perks Prairie Paradise near Stockville, having a tea party in McCook after officer's training and even a morning pajama party. Our social committees always come up with clever ideas for themes and decorations for our annual salad supper in May and BIL picnic in September. We enjoy surprising our secret sisters at Christmas and on their birthdays. Our courtesy chairman always remembers our sisters with cards for all occasions. Chapter CG sisters are always there to help with food and support when needed.

Tasting teas, card parties, silent auctions, and Christmas tours of homes, have been a fun way for CG to make extra funds. Caramel apples, sundaes, and cookies have been made, baked and sold to increase our funds. Our chapter also has auctions after some of our business meetings, bidding on all kinds of neat things that members donate. We have a basket raffle every fall to raise funds for a local scholarship.

Members have volunteered at the movie theater and at the care home. Chapter CG gives to the P.E.O. projects. We've sponsored many women for the P.E.O. Educational Loan Fund and we give to the Nebraska P.E.O. Home in Beatrice. Gifts have been sent to Cottey students and member college students. Chapter CG has also given to other worthy charitable projects.

We celebrated our 50-year members—Alta Schroeder 1971, Corrine Keith 1971, Veda Adams 1973, Bertha Wilkinson 1974, Bertha Dillman 1974, Betty Cook 1978, Neva Watkins 1981, Helen Adams 2001, Beverly Jurgens 2003, and Shirley Schroeder 2005. We have had memorial services for our members lost to Chapter Eternal.

Our chapter is so special because of the love, kindness, and support of our members. Our meetings are very enjoyable and the programs are interesting.

CHAPTER CG'S ACTIVE MEMBERSHIP IS 36; TOTAL ENROLLMENT IS 200

★

CHAPTER CH COLUMBUS
ORGANIZED APRIL 22, 1921
BY LULU WOLFORD

Chapter CH, Columbus, was organized April 22, 1921, by Lulu Wolford. Fourteen friends became sisters. Olga Webb, president; Wilhelmina Larson, vice president; Metta Neumarker, recording secretary; Alma H. Walker, corresponding secretary; Elizabeth Campbell, treasurer; Louise Whitney, chaplain; Myrtle Miller, guard; Elsie Griffith, organist; Maude Gates, Carrie Voss, Edna Robertson, Greta Rhode, Margaret Lightner, and Vera Kelly.

Chapter CH participated in the state convention for the first time in 1942. The 68th state convention was held in Columbus in 1957. The 96th state convention was held in Columbus in 1985. 2013 brought the 124th state convention to Columbus and many CH sisters were actively involved.

In 1950 Meta Neumarker sponsored the organization of a new chapter in Columbus, Chapter FJ. Thirteen Chapter CH members dimitted to the new chapter.

Chapter CH celebrated its 70th birthday in 1991 with a picnic. Our 90th birthday was celebrated April 2011 with a luncheon, photo shoot, and power point program "Then and Now" walking us down memory lane.

Laura Miller served as treasurer and corresponding secretary of the executive board of the Nebraska State Chapter. Cynthia (Uhlmann) Jarecke progressed through all offices of the executive board of Nebraska State Chapter and served as president in 2005-2006. Shirley Deyke Thompson served on the Board of the Nebraska P.E.O Home. Elsie Griffith, one of the CH charter members, was a charter resident of the Home.

Chapter CH raises funds by entertaining our BILs at a dinner combined with a silent auction. Many members participate in an annual bridge marathon with other local chapters. CH participated in the Horse Race fundraiser called the Defining Moment Campaign for Cottey College.

CH continues to assist women students with moral and monetary support. The marathon bridge proceeds benefit a non-traditional woman student at the local community college. CH assisted one such student to complete her four-year degree.

CH donated funds to the educational exhibit at the Higgins World War II Memorial. Toiletries were collected to be donated to the Center for Survivors of Domestic Abuse. A baby shower benefited the East Central Health District Center. Care packages were sent to a Cottey student and to the Nebraska P.E.O. Home. Cookies were sent to the U.S. troops in Bosnia along with supplies for the Bosnian school children.

CH sisters socialized at the BIL events, ice creams socials and coffees in the park. The longevity of our memberships and the variety of ages among our members create a diversity we treasure. Mothers, daughters and friends became sisters.

Sixty-three of our CH sisters have joined Chapter Eternal. Fifteen left us since 1995. We cherish their memory each Memorial Day by placing a floral tribute beside the P.E.O marker at their grave site. Thirty-four sisters were initiated from 1996 to the present.

CHAPTER CH'S ACTIVE MEMBERSHIP IS 73; TOTAL ENROLLMENT IS 321

★

CHAPTER CI CHAPPELL
ORGANIZED APRIL 27, 1921
BY LULU WOLFORD

Chapter CI was organized with seventeen charter members: Mabel Fordyce, president; Retta F. Brown, vice president; Bertha M. Wertz, recording secretary; Grace M. Busse, corresponding secretary; Tillie Peterson, treasurer; Nina G. Pyle, chaplain; Blanche Wertz, guard; Alice M. Peterson, Linnea Betts, Blondell Draemel, Lulu M. Colman, Agnes Grey, Hazel G. Stanley, Blanche Isenberger, Mary E. Dryden, Eunice Weigand Hall, and Ada Wolf. Anna Mitchem of Chapter H, Boulder, Colorado, sponsored the movement to organize Chapter CI. However, her dimit arrived too late for her name to be on the charter list.

An elaborate luncheon in a lavender and white theme was prepared for the state organizer, Miss Lulu Wolford. A standing joke in Chapter CI has been that Miss Wolford, after complimenting the chapter on the beautiful luncheon, very subtly remarked that in the future, their luncheons might be decorated in yellow and white.

Chapter CI celebrated its 50th Anniversary April 22, 1971, with a covered dish dinner. The same lavender dessert that the Chapter CI charter members served at their organizational luncheon was served. Three charter members were honored and a letter from a fourth member living in Idaho was read. After hearing a résumé of the past fifty years, the evening was spent with members reminiscing.

Chapter members celebrated our 85th Anniversary with a huge birthday bash on April 27, 2006. Our party was complete with balloons, favors, games, cake and ice cream. Excerpts were read from early chapter minutes and president's letters of long ago.

A longtime tradition of Chapter CI has been to honor the junior and senior girls of the local high school. We invite the girls to "tea" at our February meeting. We have a presentation about Cottey College, the P.E.O. STAR Scholarship and conclude with entertainment and lunch.

Another tradition of our chapter is to place a book in the public library in memory of each deceased sister. The chapter has outstanding talent and many interesting and educational programs throughout the year.

Chapter CI combines popular social dinners in September and December with money-making for our projects. Each member contributes cash for the meal and we also sell chances on prizes and pay to play entertaining games. Chapter CI contributes to seven projects, the newest being the P.E.O. STAR Scholarship. We also donated extra for the Cottey College "Defining Moment Campaign" as they change to a four-year institution.

A new social event is a winter dinner. We invite our BILs and friends of chapter members to enjoy an evening of dinner, fellowship and entertainment.

"The March into Chapel" was the theme for Reciprocity Groups III and X meeting on October 19, 2013, in Chappell. There were eighty-four in attendance. Included in the event were a memorial service, workshops, our annual business meeting, a luncheon and a skit telling about the aprons worn by our seven Founders when they made the 1869 dramatic announcement about their new society during chapel at Iowa Wesleyan.

We were proud in 2009 to sponsor Becky Peters, who successfully was awarded money from the P.E.O. Educational Loan Fund and also a grant from the P.E.O. Program for Continuing Education.

Chapter CI 50-year members are Maurine Lydiatt, Musa Duffield, Hilda Ray, Margaret Klingman, and Virginia Peeks.

CHAPTER CI'S ACTIVE MEMBERSHIP IS 34; TOTAL ENROLLMENT IS 209

★

CHAPTER CJ BURWELL
ORGANIZED MAY 21, 1921
BY LULU WOLFORD

Chapter CJ was organized May 21, 1921, greatly in part due to the efforts of Grace V. Wagner. Mrs. Wagner brought the dream of a sisterhood to Burwell from Chapter AB, Central City. State organizer Miss Lulu Wolford was assisted by members of Chapter BB, Ord, and initiated Effie Cram, Bess Cram, Frances DeLashmutt, Fannie Fenner, Alice Jenks, Julia Johnson, Cora McMullen, Rose Roberton, Mabel Turnicliff, Sylvia Weber, Nina White and Alice Cole as charter members. Due to a delay in receiving Mrs. Wagner's dimit, she was not listed as a charter member.

Believing in promoting education for young women, Chapter CJ works very hard raising funds to give to local scholarships and to the P.E.O. projects. Over the years, rummage sales, bake sales, cookbook sales, greenery sales, spring teas, and Christmas home tours have raised money. Local scholarships have been given since 1976 to area high school graduates. And in 1985, Rex Wagner established the Grace V. Wagner scholarship fund in memory of his mother. This four-year scholarship of $1,000 for each year has helped each young woman to graduate from college.

Honoring our high school senior young ladies has been a tradition since 1923. In the spring, a party is held to celebrate this milestone in their life. It is an evening to enjoy dessert and fellowship together, and to share with the senior girls and their mothers about P.E.O. projects.

Fellowship together as a chapter has been important for harmony and growth. From salad suppers, dress-up teas, BIL dinners, and birthday parties in May to celebrate our organization, Chapter CJ has had fun together.

Sharing with our community, the "Daisy Award" was started to recognize people who have made a difference in the community through service. It is our way of saying "you are valued" and "thank you."

Chapter CJ is honored to have a 70-year P.E.O. member, Margaret Harrod. She is a true example of the qualities of P.E.O. in the many years she has served.

CHAPTER CJ'S ACTIVE MEMBERSHIP IS 38; TOTAL ENROLLMENT IS 192

★

CHAPTER CK GRAND ISLAND
ORGANIZED MAY 21, 1921
BY LULU WOLFORD

Chapter CK was the first P.E.O. chapter established in Grand Island. Chapter CK was organized May 21, 1921, by Miss Lulu Wolford, state organizer. The work was exemplified by Chapter BI, Shelton. Charter members of Chapter CK were Grace B. Kinney, president; Blanche Stitt, vice president; Alice R. Emigh, recording secretary; Florence B. Free, corresponding secretary; Ruth D. Kendall, treasurer; Grace B. Paine, chaplain; Myra Lyons, guard; Margaret Martin, Joanna B. Firth, Lora C. Hanna, Jennie I. Martin Brigance, Mary D. O'Laughlin, Mildred E. Rother, and Marion C. Tully.

The chapter organized with six dimitted members and eight initiates. After organizing they added four members by dimit. Three of these were supposed to be charter members, but their dimit did not reach the organizer in time. The first president's letter relates: "before we were ready for our fall work we lost three members by removal." That first year the chapter never missed a meeting and "everyone has taken her part willingly and well."

Marsha Miller and Karin Miller, daughters of Marilynn Miller (past president of Chapter CK and now a nonresident member) both received loans from ELF. Also during this time we sponsored non-traditional students at Central Community College and Doane College. Today the chapter also provides a $100 scholarship to daughters of CK members at the time of their high school graduation.

During this time our chapter has had many programs. Some stand out and are long remembered. Charlotte Brown led the chapter in playing hand bells for our December meetings. That fun Christmas activity is found in president's letters several times during the last twenty years.

It seems our chapter likes pumpkins. Even many years ago we were decorating pumpkins. Programs and chapter priorities change, but Chapter CK still decorates and sells pumpkins each fall. This is a very successful monetary endeavor and decorating day is a wonderful bonding experience for all members.

Chapter CK has had two Nebraska State Chapter presidents—Florence Stewart in 1948 and Harriet Lumbard in 1960. Kathleen Gosch, state president in 1998-99, was initiated into Chapter CK. In 1997 the chapter celebrated its 75th anniversary. We look forward to celebrating 100 years in 2021. Time moves on so quickly! Hopefully our chapter moves forward with vigor and anticipation in the future of Chapter CK.

In 1993 there were four P.E.O. chapters in Grand Island—CK, EH, EZ and GP. Many of the founding members of these chapters dimitted or transferred from Chapter CK. We now have six chapters in Grand Island with the addition of Chapter HJ and Chapter II.

CHAPTER CK'S ACTIVE MEMBERSHIP IS 51; TOTAL ENROLLMENT IS 412

★

CHAPTER CL OGALLALA
ORGANIZED OCTOBER 25, 1921
BY NELLE GRANTHAM

Chapter CL begins its 94th year grateful to organizing sisters Bernice Theal and Ferne Hunt and their aunt, sponsor Nell Barnard of Stromsburg. Other charter members included Claire DeVoe, Josie Doherty, Bess Dutch, Gertrude Eymann, Gertrude Hillyer, Frances Hough, Mattie Meredith, Carrie Nelson, Vesper Nye, Lois Walsh, Blanche Woolery and Ethel Worden.

Education was of highest priority for CL during the earliest years, when they donated $1 each to the P.E.O. Educational Loan Fund, and remains so today. Members organized an annual "Educational Day" to honor local teachers, raised money for books and volunteered at the library, plus donated magazine subscriptions to local schools. A P.E.O. glee club often entertained community groups.

During World War II, members prepared food for and worked at the North Platte Canteen and at Ogallala's German prisoner of war facility, helped write letters, supervised activities, plus sponsored a recreation center for U. S. Army Guards. They also planted and subsequently carried water to trees at the local cemetery, establishing CL as community involved.

CL hosted the Nebraska P.E.O. State Convention in 1972 under the leadership of Bette Padley and Barbara Cobb, launching Mrs. Cobb through the state offices to the presidency in 1977-78. CL is pleased that five members have served on the Nebraska P.E.O. Home Board of Directors, no small feat of service given the 592 miles round trip driving distance from outstate Nebraska to the Beatrice Home site; a CL member also administered the Home for seventeen years. When chapter membership increased significantly, thirteen CL members helped establish our spin-off sister, Chapter HI.

Special events in the life of our chapter are the January Founders' Day brunch shared with Chapter HI and our summertime salad supper at a Lake McConaughy home where we enjoy casual conversations, good food, and beautiful sunsets. In addition, personal visits and offerings of assistance or meals are extended to sisters during their times of special need.

December meetings are dedicated to arranging our homemade cookies onto plates, which we deliver by hand to Ogallala area shut-ins. Firmly established as another of CL's many examples of consideration for others, we continue the activity into its sixth decade. CL also hosts two coffees for residents in local assisted living facilities where we partake of our cookies and holiday spirit together.

Today Chapter CL continues its support for education, proud of their reputation as a state leader in the number of P.E.O. Educational Loan Fund recipients. Imagine the delight charter member Ethel Worden might enjoy in knowing that through the leadership of her granddaughter, our ELF chairman, the number of approved loans has grown to 104 with never a default, sealing our leadership role within Nebraska. We have also sponsored an untold number of grants for the P.E.O. Program for Continuing Education and our members have filled numerous state P.E.O. positions.

Chapter CL honors its commitment to remain a viable community organization as we struggle to integrate our influence in a changing, more casual world. While our continued focus is on building connections within our own membership through thoughtful care and concern for each other, many members also serve our county through service on boards, foundations, schools and church leadership, always with a sincere regard for our role within our community.

CHAPTER CL'S ACTIVE MEMBERSHIP IS 53; TOTAL ENROLLMENT IS 336

CHAPTER CM CRETE
ORGANIZED NOVEMBER 3, 1921
BY NELLE GRANTHAM

Chapter CM was organized November 3, 1921, by Organizer Nelle Grantham. She was assisted by State Chapter President Elizabeth Robertson, and Chapter BR, Lincoln. Charter members included Edith Aller, Florence Bennett, Lucille Braun, Mildred Brown, Grace Carter, Ethel Collett, Helga Dayton, Edith Hastings, Carolyn Kinney, Nora Matthews, Harriet Mitchell, Margaret Mixa, Anna Taylor, and first president of CM, Eglantine Velte. Through its 92 years, members have been innovative in presenting their writing skills, sharing a variety of artistic talents, and developing absorbing and pertinent programs. Social occasions and entertainments for families and guests have been yearly highlights that strengthen our sisterly bonds.

In 1928, Chapter CM participated in the organization of Chapter DQ, Friend. Through the years, reciprocity meetings with Chapter DQ and Chapter BF, Wilber, have been enjoyed.

In 2013, Chapter CM lost two sisters to Chapter Eternal. Rowena (nee Adams) Lothrop Miller and Erma (nee Ragatz) Osterhout met at Doane College and were initiated into Chapter CM in November of 1939. Their remarkable dedication to the Sisterhood and to Chapter CM for almost seventy-five years is an incredible record of service and selflessness to all of us. The chapter currently boasts of three 60-year-plus members.

Fundraising activities, within the chapter and the wider community, have often been exceptional times for fun and fellowship thereby enabling us to provide generous gifts to our philanthropies.

Chapter CM supports all P.E.O. projects and now gives on average $1,000 per year. Money is raised in a variety of ways: silent auctions, farmer's market sales of produce and baked goods, a Brag Box, a pie event with Nebraska's famous "pie lady of Eustis," crocheted dish cloths, sales of special cleaning cloths, a food stand for the two-day Blue River Music Fest at the Benne Memorial Museum in Crete, food stands at Czech concerts and dance recitals, garage sales, and, in years past, participation in the Bed & Breakfast Program. For over ten years we had a three-mile stretch of Highway 33 that we volunteered to keep attractive and litter-free.

In 2013, Chapter CM assisted with the Nebraska State Chapter Convention in Fremont. Reciprocity meetings are always an enjoyable time to gather and share ideas with sisters. Wyladee "Billy" Pecka is serving her third term on the Nebraska P.E.O. Home Board of Directors. Chapter CM has sponsored twenty-two ELF loan recipients and nominated a P.E.O. STAR Scholarship recipient in 2012. Two CM members, Dr. Annadora Gregory and Rhoda Miller, have served on the faculty of Cottey College. Our CM sister Gertrude Brown was the first matron of the Nebraska P.E.O. Home. Another initiate, Debbie Cowan, ably served as Executive Secretary of International Chapter from August 1988 to August 1993 when ill health forced her resignation. Chapter CM sister Connie Hood served as state chairman of IPS from 2009 to 2011. Upon our chapter's recommendation, Necla Palamutlu, a native of Turkey, received a P.E.O. International Peace Scholarship for study after her 1957 Doane College graduation.

Chapter CM has celebrated numerous milestones in its nine decades. As we have **c**ultivated **m**embership and **c**reated **m**emories, our chapter has grown strong by wholehearted support of our educational projects for women. Our rich heritage and our willingness to embrace diversity gives us a firm foundation to face the challenges of the future with renewed commitment to our ideals.

Chapter CM's active membership is 44; total enrollment is 268

★

Chapter CN Osceola
Organized December 16, 1921
by Nellie Grantham

It is to Capitola Israel that we owe our gratitude for taking the steps to start a P.E.O. chapter in Osceola. Conducted by the Stromsburg's Chapter AR officers, the initiation of twelve charter members took place in Ms. Israel's home on December 16, 1921, to form Chapter CN. These initial members were president, Capitola Israel; vice president, Lillian McBeth; recording secretary, Anna L. Ludden; corresponding secretary, Margaret Inness; treasurer, Anne A. Craven; chaplain, Florence Ball; guard, Ruth Cornish; Gladys Hansen, Maurine Walrath, Leah Shaw, Mattie Olson, and Minnie Dunn. Chapter CN received its charter on May 24, 1922. This relationship with Chapter AR continues today with an annual meeting in January at which the chapters take turns presenting the Founders' Day program and enjoy a meal and fellowship before having separate business meetings. Other joint events have included social trips around Nebraska, Chapter AR's 100th anniversary celebration, and joining in October to hear the Convention of International Chapter report for many years.

Often seeking inspiration from the past, Chapter CN maintains many records. All minutes dating back to that first meeting, a complete file of yearbooks, scrapbooks of important chapter events and the presidents' letters are preserved. Among these treasures are two outstanding programs of long ago, "Notes from an Old Organ" and "A Unique Cottey Program" written by members and sold to many chapters through The P.E.O. Record. Other programs have been based on the yearbook theme for the year, focusing on "Light," "A Time for Angels," "God Bless America," "Women Who Inspire Us," and "Dancing with the Stars."

The 1988-1989 yearbook theme was "Birthdays" in honor of Nebraska State Chapter's 100th birthday and the 50th birthday of the Nebraska P.E.O. Home. This celebratory year was recognized with a donation to Nebraska P.E.O. Home making our chapter a Ten Carat Chapter. Recognizing the history and sisterhood of members in the Home, Chapter CN sends valentines to sisters in the Nebraska P.E.O. Home each year and continues to visit the Home and its residents during social outings.

Special outings have included everything from Christmas celebrations to cookouts with the BILs. During the spring, the chapter usually ventures out to enjoy lunches in area tearooms or bed and breakfasts, or tour interesting places like local wineries and museums or travel to Lincoln or Omaha with Chapter AR. Summer events often occur at the lake homes of our sisters or at the Nebraska P.E.O. Home in Beatrice. Our chapter typically celebrates the Christmas season with a Dutch-treat dinner at a local restaurant. The tradition of exchanging gifts has now turned to collecting donations for Blue Valley Health on that evening.

A lunch stand on the city square during the dedication of the Polk County Courthouse in October 1922 was Chapter CN's first monetary venture to support the P.E.O. Educational Loan Fund and other local charity work and community service. Since that time many innovative ideas have added to the treasury to support all the P.E.O. projects and to extend other courtesies. "A Christmas Tour of Homes" in 1989 was fun and profitable, making a P.E.O. Book Scholarship a reality for a deserving senior girl planning to further her education. This scholarship is now an on-going project for Chapter CN with a $50 minimum gift, which increases as funds permit and more recently has been gifted to two senior girls in the amount of $400 per scholarship. In 1991, a "Christmas Cookie Walk" was so successful that it was decided to make it an annual affair.

Other fundraising projects have included running the concessions for wrestling or track meets on a yearly basis. This has allowed Chapter CN to be generous with our funds, but it shows our giving spirit to one another as well. Supporting the advancement of women's education, Chapter CN has sponsored several women for the P.E.O.Educational Loan Fund and grants from the P.E.O. Program for Continuing Education.

Serving our sisters is a way of life in Chapter CN. Through the "Brags and Concerns Box" that began in 2006, we are able to share the concerns and joys of our sisters, which often leads to caring for one another with showers of cards, meals for families in a time of need, transportation to appointments and numerous other acts of kindness to show that we believe that "far stronger is the love between sisters." Decorating the graves of deceased members on Memorial Day and remembering sisters in nursing homes with visits and flowers are also loving traditions.

Chapter CN enjoys the legacy of two 70-year members, Catherine Norton and Zella Kepner. We continue to support all state and International projects as well as support the Cottey College with their numerous fundraisers. It is our privilege to support the "Adopt-a-Cottey Student" with our notes of encouragement and small gifts; and occasionally, members have had the honor of visiting our Cottey College student.

Chapter CN's Margaret Norton has been a delegate at many state conventions and the 1996 Convention of International Chapter. In 1989, she attended Convention of International Chapter in Arizona to observe and prepare for co-chairing the hospitality room at the 1991 Convention of International Chapter in Omaha. Margaret designed the colorful prairie aprons worn by the hostesses. The aprons were made by CN and HH, York, members.

CN's Peggy Carlson served as an usher at Convention of International Chapter in Omaha, and was an usher at the 2001 Convention of International Chapter; Jane Roberts was a delegate to the 2005 Convention of International Chapter and Becky Watts was co-chairperson of the 2013 Nebraska State Convention.

In March of 2013 we celebrated with our CN sister and Trinity University Professor Nancy Mills when she received an American Chemical Society Award for her stellar career in research.

CHAPTER CN'S ACTIVE MEMBERSHIP IS 56; TOTAL ENROLLMENT IS 181

Chapter CO Cozad
Organized March 10, 1922
by Nelle Grantham

In 1922, thirteen women, assisted by Chapter AN, Lexington, were chartered as members of Cozad's first P.E.O. Chapter. Those women had foresight regarding what this organization could bring to the city of Cozad, as well as making an impact on the community, the state, the nation and the world. Charter initiates were Etta Adams, Dorothy Allen, Hallie Allen, Mayme Cook, Ethel Good, Margaret Hecox, Susie Hord, Jessie Ralston, Mabel Ward and Adella Weldon. Three dimitting members, Margaret Martin, Sarah Pierce and Erma Scott, completed the group.

The chapter letters would be CO. If one were to think about the letters, one may believe that they are the abbreviation for Cozad, and that it was intentional that those letters be appropriate for this chapter. CO are the first letters for words that describe the sisters, who are COmpassionate and COncerned for each other and for the peoples of this COmmunity, reaching far beyond the boundaries of Nebraska.

Support for the Cozad Community is recorded as the P.E.O. sisters provide funding and donations of items for programs, such as Toys for Tots; Food Pantry; the Cozad Elementary AfterZone Program, Marsha Engel, Director; books for the Cozad Community Hospital; and United Way, including "Books for Kids."

In 1985 ten members dimitted from Chapter CO to form a second chapter in Cozad, Chapter IB. The chapters meet together at least once or twice a year.

Additional support includes two programs, chaired by Jeanne Hart. They are the annual "Coat Drive," serving over 260 children and adults during Christmas, plus the "Clothe 'Em" program, which involves sorting and packaging new clothing for over 200 families in Cozad and area communities, Eustis and Farnam.

One of the most heartfelt gifts was recorded in 2005. The women in CO provided money to purchase Christmas gifts for "children in Iraq, affected by the war."

Other offerings of P.E.O. love include delivering Meals on Wheels; providing meals for families who are grieving or need assistance due to illness; plus the annual scholarship given to a Cozad High School senior; funding for the Junior Senior Prom; and support for such programs as the 2012 National Smithsonian Exhibit, with Cozad as the host city.

Working together is the key, as in the "plant sale," amidst a downpour seeping into the garage; selling "Butter Braids"; sharing lovely cross-stitched bookmarks created by Virginia Sitorius; celebrating the 75th anniversary of Chapter CO. The luncheon was the same menu that was served in 1922, using china, crystal and silver from that era. The special touch was that the hostess Jane Kinnan is the granddaughter of one of the charter members, Ethel Good.

Chapter CO hosted Reciprocity Group I in October 2004. The theme, "Branch of the Vine," provided for elegance, with large crystal vases entwined with grape vines and leaves, and ambiance created throughout with the presentation of delicious foods, served with formality. Each guest received a jar of jam with the lid cross-stitched, denoting the "fruit of the vine."

The CO sisters continue to lead, on the local, state, national and International levels. Carol Stuckey was the delegate to the Convention of International Chapter, Baltimore, 1999. Carmen Atchison made global news, winning First at the World Wide Napa Valley Wine Festival, featuring her original South Side Mustard, 2006.

Sisters making national news include Julie Geiger, Retailer of the Year; Anne Burkholder, Feed Lot Management; Nancy Rice, Best Educator, WHO'S WHO, 1998; Marilyn Peterson, presentation, Smithsonian Institute, Washington, D.C., with Cozad named the "Poster City," 1997. Marilyn accepted the Nebraska Humanities Award, "The Sower," on behalf of the 100th Meridian Museum, 1998.

Other awards went to: Katherine Wilson, Cornerstone Society, Nebraska Wesleyan University; Judy Eggleston, Corn Growers Ambassador; Farm Families of the Year; Chamber of Commerce Distinguished Service and Community Awards: Shirley Harkness, Marilyn Peterson, Mary Jane Whiting; Norma Rhone, Poll Worker Hall of Fame; Cozad Community Healthcare Hall of Fame: Virginia Sitorius, Shirley Harkness; Marilyn Peterson, Advisory Council, Nebraska Educational Television, Lincoln, 2011; sisters are members of the Cozad Ambassadors; Chamber of Commerce; Teammates; and a variety of boards in the community. Newsmakers include Katherine and Lloyd Wilson, celebrating the dedication of the new Wilson Library, 1997.

Scholarships and support for women are noted by a sampling of the presentations of the P.E.O. Program for Continuing Education: Patty Durner, Michelle Franzen, Luella McKelvey, Tracy McKelvey, and Teresa Netherton.

On the state level, Reciprocity Group I hosted the Nebraska State Convention in North Platte in 2007. Chapter CO was in charge of decorating the main meeting hall. Marlene Geiger served as a guard.

An enjoyable event was the "Mad Hatter Tea," hosted by CO, with Chapters IB and AW as guests. The variety of chapeaus was historical and hysterical. Other fun events have included the summer picnics with the families, and the BILs reciting the "Pledge."

Throughout the years, CO sisters of fifty years or more have been honored, including Bonnie Young, Jane Kinnan, and Katherine Wilson.

CHAPTER CO'S ACTIVE MEMBERSHIP IS 52; TOTAL ENROLLMENT IS 220

★

CHAPTER CP OMAHA
ORGANIZED APRIL 15, 1922
BY NELLE GRANTHAM

Chapter CP was organized on April 15, 1922, at the home of Mae Caldwell. Sixteen dimits and two initiates formed the charter list at the first meeting. State Organizer Nelle Grantham of Kearney organized the chapter which was sponsored by Blanche George, a dimit from Chapter E. Charter members and first officers were: Blanche George (E), president; Hazel Browne (F, Wisconsin), guard; Lola Searson (BF, Missouri), vice president; Ethel Beckley (AP), recording secretary; Mary Dickey (J, Idaho); Elizabeth Wright (CD), treasurer; Frances Adams Francis (V, Iowa), chaplain; Mae Caldwell (Q), corresponding secretary; Rose Harrington (CT, Iowa); May West; Elizabeth Shaffer (BQ, Indiana); Ina Lindaman; Maude Munroe (E); Irma Bramard (E, Iowa); Edna Darner (Y); Isa Hussey (DN, Iowa); Fannie Osborn (BR); and Martha Aten (N, Iowa).

Chapter CP has celebrated many milestones over the last ninety-one years. In 1991, many of Chapter CP's members participated in the Convention of International Chapter in Omaha. We marked our 75th anniversary in 1997 with a luncheon and video showcasing the history of CP. Members who could not attend sent cards and letters. Our 90th birthday was celebrated in 2012 with birthday cake and a program highlighting advancements that have occurred since 1922. The world is different today; however, our commitment to the Sisterhood and P.E.O. projects remains unchanged.

In 1998-1999, Chapter CP members elected to switch from a day to evening meeting group. Our sisters believed this adjustment was necessary for the vitality of Chapter CP. Evening carpooling was encouraged to include members who did not drive at night. Our chapter has grown in numbers and strength due to this change. Today, our chapter is a healthy combination of women of all ages and backgrounds. We draw on the diverse talents of sisters for intellectually stimulating and fun programs on subjects like pet therapy, personal finance, health, travel, technology and many more.

Social meetings have been enthusiastically incorporated into our P.E.O. calendar. We are a chapter that loves to have fun and laugh. We've met for brunch, attended the farmer's market, held backyard barbeques with the BILs, played games, and gathered for Christmas parties. The bonds of sisterhood are strengthened when we have time to share and get to know each other better.

Chapter CP remains focused on P.E.O. projects and is proud to have supported PCE project recipients Betsy Yankie in 1995 and Bonnie Brabek in 2000. In 2002, we sponsored ELF recipient Marguerite (Meg) Serifini. Our chapter donates annually to all projects and is often able to assist with special fundraising campaigns for Cottey College and the Nebraska P.E.O. Home. Strong fundraising is essential and we've been successful in increasing our funds through silent auctions, selling Santa letters, and sending holiday donation letters to members.

A true showing of sisterhood was demonstrated when a dear member, Katrina Phillips, faced declining health. Katrina was an ideal P.E.O. and introduced P.E.O. to many current members. During her illness CP sisters delivered meals, ran errands, planted flowers, and spent time with her as a sign of our love and support. After Katrina's passing, her husband John established the Katrina Phillips Endowed Scholarship Fund at Cottey College. Chapter CP continues to honor Katrina by supporting her scholarship with fundraising and annual gifting.

CHAPTER CP'S ACTIVE MEMBERSHIP 31; TOTAL ENROLLMENT IS 188

★

CHAPTER CQ NELIGH
ORGANIZED APRIL 26, 1922
BY NELLE GRANTHAM

Nebraska Organizer Nelle Grantham and State Treasurer Harriette Salter organized Chapter CQ on April 26, 1922, in Neligh. The sponsoring chapter was Chapter BE, Pierce. The charter members and officers were: Alice Bauman, president; Mabel Williams, vice president; Georgia Melick, recording secretary; Nell Rice, corresponding secretary; Edith Friedebach, treasurer; Jennie Bliss, chaplain; Marion May Auringer-Wood, Grace Ray Spirk, Mae Auringer, Carrie Jones, Percie Best, Ruth Harrison, Marie Switzer and Bertha Melick.

During the early years of existence, Chapter CQ met on Monday afternoons without the benefit of refreshments. Five-cent fines were levied against unexcused absences, and ten-cent fines were collected from sisters who forgot to wear their pins. Chapter CQ's first anniversary celebration was held on April 24, 1923, and the chapter celebrated its 75th anniversary in April 1998.

During the past twenty years, Chapter CQ has adjusted meeting times to accommodate the sisters' busy schedules and varying lifestyles. At the same time, the chapter has continued to pursue social, literary, and philanthropic objectives.

Chapter CQ projects continue to serve the community as well as the chapter. Every year a grant is awarded to a Neligh-Oakdale High School graduate, and PCE grants and ELF loans are awarded to eligible women. The first ELF recipient was Marguerite Nyrop in 1924.

On Memorial Day weekend, sisters honor those who have entered Chapter Eternal and are interred in Laurel Hill Cemetery by placing a white daisy at the gravesite. A no-bake sale replenishes CQ's treasury annually with members' donations sent along with their yearly dues.

Past projects included clothing donations to children in need, food showers at Christmas, a contribution to the Antelope County Memorial Hospital building fund and the purchase of an iron lung during the Polio epidemic. Other projects were financing the repainting of a mural on a local historic building and contributing to a fund that allowed a student to participate in a European music tour. A Ribbon Tree project at Christmastime provided gifts for those whose names were on ribbons that decorated two trees placed in Neligh banks.

Chapter CQ has hosted PACK Picnics and Reciprocity Group IV meetings. (PACK is an acronym for chapters in Pierce, Antelope, Cedar, and Knox counties.)

With Reciprocity Group IV the chapter has hosted two state conventions in Norfolk. Sisters participated in the Cottey Challenge, and they send gifts to a student each year. They also send items to a resident of the Nebraska P.E.O. Home. The December social meeting includes BILs. Another popular social meeting is the October progressive dinner. Prospective members are invited to attend the meal.

Members who have held state P.E.O. offices in the past include Thelma Millen, Nebraska State Chapter president in 1964-65, and Kay Little who served as administrator of the Nebraska P.E.O. Home.

Several sisters have received recognition for educational service in the community and state. Gloria Christiansen received the "Sound Off for Media Award" from the Nebraska School Librarian Association. Jill Bates received the 2013 Nebraska Rural Community School Association Educational Service Unit Employee of the Year Award, and Cindy Hild received the 2013 Nebraska Rural Community School Association Secondary Teacher of the Year Award. Carol Jessen was awarded the 2013 Donald W. Miller Distinguished Service Award at the Nebraska Association of Mathematics Teachers. Judi Sigler invented MugStir (a teaspoon that hangs on the side of a cup) through the internet company Quirky. Author Marie Krohn has published three books: a biography of Nebraskan Louise Pound, a novel, and a history of Nebraska's Antelope County.

CHAPTER CQ'S ACTIVE MEMBERSHIP IS 35; TOTAL ENROLLMENT IS 199

★

CHAPTER CR OMAHA
ORGANIZED MAY 9, 1922
BY NELLE GRANTHAM
MERGED WITH CHAPTER DZ MARCH 4, 2009

Chapter CR's charter members were Cora Jackson, Eloise Virtue, Florence Wheeler, Nelle Ringer, Grace McLain, Celesta Mabery, Anna Cressey, Isabelle Barclay, Fannie Fisher, Barbara Stryker, Adeline McCulloch, Minnie Laverty, Jeanne Bishop, Cornelia Wilson, Fannie Lee, Margaret Young, Edith Cook, Ruth Wyman and Zulu Towl. Fifteen members dimitted from Chapter M, one from Chapter N, Minden, and three were initiates.

Fannie Reeves Fisher was initiated into "Original A" in 1886 and was the sister-in-law of Winona Reeves, president of Supreme Chapter and thirty-one-year editor of The P.E.O. Record.

Chapter CR was organized by Chapter M. Chapter CR later was the "mother chapter" of Chapter FD. The "birthplace" of Chapter CR was the home of Anna Cressey, charter member of Chapter M who dimitted to Chapter CR.

Chapter CR's greatest source of pride has been its two presidents of Nebraska State Chapter—Mary McCulloch Nixon in 1943-44 and Catherine Cook Andersen in 1972-73. When Catherine was president, someone said, "I wish your mother, Edith Cook, had lived to know about this." Catherine replied, "She knows."

Chapter CR merged with Chapter DZ on March 4, 2009.

TOTAL ENROLLMENT 201

Yard by yard it's very hard,
but inch by inch it's a cinch. -Anonymous

Chapter CR-DZ Omaha
Organized and merged as one Chapter, March 4, 2009

Bringing together CR and DZ has its own "P.E.O. Math":
One + One = One

Sharing many ideals and likes and with CR's and DZ's dwindling membership, Organizer Joyce Victor worked closely with both chapters to facilitate a "new P.E.O. Family."

Charter members: Beth Anderson, CR; Eden Anderson, CR; Fay Andrews, CR, now DU, Florida; Sharon Becker, DZ; Pauline Brager, CR; Dee Bruggeman, DZ; Kimberly Boyd Clure, DZ; Mary Dunn, CR; Jean Fenger, CR; Jeanette Garner, CR; Mary Geisler, CR; Marilyn Griffith, CR; Wilma Hauptman, CR; Ada Huning, CR; Lila Johnson, CR; Nancy Johnson, CR; Cindy Kadavy, CR; Karen Kozak, CR; Freda Lauritsen-Frost, CR; Verna Lucks, DZ; Susan Manuel, DZ; Georgene Marks, CR; Denise Marts, CR; Julie McCoy, CR; Charlene Brodd Morris, DZ; Marcia Ochsner, CR; Phyllis R. Ongert, CR; Deborah Peckenpaugh, CR; Aretha Peterson, DZ; Donna L. Peterson, CR; Deborah Peckenpaugh, CR; Ruth A. Shuck, CR; Suzanne Sears, CR; Barbara Steere, CR; Edith Storms, CR; Julie Tartaglia, CR; Jane M. Tinder, CR; Marge Torpy, DZ; Constance Tullis, CR; Virginia Voelte, CR. On April 15, 2009 we welcomed and initiated our first new sister, Carol Groothuis, CR-DZ.

Involvement in P.E.O. activities beyond the scope of the chapter is one of CR-DZ's strengths. For example, our care and concern for the sister-residents of the Nebraska P.E.O. Home in Beatrice has a special connection as Cindy Kadavy serves on the Board of Directors for the Home. Chapter CR was among the three chapters that gave the Home its first $800 to the Endowment Fund. Numerous CR-DZ sisters have served in higher P.E.O. capacity: Two presidents of Nebraska State Chapter—Mary McCulloch Nixon (CR) in 1943-44 and Catherine Cook Andersen (CR) in 1972-73. Cindy Kadavy (CR) served as state convention co-chair in Omaha in 2008.

Chapter members who have expanded the scope of service to P.E.O. as officers in the Omaha P.E.O. Reciprocity Association have been Jane Muffly (DZ), Aretha Peterson (DZ), Darlene Willmarth (DZ) and Cindy Kadavy (CR), presidents; Relta Starrett (DZ) and Mary Dunn (CR), treasurer; Grace Shellberg (DZ), Ruth Belmont (DZ) and Mary H. Anderson (DZ), secretaries. Our most recent delegate to International (2011) was Georgene Marks, and numerous sisters have had the privilege of attending in past years.

CR-DZ has an impressive number of successful recipients of educational assistance through ELF, Scholar Awards, Cottey College and PCE grants; as of December 2013, our recipients have received $207,736! STAR Scholars have been submitted yearly since the official inception of this program. We remember our "Gals" with gift baskets, gift cards, greeting cards, and other mementos marking finals, holidays, birthday and other special events in their lives and just to encourage them and keep in touch. Several of our candidates and recipients have been guests at our chapter meetings and we enjoy meeting them and hearing of their goals, dreams and accomplishments and letting them know the pride we have in them. In 2014 we had the great joy of sponsoring the daughter of one of our prior "double-dipper" candidates (both ELF and PCE).

Chapter CR-DZ with state officers (upper right) at merging ceremony in 2009

CR-DZ meets Wednesday noontime for dessert, with occasional luncheons, graciously prepared by several sisters with a small fee charged and proceeds going to our obligations and projects. Chapter fundraisers have included a fun and lucrative purse auction; a "Home Finder" booklet with general driving directions to each sister's home; raffles; paying a small fee for each pair of shoes, or earrings or cookies eaten during holidays. Our treasurer and technology guru, Julie McCoy, prepares a monthly newsletter to keep us in touch, with upcoming meeting information, humorous and helpful tidbits and sisterly news.

Programs have utilized talents of our members and sisters from other chapters as well as wonderful community speakers. We have done "in-gatherings" of needed items for various groups such as The Omaha Street School and the Food Bank; we've had book reviews—from the Bookworm—with the opportunity to buy books with a courtesy discount, a piano concert, Lauritsen Garden Art Walk, and travelogues.

Two sisters, Janie Tinder and Virginia Voelte, opened their homes as approved P.E.O. Bed and Breakfasts, and generated $795 in the first year.

Being P.E.O. as a merged chapter has been successful for CR-DZ, where One Great Chapter and One Great Chapter total One Great New Chapter.

Editor's Note: After much loving effort, CR-DZ disbanded June 2015.

CHAPTER CR-DZ'S ACTIVE MEMBERSHIP IS 22; TOTAL ENROLLMENT IS 87

There is no physician like a true friend -Anonymous

Chapter CS Lincoln
Organized June 6, 1922
by Nelle Grantham

A tea given by Lincoln Chapters K, BR and BY at the Lincolnshire Club preceded the organization of Chapter CS at the home of Minnie Fried Watson. Members of Chapter K assisted State Organizer Nelle Grantham in the ceremonies.

Lue R. Spencer, past state president, was instrumental in forming Chapter CS and was its first president. Other charter members were Florence Cowan, vice president; Edna Mason, recording secretary; Lucy R. Hewitt, corresponding secretary; Ferne Gustin, treasurer; Ida Allyn, chaplain; Roxy A. Kennedy, guard; V. Louise Fulmer, Elzada A. Hughes, Thea McGrew, Clara B. Ellis, Maude K. Pemberthy, Clara S. Paine, and Mabel Lindley.

From its inception a unique spirit developed in Chapter CS. Records show the first yearbook bill ($8) was allowed but there was only $7.46 in the treasury! Never a fundraising group, Chapter CS nevertheless wholeheartedly supported all P.E.O. projects. Numerous loan fund girls were sponsored, sometimes three at once. Chapter CS also is devoted to the Nebraska P.E.O. Home.

The chapter sent a blind orphan through school, a girl to Oakwood Camp, gifts to Whitehall and monthly care packages to Austria. One year Chapter CS bought a high school girl's graduation outfit and had her hair done. Chapter CS initiated a "Warm Hands; Warm Hearts" project under the aegis of Wally Dickson. Several Lincoln chapters joined CS in providing mittens, warm caps and other clothing for needy children in the Lincoln elementary schools. Willie Shafer, Chapter K, now oversees this project.

Chapter traditions included an anniversary family picnic on June 6 until the beginning of World War II. Early guest days were large affairs held at the Governor's Mansion. Members' children performed at Christmas gatherings. The annual picnic was revived as a BIL party in 1988 for Chapter CS's 66th birthday on June 6.

Chapter CS considers each member outstanding. All are active in civic, charitable, and church affairs. Gladyce Simmons was a force in the service of international understanding and a Mother of the Year. Katherine Coleman was national president of Mortar Board. Bertha Hill, long the state chairman of Mother of the Year committee, was treasurer of the State of Nebraska. Beth Miller Harrod, founder of Rocky Ridge Music Camp in Colorado and professor of piano at Nebraska Wesleyan University represented Chapter CS's talented musicians. Doris Cunningham, recognized nationally in 4-H and Extension, served as president of Nebraska State Chapter in 1975-76. Elaine Bertrand served as president of Lincoln Reciprocity Roundtable. Joann Waterbury and Barbara Dinsdale were co-founders of Prevent Blindness/Nebraska. Helen Hayes and Joyce Cartmill have been honored as Arthritis Woman of the Year.

Chapter CS is blessed to have members from three generations in three families. The challenge of maintaining membership in this changing society will always be with us. We have tried to stem the tide by changing the formats of meetings, simplifying our food service and especially avoiding the seven deadly words, "But we've always done it that way." New methods of fundraising have been explored, such as the Cake Ball sponsored by several Lincoln chapters. Individual donations to projects have increased the overall support of these endeavors instead of including the donations in the chapter budget.

The unexpected is a frequent visitor to CS meetings. One of the most memorable programs was entitled "After Easter." Full attention was being paid to the presentation of the Easter story. Each portion was illustrated with flannel board figures and appropriate piano music and songs. Just as the soloist came to the chorus of "Were You There?" she was joined in song by the resident poodle who had awakened from her nap and had come down to the landing to sing along. Tears came in the members' eyes but no one laughed. Congenial sisterhood continues to be the hallmark of Chapter CS members.

To date, we have one 70-year member, four 60-year members, and five 50-year members.

CHAPTER CS'S ACTIVE MEMBERSHIP IS 37; TOTAL ENROLLMENT IS 334

★

CHAPTER CT NORTH BEND
ORGANIZED NOVEMBER 1, 1922
BY NELLE GRANTHAM

Chapter CT was chartered on November 1, 1922, with the assistance of Chapter AJ, Fremont, and Chapter I, Wahoo. It was one of fourteen chapters organized by Nelle Grantham between 1923 and 1925. All eighteen charter members were initiates: Myrtle Eason Rand, president; Elizabeth Hoff, vice president; Mabel "Lillie" Datel corresponding secretary; Grace Sidner, recording secretary; Agnes Collins Jansen, treasurer; Gertrude Cherny, chaplain; Laura Thom, guard; Bertie Acom Eason, Sarah Acom, Lucy Walker, Margaret Watson, Jessie Emerson, Anna Kastle; Mabel Cusack; Flora Cheney; Ada Newsom and Fern Sloss.

"Chapter CT is a blend of younger and older P.E.O.s, each being a catalyst for the other. The younger members appreciate the dedication and untiring interest of the older members and the older members admire the energy and creativity of the younger women. A perfect balance!" *Spirit of the Prairie: A history of P.E.O. in Nebraska* 1874-1995, page 126.

Chapter CT continues to be a "perfect balance" of active, dynamic members of all ages and interests. We believe that contemporary P.E.O. members need the fellowship and friendships of their P.E.O. sisters more than ever and our chapter activities reflect this.

In December of 2007 we celebrated the 85th anniversary of our chapter and recognized our 50-year member, Alice Diffey. A year later, we celebrated by inviting all four of our chapter babies to join their P.E.O. Chapter CT mothers, grandmothers, and even one great-grandmother at our meeting.

The chapter has actively supported the work of the state chapter. Ellen Ann Qualsett served as president of Nebraska State Chapter in 1974-75. Recently, the chapter donated a seascape painted by Ellen Ann to the Nebraska P.E.O. Home.

The chapter helped organize Chapter HG, Schuyler, in 1977. Chalice Harvey served as president and vice-president of the Nebraska P.E.O. Home Board of Directors. Carol Bohling has served as state P.E.O. Scholar Award chairperson and is currently on the Board of Directors of the Nebraska P.E.O. Home. Our

60-year member, Maxine Arneal is a current resident of the Nebraska P.E.O. Home. Carol Clement is our 50-year member. Most of our officers serve two years in each office which contributes to our stability as a chapter.

The chapter regularly contributes financially to all P.E.O. projects and actively seeks candidates to receive grants, loans, and scholarships. One of the recipients of the P.E.O. Scholar Award was our candidate, Amy Vrana of North Bend.

The chapter also supports local community projects. Several chapter members served on the North Bend Library Foundation board which was instrumental in the construction of the new North Bend Public Library which was dedicated in 2012. The chapter also financially contributed to the project.

Because we genuinely enjoy each other's company, we schedule social meetings through the year. We started taking summer road trips when we caravanned to Des Moines to visit P.E.O. International Headquarters. Since then, we have driven to the Nebraska P.E.O. Home in Beatrice several times, to Omaha for meetings in the homes of two of our members who have retired there, into the countryside for summer brunch meetings in the homes of our rural members, and sought out interesting area restaurants. Our once-a-year BIL party has morphed into a variety of social outings: "Invite a Friend (not everyone has a BIL)," "Let's eat out," "Game Night," and "Salad Suppers." Recently, we added a "show-up-if-you're-free for Coffee at the Corner Café" on the first Saturday of each month.

Several chapter members have had generations of P.E.O.s in their families. One of our current members, Marcy Eason, is the fifth-generation of her family to be initiated by CT.

CHAPTER CT'S ACTIVE MEMBERSHIP IS 50; TOTAL ENROLLMENT IS 221

*

CHAPTER CU NORFOLK
ORGANIZED NOVEMBER 23, 1922
BY NELLE GRANTHAM

Charter members of Chapter CU consisted of fourteen dimitting P.E.O.s (ten from Nebraska): Hazel Silas, president; Marie Gadbois, vice president; Ada Hinson, chaplain; Mary L. South, guard; Carrie Lackey, treasurer; Claudia Baker; Dorothy S. South, corresponding secretary; Felice Erskine; Marguerete Dudgeon, recording secretary; Minnette Hutchinson, Chester Wilson, Lena Daubert, Jessie Nicola, and Marion Wright. Pierce Chapter BE conducted the initiatory service and Harriette Saler, recording secretary of Nebraska State Chapter, installed the officers. The first regular meeting was on January 7, 1923.

Until 1926, the membership was limited to twenty. The age range in Chapter CU is from twenties to nineties. The chapter enjoys the sharing of the talents and interests of this diverse group of sisters. Twelve sisters have been recognized for fifty years of allegiance; Gretta Barry, Fay Gordon, Ruth Brown, and Martha Adkins each were initiated over sixty years ago into Chapter CU.

Chapter CU has been continuously supportive of philanthropic work. In the past, gifts were given to many local and state organizations. Sponsoring women for the P.E.O. Educational Loan Fund and the P.E.O. Program for Continuing Education has been a priority for Chapter CU and of special interest to our members.

Twenty-six women have received loans and eighteen grant recipients have been supported in continuing their education.

Two CU members have served on the Cottey College Committee: Fauneil Pickett was one of the Cottey Area Chairmen in Nebraska and Karla Huse served four years on the Nebraska Cottey Scholarships Committee, one year as chairman.

Chapter CU sponsored the organization of Chapter DF, Stanton, in 1926 and Chapter GS, Norfolk, in 1968.

Fundraising activities have included boutiques, bazaars, bake sales, cookbooks, assessments, increase in the local dues and selling recipes used at regular luncheons and coffees. Since 2000, we have held a Christmas auction which showcases the specialties of our members from foods, crafts, or white elephants. A Founders' Day skit, "Person to Person," (written by Gertrude Burkhardt), was advertised in The P.E.O. Record in 1958. Part of the profit was used to purchase initiation robes for the officers.

In 1942, Stella Taylor's president's letter expressed a challenge which remains appropriate for 2013. "In this period in history, where so much hatred and hardship are being engendered, it is indeed a challenge to every woman who wears the Star to enter the year of 1942 more fully determined to live up to the ideals of the P.E.O. Sisterhood and to forget the froth and engage, more conscientiously, in the activities of life that are indicative of the truths shown in our initiatory service."

Today, our sisters represent the P.E.O. Sisterhood by providing leadership through service to family, churches, schools and community by sharing their many skills and caring for others.

CHAPTER CU'S ACTIVE MEMBERSHIP IS 55; TOTAL ENROLLMENT IS 354

★

CHAPTER CV OMAHA
ORGANIZED MARCH 27, 1923
BY NELLE GRANTHAM

Chapter CV, Omaha, was organized March 27, 1923, with fifteen charter members—twelve dimitting members and three initiates. Bertha Clark Hughes, president of Supreme Chapter, installed Addie Fay as president. Also present were state chapter officers: Ona Baird, president; Lulu Wolford, first vice president; Viola Cameron, corresponding secretary; and Lulah Andrews, executive secretary. Ten chapter presidents from Omaha also attended. Nellie Allen and Helen Lee formulated the plan for organizing Chapter CV. Charter members were Edith Ely, Nellie Allen, Ione Albright, Anna Clark, Addie Fay, Daisy Johnson, Helen Lee, Edna Siebrass, Josephine Sandham, Mary Sturdevant Mills, Rose Terrell, Lucille Uridil, Mary Kennedy, Lela Cole, and Laura Young.

Meetings were held the first and third Saturday afternoon at 2:30 and once a month during the summer months for social purposes. Meetings were later changed to the second and fourth Tuesday afternoon. Light refreshments were served. The attendance and interest were good. In response to roll call, a topic was assigned to each one for the year. Programs varied with music, readings, travel and many rummage sales. The chapter consented to frame one copy of the Ten Commandments for $4 to be placed in one of the public schools. Later the custom of answering roll call with a current event was initiated by the president. During the war years the chapter did Red Cross work, staffed the Service Center for Soldiers and bought war bonds. One of CV's members had a son who was a prisoner of war in World War II who, fortunately, was released when the war ended.

Chapter CV is fortunate to have a nice balance of ages, interests and activities among its members from a mother with a young child to our "senior" members.

Presently Chapter CV meets the first Tuesday of February, March, April, May June, August, October, November, and December and the second Tuesday of January, July, and September. Social meetings are held the third Tuesday of March, April and October. For many years a noon luncheon was followed by the program. In 2013 Chapter CV changed the format to allow the hostess to serve either a full luncheon or dessert only. This allows more members to serve as hostess. Programs reflect a variety of interests, are well-received and often given by Chapter CV members themselves. Chapter CV celebrated its 90th anniversary in March of 2013.

Over the years, Chapter CV has supported all of the P.E.O. projects. In 2011 the chapter began its annual flower sale. This project has provided support for all of the P.E.O. projects. A representative has attended P.E.O. Reciprocity Group II meetings and the chapter has provided a president for the Group and served as hostess for some meetings.

Conventions of State and International Chapters bring out the true measure of the Sisterhood, and Chapter CV always is delighted to meet sisters from all over the state and nation and extend P.E.O. hospitality to them. The chapter has sponsored eleven P.E.O. Educational Loan Fund recipients, two P.E.O. Scholar Award recipients, and one recipient each for PCE, IPS, and the P.E.O. STAR Scholarship. The chapter misses the many members who have joined Chapter Eternal.

CHAPTER CV'S ACTIVE MEMBERSHIP IS 32; TOTAL ENROLLMENT IS 173

★

CHAPTER CW SARGENT
ORGANIZED APRIL 17, 1923
BY NELLE GRANTHAM

All have heard the song, "*The Impossible Dream.*" No doubt, on the spring day of April 17, 1923, twelve women of Sargent, Nebraska, made the "impossible" finally the "possible" when they fulfilled their dream. Mary Lakeman of Sargent and Carrie Peterson of Aurora were acquainted, and it was through their association that the organization of Chapter CW was conceived. Carrie Peterson was well known throughout the P.E.O. Sisterhood, having served as president of the Nebraska State Chapter and also Supreme Chapter. Nelle Grantham of Kearney served as organizer of our chapter with members of the neighboring Chapter S of Broken Bow assisting. Mary Lakeman had the distinction of being Chapter CW's first president with other charter members being Merle Stouffer Kiker, Olive Fenstermacher, May Ottun, Lulu Hicks, Mattie Penny, Margaret Abbott, Etta Reir, Meta Abbott, Jeanette Scott, Lizzie Morris, Zelda Pizer and Pearl (Morrison) Leininger.

Within four years of organizing, Chapter CW's pioneers began to envision a home to care for their elderly P.E.O. sisters, and they were desirious that it be located in Aurora, Nebraska. This idea of a P.E.O. Home was first conceived with a proposal at the 1927 Tecumseh convention but the proposal was not accepted. Later, when the Nebraska P.E.O. Home was established in Beatrice, CW charter member Lizzie Morris generously furnished one of the resident's rooms. Chapter CW has over the years made many trips to the Home to visit the residents.

The members of Chapter CW strive to exemplify the P.E.O. ideals daily, along with making available the P.E.O. educational programs to the young women of the area. Close to one hundred local girls have benefited from Chapter CW's high school senior girl scholarships over the years. Thirteen women have benefited from the P.E.O. Educational Loan Fund; seven local women have appreciated the assistance provided them through the P.E.O. Program for Continuing Education grants; and five women have attended Cottey College.

Starting in 2013, our chapter has initiated a new program we call "Pat on the Back." Our members propose a woman from our local community who is attending some type of secondary education. Our chapter will vote on this person and then we send her a check for $50 and a letter describing P.E.O. in general and our chapter in particular, totally unexpected by her. We have had great response to this and hope to be able to continue the program in the future. Through this avenue, the chapter is reaching out and making P.E.O. better known in Sargent and surrounding areas.

Through the years, Chapter CW has had many different fundraisers to support our educational programs. Bake sales, afghan raffles and more recently, a large booth at the area's "Junk Jaunt" each September are just some of the ways we have raised money. Many of our members have really enjoyed the experience of meeting people traveling through the area for the "Junk Jaunt" and we have met some fascinating P.E.O. sisters from other states!

Sargent is a small, agricultural-based community but our chapter is trying to stay vital and growing. In 2013 alone we have added five new members and continue to strive to impact our community and to encourage the education of each and every woman. Chapter CW's average attendance is nine.

CHAPTER CW'S ACTIVE MEMBERSHIP IS 21; TOTAL ENROLLMENT IS 164

I long to accomplish great and noble tasks, but it is my chief duty to accomplish humble tasks as though they were great and noble. The world is moved along, not only by the mighty shoves of its heroes, but also by the aggregate of the tiny pushes of each honest worker.

–Helen Keller

Chapter CX Lyons
Organized May 2, 1923
by Nelle Grantham

Chapter CX was organized May 2, 1923, by Nelle Grantham, assisted by Ona Baird, president of Nebraska State Chapter and by Chapter AZ, Wayne. Cora Salsbury, Presbyterian minister's wife from Chapter AQ, Loup City, brought P.E.O. to Lyons and served as the new chapter's president for the first three years. Charter members include: Cora Salsbury, Carrie D. Lyon, Kathryn Newmyer, Cevilla McMonies, Clara Heyne, Mae B. Newmyer, Mabel Heintzelman, Elizabeth Jenkins, Helen Newmyer, Mathilda Calnon, Minnie Osberg, and Lola Dyson. Five generations of our charter member Lola Dyson have been initiated into our Sisterhood.

Karen Dykstra (left) and Kaelynn Castin (right), great-granddaughters of our Founder Hattie Briggs, were our guests of honor at a tea attended by thirteen chapters. Food and decorations typical of the mid-1800's were enjoyed.

Chapter CX's 50th anniversary guests included Marietta Jack, past state president, and three chapters CX helped organize: Chapter DC, Tekamah, Chapter DE, South Sioux City, and Chapter EL, Oakland. Our first 50-year members received their pins and Nina Paine wrote a very special poem.

> *Happiness is dancing feet!*
> *Music, laughter, friends to greet!*
> *Happiness is quiet too*
> *Hearth fires burning, bright and true.*
> *Happiness is work and play,*
> *Time to dream and time to pray.*
> *Happiness is fifty years*
> *Blessed with comfort through our tears.*
> *Fifty years of Sisterhood*
> *Problems shared and understood*
> *While the Star with steady glow*
> *Leads us on in P.E.O.*

Our 75th was celebrated at the 1998 Nebraska State Convention and a special meeting at a sister's home. Cake was served for our 90th celebration in May 2013. Fifteen members reached their 50-year milestone over our 90-year history.

Since 1970, nineteen women from Lyons have received financial aid from the P.E.O. projects. Teresa Fritts was named a P.E.O. Scholar Award recipient. Jantina and Teresa Fritts attended Cottey College. Esther Pond was a resident at the lovely Nebraska P.E.O. Home in Beatrice.

Chapter members enjoy a favorite guest, International President Joyce Goff

Chapter CX hosted Reciprocity VI in 1989 with a Bluegrass Prairie theme, covered wagon luncheon, and "Raisin a Ruckus" musical skit. A lively Jungle theme was used for 2006 Reciprocity VI with community youngsters singing jungle music.

Other special events include initiation of five members in one evening, and five members attending Convention of International Chapter in Vancouver, BC, where

Joyce Goff presided. Memorable meetings include a 1920's lawn party, and an evening when we came wearing our wedding attire.

Our fundraisers have included unique events such as a tasting bee, picking grapes at a local winery, silent auction of gift baskets, making and selling daisy pin holders and taking items to a consignment store for local scholarships.

Chapter CX 1920's style lawn party. Mary Lou Cram, Debbie Webster, Dorothy Shaw, Densmer McIntyre, Esther Timm Evonne Anderson, Evelyn Heideman

Chapter CX senior members revive an old skit to show the young new members they know how to have fun. Donna Jensen, Gayle Pearson, Janet Kroger, Mary Fritts, Kay Larson, Densmer McIntyre.

Community activities of our chapter include participating in the library Festival of Trees, making pillows for the local rest home, furnishing food for the

VFW, Senior Center, and school, participating in the Relay for Life, and helping with our local food pantry.

Our popular "Happiness Box" provides opportunity for sharing life and family events, drawing us into closer fellowship.

CHAPTER CX'S ACTIVE MEMBERSHIP IS 49; TOTAL ENROLLMENT IS 151

★

CHAPTER CY FALLS CITY
ORGANIZED MAY 12, 1923
BY NELLE GRANTHAM

Charter members of Chapter CY were May Maddox, president; Lena B. Moeser, vice president; Eula Chaney, corresponding secretary; Jessie Hargrave, chaplain; Margaret Falter, recording secretary; Adele Huffman, Maude Weaver, organist; Dora Fordyce, Grace Reavis, Lyde Miles, Lillian Towle, treasurer; Frances Powell, Lottie Jones, guard; and Elizabeth Davis. The organization took place at the home of Jessie Hargrave who was a member of Original A, Mount Pleasant, Iowa.

Maude Weaver, First Lady of Nebraska from 1929 to 1931, often entertained the chapter at the Governor's Mansion. Serving all offices of Nebraska State Chapter, she became president in 1952 and Nebraska Mother of the Year as well.

After a period of low attendance and difficulty finding officers in the late nineties, when disbanding was considered, we were happy to be celebrating our 90th anniversary in 2013. Changing our afternoon meetings to evenings helped put us on sure footing and we have continued to increase active membership and the amounts given to our projects.

Our project recipients: Katherine Merz Green received the Laurine Kimmel Cottey Scholarship in 1996, the Nebraska Cottey Scholarship in 1997, graduated 1998 with honors; Rachel Merz Burbach received the Laurine Kimmel Cottey Scholarship in 2000, the Nebraska Cottey Scholarship in 2001, graduated in 2002; Krista Anderson received a PCE grant in 2001; Connie Rowe received a PCE grant in 2002; Sandy Appleoff received the ELF and PCE in 2002; Carrie Ramsay received the ELF and PCE in 2008; Amy Dunn received the P.E.O. STAR Scholarship in 2010.

Keeping in touch with each member by phone and mail before each meeting keeps us informed about chapter life and enhances attendance. We often meet for a catered meal at our County Historical Museum before our meeting. We are able to support the museum and also enjoy a delicious meal.

Paper bag raffles have become a favorite fundraiser. We have two a year and with the money raised we have been able to significantly increase our support of the projects. Dinnerless dinners have also been a simple way to add to the treasury.

Taking jellies and bingo gifts to the Nebraska P.E.O. Home in December has been a continuing project of our chapter for many decades.

Social meetings have been wonderful times for getting to know our sisters better. Several members took a two-day trip to Mount Pleasant, Iowa, where they toured the P.E.O. rooms on Iowa Wesleyan College campus; we took a day trip to Kansas City to see the Nelson Atkins Art Museum and have also visited the Lauritzen Gardens in Omaha.

Rita Weaver was our delegate to Convention of International Chapter in

Baltimore 1999 and Dallas in 2013. Chapter CY's 50-year members since 1994 include Genevieve Heinzelman, Charmian Davies, Susan Eisenthal, Carolyn Joy, Elizabeth Knaup, Joyce Carter, Mary Jo Tangeman and Mildred Appleoff-Marsh. Our 60-year members include Mary Elizabeth Martin and Jane Weaver.

CY's ACTIVE MEMBERSHIP IS 47; TOTAL ENROLLMENT IS 202

★

CHAPTER CZ WAKEFIELD
ORGANIZED JUNE 5, 1923, BY HARRIETTE SALTER

"An intimate acquaintance with members of Chapter AZ, Wayne, inspired this group to seek a P.E.O. chapter in Wakefield" stated a 1939 history of Chapter CZ, Wakefield. Included in "this group" were charter members, notably Cora Beebe, who had two sisters in Chapter AZ. Chapter CZ was organized at the country home of May Montgomery with Chapter AZ assisting the organizer. Charter members were Cora Beebe, president; Lua Nuernberger, vice president; Edythe Segren, recording secretary; Stina Nyberg Johnson, corresponding secretary; May Montgomery, treasurer; Elizabeth Mathewson, chaplain; Inez Davies, guard; Marjorie Beebe Callahan, Hilda Bengston, Vena Green, Bess Hanson, Mollie Henton, Nan Nyberg Davies, Edna Sandahl Olson, Ruth Schwedhelm, Ulden Smith, and Gertrude Ware.

Chapter CZ assisted in the organization of Chapter DE, South Sioux City, in 1925. In 1972, four members of Chapter CZ again lent moral support to South Sioux City as Chapter DE sponsored the organization of Chapter GX in South Sioux City.

At the 1934 Convention of Nebraska State Chapter in Wayne, Chapter CZ presented the model meeting and Eva Francy Hinds, a Wakefield teacher, was initiated. More recently, Wakefield was among host chapters for conventions in 1970 in South Sioux City, 1984 in Blair, 1998 in South Sioux City, and 2012 in Fremont. For the 1970 Cottey College convention display, Chapter CZ dressed dolls and arranged them in scenes to represent Cottey classes and activities. This display was updated and used at several subsequent conventions.

Always willing to share our talents, CZ initiate Priscilla Moller Drayton went on to become president of the state chapter of North Dakota.

Since May 1987, Chapter CZ has presented a scholarship to a graduating Wakefield High School girl; several of these recipients have become active P.E.O. members. Chapter CZ has sponsored four women for the P.E.O. Educational Loan Fund: Mildred Nuernberger Carrier in 1933, Kristi Chase Artz and Stacey Kuhl in 1989 and Laurel Fraser in 1990. With CZ recommendation, Mrs. Deb Nicholson was awarded a P.E.O. Program for Continuing Education grant in 2001.

In June of 1973, Chapter CZ celebrated its first fifty years with an anniversary tea at Salem Lutheran Church. Guests attended from organizing Chapter AZ of Wayne as well as Chapters DE and GX, South Sioux City; DG of Ponca: and EN of Pender. Resident charter members Hilda Bengston and Stina Johnson were honored. Our 75th anniversary was celebrated with a dinner meeting and historical program at the home of Sheri Eaton.

Chapter CZ has contributed regularly to P.E.O. projects and has supported many special sisterhood endeavors. In addition, CZ has contributed to various local fundraisers including Haven House, Wayne County Relay for Life, Gardner

Public Library, and the Wakefield Heritage Organization. In the past several decades CZ has raised money by holding silent auctions, feasting at Super Scooper Salad Suppers, selling pie and coffee at Wakefield Balloon Days, and currently by helping Santa write and send Santa letters. For over twenty-five years, contributing to the "Happiness Basket" after each meeting continues to be a popular and painless local fundraiser.

Chapter CZ has four active fourth generation sisters: Terri Nuernberger Davis and Susan Nuernberger Finochiaro, whose mother, grandmother, and great grandmother were chapter members; Kristi Gustafson, whose mother is a chapter member, as were her grandmother and great grandmother; and Lisa Potter Sievers, whose mother and grandmother are CZ members as were both great grandmothers.

CZ'S ACTIVE MEMBERSHIP IS 35; TOTAL ENROLLMENT IS 173

★

CHAPTER DA HASTINGS
ORGANIZED FEBRUARY 21, 1924
BY HARRIETTE SALTER

Charter members of Chapter DA were: Emma Gilbert, Myra Snyder, Isabelle Nelson, Lena Zook, Besse Linn, Ida Lennox, Mary Yokum, Margaret Clearman, Verna Rork, Grace Krueger, Belle Heasley, Verna Brewster, Jessie Boos, Lucille Uridil, Rose Storer, Mary Elizabeth Storer, Olga Parker, Elsa Williams, Mary Brown and Dora Risberg.

Nebraska State Chapter has had three presidents from Chapter DA: Emma Gilbert in 1930-31; Isabelle Nelson, 1936-37; and Julia McDougal in 1983-84. Julia also served as historian for Nebraska State Chapter. Rhonda Pauley was chairman for the 2003 Nebraska State Convention, and Kathy Haverly was her assistant. These sisters' talents came to light, and the convention was a great success.

From the beginning Chapter DA has reached out to others. In 1928 Chapter DA established the Salter Memorial Fund for "worthy girls attending Hastings College." The revolving fund never totaled more than $450, but it helped twenty-five girls, amounting to $1,712 in usefulness. After the Depression the money was given to the Nebraska P.E.O. Home building fund. Chapter DA has sponsored girls for the P.E.O. Educational Loan Fund and for the P.E.O. Program for Continuing Education. Through chapter members' connections to Hastings College, Chapter DA supported a P.E.O. International Peace Scholarship recipient throughout her master's degree program. The chapter has also sponsored applicants for the P.E.O. STAR Scholarship. Chapter DA has donated at least $1,300 annually to P.E.O. projects and the Nebraska P.E.O. Home for the past few years.

Chapter DA's 50th anniversary was observed with a luncheon at the Clarke Hotel. Members and guests enjoyed hearing Katherine Rump read her "Chapter DA-P.E.O., The First Fifty Years," and Elizabeth Collins read Dorothy Creigh's "Fifty Years Ago in Hastings, Nebraska." At the 60th anniversary, a dinner meeting at My Place restaurant, guests and former members joined DA members in recalling "Sixty Years of Sisterhood and Fashion." To music of bygone eras, thirteen members modeled ensembles ranging from a 1924 wedding gown, bell bottoms, and mini-skirts to the new look of 1984. The chapter's 75th anniversary celebration featured a dinner at the Garden Café for members and guests. The program highlighted changes to P.E.O. through the years, with presenters attired in 1920's fashions and sharing colorful snippets from early presidents' letters.

Chapter DA is known for its talent. A choir of mostly DA sisters has sung at two Nebraska State Chapter conventions and the 1991 Convention of International Chapter, with Linda Johnson as soloist. Dorothy Creigh compiled a history of Adams County for its centennial in 1972 and wrote the state history for the U.S. bicentennial in 1976. Fairy Burt was named Nebraska Art Teacher of the Year in 1969. Reba Yeakle has spent years volunteering on behalf of others and has received the Ak-Sar-Ben Good Neighbor Award, as well as numerous civic awards. Jean Aiken headed the Hastings Literacy Program for thirteen years. Jody Jacobi has been the executive director of the YMCA and Evalyn Udlock held the same position earlier for the YWCA. Iris Sypherd made DA's officers' initiation robes. At Christmas, the chapter sings for members who are shut-ins.

Chapter DA is changing with the times, as it must in order to thrive in the future. Chapter DA embraces technology. Technology Committee chairman Joanne Seberg sends emails reminding members of meeting and informing members of births, deaths, and other news. Telephone Tree Committee chairman Flossie Sanderson makes sure that the word gets out to members who do not have email. This chapter finds great advantage in the new meeting schedule of twelve regular meetings and three social meetings each year. Our chapter uses various meeting formats and strategies to lure younger women to meetings, as well as to involve them in the Sisterhood. One of our most successful social meetings, in terms of attendance, has been a Saturday-morning Kids Against Hunger session. Members brought their children and grandchildren and assembled these meals together, while enjoying each others' company and also teaching the children about the importance of giving our time. An informal survey showed that our younger members especially appreciated this event. In addition, several special meetings for the purpose of initiation were held on Saturdays and included brunch. These were also well attended, and members enjoyed getting to know each other better over brunch. Being flexible on initiation times, especially to accommodate students in college, is essential to future P.E.O. growth. Chapter DA has also tried, and succeeded, in making our fundraisers enjoyable and financially effective. We have done white elephant sales, where chapter members brought "treasures" to share. We have had fundraiser auctions as meeting programs. Recently, the social committee has hosted a Saturday brunch or a light dinner at the same home each year. The committee donates the food and charges each chapter member a certain amount to be donated in its entirety to the projects.

Sisters of Chapter DA inspire each other by little acts of kindness and big concern for each other. They cherish the love they find in P.E.O. The chapter searches for ways to celebrate P.E.O. traditions and values, as it also seeks appropriate changes to keep the Sisterhood vital for the next generations. As we look to the future, our chapter's diversity, especially in ages and occupations, is both our strength and our challenge.

CHAPTER DA'S ACTIVE MEMBERSHIP IS 73; TOTAL ENROLLMENT IS 401

Chapter DB Auburn
Organized April 23, 1924
by Harriette Salter
Disbanded June 7, 2014

Martha Kiechel, the daughter of a prairie physician and sister of a past president of the Kansas State Chapter, conceived the idea for the organization of Chapter DB. Charter members were Martha Kiechel, president; Kate Linn, vice president; Floretta Reynolds, corresponding secretary; Lillian Hemmingsen, recording secretary; Adah Bath Wells, treasurer; Alma Armstrong, chaplain; Mary F. Howe, guard; Hettie Jefferson, organist; Lucile Cline, Lydia Harris, Maude Nordlund, Mary S. Neal, Jessie Gerlaw, Olga Thurlow, Emma Taylor, Florence Tyler and Bessie Smith.

In the early years as the prairie continued to be developed, Chapter DB projects consisted of local philanthropies (including helping with the war effort), the P.E.O. Educational Loan Fund, and the Nebraska P.E.O. Home. In the war years, baskets of fruit and toys were distributed to the needy and donations were made to the Blood Bank, the United Victory Fund, County Health Project, Infantile Paralysis Fund, Child Saving Institute and other causes. Amusing scrapbooks were compiled for convalescent soldiers. Chapter DB has continued recognizing the need in our community by offering educational assistance to local women. We sponsored and supported several women with a PCE award, the P.E.O. Scholar Award, and our annual local scholarships. A special award was given to an outstanding young woman so she could complete her training to become our local library director. This award benefitted the community as well as the recipient.

Chapter DB was one of two 50-year chapters honored at the 85th state convention banquet. Chapter DB celebrated its 70th birthday in 1994.

Members of Chapter DB who have served as reciprocity presidents are Mary Alice Grant, Marion Clarke, Juanalee Alden, Marion Gomon and Ruth Alden. Serving as Cottey Area Chairmen have been Audrey Pohlman, Helen Moody, Sarah Fairbanks, and Ruth Smith. Delegates to International Convention include Helen Holman, Victoria Berlet, Ruth Alden, Juanalee Alden and Marion Clarke.

Among the most memorable program themes of recent years were The President's Wives, American and British Literature, and "Destinations." One of the most memorable meetings was held one snowy January evening. The weather had prevented our country-dwelling president from coming into town. The sisters that lived in town decided to go ahead and meet. The meeting was conducted without the president's book as best as could be recalled, the meeting being called to order with a meat tenderizer and coaster. The hostess's cat served as the second guard and checked everyone out before taking his place on the only remaining chair. It was hilarious!

This will be the last history written for Chapter DB as we will soon be disbanding. Time changes our circumstances and lives, and we find ourselves in that situation. We all agree we are always and forever sisters, and that the loving relationship we have will continue. We are grateful for the love and lessons learned in the past and look forward to the future.

Chapter DB disbanded June 7, 2014.   Total enrollment 201

Chapter DC Tekamah
Organized March 9, 1925
by Eloine Gettys

A former Tekamah teacher, Goldie Brookings, suggested the idea of a P.E.O. chapter in Tekamah to State Organizer Eloine Gettys. With the help of the dedicated efforts of Frances D. Reimund, originally a member of Chapter AP, Saint Paul, Chapter DC became a reality. On March 9, 1925, the chapter was organized, assisted by Chapter CX, Lyons, and the meeting was held at Jenny Houston's home, which today is the Houston House, currently the Burt County Museum. The twelve charter members were Frances Reimund, dimitted from Chapter AP, president; and eleven initiates. Initiates were: Stella Latta, vice president; Jane Ellis, recording secretary; Ila P. Hopley, corresponding secretary; Faye Tunberg, treasurer; Jennie Houston, chaplain; Anne Radcliffe Bryant, guard; Ethel Wragge, Rachel Holmquist, Jessie Smith, Elizabeth Rhoades and Willa H. Chatt. A tea was held to celebrate Chapter DC's 75th anniversary in April of 2000.

Since 1995 Chapter DC has successfully sponsored seven local women for the P.E.O. Program for Continuing Education and one local woman for ELF. In 2004 we successfully recommended Lilian Ringera from Kenya for an IPS Scholarship. We have had two Cottey College students from the community accepted by and sponsored by our chapter in the last twenty years. Chapter DC continues to support and take an active part in local, worthwhile projects and organizations.

Chapter DC members continue to be and have been active in church, school, Chamber of Commerce, library, museum, 4-H and the American Cancer Society. Karen Grass has held the elected position of Burt County Treasurer since 1991. Bonnie Newell is the curator of the Burt County Museum, also known as the Houston House. Marlene Kaeding is president of both the Museum Board of Directors and the Tekamah Housing Authority. JoAnn Wragge and Sarah Chatt serve on the Tekamah-Herman Foundation Board for which JoAnn is currently serving as president. Susan Skinner is the chairperson of the Tekamah Public Library Foundation. During her tenure a 1.4 million dollar expansion project was completed. Jerris Palmer and her husband, Jerry, have recently retired from managing the Tekamah area Food Bank for a period of twenty years.

Chapter DC has had one member serve on the executive board of Nebraska State Chapter. Marietta Jack was elected to the Nebraska State Chapter executive board in 1956 and served as president in 1962-63. She served on the Amendments and Recommendations Committee at the Convention of International Chapter in Columbus, Ohio, in 1963; served twice as parliamentarian for Nebraska State Chapter, and served for two years as president of the Past Presidents Club. Laurie Elliott served on the Cottey College Committee for three years, the first two years as a member and the last year as chairperson. In 1999 Loretta Petersen was named as a "Woman of Distinction" at the state convention. Loretta educated the public in braille and how to live independently with visual impairment.

Chapter DC's program committee has interesting and original ideas for entertainment and practical ideas to meet the chapter's financial and philanthropic needs. Our most recent project was "Secret Sisters," in which sisters shared pictures of themselves and childhood memories. Every other

November we decorate the Burt County Museum School House with Christmas artwork made by Burt County fourth graders.

Chapter DC has grown and changed in many ways since that day in March of 1925, but the ideals and traditions of the charter members remain as strong as ever. We feel fortunate that our chapter has a good mix of women with varied talents, interests, and ages. Recently our chapter has attracted younger, energetic sisters.

Chapter DC's active membership is 44; total enrollment is 160

★

Chapter DD Omaha
Organized May 11, 1925
by Eloine Gettys
Disbanded June 4, 2011

Charter members of Chapter DD were dubbed "Dutiful Daughters" at the organization of the chapter and that tradition has continued through the decades. Bess Ralph was sponsor and first president. Other charter members were Evelyn Ricker, vice president; Irene Pulver, recording secretary; Constance Lowry, corresponding secretary; Anna Simpson, treasurer; Percie Best, chaplain; Matie Trott, guard; Marie Switzer; Hattie Dickinson; Priscilla Wellman; Grace Carmichael; Edith Robins and Carrie Ada Campbell.

Irene Van Brunt, daughter of charter member Anna Simpson, served as president of Supreme Chapter in 1964-65. She gave seventeen years of service to Nebraska State Chapter and to Supreme Chapter. A tea honoring Irene was held at the home of Helen Throop on February 9, 1965. Not even the ice storm early in the day could diminish the celebration! Later Irene was elected chairman of the P.E.O. Foundation Board. She was honored at the opening night of the Nebraska State Convention in June 1994, particularly for her work for the P.E.O. International Peace Scholarship project.

Chapter DD was designated a "Gold Chapter" when contributions of $50 per member were made to the Cottey College 50th Anniversary Fund.

The 1991 Convention of International Chapter held in Omaha provided opportunities for new P.E.O. friendships and service. Judy Nelson was Box Supper chairman and her team of DD sisters expected to help with tickets, food and seating. There was concern when several sisters suddenly vanished. Imagine the surprise at finding them wiping dust off Ak-Sar-Ben grandstand seats as a courtesy to those attending the outdoor opening ceremonies!

The chapter's 50th anniversary in 1975 was celebrated with a tea at the home of Mildred Curtis. Chapter DD treasures its 50-year plus members for their faithfulness, leadership and support: Mildred Cromwell ('31), Myrtle Ralph ('36) and Helen Throop ('38). Many DD sisters have moved to other cities where they continue to be active P.E.O.s. Newer members have enriched the chapter with freshness and energy.

"Dutiful Daughters" face the future with faith, hope and love, confident that each sister will continue to give her very best to P.E.O.

Chapter DD disbanded June 4, 2011.

total enrollment 138

Chapter DE South Sioux City
Organized May 15, 1925
by Eloine Gettys

On May 15, 1925, Chapter DE was organized in South Sioux City with the assistance of Chapter CX from Lyons and Mrs. Eloine Gettys, state organizer. The following charter members were initiated. Bess Swett, Alice Frum, Fannie Dixson, Ruth Hainey, Eva Graham, Gertrude Mullins, Nellie Maynard, Daisy Savidge, Besse Leamer, Vera Murphy, Dorothea Rockwell and Doris Pucelik. We are especially proud to have helped with the organization of two new chapters in South Sioux City—Chapter GX in 1972 and Chapter IC in 1986.

We take great pride in recognizing the fact that we have several two or three generations of families of sisters. We are especially pleased to have a four generation family of sisters—Meegan Burr, Chris Reed, Corrine Thacker and Margaret Thacker. Margaret Thacker was one of our charter members. Our long term members are Ruth Weeks, fifty years and Bev Smith, sixty years.

Over the years, Chapter DE has supported not only the P.E.O. projects, but also many of its own. During the Depression, the chapter adopted needy families and sponsored free movies for local children. During World War II members made bandages, learned First Aid, served dinners to soldiers, and donated to the Victory Fund. When South Sioux City was hit with a disastrous flood in 1952, Chapter DE helped the town to prepare for the flood and also to clean up after. In 1982, the chapter compiled a cookbook and sent the profits to the Cottey College Anniversary Fund. The chapter has donated to the Nebraska Children's Fund and the Child Saving Institute at Christmas.

On our 70th birthday in 1996 we hosted a party with Chapters GX and IC and celebrated with a music and candle lighting ceremony. In May of 2000 we celebrated our 75th anniversary with a tribute to our Chapter DE charter members written by Bev Smith. Treats served were those popular in the 20s.

We take great pleasure in recognizing our sisters through the years in times of both joy and sorrow. We present an engraved baby spoon to sisters who are new mothers for the first time. We attend reciprocity meetings with our sisters in Sioux City, Iowa, for Founders' Day brunches. We also attend Reciprocity Group VI meetings and have hosted several.

We hold a theme basket raffle to raise money to support our P.E.O. projects. In 2003 we started a scholarship for a local high school graduate. This has increased to two scholarships each year. We have sponsored two girls for P.E.O. STAR Scholarships. In the past we have contributed to the Council on Sexual Assault and Domestic Violence, Battered Women's Shelter and Haven House. Now at Christmas time, through the generosity of our sisters, we are able to contribute to families in need of financial assistance due to life circumstances including health issues and accidents.

Some of the highlights of our business and social meetings have been visits to the Queen of Peace, Sioux City Museum, Edgar's Ice Cream Parlor and the Lewis and Clark Interpretive Center.

Chapter DE's active membership is 45; total enrollment is 191

CHAPTER DF STANTON
ORGANIZED APRIL 3, 1926
BY ELIZABETH STEPHENS

Louise Allen, Chapter CD, Scottsbluff, who came to Stanton with her physician husband in the early 1920's, brought her love of P.E.O. By the year 1926 she had chosen fourteen lovely ladies to join her in a charter list to form Chapter DF. Louise became the first president, and her sweet and conscientious ways have pervaded Chapter DF and the ways of all the members of this chapter. Hermine Thuman (Ham) became vice president; Bess Pont, recording secretary; Daisy Robinson, corresponding secretary; Minnie Chase, treasurer; Elizabeth Pilger, chaplain; Nina Spence, guard. Other members were Viola Allen, Ethel Chace (Hollinger), Vera Chilcoat, Enid Cook, Bessie Drewelow, Jean Hollstien, Anna McLeod, and Verna McMahon. Beulah Greenslit and Vee Hicks were soon added.

Supporting education projects in all their aspects has been a major focus. Seventeen girls have been sponsored for loans from the P.E.O. Educational Loan Fund, all of whom have repaid them. Six women who wished to widen their horizons have been sponsored for grants from the P.E.O. Program for Continuing Education. One girl received Nebraska Cottey Scholarship. An initiate in our chapter, Linda Smithberger Flaherty, graduated from Cottey College.

Exceptional women of Chapter DF have contributed to the higher offices of P.E.O. Dorothy Smithberger held the office of Nebraska State Chapter president in 1955-56 and was appointed historian and chairman of the Research and Editing committee for publication of the first history of Nebraska P.E.O., *Saga of Nebraska P.E.O.*, published in 1975. Dorothy's daughter, Susan Smithberger Harr, another initiate of Chapter DF, served as Nebraska State Chapter president in 1986-87. Alice Greenslit Provost, originally of DF, held the gavel of Mississippi State Chapter in 1982-83. Lilas Brandhorst, also a DF initiate, was Missouri State Chapter president in 1961-62 and, after serving Supreme Chapter in various capacities and offices, she served as president of International Chapter in 1981-83.

Annually, Chapter DF has thirteen regular meetings and two social meetings. Salad luncheons are held twice a year (the first meetings in March and October). Many members have full time jobs so the chapter accommodates their schedules by having a morning coffee (on a Saturday, to hear convention report) and two evening meetings a year. Our chapter's social meetings are creative: one of the most interesting was the chapter's trip to the Orphan Grain Train's Norfolk warehouse, where trained helpers filled nutritious little bags with grains, meals that are sent internationally to those needing food. For another social, we met at The Uptown and heard Rosalind Lamson tell about the making of the film *Nebraska* by Alexander Payne. Roz appeared in the film, which included scenes in her restaurant.

We have saved and contributed our pocket change, met our Chapter Challenge, rather incredible for a chapter our size, and sent $1,532 to the Cottey Defining Moment Campaign. Chapter DF has recently taken in talented members who are becoming promising leaders, bringing new ideas to the chapter.

CHAPTER DF'S ACTIVE MEMBERSHIP IS 34; TOTAL ENROLLMENT IS 162

Chapter DG Ponca
Organized April 5, 1926
by Elizabeth Stephens

With love in her heart and through untiring effort, Jessie Mikesell brought P.E.O. to Ponca the day after Easter in 1926. The organizer said, "You are my Easter gift to P.E.O. I pray that you will always remember that you are an Easter chapter, and keep the ideals of our Sisterhood as pure and spotless as the Easter lilies." Elizabeth Stephens was assisted in the organization by Chapter DE, South Sioux City.

Charter members were Jessie Mikesell, corresponding secretary; Belle Mellon, president; Mattie Fales; Lillian Lynde; Margaret Logan, treasurer; Myrtle Scheffel, guard; Catherine Williams; Virginia Boughn; Edith DeBord; Pearl Richardson, recording secretary; Minnie Jones, chaplain; Esther Hart; Ethel Bauer; and Nellie Hart, vice president. The last of our charter members, Virginia Iverson, died in 2004 at the age of 101. On her 100th birthday, she played the piano for us and those in the Health Care Center where she resided in her last years.

Our chapter is eighty-eight years old, but we are young in spirit and enthusiastic for P.E.O. We keep all our members informed of meetings and activities by using email. Chapter DG is a small but loving sisterhood with twenty-one members. We continue to encourage those who are inactive to again become active. Some of our meetings are held in our homes, but some are held in the Kingsbury Room of the public library.

Raising money to support continued giving to our P.E.O. projects, and for the local P.E.O. scholarship we sponsor, has always been a challenge. We have hosted basket auctions and tried other fundraisers. A few years ago we decided to put together packets of herbs and spices which are to be used to make dips and spreads. This has been our best fundraiser. We generally make about five hundred mixes in five different flavors. We sell them at a local craft fair. We provide pretzel sticks and samples for tasting. People look forward to seeing what new blends we have each year, and stocking up. Cathy Hurley is project leader for this.

At her death, Gladys Scheffel bequeathed $1,000 to the chapter. We decided to establish a scholarship fund. This scholarship is to be given to a senior girl in high school to be used toward her education. At the start it was $100 yearly, but it has grown to $200. We also pledged $750 toward the restoration and addition to the Carnegie Library, and $300 to the Nebraska P.E.O. Home Endowment Fund.

We have sponsored three ladies to receive scholarships from the P.E.O. Educational Loan Fund. Each year we get the name of a Cottey College Student and send a small gift and an occasional note of encouragement. On June 21, 2014, Vernice Kingsbury was the honored guest of a mid afternoon tea for being a member of the Sisterhood for sixty-five years.

Our programs are varied and interesting with a different theme each year. We've learned about birds, computers, books, jewelry, gardening, the stars, national parks, the arts, mission work with the Lakota Indians, and played Patriot Jeopardy and Bible Jeopardy. We have day trips in the summer. Our BILs have journeyed with us to visit a winery in Vermillion, South Dakota.

Each year we observe Founders' Day in some new and creative way. One year it was with paper dolls, and one time we used Founders' recipes to prepare a meal.

In 2011, we hosted Reciprocity Group VI at the Ponca State Park Resource Center. We served a brunch incorporating some of our Founders' recipes. Fall was a beautiful time to gather in Ponca State Park, and a fine program was enjoyed by a large crowd of our P.E.O. sisters.

Two of our members, Christina Luebe and Heather Craig-Olson, were co-chairmen for the Nebraska State Convention in 2012.

CHAPTER DG'S ACTIVE MEMBERSHIP IS 21; TOTAL ENROLLMENT IS 116

★

CHAPTER DH OMAHA
ORGANIZED APRIL 14, 1926
BY ELIZABETH STEPHENS

Fifteen members dimitted from Chapter E, Omaha, to form the new Chapter DH. Charter members were Metta Updike, president; Zella Fitton, vice president; Lucile Carnaby, recording secretary; Zella Bryans, corresponding secretary; Louise Platt, treasurer; Alma Smith, chaplain; Dorothy Wirt, guard; May Adams; Florence Cole; Fannie Griffis; Laura Hervey; Mayme Hutchinson; Grace Kinney; Clyde Porter; and Hazel Reasoner.

Our members have attended and participated in state and International Chapter conventions, and Susan O'Donnell was a member of the state Finance and Budget Committee. We have held officer positions in the Omaha P.E.O. Reciprocity Association. One of Chapter DH's talented members, Janet Mardis, made the quilted stage back-drop for Convention of International Chapter in Omaha in 1991 (see more of "1991 International Convention Remembered" on page 577).

This quilt was made by Janet Mardis, DH, and used as the stage backdrop for Convention of International Chapter in Omaha, 1991.

Chapter interests and traditions were established by a nucleus of gifted women who gave priority to financial support of all P.E.O. projects. The Nebraska P.E.O. Home always has held a special place in the hearts of chapter members. In addition to our annual contribution to the Home, we annually give to Daisy (the Home's mode of transportation). Sally Hanley and her husband have made a donation to Merry Makers to provide entertainment for the ladies at the Home.

Over the years, Chapter DH has sponsored eleven women for the P.E.O. Educational Loan Fund. One of the first, DeLanne Simmons, became the executive director of the Visiting Nurse Association. Another is a physician. We sponsored Jane Kanchense, from Zimbabwe, for the P.E.O. International Peace Scholarship. We contributed to the ELF 100th anniversary fund, Goff's Goals, and we became part of an IPS Designated Award group. We contribute to Cottey annually, support the Cottey Bus Trips, Bucks for Beds campaign, and support the students with "care" packages.

Chapter DH's motto, "Do Heartily," has inspired members to give enthusiastically of talents and energies, not only to P.E.O., but also to the community. Our chapter members helped girls at Central High School and served as canteen workers and bought bonds during the war. Today, members share their time and talents with the community. Our involvement includes volunteering at hospitals and churches, and contributing time to the arts and service organizations.

Omaha Founders' Day Luncheon 2007
Kelly Brown, Cindy Hanley and Lori Schuster of Chapter DH portray three of our Founders at the P.E.O. Reciprocity Luncheon

Chapter DH meets the first and third Tuesdays of the month for a salad luncheon and program. Programs are given by our members, P.E.O.s from other chapters or members of the community. Mimi Alexander, Chapter Eternal, whose family came from Mount Pleasant, annually reminded the chapter of its heritage as she spoke intimately of the Founders. An inspiring program was given by our member Lida Koukol, telling how she and her mother were forced to flee their home in Czechoslovakia to escape the Communist take-over. We look forward to our social meetings—a BIL party in the summer and our Christmas auction. Our fundraisers have included garage sales, a frozen custard sale, cleaning cloth sale, the Christmas auction and the Brag Box.

We have celebrated our 85th anniversary, and we're looking forward to the100[th]. We continue to be inspired by our Chapter Eternal members who honored P.E.O. with their dedication and by our 50-year plus members who remain active and involved. The tradition of multi-generation members continues with the granddaughter and great granddaughter of Charter member Zella Bryans active in DH today. We find joy in the mutual sharing of the P.E.O. experience.

Chapter DH will disband June 2015.

TOTAL ENROLLMENT 158

★

Chapter DI Humboldt
Organized May 13, 1926
by Elizabeth Stephens

Inspiration for organizing Chapter DI was presented by Elnora Hadsell, who had moved to Humboldt from Chapter O, Geneva, Nebraska. Elizabeth Stephens presided over the organization on May 13, 1926. There were ten initiates and four dimitting members. Officers were: Eleanor Hadsell, president; Alice Pugh (AG, Kansas), vice president; Ida Sanford (EG, Missouri), treasurer; Nellie Kerns, guard; Betty Park, corresponding secretary; Winnie Philpot, chaplain; Belle Pipal, recording secretary; Rushie Hynek, organist. Other charter members were: Grace Hadsell (CF), Susie Epley, Ena Burton Arnot, Pluma Hadsell, Nellie Marburger, and Harriet Rist. Chapter AV, Pawnee City, assisted with the organization.

As a very young chapter, Chapter DI members conducted a model meeting at a Convention of Nebraska State Chapter. Many members have served on state committees, as delegates to state and International Conventions, and as assistant hostesses. Six chapters joined the Southeast Reciprocity Group organized in Humboldt in 1933. Currently twenty chapters belong to our reciprocity group.

Chapter DI's meetings are currently held on the third Thursday of each month, with three social gatherings dispersed throughout the year. These may be fellowship times for members only, but special events may include BILs as well. With the changing tenor of members' lives, it is not always convenient for members to host in their homes, and local churches or the public library have welcomed us to use their meeting rooms.

Chapter DI over the years has responded to many community needs and concerns: May Day breakfasts, teas, Cottey College programs for high school girls, holiday food baskets, Red Cross projects, war-time needs, gifts to hospital patients and shut-ins. The Nebraska P.E.O. Home in Beatrice has received special attention from Chapter DI in the form of visits, meetings in the Home, and gifts of jams, jellies, stamps and other items. The chapter continues to support the annual Cottey College weekend, the Nebraska P.E.O. Home, and hosts bingo for residents at the Colonial Acres facility in Humboldt. Every other year in the fall we sponsor a bake sale to raise money for our local scholarship. Graves of deceased members are decorated each Memorial Day.

In recent years, in addition to support for P.E.O. projects, Chapter DI has sponsored our own local scholarship by means of a monthly "Mystery Gift" raffle. Since its inception in 2007, this raffle has raised a total of $4,177.08, which has been used for local scholarships of $500 each. This past year, the Mystery Gift raffle has been used to support Cottey College's "Defining Moment Campaign."

CHAPTER DI'S ACTIVE MEMBERSHIP IS 37; TOTAL ENROLLMENT IS 177

★

CHAPTER DJ ALBION
ORGANIZED APRIL 29, 1927
BY MAE BOND

Viola Cameron, state president, accompanied Mae Bond to the home of Frances Gates in Albion where nineteen members of Chapter CQ, Neligh, had met to assist with the organization of Chapter DJ.

Fifteen women had signed the petition for the new chapter. Clarice H. Seiter, AP, headed the charter list and became president. She was assisted by Winona Hobbs, J, who became recording secretary and Hermine T. Ham, DF, who became vice president. Other charter members included Mary Doten, Olga Martin, Agnes Price, Clara Needham, chaplain; Laura Cowan, Etta Parrott, Gladys Lowenberg, corresponding secretary; Alta Krause, treasurer; Frances Gates, Florence Keister, Nell Thompson, and Sarah Postle. Chapter DJ was started on the P.E.O. highway with Mae Bond's admonition: "Drive Slowly, Daughters of Joy."

Looking back at the past twenty years we have experienced changes in the world and in our chapter. The wide range of ages, personalities and talents make us an interesting group.

The regular meetings are now all held in the early evening. Recent social meetings have included a fun movie night at the local theater, Christmas dinner at a restaurant, a BIL garden party and a brunch at a member's lakeside home. Twice a year we enjoy a cooperative dinner meeting. Most of the meetings are held in the homes of our members if possible, or at our local Bed and Breakfast that is owned and operated by our member Connie Sugden.

Chapter DJ has sponsored four recipients of the P.E.O. Program for Continuing Education. We were proud to have Rory Sallach receive the P.E.O. Scholar Award in 2007. She is the granddaughter of Lyla Levander, a 51-year chapter member. Marcia Wilcoxon, our 52-year member, is the mother of Susan Wilcoxon Major who is a past president of the Mississippi State Chapter.

We have increased our giving to the P.E.O. projects. Chapter DJ was honored at the 2004 Nebraska State Convention for our support of all the projects with our emphasis on ELF.

Chapter DJ hosted Reciprocity Group IV in 1997. Our member Elva Bartels was president of Reciprocity Group IV at that time.

The primary source of our income was selling an original robe pattern and also constructing robes for sale. This project began in 1976 and ceased in 2002. Today we volunteer at the local theater managing the concessions. This has proved to be an excellent source of income. It also provides a community service. The chapter has provided teddy bears for the EMTs to give to children in the ambulance. The Love Fund continues to be an additional source of income. At the conclusion of each meeting we can share family news and some have even been known to brag a little!

Our second Cottey College graduate was Jasmine Kai in 2010.

Chapter DJ continues to be the selection committee for the Alda Lehr Endowed Scholarship to a Boone Central High School female graduate who will attend a school in the University of Nebraska system. This scholarship is renewable at $1,500 a year.

Our 75th anniversary was observed April 29, 2002. Elva Bartels, assisted by chapter members, presented the program. The 80th anniversary was celebrated with a special meeting and group photo.

We have many outstanding members including teachers, nurses, and business owners, those that serve on various boards, foundations and do volunteer work. Pam Robinson was a delegate to the Convention of International Chapter at Baltimore in 1999. Jerene Kruse was chosen Nebraska Art Educator of the Year 2010. Jill Johnson is the current Nebraska State President of the Clinical Laboratory Managers Association. Karen Kayton is the president of the local school board.

Chapter DJ's 72-year active member Mary Minnick Nelson was initiated into Chapter BC, Cambridge, in 1943 at age 18.

Each Memorial Day we pause to remember our Chapter Eternal sisters by placing flowers at their graves.

The love and friendship among our sisters continues as we "Daughters of Joy" strive to uphold the ideals and traditions envisioned by our Founders.

CHAPTER DJ'S ACTIVE MEMBERSHIP IS 50; TOTAL ENROLLMENT IS 175

CHAPTER DK LINCOLN
ORGANIZED MAY 7, 1927
BY MAE BOND

Chapter DK was organized on May 7, 1927. Excitement was high and plans carefully made. That special day dawned with pouring rain and problems. Two dimits had not arrived and one of the initiates was not able to attend the meeting. President Floy Roper carried on bravely and gracefully. Mrs. Mae Bond, organizer, granted the charter and named DK Daughters of Kindness, a goal for all these years. By the second meeting, the problems were solved. The charter members were as follows: Enid Andrews, Katherine Barber, Margaret Burt, Margaret Cook, Margaret Edwards, Marie Gray Fordyce, Esther Roper Karo, Alice Kendall, Mary B. Lakeman, Blanche Burt Petersen, Lena Pirie, Charlotte Reynolds, Floy Roper, Alverta Simpson, and Esther Wirsig.

Floy Roper left her beloved Chapter V to mother this band, and she was loved by all. She also served the state chapter in many ways. DK members caught her spirit and responded with enthusiasm. Briefly, the P.E.O. Educational Loan Fund was the only P.E.O. project, then at Supreme Convention the same year, Cottey College became the property of P.E.O. DK was quick with support for both. In the first year, a young woman was sponsored for a loan and a second in the next year. By now there have been ten loan fund girls. DK has given generously to Cottey College, answering every call for assistance. DK claims four graduates from Cottey College.

In 1937, the Nebraska State P.E.O. Chapter was gifted with a beautiful old house in Beatrice, Nebraska, to be used as the Nebraska P.E.O. Home. Floy Roper chaired the furnishing committee and in 1938 chaired the P.E.O. Home Board of Directors. DK joined in this project and gave the home twenty-four silver place settings plus serving pieces. During the years, DK has regularly budgeted funds for maintenance, expansion and comfort. After a particular building effort, the Board recognized DK as a Golden Anniversary Chapter. Four DK members have enjoyed living in this beautiful home, and in the fall of 2013 another of our members has made the Nebraska P.E.O. Home her new home.

Chapter DK always supports a local philanthropy, and members are dedicated volunteers, many winning recognition. The minutes during World War II tell of hundreds of hours of service being done and mountains of USO cookies baked by DK members.

Chapter DK members have served P.E.O. at large. Margaret McVicker, after filling each of the state offices, was elected president of Nebraska State Chapter for 1953-54. Five DK members have served as president of the Lincoln Reciprocity Roundtable and five also took part in "P.E.O. in Bloom."

As Supreme Chapter added projects in 1949, 1973, 1991 and 2009, DK's plan to support each equally meant work. Many ideas were implemented, some more successful than others but creating bonds for members. DK claims four PCE and one IPS recipients.

Tradition is important to the members of Chapter DK. In 1976, talented members made lovely white robes which are still as beautiful today after many initiations.

Membership has ranged in age from fifty-four to twenty-nine. Various meeting dates and times have been tried to accommodate its members. Alternate day and night meetings resulted in two groups and problems. One day DK met with six pro tem officers. An emergency arose for the president and then a pro tem stepped in for her. The solution seemed to be two chapters, and subsequently Chapter IA was formed with nine DK members. With ranks depleted, a slow but successful effort was made to recover, and Chapter DK grew with the experience.

Several years ago DK fell on hard times. Spirit was down, age was up, and officers were reruns. The search was on. Three new younger women were initiated, then their friends and then their daughters. New ideas, friendships and energy was generated. Recently, however, our membership has steadily declined again due to several members entering Chapter Eternal and others becoming inactive. We have had discussions about the options for our chapter and will make that a priority for the near future.

CHAPTER DK'S ACTIVE MEMBERSHIP IS 30; TOTAL ENROLLMENT IS 259

★

Chapter DL Lincoln
Organized May 10, 1927
by Mae Bond

Chapter DL was organized May 10, 1927, by Mae Bond. Nine members from Chapter BR along with four other dimits and two initiates made up the charter list for the new Lincoln chapter. Charter members were: Margaret Brown, president; Lulu Wolford, Ada Schorr, Dora Lantz, recording secretary; Helen Leverton, vice president; Ruth Schreve, chaplain; Lena Armstrong, treasurer; Kate Linn, Grace

Curley, Mary R. Lieuwellen, Grace Walls, Grace Mayhew, Verneda Whitney, Ruth Leverton, Harriet Wallace, and Eva Curtiss, corresponding secretary. Two charter members, Lulu Wolford and Eva Curtiss, served as president of Nebraska State Chapter. Lulu served in 1923-24 and Eva, in 1945-46.

Chapter DL has seen a steady influx of new members over the last few years, which has helped us maintain our membership as one of the larger chapters in Lincoln. Ten sisters have been members of P.E.O. for fifty or more years. These are Diane Butherus, Rickie Holyoke, Shirley Martin, Jane Peters, Marian Statton, Jan Weyhrauch, and Sue Wood. Edith Wekesser Hillyer has been a member for seventy years, and Marion Larmon (also a Nebraska past state president) for sixty-five years.

Our twenty-year history begins in 1995 with the presidency of Nancy Pierce (Davis). She decided to start a quilt as she began her second term to help her get through the year as she was not only our president, but her husband was dying of cancer. She chose as the theme of her quilt, "Stars on the Prairie," a kaleidoscope of various star patterns and fabrics. The many different talents, diverse backgrounds, and personalities that make up Chapter DL are similar to the pieces of that quilt.

Chapter DL has always generously supported the P.E.O. projects. Since 1995 we have had bake-less bake sales, silent auctions of "Attic Treasures," and sales of our third chapter cookbook, *Kitchen De Lites*, published in 2007. After some discussion, the chapter decided to simply add $20 to the annual dues total so that all members contributed equally. Our most significant gifts have been for fire sprinklers at the Nebraska P.E.O. Home, funds for the renovation of a Cottey Suite, and contributions to Cottey's "Defining Moment Challenge." In 2013 we participated in the first ever Cake Ball in Lincoln. It was a very successful event and DL received over $1,000 to contribute to projects. We decided to divide the sum equally among three scholarship projects—P.E.O. Scholar Award, P.E.O. STAR Scholarship, and P.E.O. International Peace Scholarship.

Our third cookbook, *Kitchen De Lites*, was a big undertaking. The principal mover and shaker was our long time member, Jan Weyhrauch, but many members contributed recipes and helped with typing. Debbie Hedgecock also spent many hours helping to sell the cookbooks.

Our diverse backgrounds and talents have been drawn upon many times for our meeting programs. This is one thing that contributes to our excellent attendance at meetings. We've had years with themes such as "celebrating our sisters," "picture this," "finding your passion," and "a time for DL." Some years have been a potpourri of programs. We've had many interesting speakers and programs brought in, but without a doubt, the most interesting programs have been those given by our many talented chapter members.

Members of DL also willingly contribute their talents in the community through service on boards, on projects to raise money for many organizations and causes and through their churches. Our scrapbooks give testimony to these many contributions.

The year 2007 was a significant one for DL. That was the year that Linda Statton became vice president of Lincoln Reciprocity Roundtable. She then moved up for the 2008-2009 year to represent DL as president of Roundtable.

We also had a special initiation in 2008. We've had many daughters initiated into our chapter, but that spring we initiated four who represented third, and even fifth generations of P.E.O.

In June of 2008 our president, Liz Shea McCoy, and immediate past president, Debbie Hedgecock, hosted a President's Luncheon for all the past presidents of Chapter DL. This was a great way to express the chapter's appreciation for their years of service and love to DL.

For Christmas in 2010, several members of the chapter decorated the Bess Streeter Aldrich home in Elmwood. They spent many hours making a beautiful holiday mantle display and decorating a tree with ornaments that depicted themes from the books by this Nebraska author. Chapter DL has a special tie to Bess Streeter Aldrich, as she was a member of our chapter.

With our membership of talented and devoted members, Chapter DL has a bright future ahead.

CHAPTER DL'S ACTIVE MEMBERSHIP IS 82; TOTAL ENROLLMENT IS 308

★

CHAPTER DM LINCOLN
ORGANIZED MAY 11, 1927
BY MAE BOND

Chapter DM, organized in 1927 in Lincoln, celebrated eighty-eight years in 2015.

P.E.O.s met Wednesday, May 11, 1927, with the charter head, Marie Williams, state organizer Mae Bond, and with the officers of Chapter K for the purpose of organizing Chapter DM. Charter members were: Marie Williams, president; Eudora Esterbrook, vice president; Bertha Stahl, recording secretary; Josephine Ingram, corresponding secretary; Nellie Strader, treasurer; Gussie Cadwallader, chaplain; Daisy Coryell, guard; Marguerite Cadwallader Weaver, Beulah Ramel, Margaret Davis, Caroline Furgason, Ressa Shroder, Pearl Van Gilder, Emma Beckman, Caroline Eiche, and Helen Colby.

Many exceptional women contributed much to the early years of Chapter DM. Marie Williams, who was instrumental in the formation of Chapter DM, served as Nebraska State Chapter president in 1939-40. Helen Colby dimitted to Chapter DM from Original A and was related by marriage to Founder Alice Bird Babb.

Our chapter has grown stronger through the years with many active 50+ members, including Jan Leeper, Gen Schmidt, Ruth Massengale, DiAnna Schimek, Mary Ghormley, and Marjorie Dickinson. For a time, we had a three-generation family in our chapter—Gladys Chatfield, Jan Leeper and Kathy Leeper Rasmussen. Dimitting members have been welcomed and bring further strength to our chapter.

Twelve meetings are held each year with morning coffees and noon luncheons on the first and third Monday of the month. Our summer meetings are informal coffees to keep in touch and welcome guests. Attendance at our meetings will average between twenty and thirty-five members.

Our yearbook committees put together a great variety of programming. Our members have enjoyed tours of the Governor's Mansion, the International Quilt Study Center, and a special tour of the University of Nebraska Lincoln football stadium. Our guide was a chapter member's BIL, who allowed us to have our picture taken on the football field. Not too many get this opportunity! Other programs included a High Tea, a Mad Hatter party—wear a hat or bring one—book review and view a Red Wing collection. The Nebraska P.E.O. Home in Beatrice receives special attention in the form of visits, meeting in their Home, and memorials.

Social activities with our BILs each year bring great attendance! Soup suppers, a leap year party with a Texas fiesta dinner, a Place to B Barbeque, a western party, and a members' tour of her vineyard, along with a picnic dinner that was special.

Throughout our community our sisters are involved in many activities. One of our members, DiAnna Schimek has completed her term as a senator in the Nebraska State Legislature and now is serving on the Lincoln City Council. Jan Leeper has been head of Leadership Lincoln. Judy Dougherty is on the board of the Lied Center for Performing Arts. Two of our members, Meera Bhardwaj and Kiran Bhardwaj, are Fulbright scholars and are completing their years in foreign countries. A reading room at the International Quilt Center in Lincoln has been named in honor of our member Mary Ghormley.

Support of our projects is important to us each year. In the year 2000, we supported a P.E.O. Program for Continuing Education grant applicant and a P.E.O. Scholar in the year 2001. Our members have been helping provide clothing, stockings, and other items to needy children in our schools through a P.E.O. in our community. After our fundraiser project is complete we celebrate! A visit to a bed and breakfast near Lincoln was a fun excursion and one of our members won a weekend visit there.

Getting to know each other is our goal and starting a bridge group that includes twelve members is very active. A book club meets once a month which leads to a lively discussion. Marguerite group luncheons, consisting of four members, are held to strengthen our bonds of sisterhood.

CHAPTER DM'S ACTIVE MEMBERSHIP IS 70; TOTAL ENROLLMENT IS 261

★

CHAPTER DN LINCOLN
ORGANIZED FEBRUARY 25, 1928
BY BERNICE TILLETT

Chapter DN, Lincoln, was organized February 25, 1928, by Bernice K. Tillett. Mrs. Tillett designated the chapter members "Daughters of Nobility." In the presence of two former Nebraska State Chapter presidents and the officers of Chapter K, Lincoln, seventeen charter members were linked together in the intimate bond of sisterhood.

Eleven women came to DN through dimit: Margaret Cleland (BR), Pearl Kincaid (U, Kansas), Gertrude Campbell (F, Wyoming) and seven women from Chapter K, as well as Nebraska dimits Mary Miskell, Berna Ann Miskell, Clara Miskell, Kate Davis, Marguerite Davis, Iva Anderson and Eunice Darrow. Initiates were Wilma Schlentz-Hart, Alice Smith French, Margaret Fedde, Gertrude Forbes, Norma L. Carpenter, Etta Carpenter and Martha Serson.

Our chapter has a loving concern for our sisters. Forty percent of our members have come from transfers. Our members range in age from the late twenties to the mid-nineties. Several of our members have contributed to education in Nebraska. Anne Campbell was Commissioner of Education. A Lincoln elementary school was named for her. Lillie Larsen served twelve years on the Lincoln Board of Education and is currently a member of the State Board of Education. Chapter DN has had several members with outstanding service to P.E.O. Nelsine Scofield served as president of Nebraska State Chapter from 1967 to 1968. She also acted as assistant secretary-treasurer of Nebraska State Chapter from 1980 to 1990. Jeanette Johnson served as advisor for the P.E.O. College Group at UNL, nurturing young P.E.O.s during their college life. Mayme White and Clarice Hicks presided over the Lincoln Reciprocity Roundtable and several DN members have served as officers. Janet McDonald has been a Cottey Area Chairman.

Programs cover a variety of interesting subjects including history, health, computer savvy, community awareness, and getting to know each other. Recent social meetings have been tours of Homestead Monument, Grand Manse in Lincoln and Prairie Creek Inn. BILs are often included in social meetings.

A DN tradition is to hold a Harvest Festival in October of each year. Following a meal there is a raffle and silent auction. Proceeds go to P.E.O. projects. DN always chooses a philanthropy project in December. Miniature red felt stockings are passed around and are stuffed with dollars to give to our chosen charity for that year.

We enthusiastically support our projects. Member Suzanne Jouvenat was the recipient of an ELF loan. Michelle Lynn Coonrod received a PCE grant. We have sponsored three designated IPS students in recent years. We have nominated candidates for the P.E.O. STAR Scholarship and the P.E.O. Scholar Award. DN loyally supported the "Defining Moment Campaign" for Cottey College. Three DN members have lived at the Nebraska P.E.O. Home in Beatrice and we visit there on occasion and hold a meeting.

DN schedules a monthly Saturday morning coffee at various coffee shops. This is an opportunity for our members to gather in an informal setting.

In 2003 Chapter DN celebrated our 75th anniversary with a luncheon at the Country Club of Lincoln. Later in the year we were recognized at the Nebraska State Convention in Lincoln.

CHAPTER DN'S ACTIVE MEMBERSHIP IS 52; TOTAL ENROLLMENT IS 210

★

CHAPTER DO NEWMAN GROVE
ORGANIZED MARCH 29, 1928
BY BERNICE TILLETT
DISBANDED JANUARY 29, 2009

Chapter DO was organized with the assistance of Chapter DJ, Albion. The charter list was composed of all initiates since no P.E.O.s lived in the community. Ethel Hoagland compiled the charter list and the organization was held in the home of Kathryn D. Gerhart.

Charter members included twelve young ladies and four of their mothers: Ethel Hoagland, president; her mother, Hilda Hoaglund; Margaret Hastings, recording secretary; Kathryn E. Gerhart, corresponding secretary; her mother, Kathryn D. Gerhart, vice president; Louise S. Johnson, chaplain; Vera S. Johnson; Hazel Hansen, treasurer; her mother, Ida Frink; Anne E. Wyant; her daughter, Helen Finstrom; Elsie Kennedy, guard; Margaret Lewis; Dorothy Gerhart;

Alphie Jacobson and Clara Johnson.

Interesting customs from the past include a nickel fine for not wearing the pin to meetings, Christmas and Valentine teas, "heart" sisters, a silver spoon wedding gift to sisters, and a handkerchief shower for the retiring president.

Chapter DO sponsored three women for the P.E.O. Educational Loan Fund. The chapter faithfully supported all P.E.O. projects. The annual auction helped raise funds for the chapter donations.

Four Chapter DO sisters were third and fourth generation P.E.O.s.

TOTAL ENROLLMENT 115

★

CHAPTER DP BRIDGEPORT
ORGANIZED APRIL 14, 1928
BY BERNICE TILLETT

Located in the panhandle of Nebraska, Chapter DP of Bridgeport was begun on April 14, 1928, by State Organizer Bernice Tillett.

Charter members were Celia Hurd (L), Ora Burwell (Y), Ruth Canaday (N), Bessie Milmine (K, Iowa), Gertrude Spanogle (T), Mary McGee, Eulah Dunlap, Sybil Marquis, Dorothy Banta, Esther Nelson, Lyla Rice, Nell Jones and Liza Welsher. The organizer identified these charter members as "Daughters of Purity."

Through the years Chapter DP has supported P.E.O. projects, both financially and by study of their goals. We have also supported many community groups including Girls State, Girl Scouts, Campfire Girls, and our local hospital and nursing home. We have also philanthropically contributed to Meals on Wheels and our local food pantry.

Chapter DP has assisted several women in applying for and receiving grants from the P.E.O. Program for Continuing Education. Some recipients were our own members. In 2010, the chapter was privileged to award the P.E.O. STAR Scholarship to Emily Wright, daughter of member Bobbi Wright.

On April 19, 1978, Chapter DP held a commemorative tea at the Presbyterian Church to celebrate the chapter's 50th Anniversary. There were two charter members living at that time, Ruth Canaday and Nell Jones. They shared their appreciation of their years as members of P.E.O. and Chapter DP.

The 75th anniversary was celebrated on April 7, 2003, with a catered dinner at a member's home. Twenty-four members attended and 50-year pins were presented to Wilma Johnson and Fran Erickson. The chapter observed its 85th anniversary on April 20, 2013. Sixteen members enjoyed a wonderful brunch at the home of one of our sisters, followed by our regular meeting.

Entertainment of Reciprocity Group X during two significant times is a highlight of Chapter DP's happy memories. During the World War II era, with meat and sugar rationing nationwide, the sisters pooled their ration stamps and managed to have enough meat and sugar to feed everyone bountifully. In 1961, Chapter DP was privileged to entertain the Panhandle Reciprocity and commemorate that group's 25th anniversary. One hundred six P.E.O.s from across western Nebraska, together with state officers, gathered in Bridgeport amidst a backdrop of silver decorations. The highlight was place cards with tattered borders and marguerites made by Chapter DP's talented charter member Nell Jones. The chapter also hosted reciprocity in 1984.

We currently have a 60-year member and a 50-year member. Wilma Johnson was initiated in 1953 and Virginia Plummer joined Chapter DP in 1961. Our chapter remembers our Chapter Eternal sisters by placing crosses on their graves each Memorial Day. Secret Sisters has been a tradition for decades, as we take on various names such as football teams, movie stars, cities, candy bars, bath and body fragrances, magazines and famous women. Through Secret Sisters, we always know that we will be remembered on special occasions by a Chapter DP sister. We have also met jointly with Chapter EI from Bayard and held BIL parties throughout the years.

We are proud that we have several two-generation members and even a three-generation group of sisters. We continue to help with each of the P.E.O. projects. We also attend state conventions and reciprocity meetings and report back to the chapter the direction of the state leadership. Our membership has been faithful to our P.E.O. obligations and looks forward to a future of friendship, devotion, and service.

CHAPTER DP'S ACTIVE MEMBERSHIP IS 27; TOTAL ENROLLMENT IS 164

★

CHAPTER DQ FRIEND
ORGANIZED APRIL 21, 1928
BY BERNICE TILLETT

Something very special happened in Friend, Nebraska, April 12, 1928. Chapter DQ P.E.O. was organized by Bernice Tillet. Mrs. Tillett was assisted in the organization by Chapter CM, Crete. At that time there were two residents who belonged to chapters in other towns. They were Elizabeth Burnette, Chapter CM Crete and Esther Lehman, Ravenna. Charter members were Esther C. Lehman, president; Edith Teale, vice president; Margaret E. Hughes, recording secretary; Elizabeth Burnett, corresponding secretary; Gladys Southwick, treasurer; Clara S. Newcomb, chaplain; Floss M. Locke, guard; Dorothy H. Southwick; Fay H. McFarlane; Florence A. Hagelin; Minola M. Hamilton; Anna E. Barney (Elliott); Marie Wentworth (Jacobson); Arline Justice. Sister Bernice was pleased with her new group. So much so that she nicknamed them Daughters of Quality. These first charter members became 50-year members. Several years ago June Krebs was honored as a 50-year member and our latest 50-year member is Erma Clouse. Four other charter members have also been honored.

Another celebration in 2013 was our chapter's 85th anniversary.

Our meetings, as well as being educational, are informative. One of our favorites is the yearly Founders' Day program, which is always special.

As a group we have supported all of the P.E.O. projects and Cottey College. We have not visited either Cottey College or the Nebraska P.E.O. Home in Beatrice for some time. We do look forward to going again.

In the past twenty years we have taken our turn in Reciprocity Group VII and have helped with the Nebraska State Conventions in Columbus and in York.

In the early years of Chapter DQ, local community projects consisted of providing funds for Christmas baskets for the needy, milk for underweight children, swim tickets for disadvantaged youngsters, graduation clothing for two high school girls and gifts to the local hospital, Girl Scouts, Child Saving Institute and the Red Cross Bloodmobile. U.S. Savings Bonds were purchased; contributions were made to the Red Cross and CARE packages were sent to servicemen during World War II and the Korean Conflict.

We are still an organization of traditions when it comes to community projects. Among these are playing bingo at the local nursing home, participating in the local Christmas Tree Festival at which we collect cans of food for the local food bank; adopting a Cottey College student; and our "fun" thing is our Brag Box. With it we earn $1 a brag as well as learning something special about that member. Our newest community project is our Christmas in July.

In the past we have had a member gift exchange. Now we use this money to participate in the Local Schools Back Pack Program. This program works to help needy children. The back pack is filled with school supplies the first time and when it is returned to school it is filled with groceries for the weekend.

The climax to our projects is remembering our members who have gone to Chapter Eternal with a marguerite on Memorial Day.

CHAPTER DQ'S ACTIVE MEMBERSHIP IS 48; TOTAL ENROLLMENT IS 143

★

CHAPTER DR OMAHA
ORGANIZED APRIL 28, 1928
BY BERNICE TILLETT
DISBANDED JUNE 6, 2006

No history today seems complete without a look back at the "pre-historic" days of Chapter DR. Therefore, the opening chapter of DR's history delves back to the fall of 1923 when Anna McClelland of Chapter AG, Fullerton, came to teach at Omaha Technical High School. There, she met another teacher, Adah Lonneker of Chapter AL, Madison. Having become fast friends, their talk would often turn to the desire for an Omaha P.E.O. chapter which met at a time available to teachers and business women. It seemed that young, enthusiastic P.E.O.s had professional and business careers which precluded attending luncheons and afternoon meetings of the twelve Omaha chapters. Two of their friends of Chapter BY, Lincoln, Virginia Zimmer and Matilda Peters, and the president of the Omaha P.E.O. Association, Martha Aten, assisted the two teachers in organizing the first evening chapter in Omaha, Chapter DR. Chapter CP, Omaha, assisted with the organization.

The original dimitting members consisted of Anna McClelland (AG); Adah Lonneker (AL); Lillian Meyerhoff (CH, Iowa); Elizabeth Farrell (FL, Iowa); Esther Butts (M, Wyoming); Bertha Neale (Z); Bess Bedell (AU); Mildred Butler (K); Leona Wood (Z); Adeline McCulloch (M); Lula Haskell (BJ); and Louise Matthews (BD). Maud Poley, Lena Hosman and Maud Smith were the three new initiates. A luncheon at the Blackstone Hotel preceded the organization with honored guests from Nebraska State Chapter attending: Jenny Bryant, first vice president; Mae Bond, president; Bernice Tillett, organizer and Viola Cameron, past president. Organizer Tillett spoke of cherishing the history and idealism of P.E.O. and warned against letting the chapter become "another club." She christened Chapter DR "Daughters of Radiance."

Traditionally, DR memorialized their sisters through generous gifts to the P.E.O. projects and gifts to the Centennial Fund. They also supported the Cottey Bus Trip and sent money to new chapters in the Omaha area. A special memorial also was sent to the Omaha Boys' Home in honor of the husband of DR member Kathryn Kendall.

Chapter DR's history was richly steeped in tradition. Strong ties of warm affection and genuine appreciation endured not only with DR's sponsor, Martha Aten, but also with their organizer, Bernice Tillett. Every yearbook carried the names of these two guardian sisters and they also were remembered at chapter birthday parties which have become yearly tradition. DR charter member Anna McClelland composed an impressive Founders' Day Memorial Service that has been shared with the Omaha Reciprocity Association.

Two simple customs which displayed the concern among DR sisters were the hostess reports after roll call concerning absent members and the frequent use of the "marguerite chain" (telephone calling tree). The Philanthropic Committee passed at each meeting a three-compartment box (made by DR sister June Tipton) to collect pennies, birthday money and a ten cent fine for not wearing the pin. One of DR's more legendary traditions was the dispensing with ALL refreshments. This took place during the war and DR sisters were ready to sacrifice! At the first meeting following the motion to do away with refreshments, members were treated to the aroma of coffee and presented with paper plates with pictures of luscious desserts and paper cups—SANS COFFEE!

DR sisters reported that a beautiful spirit of love and understanding pervaded the chapter. Dedication, helping hands, and loving concern were abundant.

Chapter DR disbanded June 6, 2006.

TOTAL ENROLLMENT 127

★

CHAPTER DS SUPERIOR
ORGANIZED JUNE 2, 1928
BY BERNICE TILLETT

Fourteen women came together to become charter members of Chapter DS, Superior. These women were dimitting members: Dora Baumbach Jones (J), president; Marvella King (V), vice president; Maude Furrey (BG), recording secretary; Nellie A. Barnard (AR), treasurer; Lee T. Petit (AU), chaplain; Carterette Ebersole (J), guard; Kate Meek Scoular (disbanded D), corresponding secretary; and Jennie F. Fisher (disbanded D). Initiates were Josephine Day Mendell, pianist; Dorothy E. Jones (Haber), Ruth Ebersole, Margaret L. Furry (Knaup), Mary Lyndall Fisher (Newens), and Martha Rose King (Carroll).

The seeds for Chapter DS had been sewn earlier with the formation of Chapter D in Superior. This chapter, organized in 1889, had as a charter member Alice Cary Briggs, sister-in-law of founder Hattie Briggs. The chapter was disbanded in 1909 for unknown reasons. However in its brief existence, it figured prominently in early Nebraska P.E.O. formation. Mrs. Briggs was the first president of Nebraska Grand Chapter in 1890, as well as the president of Supreme Chapter in 1893.

With such a historical background, it was only fitting that at the 1989 convention in Hastings, Chapter DS, along with Chapter J, presented a skit depicting the organization of Nebraska Grand Chapter in 1890. Another memorable event in chapter history was the celebration of a 50th anniversary tea at the home of Iva Mae Upton on June 2, 1978.

Appreciation for its heritage continues to the present in Chapter DS. A long-standing tradition is the annual reciprocity dinner with Chapter J, Nelson. Another cherished tradition is the December meeting complete with a salad supper. Christmas greetings are sent to nonresident members with each sister writing a personal greeting. Each member also participates in the local "Giving Tree" and at the Christmas meeting we share what we purchased and wrap them as a group. The March meeting prepares the chapter for a change in leadership. Chapter members gather for a meal and participate in the election and installation of new officers.

Chapter DS supports all P.E.O. projects and provides a scholarship for a senior girl graduating from Superior High School. We raise the scholarship money by having a basket of goodies raffled off at each meeting, the winner gets to bring the basket to the next meeting. Our chapter also donates each year to the "Coats for Kids" project in our area.

The past few years a successful fundraiser has been preparing breakfast in the park on the 4th of July which coincides with the local "Firecraker Run" which has been held for over thirty years. The participants and the crowd are very supportive of our breakfast. Our previous fundraisers have been auctioning baskets at our Christmas meeting, selling blanket throws with our town history on them, and garage sales.

Our social meetings consist of a bunco night, bowling, dining out, enjoying a local winery, and actually having a slumber party. Our members are a very special group of women that are all very busy with their careers and families. All of our members are influential and active in their church and community. One of our current members, Sonia Schmidt, is our town mayor.

Chapter DS is a proud group of dedicated members and will continue to grow, support projects, and also be an influence in our community.

CHAPTER DS'S ACTIVE MEMBERSHIP IS 40; TOTAL ENROLLMENT IS 206

★

CHAPTER DT KIMBALL
ORGANIZED MAY 28, 1929
BY BERNICE TILLETT

Charter members of Chapter DT were Marie Goodhand (BB), president; Minnie Neeley (EP), vice president; Elizabeth Cromwell (BB), recording secretary; Jessie Reid (AC, Illinois), corresponding secretary; Vera Rodman, treasurer; Lillie Wilcox, chaplain; Edith Larson, guard; Mary Smith, Helen White, Nellie Alden, Eliza Barfoot, Ruth Graves, Marjorie Rodman, and Irma Grosshans. Irma, the last living charter member, entered Chapter Eternal in 1987.

Chapter DT, historically an afternoon chapter, has experienced a transition to evening meetings to accommodate schedules of a greater number of sisters. Members enjoy program topics which are stimulating and varied; the 60th anniversary was a gala occasion celebrated with a candle-laden cake; a festive December meeting includes Christmas dinner, ornament exchange, gifts for the

Nebraska P.E.O. Home residents, and carols sung by Junior High students.

Lucrative annual rummage sales have traditionally been Chapter DT's major fundraiser. Donations of time, effort and "sisterpower" have made possible generous support of the P.E.O. projects, including furnishing a room at the Nebraska P.E.O. Home, becoming a Cottey College Golden Anniversary Chapter, refurbishing a room at Cottey, giving a $500 gift honoring State President Jean Johnson at her convention, sponsoring Nebraska Cottey Scholarships for five Kimball girls, becoming a Nebraska P.E.O. Home 50th Anniversary Solid Gold Chapter, and giving $100 in honor of 1988 Nebraska State Convention Chairman Donna Linn. A tradition is being established of honoring selected chapter members with a donation to the project of their choice. Summarily, Chapter DT proudly supports projects international, state and local in scope. Locally Chapter DT assists the community blood drive for United Blood Service of Cheyenne, Wyoming.

Eighteen women have been sponsored for loans from the P.E.O. Educational Loan Fund and three women have received grants from the P.E.O. Program for Continuing Education. Chapter DT members show loving concern to these women through cards, telephone calls and special remembrances throughout the year.

Chapter DT members who have served on Nebraska State Chapter committees include Vera Rodman, Admission Committee of the Nebraska P.E.O. Home in 1938; Bernice Linn, Post War Activities in 1953; Jean Johnson, Nebraska State Executive Board 1962-69 and president of Nebraska State Chapter in 1968-69. Two members have been Cottey College Area Chairmen—Wilma Gilliland in 1969-72 and Donna Linn in 1983-85. Wilma Gilliland also served as chairman of the Amendments and Recommendations Committee in 1980 and Shelby Warrington served on the Nominating Committee in 1989.

Evangel Wisdom, Dorothy Alden and JoAnne Burke served as presidents of the Panhandle Reciprocity Group III and Isabel Linn and Maurine Kennedy as treasurer. Chapter DT often hosts Reciprocity Groups III and X.

Convention of International Chapter delegates include Vera Rodman, Edith Larson, Carolyn Harkins, Evangel Wisdom, Jean Johnson, Dorothy Alden, Wilma Gilliland, Sharon Olsen and Donna Linn.

In March 1966 six members dimitted to form the nucleus of Chapter GN, Kimball. Chapter DT officers assisted Organizer Jean Johnson with the initiation. Joint activities with Chapter GN include International Convention reports, Founders' Day programs, BIL parties and an occasional social function.

Chapter DT and other chapters of Reciprocity Group X hosted the 1988 Nebraska State Convention in Kimball. The bustle of preparation for this event gave DT president Shelby Warrington and sisters a sincere warm regard and appreciation for their multi-talented sisters. Artists Pris Gilmore (DT) and Frances Campbell (GN) provided a beautiful backdrop for the stage. Donna Linn served as State Convention Chairman. Of those from Chapter DT attending Convention of International Chapter in Omaha in 1991, three served in official capacities: Donna Linn, Executive Committee, Wilma Gilliland, guard, and Sharon Olsen, delegate.

In 2001 the chapter welcomed P.E.O. Scholar Award recipient Pamela Olsen as a member. Pamela has served in many offices including three years as president of Chapter DT.

CHAPTER DT'S ACTIVE MEMBERSHIP IS 50; TOTAL ENROLLMENT IS 220

Chapter DU Omaha
Organized May 29, 1929
by Bernice Tillett

One's sister is part of one's essential self, an eternal presence of one's heart and soul and memory. -Susan Cahill

On May 29, 1929, Bernice Tillett, state organizer, organized thirteen women into a new P.E.O. Chapter in Omaha, Nebraska. Chapter DU began with thirteen charter members, ten were received by dimit and three were new initiates. Charter members were: Ann Hyson (P, Illinois), president; Helen Prouty Adamson (BV, Iowa), vice president; Anna Tighe (AL), treasurer; Lexie Finch (V); Margaret Olson (CP, Iowa); Helen Pierce Stuart (AP, Iowa); Hazel Muzzy Herring (P); Kate Hoffman (U); Gladys Schabinger (AU, Kansas), May Stewart Skinkle (O), corresponding secretary; Hazel Dunbar, recording secretary; Mary Ellen Wallace and Abigail Manning. These women gave Chapter DU a firm foundation upon which the sisters have been building for eighty-five years.

Hazel Dunbar later reported she knew little of P.E.O. before her initiation but was intrigued by the gold star with black initials on it worn by a favorite aunt. The aunt told her it was from a "lovely organization" and the letters meant "Pretty Every One"—not only pretty appearances, but pretty words and pretty deeds.

As with all things in life, Chapter DU celebrates its gains and mourns its losses. Forty-three gifted sisters have transferred to bless other chapters and forty cherished sisters have gone to Chapter Eternal.

Chapter DU - Front Row (L to R) Ardith Vickery, Barbara Ford, Marjorie Quinlan, Erica Marburger, Andrea Marburger, Carolyn Reade. Back Row (L to R) Susan Marburger, Mardel Bridgman, Jessica Reade, Alison Rider, Janelle Davis, Connie Woodward. Not pictured- Lanni Branch, Mary Ann Folchert, Geneva Johnson, Marcene Johnson, Rana Scarlett-Johnson, Joyce Kronberg, Kathy Leach, Barbara McNeal, Charlene Meyer, Kathlyn Ramsell, Sherry Smith, Dorothy Stern, and Connie Sydzyik.

In 1936, Chapter DU sponsored the organization of Chapter EK in Omaha.

Chapter DU is proud of its record of community service. During World War II, the chapter purchased $44,610 in bonds and gave 1,350 hours of service. Later, chapter members volunteered to the Thrift Shop at Uta Halee Home for Girls and at the Visiting Nurses Association project for the handicapped. Today many volunteer in Omaha's community projects and foundations.

DU has a rather unique fundraising tradition which includes their beloved BILs. Each year they hold a pot luck dinner which is centered on a particular theme. We have gone from the "ranch," with hay bales, a saddle and stick horses to the "super bowl." The BILs really enjoyed that one.

In the past we had a Nebraska P.E.O. Home Christmas project. At every December meeting, each member was asked to bring a gift for the sisters in the Nebraska P.E.O. Home. Items given have included stamps, stationery, tissues, perfumed soaps, games, puzzles, bud vases, candy and candles. These gifts were always appreciated by the P.E.O. sisters in the Home. We also support Cottey College students with gift cards and notes of encouragement.

We have enjoyed the programs presented at each meeting. We never stop learning about our city, state and country as well as our world through these informative programs given by our members and guest speakers.

Within the last twenty years, no anecdote involving Chapter DU could top an incident which occurred in the '70s. A brand new member had just been installed as chaplain. At the very next meeting, which was initiation, the new chaplain was so anxious to have the ritual go so smoothly that every time there was a lull, she would say "Let Us Pray" and the president had to say, "No, Not Yet!"

Our Delightfully Unique members of Chapter DU are Definitely United in the spirit of P.E.O.!

Chapter DU lives the following two quotations.

A sister always knows when to listen and when to talk,
when to laugh and when to cry. -Unknown
She is my sounding board, my confidante, my keeper of secrets and my best friend.
-Kathleen O'Keefe

CHAPTER DU'S ACTIVE MEMBERSHIP IS 27; TOTAL ENROLLMENT IS 144

★

CHAPTER DV ST. EDWARD
ORGANIZED APRIL 22, 1930
BY JOSEPHINE WADDELL

According to early accounts, Edna E. Simms from Broken Bow, Chapter S, brought P.E.O. to St. Edward. Chapter AG, Fullerton, assisted with the organization. Charter members were: Minnie Leach (AG), treasurer; Edna Simms (S), president; Nellie Hasselbalch (AX), recording secretary; Katherine Knudsen, corresponding secretary; Mary Myhre; Lola Frank, pianist; Carrie Baldwin, chaplain; Fern V. Burn, guard; Iva Wells; Jennie Powell, Zella Scriven, Hettie Hehnke, Olive Lightner, vice president; Winifred Duncan and Alma Kennedy.

Chapter DV has grown stronger during the past eighty-three years through a commitment to P.E.O. Over the years, programs have been as interesting and varied as the members. Chapter DV members have been honored by serving at reciprocity, state, and International Conventions. In both 1987 and 2004, Chapter DV hosted the Reciprocity Group VII with Marion Clark serving as reciprocity president each time. Marion Clark was a guard at the 1985 Nebraska State Convention in Columbus, Stephanie Dawson served as a teller for the 1991 Convention of International Chapter in Omaha. Tami Nauenburg was a guard at the 1999 Nebraska State Convention in York, and Pam Carlson was a guard at the 2013 Nebraska State Convention in Columbus.

A birthday dinner always has been one of the highlights of our P.E.O. year. In April 1980, "Our Golden Year" was the theme chosen for the 50th anniversary year of Chapter DV. The dinner was held on the exact day Chapter DV was organized fifty years before. A skit titled "This is Your Life" highlighted Chapter DV's first fifty years. Favors were porcelain thimbles, hand-painted with the marguerite by Elizabeth Merrell. Our 75th anniversary year was celebrated in 2005 with the year's theme being "A Look Back at 75 Years of Sisterhood." Elizabeth Carder made beautiful painted china teacups for each member to commemorate the occasion.

Chapter DV has relied upon a Harvest Auction to replenish its treasury each year. Members bring produce from their gardens, baked goods, and handmade crafts to a fall chapter meeting and each item is auctioned. We have also worked a few summer weekends for the past ten years at the Gateway Theater in Albion to be able to increase our giving to the projects. Farmer's Market sales and sales of porcelain P.E.O. commemorative plates have benefitted our treasury, as well.

Annual gifts to the projects have been a priority for Chapter DV. Chapter DV became a Cottey Golden Anniversary Chapter in 1984. Our chapter has contributed to Cottey College's Academic Center and the "Defining Moment Campaign." Chapter DV members are currently saving pocket change in pink and yellow socks to "Sock It Away for Scholars" with the goal of earning the P.E.O. Scholar Awards Laureate Chapter status. We have been pleased to sponsor Kim Good, Dee Wurtz, Audrey Robertson, and Megan Schiner as recipients of PCE grants. In addition, we have participated in the Nebraska P.E.O. Home "Adopt-a-Resident" and the "Adopt-a-Cottey-Student" programs.

In 1990, Chapter DV began to give an annual scholarship to a female graduate of St. Edward High School. Since that time, twenty-four young women have been recipients of our local scholarship awards.

Our annual BIL social event has evolved into a family and friends gathering. Sharing a meal and games with these special people in our lives has been a fun and relaxing way to show our appreciation.

Over the years, Chapter DV has initiated wonderful new members and watched them grow in P.E.O. Some members have left the chapter through dimits and others through changes in their lives. The chapter is saddened by the loss of members to Chapter Eternal. Change constantly has altered the makeup of Chapter DV, yet the spirit of P.E.O. has grown in the chapter and loving concern is always shown.

The spirit of Chapter DV can best be expressed through a poem written in 1981 by Chapter Eternal member Lenna McKay:

A TRIBUTE TO US

Chapter DV, now aren't we nice. We are sisters, indeed, everyone.
We can be serious and do worthwhile things,
But we also can have lots of fun!
And in reading the minutes compiled by the girls,
One thing that I observed that was neat,
Was the lovely food that everyone served. So it's plain, we all like to eat!
Two more meetings this year, then good-bye for a while
But we'll be close together in heart and pray for each other.
May God bless us all, and the Sisterhood of which we are a part.

CHAPTER DV'S ACTIVE MEMBERSHIP IS 20; TOTAL ENROLLMENT IS 97

★

CHAPTER DW RUSHVILLE
ORGANIZED MAY 9, 1930
BY JOSEPHINE WADDELL

Chapter DW of Rushville was organized May 9, 1930, by Josephine Waddell. In 1929, Rushville applied to become a P.E.O. chapter. Disappointingly, the population of Rushville was slightly less than the required 1,000. When the 1930 census showed a population of 1,015, Rushville again applied and permission was granted. On May 9, Myrtle Musser received a telegram from Organizer Josephine Waddell saying she would arrive in Rushville on the afternoon train and would like the ceremony that afternoon. Some of the ladies were involved with the Junior-Senior banquet that night. Pearl Edgell offered her home decorated with lovely spring flowers. The train was two hours late, and when Mrs. Waddell arrived, she learned her supplies had not been delivered. Myrtle Musser and Hertha Bates hurried to the depot. After much searching, the package was located. Due to Mrs. Waddell's allergies, all the flowers had to be removed! Despite the confusion, fifteen initiates became P.E.O. sisters by midnight. Charter members of Chapter DW were: Myrtle B. Musser, president; Marie Aplan, vice president; Amy Stewart, recording secretary; Maude Rosseter, corresponding secretary; Myrtle E. Musser, treasurer; Dora Marcy, chaplain; Olga Wilhite, guard; Mollie Ellsworth, pianist; Marie Smaha, Hertha Bates, Beatrice Stookey, Pearl Edgell, Josie Boyer, Ivy Reed, and Emma J. Veach.

In May 1980, Chapter DW celebrated its 50th anniversary. Area chapters helped share their special "golden" day. In 1981, Chapter DW served as one of the hostess chapters for the Nebraska State Convention in Chadron. In September 1986, Chapter DW held the 50th Anniversary meeting of Panhandle Reciprocity Groups III and X. Over 120 P.E.O.s from the Panhandle attended this special celebration. Mary Hewitt, the first initiate of Chapter DW, celebrated her sixtieth year as a P.E.O. in May 1991. Chapter DW's 75th anniversary was in May of 2005 and was celebrated in July with guests from northern Panhandle chapters. Our theme was hats and the room was decorated accordingly with guests invited to wear hats and gloves for the occasion.

Other noted anniversaries celebrated during the last twenty years include: Jerene Smith 55 years and Gwen Hook 50 years in 1994; Ruth Johnson 50 years in 2008; Doris Winter 50 years in 2009; and Addis King, 60 years in 2010. In 2012-2013, we lost the two longest standing members of our chapter, Doris Winter and Addis King. Addis was still hosting meetings until the time of her death.

We are proud to have had Glenna Vodicka serve as Cottey College Area III Chairman and State Cottey College Chairman for a number of years. Glenna also graciously offered her home as a P.E.O. Bed and Breakfast.

Our P.E.O. meetings are continually enhanced by clever programs given by sisters. Programs have included skits, readings and poetry including one sister's Easter dramatization of the thoughts and feelings of the mother of Judas, a presentation on area Hospice services, and more. We learned much about our sisters from personal items each member put in a special bag. Each meeting, the contents of one bag would be revealed and the identity of the sister guessed. Other personalities were shown by secret sister gifts given during a year's time. A lunch for three randomly selected sisters was held during summer months to give members an opportunity to become better acquainted. Learning more about each other gives us strength as a chapter and draws us closer as we share in the cares and concerns of our sisters and their families.

Chapter DW has made annual gifts to the P.E.O. projects a priority. When our brag box contains twenty dollars, a member's name is drawn and that money is given to the project of her choice. This has helped increase our contributions to the projects. Bakeless bake sales are also used as a money maker. One Christmas we broke balloons containing an amount which was our required payment for supper. It generated a lot of laughter as we tried to break the balloons and provided a nice sum for our projects.

We had such fun at our Christmas party this year. Each sister was to bring a gift representing the letters P.E.O. It is amazing the creativity sisters used.

Christmas donations of gloves and hats to our local Community Action have become an annual tradition, as well as giving canned goods and food pantry items. Our chapter has supplied our medical clinic's waiting room with children's books and toys.

A Spring Salad Luncheon with high school girls modeling their prom dresses and little girls modeling their Easter finery has been a favorite social event. Sisters from neighboring chapters and community members are invited. In the fall, we host an ice cream social to acquaint area high school girls and their mothers with Cottey College. Chapters FO, Hay Springs, and BZ, Gordon, are also included.

Chapter DW is proud to have sponsored several special women for scholarships. These include awards for the PCE, ELF, STAR and Cottey Scholarships. We were honored to have one of our PCE grant recipients, Rena Krotz, selected to present her story at state convention. Our chapter has sponsored three Cottey College attendees: Gretchen Plantz, 1962, Sheryl Orr, 1992, and Arielle Tiensvold, 2011. This year Danielle Thies, whose goal is to become a medical doctor, was a recipient of the P.E.O. Educational Loan Fund.

We are proud of the fact that we have increased our membership by nineteen in the past five years and continue to grow and thrive. Chapter DW strives to continue the spirit of our founding sisters and their passion for P.E.O.

CHAPTER DW'S ACTIVE MEMBERSHIP IS 38; TOTAL ENROLLMENT IS 143

★

CHAPTER DX LINCOLN
ORGANIZED MARCH 20, 1931
BY JOSEPHINE WADDELL

Chapter DX was organized primarily to welcome University P.E.O.s through the efforts of Clara Prouty, president, and Harriet McMillen, vice president. Other charter members were: Zena Hiner, recording secretary; Mildred Hill, corresponding secretary; Ethelyn Colwell, treasurer; Essel Bimson, chaplain; Helen Prouty (past Supreme President Helen Drake's daughter) guard; Tillie Wright, Zazel Sloniger, Vaunie Black, Laura Ryons, Carrie Webster, Myrtle Dean and Augusta Baer.

Annual traditions of Chapter DX include the inviting of campus P.E.O.s to a meeting devoted to their entertainment (all Lincoln chapters now share this tradition), BIL activities, often with humorous initiation skits, annual chapter birthdays where history is reviewed and messages from nonresidents read, monetary gifts to the Nebraska P.E.O. Home (a grandfather clock was given with Chapter DL), and an annual Christmas gift exchange.

In 1959, upon the death of Clara Prouty, Chapter DX received her jeweled guard and it has been worn by every president in her term since that time. Minnie Stuff, a 60-year member, was state president prior to being a 30-year member of Chapter DX. DX member Nina White designed the guard's lock box and Pearl Seaton originated the "Bride's Box," a project which provided items to needy brides and others.

Notable DX members include Nettie Brown, who served as P.E.O. Home Superintendent 1948-1964; Helen Wallace, who served as P.E.O. Home Superintendent, 1964-82; and Marjorie Hewitt who helped organize the UNL Campus P.E.O.s and served as its sponsor for four years.

In 1983, many DX members acted as chairmen for convention committees. Jean Patoka wrote the invitational skit in 1982 and "*P.E.O. in Bloom*" in 1983 and also served as convention pianist and music chairman. In 1984, the video tape of Jean Patoka's "*P.E.O. in Bloom*" was rented nationally and the proceeds of over $2,100 were given to Cottey College and the Nebraska P.E.O. Home.

Fundraisers the past years have included garage sales and a boutique of crafts and paintings by Colleen Eubanks. These events raised sufficient funds for Chapter DX to qualify as a Cottey College Golden Anniversary Chapter.

DX member Jean Patoka served as a member of the state Centennial Committee in 1987-90 and composed the guard's march "*Centennial Melody*" (see page 592). Jean also chaired the 1991 Convention of International Chapter invitation skit which was presented in Phoenix, served as pianist for the 1990 Centennial Convention of Nebraska State Chapter in Lincoln and served as an usher at Convention of International Chapter in Omaha.

Past Lincoln Reciprocity Roundtable Officers from Chapter DX have included Helen Wallace, Caroline Taylor, Martha Wier, Margaret Smith, Louise Rowe and Marsha Glover.

Chapter DX continues to support all of our P.E.O. projects. A fundraiser luncheon in the Fall with generous donations is a welcome yearly event.

We have recently designated our members who can no longer participate actively as hostesses, or committee members, or officers as Chapter DX Marguerites. Age and health problems are the main reasons they cannot participate except by remaining as active dues paying members. They still can participate with ideas and input and sometimes with attendance. We value their membership and designation as Marguerites.

We are also working on the officer position by having a president who has served two years become the vice president and help the new president if she needs help. The experienced vice president is not the yearbook or program chairman which has a committee designation.

Chapter DX members provided leadership with Colleen Eubanks and Susan Brouse and others working on the inaugural Cake Ball in February 2013. Money for projects was raised by several chapters involved in this event.

Interest groups within the chapter started by Joyce Vosteen have been formed with reading and reviewing books, walking, biking, and playing bridge. These groups are open to all the sisters in the chapter. In a large city, this helps members get to know one another better.

CHAPTER DX'S ACTIVE MEMBERSHIP IS 55; TOTAL ENROLLMENT IS 290

★

CHAPTER DY OMAHA
ORGANIZED MAY 13, 1931
BY JOSEPHINE WADDELL

A group of eighteen women, all P.E.O.s, saw the great need for a second evening chapter in Omaha. Charter members were M. Jane Hughes, president; Frances S. Reimund, vice president; Margaret Mines; Grace McLain, corresponding secretary; F. Ethel McAfee, recording secretary; Lucille Airy, F. Ruth Forbes, Florence Frohnen; Katherine Cadwell, guard; Dorothy Ware; Aileen McGee; Dorothy Kimmel; Edith Wagner, chaplain; Elta Moore, treasurer; Mary E. Cadwell; Nelle V. Rogers; Faye Brittain; and Olive A. Campbell. The chapter proudly acknowledges the role played by Bertha Clark Hughes in the early life of the chapter. A sister-in-law of Jane Hughes, she graciously opened her home for chapter meetings. Her wishes, love and guidance were of great benefit to this chapter in its infancy.

In 1933, the chapter held its first president's tea at the Blackstone Hotel on the day President Roosevelt closed the banks throughout the country. Had plans not already been complete, the chapter might not have had the courage, nor the funds, to proceed with its party.

Much interest was shown by the chapter members in establishing a Nebraska P.E.O. Home. Jane Hughes served three years on the Promotion Committee for the Home. Interest was sustained through the years by keeping in touch with members who resided at the Home. The chapter has also held three meetings at the Home in Beatrice, allowing the members to tour the facility and to get to know the residents better. For many years the chapter has sent boxes of gifts to the Home in addition to its financial support.

During World War II, members volunteered many hours of service making surgical dressings, serving food at the Service Men's Center at Union Station, staffing War Bond booths, and serving on rationing boards.

In 1980, the chapter amended its bylaws to adjust to the problems of winter travel in Nebraska. The chapter met earlier in the fall, later in the spring and only met once a month during December, January and February. In 2013, the chapter again decided to meet the changing needs of our group by meeting only on the first Thursday of the month year round, except for the January and February meetings when the meetings would be on Saturday mornings. The chapter also plans to have three social events during the year.

Chapter DY celebrated its 50th anniversary in 1981 by making new robes for initiation. These robes served the chapter well until finally replaced in 1992 with professionally made robes.

Chapter DY has sponsored five women for loans from the P.E.O. Educational Loan Fund and one woman for a grant from the P.E.O.Program for Continuing Education.

Every year, Chapter DY has supported all of the P.E.O. projects including the Nebraska P.E.O. Home. The chapter is proud to have achieved Cottey Golden Anniversary Fund Chapter status. Fundraising has been accomplished in many ways—silent auctions, recipe books, garage sale, beans for soup, sale of plants, sale of coupon booklets for a local business, and passing around a silver pig to collect loose change as a contribution to be used for gas for the Nebraska P.E.O. Home's van.

Chapter DY's membership has remained fairly constant—though the average attendance has fallen in the past few years to eight to ten members. New members have joined the chapter every year, either by initiation or transfer. Chapter DY has been blessed with women who are a variety of ages and have had many different life experiences. The chapter is proud of their member-given programs. Over the years, they have reflected the interesting diversity in the members' lives and interests. The programs given by visitors have greatly expanded our horizons.

Over the years, Chapter DY sisters truly do all they can "to Devotedly Yield in expressing a loving concern for each sister."

CHAPTER DY'S ACTIVE MEMBERSHIP IS 35; TOTAL ENROLLMENT IS 176

Chapter DZ Omaha
Organized May 14, 1931
by Josephine Waddell
Merged with Chapter CR 2009

Since its organization on May 14, 1931, Chapter DZ, Omaha, has conscientiously put into action the charge of the organizer to "Do Zealously." Starting the chapter off in P.E.O. participation were charter members Esther Bloom, Ida Dickey, Maurine Kilgore, Regina Rooker, Elizabeth Lucke, Sarah Valder, Blanche Burke, Emma Powers, Emma Gibbs, Rose Bloom, Marion Dickey, Grace Frahm, Grace Heath and Dorothy Kain.

Traditions unique to Chapter DZ knit the chapter together and add verve to programming. A cherished gift in 1933, a powder box topped by a lazing flapper dubbed "Minnie," has been passed along to an unsuspecting member each Christmas. A packet of verses accompanies "Minnie" detailing her year with that P.E.O. sister. Roberta Olson has further enlivened the holiday celebrations with her witty poem characterizing each sister. Seven dolls dressed in 1860s style and depicting the Sisterhood's Founders are a treasured endowment made in 1961 by Ruth Coffin. A stile and picket fence provide a background for a set-piece showcased at Chapter DZ's Founders' Day observances. An article in an issue of the 1966 P.E.O. Record brought numerous requests to borrow the dolls. A recently-added tradition recognized a member whose zeal exemplifies true sisterhood. The DZ pin guard of the late Daisy Martin has been mounted, framed and designated the "Spirit Award." Recipients have been Dorothy Christensen, Aretha Peterson, Mary H. Anderson, Charlene Brodd and Kay Thorson.

Chapter members who expanded the scope of service to P.E.O. as officers in the Omaha P.E.O. Reciprocity Association were Jane Muffly, Aretha Peterson and Darlene Willmarth, presidents; Relta Starrett, treasurer; Grace Shellberg, Ruth Belmont and Mary H. Anderson, secretaries. At the 1975 Omaha Founders' Day luncheon, a program based on music inherent to the era of P.E.O.'s founding was written by Mary H. Anderson. A costumed chorus of members from other chapters harmonized beautifully. Narrator, DZ's Charlene Brodd, decked out in plumed hat and lacy shawl, completed the scene.

During the 1973, 1981 and 1987 Nebraska State Conventions in Omaha, Chapter DZ members volunteered as hostesses, choir members, guards, skit participants and transporters.

Five DZ sisters served as delegates to Conventions of International Chapter: Blanche Burke, Daisy Martin, Ruth Coffin, Dorothy Sheffield and Dorothy Christensen. For the 1991 International "Spirit of the Prairie" Convention, Chapter DZ members made decorations, shared display quilts, found lost articles, hosted meals, registered delegates and provided transportation.

In 1937, Chapter DZ sponsored a woman for the P.E.O. Educational Loan Fund. A donation of $100 was made in 1967 to the Centennial Building Fund. The P.E.O. International Peace Scholarship Fund received a gift in 1963 in honor of Irene Van Brunt and in 1964 in honor of Dorothy Yeager. A contribution was made in 1965 to the Uretta M. Hinkhouse Memorial and in 1989 a pledge to the Bobbie Koefoot Fund was fulfilled. Total enrollment prior to merge 135

Chapter EA Randolph
Organized May 25, 1931
by Josephine Waddell

Chapter EA was organized May 25, 1931, by Josephine Waddell. Present members are forever grateful to Fauneil Carhart who instigated the organization at the home of Mary Randall. Chapter AZ of Wayne assisted. Charter members included Fauneil Carhart, Mary Randall, Elizabeth Stewart, Alma Hahn, Cleo Hoile, Elsa Dawson, Velna Hancock, Olivia Buol, Eva Hill, Elly Sherwood, Efia Nelson, Helen Cook, Marie Wilcox and Edith Graham.

Chapter EA takes advantage of our members' talents and resources to give a program at the meetings. We usually have a wide variety of topics we cover as our members have varied talents and knowledge on many subjects. They are entertaining and educational. Some examples this year in which our program title was *"Make Time for You,"* we covered entertainment, travel, health, education, creativity, going green and reading. We also had three social meetings, one of which is our silent auction at a fall meeting that serves as our fundraiser for our projects. Our members bring crafts, baked goods or anything in between to auction off to the highest bidder and it has proven to be a good fundraiser as well as a social time.

During 2011, one special project for our town's quasquicentennial celebration was the sponsoring of the queen contest. Chapter EA hosted interviews as well as a tea in which all the candidates were introduced and were required to decorate a table and serve those in attendance. The tea was well attended and proved to be a success. Chapter EA had three candidates and our very own Peggy Leiting was crowned Queen. Chapter EA also supports community projects such as our library and our county's Relay for Life walk as we have members who have had health problems or are now struggling with gaining their health again.

We attend and take turns hosting the area PACK picnic each year. This includes chapters from nearby Pierce, Antelope, Cedar and Knox counties. We also attend and take turns hosting Reciprocity IV meetings each year. Both of these annual events give us a chance to touch base with other women in P.E.O. Chapter EA also participates in the Adopt-a-Cottey student program each year and we enjoy hearing from the girls about their Cottey College experiences. Four members from Chapter EA have attended Cottey: Ann Sellon, Roberta Sellon, Lynell Jensen and Rebecca Lackas.

Chapter EA has three members who have belonged fifty to sixty years including Virginia Sellon, Ruth Ellen Truby and Virginia Weber. We celebrate them with cards and a gift. We just recently initiated two college aged young women who are 3rd and 4th generation P.E.O.s. What a pleasure to see their fresh faces and to know that Chapter EA will make a lasting gift in their lives. Also, we are pleased that Nicole Berner, an active member of our chapter, was elected to the Executive Board of Nebraska State Chapter in 2012 and will serve Nebraska P.E.O. as its president in 2016. We are so very proud of her. Virginia Sellon was a member of the Executive Planning Committee for the 1991 Convention of International Chapter and she has served as the Cottey Area Chairman for many years.

Chapter EA assisted with the organization of Chapter HZ, Hartington, on

November 19, 1983.

Although our roots run deep, we are still reaching out to the next generation. The ages of our members is balanced out to include 90-year-olds to 19-year-olds and each decade in between.

CHAPTER EA'S ACTIVE MEMBERSHIP IS 34; TOTAL ENROLLMENT IS 158

★

CHAPTER EB NORTH PLATTE
ORGANIZED MAY 27, 1931
BY JOSEPHINE WADDELL

Chapter EB, North Platte's second P.E.O. chapter, received its charter at the 1931 Convention of Nebraska State Chapter in Gothenburg. The thirteen charter members included: Lue Spencer (CS, Lincoln), president; Rebecca White (Z, Colorado), chaplain; Nell Highleyman, (S, Wyoming), corresponding secretary; Helen Butzirus (AK); Janet McDonald (AK); Maude Hendy (AK); Grace Mooney, treasurer; Nell Edwards, vice president; Ruth Patterson, recording secretary; Onetah Tramp, Sybil Yost, Grace Krause, guard; and Grace Tramp. Dimits of Alice O'Connor, Dorothy Woods, Helen Hinman, Edna Nisley and Una Donnels were accepted the first year. Mary Neville was a new initiate. Maude Hendy, assumed the presidency of Chapter EB when Lue Spencer moved. Lue Spencer served as president of Nebraska State Chapter in 1916-17.

Chapter EB sponsored Chapter GO when they organized in 1966. Also, Chapter EB helped to organize Chapter HO in 1979. It has been rewarding to grant permission to several nonresident members as they have helped organize new P.E.O. chapters elsewhere.

Chapter EB has extended its support to the P.E.O. projects and they are pleased to have sponsored several women for loans from the P.E.O. Educational Loan Fund. We have also sponsored women for grants from the P.E.O. Program for Continuing Education. Chapter EB is especially proud to have sponsored two Scholar Award recipients and also participated with the other North Platte chapters in sponsoring IPS designated scholars. Participation in awarding these grants and loans has been a rewarding experience for the recipients as well as the chapter members.

A few years ago, a highlight for the chapter was a bus trip to the Nebraska P.E.O. Home in Beatrice. Chapter EB has had one of our members, Carol Ann Huckfeldt, serve on the P.E.O. Home Board of Directors.

Chapter EB has supported Cottey College in many different projects including the remodel of the Nebraska suite, Bucks for Beds, and most recently "Green Team" Cottey Challenge horse race during the Defining Moment Campaign. We have adopted Cottey students and sent students on the Cottey Bus Trip. The chapter has been rewarded hearing from members, daughters and granddaughters who have been students at Cottey College. Our chapter has been honored to have a state Cottey Chairman and several Cottey Area Chairmen.

In order to financially support the projects, as well as to help finance Reciprocity meetings and state conventions, Chapter EB has had some exciting fundraisers. These have included garage sales, bake sales, book sales, raffles, "kitties," fines, silent and regular auctions, "Star" bear sales, and our annual Christmas pecan sale.

Chapter EB sisters have been involved and active as individuals also. Particularly rewarding were participation in the World War II North Platte Canteen and the Red Cross activities. Helping to host the 1943 state convention during those "rationing years" provided real challenges. More recently members have also been active in the Community Playhouse, Hospital Guild, Goodfellow Shoe Fund, and the Prairie Art Center.

One of EB's charter members, Maude Hendy, served as president of Nebraska State Chapter in 1924-25. Mary Neville served as Nebraska's First Lady when her husband Keith was governor.

Chapter EB has nationally known artists, business women, authors, musicians, state and nationally-recognized leaders, as well as a Nebraska Mother of the Year (Helen Adams) to cite only a few of the sisters' accomplishments.

Some fun chapter activities have included family picnics, BIL parties, barbecues, anniversary teas, mother-daughter Christmas and Valentine parties, monthly birthday lunches, bunco and our famous Kentucky Derby parties.

Highlights include lighting 100 candles at the 100th birthday Founders' Day meeting, doing the model meeting and exemplification at state convention, honoring those special sisters who have been in P.E.O. for fifty, sixty and seventy years, receiving a white gavel and initiatory cloth from Maude Hendy, buying initiation robes for the chapter, and being invited into the sisters' homes for the many special programs presented by the members.

Chapter EB meets year round to better accommodate all of our members, especially our snow bird sisters. Informal social meetings help the chapter to become better acquainted.

Remembering those deceased sisters by decorating graves on Memorial Day is an ongoing tradition, as is sharing Founders' Day luncheons with all the North Platte chapters.

P.E.O. was, and still is, an inspiration for all those who are members. May all P.E.O.s provide leadership and understanding well into this 21st century.

CHAPTER EB'S ACTIVE MEMBERSHIP IS 79; TOTAL ENROLLMENT IS 355

★

CHAPTER EC OMAHA
ORGANIZED JUNE 2, 1931
BY JOSEPHINE WADDELL

Chapter EC, Omaha, was organized June 2, 1931, by Josephine Waddell. Sylvia Clow of Chapter M and president of the Omaha P.E.O. Association, was instrumental in bringing sixteen not locally affiliated P.E.O.s together. Muriel Smith succeeded Mrs. Clow as president of the Omaha P.E.O. Association and consummated plans for the new chapter. Eight were from Nebraska, six from Iowa and two from South Dakota. Sylvia was then persuaded by this group to head the charter list as EC's first president. With seventeen active members, a chapter of unusual strength was formed.

Organization took place at Mrs. Smith's home. Guests extending greetings were Past President of Supreme Chapter Bertha Clark Hughes; Past State Presidents Lulah Andrews and Viola Cameron. The charter members of Chapter EC were Sylvia Clow, president; Marie Williams Bossert, vice president; Alma

Cutler Brown, Nellie Burress, Fern McConney, Alice Bennett; Rita Drews, guard; Blanche D. Bradley, Bessie Coye; Pauline Reed, treasurer; Marguerite Shainholtz, recording secretary; Berenice N. Theal; Pearl Hancock Woods, chaplain; Grace Bailey Haskell, Julia Coye Delaney; Edna O. Hughes, corresponding secretary and Blanche Epperson.

Since that day, Chapter EC has been a vital and growing chapter, always enjoying a wide variety of programs and opportunities that our community allows. Over the years, Chapter EC has sponsored many girls for the P.E.O. Educational Loan Fund, and nominated many others for the P.E.O. Program for Continuing Education and the P.E.O. STAR Scholarship.

In Fern McConney's 1937 annual president's letter, she said, "we gave $1 per capita to the Educational Fund and $10 to Cottey. We held one of our meetings at the Child Saving Institute, sewing and mending for the children and leaving $2 for milk. We also gave $5 to the Community Chest and $3 to the Red Cross Flood Fund." And during the war there were many hours serving as Grey Ladies and at the USO.

Since the last printing our fundraising has increased dramatically. We have doubled the amount that we are able to annually donate to our projects. This is due to the sale of our magnetic P.E.O. pin holders and our Podiums-In-A-Bag and other creative efforts our sisters have devised. Through their efforts we have raised even more monies that we have joyously shared with local, state and International projects.

But the heart of our chapter has always been the joy we have with each other. We gather over a delicious meal, sharing our lives, and enjoy the many wonderful programs and opportunities that our Sisterhood brings us. We've traveled the city to wonderful art galleries, enjoyed BIL socials in our homes or at the Omaha Community Playhouse. We have invited speakers from local non-profits that focus on education, women and children. Our sisters who travel or have special interests willingly share the "right exercise of any talents they possess." And when one of our sisters or her BIL is sick or passes away, we truly know the value of a sisterhood as we jump into action to help her in time of need.

Historically, there have been three members of Chapter EC who have served as president of the Omaha P.E.O. Association: Sylvia Clow, 1930; Flora Smiley, 1949; and Lillian Eglehoff, 1970. Other Chapter EC members have served in other Association offices.

Currently Chapter EC has four active 50-year members: Elizabeth Brchm, Patricia Clow, Mary Lueder, and Loy Nebergall.

As most chapters of 80-plus years have learned, you need to infuse new life into your chapter or die on the vine. We are delighted to have chosen the former rather than the latter path. In 2012, we initiated five new young members and are always actively seeking more women who believe in providing educational opportunities for woman and at the same time have the qualities that will "share a loving concern for each sister."

At the time of this printing our chapter has celebrated its 83rd anniversary. We look forward to the next eighty years!

CHAPTER EC'S ACTIVE MEMBERSHIP IS 36; TOTAL ENROLLMENT IS 189

Chapter ED Omaha
Organized April 7, 1934
by Isabelle Nelson

Chapter ED, Omaha, was organized April 7, 1934, by Isabelle Nelson. The fifteen charter members included Charlotte Wilkerson, the chapter's first president, as well as Belle Metzger, Annie Jones, Docia Mockler, Lois Irwin, Franc Hunter, Lillian Tancock, Alma Steffen, Mildred Mockler, Louise Stimson, Marguerite Metzger-Hall, Hortense Eads, Mabel Rose, Mayme Bulla and Merle Cheek.

Throughout the years, Chapter ED has been honored to participate in P.E.O. activities at all levels. In 1937, only three years after organization, Chapter ED presented the model meeting at the state convention. Chapter ED participated in establishing the Nebraska P.E.O. Home in Beatrice. The chapter also was a proud host at the 1991 Convention of International Chapter in Omaha. Chapter ED has actively contributed to all P.E.O. projects each year.

The volunteer spirit of Chapter ED is alive and reaches beyond its own chapter and projects. Members have shared their abundant talents with local philanthropies, civic endeavors and volunteer activities. Members have served in leadership roles for the Junior League of Omaha, the Assistance League of Omaha, Omaha Symphony Guild, Omaha Community Playhouse, Joslyn Art Museum, Lauritzen Gardens, the Omaha Public Library (the Board and the Foundation), and more. Local hospitals benefit from volunteer support of our members. Top honors from some of these organizations have been given to Chapter ED sisters.

Chapter ED frequently enjoys a themed auction, as well as other fundraisers, with proceeds benefiting P.E.O projects, with special efforts for Cottey. An annual Christmas event is a festive way to enjoy time with our sisters and their BILs. Our meetings focus on learning about the cultural, educational and social services of our community, discovering new interests and visiting local points of interest. One popular visit was to the Metro Community College Culinary Arts for an extensive tour and lunch.

Chapter ED celebrated its 80th anniversary in April 2014. Over the years, the chapter was privileged to have many three-generation members. Now there is a member who is a fourth-generation P.E.O. on her mother's and her father's side. The thread of loyalty, devotion and cooperation has run even and deep among the sisters since 1934. Even though the times and events change with regularity, the spirit of sisterhood has remained constant and true in Chapter ED.

CHAPTER ED'S ACTIVE MEMBERSHIP IS 28; TOTAL ENROLLMENT IS 142

★

CHAPTER EE LINCOLN
ORGANIZED APRIL 8, 1935
BY ADA MEAD

Upon petition from a number of unaffiliated P.E.O.s in Lincoln, a dispensation for a new chapter was granted by Nebraska State Chapter. Chapter EE was organized on April 8, 1935, by Ada Mead. Chapter DX, Lincoln, acted as sponsoring chapter. Charter members of Chapter EE who served as officers were: Grace Banta, president; Irene Roberts, vice president; Georgia Owen, recording secretary; Bess Mitchell, corresponding secretary; Stella Gillespie, treasurer; Vera Hulac, chaplain; and Anna Elliott, guard. Other charter members were Margaret Adams, Grace Follmer, Lette Linderman, Ruth Lucke, Bernice Theal, Kathryn Watkins, Mabel Vaughn, and Ruth Haberly Harper.

Eva Schmadeke, 1959, Phyllis Acklie and Kay Hesse, 1964, are 50-year members and one member, Evelyn Donaldson, 1946, is a 60-year member. Chapter EE has lost seventy-eight members to Chapter Eternal.

Through the years, many members of Chapter EE have served as officers of Lincoln Reciprocity Roundtable. Five Chapter EE past presidents have served as Roundtable president: Ida Frey, 1947; Dorothea Holstein, 1966; Marie Frey, 1981; Jane Polson, 1999; and Judith Duff, 2002. Chapter EE was proud to include in its membership Adele Reed, Chapter Eternal, past president of the State Chapter for the District of Columbia. Members of Chapter EE have served on state committees and have been chairmen of convention committees when Lincoln hosted the state convention. Kathy Olson and Judy Workman both served on the P.E.O. Home Board of Directors for nine years. Kathy was president of the board from 2007 to 2009.

Early chapter philanthropies mainly were civic projects outside of P.E.O. concerns. In the l940s, volunteer work loyally supported the war effort. Today, the chapter's efforts focus on the P.E.O. projects, supported annually through budgeted donations and other gifts. Outside of the projects today's sisters give "of their time and talent" to efforts for the homeless, abused women, and hungry school children.

Chapter EE has been a continuous supporter of the Nebraska P.E.O Home since its dedication in 1938. A number of Chapter EE sisters have served on the Home Board of Directors. A contribution to the P.E.O. International Peace Scholarship was first made in 1952, and the first sizable contribution to the P.E.O. Program for Continuing Education was made in 1978. Chapter EE has sponsored a number of young women to further their education with help from grants and loans through our projects and has submitted candidates for the P.E.O. Scholar Award and P.E.O. STAR Scholarship projects. The chapter displays ongoing interest in and support of Cottey College and has contributed over the years to special fundraisers for Cottey and its campus facilities. Chapter EE remembers its sisters who have departed to Chapter Eternal with a gift to a project that this sister has designated in her P.E.O. Wish form. Several large contributions have been made to the projects by families in their memory or from the estates of Chapter EE sisters.

Chapter EE celebrates its birthday each year with a special event. The chapter's 50th birthday in 1985 included lots of memories and a BIL dinner. The chapter's 75th birthday was celebrated at the Honor's Luncheon at the 2011 Convention of Nebraska State Chapter in Lincoln that allowed many EE members to attend. Members took advantage of the rare opportunity to attend Convention of International Chapter in Omaha in September 1991. Some served on committees to help in the preparation and creation of this special event and it was an inspiration to be a part of an International Convention.

Chapter EE meets throughout the year with a total of 12 business meetings and three social meetings. Programs can be educational, thought provoking or entertaining. Our social meetings have been soup suppers, trips to the Nebraska P.E.O. Home preceded by lunch, our birthday celebrations, and BIL picnics. An effort has been made recently to have informal get-togethers focusing on such interests as books, crafts, movies, golf and exercise as a means of becoming better acquainted with our sisters. For a number of years the newsletter committee has written and distributed a quarterly newsletter as a means of keeping members informed. It is sent out to all members and nonresident members electronically or U.S. mail and is appreciated by those who for whatever reason are not able to attend meetings regularly.

Chapter EE is a multi-generational blend of sisters. Our strength comes from our new, young and enthusiastic sisters along with the knowledge and experiences of our seasoned P.E.O.s. A wonderful spirit of love and cooperation continues to prevail in Chapter EE.

CHAPTER EE'S ACTIVE MEMBERSHIP IS 71; TOTAL ENROLLMENT IS 258

Dreamer. Realist. Critic.
When the dreamer's working, tell the critic to get lost!
-Walt Disney

Chapter EF Omaha
Organized April 24, 1935
by Ada Mead

In 1935, Florence Wilson, president of the Omaha P.E.O. Association, was asked to dimit to the new Chapter EF in order to assume its leadership. She lovingly agreed and stayed with Chapter EF for eighteen years before returning to Chapter BN.

Chapter EF was organized with twelve dimitting members and three initiates. Charter members and first officers were: Florence Wilson, president; Gail Heaton, vice president; Georgia Wolcott, recording secretary; Bessie Thornton, corresponding secretary; Alice Peterson, treasurer; Mildred Eyer, chaplain; Burdette Norton, guard; Henrietta Cramer, Cordia Fisher, Alice Eyer, Josephine Eyer, Marguerite Hetherington, Eva Wilson, Grace Willsie and Mabel Kopperud.

Chapter EF's song began on April 24, 1935. Thus at this 2015 printing, the chapter has existed for eighty years, putting its existence well into the fourth quarter of a century. Its birthday is recognized by its members each April and the chapter rejoices and reflects on the many recognitions and successes which have been achieved by sisters personally as well as by the chapter as a whole.

EF—'Ever Friendly'—is a most congenial group. Meetings are held in homes, which is special because it is truly a way to become even more familiar with each other as well as observing just what is important to each. Occasionally, another venue is required when space is a necessity. Luncheon is provided each meeting and this practice has continued for eighty years.

Luckily, the membership is diverse in ages and also in interests. Each sister either gives a program herself or provides for the subject to be presented by another. Programs reflect a variety of subjects, therefore, each program becomes both a learning and entertaining situation for the members.

P.E.O. projects are stimulating and enlightening to the sisters each time that information relating to a project is presented. It is at this time that the chapter makes its decision as to the amount of chapter monies to be donated for the year. Chapter EF is a generous group and proud to be associated with an organization that financially supports such outstanding projects of its own.

Since the year 2000, EF holds one fundraiser per year. The Holiday Auction is held the first Tuesday in December. In November invitations are created and posted to all EF members. A friend may be invited to attend if a member wishes to do so. Items to sell can include a holiday gift, a 'handmade' specialty, a favorite holiday treat, a very special 'white elephant' or another Christmas surprise. Members are asked to be creative! Two members act as the auctioneers. They show up in their Christmas hats and aprons and their 'pitch' adds great fun to the event. Everything gets sold! If a sister is unable to physically participate in any way, then she is invited to send a contribution to the treasurer because everyone's participation is necessary for a financially successful fundraiser.

Brothers in love known as 'BILs' are special to all of the members even though there isn't always one to accompany each sister. Nevertheless, the tradition is celebrated once a year with a special social meeting known as "The BIL Party." Usually this event is scheduled in early October. The committee responsible makes all of the plans and the chapter has never been disappointed. Recently one of the sisters and her husband hosted a casually elegant dinner for the chapter and their BILS at their beautiful Party Barn. Yes, "The Barn" is beautiful and so is the venue overlooking the scenic rolling hills surrounding Lake Cunningham north of Omaha. Of course, it was a wonderful event, and many new and special P.E.O. memories were created.

Another time a BBQ dinner was planned at the Fair Hills Farm near Nashville, Nebraska. Guests could tour the farm's stables and gaze at the lovely countryside. The accomplished twelve-year-old granddaughter of one of the sisters gave a riding demonstration in the outdoor riding arena before dinner. This was an entertaining and educational experience for everyone. The BIL party tradition carries on.

The distribution of chapter talent is varied and wonderful. Chapter EF claims church and civic leaders, artists, designers, poets, educators, business women, two professional registered parliamentarians, students and outstanding university alumnae. Many organizations have enjoyed the leadership of EF members, and through the years chapter members have been the recipients of numerous community recognitions.

Beginning with EF Charter Member Eva Wilson, the chapter claims one four generation family—all EF members. Also through the years the chapter has been blessed with several mother-daughter combinations.

Chapter EF celebrated "Fifty Golden Years" in 1985 and has now reached its "80th Year" in 2015. It has been celebrating ever since—celebrating its heritage, its present and its future—the golden thread of P.E.O. binds us together and becomes stronger with each passing year. EF has a fine spirit and continues to look to the future with great anticipation.

Also, EF has long enjoyed the contributions of its 50-year members. Currently, there are six 50-year members and one 60-year member participating on a regular basis. They are the brightest "stars" in the galaxy.

P.E.O.'s Chapter EF is truly special! It offers so much and asks so little—the reinforcement of the spirit through beautiful rituals, the endless love and support through association with sisters representing a variety of ages, the opportunity to grow intellectually through the sharing of knowledge and experiences are but a few of its offerings. In return, Chapter EF P.E.O. only asks for one's loyalty in attendance and one's commitment to leadership when called upon. "One becomes a P.E.O. not by initiation but by participation!"

It has been said many times: Chapter EF is people—"those who can give without remembering and take without forgetting."

Chapter EF's active membership is 72; total enrollment is 207

★

Chapter EG Kearney
Organized April 25, 1935
by Ada Mead

Chapter EG, Kearney, was organized by twenty-four dimitting members, twenty-two of whom were from Chapter AS, Kearney. State officers Ada H. Mead, organizer, and Anna Loutzenheiser, first vice president, officiated at the organization of Chapter EG. Past President of Supreme Chapter Bertha Clark Hughes presented the charter to Ruth Dryden Kendall, EG president, at convention in Ord. Charter members were: Ruth Kendall, president; Lucille Denzler, Amelia Jester, Faye Clem, Florence Sidwell, Helen Dryden, Emma Jane Gilmore, Mary Elliott, Lucille Cary, Katherine Major, Hallie Dryden, Helen Jensen, Anna Henline, Metta Ayers, Mildred Randolph, Margaret Hostetler, Clara Spencer, Urilla Stimfig, Margaret McGrew, Minta Todd, Nelle Grantham, Theresa Champagoe, Mildred Housel (AN, Lexington), and Mattie Penny (CW, Sargent). Nelle Grantham was state president in 1925-26. Chapter EG lost its last charter member, Hallie Dryden, age 100 in 2004 to Chapter Eternal. She was a P.E.O. for 74 years.

Chapter EG Kearney bell choir

Chapter EG meets on the second Thursday of each month for twelve months with a social time at 7:00PM Most of our meetings are held in members' homes. We have also held meetings at the UNK Alumni House, the Kearney Public Library, the Kearney Women's Club Home, Northridge Retirement Center, the First Presbyterian Church and the First United Methodist Church. Our three social meetings are held with the other five Kearney chapters: AS, FN, GG, HB and IX. We also have a social BIL party.

The past twenty years—1995 to 2015—have brought many changes to Chapter EG while the spirit of P.E.O. remains our chapter goal. Chapter EG has sponsored women for the P.E.O. Educational Loan Fund, the P.E.O. Program for Continuing Education and P.E.O. Scholar Award. We participated in Goff's Goal, Adopt a Cottey student, Cottey Bucks for Beds, the Nebraska P.E.O. Home and an honorarium to our state president at convention in 2013. Monetary gifts are given to all the P.E.O. philanthropies each year. Auctions have been held to supplement the local dues to raise money for the philanthropies. We also have had two other fundraisers that help with the philanthropies. We have a Brag Basket that you can brag about your family for a dollar a boast. It provides additional funds for the Remembrance Committee to purchase flowers and cards for our sisters. We also have a decorated Gift Box with items inside. You can buy a chance to win the box and then fill it and return it to the next meeting for someone else to win. This fundraiser was used for the state president's philanthropy.

In 2005 Chapter EG began publishing a newsletter twice a year entitled "E"nterprizing "G"roup Gazette. Technology has permitted many sisters to receive the newsletter by email. Dorann Bartels is the editor and publisher. Our Notification

Committee also uses email to inform members of meeting times and places and other pertinent chapter communication.

A nucleus of EG members formed FN, Kearney, in 1951. In April 2009, Chapter EG sponsored the sixth chapter in Kearney. Seven Chapter EG sisters dimitted to Chapter IX and organized the new chapter.

State officers at Presidents' Tea hosted by Chapter EG honoring newly-elected State President Terri Ridgway

L to R:
Patti Cowher, Karen Blair, Merikay Berg, Nicole Berner, and Terri

Chapter EG celebrated its 75th anniversary at the 2011 Nebraska Honors Luncheon in Lincoln. Six 50-year members and one 60-year member were present.

Terri Ridgway, Chapter EG, was installed as president of Nebraska State Chapter at the 2012 convention in Fremont. Chapter EG is very proud of Terri and honored her with a tea on September 9, 2012. She presided at the 2013 convention in Columbus using the theme, *"When You Wish Upon a Star."*

Music has always been a trademark of Chapter EG. For many years Mary York directed the Vocal Chords. Natalie Radcliffe directs the bell choir consisting of several members of Chapter EG. We are fortunate to have many talented musicians in our chapter.

Three Chapter EG sisters have served as Reciprocity Group XIV president in the past twenty years. They are Marsha Stewart, Terri Ridgway and Jane Jossi. In 2000, Chapter EG sister Fran Lane wrote an original program for Founders' Day entitled "Our Founders After 1869 Into the New Millennium."

The virtue upon which P.E.O. is founded instills a spirit of helpfulness and devotion to our Chapter EG members. The giving, caring spirit of our chapter is especially evident in those who serve on the Remembrance and Calling Committees. The loving care and concern shown to our members through recognition of special occasions, monthly visits to shut-in members, and meals and cards of concern during difficult times truly exemplify the spirit of the Sisterhood.

Our officers serve faithfully and our chapter serves the community in many areas. We continue to seek new members and support women applying for the P.E.O. philanthropies.

Chapter EG will celebrate its 80th anniversay in 2015.

CHAPTER EG'S ACTIVE MEMBERSHIP IS 65; TOTAL ENROLLMENT IS 367

Chapter EG President's Tea honoring new state president Terri Ridgway

★

CHAPTER EH GRAND ISLAND
ORGANIZED FEBRUARY 15, 1936
BY HATTIE ENGLEMAN

Chapter EH, Grand Island, was established when four members from Chapter CK petitioned to start a new chapter. Marie Yokum, Pauline Hanson, Margaret Firth and Alice Payne were the charter members who met at the home of Mrs. E.W. Augustine to initiate seven new members. Additionally, eleven others dimitted into the chapter that winter evening of February 15, 1936. Charter members were Marie Yocum, president; Pauline Hanson, vice president; Dorothy Curtis, recording secretary; Alice E. Paine, corresponding secretary; Selma Moulton, treasurer; Margaret Dean MacFarlane, chaplain; Marion Parson, guard; Marguerite Worden, Lucille Evans, Margaret Firth, Florence Reese, Marie Overturf, Mabel Hutchins, Mercedes Augustine, Flora Sorensen, Margaret Roenfeldt, Dorcas Hoge, and Florence Michelmarm. President of Nebraska State Chapter Anna Loutzenheiser christened the group's nickname as "Eternal Happiness" and they truly were sisters.

In the early years our first meeting each autumn always began with a family picnic, which later evolved into a BIL dinner. As the membership grew to over fifty, it became necessary to limit the meal to members only. Quoting from the *Saga of Nebraska P.E.O.*, "Anniversaries were always observed—the tenth was held at Riverside Country Club, while the twenty-fifth anniversary was celebrated at the Women's Club with a buffet supper. Nebraska State Chapter Organizer Jean Johnson, former member of Chapter EH, was a guest at our thirtieth anniversary which was celebrated with a musical program at the Howard School foyer." Our fiftieth anniversary celebration was delayed a few weeks, until April 28, 1986, with a special dinner, meeting and program at the Holiday Inn. There were forty-seven chapter members, four former chapter members, and state officer Joyce Goff present. We were proud that four of our charter members were still actively participating in meetings at that time.

We have always raised funds to support our projects by participating in the Bed and Breakfast program for many years as well as our highly successful Awesome Auctions and Soup and Pie suppers. We sold hand-made stationery, home-made raspberry jam, and 5-bean soup packets; our lovely hand sewn aprons are well known. Our chapter was proud to have been able to give major support to the establishment of Grand Island's sixth chapter—Chapter II in 1990. We have always been a night meeting chapter with many teachers and working members from our earliest years. We have visited the Neraska P.E.O. Home in Beatrice several times and always send holiday surprises to them.

We have experimented with our meeting times, trying some Saturday mornings; we have varied our starting times and reversed our coffee and business meeting times. Our membership numbers reached into the nineties, but have declined with the addition of more local chapters. Some of our members have become snowbirds. As the times have changed, we have revised our yearly schedule from two meetings monthly during the school year only to meeting once a month all year long and including three social events as well. We look forward to our century celebration in 2036.

CHAPTER EH'S ACTIVE MEMBERSHIP IS 46; TOTAL ENROLLMENT IS 272

★

CHAPTER EI BAYARD
ORGANIZED APRIL 18, 1936
BY HATTIE ENGLEMAN

Chapter EI of Bayard was organized by Nebraska State Chapter Organizer Hattie Engleman of Crawford, who was assisted by officers of Chapter AH, Alliance, on April 18, 1936.

The thirteen charter members were Fern Prince, president; Fannie Moore, vice president; Vada Comstock, recording secretary; Margaret Davenport, corresponding secretary; Zella Rae Rystrom, treasurer; Grace Pugsley, chaplain; and Maude Moberg, guard; Helen Ericson, Werdna Ginn, Eileen Moore, Fannie Moore, Willamette Moore, Maude Moberg, Fern Prince, Grace Pugsley, Thelma Raymond, Zella Rae Rystrom, and Edna Stelk.

The new chapter immediately became very active, supporting the P.E.O. projects and helping host the state convention after only three years of existence. Over the years, they hosted the Panhandle Reciprocity Group and also provided it with its president four times: Zella Rystrom, Margaret McKibbin, Thelma Raymond and Connie Langhofer.

The attack on Pearl Harbor on December 7, 1941, brought the EI sisters much closer in sisterly love and support in the face of war. One of the sisters, Werdna Ginn, lost her only son in this attack. Her grief became the grief of the chapter and the sisters worked tirelessly in so many ways to support the war effort. They also continued devoting much to the war effort during and after the Korean War by contributing funds and sending CARE packages.

Chapter EI was honored for their 75th anniversary at State Convention in Lincoln, June 4, 2011. Pictured l to r: Phyllis Reifschneider, Tula Cundall, Barb Kniss, Connie Langhofer, Laura Krantz.

On September 11, 2001, state officer Joan Fink came for a scheduled visit and it is a day that will never be forgotten. Nothing could have prepared everyone for the horrible events that took place in our country that day and, when she arrived, everyone was uncertain whether to continue with the plans. After much discussion, it was decided to proceed and members would be able to comfort and take comfort from each other in sisterly love.

The chapter has sponsored four girls who attended Cottey College. One was a member of EI and later became a counselor at Cottey.

Through the P.E.O. Educational Loan Fund, Chapter EI has, over the last twenty years, sponsored thirteen recipients of loans from the fund. EI also sponsored one recipient for a grant from the P.E.O. Program for Continuing Education.

Chapter EI celebrates their anniversary each year at a meeting in April, complete with birthday cake. In April 1986, a special celebration was held to honor the chapter's 50th anniversary. A reception was held with EI members, BILs and members of neighboring chapters in attendance.

In April 2011, Chapter EI celebrated their 75th anniversary at a meeting at which there was lots of reminiscing; old president's letters were read and birthday cake was served. In June several members traveled to join their delegate for the Honors Luncheon at state convention.

The chapter enjoys an annual Christmas dinner each December at which the menu has stayed the same for many years. Members reveal their secret sisters with a Christmas gift and then draw names for the coming year. Before the dinner, members visit the local nursing home to sing Christmas carols and leave a fruit basket. They also stop at homes of any shut-ins, singing carols and bringing dinner.

A BIL party is held almost every year. This has ranged from a Valentine party, a picnic or concert, to just having dinner out. New BILs are usually initiated at this time using a special BIL initiation ceremony written by BIL Fea Raymond in 1976.

Over the years, the chapter has enjoyed many annual dinners or desserts with Chapter DP, Bridgeport. After the dinner, the host chapter would entertain with a wonderful program or the International report.

Chapter EI's special program on November 18, 2013, by Miss Nebraska 2013, JaCee Pilkington, and Kyle Van Newkirk, tap dancer and musician.
Pictured back row l to r: Elaine Kuxhausen, Laura Krantz, Connie Cordes, Cynthia Trimble, Shawna Reish, Kim Kildow, Diane Coon, Anne Schmall, Barb Kniss, Connie Langhofer. Front row: Pat Lind, Marilyn Wimmer, Miss Nebraska, Kyle, Tula Cundall

Chapter EI has given consideration to its influence in the community in a variety of ways. The chapter has hosted a birthday party one month every year at the nursing home, provided funds to help create a park on Main Street, planted flowers in pots in front of local businesses, had floats for several years in the local Pioneer Days parade, conducted a Clean Up Main Street Day and have adopted the history museum as a primary project.

A variety of fundraising projects have been held over the years with a recent one having been a lot of fun. Pinky, the flamingo, was placed on the lawn of various members; to get it removed, $6 had to be paid to the chapter. After the project was completed, the Nebraska State Chapter was enlisted to use Pinky to raise funds for the P.E.O. STAR Scholarship fund. Pinky was placed on the lawn of a chapter's president, and continued to be moved about until it made it all the way to the state convention in Norfolk one year later. Each chapter made a donation as it moved Pinky to another president's lawn.

Chapter EI has a wonderful diversity of talent, personality and inspiration to create some spectacular programs over the years, most of which have been given by the members themselves. However, a recent program was a visit by Miss Nebraska 2013, JaCee Pilkington, a Bayard High graduate, and Kyle Van Newkirk, a very talented musician and tap dancer who has competed nationwide. This was a wonderful and entertaining program from very talented young people of our area.

The members of Chapter EI strive to maintain the ideals of the P.E.O. Sisterhood and cherish the very special love and friendship among their sisters.

CHAPTER EI'S ACTIVE MEMBERSHIP IS 25; TOTAL ENROLLMENT IS 150

★

CHAPTER EJ CREIGHTON
ORGANIZED DECEMBER 8, 1936
BY MARIE WILLIAMS

Chapter EJ was organized December 8, 1936, by Marie J. Williams. She was assisted by Isabelle Nelson, state president, and sponsored by Chapter DG, Ponca. Twelve Creighton women were initiated as charter members of Chapter EJ. They were Verna Rice, president; Edna Brown, vice president; Doras E. Rupert, recording secretary; Maude Tarbell, corresponding secretary; Maude Kile, treasurer; Agnes Mann, chaplain; Bernice Riisness, guard; Elva VanDeVeer, Helen Condon, Adela Horn, Louise Petersen and Lilles Turner.

The hand-engraved charter was presented by State President Bertha Clark Hughes at convention in Omaha in 1937 to Verna Rice. Verna had borrowed a beautiful hat from her sister for the occasion, only to find out the P.E.O.s do not wear hats to meetings!

Chapter EJ has assisted in the organization of Chapter EM, Bloomfield, and Chapter FE, Plainview.

Chapter EJ has sponsored many women for loans from the P.E.O. Educational Loan Fund. The first one went on to be a missionary and many have gone on to get their degrees in all walks of life. We seem to always have a member that is a local high school teacher or counselor. This has proven to be very helpful to keep us in touch with the young women in our community who will be going to college soon and may need help. We also give a $500 scholarship to a local senior every year.

Chapter EJ celebrated its 50th anniversary on December 7, 1986, at Bruce Park Social Hall. Second Vice President of Nebraska State Chapter Catherine Hutton was guest speaker. Chapter EJ celebrated its 75th anniversary in December of 2011 with a wonderful meeting and party, including ice cream and cake. It was also our annual Christmas party and ornament exchange—a very festive evening.

Chapter EJ has recently changed meeting night to the third Wednesday of the month with the exception of March, July and October when they also meet the first Wednesday of the month in order to have the scheduled fifteen meetings in a year. We usually have a social meeting in those months, which includes a prom show in March at the nursing home, a summer activity, and another activity in October. Chapter EJ has a patio picnic in August and a May dinner in May. We have BIL parties to celebrate the 50th wedding anniversaries of our members. We always have a Christmas party in December which includes an ornament exchange and we assist with bingo and furnish refreshments at the nursing home every Monday in November.

We have fundraisers throughout the year, and also an annual donation of $20 from every member to ensure money to give to our projects. We do a philanthropic fundraiser to help a needy family in the area every year. We have a Brag Box which sisters can donate to and then share their stories of what their families are up to. This keeps us up to date on our sisters' worlds and brings us closer to each other.

CHAPTER EJ'S ACTIVE MEMBERSHIP IS 35; TOTAL ENROLLMENT IS 143

CHAPTER EK OMAHA
ORGANIZED APRIL 22, 1937
BY MARIE WILLIAMS

Chapter EK was organized on April 22, 1937, by Marie Williams and Chapter DU. Charter officers were Ruth Francis Townley (DX, Iowa), president; Mae Patterson (CD, Iowa), vice president; Kathryn Hoehne (DF), recording secretary; Mattie Meredith (HG, Iowa), corresponding secretary; Vina Carter (BJ, Iowa), treasurer; Sarah Hudson (CS), chaplain; and Della Bailey (DI, Iowa), guard. Other members were Clara Pattison (N), Metta Ayers, Georgetta Coon (Y), Veta Pickard (AF, Iowa), Florence Sherman (DG, Iowa), Norma Norton (AP), and Clara Day Whelan (AK). These women came together, along with special guest Past President of Supreme Chapter and Nebraska State Chapter Bertha Clark Hughes, and the Ever Kindly (EK) chapter was founded as the twentieth P.E.O. chapter in Omaha. The theme for that first year was "Know Omaha," and over the last seventy-seven years our members have indeed gotten to know Omaha as well as other places around the globe through the experiences shared with and by sisters.

Chapter EK's meetings were initially arranged at the convenience of the majority. After various combinations of meeting days and times were tried, EK now has the unique distinction of being the only chapter in Nebraska to hold regular business meetings on Saturdays. There has only been one drawback to the Saturday meetings in Nebraska...in the fall, nothing competes with Big Red football!

First and foremost, the sisters of Chapter EK value the camaraderie and diversity of our group. We have women who truly inspire us with their personal and professional lives. Throughout EK's history there have been many second generation members in addition to sisters, cousins, and other relatives. We have enjoyed celebrating several 50-year members through the years. Many members have lived well into their nineties, and we celebrate each of those birthdays with a cake. Currently our sisters range in age from twenty-five to ninety-six. Talented sisters have penned poems for our yearbooks; most recently our poet has been one of our 96-year-olds, Dorothy Ebener! The opportunity to interact with sisters of diverse ages is a source of inspiration for us all.

Attention to philanthropy has always been a focus. Chapter EK BIL Ivan Fletcher donated funds to purchase Bing and Grondahl plates for the Nebraska P.E.O. Home in Beatrice. Also, in memory of his wife Kay, a sizeable donation was made to purchase a half-bath for each room at the Home. In the early years chapter funds were sparse, so most of the donations were of time rather than monetary. Donations totaling $2.50 were sent to two projects in 1941. Fortunately,

Chapter EK made a commitment to give to all P.E.O. projects, supported by various fundraisers. Some involved chapter activities that helped us get to know each other better, such as white elephant auctions. And more recently we've enjoyed success selling "boutique items" such as hand-made scarves and P.E.O. "blinged" clutches, again thanks to the talents of our sisters.

Over the years, Chapter EK has sponsored women for ELF, PCE, Cottey College, the P.E.O. Scholar Award and the P.E.O. STAR Scholarship. Recent ELF recipients include Susan Rodenburg and Heather Clark. While other applications were unsuccessful, the women we sponsored were honored that EK believed in them, and we were inspired by their talents and drive. Chapter EK has been active at all levels of P.E.O. with officers serving Omaha Reciprocity Association, including Deb Scharf as president, Karen Adams as treasurer, and Connie Johnk as corresponding secretary; delegates and other workers for state and International conventions; and Kris York who served as state P.E.O. Educational Loan Fund chairman in 2007-2008. The work continued as Heather Adams prepared for the 2015 State Convention in Omaha as a co-chairperson. We are proud and supportive of the members who take on these endeavors.

Special EK anniversaries have been celebrated with tea parties, which were initially held in the homes of sisters. In April 2012 we continued this tradition for our 75th anniversary with an outing to the Mount Michael campus in Elkhorn for our tea. We also had seven members in attendance when we were recognized at the Convention of Nebraska State Chapter in June 2012. Our thirty-two active members continue to bring any talents we possess to our chapter. We celebrate the gifts of our sisters over the past seventy-seven years, and with the addition of technology and social meetings that take us to various landmarks and events, we continue to get to "Know Omaha!"

CHAPTER EK'S ACTIVE MEMBERSHIP IS 34; TOTAL ENROLLMENT IS 146

★

CHAPTER EL OAKLAND
ORGANIZED SEPTEMBER 1, 1937
BY EDNA CASPER

Chapter EL was organized in the Methodist Parsonage, home of Lillian Parkin, who was instrumental in organizing the chapter with the assistance of Chapter CX, Lyons. Fourteen women signed the charter. State President Ada Mead was in attendance and installed the officers. Charter members were Ida Swanson, president; Ann Anderson, vice president; Mae Latch, recording secretary; Nellie Stauffer, corresponding secretary; Minerva Holmquist, treasurer; Elizabeth Peterson, chaplain; Laura Alexander, guard; Ora Holmquist, Lola Lofgren, Lillie Steinbaugh, Mildred Holmquist, Vivian Hanson, Marion Harding, and Marjorie Harding.

The first three initiates were daughters of charter members. Our chapter continues this very strong family connection. One of our sisters is the daughter of a charter member; her niece and grandniece are also active members of the chapter. We have another family of sisters with a five-generation P.E.O. history.

Three of our sisters graduated from Cottey College: Patricia Holmquist Anderson, Sandra Peters Snoke, and Teresa Hilderman Clark. Pat Anderson (a 1949 graduate) is celebrating sixty-five years in P.E.O. and still is very active in our chapter. Our current connection with Cottey College is through our chapter member, Darla Nelson, who is serving as Cottey Area Chairman.

Chapter EL takes great pride in sponsoring women for the P.E.O. Educational Loan Fund. Our first recipient, Marjorie Harding Hegstedt, was a charter member and received her loan in 1938. We have sponsored a total of twenty-five women in our seventy-eight-year history. In 2007, we initiated a scholarship for our local high school girls. We designate a fundraiser for this cause, and can give up to four $100 scholarships. We are proud to help girls in the local area, and at the same time we are promoting the benefits of P.E.O. for women.

Chapter EL donates our time to support local chamber events and to show appreciation for our hard working educational professionals. We have sold coffee and rolls to support our Swedish Festival and had ice cream sundaes for BRAN riders who rode through our town. We honor our teachers with a meal sometime during the school year.

Our most successful fundraisers usually involve our BILs and a social meeting. One of our favorite events was a lasagna dinner and a silent auction. Every member donated a basket for the auction and contributed to the meal. Most of the donations sold at or above their retail value, and it was a lot of fun to win a basket.

Chapter EL is adapting their meetings and times to fit the needs of the members. We now meet in the evening and have a blessing basket. After the close of the meeting, we pass a basket, and each member donates $1 and shares something they are thankful for, or in some cases, something they need help and support with. We learn more about our sisters this way and we use this money to support our courtesy committee. This committee sends get well greetings, visits shut-ins, buys gifts for those in the hospital, new babies, and weddings. This committee also provides help for funerals for sisters entering Chapter Eternal.

In 2011, we hosted our Reciprocity group for a Swedish luncheon, and showed them "How Swede it was to be a P.E.O." In 2012, Chapter EL was honored at the state convention in Fremont as a 75-year chapter. In the fall we celebrated our special anniversary with a casual fiesta at our local golf club. Thirty-two active members were in attendance, and four out-of-town members and past members joined us.

CHAPTER EL'S ACTIVE MEMBERSHIP IS 66; TOTAL ENROLLMENT IS 179

★

Chapter EM Bloomfield
Organized March 12, 1938
by Edna Casper

Chapter EM was organized on March 12, 1938. Jean Anderson, an initiate of Chapter AY, Iowa, was the sister who got our chapter together and state Organizer Edna Casper was present to do the honors. Our sponsoring chapters were EJ, Creighton, and EA, Randolph. The charter members were Jean Anderson, president; Lydia Ann Borin, vice president; Leila High, recording secretary; Mae McQuistan, corresponding secretary; Elaine Borin, treasurer; Alta Swanson, chaplain; M. Lola Simmons, guard; Marvel Feldman, Iola Solso, Beth Peter, Ella Suckstorf, Frances Dart, Bertha Settell, Clare Baker, and Arlene Borin.

Although only a year old, Chapter EM helped Group IV at the Convention of Nebraska State Chapter held in Norfolk. On the second day, all fifteen members of Chapter EM were present.

When EM held a meeting, the members walked in roundabout ways, so no one could figure out where the meeting was being held. The first year our chapter donated cod liver oil to a family of undernourished children. We sent $2.50 to Cottey College and also to the P.E.O. Educational Loan Fund. The Child Saving Institute was given $1.

The chapter has supported all of the P.E.O. projects and sponsored eleven women for the P.E.O. Educational Loan Fund and two women for the P.E.O. Program for Continuing Education.

BIL parties and Christmas parties, PACK picnics and our annual buffet suppers are things that we all look forward to. Each year at our annual spring buffet supper we invite the daughters of our members who are seniors in high school and celebrate their accomplishments. We have a tradition of putting flowers on the graves of our deceased members in the Bloomfield Cemetery on Memorial Day. This year we will be replacing the flowers with a P.E.O. Star on a stake.

Each of the members of our chapter has a heart-shaped pillow made of the same material as our initiation robes. The star, trim, marguerites, and ribbon bows symbolize the love of P.E.O. and our connection as a loving sisterhood. Each new initiate is presented one and so are the visiting officers. Betty Busskohl-Peters started making them and now other members have taken over the task.

We have two 50+ year members, Bell Scott and Kathleen Canaday. We cherish their knowledge and guidance. They are wonderful members of our chapter.

We have always had excellent attendance, with some having perfect attendance and others only missing a meeting or two. Our chapter is very small with sixteen members and four nonresident members, but we are able to fulfill our duties and we all have become very close to each other. Our programs have been very interesting and educational, and that keeps our attendance up for each meeting.

CHAPTER EM'S ACTIVE MEMBERSHIP IS 20; TOTAL ENROLLMENT IS 115

★

CHAPTER EN PENDER
ORGANIZED APRIL 8, 1938
BY EDNA CASPER

Edna Casper, organizer, and Chapter AZ, Wayne, conducted the initiatory service for Chapter EN. Pauline Moseman was hostess. Charter members were Mary Surber, president; Nellie Craven, vice president; Dora Carlberg, recording secretary; Edna Mittelstadt, corresponding secretary; Frances Boughn (Meyer), treasurer; Genevieve Owens (Beerman), chaplain; Marcella James, guard; Anna Biles, Nellie Fuhrman, Pauline Moseman, May Benson and Hattie Mutz. A very early initiate, Helen Davis, WI, Iowa, is a past president of Iowa State Chapter.

In 1963, the chapter celebrated its Silver Anniversary with area chapters attending a tea hosted by Chapter EP, Wisner. Past President of Nebraska State Chapter Ada Mead gave the program. Edna Casper, EN's organizer, was also present.

On April 14, 1988, Chapter EN celebrated its Golden Anniversary at the Presbyterian Church. Hand-crafted star necklaces bearing the chapter's name and organization date are treasured favors.

As this history is being written, our minds are full of wonderful memories and our hearts are full of gratitude for all that P.E.O., Internationally and locally, means to "We who are Sisters." We have a strong belief in providing educational support for women around the world and are humbled by that opportunity.

Chapter EN

We have been active in supporting our P.E.O. projects each year with a number of fundraisers including the following: BIL-served Christmas dinners (BILs delivered us to our destination in a limo), The Wine (Nebraska-produced) and Wellness Kickoff, silent auctions, beef brisket dinner, a lovely Christmas dinner topped off with entertainment by a group of Shrine Chanters.

In the greater community, we have supported the Siouxland Blood Bank, Hospice of Siouxland, a local non-profit store called Main Street Thriftique which donates funds to worthy causes in Pender, the Pender Community Hospital Gift Shop, House Memorial Library (with yearly donations of books in memory of our Sisters Eternal), scholarships for high school senior women and financial support for our North Dakota sisters following a major flood in 1998. Pender Elementary School received a financial gift when two of our sisters were awarded the Peter Kiewit "Presidential Monetary Scholarship Award" for outstanding contributions to the teaching profession.

We love spending time with and caring for our sisters. Each sister is responsible for one week during the year at which time she sends cards to sisters who are unable to attend our meetings. Our Courtesy Committee is diligent about watching over sisters who are in our thoughts. When one of our sisters was no longer able to drive, she purchased a motorized scooter. A contest among sisters was immediately organized to name the "vehicle," which was subsequently christened "Lady Bug." Later, we joined this sister as she celebrated her 100th birthday in an area care center. For six years, one of our 50-year member sisters living in Sioux City created social events for all of us. We visited a TV station, the Sioux City Museum (where we celebrated her 90th birthday), Palmer Candy

Company, Goodwill Industries, the Sioux City Art Center and Ponca State Park. At each meeting we take the opportunity of sharing special events in our lives, and we rejoice in the happiness of our sisters!

In 2012, our chapter was recognized for its seventy-five years at the state convention in Fremont. We have three 50-year P.E.O.s in our chapter. One of them graces us with her presence at most of our meetings—at age 90! P.E.O. continues to be vital in our lives as we strive "to consider thoughtfully the full import of P.E.O." and we hope to remain active for many years as we "radiate all light possible and express a loving concern for each Sister."

CHAPTER EN's ACTIVE MEMBERSHIP IS 59; TOTAL ENROLLMENT IS 170

CHAPTER EO WEST POINT
ORGANIZED MAY 7, 1938
BY EDNA CASPER

Chapter EO was organized at the home of Lillie Kerl. Charter members were: Maria Thompsen, president; Margaret DeWald, vice president; Helen Williams, recording secretary; Elizabeth Von Seggern, corresponding secretary; Clara Korb, chaplain; Lillie Kerl, guard; Grace Anderson, Mame McDonald, Verna Reier, Esther Ellwood, Lillian Benedict, Nada Ellyson, Pearl Daniel, Bessie Walla, Clara Moodie, Kate Moodie, and Alvina Frahm. Five members were initiated the next year.

The influence of the charter members and first initiates continues. Clara Moodie was involved in the chapter for almost sixty years, and technology has allowed us to capture her pleasant memories of early history with a taped interview in which she describes with loving detail the women who guided EO through the first years. A video interview with first initiates Marie Lofgren and Margaret Graves was created in 1997, and they each provided inspiration and influence for over fifty years. Second and third generation members Jane Moodie, Susan Moodie Sheppard and Glenda Graves continue an active role in the chapter.

Support of P.E.O. projects has been ongoing for over seventy-five years through a variety of means. From the sale of 250 flashlights for the Cottey College 50th Anniversary Fund, at least two community garage sales, one book sale for the Nebraska P.E.O. Home, personal donations, an annual silent auction, a weekly 'Brag Basket', honorariums for visiting state officers and organizers, memorials for Chapter Eternal and a bequest from Ralph and Mildred Eby to benefit the Nebraska P.E.O. Home, the chapter continues to honor the financial commitment.

Since 1938, chapter members continue to give in other ways, from wrapping bandages for WWII service hospitals among other war work activities; local assistance efforts; sending annual 'Care Packages' to college daughters and our adopted Cottey student; gift cards sent to P.E.O. sons serving in the military; providing blankets for service members in field hospitals in Iraq; donating our 'slightly used' purses, filled with basic needs, for womens' shelters and personal donations to a local Crisis Center. Two chapter members, Linda Cihacek, P.A., and Mary Lauritzen, were among the group that organized the 'Humble Heroes Project', and escorted local WWII Veterans to Washington D.C. to visit the WWII Memorial in 2008. Each year since 2000 our chapter has given a scholarship to a graduate of both West Point-Beemer High School and Guardian Angels Central Catholic High School.

The chapter has four members who have been honored by the city of West Point with its highest recognition, the 'Community Service Award'. Recipients are Shirley Schlueter, Audrey Maack, Darlene Strehle and Jane Moodie.

Chapter EO celebrates anniversaries: the 25th Anniversary was held in the home of Marie Lofgren, our first initiate. The 50th Anniversary was held at the Neligh House restaurant in West Point, and the 75th Anniversary was recognized at the state convention in Fremont in 2012, with almost all chapter members in attendance, and at a special evening at the home of Susan Moodie Sheppard, the granddaughter of a charter member, to which inactive members were also invited.

Entering Chapter Eternal in the past twenty years: Lynn Hartmann, Mary Chantry, Marie Lofgren, Clara Moodie, Lydia Young, Mildred Eby, Margaret Graves, Ruth Moodie, Leona Yarger and Alice Lubker.

Chapter EO provided workers for the Convention of International Chapter in Omaha (1991). Chapter member Mary Lauritzen served as state convention chair (1998) with the entire chapter taking part. EO was among the host chapters for the 2012 state convention. Reciprocity Group VI came to West Point in 1997 and 2013. We have pledged to grow our chapter with an effort toward encouraging new initiates to share in the good work and sisterly love of P.E.O.

Chapter EO's active membership is 33; total enrollment is 169

★

Chapter EP Wisner
Organized May 9, 1938
by Edna Casper

Chapter EP, Wisner, was organized May 9, 1938, by Edna Casper. Chapter AZ, Wayne, assisted the organization of Chapter EP. Charter members were Marie Alice Pumphrey; Helen Oleson, vice president; Eleanor Oleson Anderson, Gladys A. Albers; Gladys Evans, corresponding secretary; Faith Philleo Friest, chaplain; Margaret Wupper Ziegenbein, president; Hazel V. Emley, recording secretary; Mabel Mansfield, treasurer; Lillian McMaster, guard; Hazel Oleson, Adelaide Hull, Helen Griffith, Mae McGinnis, Aletta Thompson and Isabelle Howe. President of Nebraska State Chapter Ada Mead attended.

Marie Alice Pumphrey served as treasurer of the 1949 state convention, as a Group VI representative on the Nebraska P.E.O. Home Building Committee, and was a member of the Nebraska P.E.O. Home Board of Directors from 1958-1972. Her special talents are reflected in the beauty and charm of the entire Home. Two charter members, Helen Oleson and Isabelle Howe, have received loving care at the P.E.O. Home.

Betty McMaster was treasurer of the 1970 state convention. Appointed in 1970 to fill a vacancy on the state executive board, Penny Dinklage completed the term as recording secretary. Ina Glaubius, 1970 Cottey Area Chairman, informed chapters of new Cottey College developments. Karen Hunter served on the nominating committee for the Nebraska State P.E.O. convention in 1985. This was the first year a nominating committee was used to present a slate of officers.

Chapter highlights include the 25th Anniversary Tea, with Ada Mead as guest speaker. At our 40th anniversary, charter member Gladys Albers shared information about the first meeting. Our 50th was observed with special programs during the year. We celebrated our 69th with our two 60-year members being driven to the meeting in a 1947 black sedan. In 2012, we celebrated our 75th chapter anniversary with a dinner and several programs throughout the year. Chapter EP was honored at the 2012 convention for seventy-five years of a shining tradition.

To help support P.E.O. projects we have had creative fundraisers, which now include a turn at the concession stand at the local high school. In 1982 we held a Harvest Festival to begin our local scholarship funds. BIL Keith Glaubius created a two-story Victorian dollhouse, which was raffled. Our first scholarship was valued at $200, and we have since raised the amount to $500.

Since 1938, we have sponsored nine women for the P.E.O. Educational Loan Fund and two for the P.E.O. Program for Continuing Education. We have nominated three for the P.E.O. Scholar Award and two for the P.E.O. STAR Scholarship. We have had two girls attend Cottey College. Two sisters have enjoyed living at the Nebraska P.E.O. Home in Beatrice. Currently, chapter member Joyce Mesmer resides at the Colorado P.E.O. Home.

In 1970, our chapter did the model meeting at state convention. State Organizer Catherine Anderson presented us with an engraved white gavel, which we only use at initiations. Charter member Marie Alice Pumphrey served on the Nebraska P.E.O. Home Board for several terms, and others have served on reciprocity and/or convention committees. In 2001 a flag and stand in memory of Alice Marie Griffith Hansen was given to the Nebraska P.E.O. Home.

With numerous sisters working outside the home, our meetings are now at 7:00PM, the first Monday of the month. We often receive chapter updates via email. The many talents of our sisters provide interesting and educational programs. We continue to support not only P.E.O. projects and activities but also community organizations, schools and churches as well.

The EP sisters range from two-year memberships through sixty-seven years. We continue to grow not just in membership, but also personally through the Objects and Aims.

CHAPTER EP'S ACTIVE MEMBERSHIP IS 36; TOTAL ENROLLMENT IS 134

★

CHAPTER EQ BLAIR
ORGANIZED MAY 19, 1938
BY EDNA CASPER

On May 19, 1938, at the home of Lila Dixon and in the presence of guests from five neighboring chapters, fifteen Blair women who had responded favorably became the charter members of Chapter EQ.

With Edna Casper, state organizer and mother of our current active member Dorothy Harrison officiating, Louise Bellows became the president of the charter membership. Other officers included Dorothy Schmidt, recording secretary; Lucille Rhoades, corresponding secretary; Perna Lundt, treasurer; Vera Hunt, chaplain; and Frances Murdoch, guard. Madge White, Alice Fahrney, Lola Hemphill, Louise Grimm, Lila Dixon, Verna Gutschow, Dorothy Gray and Jean Vinton completed the membership.

We observe the date of the organization of Chapter EQ annually and recognize each sister as she becomes a 50-year member. In 2013, on our 75th anniversary, we celebrated with a lovely dinner party hosted by Nancy Gabby and her committee.

Although the projects and programs of our early years tended to focus on local concerns, the years of World War II and the widening of women's roles and issues outside the home brought about heightened interest in the welfare and education of women everywhere. In response, Chapter EQ has directed more attention to programs emphasizing scholarship and the support of women in continuing education programs. Six young women, one in computer information science, four in nursing programs and another in teaching have received help from our chapter and we sponsored Haley Smith as a P.E.O. STAR Scholarship recipient from International Chapter.

Robley Garrigan, who was initiated into Chapter EQ and later dimited to HL, and EQ member Jane Gilbert co-chaired the 1984 state convention in Blair. It was at that time that Robley, a third-generation P.E.O., became treasurer of Nebraska State Chapter. She must have taken the convention theme *"P.E.O.—A Star To Guide"* seriously, because she followed hers all the way to the presidency of Nebraska State Chapter in 1990-91.

As a chapter, EQ continues to be actively involved in state and International business. In 1984, combining the talents of both Blair chapters, we hosted the state convention, and since then have provided support as pages, hospitality hostesses, and even taxi drivers and cookie bakers for state and International conventions. One of our members, Candace Suverkrubbe, served as a page at the 2013 Convention of International Chapter in Dallas, and we hosted the hospitality room for the Honors Luncheon at the 2012 state convention in Fremont. Our efforts leave us "tired but inspired."

Our EQ chapter meetings reflect our varied interests, and we enjoy them all: musical programs, book reviews, travel experiences, and art appreciation. A highlight of our programming this year featured a one-man exhibition of paintings by Kent Bellows, grandson of our charter president, at Joslyn Art Museum in Omaha—a memorable afternoon for Chapter EQ.

Our silent auction of Christmas goodies ushers in the Christmas season each year and also fattens our treasury, and our "Brag Box" appears at every meeting, giving us a chance to share family news with our sisters.

Our chapter membership has grown from the 15 charter members to 57 active resident members and 9 nonresident members.

For several years after the organization of Chapter EQ, Fanny Grimm was the only member of Chapter Eternal, which now numbers forty-four. In 2013, past president Ellie O'Hanlon Noble and Fern Rhoades, our 100-year-old member, joined its ranks.

As we mourn the loss of these two sisters, we are reminded again of the Longfellow lines which appeared in the history *Saga of Nebraska P.E.O.*, dedicated to that grand lady Bertha Clark Hughes:

"The light she leaves behind her, lights our mortal paths again."

May the "essence of the Sisterhood" live in our hearts as we remember these words.

CHAPTER EQ'S ACTIVE MEMBERSHIP IS 64; TOTAL ENROLLMENT IS 241

Chapter ER Benkelman
Organized April 22, 1939
by Mary Koupal
Disbanded January 29, 2009

Chapter ER was organized upon the instigation of Nora Radcliff, who dimitted from Chapter P, Stanbury, Missouri. The charter list, with twelve initiates, included Nora Radcliff, president; Marie Mason, vice president; Anna Gorthy, recording secretary; Mabel Lewis, corresponding secretary; Minnie Hester, treasurer; Ethel Boswell, chaplain; Helen Phelps, Guard; Verna Freeman, Margarette Finny, Elizabeth Our, Eleanor Ough, Keturah Hines and Caroline Boswell.

Chapter ER's success was due largely to the efforts of Nora Radcliff. She expected every member to be present at each meeting. Her high standards set the bar for ER members. In turn, those members were wonderful P.E.O.s.

Chapter ER members hosted teas for the junior class girls from the high school in order to introduce the students to Cottey College. Donna Laughlin, Muriel Morehouse, Paige Powell, Allison Kitt and Dorthea Bauerle attended our wonderful college. We had two P.E.O. Program for Continuing Education recicipients, two ELF recipients and one P.E.O. Scholar Award recipient. In addition to our International projects, we also raised funds to provide a scholarship each year to a graduating senior from our local high school. Occasionally we assisted college students with financial gifts. Once we gave a generous gift to a young man who had been a foster child in our community whose goal it was to become a veterinarian. We all cheered when he graduated from veterinary school.

Chapter ER members after Anita Kitt's President's Tea.
Front Row: Barbara Waters, Julie Jones, Anita Kitt, Betty Parman, Amy Shillington, and Betty VanDike. Back Row: Dee Fries, Margaret Powell, Velda Wright, Carol Peterson, Shirley Adkinson, Doris Tecker and Kim Wright.

Our members were resourceful in their efforts to raise money to support our projects. We did the usual garage sales and food sale. One year we had goose drop bingo at our county fair when our county could no longer afford a carnival. Chapter ER members graciously hosted numerous Reciprocity meetings.

In 1991 several of our members attended and assisted with the Convention of International Chapter held in Omaha. The work and planning of *Spirit of the Prairie* was a load that was carried by all of the P.E.O. chapters in Nebraska. Anita Kitt was chairman of sales with Betty Parman, co-chairman. It was great fun working with other Nebraska P.E.O.s. By the end of the convention, although our feet were tired, we knew we had come together and hosted a wonderful, long remembered convention.

In 1993, Reciprocity Group I hosted the state convention in McCook. Anita Kitt was the convention chairman. We had every hotel full plus a few rooms in the college dorm. Mother Nature worked with us and provided relatively cool weather for the convention. This was a concern as the auditorium was not air conditioned. Mary Owens presided at the convention with the theme *"The Plus of P.E.O."* Anita Kitt was elected treasurer to the state board at the McCook convention. She served as president of Nebraska State Chapter in the millennial year 1999-2000 at the convention held in Beatrice, exemplifying the theme *"Star Gazing, Star Raising, Star Amazing."*

Chapter ER members with assistance from other P.E.O. sisters perform *"A Star in the Window"* at a Reciprocity Group I luncheon. Standing: Carol Peterson, Jean Matthews, Christy Tecker, Allison Sandman, FA, Julie Jones, Chris Schrader, Velda Wright, Jana Mintling, IG, Barbara Waters, Nichole Sis and Anita Kitt.

Chapter ER's members were a multi-faceted group of women with many interests. We had wonderful programs. There were even a few instances when ALL of our members were present at meetings. We often had meetings at our local retirement home so that our members who resided there could be a part of our meetings and share in the fellowship. Our members lived as far as forty miles south to thirty miles north and twenty-five miles west of Benkelman, crossing state lines and time zones. But we made it work and always chuckled about "fast time or slow time."

Slowly we began to lose our charter members to Chapter Eternal and then our older core members entered Chapter Eternal. In one year we lost five of our sisters. Although our members had been diligent in giving the gift of P.E.O. to friends and daughters, too many of these friends and daughters were moving away. Chapter ER was the recipient of only two dimits in thirty years. We were initiating but these new members weren't staying in the area. Out of all of the daughters who were initiated only two were still in Chapter ER. Soon our attendance was ten or fewer members and often times we didn't have a quorum. Our "core" group dwindled down to five members who would regularly attend meetings and take an office. The population in Benkelman had declined by 30 percent and our county by a larger percentage. Gone were the days when our membership was forty members strong and our chapter enjoyed a high profile in our community. It was a sad day for our chapter when the question to disband was put to a vote.

Some of our members decided to go inactive, three of us dimitted to different chapters and a handful continue to pay their dues as members of a disbanded chapter. Losing Chapter ER left Benkelman and the area with less to offer and a loss of luster.

Chapter ER disbanded January 29, 2009.   TOTAL ENROLLMENT 137

CHAPTER ES LINCOLN
ORGANIZED MAY 6, 1939
BY MARY KOUPAL

Chapter ES was organized in Lincoln on May 6, 1939, by organizer Mary Koupal, with fourteen unaffiliates. Charter members were: Maud Barker, president; Nellie Duffield, vice president; Annis Wolfe, recording secretary; Berta Dean, corresponding secretary; Margaret Haubensak, treasurer; Marguerite Davis, chaplain; Edna Olson, guard; Grace Finch, Marjorie Allen, Hope Wilbur, Olga Dvoracek, Virginia Van Decar Raasch, Esther Fruhling Naden, and Nettie Anderbery.

Currently, Chapter ES has five 50-year members: Jan Loftin, Mary Alice Park, Georgia Payne, Helen Weber and Karen Simopoulos. In our 75-year history, ES has had over twenty 50-year members, including Clara Higgins, who also celebrated eighty years with our chapter in 1993. We have had several families dating back four generations. ES has had a total enrollment of 178 with an average meeting attendance of 22.

Chapter ES celebrated its 50th anniversary at East Campus Student Union in Lincoln on May 6, 1989, with twenty-six members having lunch together. ES celebrated their 75th anniversary during the May meeting in 2014 with a history program.

Chapter ES became a Solid Gold Chapter with a contribution to the Nebraska P.E.O. Home. The chapter also enjoys status as a Cottey College Golden Anniversary Chapter.

The chapter is proud of having two past state presidents. Helen Curtiss served as president of Nebraska State Chapter in 1982-1983. Her convention theme was "*P.E.O.—A Garden Where Love Grows.*" Our second past state president was Jan Loftin, who presided in 2010-2011. Her theme was "*P.E.O.—A Network of Love.*" Throughout the years Chapter ES has had several past presidents and officers of the Lincoln P.E.O. Reciprocity Roundtable, including presidents Lee Ora Benton, 1948; Janet Huffman, 1973; and Jan Loftin, 1997. ES has sent many delegates to Supreme and International Conventions. There have been four ES daughters who attended Cottey College: Kim Heikes, Kay Heikes Butler, Karyn Dewey Flesch, and Robin

Peterson Everts. The chapter has sponsored women for ELF loans and PCE grants.

Chapter ES has had many cherished traditions, some of which still continue today including: Spring picnics, Christmas parties, teas and luncheons. For many years, Helen Curtiss hosted the covered dish supper in her home the night of election and installation of officers. The Souther sisters held a Presidents' Tea for the Lincoln chapter presidents in their lovely home for many years. It was considered quite the social event of the season complete with hats and gloves.

Chapter ES 75th Anniversary celebration in May of 2014

Members have enjoyed numerous visits to the P.E.O. Home in Beatrice for chapter meetings and socials. Elsie Rice donated her silver coffee and tea service to the home. Three chapter members, Grace Finch, Marguerite Davis and Nellie Turner, received loving care at the Home. Since 1947, ES has sent a Christmas basket to the Home containing everything from canned goods to bingo prizes.

In 1940 the chapter began to raise money for the P.E.O. projects, raising $12 in that first year. Chapter funds have been supplemented by garage sales, auctions, magazine sales, contributions for rides, tax for failing to wear P.E.O. pins to meetings, Brag Bag, Pennies for Projects and by stuffing a sock full of change. By far our most successful fundraising event is the "Nuts to You" program.

Past State Presidents Jan Loftin, right, and Cindy Biehl, left, proudly display Nebraska parphernalia at International Convention

ES has raised thousands of dollars, supporting two state presidents and the P.E.O. projects through the years. Some of ES's philanthropic projects include the Lincoln Malone Center, Friendship Home, Tabitha Nursing home and for many years the Child Saving Institute. ES also supported the Red Cross and USO starting with World War II from knitting blankets, making first aid kits and bandages to writing soldiers. Helen Weber received the Distinguished Service to Nursing Award from the University of Nebraska Medical Center for her work through the Red Cross.

Chapter ES looks back with happy memories and appreciation of how P.E.O. can enrich the lives of its members. We continue to be "Extra Special."

CHAPTER ES'S ACTIVE MEMBERSHIP IS 43; TOTAL ENROLLMENT IS 178

Chapter ET Scottsbluff
Organized December 2, 1939
by Florence Davis

Chapter ET was organized on December 2, 1939, at the home of a gracious member of Chapter CD, Mary Halley. ET is the second oldest chapter in Scottsbluff. There were fifteen charter members. Dimitting from Chapter CD, Scottsbluff were: Mable Bomgardner, Camille Elliott, Sara LeRoy, Irene Neighbors, Miriam Riddell, and Edith Stoops. Dimits were Dorothy Weeth, Margaret Clark, Natalie Stockfleth and Fay Clem. Five daughters of P.E.O.s initiated that morning by Chapter CD were Virginia Barron, Jane Bomgardner, Betty Elliott, Barbara Stoops and Shirley VanDecar. A luncheon was held at the Scotts Bluff Country Club and in the afternoon Chapter ET held its first meeting and elected its officers. Our chapter celebrated its 75th anniversary on December 2, 2014. Betty Elliott Metcalf will be a 75-year member and is still very active.

Chapter ET meets the second and fourth Wednesday of each month for a noon luncheon in members' homes. The average attendance is twenty-one. The programs are very inspiring and usually given by ET members or community organizations. We have very successful social meetings. They give us more time to have fellowship and form closer friendship in the P.E.O. Sisterhood. Our inactive members are invited.

Our money-making project each year is an auction in the fall. The auction consists mostly of baked goods, jellies and pickles. A pie may go for $40. The money raised is used to assist in local projects, such as the Panhandle Youth Shelter, Riverside Discovery Center (Zoo where we have an Adopt A Spot for flowers), Cat Packs (backpacks of food go home with students who need food for the weekend), Library, Red Cross and Humane Society. In addition, Chapter ET supports all of the P.E.O. projects. Since 1992, the chapter has sponsored several students who received loans from the P.E.O. Educational Loan Fund. In 2013 we sponsored a young woman who received the P.E.O. STAR Scholarship. Our chapter is honored to have a local woman be a recipient. We stay in touch with her and send gift cards and gift baskets throughout the year. The chapter also sponsors a student that lives in the Nebraska suite at Cottey College.

We have reactivated our summer picnic to entertain the BILs. The members remember their shut-ins with plants and cards, and they take complete dinners to bereaved P.E.O. families or when members go home from the hospital.

We are a very caring chapter.

Chapter ET celebrates Founders' Day every year with the other five Scottsbluff chapters, two Gering chapters and one Mitchell chapter, with a brunch at the Gering Civic Center. The eight chapters rotate responsibilities and the brunch is always well attended.

P.E.O. is very important to the members of Chapter ET and we do our best to maintain a viable, energetic presence in our community.

Chapter ET's active membership is 45; total enrollment is 265

Chapter EU Mitchell
Organized May 20, 1940
by Mary Nixon

Chapter EU is a living legacy of loving sisterhood. It was organized May 20, 1940, under the sponsorship of Bernice Tillett of Alliance. Charter members were Dorothy Bronson, Mable Hoffman, Helen Delahoyde, Faye Parrish, Myrrh Attebery, Elizabeth Newell, Florence Strachan, Dorothy Vorpahl, Susan Ashbrook, Lillie Whitehead, Helen Simpson, Lillian Jones, Myrtle Jones, Texa Herring, Mary Eastman, Mabel Watson, Catherine Cannon, Geneva Lindsay and Mayme Hanson. Dorothy Bronson served as the first president.

From nineteen charter members in 1940, EU now has twenty-four active sisters with 184 members enrolled. EU is proud to have three 50-year members as well as two members under the age of twenty-five.

During EU's first years, all meetings were held in the afternoon. During the war years, many members joined the work force and the chapter alternated afternoon and evening meetings. Since 1986, all meetings have been held in the evening, with the exception of the state convention report given at a brunch in June.

Our letters EU stand for Ever Useful. Our sisters exemplify this in service to the Sisterhood with yearly support of the P.E.O. philanthropies, the Nebraska P.E.O. Home and Cottey College. Chapter EU recently supported the Cottey College capital building project and the Cottey College suite renovation; and held a Nebraska P.E.O. Home shower collecting thirty-two items to share with our sisters.

Emma Sanderson, President of Nebraska State Chapter in 1957-58, was a member of Chapter EU and began her climb to state offices during the Scottsbluff convention. Vera Clouse in 1954, Jane Bowman in 1970, and Helen Reiber in 1989, were all members of Chapter EU when they served successful terms as president of Panhandle Reciprocity.

Chapter EU has nominated women for PCE and the STAR Scholarship and supported the women who received these in many ways.

EU sisters have enjoyed many fundraising activities such as daisy sales, which included helping a sister who generously provided these plants to pot them for sale; a traveling basket for silent auction at meetings; and selling, assembling, and decorating packaging for bread kits.

Chapter EU was "Ever Useful" when the 2009 state convention was held in Gering, as the chapter provided flowers and carried out the work of the Property and Site Preparation Committee. Sisters are "Ever Useful" as they step in to fill offices, travel to workshops and conventions, and as past officers stand in when needed during initiation.

Sisters provide inspiring, informative and entertaining programs as varied as their individual interests. Some have included trivia about our Founders, comparisons of fashion and popular culture through the decades of P.E.O., fun facts about each sister, and travel with sisters around our nation and our world.

Chapter EU's sisters also enjoy informal social time together. These social meetings have included our BILs in picnics and a Valentine dinner, a tour of a winery located in Mitchell, a mother-daughter tea, and attending another chapter's themed table brunch.

Perhaps Chapter EU's greatest legacy is found in the loving way older sisters mentor younger members in the goals of our chapter and the duties of our offices, while younger sisters often provide service by spearheading activities and driving to meetings and other events.

We lovingly honor our sisters who have passed to Chapter Eternal by placing a P.E.O. marker at their gravesite each Memorial Day. While Chapter EU's legacy connects us to a treasured past, our sisters continue to grow a legacy for the future.

CHAPTER EU'S ACTIVE MEMBERSHIP IS 37; TOTAL ENROLLMENT IS 184

★

CHAPTER EV GERING
ORGANIZED MARCH 13, 1943
BY EVA CURTISS

Chapter EV (Ever Victorious), was organized March 13, 1943, by Eva Curtiss with the sponsorship of Chapters CD and ET, Scottsbluff. The chapter began with eleven members received by dimit and four by initiation. The first officers were Frances Fields, president; Olga Thurlow, vice president; Verna Metzger, recording secretary; Myrtle Carey, corresponding secretary; Evelyn Sandall, treasurer; Emily Gentry, chaplain; Alice Christian, guard; and Iva Lyda, musician. Other charter members were Hazel Adams, Sady Grimm, Esther Gentry, Ethel Meinzer, Mary McMillan, Helen Weaver, and Myra Wolcott.

The 50th Anniversary was celebrated March 10, 1993, with personal remembrances of charter members Emily Gentry and Alice Christian, as well as a letter from Myra Wolcott Scriven. Other longtime members shared their special memories of Chapter EV. The officers were very fetching in their 1940's hats.

In 1964 Chapter EV helped with the organization of Gering's second chapter, Chapter GI. Through the years the two chapters have shared many social functions. Currently, we enjoy a June salad luncheon which the two chapters take turns hosting. The report of the state convention is the featured program for this joint meeting.

For the past three years, EV's most successful fundraiser has been a card party held on the last Wednesday in June. Hosting up to twenty-two tables, members provide a wide variety of delectable confections to create a dessert buffet. Prize drawings throughout the afternoon add to the enjoyment. The second big fundraiser is a silent auction of craft items and baked goods held with the November meeting. At the end of each business meeting, members are given the opportunity to share "Happy Bucks" by giving a dollar to celebrate the happy occasions and milestones in the lives of members and their families. Years ago, Emily Gentry served as chairperson of the Magazine Fund which contributed over $900 to the chapter over thirty years. All money is contributed to the P.E.O. projects which we actively support financially and by encouraging local women to utilize the various P.E.O. grants and scholarships. Through the years we have had a number of successful recipients of our philanthropies.

Our members participate in many local organizations and churches, serving in leadership positions when called upon. Susan Wiedeman served as Gering's mayor. Along the way, our members have received special honors. In 1951 Emily Gentry served as Nebraska Mother of the Year, and in 1960 Ruth Bassett served as

Scotts Bluff County Mother of the Year.

After each business meeting, EV is enlightened or entertained with a wide variety of programs. Recent programs included "Festival of Hope," "Golden Halo Foundation," and the "Gering Speech Team." Members are encouraged to support these groups individually, but as a chapter we are committed to supporting P.E.O. projects. We do award a scholarship to our P.E.O. STAR Scholarship applicant.

We meet the second Wednesday of each month throughout the year with two meetings in March for election and installation of new officers. A favorite activity is "Lunch Bunch" held whenever there is a fifth Wednesday in the month. We celebrate by sharing lunch at different local restaurants.

CHAPTER EV'S ACTIVE MEMBERSHIP IS 45; TOTAL ENROLLMENT IS 225

★

CHAPTER EW GENOA
ORGANIZED MARCH 17, 1944
BY REBECCA LEE

March 17, 1944, Chapter EW was launched by Organizer Rebecca Lee who was assisted by President of Nebraska State Chapter Mary Nixon; Jean Harvey, M, Omaha; Lois Hawkes, DY, Omaha; and the following members from Chapter DJ, Albion: Thelma Millen, Gertrude Burt, Velma Krause, Alta Krause, Marie Reed, and Neva Robinson.

Charter members were Stella Krause, president; Helen Brown, vice president; Catharine Nore, recording secretary; Lois Hawkes, corresponding secretary; Edith Senften, treasurer; Lillian Pearson, chaplain; Lucille McKillip, guard. Other chapter members were: Anna Krause, Althea Winell, Linnea Winell, Minnie Johnson, Agnes Shotkoski, Ethel I. Kenner, Gladys Wright, Lucia Spear, and Maude I. Welch.

Interest in war and post-war activities and sponsoring the Genoa Youth Canteen have been followed by constant support of all the P.E.O. projects.

Prior to 1995, EW had gained 82 initiates and 8 members by dimit. Thirty have dimited to other chapters, thirteen have joined Chapter Eternal and eleven are inactive.

Since 1995, 21 have been initiated, 7 are inactive, and 3 have entered Chapter Eternal. A highlight of one initiation was when three daughters of members were initiated. One was a third generation P.E.O. and her grandmother was in attendance and all three mothers were serving as officers that year.

Chapter EW has assisted with six state conventions and has had five delegates to Convention of International Chapter. EW has had one member serve as a guard at International convention and one member serve as vice-chairman of a state convention. We have also hosted Reciprocity and the theme for the event was "*P.E.O. For All Seasons.*"

Chapter EW has been fortunate to have several young ladies graduate from Cottey College and another serve in the Peace Corps. Chapter EW has sponsored a grant recipient through the P.E.O. Program for Continuing Education.

Through the years Chapter EW has supported various community events. Genoa has an "Old-Fashioned Christmas" event every year and P.E.O. has a tree at the "Festival of Trees" and had a white elephant booth to help raise money for our scholarship fund. During Pawnee Days in the summer, P.E.O. has sponsored a fun-run. Chapter EW also sponsors a local scholarship to a female high school senior.

One thing the chapter tries to do is highlight our members' various talents in our programs. Some of the programs presented by our members have focused upon archeology, technology, cross-stitch, scrapbooking, and genealogy.

Throughout the years the sisters have gone on various small excursions for a day of friendship, fun and laughter. Some of those trips have taken us to a craft show, a tea room, art gallery, and a winery (where we acquired the nickname of Luscious Lovelies). One event the sisters look forward to every year is our annual salad supper and our anniversary luncheon. Both these events give the opportunity for sisters to share memories with each other.

A monthly newsletter helps the members to stay in touch with all of the sisters whether they are far away or unable to attend meetings, and lets them know what's going on in the chapter.

Chapter EW's active membership is 29; total enrollment is 119

Chapter EX Fremont
Organized March 20, 1944
by Rebecca Lee

In the shadows of 1944, as World War II was winding down, perhaps Chapter AJ was feeling the pangs of becoming too large. Regardless of the reason, with the blessing of Chapter AJ and the help of Organizer Rebecca Lee, Chapter EX of Fremont was formed with the leadership of Marie Hansen. Charter members included Hannah B. Stephens, Marie Hansen, Dorothy S. Zimmerman, Katherine S. Sudman, Jessie Johnson, Myrtle I. Sidner, Jessie A. Fleming, Augusta Switzer, Ruth Fredrickson, Dorothy Thomas, Mildred P. Winn, Emma Noerenberg, Dorothy Gray, Anna Maben, Mary Follen, Florence S. Reckmeyer, Alma Christensen, Jeanette D. Young, Helen Wiles, Muriel Freeman, Edith Colley, Minne L. Toole, and G. Ellen Taylor. Since then, we have celebrated our 50-year anniversary at the 1994 state convention, had one member celebrate her 100th birthday at a meeting, initiated two fourth-generation P.E.O.s and celebrated as one member's daughter was awarded the P.E.O. Scholar Award.

We have a plethora of talents in our chapter and they are generously shared for programs. These include gifts of voices, bettering our health, and learning more about ourselves and our community. All of this is what it takes to make Chapter EX "EXtra" special.

Chapter EX continues to support the projects in many different ways, and we have kept our P.E.O. educational projects in the foreground in order to keep our Sisterhood vital and growing. One way we do so is to participate in a bridge tournament that three of the Fremont area P.E.O. chapters sponsor. We also receive a yearly donation from a family in memory of one member with the intention that it be used for one of our projects.

Other fundraisers have included (but are not limited to), BIL parties and auctions, a December silent auction of food and crafts made by our sisters, the selling of pre-packaged bean soup, auctioned boxed lunches, and the Precious Moments' donations that are shared at meetings. Additionally, a photo book of the members of Chapter EX was made and sold (and is fun to look at even now). One year, talents were sold and the result was much merriment and bonding in addition to fundraising. Finally one of our sisters organized, printed and sold a city-wide P.E.O. directory of all four of the Fremont area chapters. It has been invaluable as a reference for all.

In the remembrances from our presidents, a common thread was the feeling that each received much more than they gave! There was always support from members and officers that gave her a sense of confidence. The warmth and love shown to each sister in times of need and times of joy have made us into the loving sisterhood we are today. We have snowbirds, travelers, volunteers, authors, and all are women of the world in their own right.

> We strive to give gifts
> Of heart, spirit or mind,
> To help make the world better for all human-kind.
> For life is a quest
> For the noblest and best,
> And we pray to God
> That we each meet the test.

CHAPTER EX'S ACTIVE MEMBERSHIP IS 62; TOTAL ENROLLMENT IS 298

★

Chapter EY Omaha
Organized March 27, 1944
by Rebecca Lee

Chapter EY, Omaha, was organized by state organizer Rebecca Lee with the assistance of state president Mary Nixon, Past Supreme President Bertha Clark Hughes, and past state presidents Viola Jennings Cameron and Ada Mead. After a morning meeting and luncheon at the home of Viola Jennings Cameron the officers were installed and Chapter EY's organization was complete. The charter members were: President Ona M. Scroggs, vice president; Katherine Barber, recording secretary; Effie Johnson, corresponding secretary; Caroline Hill, treasurer; Beth Obye, chaplain; Sara Bahr, guard; Mildred Swan, Wilma Bunney, Mary Eunice Dayhoff, Lorene Ellingson, Frances Eubank, Harriette Ford, Margaret Gilbert, Carol Johnson, Jessie Schaberg and Reba M. Stocks. After installation a short business meeting was held, and the second and fourth Tuesdays of each month were chosen as meeting dates to be held in members' homes.

For years, regular meetings were noon luncheons, but in recent years regular meetings have alternated between morning coffee and afternoon dessert with a few social noon luncheons. One of a number of memorable meetings was an elaborate Victorian Tea at the home of Betty Beach when members were encouraged to bring a favorite tea cup. Each P.E.O. project is a topic scheduled for a report or update during the year. Other monthly topics include informational and educational subjects with discussion led by an EY member or an invited speaker. To encourage personal growth, EY presidents choose uplifting and inspirational themes to be carried throughout the year.

Some significant events and activities since 1995 include the 100th birthday of charter member Mildred Swan. Mary Brown, Barbara Raffensperger, and Jean Lippold received Awards of Achievement as charter members of the "Order of the Star" for holding all seven elected offices. Members have enjoyed using their organizational and creative skills as they served on state conventions held in Omaha. President Bev Traub was a delegate for the Convention of International Chapter held in Vancouver, Canada. Carol Schroeder served as Omaha Reciprocity Association president. Sally Domet received a Buffet Award for Outstanding Omaha Public Schools Teacher. Debby Hanlon served as president of the Nebraska P.E.O. Home Board in Beatrice and obtained a Cottey Brick for EY. Members have organized visits to the Nebraska P.E.O. Home and made lap robes for the residents.

Our primary and traditional fundraising project has been an auction held in the fall in alternate years. Mostly, unique handmade/homemade items are donated by members. Donna Wilcox has been our auctioneer for a spirited bidding process. EY sisters have had jolly times while keeping in mind that the auction proceeds would be directed toward important P.E.O. projects. Another successful fundraising project has been the sale of handcrafted Venetian glass daisy hearts to be worn as necklaces. The hearts have been offered for sale on the Nebraska P.E.O. website and whenever allowed at P.E.O. gatherings. A penny pot is passed at each meeting for members to contribute spare coins and a time for "brags" provides an opportunity for members to share our lives and to contribute a dollar to the EY treasury.

Some of our members live far apart and we have various interests and talents, but the Objects and Aims knit us together and the spirit of good will extends far beyond our immediate circle.

Chapter EY will soon celebrate its 70th anniversary as members look forward to future years of friendship and memories.

CHAPTER EY'S ACTIVE MEMBERSHIP IS 39; TOTAL ENROLLMENT IS 204

★

CHAPTER EZ GRAND ISLAND
ORGANIZED APRIL 3, 1945
BY FLORENCE STEWART

In 1944, Blanche Wellensiek of Chapter CK, and Nebraska State Chapter Organizer Florence Stewart presented the charter list of Chapter EZ. The chapter was organized on April 3, 1945.

Initiates were Ila Anderson, guard; Berenice Belford, Alma Cunningham, Jessie Farnsworth; Louise Funk, treasurer; Frances Grayson, Gertrude Lanigan; Frances Jensen, recording secretary; Myrle Menck, Belva Ruby, and Roseanne Snygg. Dimitting members were Eloise Lindgren, vice president; Ruth Spelts, chaplain; Gertrude McLaughlin, corresponding secretary; and Blanche Wellensiek, president. Florence Stewart said, "Chapter EZ is easy to look at, easy to love and easy to live with."

Educational projects have been emphasized by Chapter EZ. From 1951 to 1956, Chapter EZ sponsored Helen Tsista of Greece under the Post-War Foster Parent Program. She was provided with $8 monthly, gifts and clothing. These enabled her to become an apprentice seamstress. Helen was visited in Athens by two members of EZ.

Our chapter is represented by sisters ranging in age from their twenties into their nineties. We meet on the second and fourth Wednesdays for twelve business meetings and enjoy three socials a year. Our socials include a Christmas brunch, a fall road trip, and a Valentine dinner with our BILs. We do not meet in July and August. We further our education with informative programs, often given by our own sisters. Topics include the creative arts, healthy living, gardening, travelogues, volunteer opportunities, and much more. Our occasional trips to the Nebraska P.E.O. Home are enjoyable for us and for the residents as well. We join our sisters from other chapters twice a year at our Founders' Day brunch and our annual Reciprocity XIII meeting. The presidents from each chapter in Grand Island also meet quarterly to share ideas and support one another for a stronger Sisterhood.

Chapter EZ Christmas social - 2012

Since the publishing of our last P.E.O. History book, we have sponsored several outstanding young women to receive International P.E.O. grants and loans. Financially, we provide $75 each to the seven projects of P.E.O. Every year our chapter also provides a $500 local scholarship to a college-bound high school senior from our area. Our fundraiser for the past six years has been selling frozen cookie dough, and this has proven very successful. The past two years, all six Grand Island chapters have come together for a fundraising dinner and raffle to assist Cottey College in becoming accredited as a four-year institution.

CHAPTER EZ'S ACTIVE MEMBERSHIP IS 42; TOTAL ENROLLMENT IS 235

*There are no rules.
Just follow your heart.*

-Robin Williams

Chapter FA McCook
Organized April 1, 1946
by Helen Riddell

Chapter FA was organized April 1, 1946, by Helen Riddell. Five members of Chapter X, McCook, transferred and became charter members of Chapter FA. The first chapter officers were: Marjorie Johnston, president; Eunice Larson, vice president; Alice Wolfe, recording secretary; Irma John Stetzel, corresponding secretary; Viola Hiatt, treasurer; Frances DeForest, chaplain; and Rose Horton, guard. Other charter members were Lucile Noyes, Evelyn Donaldson, Verda Wiley, Maurine Hofferber, Pauline Stetzel, Hope Reese, and Martha Watson Greene.

In 1951 Chapter FA assisted with other Reciprocity Group I chapters to host the state convention in McCook. Irene Van Brunt, DD, presided at the convention and Flora Stevens, X, was convention chairman. In 1979, Chapter FA again assisted other chapters in hosting the state convention in North Platte. McCook hosted the 1993 convention with Chapter FA in charge of Arrangements and Properties. Mary Owens, BT, presided at this convention and Anita Kitt, ER, served as convention chairman. Once again in 2007, Chapter FA helped host the state convention, this time in North Platte with Joan Fink, AT, presiding.

At the 1997 state convention held in Lincoln, Chapter FA celebrated its 50th anniversary. It only seemed appropriate that the theme for the Honor's luncheon was, "*A single seed planted fifty years ago...what a flourishing garden today!*" That theme most accurately described our chapter's beginning and subsequent growth.

Chapter FA's annual money making project is a Harvest Sale in November. Members bring homemade food, crafts, prepared baskets and other wonderful goodies, which are auctioned off. Our Harvest Sale enables us to give generously to our P.E.O. projects and also support some local philanthropy as well. This is part of our chapter's outreach in our community and helps to illuminate our Sisterhood's generous spirit and caring nature.

Our chapter's members are always seeking women who are working toward higher educational goals. We have recently and successfully nominated several ELF recipients. One is now practicing dentistry and another one is a veterinary student at the University of Nebraska-Kearney. In 2011, the pilot year for the P.E.O. STAR Scholarship, we successfully sponsored Amy Been, whose intention was to become a math teacher. Amy is now in the master's program for mathematics in Arizona. Emily Tolliver was awarded the P.E.O. STAR Scholarship two years later in 2013. We continue to sponsor other high school ladies for this scholarship, and if they are not successful at the International level, our chapter provides a small scholarship for each one. Our chapter has also promoted Cottey College and has had several area women attend Cottey. One of these students was later awarded the P.E.O. Scholar Award for her studies in pharmacology.

A member of our chapter who is a retired military officer's wife, took on the Adopt-a-Chaplain project. During the past five years, Ann Trail has received increased support from area clubs, churches, school children and local business and gathers up a variety of personal care items: hand and foot warmers, types of games, convenience foods, etc. This year she sent off 200 boxes to five U.S. military chaplains stationed in the Middle East, just before Thanksgiving so that they will be distributed to our soldiers before Christmas. Chapter members have supported this project with donations of items, money, and their time, especially when it comes to packing boxes.

Over the years, FA has celebrated Founders' Day by sharing with the other two McCook chapters this special evening by gathering together. Each chapter rotates the duties of being hostesses, providing decorations, or the entertainment about our Founders.

P.E.O. has entered into the era of website technology, with Allison Sandman leading the way and keeping us informed. Her expertise has been invaluable helping us with web page correspondence.

We have extended invitations to sisters of a recently disbanded chapter for them to join us.

Our Sisterhood is blessed to have women of all ages, who are leaving "footprints" in several communities in southwest Nebraska, as our chapter membership is not limited to just McCook. Our members serve in all levels of their communities as community leaders, educators, healthcare professionals, fundraisers, artists, and philanthropists in their own right.

CHAPTER FA'S ACTIVE MEMBERSHIP IS 58; TOTAL ENROLLMENT IS 277

★

Chapter FB Lincoln
Organized January 18, 1947
by Bessie Buchanan

Chapter FB owes its beginning to Janet Johnson who energetically sought to organize a chapter which could include many of the unaffiliated members in Lincoln in 1946. Charter members were June Misko, Janet Johnson, Charlotte Ralston, Fern Brown, Esther Sloan, Jessie Moyer, Lila Chard, Jean Fossland, Hermine Hamm, Catherine Ham Munson, Martha Heminghaus, Carmen Hornby, Irene Mikkelsen, Lillian Parkin, Dora Whitford and Gladys Churchill.

In 1990, FB member June Brunmeier led Nebraska State Chapter as its president. Chapter FB has had three presidents of Lincoln Roundtable, including June Misko, Marilyn Hansen and Diane Conley.

Updating our chapter history is a wonderful time to reflect on all the traditions and changes in the last twenty years.

There are traditions we have kept and new ones we've made. For this particular edition, one could describe our chapter in these few words: Chapter FB is thoughtful, flexible, and innovative.

Thoughtful is an adjective meaning thinking deeply, thought out carefully, considerate. Following initiation, a new sister receives calls for rides to the meetings; and an established member sits with her to help her match names to faces, and to understand the proceedings. We adopt Cottey College students as well as Nebraska P.E.O. Home residents. We have had programs on City Impact and other agencies, as well as multicultural issues.

Chapter FB is always there for each of our sisters. When Edus Conley passed away, three FB sisters went to her house to clean and make up beds for out-of-town relatives; and a host of other sisters brought food and served those relatives in a pre-funeral luncheon in her home. This story of caring could be repeated many times, just by changing the sister's name. Ask any member of the chapter who has been ill, had surgery, or lost a family member, and she will tell you of the flowers, food, cards, calls, and caring.

Flexible could very easily be the "F" in FB. Cancer seems to be more prevalent with each passing year. A few years ago, when we had our officers all elected and installed, cancer struck. Four of our officers were diagnosed with cancer within a few months of each other. Our president was first, facing surgery, radiation and chemo. She asked the chapter for their prayers, and wanted to continue to serve. With her blessing we elected a co-president. Right now you are thinking, "isn't that what a vice president is for?" Yes. The vice president was diagnosed next, followed by two more sisters. Besides the love, prayers, and caring that poured out of the chapter, the entire chapter showed its flexibility and willingness to serve wherever needed. It made for a memorable year that went as smoothly as if we were swans. To be like a swan, one glides effortlessly across the top of the water, while the feet paddle rapidly beneath the surface.

Innovative is to introduce something new. This is a concept that Chapter FB embraces. It is a new millennium, an age of technology and innovation, an integral part of any chapter. Nikki Isemann asked members to bring their laptops to share at a meeting. We logged in and proceeded to have a most informative meeting as we navigated our way around the P.E.O. websites. The recording secretary now sends emails with chapter updates attached. Her emails also remind us of "Sister Saturdays" or ask whether anyone needs a ride to a meeting. Many of our programs incorporate PowerPoints, computer slide shows of trips, or some other technology.

The quote "Beauty is in the eye of the beholder" could never be more truthful than when we look at our own chapter's scrapbook and get a new appreciation of the different qualities of our historic sisters. One of our sisters, years ago, secured the chapter scrapbook box with a black nylon stocking, which is still used today.

Now the secret: FB stands for "Fabulous Babes," innovated from last century's "Femme Beautiful."

CHAPTER FB'S ACTIVE MEMBERSHIP IS 40; TOTAL ENROLLMENT IS 176

★

CHAPTER FC SCOTTSBLUFF
ORGANIZED MARCH 13, 1947
BY BESSIE BUCHANAN

On March 13, 1947, twenty members of Chapter CD met at the home of Edith Emery. State President Rebecca P. Lee, State Organizer Bessie Buchanan, and State Historian Bernice K. Tillett were on hand to guide the organization of Scottsbluff's third chapter.

Charter members were: Ethel Green, sponsor; Kathryn VanDecar, president; Helen Haworth, vice president; Carrie Heldt, recording secretary; Lenore Everett, corresponding secretary; Dorothy Warrick, treasurer; Lucretia Green, chaplain; Florence Strachan, guard; Mary Jo McMillan, Lillian Jones, Carrie Hun, Margaret McKinley, LaVerne Benda, Hazel Fuller, Elizabeth Wright, May Halley, Ruth Hooper, Edith Patterson, Cora Pengelly, and Lois Schrock.

Three of our dimitting members were charter members of Chapter CD. They were Carrie Hunt, Lois Schrock, and Elizabeth Wright. Elizabeth became a charter member of a P.E.O. chapter for the third time, being on the charter roll of chapters CD, CP of Omaha, and FC.

Unable to be at the charter organization, three Chapter CD members were accepted by dimit at the first meeting.

Lucretia Green is our only surviving charter member. She was chaplain in the newly formed Chapter FC in 1947. She is an 80-year member and is 98 years old. Lucretia was honored during Founders' Day 2013. She played a remarkable piano solo for all the attendees to enjoy as they celebrated P.E.O. milestones.

Early programs were held on religions and foreign countries. Families were adopted in other countries and Chapter FC sent monthly packages and money. An early committee was philanthropic and post war. Later programs emphasized nature, arts, books, study, and society. Programs also covered education, women, personal talents, finance and a multitude of fascinating ideas.

Chapter FC celebrated their 50-year anniversary in 1997 and their 60th anniversary in 2007. We hosted the state convention in 1995 in Scottsbluff.

Chapter FC has maintained a flower plot at the Riverside Zoo for many years. In addition to donating to the P.E.O. projects every year, we also give to the library, youth shelters and Jeremiah House, Farm & Ranch Museum, the Backpack program for families in need, and the Cradle Book Catchers Project which gives books to newborns.

Our chapter is special, and we've been known as the friendly chapter from the beginning. Chapter FC has always had fun at all our events, but we do take it seriously and emphasize the qualities of faith, love, purity, justice, and truth.

Project recipients since 1995: 1995 Brooks Ehler, ELF loan; Brooke Simpson, P.E.O. Scholar Award nomination; 1996 Cara Haney, ELF loan; 2005 Shelly Leeper, ELF loan and Kierstin Aman, ELF loan; 2012 Maggie Skiles, PCE full grant to John Hopkins University; 2013 Maggie Skiles, ELF Loan.

We have also sponsored several women for P.E.O. Program for Continuing Education grants: Jillian Rutan, Kristin Avila, Katherine Eich, Rachel Griner, Laura Marie Gill, Mary Elizabeth Stephen, and Anne Elizabeth Walter.

Chapter FC has had many successful social meetings. We have annual BIL picnics in the summer. We have a Christmas ornament exchange and recently started a white elephant re-exchange. We have a Valentine's Day card exchange. We have a fairy godmother, secret pals, and a crystal ball to observe the Nebraska P.E.O. Home.

Our fundraisers include an annual bake and craft auction, which, in the spirit of fun and giving, is a special and successful event. We sell UV protective sunglasses, and it has been a steady and reliable long time fundraiser.

CHAPTER FC'S ACTIVE MEMBERSHIP IS 56; TOTAL ENROLLMENT IS 228

"If you don't know where you're going, any road will take you there."

-SUSAN SELLERS, P.E.O. INTERNATIONAL OFFICER
VISITING NEBRASKA

Chapter FD Omaha
Organized March 17, 1948
by Irene Van Brunt

Chapter FD organized with thirteen members—all of whom dimitted from Chapter CR—on March 17, 1948. They were Anne Armstrong, president; Nelle M. Ringer, vice president; Mary A. Irwin, recording secretary; Gretchen Daugherty, treasurer; Florence Dunham, chaplain; Dorothy Combs, guard; and Cordie Burdic, Jane Buntz, Maude Gates, Leita Hill, Grace Nixon and Mary Nixon. The newly formed chapter was honored with the presence of Past President of Nebraska State Chapter and Past Treasurer of Supreme Chapter Rose Owens, who was at the time serving as chairman of the Finance Committee of Supreme Chapter; Past State President Rebecca Lee; and state officers: President of Nebraska State Chapter Florence Stewart; Vice President Helen Riddell; and Organizer Irene Van Brunt, who presided at the organizational meeting.

Chapter FD continues to honor the principals of the Founders and organizing members, however times have changed. LeClare Steffen and Bev Karrer, both 50-year members, presented programs which remarked on the evolution of Chapter FD. Recognition of the 50-year anniversary of Chapter FD's organization was given at state convention in 1998 and marked in the chapter with a special celebration.

Our focus is on diversity of membership, talents of our members, recognition of our Founders with creative programs in January, philanthropies, and a loving concern for those who cannot be present at meetings. To accommodate many younger members we offer meetings as coffee or luncheon, innovative speakers including our own members on travel, missionary experiences and forgotten arts. To aid in increasing communication we initiated a Daisy newsletter, calling committee and Marguerite programs. Chapter FD's membership continues to be a warm and loving group of women who genuinely respect, honor and enjoy each other, thus creating a special bond. One of our primary goals is to always have a loving bridge that joins the fifty-year span of our ages.

Chapter FD is pleased that two members have served as officers of Nebraska State Chapter. In 1943-44, Mary Nixon served as president and in 1993, Beverley Karrer was installed as president, having previously served fourteen years on the Nebraska P.E.O. Home Board, as general chairman of Convention of Nebraska State Chapter in Omaha in 1987, and in the other offices of the Executive Board of Nebraska State Chapter.

Four members of Chapter FD have served in Omaha's P.E.O. Association as presidents: LeClare Steffen, Dorothy Nicholson, Beverley Karrer and Brenda Nicholson. Laura Reavis served as state PCE chairman in 2009-2010 and continues with active involvement.

Chapter FD has supported three Cottey College students as well as adopted a resident of the Nebraska P.E.O. Home. Through the philanthropies we supported two students, both of whom received scholarships. Chandler Pritchett received a PCE grant and Jill McGinnis received the P.E.O. STAR Scholarship. As a chapter we received the Above and Beyond Award for Bucks for Beds for Cottey College and were recognized as a 2011 Laureate Chapter.

Chapter FD's social functions have included outings to the Durham Museum, Botanical Garden, picnics at the lake, visits to the Nebraska P.E.O. Home, Christmas Special with our BILs and Canvas and Cabernet. In conjunction with Chapter FL a group of six foreign students from UNO presented a very interesting program on "Glad to Live in the USA." We are so blessed with our freedoms.

As fundraisers for Chapter FD we have Bed and Breakfast, Santa letters, recipe card and our ever popular Holiday Market in November. During Holiday Market bake sale items and holiday gifts are auctioned. This has always been very successful. With our fundraising efforts we are very proud to have placed in the top ten of per capita giving in the state.

CHAPTER FD'S ACTIVE MEMBERSHIP IS 39; TOTAL ENROLLMENT IS 161

Chapter FE Plainview
Organized April 10, 1948
by Irene Van Brunt

Late in the 19th Century, P.E.O. created a unique Sisterhood for women. During this time, many charming customs were observed by the original Founders. One of these customs was the creation of "button" or "memory" strings. The rules were simple: the buttons on the string had to be one-of-a-kind gifts or free trades between friends, family, or well-wishers. Unfinished strings were kept in "plain view" so as to encourage and inspire contributions to the string.

Chapter FE Nebraska started a memory string a mere seventy-nine years later.

The large "touch button" was first tied on FE's string on April 10, 1948, by Irene Van Brunt, organizer. The foundation buttons strung honor FE's Nell Fickling, president, Clara Wade, vice president, Helen Johnson, Lenita Sehnert, Edith Bush, recording secretary, Mildred Kraemer, corresponding secretary, Lu Jeffrey, treasurer, Ruth Gates, guard, Alfreda Chase, chaplain, Anna Peterson, Mabel Trump, Helen Webster, and Ruth Craig. Chapter EJ, Creighton, provided the second largest button by assistance with the organization.

Soon after organization, Chapter FE invited P.E.O. chapters from Pierce, Antelope, Cedar and Knox counties to a picnic named PACK (from initials of member counties). This tradition exists unbroken today, adding sixty-five one-of-a-kind button memories to FE's string, most recently a murder mystery evening.

On our button string are buttons representing members who have served both state and International Conventions. Three floral buttons represent International delegates and four themed buttons denote sisters who have served as guards at state and International Conventions.

Along our string at intervals over the sixty-five years are buttons of projects recipients sponsored by FE—a total of thirteen PCE, four ELF and one Nebraska Cottey Scholarship. A button is in reserve for the local girl to claim the Chapter FE Cottey Scholarship. Three special buttons remind us of three area girls who have attended Cottey College.

Chapter FE counts among the memories administration of two scholarships for local girls founded in memory of FE members: the Theresa A. Peterson Memorial, founded by her daughter, Ranae Marks, and the Marion Brunke Scholarship founded by her daughter, Judy Rada.

Along the string are button memories of accomplishments of pride for Chapter FE. One golden button denotes our status as a Golden Anniversary Chapter. A particularly spunky button is for sister Dorothy Kuhl, who joined P.E.O. in later life and served as president when well into her 80's. Yet another notes that Chapter FE existed for sixty years without repeating an elected president, a testament to the dedication of FE's devoted sisters.

Star buttons shine for two 50-year members, Dorthalie Kuhl and DoLores Larson, who we rejoiced with before they joined Chapter Eternal. Happily, another 50-year button, Ina Beth Engel's, was added in 2014. Most recently, buttons were added for having the fewest inactive members in Nebraska's chapters and meeting our challenges from state and International projects with funding from auctions, mint mold sales, bake sales, and clothing donations.

A curious set of buttons strung along the string are from our FE birthday salad luncheons, BIL parties, and social meetings, including a bone button from a visiting Mountain Man and a glass button from a visiting local gaffer.

Buttons of rare beauty have been donated by sisters who state that FE's most enduring quality is the loving, caring concern among our members who each have unique circumstances, ages, and interests.

Interspersed among all these memories are the FE member buttons. They number a total of 123 unique buttons, forty of which are active members.

CHAPTER FE'S ACTIVE MEMBERSHIP IS 40; TOTAL ENROLLMENT IS 123

CHAPTER FF LINCOLN
ORGANIZED APRIL 21, 1949
BY MAUDE WEAVER
MERGED WITH CHAPTER IA MARCH 27, 2011

Six officers of Nebraska State Chapter were present at the organization of Chapter FF, including Organizer Maude Weaver, President Helen Riddell, Corresponding Secretary and sponsor, Margaret McVicker. Also present were Lincoln Roundtable President Leora Benton, (ES), the presidents of the Lincoln chapters, and guests.

All charter members were dimits from sixteen chapters in five states. Chapter FF's charter members were Ruth Engel, president; Esther L. Pratt, vice president; Donna Jean Pratt, Marion Nisley Kline, Doris Childs, treasurer; Nellie Lippett Mercer, Anne Crosby Kline; Virginia Pierce Manrose, chaplain; Annalee Lawson Sheldon; Esther Lehman, guard; Patricia Wendelin; Esther Schwerdtfeger, recording secretary; June Riggins, Joan Castle Bauer, Helen Gardner Simpson, Barbara Engel Johnson, Mildred Ballou, Carol R. Stevenson Eaton, Margaret Hughes, Bina Day Jordan Gulbrandse and Arlene (Sue) Tidball.

Favorite traditions of Chapter FF have included a dinner for the March election meeting, gifts for brides and first babies, a Christmas cookie party, ornament exchanges, collecting hats and gloves for Willie Shafer's project in the elementary schools, a basket silent auction, and hostess reports after each meeting to keep up-to-date on our sisters. Many of the talented members have given chapter programs through music, education, inspiration, community activities and projects, humor and hobbies. The chapter also keeps scrapbooks of items of interest about our members.

Chapter FF has special interest in the beautiful Nebraska P.E.O. Home in Beatrice. Birthday cards and carnations are presented to each resident on her birthday from Chapter FF.

Chapter FF contributes to all P.E.O. projects and is proud to have helped several recipients of the P.E.O. Educational Loan Fund, P.E.O. Program for Continuing Education, Nebraska Cottey Scholarship, P.E.O. Scholar Award, and the P.E.O. International Peace Scholarship reach their educational goals. Chapter FF passes around the "project money container" at each meeting to assist with all the P.E.O. projects.

Members of Chapter FF have been guards, tellers and delegates for Conventions of International Chapter and many have had major involvement when Nebraska State Chapter has convened in Lincoln. The chapter has been involved with Lincoln Reciprocity Roundtable with hosting and by serving as officers, hosting girls from the College Group, and being involved with the Cottey Bus Trip.

Chapter FF cherishes their 50-year and 60-year members. Thirty-three sisters have joined Chapter Eternal.

Chapter FF was excited to merge with Chapter IA and to become Chapter FF-IA on March 27, 2011.

TOTAL ENROLLMENT 175

★

CHAPTER FF-IA LINCOLN
MERGED MARCH 27, 2011
BY MERIKAY BERG

Chapter FF-IA began as a newly formed chapter on March 27, 2011, with the Nebraska State Chapter officers, local chapter presidents and many guests present for the ceremony. Past State President Cindy Biehl was assigned to mentor and advise Chapters FF and IA through the merger process.

At the merger ceremony, each member of Chapter FF and Chapter IA received a daisy as she came into the meeting, and as roll call was read, each sister brought her daisy to the front of the room and put it into a vase creating a bouquet of sisters of Chapter FF-IA. Chapter FF-IA started with a membership of sixty-three resident and seven nonresident members. During our first year, two sisters transferred into Chapter FF-IA and one sister was reinstated. One sister entered Chapter Eternal and two sisters transferred out of Chapter FF-IA. It was exciting to receive our charter in June at the Convention of Nebraska State Chapter held in Lincoln. Quite a few of our members were recognized at the convention.

The process for the merger started with the two chapters getting together for socials and meetings, and to get to know each other. The chapters had a lot of common interests and ties among sisters which helped to start the merger process. Both chapters obtained the 2/3 vote of their active membership needed to proceed with the merger. Both chapters worked to write new bylaws, preserving traditions held by both chapters. The chapter adopted the motto "Fast Friends In Action," in tribute to its merged letters. The new officers were from both Chapter FF and IA, which completed the uniting of the sisters. The first officers of the merged chapter were Cheryl Peterson, president; Kim Hachiya, vice president; Karen Williamson

Conway, recording secretary; Nila Jacobson, corresponding secretary; Alysa Haack, treasurer; Nancy Larimer, chaplain; and Barbara Gaiter, guard.

Chapter FF-IA merger at St. Mark's United Methodist Church – March 2011

Chapter FF-IA contributes to all the P.E.O. philanthropies and members were excited that in our first year we successfully sponsored a recipient for the P.E.O. Program for Continuing Education. Our goal is to continue to look for deserving women for all of the projects. We are also working with some high school girls as they consider Cottey College.

There has already developed a spirit of harmony, enthusiasm, devotion and love among Chapter FF-IA's members, which will help to reach goals and ideals of the Sisterhood.

CHAPTER FF-IA'S ACTIVE MEMBERSHIP IS 51; TOTAL ENROLLMENT IS 129

★

CHAPTER FG LINCOLN
ORGANIZED APRIL 22, 1949
BY MAUDE WEAVER

Chapter FG was founded on April 22, 1949. Maude Weaver, former state president, was the organizer. Charter members, all by dimit, were: Elsie Rosenlof, Mary Jane Hughes Joy, Marguerite Metzger Hall, Clara Jean Doubt, Ruth Brown, Helen Kent, Agnes Meves, Elizabeth Wright, Gail Stephens, Marion Calder, Bonnalyn Rodwell, Alice Mae Prouty, Manette Wisman, Navada Howard, Elizabeth Ann Rosenlof DuTeau, Carolyn Platt Thornton, Evelyn Struble and Dorothy Weaver Morgan. The first president of Chapter FG was Elsie Rosenlof. Bertha Clark Hughes, whose daughter Mary Jane Joy was a charter member, was unable to attend because of illness. She did attend frequently in the coming years.

FG's 50th anniversary was celebrated on April 22, 1999, with a luncheon. Members were invited to wear hats and clothing of the '50s. Selected photos and clippings were on display. Each member received a small gift from the planning committee. Songs of the era were sung and our oldest charter member, Ruth Brown, shared her memories of that first meeting.

Member Beth Jantzen served as a Cottey College Area Chairman from 2009 to 2014. In 1965 Elsie Rosenlof served as president of Lincoln Reciprocity Roundtable, and in 1985 Nancy Fletcher served as Roundtable president.

Lorie McClain, DeEtte Wilhelm and Lyubov Berzin (from USSR) were awarded PCE grants, and Karen Harris received an ELF loan. We helped an IPS student, Doreen Moya, with a monetary gift to assist her while working on her doctoral degree.

We have written a booklet, "Sharing with Sisters," as a way for each member to know her sisters. A copy is given to our new sisters as an introduction to the chapter when they join.

Some of our money-making projects were garage sales, lipstick sales, flower deliveries on Valentine's day, raffling items from members returning from trips, bake sales, selling dish cloths crocheted by members, pin jackets and note cards.

We have enjoyed many social events. There were Christmas parties with BILs, an outing to the Lauritzen Gardens in Omaha where we also viewed member Valery Wachter's artwork on display, trips to the International Quilt Study Center, the Sunken Gardens and Rose Garden in Lincoln and the Lewis and Clark Interpretive Center and the Lied Lodge in Nebraska City. We also traveled to Beatrice where we enjoyed lunch at the Black Crow, a visit to the Nebraska P.E.O home and shopping at Cedar Creek Pottery. One of our biggest social events was the "Royal Wedding Tea Party" at Eastmont Towers with beautifully decorated tables and elegant linens, china, silver and flowers. P.E.O.s from the facility and guests were invited to attend and encouraged to wear lovely hats. The Bingorama event brought lots of fun and each year we have a lovely Christmas luncheon.

Chapter FG is a small but strong chapter. Our love and concern for each other and the fun we have together makes it very special. Along with our meetings we have Knit at Night and Lunch Bunch groups that meet for fellowship each month.

CHAPTER FG's ACTIVE MEMBERSHIP IS 36; TOTAL ENROLLMENT IS 167

When I stand before God at the end of my life,
I would hope that I would not have a single bit
of talent left, and could say,
'I used everything you gave me'.

-Erma Bombeck

Chapter FH Hastings
Organized May 18, 1949
by Maude Weaver

Sixty-four years ago, amid inclement weather, an electrical outage and rescued by the glow of candles, a new evening P.E.O. chapter for Hastings was formed. Chapter FH! State Organizer Maude Weaver, assisted by State President Helen Riddell, State Corresponding Secretary Margaret McVicker and State Treasurer Ruth Gellatly, made Chapter FH a reality. Helen Kucera, dimitting from Chapter DA, became the first president, with Genevieve Boslaugh, DA, vice president; Cecilia Gass, DA, recording secretary; Lura Hartquest, DA, corresponding secretary; Pauline Collier, DA, treasurer; Constance Steele, DA; chaplain, Mary Brower, DA, guard. Other dimitting members from Chapter DA were Peggy Lou Gedney, Marcella Krieger and Selma Moulton, along with Miriam Dearborn, I, Alice Grosshans, BH, and Katherine Mummey, W.

This year our remaining charter member Marcella Krieger celebrated ninety years young and seventy years in P.E.O. We have eight members who have enjoyed the Sisterhood for over fifty years.

We have adapted to changing lifestyles by moving our meeting time to 7:00 PM for social time, and our meetings start at 7:30 PM. With the advent of the electronic age, the use of the calling tree to remind members of meetings has morphed to emails on the computer.

Our yearbook, measuring 4 ½" by 6" is our lifeline to each year's meetings and activities. It provides vital information and tidbits—both past and present—on members, committee positions, P.E.O. projects and our standing rules and bylaws. We celebrate our birthday every year with a restaurant meal and treat before our meeting in May.

We thrive on our moneymaking projects. To name a few—cooking classes, remembering the good old days social, Halloween lunch, children's birthday party, most money in a sock, bridge outing, white elephant gifting and auctions. We also have a Brag Box at the end of each meeting that is never short on dollars. When our young members get married we share recipes and a recipe box and at Christmas we enjoy the cookie meeting and sharing an extra portion of them with our members unable to attend. We are also aware of the importance of being there for our members in times of need with a meal, and find our members are always eager to volunteer. Sharing time with a book club, sharing time with our ice cream social and sharing time with a BIL's "pot luck on the farm," all add an extra dimension to nurturing our relationships.

We strive to keep our membership thriving and find the initiation ceremony different without the necessity of memorization but still as meaningful. Using the "transfer" instead of "dimit" is definitely a great change in vocabulary.

In our support of the projects we have sponsored women for the P.E.O. Educational Loan Fund, Cottey College, P.E.O. Program for Continuing Education and the P.E.O. STAR Scholarship. We continue our own education every time we help them through the process. Holding a special place in our hearts are the Cottey College students that are our "Stars" and we enjoy sending special "thinking of you" packages.

The Nebraska P.E.O. Home in Beatrice is also on our list to send special packages to the residents through the year.

CHAPTER FH'S ACTIVE MEMBERSHIP IS 75; TOTAL ENROLLMENT IS 257

CHAPTER FI OMAHA
ORGANIZED APRIL 10, 1950 BY LUCY LIVINGSTON
MERGED WITH CHAPTER IK SEPTEMBER 10, 2006

The nineteen charter members of Chapter FI, dimitted from seven states, included Muriel Nye, president; Janice Smith, vice president; Betty Leeds, recording secretary; Janice Beck, corresponding secretary; Elizabeth Kidwell, treasurer; Vera Martin, chaplain; Betty Rubelman, guard; Betty Aenchbacher, Georgia Martin, Virginia Harris, Helen Kay, Elva Gillaspie, Winnie Mann, Ruth Minnick, Maude Dewey, Rosemary Hansen, Mary Martin, Ruth DeMay, and Peggy Lou Gedney. One would-be charter member, Frances Lloyd, was snowbound in Minnesota. Bertha Clark Hughes, then doing research on the Federal Bureau of Investigation, installed the officers as those of "Chapter FBI."

Chapters FI and IK merged to become Chapter FI-IK on September 10, 2006.

TOTAL ENROLLMENT 142

CHAPTER FI-IK OMAHA
MERGED SEPTEMBER 10, 2006
BY CINDY BIEHL

This marked a milestone for P.E.O. in Nebraska as these two former Chapters FI and IK were the first merged chapters. Charter members were: President Stephanie Maciejewski, Vice President Dicksy Mobley, Recording Secretary Alice Norris, Corresponding Secretary Susan Nelson, Treasurer Marty Magee, Chaplain Helen Mead, Guard Shirley Shepherd, Jean Ackerman, Cher Anderson, Janice Beck, Marcia Beck, Katie Casey, Linda Cumbee, Jan Daniels, Tammy Day, Bev DeBoer, Cyndi Ferguson, Rebecca Ford, Shawna Forsberg, Diane Fowler, Carol Gregory, Shelly Grote, Rosemary Hansen, Margaret Hold, Shelley Homa, Helen Howell, Kristin Huber, Ann Hustable-Scates, Lori King, Shari Kresha, Pam Knapp, Laura Lentz, Elizabeth McCluskey, Nancy Mangus, Michele Millard, Rondi Mitchell, Jamie Morse, Suzanne Raabe, Catilyn Ramey, Denise Reed, Peggy Rupprecht, Julia Russell, Cyndy Salzmann, Stacy Schutte, Wendy Smalley, Chris Stalder, Dawn Starr, Cheri Stevens, Beverly Swanson, Ellen Thompson, Rena Van Pelt, Donna Van Riper, Annette Volberding, Carol Walters, Lynn Weibel, and Pauline Wilcox.

Nonresident members were: Deanice Beck, Debi Meuret, Carrie Turpin, and Lisa Fahien-Uldrich. Since its organization, Chapter FI-IK has initiated five women. Several have been welcomed by transfer. Chapter FI-IK is active in inviting unaffiliiated members to meetings.

Chapter FI-IK—organized as an evening chapter—strives to meet the needs of chapter members. Its membership includes business, professional and retired women. The chapter has varied its meetings to include early supper meetings, Saturday morning coffees and social gatherings at restaurants.

Chapter FI-IK Merger Meeting

Chapter FI-IK gives active support to P.E.O. projects and has sponsored women and recipients of both the P.E.O. Educational Loan Fund and the P.E.O. Program for Continuing Education.

Ways and Means projects have included several shopping trips to retail stores that give the chapter a percentage of the proceeds and used book, CD, and movie sales.

All members of FI-IK have given service to P.E.O. by attending meetings and supporting chapter programs and activities.

Chapter FI-IK celebrates its birthday each year with a potluck meal and birthday cake. The chapter's history is shared with the members at that time.

CHAPTER FI-IK'S ACTIVE MEMBERSHIP IS 41; TOTAL ENROLLMENT IS 126

CHAPTER FJ COLUMBUS
ORGANIZED APRIL 19, 1950
BY LUCY LIVINGSTON

Growth for P.E.O. in Columbus was made possible when thirteen sisters from Chapter CH organized Chapter FJ. Metta Neumarker, a charter member of CH, became the sponsor and the organizational meeting was held in her home.

Charter members were Rosalie Clement, president; Laurel Johnson, vice president; Gretchen Ellefson, recording secretary; Betty Bunting, corresponding secretary; Joyce Schultz, treasurer; Fyanna Brooks, chaplain; Lois Loomis, guard; Marie Boerio, Wilma Carlson, Martha Fish, Frances Jacobsen, Irene Mulick, and Emma Magnusson.

There are many memories of this era. Active membership and attending membership has grown especially after the creation of a chapter membership committee in 2004 and with the dedication of its various chairmen and committee members.

Several activities which began in later years have helped membership. In 2007 the chapter started monthly birthday parties which have helped members become better acquainted outside of regular chapter meetings. Also, our chapter started a 'Brag Box" where for a mere twenty-five cents or whatever a member wants to contribute she shares with the attending members what has been happening in her life. Besides being a good sharing tool, the chapter treasury benefits too. Over a period of two or three years each member was asked to share their history at a chapter meeting. This sharing wasn't the program but still added to the meetings and to the knowledge of a sister.

Chapter FJ joins with other Columbus chapters, HA and CH, for an annual "Sisters' Night Out." The social outing has included dinners, golf, music, bridge, and a tour of an historical building which earlier housed a local "speakeasy" called the Bunny Club.

These outings are well attended and the members from the three local chapters mix, share ideas and friendships.

Another popular activity sponsored by the three local chapters is a bridge marathon where all the money raised by playing partners joining the marathon is given to a woman student attending Central Community College at Platte. At the end of the marathon season, the scholarship recipient addresses the group at the last card party.

During this era there have been a variety of fundraisers such as a garage sale, silent auctions for gift baskets, boisterous auctions for our crafts and baked goods, making and selling a cookbook, passing the 'hat', literally a golf hat. The monies raised have been divided among the P.E.O. projects and the Nebraska P.E.O. Home in Beatrice. Once a brick bank was passed for the P.E.O. Home Endowment.

Chapter FJ has revived the BIL socials, established a technology committee, and has adopted email notification of meetings.

Our chapter has been active in two state conventions: York in 2000 and Columbus in 2013.

The majority of meetings are held in members' homes but with a larger attending membership several host members have elected to host at various churches and the community rooms of retirement centers. We still have evening meetings and one day meeting.

There have been many interesting programs and meetings but several stand out: a Founders' Day celebration, which was written by Helen Galley in the 1950's, was presented as a radio program. A memorable meeting was the hosting of the state representative and being one robe short for the exemplification so the hostess found a white linen tablecloth and it served as the president's robe. During this time one program was a road trip to Beatrice to tour the Nebraska P.E.O. Home. FJ has been a strong supporter of the P.E.O. projects. During this time we have nominated and supported five recipients of loans and grants.

Our chapter through this era has had many members recognized for long term membership: Lois Loomis, Ruth Sherfey and Francis Jacobsen received 60-year membership recognition and Gretchen Ellefson, Wilma Floyd, Dorothy Grosz, Marie Kuper, Charlotte Moran, Alice Mae Nelson, Betty Reed, and Roberta

Saalfeld received 50-year membership recognition. Our final three chapter charter members joined Chapter Eternal during this interval: Francis Jacobsen, Gretchen Ellefson, and Lois Loomis. Through the leadership and examples set by these members, Chapter FJ has been blessed.

CHAPTER FJ'S ACTIVE MEMBERSHIP IS 56; TOTAL ENROLLMENT IS 232

CHAPTER FK OMAHA
ORGANIZED JANUARY 30, 1951
BY MARGARET MCVICKER

Chapter FK was founded January 30, 1951, in Omaha. Eleven members dimitted from the "mother chapter" M: Louise Moore, president; Leola McKie, Frances Key, Alma Jensen, Irene Savidge, Ernestine Bergquist, Edythe Moore, Catherine Gleason, Vesta Watkins, Lucille Clow, and Edna Cherry. There were also three members from other chapters: Helen Latta, CG, Nancy Mines Peter, AZ, and Marolyn Merchant, V. Our most recognized name is Frances Key who entered Chapter Eternal December 12, 1996. She not only served as president of our chapter but also president of Nebraska State Chapter in 1979-80. Frances Key was a drama teacher at Central High School in Omaha, director of the Omaha Community Playhouse, and author of many P.E.O. plays and skits through the years. One of her plays, "*A Star in the Window,*" was performed at the Centennial Convention in Des Moines, Iowa.

Our members have served their community in various ways. They provide interesting and timely programs and outings ranging from tours of local businesses to matters of healthcare.

As a rule we have ten to thirteen members in attendance monthly. We are trying to stay current and care for our community and each other.

CHAPTER FK'S ACTIVE MEMBERSHIP IS 35; TOTAL ENROLLMENT IS 122

CHAPTER FL OMAHA
ORGANIZED FEBRUARY 13, 1951
BY MARGARET MCVICKER

Chapter FL was organized February 13, 1951, by Margaret McVicker, state organizer. The meeting was held at the home of Lyle Eilers. Bertha Clark Hughes, past president of Supreme Chapter attended, along with officers of Nebraska State Chapter, Irene Van Brunt of Omaha, president; Lucy Livingston of Fairbury, second vice president; Ruth Gellatly of Hastings, recording secretary; and Dorothy Smithberger of Stanton, corresponding secretary. Charter officers were Eleanor Danielson, president; Myrtle Carey, vice president; Helen Kingsbury, recording secretary; Lyle Eilers, corresponding secretary; Alma Welk, treasurer; Ruth Ekwall, chaplain; and Margaret Cortelyou, guard. Other members were Wilma Abart, Verna Binkerd, Winifred Froyd, Bertha Hoffman, Gladys Husted, Stina Johnson, Marjorie Johnson, Wilma Jones, Lyle Keeling, Mary Nomland, Mildred Propst, Mary Louise Rasmussen, Lillie Steinbaugh and Mina Dawson.

One of Chapter FL's charter members, Helen Kingsbury, was the originator of a little figure called "Dottey Cottey." "Dottey" was originally drawn to illustrate the student newspaper of Cottey College and later became the model for ceramic dolls made by Helen.

On our golden 50th anniversary, February 13, 2001, charter members Lyle Keeling attended, and Wilma Jones sent taped greetings. The minutes of Chapter FL's organization were read as part of the program. We received a lovely white gavel with an inscribed gold band from Caroline Hosier.

Our 50-year members are: Carol M. Brown, Sally Goodman, Ann Rutherford, Charlene Srb, and Diane Weitz. Our 60-year member is Carrie Humphry.

Since 1979, Chapter FL has actively sought and sponsored more than twelve P.E.O. Educational Loan Fund recipients. We have sponsored three young women for the P.E.O. Program for Continuing Education. In 2011, for the first time Chapter FL was able to sponsor a P.E.O. International Peace Scholarship recipient from Mongolia with a $500 Designated Award. We have met our pledge of $3,000 to the "Defining Moment Campaign" for Cottey College. We continue to support the Nebraska P.E.O. Home and enjoy giving special gifts to the residents at Christmas.

Chapter FL - 2005

Starting in 2000, our annual fall fundraiser has been the "Santa Letter Project." Personalized letters, printed on Christmas stationery, were mailed to children eager to hear how Santa was preparing for his visit. In 2013, the spring fundraiser was entitled "Plant Your Roots with P.E.O." Each sister received a packet of seeds with an invitation to contribute. Also, we enrich our treasury with a $1-per-Brag donation at each meeting and offer delicious luncheon-tested recipes duplicated and sold for 25 cents. Recent social events have included a luncheon at Art Chicks in Louisville; a BIL event with miniature golf and dinner; a tour of the Institute for Culinary Arts at Metropolitan Community College and lunch. Our 2012 holiday party at the Champions Run Country Club was a luncheon shared with Omaha Chapter FD. Chapter FL hosted a discussion with six young women who are students at the University of Nebraska at Omaha. They were from Africa, Bangladesh, China, Iran, Brazil and Kazakhstan.

Other social events have included a behind-the-scenes tour of Nebraska's Wildlife Safari Park with lunch at Mahoney State Park; a book discussion and tour at Joslyn Art Museum; a tour of the Lauritzen Gardens; a BIL party and pontoon boat ride at the lakefront home of Judy Miller; and a trip to Beatrice to visit with the Nebraska P.E.O. Home residents.

Cara Humphry Brown was initiated at a special meeting on August 31, 2012. Cara's mother, Cheri Humphry, was chapter president. Cara's grandmother, Carrie Humphry, has served as chapter president and as Omaha P.E.O. Reciprocity Association president. Carrie celebrated her 100th birthday on January 18, 2013.

Chapter FL was saddened when our only graduate of Cottey College, Marybel Voss, entered Chapter Eternal May 31, 2012. Marybel had been a P.E.O. since 1932.

In the 2001 July-August issue of The P.E.O. Record, Esther Kauffman was acknowledged when a new building at the University of Nebraska-Lincoln campus, the Kauffman Center, was named in her honor. In the 2001 January-February issue, Donna Gresham was highlighted in a feature story about china painting. In the 2005 July-August issue Carol Russell was in the "P.E.O. in the Spotlight" article when she received the International Volunteer Fundraiser of the Year award from the Association of Fundraising Professionals.

Chapter FL - 2012

Virginia Stuart's picture and biography were displayed at the state convention in 1999 as our chapter's Outstanding Woman for her participation as co-founder of Lauritzen Gardens. Joan Hackett and her husband opened their home to a refugee family from Bosnia, for which the Hacketts received the 2006 Aksarben Omaha World-Herald Good Neighbor Award.

We are pleased to have shared our talents with the Omaha P.E.O Reciprocity Association. At the 2008 Nebraska State Convention in Omaha, we hosted the "Ask Me" desk. Chapter FL was listed in the program as a successful "We Imagined—We Achieved" chapter.

In reading the minutes from our charter meeting, mention was made that Chapter FL sisters are truly "Forever Loving." That quality has permeated this chapter for sixty-three years, and without exception, our members exemplify this theme along with their commitment to our P.E.O. ideals.

CHAPTER FL'S ACTIVE MEMBERSHIP IS 51; TOTAL ENROLLMENT IS 194

★

CHAPTER FM BEATRICE
ORGANIZED MARCH 17, 1951
BY MARGARET MCVICKER

Chapter FM, the second chapter in Beatrice, was organized at the Nebraska P.E.O. Home with the assistance of Chapter Z. Charter members were: Leah Drishaus from Chapter Z, president; Winona Seng, Z; May Wheeling, Z; Mary A. Irwin, FD, vice president; Vivian Harman, Z, recording secretary; Pearl Rice, Q; Florence W. Burns, AN, Texas; Mildred Barber, Z, corresponding secretary; Bertha Meshier, AT; Phyllis Chamberlin, Z, guard; Frances Goble, Z; Beth Kline, Z; Mildred Bussell, Z; Mildred Decker, Z; treasurer; Janet Bagby, Z, chaplain; Genevieve L. Dunlap, Z; Grace Souther, Z; Rhea L. Pickett, Z; and Loretta Metcalf, Z.

Guests of honor included Nebraska State Chapter President Irene Van Brunt; Nebraska State Chapter Second Vice President Lucy Livingston; Past President of Supreme Chapter Bertha Clark Hughes; Rose Owens; Mae Bond and Superintendent Nettie Brown of the Nebraska P.E.O. Home. The Happy Hour Club of the Nebraska P.E.O. Home honored the new chapter with a coffee, serving more than eighty guests who arrived under hazardous ice-storm conditions. Special gifts were the $25 charter fee and initiatory tablecloth from Chapter Z, and a history book from Chapter Q, Wymore.

Cherished traditions include the annual anniversary celebration with a dinner and cake for Founders' Day with Chapter Z, and the December meeting held at the Nebraska P.E.O. Home with Christmas festivities and the residents as guests. The chapter presents a pin guard to the retiring president and 50-year members, and the placing of flowers at the grave site to remember our sisters on Memorial Day. Pauline Spence was initiated into Chapter M, Wyoming, sixty-nine years ago and has been a member of FM for sixty-four years.

At the 60th birthday celebration the first president's letter was read. Since 2008 Chapter FM and Chapter Z have granted a $500 scholarship to a Beatrice High School graduating student.

In 2004 Linda Bierman served as secretary/treasurer for Reciprocity Group VIII and later was president in 2007.

The sisters in Chapter FM are proud that its membership continues to grow, is diverse in age, interests and careers. Its members have varied and outstanding talents and personalities to enrich the Sisterhood, and are involved in the community and church. Members give of their time to help with Meals on Wheels, summer reading programs at the Beatrice Public Library, donate items and financial assistance to the

Hope Crisis Center and Beatrice Community Food Pantry. Chapter FM has always pursued the ideals of the Sisterhood, and their main support has been given to the P.E.O. projects and the Nebraska P.E.O. Home. Since the Home is in our hometown, Chapter FM hosts summer coffees on the verandah and tours the lovely flower gardens, hosts Valentines parties, delivers May baskets, trick or treat at Halloween, pajama parties and Christmas caroling. Most Friday afternoons several members and their young children entertain the ladies by playing bingo.

The membership of Chapter FM is proud of their constant involvement in sponsoring women to continue their education. Kelley Perkins was a recipient of the P.E.O. Educational Loan Fund in 1996 and 2005, Dana Whaley in 2002 and Kathryn Claassen in 2004. Connie Rock was the recipient of the P.E.O. Scholar Award in 1997 as was Carrie Riha in 2005.

Our socials have great participation, and have included a wine tasting event and visiting the Schilling Bridge Winery. Sisters wearing Halloween costumes made for a fun time at the James Arthur Vineyard. Tours included Sunny Slopes organic farm, Erv Dixon's Pottery, and the Filley Stone Barn all near Beatrice. Yesterday's Lady was an entertaining social as the owner gave a presentation on her collection of vintage clothing and spoke of the haunted building in which she lives in downtown Beatrice. Summer tea parties, brown bag luncheons, and a box social where each sister brought a box lunch which was auctioned off to lively bidding were all well attended. Sisters enjoyed the Farmer's Market in Lincoln, a tour of the Governor's Mansion, and the International Quilt Gallery in Lincoln.

Fundraisers over the years have been varied and successful. Star Tax Plan was implemented in the 1990's, auction of crafts and food items, "Sand Art Brownies" made by the sisters, and a "No Bake" bake sale where each sister donated $10 were ideas to raise the needed funds. A sister made postcards from her photos, money in a box for not wearing her P.E.O. pin, a raffle and whoever won the prize brought a gift to the next meeting and the very successful garage sales where sisters donated the items for sale.

Chapter FM is proud of our growth, devotion to our sisters, and involvement in the community of Beatrice.

CHAPTER FM'S ACTIVE MEMBERSHIP IS 71; TOTAL ENROLLMENT IS 245

★

CHAPTER FN KEARNEY
ORGANIZED APRIL 17, 1951
BY RUTH GELLATLY

Chapter FN was organized at the Kearney Country Club April 17, 1951. Fourteen P.E.O.s from Chapter EG, Kearney, and three from other chapters launched this new chapter with the gracious assistance of five Nebraska State Chapter officers and a past state president.

The first seventeen "Friendly Number" FN members were: Martha Jensen, president; Genevieve Welch, vice president; Virginia Lancaster, recording secretary; Helen Wallace, corresponding secretary; Helen Marshall, treasurer; Geraldine Neustrom, chaplain; Isabel Kruse, guard; Lucile Cary, Amelia Edwards, Mary Elliott, Elizabeth Elliott, Edith Gunlicks, Bess Grantham, Edith Geisler, Stella Hill, Jeanette Nye, and Emma Jane Wilder.

A quote from a past president's letter says, "Chapter FN was started from a P.E.O. spark in 1951. That spark has never died and glows a warm spirit of ember love from meeting to meeting and sister to sister."

On the chapter's 25th anniversary in April 1976 they met at the Kearney Country Club to share memories of the past. On the Chapter's 50th anniversary in April 2001, they again met at the Kearney Country Club.

Presently, the chapter boasts of one 76-year member, Helen Marshall; one 71-year member, Emma Jane Wilder; and nine 50-year plus members: Audrey Nelson (66), Barbara Bush (62), Wilma Wolford (62), Jo Erickson (61), Verna Barney (55), Kari Anderson (54), Joan Hartman (54), Emily State (53) and Artie Hobbs (50). Four young women have received loans from the P.E.O. Educational Loan Fund and grants from the P.E.O. Program for Continuing Education under Chapter FN's sponsorship. Chapter FN was also a sponsor for a P.E.O. STAR Scholarship recipient in its inaugural year.

Chapter FN properly supports all the P.E.O. projects and the Nebraska P.E.O. Home. Many gifts have been given to the Home by Chapter FN sisters, including a garden fountain from Lucile Cary in memory of Jeanette Nye; a knee-hole desk on casters and a large print Bible from Chapter FN; and knitted bed socks from Dorothy Richards. Also, the chapter has held meetings at the Home as well.

The chapter's annual basket auction notably showcases chapter talents and has increased gifts to the projects. In 1952, FN was able to give only $5 to the Home. However, in 2013, the auction yielded $1,500 to share with all of the projects.

At holiday time, FN members are quite generous with their gifts, with both monetary and donated goods provided to struggling families in the community. Gifts given to Chapter FN by chapter members are many, including: organizing a chapter portrait, a podium and gavel block for the president's use, small quilts and knitted sweaters for money-making raffles, a beautiful, hand-made table cover for initiations, and star necklaces that are worn for initiations along with new robes.

Many hours were spent by Chapter FN members as they helped with registration for the 2007 Nebraska State Chapter Convention held in Kearney. Chapter FN was also honored with sending a delegate to the 2007 International Convention held in Minneapolis, Minnesota.

Chapter FN is a special group of multi-talented women. There are writers, actors, artists, musicians, honors recipients, youngsters, seniors and in-betweens, humorists, serious ones and those who are quietly "the wind beneath our wings." The members are also mothers, grandmothers, career women and can fit in any other niche one might name.

Chapter FN has recognized the changes in the role of women in today's society and is striving to meet the needs of its membership in the face of these changes. Attempts include meeting year-round in the evenings, encouraging lateral transfers, and having those willing to serve as chapter president for consecutive terms. Chapter FN is definitely "alive and well" in 2013.

CHAPTER FN'S ACTIVE MEMBERSHIP IS 60; TOTAL ENROLLMENT IS 283

*Start where you are, use what you have,
do what you can.*
-Arthur Ashe

Chapter FO Hay Springs
Organized April 24, 1952
by Ruth Gellatly

We have an amazing chapter! I know everyone feels that way about their own, but I believe ours is truly special. In this small community in the northwest corner of Nebraska we are a close-knit group, truly devoted to the support of our projects and to each other. Each member is equally and vitally important in making our group a success. We rely on and trust each other. With this solid foundation of support we empower women, embrace change and energize our chapter.

In 1950, interest in P.E.O. was high in Hay Springs, but a chapter could not be organized until the town's population reached one thousand. Chapter FO finally was organized with charter members including Ella Hagedorn, recording secretary; Nelle Johnston, vice president; Irene Peck; Elvah Molzahn, treasurer; Pearl Riley; Velma Larson; Helen Marshall; Helen M. Gilmore, corresponding secretary; Elinor Jentges; Gladys Hardin; May DeCastro; Stella Powles; Minnie Horn, guard; Edna Chamberlin; Ethel Morgan; and from Chapter DW, Rushville, Jane Horn, president; and Dora Marcy, chaplain. Claire M. Moody was the first initiate after the chapter was organized.

We continue some of the original traditions begun by our founding sisters such as Christmas dinners, which now include White Elephant exchanges, annual observance of Founders' Day and BIL suppers.

Our programs continue to be mainly given by our own sisters. They are entertaining, educational, interesting and inspiring. The hidden talents of our sisters continue to shine.

We have held various fundraisers, notably bakeless bake sales, monthly filled basket auctions, garage sales, catered meals, a "Unique Antique" fashion show, and cookbooks. Our most recent success was an evening of "Wedded Bliss & Tattle Tales" game show versions during our town's Hay Springs Friendly Festival with homemade concessions.

One of our great enjoyments is our correspondence with a Cottey College adoptee and our support of the college with our monetary donations. We encourage local girls to take the Cottey College Bus Tour each year.

We hold at least two socials a year which range from BIL /family picnics to game nights, attending Fort Robinson Play House, entering our town's local Soup Cook Off, movie parties, quilt shows, stained glass workshop, and even touring a local pumpkin patch.

We have sponsored four girls for the P.E.O. STAR Scholarship, as well as one P.E.O. Scholar Award candidate, six PCE grants and four ELF loan recipients since 1995. We have begun giving a local high school senior girl a scholarship, and look forward to continuing this each year.

From our chapter, Patsy Bridge served on the Nebraska P.E.O. Home Board and Kim Marcy served as chairman of IPS. In 2001, we joined with Highway 20 chapters to sponsor an IPS applicant.

We voted in 2010 to have an initiation team, which has worked so well because, best of all we are growing! To each new sister we assign a twin P.E.O. sister who is there for any questions and meeting reminders.

Chapter FO donates to our local Good Neighbor Center. Many of us adopt residents at a local nursing home. We have made "Bags of Love" for children taken from meth homes and have helped a needy family with a welcomed food box.

In 2003 members from Chapter FO helped our neighboring town of Hemingford begin their chapter. That was a very special time.

We have a very active and close sisterhood which varies in age from 20's to 80's among thirty-eight active members. This span in our ages just seems to enhance our meetings with love and laughter. I must say I have never attended a meeting where I haven't laughed, shared at least one hug, and of course, staying with true P.E.O. sisterhood, have never left hungry.

CHAPTER FO'S ACTIVE MEMBERSHIP IS 41; TOTAL ENROLLMENT IS 111

★

CHAPTER FP CHADRON
ORGANIZED JULY 8, 1952
BY RUTH GELLATLY

Chapter FP was organized on July 8, 1952, by Ruth Gellatly with ten members dimitting from Chapter BL to form an afternoon chapter; there were five initiates. Charter members were Dixie (Ruth) Ruff, president; Hazel Hays, vice president; Eunice Hoevet, recording secretary; Vera Otteman, treasurer; Vera Lee Hamer, corresponding secretary; Claire Reed, guard; Rhoda Rouse, Natalie Stockfleth, Ruby Armstrong and Jeanette Zink. Initiates included Hildred Brewer, Bernice Carroll, Alice S. Moeller, chaplain, Margaret Couch and Margaret Lucke.

White satin robes were made for the officers and a four-foot gold satin star centered with the letters P.E.O. was made and used at the 1981 Nebraska State Convention in Chadron and when Chapter FP or Chapter BL host the Panhandle Reciprocity Group. Our robes were replaced in 2007. In 1988 the chapter began having evening meetings in order to accommodate the members who worked in the afternoons. Also the chapter meets year around, again to accommodate members. Three of the fifteen meetings during the year are social meetings and at least twice a year the chapter meets with Chapter BL. Chapter FP's active membership has remained constant and diverse.

Chapter FP has honored five members as 50-year members: Bessie Helzer in 1976, Eunice Hoevet in 1994, Margaret Larson and Carolyn Thackam in 2004 and Marlene Myers in 2011.

Over the years, BIL parties included skits and stunts for their initiations, family picnics, attendance at the Post Playhouse, and breakfasts and dinners to introduce BILs to each other, as well as to members.

Early money-making projects have included rummage sales, food sales and an "Iced Tea and Ginger Snap" booth when Chadron celebrated its Jubilee Year. Other fundraising for the P.E.O. projects has included the sale of bean soup mix, the sale of vanilla, a Brag Box, a Recipe Box, birthday offerings and at one time three members hosted bed and breakfast P.E.O. guests and their families. Recent fundraisers include garage sales, silent auctions, filling baby socks with coins and a family "Picnic for the Projects" where members pay to play board games and golf.

Most years we sponsored a student(s) for scholarships or grants. These women have become medical technologists and doctors and some earned education or administrative degrees. It was decided to grant a small award to girls we submitted for the P.E.O. STAR Scholarship if they did not receive the scholarship. Each year we support our seven projects as well as the Nebraska P.E.O. Home.

P.E.O. daughters Judy and Nancy Larson attended Cottey College and helped stimulate interest in the college. Yearly, members visit with high school women about attending the college.

Special events for Chapter FP have included hosting the first Panhandle Reciprocity meeting in 1970 where Supreme Chapter President Irene Ken from Wyoming was an honored guest, observing the 40th Anniversary in 1992 with Nebraska State Chapter President Mary Owens and three charter members in attendance; and hosting the 1981 Nebraska State Chapter Convention in Chadron with Mary Ruth Wilson as president. Chapter FP's Elva Bartels served as chairman of the tellers for the 1991 Convention of International Chapter in Omaha. Chapter FP was especially happy to have Beverly Karrer, president of Nebraska State Chapter in 1993, attend the Panhandle Reciprocity Group in Chadron that year. Our Reciprocity Group III helped with the 1995 and 2009 Nebraska State Chapter Conventions in Scottsbluff. Members served as guards, produced table decorations and helped plan entertainment. We celebrated our 50th anniversary in 2002 and the 60th anniversary in 2013.

Annually, Chapter FP meets with Chapter BL for Founders' Day programs and the reports from state convention and in the past for reports of International Conventions. Our creative Membership Committee presents reports at most meetings and plans small group activities. Chadron State College student P.E.O.s are invited to attend our meetings.

Chapter FP members have been active in community service and we are proud to share the honors awarded to our members and their families. A large chapter scrapbook stores pictures and clippings which tell their stories. P.E.O. markers are placed on the graves of members and flowers decorate them each Memorial Day. Our chapter displays loving concern in many ways for its members and families.

CHAPTER FP'S ACTIVE MEMBERSHIP IS 36; TOTAL ENROLLMENT IS 158

★

CHAPTER FQ LINCOLN
ORGANIZED JANUARY 13, 1953
BY RUTH GELLATLY

The charter members of Chapter FQ, all dimitted, were: Barbara Allen, AP, South Dakota; Jane Bauder, DA; Lucile Davidson, DA; Mary Dovel, DB; Florence Dunham, FD, president; Ruth Frahm, EO; Leigh Ganzel Harding, GE, Missouri, vice president; Vera C. Martin, FI, recording secretary; Marjorie Peterson, EM; Glaideth Pfeiffer, DI, chaplain; Eloise Pool, BT; Betty Rohde, CQ, treasurer; Florence Rowley, G, guard; Marjorie Scofield, CQ, corresponding secretary; Florence Spearman, W; Emma Jane Wilder, FN; Elsa Williams, CC; Janet Williams, BG.

Florence Dunham selected the charter list since each member already had the key to the spirit of P.E.O. At our organization on January 17, 1953, at the Orthopedic Nurses' Home, guests included state officers, three past state presidents, Lincoln Reciprocity Roundtable officers, Lincoln chapter presidents and friends. Ruth Gellatly, second vice president of Nebraska State Chapter, presided in the absence of Dorothy Smithberger, organizer (quarantined when her daughter developed scarlet fever) with the help of Florence Davis and Eva Curtiss, past state presidents plus a welcome by Bertha Clark Hughes. These state officers gave us the name of "Fairy Queens." We have lived up to our name by having many "Fairies" who have helped our own members as well as countless others in the community. "Queens" have served as members and officers not only for our chapter, but for Roundtable and for Nebraska State Chapter, as well as many other organizations that support very worthwhile philanthropic projects. Roundtable presidents include Marian Waldron in 1964, and Betty Kirby in 2000.

Our sisters have represented a wide variety of professions and ways of life. The many teachers have made differences in countless numbers of youth here and wherever they taught. We have pharmacists, librarians, bankers, accountants, audiologists, ministers, public defender, hospital supervisor, department store buyer, reporter, airline hostess, homemaker, plus many other chosen paths. Recognition of many sisters has been well earned by serving on national boards and publications such as *Who's Who in American Teachers*. Our sisters' travels have taken them all over the world and we have been able to be educated about these places.

Our chapter has: provided clothing and supplies to families in desperate need, adopted a men's ward at the State Hospital and a girl's cottage at White Hall, and now concentrate on P.E.O. projects.

We have supported IPS as well as Cottey students, plus hosting the UNL students who are P.E.O.s. We have sponsored students through ELF and the P.E.O. Program for Continuing Education and other scholarships and loans. We have taken part in challenges from Cottey College and the Nebraska P.E.O. Home in Beatrice. Our visits to the Home are a continuing delight to us since we meet the residents and see OUR Home. We have enjoyed sending birthday cards to each of the residents as well as providing gift sacks during our visits.

All of these connections have helped each of us to see the delight P.E.O. can bring to our lives.

CHAPTER FQ'S ACTIVE MEMBERSHIP IS 42; TOTAL ENROLLMENT IS 147

★

CHAPTER FR SIDNEY
ORGANIZED DECEMBER 7, 1953
BY FLORA STEVENS

At the organization of Chapter FR, lovingly sponsored by Chapter BO, Chapter BO provided eleven of the fourteen charter members in Sidney, Nebraska. Charter members included Isabel Kokjer and Sylvia Weber who were credited with particular dedication and enthusiasm for organizing Chapter FR. Other charter members were Dorothy Castner, Dorothy Weymouth, Carrie Wise, Ruth Cook, Jean Siebken, Betty Knicely, Patricia Killion, Elizabeth Jones, Jane Powell, Kathryn Wait, Helen Anderson and Sally Lowe. Daisy Uptegrove was also instrumental in the organization of FR although she was taken in by dimit a week after the organization. Nebraska State Organizer Flora Stevens presided and Dorothy Castner served as the first president of Chapter FR.

The decades of the 50s and 60s brought a steady growth in chapter membership, and during this time three students were sponsored for loans from ELF. Joint observation of Founders' Day with Chapter BO has continued for the past sixty years. In 1961 Betty Knicely served as a delegate to the Supreme Chapter Convention and in 1967 the chapter served as hostess for the Nebraska State Convention in Sidney.

During the 70s, Willie Fankhauser began service on the Panhandle Reciprocity Group board; Dorothy Nelson was a delegate to Supreme Convention in Detroit. Chapter FR conducted the Memorial Hour for the Reciprocity meeting in Sidney and in 1976 the annual Christmas auction began and has continued every year since that time. The annual Christmas auctions have provided funds for P.E.O. projects for the past twenty years and have become quite a lively event for the chapter.

It was in this era that Lee Ellen Matzke became the first woman mayor of Sidney, Nebraska.

The 1980's brought a flurry of special occasions to celebrate along with a deepened commitment to both ongoing and special P.E.O projects. The chapter acquired robes for officers; became a Cottey Golden Anniversary Chapter; sponsored three more women for loans from ELF; contributed to the Nebraska P.E.O Home and IPS funds and supported the Cottey College Bus Trip with both contributions and interested young women. Member Carrie Balfour attended Cottey College in 1952-53. A special event was the initiation of the fifth-generation P.E.O. daughter of Sue Preston.

Chapter FR President's Tea honoring Rosella Mehling

Chapter FR began the 90s by joining with Chapter BO to provide the signs for the Convention of International Chapter in Omaha in 1991. Chapter FR gave a monetary gift to a new Lincoln chapter and three FR daughters have been active in the organization of other new Nebraska chapters. Willy Lowe was honored as a 55-year member in 1993 and Arlene Holecheck became Reciprocity Group treasurer.

In 1996 Willie Fankhauser was honored as the State Regent of Daughters of the American Revolution.

Carol Mason served as a delegate to the 1997 Convention of International Chapter held in Seattle. Also in 1997, Lee Ellen Matzke was elected to the Board of Trustees of Nebraska State Colleges.

When the state convention was held in Kimball in 1988, Rosella Mehling began her commitment to Nebraska State Chapter with her election as treasurer. Rosella served in all of the offices of the executive board and served as president in 1994-95. Chapter FR is proud of Rosella's accomplishments at this level of our P.E.O. history. Rosella has attended every Convention of International Chapter from 1989 to 2013.

Chapter FR Sidney 50- and 60- year members. Lois Thayer, Dorothy Nelson, Lee Ellen Matzke, 50-year members, with Diane Merritt and Carrie Balfour, 60-year members.

Fifty-year members include Dorothy Nelson (2006), Lee Ellen Matzke (2007), and Arlene Holechek (2012). Diane Merritt was recognized and honored as our 60-year member in 2012 and Carrie Balfour became a 60-year member in 2013.

In 2011 Chapters BO and FR teamed up for another special project to raise money for a $750 scholarship to be awarded to a local area graduating high school senior who plans to continue her education at the college level. This social event enables the two chapters to enjoy special camaraderie in P.E.O.

Summer socials and BIL holiday parties have added zest to the life of Chapter FR as well as inspiring and creative programs given by the sisters. Chapter FR's goals continue to be increased membership and participation in all of the P.E.O. projects. Two individuals were recipients of the P.E.O. Program for Continuing Education grant and the P.E.O. Educational Loan Fund, one becoming a teacher and one becoming a physician's assistant.

Many members of FR are active participants in the community and have been honored for their service, business ownership, and professional lives for the past 20 years, and Chapter FR celebrated its 60th year of existence in 2013.

CHAPTER FR'S ACTIVE MEMBERSHIP IS 49; TOTAL ENROLLMENT IS 188

Chapter FS Lexington
Organized February 5, 1954
by Flora Stevens

P.E.O. has been generous in sharing with the women in Lexington. Each time the chapters outgrew the capacity for entertaining in the homes, new chapters have been formed. From the first Lexington chapter, AN, eleven members signed a letter agreeing to dimit. Those women were: Helen Barrett, Joan Stuckey, Vere Olsson, Marian Kline, Nadine Howell, Ethyle Wisda, Doris Jeffrey, Marjorie Barrett, Dorothy Beatty, Nina Miller, and Louise Kugler.

On February 5, 1954, under the guidance of Organizer Flora Stevens, the eleven dimits, one unaffiliate, Jean Strickland from California, and five initiates, Naomi Bacon, Patricia Loudon, Ann Reutlinger, Cleo Dunlap, and Delphine Sanks, formally met to organize Chapter FS. There were sixty-five guests. Helen Barrett became the first president. FS was granted its charter on April 28, 1954, at the Nebraska State Convention in Norfolk. All seventeen members were present to receive the charter. Two members were initiated in the first year. By the seventh year, there were thirty members, and by the tenth year, Chapter FS had grown to fifty-two. Currently the average attendance is twenty-four. Although FS was organized as an afternoon chapter, there are now two meetings held at night and two during the summer months in an effort to accommodate young mothers and employed members.

As P.E.O. expanded, eight members dimitted to help organize Chapter GR in 1967. In 1982 eleven members dimitted to Lexington's fourth chapter, HV.

Chapter FS has developed its own traditions. Among them has been the carrying-in of meals for members and their families in times of sickness, death or other crises. Each new baby has been welcomed with a silver spoon and the chapter presents a gift of a pin guard to each retiring president. In addition to regular gifts to each P.E.O. project, the chapter gives honorariums on special occasions.

On the lighter side, Chapter FS has had secret pals, "Let's Coffee" friendship sharing, BIL parties, auctions and box socials for fundraisers. One 40-year tradition has been to sell pecans and walnuts. This project has provided the chapter with a major source of funds year-round.

Three local girls have attended Cottey College through P.E.O. encouragement. As many as eight women have been loan recipients sponsored by Chapter FS.

The chapter boasts of six 50-year members, one 60-year member and one 70-year member.

In 2007, Chapter FS's Merikay Berg was elected treasurer of Nebraska State Chapter and served as president for the 2013-2014 term.

Because it has a diverse array of talents and personalities and a variety of age differences, Chapter FS continues to have interesting, informative and inspirational programs. In February of each year the sisters celebrate a birthday—the birthday of Chapter FS, P.E.O., in Lexington, Nebraska!

Chapter FS's active membership is 63; total enrollment is 210

I have not failed. I've just found 10,000 ways that won't work. -Thomas A. Edison

Chapter FT Omaha
Organized April 22, 1955
by Emma Sanderson

Chapter FT, Omaha, with a nucleus of eight dimits from Chapter BS, was organized on April 22, 1955, with a total membership of eighteen. Charter members were: Herma Baggley, Doris Baker, Charlotte Barker, Marion Brown, Elizabeth Chase, Gertrude Evans, Elva Krause, Jeannette Magnussen, Ada Mecham, Anna Nordell, Helen Payne, Elizabeth Reagan, Lena Lee Smith, Patricia Swanson, Jeannette Waechter, Florence Wyman, Lucile Wyrens and Mary Young. All but one of the original eighteen charter members have entered Chapter Eternal.

Chapter meetings are held monthly, plus three social meetings planned annually.

Chapter FT has continuously supported the P.E.O. projects. One of our members has provided a Bed and Breakfast venue which has enabled us to sponsor several IPS students. This gave us an opportunity to get to know our international students personally. Recently we've sponsored three young women for the P.E.O. Program for Continuing Education, two students for the P.E.O. Educational Loan Fund, and one P.E.O. STAR Scholarship.

The internet has replaced our telephone tree for keeping members informed about sisters' needs, reminders of P.E.O. meetings and events, and information on our sponsored students.

Fundraisers besides our B&B include sales for gently used books, birthday raffles, and a "Sock-It-Away" project where we save our loose change in a sock decorated with P.E.O. symbols. These funds are used for the P.E.O. projects.

Our Yearbook Committee has worked hard each year providing interesting and stimulating programs which have been presented by our members as well as guests.

When Chapter FT was organized, Bertha Clark Hughes (Nebraska Grand President, 1913–1914 and Supreme Chapter President, 1921–1923) gave us our motto, "Friendly, True," and we've tried to live up to her expectations.

Chapter FT's active membership is 34; total enrollment is 134

Chapter FU Grant
Organized March 16, 1956
by Marthena Stevens

We owe a deep gratitude to the founding members of Chapter FU. They had to wait several years for the population of Grant to reach 1,000 before permission was granted to Ruth McQuiston to select a charter list, with the help of Hattie Klinck, a 64-year P.E.O. member. When Hattie joined Chapter Eternal she was a 75-year member, which at that time was the longest membership in the nation. With eighteen initiates and one dimit we became a P.E.O. chapter on March 16, 1956. Chapter CL, Ogallala assisted Organizer Marthena Stevens. The following were charter members: Ruth McQuiston, president; Dora Collier, vice president; Mabel Moser, recording secretary; Arlene White, corresponding secretary; Irene Bancroft, chaplain; Dorothy Hastings, treasurer; Gertrude Hundhausen, guard;

Ruth Dodge, Gladys Fitzgerald, Virginia Floyd, Genevieve Hastings, Clara Holoway, Ruth Jackman, Elsie Klinck, Faye Lyon, Mary Lyon, Etta Pankonin, Evelyn Todd and Vera Van Wagenen.

Through the years our chapter has faithfully donated annually to the P.E.O. projects. We've hosted reciprocity meetings and in 1990 we held a Friendship Tea with several area chapters attending. We've been part of several state conventions. Perhaps our favorite was the 1993 Nebraska State Chapter Convention held in McCook where we were responsible for the music during the convention. Several of our members have been honored to be delegates to Conventions of International Chapter.

We've sponsored one woman for a grant from the P.E.O. Program for Continuing Education. We've also sponsored several woman for loans from the P.E.O. Educational Loan Fund. Two PCE grants were awarded to two women in our area. In 2002 and 2003 we combined with Chapters CL and HI, Ogallala, and gave $600 to sponsor a designated scholar. We've also submitted names to the P.E.O. STAR Scholarship.

In 1999 Trudy Hundhausen (one of our charter members) was elected president of our Reciprocity Group X. Sherry Erlewine, a graduate of Cottey College, serves on the Nebraska Cottey Committee.

In 2007 we celebrated the 50th anniversary of Chapter FU. Each Memorial Day we place star memorial markers, commissioned and designed by a member, on the graves of sisters who have entered Chapter Eternal.

We've entertained our BILs, enjoyed brunches and potluck suppers, held garage sales, decorated pumpkins to sell, enjoyed "basket suppers," held fashion shows, Christmas parties, hosted soup suppers for a retirement home, decorated Christmas trees for the local historical museum, held a Friendship Tea for prospective members, enjoyed a "Marvelous Mystery Trip," and entertained the Ogallala and Imperial chapters with a Cinco de Mayo supper.

Through the years, chapter FU has given each sister loving support and friendship. May the love and spirit of P.E.O. continue to grow!

CHAPTER FU'S ACTIVE MEMBERSHIP IS 22; TOTAL ENROLLMENT IS 108

★

Chapter FV Nebraska City
Organized April 7, 1956
by Marthena Stevens

In 1956, seventeen charter members of Chapter FV began the weaving of a memory tapestry, using golden threads begun by their "mother" chapter, CF, who sponsored the new chapter. President of Nebraska State Chapter Dorothy Smithberger installed Josephine Davis as president, Eleanor Kropp as vice president, Amelia Peterson as recording secretary, Edith Fenstermacher as corresponding secretary, Bonnie Herndon as treasurer, Ruth Asboe as chaplain, and Betty Sharp as guard. Other charter members were Ellen Alber, Cordelia Conkling, Mary Ann Hall, Helen Morton, Wealtha Nelson, Dorothy Nicholas, Betty Peterson, Maxine Romjue, Genevieve Schulz, and Emily Wilson.

Each April we celebrate the birthday of our chapter. We have wined and dined at the Lied Conference Center, Table Creek Clubhouse, Embers, Lewis and Clark

Visitor Center, Camp Catron, Union Orchard and Winery, and Arbor Links Clubhouse as well as various other venues.

When Chapter FV celebrated their 57th birthday in April 2013, the group reflected on the legacy and milestones they have accomplished over the years. Both Ruth Asboe and Betty Peterson, charter members, retain their membership. Ruth is an active member who attends almost every meeting. We celebrated her 96th birthday at our March 2013 meeting. Josephine Davis, Chapter FV's first and only state president (1965-66), and a Nebraska P.E.O. Home Board of Directors member, passed to Chapter Eternal in 2006.

Through the years our chapter has had clever themes to guide our programs. Various programs given by our members have been "A Slideshow on Ancient Greece," "A Trolley Tour of Nebraska City," "A Day in the Life of an Australian Teacher," "An International Wedding," "Decorating Homes," "Tour of the East Coast including Presidential Inauguration," "An African Safari," and "Korean War Experiences" presented by BIL Sam Kellogg.

Our constant fundraising project has been selling pecans. The money earned funds for our gifts to the P.E.O. projects, as well as our chapter expenses. In 1995 we sold twenty-seven cases of pecans. In 2013 the number rose to thirty-two cases.

Our chapter and our sister Chapter CF took a road trip to DesMoines to the P.E.O. International Headquarters in 1995. We get together once a year with our sister chapter and enjoy food and company. In 2008 a group of sisters visited the Nebraska P.E.O. Home in Beatrice where they visited a sister from our chapter.

It is always the goal to support the P.E.O. projects, not only financially, but also through nominations. Kathy Badberg White was our 2000 PCE recipient. Amanda Drake was the 2001 ELF recipient from our chapter. Abby Reese, daughter of sister Jill Reese, was our 2011 ELF nominee. Alexa Salansky, daughter of sister Deborah Salansky, attended Cottey College 2003-2005. Abby and Alexa were both initiated into our chapter. Our chapter has also sent care packages to students at Cottey College.

As a way of staying involved in the Nebraska City community, each Christmas the chapter participates in a service project. We have donated to Project Response, the local food pantry, Child Saving Institute, Head Start, and our local fire and rescue squad departments.

In 2011, our chapter began membership interest groups. These small groups (coffee, golf, historic tours, shopping, book club, etc.) have given our members a chance to meet socially and get to know each other better.

Our chapter continues to thrive as a sisterhood and cherish the P.E.O. spirit and our rich tradition. It is our goal to make a difference by contributing to education of women around the world, as well as make a difference in the hearts of each sister at home.

In 1995 our chapter consisted of fifty-seven resident and ten nonresident members. Through the years we have initiated new members, dimitted members and have lost members to Chapter Eternal.

CHAPTER FV'S ACTIVE MEMBERSHIP IS 60; TOTAL ENROLLMENT IS 184

Chapter FW Lincoln
Organized January 10, 1957
by Harriet Lumbard

Charter members of the chapter who continue to grace our meetings have every reason to feel right at home with Chapter FW's unchanging security of ritual, philanthropy, and friendship. However, they and all chapter members since 1957 have also welcomed the challenge of change along with the comfort of continuation. Those changes include, among others, the P.E.O. website with its up-to-the-minute communications and forms, the streamlining of voting procedure, the expansion of Cottey College from two to four years, and the use of notes for rituals. The old ballot box lives on in the shape of a centerpiece-sized black piano.

Charter members, women who responded in 1957 to Lincoln Roundtable's expression of the need for a new chapter were dimits Marie Allen, Mary Barnes, Harriet Claypool, Verna Edington, Meredith Hachiya, Helen Hale, Isabel Kruse-Hatfield, Clare McGannon, Helen Porter, Joanne Prien, Kathryn Robson, Lucille Rosewell, Bess Sperring, Mary Swett, Thelma Wainscott, and Margaret Wirth, who served as the first president. Current chapter membership includes charter members Meredith Hachiya DuBois, Helen Porter, and Kathryn Robson. Initiates at the organizational meeting were Patricia Finke and Dorothy Thompson.

We became a 50-year chapter in 2007. Always an afternoon-meeting chapter, the average age of members has increased as the majority remained in the chapter and moved from young adulthood to retirement age. "For the Good of the Chapter" now resounds with news of grandchildren and great-grandchildren in contrast to the news of children of earlier years. As members have downsized their homes and moved into retirement lodgings, meetings have moved from private homes to churches, banks, libraries, and retirement homes. Chapter dues have been increased to pay for spaces requiring rental.

The chapter takes pride in contributing to all P.E.O. projects, and having increased our contribution to them over the years. Various fundraisers have provided the benevolence funds: garage sales, pay-to-attend luncheons hosted by members, raffle of a member-made quilt, and hosting of bed-and-breakfast travelers. In addition to supporting P.E.O. projects, Chapter FW has been generous to local charities, which have included, over the years, the Food Bank, the Friendship Home, and collection of emergency clothing for public school students. We sponsor a Cottey student each year, learning about her and her aspirations, and remembering her at Christmas. We nominate worthy women for P.E.O. scholarships and encourage and support them in their applications. Chapter FW is always represented at Lincoln Reciprocity Roundtable and state convention, and sometimes at International Convention. Four members have served as Lincoln Reciprocity Roundtable officers, with two having served as president: Edna Chamberlin in 1977 and Meredith Hachiya in 1990. When it was the turn of Chapter FW to present the Founders' Day program to Lincoln Roundtable, members created costumes appropriate to the Founders' student days and enacted events in their lives, to the accompaniment of a narration interspersed with parodies of popular songs for the audience to sing along.

Fellowship has grown more precious over the years, supported by purely social activities such as summer coffees, BIL events, and an annual Christmas luncheon.

A few years ago, a Star Sister project involved notes, calls, and thoughts for one other member for one year. The Courtesy/Crisis committee provides welcome meals and support to members suffering loss or illness.

Chapter FW is fortunate in the breadth and depth of programs it has offered at meetings over the years, including some from the community, such as presentations by school singing groups, the administrators of the local Food Bank, and the City Mission, and some that feature members, such as reports from a retired fashion consultant, a foreign missionary, and an inveterate reader. An innovative "Bag Lady" program each meeting invites one member to tell the chapter about herself by means of a bag-full of artifacts such as photographs and souvenirs from her life. One month's "Bag Lady" who had lived in Canada provided information about her family's involvement in "curling," a sport hitherto unknown to any depth by the membership. Tours have included visits to the Nebraska P.E.O. Home in Beatrice, historic Wyuka Cemetery, and a student fashion exhibit at the UNL East Campus.

Although our membership and attendance have diminished over the years, we have grown in affection for one another and for P.E.O. philanthropies.

CHAPTER FW'S ACTIVE MEMBERSHIP IS 42; TOTAL ENROLLMENT IS 178

★

CHAPTER FX LINCOLN
ORGANIZED JANUARY 10, 1957
BY HARRIET LUMBARD

The rays of light from the shining star of the P.E.O. Sisterhood led nineteen dimitting members to join together on January 10, 1957, to form Chapter FX in Lincoln. Officers of Nebraska State Chapter were assisted by Chapter BY of Lincoln to formally organize Chapter FX and its twin chapter, Chapter FW on the same day. The Lincoln P.E.O. Reciprocity Roundtable had contacted all unaffiliated members in the city in the hope of forming a new chapter. Subsequently, it was decided to form two new chapters in the city. Eleanor Anderson of Chapter H, Holdrege, became the first president of Chapter FX. She had been granted consent to select the charter list, which included Alice Keefe, Ann Paden, Ruth Hurst, Thelma Landgreen, Musetta Gilman, Sarah Jane Adams, Caroline Boswell, Margaret Campbell, Margaret Coffey, Zelma Coffey, Ann Goldsberry, Mary Ann Daly, Anna Marie Hall, Catherine Hasselbalch, Mildred Rengler, Elizabeth Rodgers, Jean Stange, and Nancy Vandel. Of these, Caroline Boswell remained an active member until her death at the age of 102 in 2007.

Because the late Eva Curtiss had been instrumental in the initial plans to contact unaffiliated P.E.O.s in Lincoln, the Lincoln Roundtable gave the chapter its $25 fee as a memorial to Eva.

By the fifth year, the chapter was thriving and in 1982, the "twin" chapters FX and FW celebrated twenty-five years of P.E.O. with a joint gathering of members. We celebrated our 50th anniversary at state convention in Omaha in 2007. We have several 50-plus year P.E.O. members in Chapter FX.

Chapter FX has sponsored several individuals for the P.E.O. projects and a few were honored in receiving them. Some of these are Melissa Stone, who received a P.E.O. Scholar Award in 1999, Kelly Crowley, who received a Cottey Scholarship in 1999, Jennifer Frye, who received a PCE grant in 2013, and Linda

Kattes, who received a PCE grant in 2013.

Our members have also served in the larger P.E.O. Sisterhood including Madelyn Massie who served as Roundtable vice president in 1974-75 and president in 1975-76; Mary Caudy who served as Bylaws Chairman for International Convention in 1991 and as Roundtable recording secretary from 1997-99; and Marty Link who served as Roundtable vice president and president from 2003-2005.

Our members especially treasure the friendships that P.E.O. provides. Several members participate in a first Thursday lunch group and a regular walking group. We consider ourselves a progressive chapter in recently implementing an initiation team and the option of "co-officing." We also enjoy our regular "brag time" during meetings which helps to fund our courtesy committee. Our usual fundraisers have included silent auctions, various sales, raffles, and "count your blessings" fund appeals. We enjoy regularly giving to all the P.E.O. projects.

We have thirty-nine active members including Gertrude Cekal who is a resident of the Nebraska P.E.O. Home.

CHAPTER FX'S ACTIVE MEMBERSHIP IS 39; TOTAL ENROLLMENT IS 131

★

CHAPTER FY OMAHA
ORGANIZED JANUARY 14, 1958
BY MILDRED ROBERTSON

Chapter FY is the blending of loving P.E.O. sisters who came to Omaha from a variety of backgrounds and locations only to find "no room at the Inn." Inexperienced but enthusiastic, the nineteen charter members took Organizer Mildred Robertson's words to heart. Her significant interpretation of the chapter letters to mean "Faithfully Yours" set the theme for Chapter FY's growth. The bonds in Chapter FY have grown strong and binding.

The nineteen charter members who were selected by sponsor Nina Alleman of IC, Iowa, were Gladys Percy, president; Ruth Nicholson, vice president; Athene Alsmeyer, recording secretary; Nina Alleman, corresponding secretary, Nancy Geer, treasurer; Eileen Galloway, chaplain; Margaret Brader, guard: Dorothy Akin, Alice Alden, Carolyn Black, Kathy Califf, Constance Davis, Dorothy Harris, Hazel Kelley, Martha Nueller, Josephine Ready, Wanda Schwartz, Nathalia "Nikki" Zimmerman and Betty Symonds. Two are still active resident members of this chapter.

Many delightful and talented sisters have passed through the portals of Chapter FY. There is one four-generation family set within our chapter, one three-generation family set, several two-generation family sets, and six 50-plus year members.

Eight chapter members or daughters have attended Cottey College. Two sisters have received a loan from the P.E.O. Educational Loan Fund, and a sister's granddaughter received a P.E.O. Scholar Award. The residents of the Nebraska P.E.O. Home have benefited from the many special gifts and extra support that Chapter FY gives to them. Many FY members are actively involved in community and religious outreach programs.

Through the year FY has a variety of speakers/programs, a friendship coffee to share P.E.O. love with others, BIL functions and a Christmas gathering Brunch/Auction which provides good food, fellowship, and raises funds for various P.E.O. projects.

CHAPTER FY'S ACTIVE MEMBERSHIP IS 39; TOTAL ENROLLMENT IS 147

CHAPTER FZ OMAHA
ORGANIZED APRIL 29, 1959
BY LOIS NEWELL

Plans and preparations for the birth of Chapter FZ were appropriately formulated at Clarkson Hospital by State Organizer Lois Newell and Omaha Unaffiliate Chairman Flora Smiley. The blessed event materialized April 29, 1959, when twenty-three dimitting members were organized and assisted into the P.E.O. family. In attendance were Past President of Nebraska State Chapter and Supreme Chapter Bertha Clark Hughes, and Past President of Nebraska State Chapter and Supreme Organizer Irene Van Brunt.

First officers were: E. Jean Morrison, president; Barbara Shurtleff, vice president; Emogene Nieman, recording secretary; Marjorie Parks Neukam, corresponding secretary; Jacqueline P. Johann, treasurer; Margaret Sorensen, chaplain; Betty Thai, guard. Other charter members were Barbara Grundman Sasse, Doris Goodrich, Ruth Lear, Betty Jean Williams, Barbara Finley, Marjorie Newquist, Charlene T. Wolsmann, Marjorie Elias, Mary Blanchard Rohn, Mary Lynn Anderson, Nancy Chittenden, Carolyn Conkling Balfour, Betty Morrison Stratbucker (Zachariae), Sally Bearden Rowland, Elizabeth Armstrong and Sally Kjelsen. Five charter members remain active today: Jean Morrison, Jacqueline Johann, Sally Kjelson, Marjorie Newquist, and Betty Stratbucker Zachariae, all who have served as president at least once.

In April of 2009, Chapter FZ celebrated its 50th anniversary. We were honored as a 50-year chapter at the 2008 state convention in Omaha, which Chapter FZ helped host. There have been many special memories over the fifty years. One funny memory that has been passed down was the time a dog took his place beside a new initiate during the ceremony of initiation. This may be the first time a male was part of a P.E.O. initiation!

Helping women further their education remains a priority for our chapter. To this end we have sponsored over fourteen women with loans, grants or scholarships. Some of our own members (and their daughters) have benefitted from our projects, too.

We have had many different fundraisers over the years including auctions, raffles, garage sales, bridge marathons, bingo games, bake-less bake sales and compiling a recipe book we sold to members and friends. At the closing of each business meeting the chapter raises money through "buck-a-brag," which is successful because everyone has a lot to brag about!

We continue to have interesting, informative and entertaining programs often using the talents of our own sisters. Our social meetings are often held at various restaurants around Omaha where we can relax and enjoy each other's company more fully.

Chapter FZ remains special because of our personal connections. An FZ sister who had a mother residing at the Nebraska P.E.O. Home keeps us informed about their residents, and we remember them with cards throughout the year. We are proud to have an alumnus of Cottey College, and the personal connection we feel from her. Chapter FZ keeps in contact with our sisters we have not seen recently or those who need encouragement by passing cards around at each meeting with members adding personal notes. We also have a fabulous membership committee who contact unaffiliated members to attend meetings. The committee also makes an effort to invite potential new members to all our social events.

In 2013, Chapter FZ remains a diverse group of women with many different ideas, talents and ages that continues to makes us "Fine and Zesty!"

CHAPTER FZ'S ACTIVE MEMBERSHIP IS 57; TOTAL ENROLLMENT IS 169

CHAPTER GA SCOTTSBLUFF
ORGANIZED DECEMBER 4, 1959
BY MARIETTA JACK

Chapter GA was organized in response to a need for an evening chapter in this area. Preliminary steps necessary to form the new chapter began in January 1959 and reached fruition on December 4, 1959, when State Organizer Marietta Jack and State President Harriet Lumbard flew to Scottsbluff for the organizational meeting. Dimits were accepted for eleven members from other chapters and three initiates brought the total members to fourteen. Lucille Crumbliss was elected the first president of Chapter GA. The charter for this chapter was presented at the state convention in May 1960.

Charter members were Josephine Forbes, Lucille Crumbliss, Alice Carter, Jeannette Shehein, Nancy Lehr, Berneda Ashburn, Edith Haney, Marie Henry, Edna Reiser, Ellen Taylor, Hazel Pugsley, Ruth Hopkins, Ruthann Hooper, and Irene Baumgartner. There are no longer any charter members in our chapter.

Chapter GA has always been a strong supporter of the P.E.O. philanthropic projects and continues to inform and enlighten our sisters about these projects through programs filled with information presented in a variety of ways. One of our initiates was an IPS Scholarship recipient, Ruth Soong of China. We celebrated with her when she became a citizen of the United States.

Because we are an evening chapter, we have initiated interesting and energetic business and professional women to complement our retirees and others who continue to enjoy evening fellowship and friendship.

The varied backgrounds of our members bring wonderful knowledge and resources in presenting outstanding programs at our meetings. Not only do we draw on the talents of our sisters, but we are fortunate in bringing in community persons to share their information with us—thus honoring our objects and aims.

From the beginning, Chapter GA has always closely followed our traditions. Our annual summer social, fundraisers, Christmas party, and salad supper are important in the life of our chapter. And while we feel those traditions are important, we have moved forward into the 21st Century with some new ideas to appeal to our sisters.

Our annual Christmas party has changed over the years. While we still enjoy our dinner and poems written by our members, the poems are now an optional thing and instead of our gift exchange we chose to support a Christmas Project that benefits the needy.

Chapter GA fundraisers have been varied from year to year. We have enjoyed silent auctions, bunco parties, ice cream socials, and no bake pie sales, to name a few. We always encourage our sisters to brag, but at the cost of one dollar a brag.

With our group of working women and retirees we have gone from salads provided by our members to having a catered salad supper before our March election and installation of officers. This makes it easier for all and our catered meals are always enjoyable.

Our chapter was honored as a 50-Year chapter at the state convention in Gering in 2009.

CHAPTER GA'S ACTIVE MEMBERSHIP IS 34; TOTAL ENROLLMENT IS 187

★

CHAPTER GB OMAHA
ORGANIZED APRIL 3, 1961
BY DOROTHY KAIN

Chapter GB was organized April 3, 1961, with Nebraska State Chapter Organizer Dorothy Kain as presiding officer. Charter members were Marjorie Sargent, president; Anne Ritchie, vice president; Paula Hendrich, corresponding secretary; Bonnie Finck, recording secretary; Betty Lou Smith, treasurer; Frances Halla, chaplain; Florence Davidson, guard; Marion Moore, Delores Mills Opland, Jean Aiken, Eleanor Day Greene, Karen Turner Gaines, Betty Jackson Rohde, Gladys Anderson, Jeanne Walcott Fitch, Elthea Saxvik, Pearl Currier, Virginia May Fletcher, Mildred Jacobson, Janet Hockenberry, Marian Blue, Martha Krismer, Joanne Mlinar, Wilma Merrill Lindgren, Jeanne Jewett Mobley and Bette Townsend Maughmer. The only charter member of the "Great Bunch" still a member is Eleanor (Greene) Tingwald, who now lives in Beatrice, Nebraska, near her daughter. All the charter members were already P.E.O.s and dimitted to GB. Several have passed away. Many moved from the Omaha area. Others dimitted to other chapters that met when they were able to attend more frequently.

During the early years of Chapter GB there were several member weddings and several new babies. There were many new members, both members who moved from other locations and new initiates. And there were many who moved away and later dimitted to other chapters.

God's Blessing was bestowed on the twenty sisters who have served as GB's chapter president. One became a president of Texas State Chapter; one, an author reviewed in The P.E.O. Record; one, a missionary; and one became a recording secretary of Texas State Chapter.

Can it possibly be nearly twenty-five years since Omaha had the honor of hosting the convention of International Chapter in 1991's *Spirit of the Prairie*? Many of our active members from that time have moved away or joined Chapter Eternal. Current members have fond memories of that time.

Over the years the Good Bunch has helped Nebraska State Chapter host conventions in Omaha a number of times. We have had members who served as guards and have hosted refreshment rooms and supplied goodies.

We have also hosted meetings of the Omaha Reciprocity Association. Until the last few years of meetings, they were held at the Dundee Presbyterian Church near Happy Hollow Boulevard and Underwood Street.

The Great Bunch celebrates our chapter's birthday each year at our April meeting. In some years we have had programs relating to history but we always manage to have a white and yellow birthday!

From time to time we have had various fundraising activities. Of course, rummage sales have brought in funds. For the past several years we have had an ongoing raffle at each meeting. Members sign up to bring an item, usually valued at $10 to $15 or perhaps a "White Elephant." Tickets are sold for $1 each. Near the end of our meeting, a winning ticket is drawn.

We also have a cookie sale at our December meetings. Each participant brings several dozen cookies. They are purchased for $5 a dozen; buyers may purchase one kind or may make a selection of a number of kinds of cookies. We also have a fun gift exchange at the December meetings.

Each year we donate generously to the P.E.O. projects. We have "adopted" a Cottey student and send goodies especially before finals week. Worthy community causes also are helped with money donations, as well as members volunteering.

A highlight of the last twenty-five years has been our sponsorship of recipients of the P.E.O. Program for Continuing Education grants and the P.E.O. Educational Loan Fund: Alicia Barna, Rae Smith, Amy Hammond, Rachel Ahrens, Jennifer Kaminski, Martha Partida, Kristen Mollner, Lisa Lounsbury, Andrea Turner, Sue Petersen, Paula Shearer, Devon McMullen Kucuisky, Gretchen Gfeller, Mary Shearer, Elizabeth Loghry, Kimberlee Miller, and ELF for Rachel Ahrens.

At many of our meetings we have interesting speakers and other types of programs, such as demonstrations, sometimes by our own members and sometimes other people who provide fascinating information about topics of importance to all of us. And we always enjoy the opportunity to chat and keep up-to-date on our activities.

Several of our members are "snow birds" and spend parts of the year away from Omaha. In order to handle the situation, we have co-officers in some cases. It seems to work out well.

It is hard to know what the future will be like. We are hopeful that Chapter GB will prosper with God's Blessing for another twenty-five years and more.

CHAPTER GB'S ACTIVE MEMBERSHIP IS 29; TOTAL ENROLLMENT IS 178

★

Chapter GC Alliance
Organized December 28, 1961
by Dorothy Yeager

Chapter GC was organized on December 28, 1961, by Dorothy Yeager with fourteen dimitting members from Chapter AH and seven initiates. Charter officers were Phyllis Neuswanger, president; Kitty VanDecar, vice president; Lois Gorder, recording secretary; Marjorie King, corresponding secretary; Opal Saum, treasurer; Mary Hood, chaplain; Pearl Neuswanger, guard; and members Mildred Kuncl, Maude MacNeill, Ruth Burnham, Ruth Shaw, Katharine Schill, Edna Chamberlain, Sandra Chamberlain, Helen Jean Fricke, Genevieve Merdinger, Alberta Olson,

Eunice Petersen, Carolyn Toenjes, M. Jane Hunter and Jane Gorder. The meeting began with a one o'clock luncheon, followed by the organizational meeting. The day's festivities ended with a dinner at the Drake Hotel.

Through the years, Chapter GC members have served P.E.O. in various capacities. Marie Sorum has served on the Nebraska P.E.O. Home Board of Directors, Janet Williams on the Nominating Committee during the 1998 convention, and Jan Hofmann served as president of Reciprocity Groups III and X in 2000. Janice Lawrence served as delegate to Convention of International Chapter in 2006 and in 2009 Joni Merrigan was Chapter GC Convention co-chairman and Tammy Suit served as a convention guard.

Since 1995, Chapter GC sponsored students Brenda Manion and Leigh Shreve for PCE grants. We have also supported Amy Harris, a STAR Scholarship recipient and awarded a P.E.O.Program for Continuing Education grant to Ann Weishaar, both in 2010.

Chapter GC - Front row, left to right: Gina Briggs, Margaret Koch, Janet Williams, Natha Wilkinson, Alberta Olson. Top Row, left to right: Amy Gullion, Judy Moss, Ellen Lierk, Jerri Mathistad Carla Block, Janet Jaggers, Susan Cummings, Pat Nelson, Mary Jo Hoffman, Cheryl Harris, Peggy Jensen, Janice Lawrence

Chapter GC celebrates the successes of our individual sisters as well as our chapter anniversaries. Following our monthly meetings, time is set aside for "bragging" about the successes and accomplishments of our sisters and their family members. Members for fifty years and more are honored, as are new brides, new babies, special anniversaries, and birthdays. Our current 50-year members include Alberta Olson, Natha Wilkinson, and Janet Williams. GC also lends support and encouragement by providing funeral dinners for our sisters' families at their time of loss.

Fundraisers have historically been not only a source of income for our projects in GC, but also a source of entertainment. Besides the standard garage sales and auctions, fundraising has included collecting loose coins, sweats nights, bridge marathons, selling GC cookbooks, a brag basket, friendship basket and even a bathing suit competition! This competition encouraged sisters to donate $5 not to "see" their president in a swim suit and whatever they chose over that amount not to have to model their own swim suit. P.E.O. sisters can be very creative when raising money for a good cause.

Chapter GC looks forward to celebrating Founders' Day every year with the other local chapters. We rotate hosting this event every year and love the fellowship and camaraderie it offers our Sisterhood. Our local chapters recently erected a highway sign entering Alliance in an effort to promote the P.E.O. Sisterhood.

Joyce Goff was elected treasurer of the Executive Board of Nebraska State Chapter in 1981 and moved to Grand Island before she became president of Nebraska State chapter. However, Chapter GC still claims her as one of our own and presented her with a friendship quilt containing a block from each GC member. Chapter GC "reJoyced" with Joyce when she was elected recording secretary of International Chapter in September 1995. The chapter also gave a donation in honor of Joyce to the Nebraska P.E.O. Home for their 50th anniversary.

Social meetings are always fun, and one of the reasons our chapter is so special. This is a time for members to connect with one another and enjoy each others' company. BIL/family picnics are held every summer, followed by attending a play presented by the Fort Robinson Playhouse. Christmas is usually celebrated by enjoying a dinner together. Chapter GC has started a tradition with the "Guess Who's Coming to Dinner" theme. The fun of this dinner is that the hostesses do not know who is coming to their house and the members do not know who else will be there. Members who attend this activity provide the food for the meal. We have also been on a dinner train, played bunco, had a hula party, decorated Easter eggs, a Halloween party, and participated in a yoga workout! Members also participate in monthly no-host luncheons and annual salad supper meetings. An upcoming social meeting will include a talent show! P.E.O.s do not lack creativity or fun!

Of course, the members are the real reason Chapter GC is special. The support, love and encouragement our sisters demonstrate not only to each other, but to our local, state and International chapters is the driving force behind the success of Chapter GC.

CHAPTER GC'S ACTIVE MEMBERSHIP IS 32; TOTAL ENROLLMENT IS 170

★

CHAPTER GD LINCOLN
ORGANIZED FEBRUARY 3, 1962
BY DOROTHY YEAGER
DISBANDED JUNE 10, 1995

Chapter GD, Lincoln's 20th chapter, was organized Saturday, February 3, 1962, by Nebraska State Chapter Organizer Dorothy Yeager. All state officers were present that day, plus other P.E.O. guests and friends from Lincoln chapters. The event was held in the Georgian Room of the Cornhusker Hotel at 10AM and was followed by a luncheon. It was an unusually warm mid-winter day. June Misko, Lincoln Reciprocity Roundtable president, and Nebraska State Chapter President Lois Newell guided the group of eighteen unaffiliated members during the preceding months of preparation.

The chapter's first president, Elaine Smithberger Fuller, obtained consent from her chapter in Stanton to select the charter list. Unfortunately one of the eighteen (Mary Cresse) was called out of town at the last minute and was unable to attend. She became the first dimitting member shortly afterward. Betty Bell's daughter, Virginia, and Glenna Roper were the first two initiates. Elaine Fuller and Ann Fate are daughters of past presidents of Nebraska State Chapter. Charter members, all dimitting members, were Betty Bell, Helen Frisbie, Helen Holdorf, Mary Alice Park, Maxine Rolofson, Pauline Douglas, Beth Douglas, Connie Ryan, Katherine Schumacher, Thelma Stewart, Marcia Wythers, Frances Enevoldson, Elaine Fuller, Ann Fate, Marguerite Babcock, Willa Hewitt, and Shirley Schmoker.

On organization day, Emma Sanderson (Ann Fate's mother) gave a quote in her devotion: "P.E.O.—an adventure in friendship." This phrase aptly described the years that followed, for Chapter GD grew steadily and the bonds of sisterhood were strong. Families moved in and out of the community and the chapter experienced the ebb and flow of a mobile generation.

On their 10th anniversary, Chapter GD had a sweetheart party for their BILs. In 1987, on the occasion of the 25th anniversary, the chapter visited the Nebraska P.E.O. Home in Beatrice. Treasured chapter traditions were summer picnics, September salad suppers, special Christmas meals and programs, fundraising auctions, and little thoughtful acts of kindness. These all were parts of the whole history of Chapter GD.

Friendships within the chapter remained strong in spite of the changes and challenges the chapter faced. Women were meeting new challenges, new roles, joys, losses and uncertainties. Before its disbanding, four women received 50-year membership pins: Betty Bell, Edna Reiser, Helen Ray and Helen Frisbie.

Unfortunately, problems in Chapter GD seemed insurmountable and the "adventure in friendship" ended. On April 1, 1995, Chapter GD petitioned Nebraska State Chapter to disband. At the following convention, the charter was revoked on June 10, 1995, and the chapter was formally disbanded. However, the spirit of P.E.O. lives on in quite a few GD members, as many have dimitted to other Lincoln chapters. At the time Chapter GD was disbanded, its active membership was 33 and its total enrollment was 120.

TOTAL ENROLLMENT 120

★

CHAPTER GE OMAHA
ORGANIZED MARCH 31, 1962
BY DOROTHY YEAGER

Chapters GE and GF, both in Omaha, were organized on the same day. The dream of forming two chapters in Omaha at the same time was fulfilled on March 31, 1962, with Organizer Dorothy Yeager presiding. Chapter GE, with its preference for afternoon meetings, was attended to first. Meetings were held on the first and/or third Tuesday of each month and the schedule remains the same today. Twenty-three charter members dimitted from far and near to form Chapter GE. These charter members were: Evelyn Janke, president; Catherine H. Larson, chaplain; Elva A. King; Betty J. Vifquain, vice president; Irma Henderson, treasurer; Darlene S. Reynolds, Vera Janke Kahl, Ruth Annette Neel Miller; Mary Ringstrand, recording secretary; Helen Fuller Williams, Shirley Sorenson Mitchell, Carolyn Brake, Greta N. Graham, Mary Ann Kelly, Patricia Shellenberger, Nancy Tritsch; Maude Harriet Hutchins, corresponding secretary; Lucy Ann Robertson, Jean M. King; Mary Burkgren, guard; Dorritt

Grant, Kathryn Mummey, and Patricia Dobney. Shirley Sorenson Mitchell and Nancy Tritsch remain as charter members of Chapter GE.

We have three special events which have been held annually since Chapter GE was organized. One is the April birthday salad luncheon which includes a special birthday cake. The annual Christmas luncheon and auction is an event highly anticipated. Sisters invite guests and prospective members. Hand-made or "hand-selected" gifts are auctioned. Bidding becomes quite spirited when two or more sisters desire the same gift. Money that is raised is used for P.E.O. projects. The first BIL event was held in June of 1962, and has been held yearly since that time.

At the 2012 state convention in Fremont, Chapter GE was recognized as a 50-year chapter at the Honors Luncheon. In addition, on April 22, 2012, Chapters GE and GF—who were chartered on the same day in 1962—held a joint celebration honoring fifty years of sisterhood. Chapters GE and GF, along with a couple of other Omaha chapters, gave $750 toward an IPS Designated Award in honor of our fifty years in P.E.O.

Our members lead active, varied lives, participating in many events in the Omaha area. During "brag time" it is fun to hear about the latest accomplishments of family members. And, of course, we are a very caring group, always sympathetic when members need a kind word or a helping hand.

CHAPTER GE'S ACTIVE MEMBERSHIP IS 41; TOTAL ENROLLMENT IS 147

★

CHAPTER GF OMAHA
ORGANIZED MARCH 31, 1962
BY DOROTHY YEAGER

In a unique beginning, Chapter GF participated with GE in Omaha's first double organization. It was a gala gathering including state and national officers, fourteen "unaffiliates" and two initiates. Chapter GF was organized with sixteen women. Nebraska State Chapter Organizer Dorothy Yeager organized the chapter. Charter members were Carroll Lea Anderson, Fern Edmiston, Opal Ellis, Viva Fuerst, Janet McDole, Jane Stowell, Shirley Pagel, Marjorie Limes, Sharon Fisher, Sonja Brueland, Corrine Ellingham, Norma Wright, Ruth Krafka, Nancy Rice, Helen Ray, Marilee McAuley and Helen Nelson. Six charter members remain in Chapter GF and five members have been lost to Chapter Eternal. Cleo Parde, Omaha Reciprocity Association's unaffiliate chairman, helped with the organization of Chapter GF. Beloved charter members Janet McDole and Viva Fuerst remain active members of Chapter GF. They recall the excitement Chapter GF brought to Omaha. This new evening chapter offered career women the opportunity to attend P.E.O. meetings. Over fifty years later, Chapter GF continues to be a vibrant chapter with sixty-one members. Chapter GE and Chapter GF celebrated their mutual 50th birthday together on April 22, 2012, with an open house complete with birthday cake, a display of memorabilia from each chapter and musical entertainment.

Chapter GF has had the privilege of sponsoring recipients for ELF and PCE and candidates for the P.E.O. Scholar Award and P.E.O. STAR Scholarship. In just the past four years, three PCE recipients were sponsored by Chapter GF and supported in their educational efforts by the chapter. Visits have been made to the Nebraska P.E.O. Home. Chapter GF is honored to have members who have attended and graduated from Cottey College over the years.

Warmth of spirit and a wealth of cooperation are evident in successful fundraising to support P.E.O. projects. The primary revenue source for the chapter for a number of years has been a Bed & Breakfast at the home of Jeanette Ekberg. Norann Behnken continues the GF Bed & Breakfast tradition for the chapter. She recently welcomed P.E.O. sisters from Canada into her home.

Chapter GF is composed of talented and ambitious women who have had many different career paths and avocations. Membership ages range from twenty-one to ninety-six. Even with these varied interests and ages, there is a close relationship among the sisters in Chapter GF.

Members of Chapter GF have contributed to P.E.O. beyond their own chapter. GF members have written and participated in skits and programs for the Omaha Reciprocity Association and for conventions of Nebraska State Chapter. A member made a huge gold P.E.O. star used at two state conventions and the 1991 Convention of International Chapter held in Omaha. Two GF members participated in a skit at the 1981 Convention of International Chapter in Kansas City. Chapter GF members have served as Omaha Reciprocity Association board members, on state project committees and as guards for conventions of Nebraska State Chapter. Chapter GF sisters have provided informative programs for other chapters.

Chapter GF is so very proud of its first Nebraska State Chapter officer, Lisa Helmick. Lisa was installed as secretary at the 2013 Nebraska State Convention. Lisa has implemented many innovative ideas to strengthen our chapter membership. For example, after every meeting Lisa writes "GF Highlights." These newsy meeting synopses are emailed or mailed to the entire membership. This keeps our sisters connected even when we aren't able to attend every meeting. Chapter GF is happy to share our sister Lisa Helmick with our Nebraska P.E.O. sisters!

Chapter GF has accomplished a great deal during its first fifty years and hopes to continue to exemplify the ideals of P.E.O for the next fifty years and beyond!

CHAPTER GF'S ACTIVE MEMBERSHIP IS 60; TOTAL ENROLLMENT IS 132

★

CHAPTER GG KEARNEY
ORGANIZED JANUARY 22, 1963
BY JOSEPHINE DAVIS

Although a raging blizzard played the accompaniment for the organization of Nebraska's 182nd chapter, all Nebraska State Chapter officers were present as seventeen P.E.O.s became charter members of Chapter GG on January 22, 1963. The seventeen charter members were: Beverly Kimball, president; Alta Munro, vice president; Ruth Swalley, recording secretary; Janet Ayers, corresponding secretary; Amelia Edwards, treasurer; Beverly Wolf, chaplain; Shirley Edwards, guard; Raquel Cary, Evelyn Cullen, Elizabeth Elliott, Delight Fox, Greer Fox, Ethel Lowe. Carrie Meston. Ruth Miles. Grace Moore. and Genevieve Welch. When Amelia Erickson dimitted into Chapter GG, the number of members was eighteen. "Gigi Snow" was initiated during the model meeting. Organizer Jo

Davis dubbed Chapter GG her "Good Girls."

A silk floral star was given by Shirley Walker for use by all Kearney chapters. Chapter GG lovingly remembers "Shoo" and their ten other members in Chapter Eternal.

Delegates to Supreme and International Conventions have been Alta Munro, Beverly Kimball, and Evelyn Cullen. Delight Fox has been a faithful member of the Nebraska P.E.O. Home Board and Nebraska Cottey Scholarships Committee.

Chapter GG instigated the Kearney Reciprocity summer coffee. Their "silent prayer for peace and for those near and dear who are away from them" was suggested by Ruth Miles in 1968. The idea for a P.E.O. bicentennial quilt originated in Chapter GG.

Chapter GG at Rowe Sanctuary, February 2009

Chapter GG shower restocks Jubilee Center shelves, April 2007

GG has sponsored several women for loans and grants from the P.E.O. educational projects. Six women have received loans from the P.E.O. Educational Loan Fund, one woman sponsored for IPS, and four women have received grants from the P.E.O. Program for Continuing Education. Three members are Cottey College graduates: Beverly Murray Kimball, Sandy Lantis and Jill Norblade. The chapter has sponsored two other Cottey College graduates and two first-year students. Proceeds from food coupons, auctions, cookbooks and crossword puzzles have increased the annual giving substantially.

Ruth Swalley presented a family tree for the 25th Anniversary. Jo Davis, Nelsine Scofield, Joyce Goff and "Bobbie" Koefoot were honored guests. A leaf bearing the name of each guest, charter member, initiate and dimitting member was added as the chapter history unfolded.

Beverly Wolf wrote and narrated *"Once Upon a Time"* for the 29th birthday. Six resident active charter members formed the cast with appropriate props (snowflakes, dollar bills, toy phone, letters) to enhance the story of GG's organization.

President Kay Bowman, Marian Kotas and Linda Younes ably directed GG's responsibilities for Omaha's Convention of International Chapter and Kearney's state convention. Those were two busy years!

Carolyn Richards and Beverly Kimball have been honored for 50-year memberships in P.E.O. The 1992 Kearney Reciprocity Founders' Day program was dedicated to Carolyn's memory. Carolyn co-authored *"Simple Gifts"* and made the one-shouldered apron which was assembled as the story of the Founders was retold. Carolyn was with GG such a short time but they remember her words, "When you're a P.E.O., you have friends wherever you go."

One of Billie Pahl's annual president's letters states: "Our chapter has a special closeness and bond to each other which every member values. We have not moved mountains but we have moved hearts."

Grace Moore, GG's warehouse of verse, once recited:

> *To each is given a bag of tools,*
> *A lump of clay and a book of rules.*
> *And each must make 'ere life has flown*
> *A stumbling block or a stepping stone.*

Josephine Davis gave GG that lump of clay and her "Good Girls" strive to make stepping stones for themselves and the Sisterhood.

CHAPTER GG'S ACTIVE MEMBERSHIP IS 76; TOTAL ENROLLMENT IS 183

Today is not yesterday; how can our works and thoughts, if they are always to be the fittest, continue always the same?

Change, indeed, is painful, yet ever needful.

–Thomas Carlyle, mid-1800s

Chapter GH Fremont
Organized May 3, 1963
by Josephine Davis

Due largely to the enthusiasm and organizational skills of Elsa Frick, Chapter GH came into being. Organizer Josephine Davis dubbed the chapter the "Glory Hallelujah" chapter. The charter was received at the Hastings convention from Irene Kerr, representative from Supreme Chapter and friend of GH president, Elsa Frick. Charter members were Elsa O. Frick, president; Maxine Mitchell, vice president, Marilyn Kock, treasurer, Marcia Day, corresponding secretary; Veryl Fowler, recording secretary, Shirley Parke, chaplain, Adilee Settje, guard; Vera Clouse, Jane Morse, Jo Ann Lemons, Gene Haynes, Bernice Evans, Dorothy Johnson, Geneve Phillips, Alma Christensen, Margaret Paden, and Ann Goble Sherman.

GH's first opportunity to help entertain the state convention came in 1970. JoAnn Daniel was the banquet chairman. A vocal trio from Chapter GH—Jo Ann Lemons, Imogene Bridges and Bonnie Schilke—has sung at two state conventions and at the Convention of International Chapter in Omaha in 1991. In 1999 we provided table decorations for the state convention. In 2012 we entertained the state convention at Midland University. At that time we celebrated our 50th anniversary, and 50-year plus members, Marilyn Koch, Jo Ann Lemons and Maxine Mitchell were recognized. For this convention's Honor's Luncheon, we converted old ballot boxes into "Grand Pianos"—the creative idea of Mary Collins.

Among our outreach activities we completed our pledge by giving $1,000 to the Nebraska P.E.O. Home; we sent Christmas packages to a foreign exchange student at Cottey College; hosted a P.E.O. from western Kansas while her husband was hospitalized at Fremont Area Medical Center; sent letters to chapters in Washington D.C. and New York City expressing concern for them because of the 9/11 tragedies in their cities.

Chapter GH has sponsored five women for the P.E.O. Educational Loan Fund, and successfully sponsored a P.E.O. Program for Continuing Education grant recipient. In order to raise funds for P.E.O. projects, we sponsor an all-city bridge marathon.

In January 1976, Chapter GH was devastated by the deaths of two valued past officers, Eunice Sexton and Muriel Swearingin, and the injuries of other members who were arriving for a Founders' Day program rehearsal and were caught in the Pathfinder Hotel explosion. At the state convention in May 1976, GH president Imogene Bridges gave a memorial tribute to these sisters.

Another sad parting for us was the sudden death of sister Imogene Bridges in January 2012. She had been an outstanding leader in all activities of our chapter for forty-four years. After her death our president needed to assign six sisters to fulfill Imogene's committee duties.

We are proud of our members' many contributions to our city and state, including the major donation of the Neil and Bonnie Schilke Fields baseball and softball complex donated by our sister Bonnie and her husband, and the major donation by Marie Anderson which helped to build Midland Lutheran University's center for business, journalism and administrative services named in her honor.

We are an engaged chapter, sharing with one another both many sorrows and joys.

Chapter GH's active membership is 49; total enrollment is 187

CHAPTER GI GERING
ORGANIZED MARCH 21, 1964
BY HELEN NOBLE

On February 11, 1963, Virginia Wiley, member of Chapter EV, Gering, wrote to Josephine Davis, state organizer, concerning the possibility of a new P.E.O. chapter in Gering. Virginia, who had been the head of a committee studying this possibility for two years, stated that Gering had passed the 4,000 population mark at the last census and that several deserving members of EV were unable to hold an office because EV's meetings were in the daytime and many members of EV worked.

In the spring of 1963, consent was granted by Chapter EV and they agreed to sponsor the new Chapter GI.

In August 1963, the nine members of EV who formed Chapter GI were: Jean Speedlin, Theone Zalman, Maxine Davis, Gladys Bryan, Grace Good, Harriet McDonald, Hazel Adams, Eleanor Peterson, and Dorothy Kortum. Catherine Fosket, DP, Bridgeport, also was a charter member. These ten dimitting members then suggested names of women in the community who would be good initiates. The names selected were: Gail Barnwell, Luan Knauss, Lu Hide, Marie O'Connor, Pauline Larsen, Helen McCosh and Jean Howard.

On the morning of March 21, 1964, Chapter GI was officially organized by Organizer Helen M. Noble in the home of Mrs. William Gentry. This meeting was especially memorable because the organization of GI's mother chapter, EV, had taken place in the same home twenty-one years earlier. Bernice Tillett, who organized Chapter EV, was present. Members of EV assisted Helen Noble in the initiation of seven new charter initiates. After initiation, there occurred the renewal of P.E.O. vows by the dimitting members. Election of officers followed. Jean Speedlin was GI's first president. Several state officers were present at the morning meeting. Lunch followed at the Town Park Hotel and at 2:30PM. Chapter GI had its first meeting in the home of Pauline Larsen.

Since forming our own chapter, we continue to meet annually with our sister Chapter EV at a summer picnic in June where we have time to enjoy fellowship with sisters we know so well and share the reports from members of both chapters who have attended the state convention. We welcome Founders' Day as it gives us the chance to interact with other chapters in our area.

Chapter GI continues to meet in the evenings, giving those who work an opportunity to be involved. Spouses were initiated with great ceremony into the mystic circle of BIL. One memorable event was an *"Evening in Tuscany"* dinner party with BILs and nearly fifty "people" attending. Another occasion was a delightful Saturday morning brunch.

We have initiated social activities in any month containing five Mondays, with a variety of programs including luncheons and visits to local points of interest.

Each Memorial Day our chapter honors our Chapter Eternal sisters by placing daisies and yellow ribbons on the grave site P.E.O. markers. Yearly, we also design and maintain a portion of the garden at the local zoo as part of the Adopt-A-Spot program.

Yearly we participate in fundraising activities, among the most memorable being Community Days coupon book sales at a local department store, making and selling fleece blankets, holding "bake-less" bake sales, enjoying Christmas auctions at the Legacy of the Plains Museum, and sponsoring geranium sales in the spring. The proceeds from these activities help to fund our contribution to the Nebraska P.E.O Home and other P.E.O. projects.

A very unusual circumstance occurred when the state convention was held in Scottsbluff. One of our local hotels cancelled reservations for attendees at the very last moment. Chapter GI members pitched in and provided housing for more than 40 out-of-town sisters. Those who stayed in various houses were entertained by their hostesses and were treated to the unexpected experience of a tornado.

Peggy Bays became a 50-year member in 2012 and was honored with flowers and a shower of congratulatory cards and her 50-year pin.

Jean Howard and Gail Barnwell attained their 50-year membership in 2014. Jean and Gail were among the original sisters who were invited to join Chapter GI when it was organized.

Under the dedicated leadership of Scholarship Committee Chairman Patti Ediger, Chapter GI has sponsored four young ladies for the P.E.O. STAR Scholarship—Erika Neugabauer, Katie Rueb, Alexa Anderson and in 2013, Katherine O'Boyle. Our chapter also awards a small scholarship to each candidate as a pledge of our support.

It was our pleasure and honor to be recognized at the 2014 Nebraska State Convention in Peru for Chapter GI's 50th anniversary.

Chapter GI was left a legacy by Bernice Tillett when she named the chapter "Genuine Idealists."

CHAPTER GI'S ACTIVE MEMBERSHIP IS 54; TOTAL ENROLLMENT IS 160

"There's always a good reason when something survives and attains greatness... the reason for our remembering them and their heritage to us is their ideals!... they built a foundation that was to last... sincerity, love in thought and action, not only for today, but for the yesterdays and the tomorrows..."

-Bernice Tillet, Past State President and first P.E.O. historian

Chapter GJ Lincoln
Organized December 5, 1964
by Nelsine Scofield

Chapter GJ (Great Joy) P.E.O. was organized on December 5, 1964, at the Cornhusker Hotel in Lincoln. State Organizer Nelsine Scofield and Lincoln Reciprocity Roundtable advisors Lois Newell and Leona George prepared GJ for its "birth."

Charter members were: Lorraine Adolphson, vice president; LaToi Aron; Phyllis Blanke, president; Phyllis Brockoff, Renee Cunningham, Kathryn Davis, Priscilla Drayton, Judith Jacobson Adams; Elizabeth Hart, treasurer; Sara Hough, Patricia Hyland; Sylvia Jay, chaplain; Josephine Kroeger, Elizabeth Little, Frieda Marx, Ruth Alice Maurice; Carolyn Hein McCall, recording secretary; Jo Carolyn McGurk, Carrie Meston Bence, Janet Norris, Carolyn Roper, Eileen Slaughter, Diane Snook; Elaine Stoller, corresponding secretary; Julia Taylor, Peggy Thornton, Betty Wiley; and Charlene T. Wolsmann, guard.

At the time of organization, the meaning of the marguerite was explained, as it relates to P.E.O.

Our chapter has had many long lasting traditions, including a salad buffet at our first fall meeting, remembering our loan and grant recipients with monetary gifts at appropriate times, "adopting" a Cottey College student and sending her useful items periodically, occasionally visiting the Nebraska P.E.O. Home, inviting our most recent initiates as guests to the Founders' Day luncheon, recommending, since its inception, a candidate for the P.E.O. STAR Scholarship, and contributing to various Cottey College fundraisers.

In 1974 Phyllis Blanke served Lincoln Reciprocity Roundtable as its president and went on to serve Nebraska P.E.O. as state president in 1996-97. Due to her recovery from a life-threatening aneurism, Phyllis was unable to preside at her state convention, but her devotion to P.E.O. never wavered and is known throughout the state.

In 1988 Lois Wilson served as Lincoln Reciprocity Roundtable president.

Our primary fundraiser, which we have held every year since 1965, is the Holiday auction where we bring handmade and other items to share. Its proceeds benefit various P.E.O. projects. At regular meetings we also have drawings for items that our members bring back from our travels. That money goes toward funding our local continuing education grant established in 1987. At each meeting we also have a "Brag Pig," where members can tell about a special event concerning a family member. That money partially funds our Courtesy Committee.

It has been our pleasure to sponsor nine P.E.O. project recipients: five women for the PCE, one for IPS, one for the P.E.O. Educational Loan Fund, two for Cottey College, and one for the P.E.O. STAR Scholarship.

Over the past five years we have also sponsored two new chapters, IV and IY, giving them support through our time and gifts.

Beyond our local chapter, we have annually sponsored a Cottey College student, and have given or helped to give a Roundtable program, plus hosting one of its meetings. New within the last two years is a "Cake Ball" sponsored by

Lincoln chapters. Our contribution in 2014 was a donation of two theme baskets and providing some volunteer help. Proceeds from this were distributed to P.E.O. philanthropies.

We are also proud to have had a delegate in 2001 to Convention of International Chapter, one member of the Nebraska State Executive Board, and one member as State Convention Chairman in 2004, and the same member as co-chair of state convention in 2011.

As we were christened "Great Joy," that is what we hope to bring to our fifty-four active members in caring for each other.

CHAPTER GJ'S ACTIVE MEMBERSHIP IS 54; TOTAL ENROLLMENT IS 182

★

CHAPTER GK HASTINGS
ORGANIZED JANUARY 10, 1966
BY JEAN JOHNSON

Chapter GK has always been comprised of amazing, energetic, committed, and compassionate women, a tradition begun by the charter members: Ruth Gellatly, a former state president of Nebraska P.E.O., set the tone followed by Marguerite Dunmire, Nancy Goodrich, Mary Jane Gray, Elizabeth Guildner, Carolyn Irby, Helen Jacupke, Eleanor Jorgenson, Patty Kenney, Gladys Kuehn, Mary McCall, Edith Meredith, Henrietta Morhart, Joyce Ohlsen, Dorothy Shiffler, Ella Mae Short, Berdina Strayer, Mary Walley, Jacqueline Werner and Lois Weyand. Five of the original charter members—Helen Jacupke, Eleanor Jorgenson, Joyce Ohlsen, Dorothy Shiffler, and Jacqueline Werner—continue to participate and inspire us all.

Three Chapter GK 50-year members, Ruth Warren, Carole Storer and Eleanor Jorgenson, taken in 2003

Throughout its history, GK has focused on member relationships as well as on support for the P.E.O. projects, Cottey College, and the Nebraska P.E.O. Home. The Ways and Means committees have designed creative, enjoyable projects to raise money each year. One of the most successful was producing a cookbook of GK members' favorite recipes.

The cookbook reflected that year's theme: *Our Heritage...Getting to Know You... and You...and You*"! Other Ways and Means projects have included silent auctions; production and sales of a Greater Hastings P.E.O. Directory of members in all six Hastings chapters; and, last but not least, spectacular raffles, with prizes such as

Christmas wreaths, a hanging quilt piece, a dinner for eight, baskets of various items and an array of purses. GK sisters have been very generous with both time and financial support every year. Special project donations are made in memory of those who have entered Chapter Eternal and in honor of each GK president at the end of her term.

More 50-year members grace Chapter GK

GK visits P.E.O. Home in Beatrice - Donna Minnick, Connie Yost, Barb Jenkins, Ellen Loughran, Mary Jeanne Cook, Honey Lou Bonar, Mary Kay Anderson, Fran Mulvaney (GK's adopted resident) and Ginny Locke, GK president

GK's focus on membership has included ways to stay connected. Before every meeting and social event, each member receives a phone call or email reminding her of the date, time, location and program. Until two years ago a newsletter titled *The Daisy Chain* was written four, then three times a year and mailed to each member. It included background about new sisters, joys and concerns of all sisters and program information. This year one of our dedicated members is sending a brief newsletter via email or regular mail each month.

The Membership Committee presents unique ideas to help everyone get better acquainted during each meeting. In addition, small interest groups have enhanced chapter friendships. The Courtesy Committee sends cards to sisters with special sorrows or joys and flowers to members who are hospitalized. The loving support and relationships between GK sisters make our chapter very special. Every sister who has ever belonged to GK is honored with a full page, complete with photo, in the chapter scrapbooks; these scrapbooks are displayed at our annual Founders' Day luncheons.

Marlene Mullen has served on the Nebraska State Chapter Bylaws and Standing Rules Committee.

Chapter GK Ways and Means Committee

GK has completed five applications approved for P.E.O. projects: in 1997 Barb Broadwell, PCE; in 2006 and 2007 Rebecca Burks, ELF; in 2006 and 2007 Christine Lee, ELF; in 2008 Cherie Theesen, PCE; in 2012 Lacey Uden, STAR Scholarship.

GK has recommended an outstanding local senior for consideration each year since the P.E.O. STAR Scholarship has been offered. Beginning in 2013, STAR chairmen from each of the six Greater Hastings P.E.O. chapters meet to review applications from local senior girls and then to assign those applications to various chapters so all deserving candidates can be advanced. GK is chairing this committee. GK has also sponsored two women to Cottey College: 2005/2006 McKay Knight and 2003/2004 Tamara Heilman. GK has had a designated Cottey College student and adopted a resident at the Nebraska P.E.O. Home to support through cards and small gifts.

GK's ACTIVE MEMBERSHIP IS 68; TOTAL ENROLLMENT IS 209

★

Chapter GL Omaha
Organized January 19, 1966
by Jean Johnson

Chapter GL of Omaha was founded on January 19, 1966. The letters GL were suggested to signify the "Great Love" which is nurtured and shared by each sister. There were eighteen charter members. Fifteen members were from out-state Nebraska and from other states. There were three members from Omaha—two from Chapter DY and one from Chapter EC.

Charter officers were Julia Anwyl, Mary Margaret Bieber, Eileen Damhoff, Gertrude Hundhausen, Thelma McGuire, Freda Underwood, and Mary Wiese, along with members Dorothy Adams, Dorothy Becker, Dale Cleveland, Geraldine Fritzmeier, Betty Gathman, June Gautier, Nathalie Hart (Chapter FG, Kansas), Helen Putzier, Helen Robbins, Delores Witherbee (Chapter DY, Lincoln) and Mary Warnemunde. Kay Murrell of Chapter ED in Missouri desired membership but was unable to attend the organizational meeting. A dimit was granted to her in April of 1966.

The first meeting was held in the home of the president, Mary Margaret Bieber. State Organizer Jean Johnson was in attendance. It was a 10AM meeting with a buffet luncheon to follow.

To date there have been 168 Chapter GL members. GL was Omaha's 32nd Chapter of P.E.O. GL received its charter in the P.E.O. Sisterhood at the state convention in Omaha.

The meetings have almost always been in the daytime with few exceptions. There was some flexibility allowed in attempting to increase attendance of working women and to accommodate women with young children. Later meetings were changed to a 12:30 luncheon with the business meeting to follow. Currently we meet at 1:00PM with a dessert luncheon.

P.E.O. projects have been funded by numerous activities. There have been Christmas auctions, spring plant sales, bake sales, white elephant sales, etc. Recently, the chapter's "Silver Tea" at Christmastime was changed to an October "Project Tea." This allows members to make monetary donations.

Chapter socials have included guest days, mother/daughter teas, BIL progressive dinners, BIL initiations, and outings of interest, tours of local institutions, and visits to the Nebraska P.E.O. Home in Beatrice.

Programs have been arranged in conjunction with the "theme" of the current year. They have included outside speakers from the community as well as programs by Chapter GL members and guest P.E.O. chapter members.

Chapter GL — Standing back row left to right: Sooz Edwards, Faye Couch, June Schweiger, Annette Lyman, Pat Billings, Marilyn O'Gara, Bernice Hall, Mary Jane Nelson, Sharon Sievers, Mary Patterson, Jacque Jacox, Louise Nelson, Sharolyn Lager, Gretchen Vondrak, Donna Short, Nathalie Hart, Carol Gates. Front row: Nancy Sherwood, Mary Mayfield, Ginny Petersen, Jackie Sojka, Marian Leach, Lois Wohlner, Judy Yingst.

Scholarships have sponsored continuing education for numerous local recipients.

Emphasis has been placed on support of the Nebraska P.E.O. Home in Beatrice and of Cottey College in Nevada, Missouri. Recently, GL members have simplified our emphasis on food. There are two meetings with a luncheon at 12:00 noon—at Christmastime and in the spring of the year. This change in venue was made to encourage more time for membership socialization and ease in hosting.

For the past several years Chapter GL has proudly published a "Great Love Newsletter," four times a year. It is sent to all members.

We have five 50-year members in our chapter: Dorothy Becker and Marjorie Padgett are in Chapter Eternal. Nathalie Hart, Dolores Witherbee and Sharolyn Lager are currently active and have celebrated fifty years of membership.

CHAPTER GL'S ACTIVE MEMBERSHIP IS 43; TOTAL ENROLLMENT IS 168

★

CHAPTER GM OMAHA
ORGANIZED JANUARY 23, 1966
BY JEAN JOHNSON

Organization of Chapter GM began in early 1965 in Omaha as Nebraska's newest chapter—the "Golden Melody" chapter—took shape. It was organized as one of the first evening P.E.O. chapters. Past State President Dorothy Yeager, Pat Shellenberger, and Omaha Unaffiliate Chairman Cecilia Nelson worked in harmony with the unaffiliated members throughout the year. In October, Organizer Jean Johnson met with nineteen P.E.O.s who signed a petition. Eighteen women became charter members of Chapter GM: Barbara Wetherell, president; Mary Lue Hicks, vice president; JoAnn Alexander, corresponding secretary; Louise Witzenburg, recording secretary; Anita Mitten, treasurer; Frances Coffin, guard; Sandra Allen, Jean Bancroft, Nancy Callas, Sara Dillow, Meredyth Gentry, Marcia Hansen, Mildred Johnson, Janet Kragh, Mildred Nisley, Ann Pettine, Susan Smithberger, and Marjorie Vanderlippe. Illness of Joan Nelson necessitated her later entry by dimit. One charter member, Anita Mitten Bernstein, remains an active member in Chapter GM.

Special milestones in the chapter include 50-year memberships for Anita Bernstein, Betty Lou Smith, who dimitted to Chapter AI, Nevada, and 60 year membership for the late Mary Lue Hicks. Chapter GM observes its 50th anniversary in 2016.

Chapter GM members have been active at the local, state, and International levels. Members who have served on the Omaha Reciprocity Association board include Linda Ridgway, Dee Ann Bowen, Becky Dietle, and Donna Lammert. Dee Ann Bowen has served as Nebraska State Chapter Unaffiliate Chairman and chairman of sales at state convention. Jody Botsch has served as Cottey Area Chairman for the Omaha area. Many chapter members have helped with state conventions. The late Mary Bowen served as president of the New Mexico State Chapter and secretary of Supreme Chapter. Dee Ann Bowen, Becky Dietle and Pam Kregg have been delegates to Conventions of International Chapter. Pam Kregg has served on the Nebraska State Executive Board and as president of Nebraska State Chapter in 2008. She served three years on the Ohio State P.E.O. Amendments and Recommendations committee, and as secretary of the Nebraska State Planning Committee for the 2001 convention. She has also served on the state Finance and Budget Committee, Membership Committee, Board of Directors of the Nebraska P.E.O. Home, and Special Committee for Membership Advancement for International Chapter.

Project support includes P.E.O. Educational Loan Fund and PCE grant recipients, Nebraska Cottey Scholarship winners, Cottey College students, and many loving gifts made to the Nebraska P.E.O. Home residents.

Chapter GM has enjoyed many social events with chapter members, guests, and BILs. Socials include tours of the Governor's Mansion in Lincoln, a trip to Nell Hill in Kansas, visit to the Holy Family Shrine, Soaring Wings Winery, South Gold Coast Trolley Tour, the Lucky Bucket Brewery, a Storm Chasers baseball game, and the Omaha Lancers Hockey. Krista Cox has planned many great socials for Chapter GM members and our guests!

We have had a variety of different fundraising activities to sponsor our P.E.O. projects and also charitable causes at home and abroad. Fundraising ideas have included gift bag sales, raffles, garage sales, auctions, cookbook sales, plus the sales of coupon books, poinsettias, Rada knives, and KB cloths. One idea shared from The P.E.O. Record was "Bags, Baubles, and Baked Goods" which raised over one thousand dollars within three hours! Chapter GM is very proud of our donations to the P.E.O. projects over the years plus donations to the Red Cross, Open Door Mission, Lydia House, Youth Emergency Services, Omaha World Herald Goodfellows, Uta Halee Girls Village, and Cottey College's Bucks for Beds project. We have supported the Naivasha Women's Health Care Centre in Africa, organized by member Cindy Berkland.

Chapter GM is special because we are constantly evolving—adding new members through initiation or transfer. We are a chapter of friendly, enthusiastic, and caring sisters.

CHAPTER GM'S ACTIVE MEMBERSHIP IS 58; TOTAL ENROLLMENT IS 197

★

Chapter GN Kimball
ORGANIZED MARCH 5, 1966
BY JEAN JOHNSON

Chapter GN of Kimball was organized on March 5, 1966, by Jean Johnson. The chapter consisted of seventeen charter members: Jean Long, president; America Linn, vice president; Gladys Borne, recording secretary; Salma Hammond, corresponding secretary; Anna Margaret Petersen, treasurer; Mary Moore, chaplain; Maxine Flohr, guard; Peggy Atkins, Elizabeth Eastman, Edith Haines, Dorothy Hein, Cynthia Jennings, Marian Johnson, Ruth Linn, Bonnie McNees, Shirley Ohlemeier, and Winifred Peterson. Six of the charter members were dimitting members, while eleven were initiated into Chapter GN. Since the organizing of Chapter GN, seventeen sisters have entered Chapter Eternal. Also, two sisters of Chapter GN have been members of P.E.O. since 1942 and 1944.

When Chapter GN sisters were asked to describe our chapter in one word, the most common response was 'sister,' which demonstrates the spirit of camaraderie within our chapter. Other responses included supportive, fun, and awesome. Laughter is a common trait of our chapter, and is demonstrated by the sisters whether we are laughing about wearing feather boas to a meeting, eating a fellow sister's rolls while waiting in her car, or opening a 50-cent gift at our Christmas gathering. Chapter GN truly displays the heart of P.E.O.

Every year we support the seven projects supported by P.E.O. During each Christmas season, we collect donations for the Nebraska P.E.O. Home by "Trimming the Christmas Tree" at our annual Christmas gathering. In 2004, we joined with Chapter DT in Kimball and invited high school girls to a pizza party to educate the girls about Cottey College. In 2013, we adopted a sister from the Nebraska P.E.O. Home.

Chapter GN meetings are full of laughter and the building of meaningful relationships. Each sister opens up her home to host meetings, and her generosity only strengthens our Sisterhood. During meetings, sisters provide a wide variety of programs. Programs range from educational topics about health issues to exploring the world together through vacation photos. One sister presented a program with the assistance of a parrot while another sister shared how the shape of our lipstick can teach us about our individual personalities. The local high school Shakespearean players were invited to perform. We have learned the art of carving a turkey by using a map of the United States. Another sister shared about bees and presented each sister with locally grown honey. Each unique program provides opportunities for us to grow closer together as sisters.

Our sister Frances Campbell, who entered Chapter Eternal in 2011, is the artist who painted individual portraits of our seven Founders. The portraits were displayed at state convention in 1995, and again at our Spring Tea in 2012. Another chapter highlight was hosting Reciprocity in Kimball at the Country Club in 2000. A yearly highlight is our joint celebration of Founders' Day with Chapter DT. Chapter GN has organized various fundraisers over the past years including rummage sales, Spring Tea, and passing May Day baskets amongst our sisters.

Chapter GN continues to strive to display the characteristics to P.E.O. within our Sisterhood and around our community. Each sister contributes different strengths to our chapter to make Chapter GN the successful and joyous chapter it is today.

CHAPTER GN'S ACTIVE MEMBERSHIP IS 39; TOTAL ENROLLMENT IS 110

★

Chapter GO North Platte
Organized March 26, 1966
by Jean Johnson

Without an evening chapter, working women in North Platte were unable to participate actively in P.E.O. In response to their needs, Chapter GO was organized on March 26, 1966, with Jean Johnson as organizer. It had been thirty-one years since a new chapter had been organized in the city. Chapter initials have been used creatively. One president wrote that GO sisters like to GO. Another used GO people as her yearbook theme.

The new chapter was chartered with eleven dimitting and six initiated members. Officers included Barbara Shurtleff, president; Beverly Peterson, vice president; Helen Darby, recording secretary; Maurine Haines, corresponding secretary; Margaret Morton, treasurer; Virginia Hornbacher, chaplain; and

Mary Tollefson, guard. Other charter members were Gladys Adams, Marjorie Christianson, Ellen Craft, Lillian Eberhart, Marian Miller, Mabel Oakes, Mary Kay Stevenson, Anita Swanson, Kay Toillion, and Maxine Watson. Virginia Hornbacher, and Kay Toillion, a 50-year member, are still resident members. The historian's book was a gift from Maude Hendy (Chapter Eternal 1978), past state president, Chapter AK initiate, and charter member of Chapter EB.

GO members are proud of their good attendance and strong leadership. Thirty-one members have served as president. Fifteen past presidents are still resident members. In 1979 Winifred Swanson was co-chairman of the Nebraska State P.E.O. Convention in North Platte; Carol Norgaard, Susan Altig and Laurie Morrison have served as guards for state and International Conventions. Delegates to Convention of International Chapter have been Winifred Swanson, Ruth Holm, and Laurie Morrison.

In 2000, Chapter GO hosted the annual meeting of the Panhandle Reciprocity Group. The theme of the luncheon was "*P.E.O.—Our Special Brand of Love.*" In 2002, GO members helped with the Nebraska State P.E.O. Convention in North Platte. Linda Rousey, who was president of the Panhandle Reciprocity Group, led a workshop at the 2003 convention in Hastings.

GO's involvement with P.E.O. projects has been exemplary. The chapter has contributed every year to all the projects and to special P.E.O. campaigns and endowment funds, with loving gifts to the Nebraska P.E.O. Home at Christmas and annually to our P.E.O. philanthropies. GO has sponsored thirteen young woman for ELF loans and eight for PCE grants. Since 1995, Chapter GO has sponsored Kendra Burkholder, Elaine Besthorn, and Shannon Anslover for ELF loans. Kendra also received a PCE grant.

Chapter GO North Platte gathered to celebrate its 25th anniversary on April 4, 1991

Fundraising activities have included silent auctions, rummage sales, "bakeless" bake sales, auctions of mystery gifts, and soup suppers for members. In addition, GO has earned money by serving reciprocity or Founders' Day luncheons. In 2013 Chapter GO joined four other North Platte P.E.O. chapters for an "all-girl" mystery dinner to raise funds for the Cottey College Campaign.

When Linda Clough, a beloved GO sister, died in 2012, Chapter GO received a generous memorial gift. Honoring Linda's wishes, Chapter GO is awarding scholarships to four deserving students whose mothers are GO members. (Two students also have grandmothers in Chapter GO, and one is a GO sister.) In memory of Lillian Eberhart, a charter member who died in 2001, her husband gave Chapter GO a generous bequest, which was used for a donation to the P.E.O. Educational Loan Fund and a table for the library at North Platte High School where Lillian taught for many years.

Chapter GO members enjoy sharing not only their service as P.E.O. sisters but also their good times. Favorite social meetings have been special meals with sisters or BIL events like a backyard cook-out, a progressive supper, and ice cream socials. In August 2009, GO sisters took a memorable bus trip to the Nebraska P.E.O. Home in Beatrice.

GO sisters celebrated their 10th anniversary in 1976, their 25th in 1991, and their 40th in 2006.

CHAPTER GO'S ACTIVE MEMBERSHIP IS 49; TOTAL ENROLLMENT IS 155

Chapter GP Grand Island
Organized November 21, 1966
by Sheila Shreck

A happy year of planning preceded the organization of Chapter GP, Grand Island. Officers of Nebraska State Chapter groped their way to Grand Island through dense fog, and Chapters CK, EH, and EZ sponsored a coffee at the Woman's Club. Charter members of Chapter GP were Charter Head, Joan Donley, president; Arelene Hillis, vice president; Mary Reitan, recording secretary; Marval Hornady, corresponding secretary; Vera "Bobbie" Koefoot, treasurer; Joyce Schultz, chaplain; and Harriette Francis, guard. Other charter members were Cathryn Armstrong, Jean Armstrong, Ruth Gates, Adaline House, Suzanne Kirkendall, Prue Luers, Blenda Reynolds, Margaret Steadman, Harriet Wenger, Lorayne Wrenn and Harriet Lumbard. A luncheon at the home of Marval Hornady was followed by the first meeting at the home of Arelene Hillis.

Chapter GP abounds with P.E.O. notables. Harriet Lumbard was a past president (1959-60) of Nebraska State Chapter when she joined Chapter GP. Vera "Bobbie" Koefoot, also a past president (1976-77) of Nebraska State Chapter, was vice president of International Chapter at the time of her death. Alice Fisher was a past state president (1997-98) and had served as General Chairman of the Convention of Nebraska State Chapter when it was held in Grand Island in 1991. Joan Donley was a ten-year member of the Nebraska P.E.O. Home Board of Directors. Chapter GP is so proud of the accomplishments of Harriet, Bobbie, Alice and Joan. Their devotion to the Sisterhood has been exemplary.

Each year the members of Chapter GP join together in a fundraising activity to support all the projects. Putting together bags of soup mix, cookie mix, and making greeting cards have been enjoyed by most members, but a series of small group luncheons hosted by sisters which included a bake-less bake sale have been very successful, as well. Our chapter has sponsored three PCE, two ELF, one IPS and two P.E.O. STAR Scholarship winners.

Three of the charter members continue to be active and we are proud to have five sisters who have been P.E.O.s over fifty years and one sister who celebrated seventy years in 2013.

The members of Chapter GP enjoy a yearly road trip which includes lunch, three of which have been to the Nebraska P.E.O. Home in Beatrice. There are also dinner parties with our BILs, many of which have included musical programs or tours of new local facilities. One year the men were exposed to a special initiation ceremony. The loving spirit of our chapter is evident in the camaraderie and caring we all enjoy.

CHAPTER GP'S ACTIVE MEMBERSHIP IS 43; TOTAL ENROLLMENT IS 203

★

CHAPTER GQ LINCOLN
ORGANIZED JANUARY 28, 1967
BY SHEILA SHRECK

Chapter GQ was organized January 28, 1967, at the home of Marjorie Martin with Shelia Shreck presiding. Charter members of Chapter GQ were Judith Olson, president; Nancy L. Schepler, vice president; Patricia Winkler, treasurer; Mary Ann Bede, chaplain; Margaret Peterson, corresponding secretary; Mary Elizabeth Hayek, recording secretary; Cynthia Fitchett, guard; Priscilla Whitehead, Mary Jane Bienhoff, Charlotte C. Robins, Evelyn S. Cameron, Marlis Hemphill, Marcia Hollestelle, Edith R. Dunn, and Betty Whitney. Shirley Springer should have been a charter member, but her dimit did not come through in time. Shirley was with these girls in their planning and with their formation.

Charter members active today are Marcia Hollestelle, Betty Whitney and the first chaplain of GQ, Mary Ann Bede. In these forty-seven years we have welcomed 180 members and at the printing of this history we enjoy the friendship, joys and news from fifty-eight active members and six nonresident members. Our chapter focuses on reaching out for new members, reaching elsewhere in our project support and reaching around our sisters in supportive attention. We are close-knit. We have initiated many daughters and sought young women to keep our chapter vibrant. We support new ideas, information and projects through programs and activities that are timely, educational, entertaining and young at heart.

Chapter GQ is ardent in supporting our P.E.O. projects. To finance this outreach we have held an annual raffle for a meal. For a couple of decades this meal was a gourmet affair for eight served in the winner's home. Then we simplified to a picnic for the winner's family and now we find recipients very pleased with a winner's gift card for their choice of venue. This raffle provides increased amounts for our gifting to the projects. In addition, our chapter is blessed with several women who for years have hosted Bed and Breakfast guests; notably JoAnn Sharrar, who started this activity, Joyce Bumsted and Diane Stofferhan. Darlene Jansen's artistry has added money through sales of her beautiful paintings on greeting cards and porcelain objects, and portions adapted for the cover of the very book you are reading. She provides us with very special marriage and baby gifts.

Chapter GQ has demonstrated a special concern for recruitment of applicants for our loans, grants and awards. We have been blessed with a healthy number of awards and reports of repayment of loan monies and accomplishments by the women we have encouraged. In 2000, we enlarged our world-view with our P.E.O. International Peace Scholarship recipient, Juan Xu, from China. We rejoice in this avenue of service.

We have a special love for the sisters living at the Nebraska P.E.O. Home in Beatrice and were privileged to contribute to the Home's endowment fund. We usually visit the Home annually presenting programs, gifts and our affection for the guests and staff. Each year we send gift cards or small gifts to a young woman at Cottey College showing our supportive affection.

We feel our Family P.E.O. Album is a keystone of our caring outreach. We update this charming book with pictures and stories. As we approach our fifty years as a chapter we truly realize the heartfelt meaning of our support for each other and our families. Our presidents and newsletter editors keep us informed with timely email.

Our chapter makes special efforts to energize and become better acquainted. Over the years Pat Ball has organized "GQ Lunch Bunch" and we now have casual groupings for lunch bunch, reading books, playing bridge, stitching together, doing art or walking!

These are our gifts and graces in a history that truly shows the unique character of Chapter GQ. It is all about empowering women, embracing change and growing together. Our first half-century has been wonder-filled and wonder-full! We look forward to the next fifty years with goals of growth and good works.

CHAPTER GQ'S ACTIVE MEMBERSHIP IS 61; TOTAL ENROLLMENT IS 180

★

CHAPTER GR LEXINGTON
ORGANIZED APRIL 5, 1967
BY SHEILA SHRECK

The 200th P.E.O. chapter in Nebraska was formed in Lexington from members of Chapter AN and FS. Dorothy Kain from Chapter AN was the charter head and helped to guide the group through the maze of pre-organization details. Charter members were Elaine Smith, president; Delphine Sanks, vice president; Nancy Long, recording secretary; Jeanne Kelly, corresponding secretary; Barbara Roberts, treasurer; Artie Hobbs, chaplain; Paula Knapple, guard; Dorothy Ayers, Gladys Benthack, Marjorie Burnett, Ruth Fagot, Dianne Jeffrey, Sonya Landholm, Marialice Renard, June Reynolds, Shirley Reynolds, Athea Roberts, Olga Sheldon and Genevieve Welch.

At a birthday party in 1992, Chapter GR observed our 25th anniversary, reminisced about the past and made plans for the future. GR was organized as an afternoon chapter, and remains one but we have occasional 4PM and 7PM meetings to accommodate members.

In 2007, we celebrated our 40th anniversary and had four charter members in attendance: Shirley Reynolds, Paula Knapple, Jeanne Kelly and Ruth Fagot.

Chapter GR is always looking for new project recipients. We have sponsored numerous applicants for the P.E.O. STAR Scholarship, P.E.O. Scholar Award, PCE and ELF in the past twenty years and we have had nine PCE recipients and two ELF recipients. As in the past, we continue to have our annual fundraiser, the Ways and Means Auction, during which members pay outlandish prices for their sisters' gifts, baked goods and crafts that each sister has donated. Because of our successful fundraising efforts, we have been able to continue to increase our project giving.

A special activity for Chapter GR is supporting our Nebraska P.E.O. Home by sending hand crafted Valentine cards, Christmas cards, card game prizes, occasional visits, and monetary gifts for special projects. Two Chapter GR members have resided at the Home.

Social activities are important for GR to keep our members connected. We have a BIL social every year, along with a Valentine's party, a salad luncheon in the summer, Christmas ornament exchange and the Ways and Means auction. Recently we have added a golf scramble for interested members.

We are proud to have a five-generation family in our membership. They are GR charter member Athea Roberts, Athea's daughter-in-law charter member Barb Roberts, granddaughter-in-law Tempie Roberts and great-granddaughters Kelsey and Riley Roberts. Athea's mother Carrie Hine was also a P.E.O. member in Chapter AN, thus making the five generations.

We presently have three 50-year members: Shirley Reynolds, Jeanne Kelly and Ruth Fagot. Our sister Cathy Fagot served as state ELF chairman from 2012 to 2014.

Each year we honor our members in Chapter Eternal by decorating their graves.

CHAPTER GR'S ACTIVE MEMBERSHIP IS 48; TOTAL ENROLLMENT IS 165

★

CHAPTER GS NORFOLK
ORGANIZED JANUARY 27, 1968
BY KATHRYN WHITE

Norfolk Nebraska was a growing community in 1967 with only one P.E.O. chapter. The ladies of Chapter CU and some of the new residents that were unaffiliated decided that the time was right for a new P.E.O. chapter.

On a cold January 27, 1968, Chapter GS was formed. Eight members from Chapter CU and eight unaffiliated members received their charter for Chapter GS at the 1968 Convention of Nebraska State Chapter in Valentine. The state organizer was Kathryn White and the first president of GS was Beverly Scarpolino. Three of the charter members, Eunice Mohl, Betty Lou Walz and Deanna Theisen, are still very active in Chapter GS. They are all 50-year members and past presidents of Chapter GS. The other charter members were: Mary Dewey, Elaine Fortner, Catherine Hutton, Mae McGinnis, Helen Maclay, Lavon Neuhaus, Garnet Pelter, Thiel Reynolds, Margaret Ann Ritchey, Marcella Settell, Valerie Young and Margaret Ziegenbein.

Our robes for initiation were purchased thanks to the generosity of our members and sisters of Chapter CU. Our dues were $12.50 a year. We met with our sister chapter once a year for a luncheon or social. We sponsored our first P.E.O. Educational Loan Fund candidate in 1975 and in 1978 at our ten-year anniversary, our membership was forty-five sisters.

Chapter GS was growing and we were meeting during the daytime which was difficult for our employed membership. Fourteen of our members dimitted on February 24, 1982, to form Chapter HU where they could be active in evening meetings. In January of 1983, the Norfolk Reciprocity Group was formed uniting the three Norfolk chapters. We meet every year in January for a delightful morning to socialize and share our chapter experiences.

The state president in 1988-89 was our sister Catherine "Cay" Hutton. This was a highlight for our chapter! At the state convention in June of that year, Chapter GS gave a donation to the P.E.O. Program for Continuing Education in her honor. She was a valued member that entered Chapter Eternal on January 14, 2002.

We have always enjoyed our social times together and especially when our BILs join us. We entertained our spouses at Christmas dinners for many years and most recently BarBQ's at the lake home of Jeri Egley. These are always well attended and enjoyed by everyone.

Since 2007, at the encouragement of Dottie Mckeever, we began participating in "Herberger Community Days" where each member of the chapter sells coupon books for Herbergers' fall sale days. This has proven to be a profitable and easy money maker. In the past we have had auctions, garage sales, and a used jewelry sale among other fundraisers.

The last few years the yearbook committee has dedicated the yearbook to a 50-year member. Our programs have been varied and interesting. We have had speakers from the community on current affairs, tours of our homes and gardens, a piano duet by two members of Chapter CU, cooking demonstrations, craft fairs, encouragement on health issues, and one beautiful fall day a bus trip to the Nebraska P.E.O. Home in Beatrice. We enjoy the opportunity to become closer as sisters in P.E.O. by sharing these times. We are very fortunate to have a talented member Verona Simons who has printed and organized our yearbook. This is true dedication!

We have been privileged to sponsor sixteen women for the P.E.O. Program for Continuing Education and P.E.O. Educational Loan Fund. Seven girls have received our P.E.O. 9th grade Girl Leadership Award.

CHAPTER GS'S ACTIVE MEMBERSHIP IS 48; TOTAL ENROLLMENT IS 186

★

Chapter GT O'Neill
Organized April 19, 1969
by Helen Magill

Chapter GT of the P.E.O. Sisterhood was organized in O'Neill on Saturday, April 19, 1969. The organizational meeting was held in the First United Methodist Church with Mrs. Helen Magill of Holdrege presiding. Members of Chapter BU of Atkinson conducted the initiation ceremony for the sixteen charter members. In attendance were ninety-nine P.E.O. members from Nebraska, Iowa, South Dakota and Colorado.

Charter members of Chapter GT were Helen Rooney, Joan Bauer, Olive Skrdla, Ann Nelson, Nancee Burbank, Mary Langemeier, Elizabeth Spelts, Mary Chantry, Elizabeth Schaffer, Emily Herley, Helen Gillespie, Nancy Grady, Rachel Simpson, Lillian Drayton, Mary Lundgren and Mary Ann Rasmussen.

The chapter has had many memorable programs and socials including a tour of a barn converted to a home and featured on HGTV, a wine tasting party, a program held at a local museum, holiday parties and a picnic at a beautiful property known as Fitchland. Because we have a very talented group of ladies, our socials have included musicals where we were able to enjoy watching members perform as well as attending dance reviews directed by members. We enjoy recognizing each member's talent. Each year we celebrate the chapter's organizational anniversary with a birthday dinner at a local restaurant.

GT continues to donate to all P.E.O. projects. We have had many recipients of grants from the P.E.O. Program for Continuing Education. Some young ladies have received loans from the P.E.O. Educational Loan Fund. We were honored when one of our P.E.O. STAR Scholarship applicants, Heidi Hostert, was selected in 2011. We also recently sponsored a student from our area who chose to attend Cottey College.

Chapter GT member Shari Brosz served as chairman of the state P.E.O. Program for Continuing Education as well as on the state convention committee. We were also very proud when Shari became a bone morrow donor for a young woman from Iowa.

Chapter GT has found community involvement to be very rewarding. Our main fundraiser for our chapter is the annual P.E.O. Christmas Tour of Homes. It serves as a fundraiser for our chapter and a social event the whole community looks forward to. With the funds raised from this function, each year we are able to offer four to six scholarships to girls from this area. In addition, we have contributed to the area Food Bank and the police K-9 unit fund drive. We have provided Thanksgiving dinners for an underprivileged family, and school supplies for the elementary schools in O'Neill.

Chapter GT was privileged to participate in the Nebraska State Convention at Norfolk in 2010 where Shari Brosz lent her voice to several musical numbers and our chapter provided the memorial service which included a liturgical dance.

In 2013, Mary Ann Rasmussen was among those honored at the state convention for fifty years as a P.E.O. member. She remains active as a member and is a mentor to the entire chapter.

CHAPTER GT's ACTIVE MEMBERSHIP IS 33; TOTAL ENROLLMENT IS 124

★

Chapter GU Omaha
Organized December 6, 1969
by Catherine Andersen

Chapter GU was the last Nebraska chapter to be organized in P.E.O.'s first century. There were twenty-one members, of which three still remain active members. They are Maurine DeRoin, Beverly Donaldson, and Barbara Mitchell.

To establish the chapter, Maurine Hintz chose the charter list and led the group for nine preparatory months, advised by Dorothy Yeager of Chapter E and state officers Helen Magill and Catherine Andersen. Charter members were Phebe Smith, president; Maurine DeRoin, vice president; Barbara Pyle, recording secretary; Sharon Schafer, corresponding secretary; Carolyn Spaedt, treasurer; Ruth Rinde, chaplain; Carole Smiley, guard; Maurine Hintz, Nancy Ernst, Janet Garden, Barbara Mitchell, Anne Piper, Deanna Smith, Velma Wilson, Marie Wolfe, and initiates Beverly Donaldson, Lois Hawkins, Janet Trotter and Roma Wilson. Maxine Miller and Celia Smith entered by dimit immediately thereafter.

Because of our growth, it has become necessary at times to meet in places other than our homes. We also have small groups that we call "Our Star Sisters" that meet between meetings. There are five groups representing the five points of the star and are reorganized at the beginning of each P.E.O. year.

Chapter GU's participation in the P.E.O. projects consists of the following: P.E.O. Scholar Awards in 1995, 2000 and 2011; PCE grants in 1998, 1999, 2002; P.E.O. Educational Loan Fund in 1995; IPS in 2003; Cottey College 1997. Our chapter made a donation for the recovery of Greenberg, Kansas, tornado victims and makes donations to our local Food Bank, Toys for Tots, and Hope Center.

In the year 2000, Chapter GU celebrated our 30th anniversary. Beverly Donaldson wrote a song titled *"The Anniversary Song."* State Convention was held in Omaha in 2008 and our chapter had two guards and several members participating in registration. We also had two 50-year members honored. They were Mary Jane Bienhoff and Lynn Woodruff. Our BIL parties are always a fun time with our husbands who are good sports with their initiation. At the Founders' Day celebration on January 20, 2013, Chapter GU's two 50-year members were honored. They are Joann Collins and Dorothy Lower.

Relatively new committees consist of Membership, Technology, and Ways & Means. Membership is ongoing with recruiting new members, reinstating members, and just keeping in touch. Technology has really been a great tool and we have an excellent member leading us in that area. She sends out bi-monthly newsletters and also keeps us informed of any changes in regard to members or meetings, etc., via email. We mail to sisters without email addresses. Our Ways & Means committee is doing an excellent job with notepaper designed by Barbara Mitchell, book sales, and "Birthday Bonanza," where a gift is donated by the birthday sister to be given to the winning number drawn.

Chapter GU is a vibrant group that enjoys the friendships and our time together.

CHAPTER GU'S ACTIVE MEMBERSHIP IS 55; TOTAL ENROLLMENT IS 195

★

Chapter GV Lincoln
Organized April 4, 1970
by Catherine Andersen

It was a special day, that Saturday, April 4, 1970, as women were arriving at the Country Club of Lincoln for a very special event...the organizing of a new chapter of P.E.O. It would be the first chapter organized in Nebraska in P.E.O.'s second century, the 197th in the state of Nebraska, and the 23rd chapter in Lincoln— Chapter GV. Charter members dimitting from Chapter K were Helenlee Jones, Katheryn Baer, Elizabeth James, Mildred Linch, Marilyn Edgecomb, Greta Mulligan, Louise Hale, Jeanne Cuda, Marilyn Armagost, Marguerite Van Horn, Dorothy French, Marjorie Brice, Candance Brice, Janet Asman and Suanne Stange. From other chapters came six additional dimitting members: Evelyn French, Janet Knight, Betty Bottger, Betty Brittenham, Mary Jo Cranwell and Sibyl Ramage. Of the nine initiates, three were daughters of charter members: Nancy Baer, Sue Jones and Emily Edgecomb. The other initiates were Jan Brockley, Helen Traudt, Elizabeth Wallace, Marjorie Folger, Marion Petersen and Audrey Wiegert. Following the meeting there was a luncheon for the charter members and the special guests. Elizabeth Wallace designed a ceramic vase in the outline of the P.E.O. star to be given as a gift to each charter member. Chapter K, the mother chapter, gave

Chapter GV a white gavel. Margarie Brice made the white tablecloth to be used for Chapter GV initiations

On May 12, 1969, charter head Helen Lee Jones was granted permission to form the new chapter. At the first meeting of the pending chapter on June 24, 1969, meeting times were set for the first and third Tuesdays at 9:30 AM, making GV the first morning chapter in Lincoln. Marjorie Brice designed our robes. Helen Traudt sewed them to be used in our first initiation in 1973. In 2011 Shirley Gibson made new robes for Chapter GV. They were worn for the first time that very year to initiate a new member. The old robes were sent to Africa with Jan Brockley on her annual African mission trip.

Within a year of organizing, Chapter GV recommended and successfully sponsored a P.E.O. Educational Loan Fund student. To date, Chapter GV has sponsored thirteen educational scholarships/grants which include: P.E.O. Educational Loan Fund, P.E.O. International Peace Scholarships (IPS), Nebraska Cottey College Scholarships, P.E.O. Program for Continuing Education grants and the chapter endorsed an applicant for the P.E.O. Scholar Award.

Katheryn Baer served as president of Lincoln Reciprocity Roundtable in 1980/81 and Jeanne Cuda in 1987/88. Helen Lee Jones, Elizabeth James and Mary Alice Jones have served as Roundtable secretaries. At the 2004 Convention of Nebraska State Chapter Willa Foster Jones directed the choir with Cathy Maasdam as accompanist. Delegates to International Convention include Katheryn Baer, Chapter GV's first representative in 1974; Jeanne Cuda in 1986 and Mary Alice Jones in 1999.

Our interest in the Nebraska P.E.O. Home and Cottey College remains constant. We have contributed to the Nebraska Suite at Cottey College and raised monies for the Building Fund. Many visits have been made to the Nebraska P.E.O. Home. In the event of a death of one of our sisters or a sister's family member, a memorial gift is given to the Endowment Fund of the Home.

Chapter GV

Fundraising—including silent auctions, calendar sales, raffles and bean soup mix sales—has been directed exclusively to our educational projects. Hosting out-of-town P.E.O.s at our Bed and Breakfasts has provided another source of revenue. One cookbook and a book entitled *Ribbons of Intention* have been sold. Shirley Gibson organized and chaired our annual Luncheon/Fashion Show for the third year. We have participated in the annual Cake Ball with our Lincoln sister chapters. As a result of our successful fundraising, Chapter GV is honored to give grants to three local seniors.

We have honored eleven 50-year sisters, one 60-year sister and one 70-year sister. Thirty of our sisters have entered Chapter Eternal. We have felt the losses of these faithful sisters who were our leaders and mentors.

Chapter GV's birthday is an event to which we all look forward. Our past social gatherings with the BILs have included pot luck dinners, picnicking at the lake, visiting the Governor's Mansion and dinner socials at local restaurants with programs of interest.

CHAPTER GV'S ACTIVE MEMBERSHIP IS 43; TOTAL ENROLLMENT IS 143

★

Chapter GW Lincoln
Organized January 30, 1971
by Janet Atkins

On a cold January 31st in 1971, twenty-three P.E.O.s and two initiates were organized by Janet Atkins as members of Chapter GW. These "Great Women" later received their charter at the Convention of Nebraska State Chapter in York. Members were Susan Russell, president; Grace Isaacson, vice president; Janet M. Cutshall, recording secretary; Fredrena Pappas, corresponding secretary; Mary Tous, treasurer; Stanley Rediger, chaplain; Carol Burtz, guard; Karen Curtis, Janet L. Cutshall, Shelley Edson, Rose Ann Ellison, Sally Haywood, Annette Kaplan, Connie Krohn, Connie Matzen, Mary Jane Nelson, Pamela Prater, Karen Riedman, Harriet Rome, Jayne Sandelin, Margaret Schere, Bernice Thornton-Trump, Marlene Viterna, and initiates Susan Harris and Lucille Lipps.

Chapter GW's first meeting was re-enacted in 1996 when celebrating our 25th anniversary, along with special lyrics written by Joyce Christensen to a song "My Favorite P.E.O. Things." The 40th anniversary of Chapter GW was celebrated in 2011 with five charter members still active.

P.E.O.'s focus is on projects to advance the education of women. Stanley Rediger served as state chairman of ELF, 1995-96; we have sponsored six ELF recipients, three PCE recipients, four P.E.O. Scholars; the chapter made donations of "care packages" to IPS and Cottey College students, and more. Fundraisers for projects included our annual Christmas auction of mostly homemade items, a photo raffle of professional nature photographer Chris Helzer's works, sale of sand art brownies in a jar and bean soup ingredients in a jar, making and selling stenciled aprons and tote bags, a Pillsbury Bake-Off cookbook raffle with a winning recipe by one of our members, sale of RADA Cutlery, the sale of artist/member's trivets, note cards and canvas totes, participation in the city-wide Cake Ball, and the sale of marguerite scarves.

Our chapter has been attentive to the Nebraska P.E.O. Home in Beatrice just forty minutes south of Lincoln. Members have visited residents of the Home regularly, taking part in a picnic one time, dessert other times, along with tours of the Home. We have sent jack-o-lanterns carved by GW members and greeting cards made by our "Great Women" for the Nebraska P.E.O. Home residents to send to others. Pam Prater gathers items from our members, such as toothpaste, note pads and cards, and small Kleenex packets, and delivers them in person.

Chapter GW has catered to everyone's interests with a variety of social events and meeting programs. Members have had the pleasure of entertaining University of Nebraska P.E.O. students at dinners in our homes. We have celebrated Christmases in our homes and at restaurants and rented facilities. BILs were included in country dance lessons, picnics, and watching a Husker football game at a sports bar.

Members have played golf and bunco, toured the International Quilt Study Center, Memorial Stadium, and the Nebraska State Historical Museum. Besides Founders' Day and International Convention programs, we have had programs about members' travels to England and Wales, Japan, Africa, Israel, and Italy. We have learned more about Nebraska State Parks, the Orphan Train, Peace Corps, the Golden Days of Radio, the Friendship Home and the Food Bank, financial matters and life transitions, wind energy, Taiko, and Teammates. We have compiled several recipe booklets after salad suppers, soup and sandwich suppers, and holiday parties. GW contributes annually to Willie Shafer's "underwear project"—collecting underwear, socks, hats and mittens for children in the Lincoln Public Schools.

GW takes its turn hosting the Lincoln Reciprocity Roundtable, and some of our members have served as Roundtable officers, including Pam Prater as president in 1982, Pam Stream as president in 2005, and Sharon Schnasse as reservations chairman.

Notable changes from our first twenty-five years include News for the Good of the Chapter, when reports about our sisters finishing college degrees, getting married, beginning careers and having babies has changed to our second twenty-five years news reports about our children's high school and college graduations and weddings, births of our grandchildren, and our own joint replacements. Other changes from the past to the present include meeting reminders and member information sent by email rather than by postcards and telephone, wearing name tags at meetings, serving dessert before the meetings rather than afterwards, and meeting once a month. A change for all P.E.O.s is not having to memorize initiation parts.

We have lost four sisters to Chapter Eternal: Fredrena Pappas, Sue Helzer, Pat Klein, and Lucille Lipps.

CHAPTER GW'S ACTIVE MEMBERSHIP IS 44; TOTAL ENROLLMENT IS 137

★

CHAPTER GX SOUTH SIOUX CITY
ORGANIZED JANUARY 15, 1972
BY ELLEN ANN QUALSETT

On January 15, 1972, the formation of Chapter GX was presided over by Nebraska State Organizer Ellen Ann Qualsett. The charter list consisted of thirteen initiates and seven dimits: Naomi Antrim, Nancy Bartels, Mary Kay Bohan, Deanna Bomar, Helen Brower, Arline Broyhill, Laurene Clark, Beverly Engelbart, Sandra Harris, Helen Hayes, Nancy Heitshusen, Gretchen Hirschbach, Sally Hodges, Virginia Horak, Beverly Hubbard, Jane Krogh, Bonnie Lott, Shirley Rager, Jane Rapp, and Margaret Trysla.

We participated on the State Amendments and Recommendations Committee. Each April members attend the Sioux City Reciprocity P.E.O. Founders' Day celebration. Our sisters across the river perform superlatively and a delightful brunch is enjoyed by all.

Moving into the technical age, using email has enabled the chapter to keep in contact and to be informed of events and activities. The few who do not have email access are kept in the loop via telephone call or face-to-face interaction. Technical progress has eased the task of updating yearbooks as well. Being able to access www.peointernational.org has also been a blessing.

Over the past two decades Chapter GX's yearbook committees have worked tirelessly to organize the logistics of the location, co-hostess, and program provider for our meetings. A few of the yearly themes chosen by our presidents include "Blessings of the Sisterhood," "Look to the Future for Fun and Friendship in P.E.O.," "Seeking Growth," "Celebrating the Journeys of Our Lives," and "Stick a Daisy in Your Hat and Be Happy." As we are a multi-talented group of women, our programs are varied and always interesting. Since musicians, artists, gardeners, travelers, a cowboy poet, and several women who are, or have been, actively involved in community affairs are in our midst, we have experienced a great many memorable programs.

One sister told us the history of a local church pipe organ then treated us to an organ recital. We have been introduced to the beautiful glass sculptures of Chihuly, and the paintings and history of such artists as Grandma Moses and Georgia O'Keeffe. Members have shared their travel experiences to such places as India, Australia, Italy, Tanzania, and Haiti. We have learned about making truffles, methods to deal with garden pests, and how to play dominoes. Our more serious programs have contained information concerning financial planning for women, measures against identity theft, navigating Medicare Part D, and living with breast cancer.

We relish social times, especially those involving local restaurants. We have enjoyed the company of our BILs, engaging in such activities as an historical bus tour of Sioux City and surrounding area followed by an ice cream social, our version of the Olympics, golf outings, and potluck cookouts on the river. Recently we have begun "Saturday Morning Coffee" with our sisters in Chapters DE and IC. On the last Saturday of the month, those who wish to gather at an eatery formerly owned by a Chapter GX sister. Coffee, conversation, laughter and fellowship abound. Many of our snowbirds even get together in Arizona.

Our philanthropy begins with our dues. We also give extra donations to the P.E.O.Educational Loan Fund and to the P.E.O. Program for Continuing Education. We have given back to our community through the Toys for Tots campaign, and Pete's Feeders which helps feed the less fortunate in our locale at Christmas time. Another Christmas favorite is the collection of paper products, toiletries, children's clothing and such for our local women's and children's shelter. We have given scholarships to several deserving young women graduating from South Sioux City High School upon successful completion of the first semester of college.

Our Courtesy Committee is the heart and spirit of our chapter. A meal program has been designed to aid any sister in need. Team members are assigned in advance to a calendar month during which they may be called upon to deliver a meal. A telephone call to a team member sets the process in motion.

The success of Chapter GX is due to the competence, dependability and cheerfulness of its membership. This is a group which honestly exemplifies the meaning of sisterhood. Timid though some may be when asked to serve as an officer, our women always step up to the challenge of learning and growing. Committee chairmen are quick responders when called upon because we are happy to help each other. Chapter GX is blessed with wonderful sisters who are most capable of hard work, ingenuity, love, caring, and fun. We also appreciate the visits by Nebraska state officers, and our past and present organizers. Their kind words and positive recommendations are always taken to heart.

Our goal for the immediate and long-term future is to enhance and invigorate our membership. We realize that the growth and sustenance of Chapter GX depends on enticing back inactive sisters as well as inviting new and younger women. In January 2014, we celebrated our 42nd anniversary, and also the 90th birthday of a charter member, Shirley Rager.

CHAPTER GX'S ACTIVE MEMBERSHIP IS 43; TOTAL ENROLLMENT IS 120

★

CHAPTER GY McCOOK
ORGANIZED APRIL 7, 1973
BY DORIS CUNNINGHAM
DISBANDED JUNE 8, 2013

Realizing the need for a daytime chapter, seven members from Chapter X and six members from Chapter FA came together to form Chapter GY. The organizational meeting took place on April 7, 1973, in McCook with Doris Cunningham, CS, serving as organizer. The charter members were Evelyn Donaldson, Flora Stevens, Irma John, Marilyn Shepherd, Ruth Morgan, Rose Horton, Joan Hartman, Lois Messinger, Sarah Binderup, Ruth Hileman, Teckla Allen, Jessie Brown, Lydia Webster, Judith Rueb, Gayle Hileman, Ann Allen, Lorene Glenn, Francis Kasl, Dorothy Nicholson, Helen Frick, and Gladys Aldrich. With the addition of eight initiates, the total membership was twenty-one. Chapter GY received its Charter in Omaha on May 22, 1973.

The chosen theme this first year was "In the Beginning" which gave members an opportunity to become better acquainted with each other. The membership consisted of poets, musicians, artists, teachers, public speakers, a seamstress, church leaders and business leaders, as well as homemakers.

We are proud to have had two state presidents in our chapter. Flora Stevens served as president of Nebraska State Chapter in 1956-1957. When Past State President Marion Larmon (1985-86) was ready to move to a daytime chapter, Chapter GY welcomed her as a transfer from Chapter FA. We helped Flora Stevens celebrate her 100th birthday in 1999. Her party was held at the Elks Club and several hundred people attended.

Along with Chapters FA and X, Chapter GY hosted the Convention of Nebraska State Chapter in 1993. Due to a shortage of motels, some visiting members stayed in the dormitory at McCook Community College. Since it was in the summer and college was not in session, local members were in charge of making up all the beds in the dorm and will regale you with stories of doing so on a very warm day.

In 1998, we celebrated our 25th anniversary. Evelyn Donaldson, former GY charter member, presented the program on the organizational meeting of Chapter GY and each charter member present received a marguerite corsage.

Chapter GY is proud to have sponsored several young ladies for various educational loans and grants. The chapter made it a point to stay in touch with each of them to offer encouragement and we enjoyed hearing of their progress. One ELF recipient studied radiology at the University of Nebraska Medical Center. Another young lady was able to complete her education in women's ministry through the help of a PCE grant. Our own member, Lisa Beckenhauer, was a recipient of an ELF loan. Our chapter also presented Lisa with a monetary donation to help with her mission trip to China.

A technology committee was formed in order to keep up with the ever changing technology. Very few of our older members owned computers and it became necessary to order forms and receive information electronically so this committee was of great importance to the chapter. We also formed a membership committee and they worked tirelessly to re-activate inactive members and to attract new members. One imagines that the "forward-thinking" seven Founders would have enjoyed the new technology.

We have contributed every year to each of the projects and to the Nebraska P.E.O. Home. In 1995, we fully funded our commitment to the Nebraska P.E.O. Home Endowment Fund. We made it a point to stay in touch with our Cottey College student and were faithful in sending her a gift card for Christmas. We donated annually to our local food pantry. We helped prepare and serve a hot meal for anyone in need of it for the "Feeding His Flock" ministry at the United Methodist Church.

Our "C-3" sister Cheri Beckenhauer and her co-chair Sandy Graves made it possible for us to fund our obligation to the Defining Moment Campaign for Cottey College. To get us started, two members purchased two autographed copies of Cottey College's chef Michael Richard's cookbook and auctioned them off at a meeting, raising $150. A box was placed at each meeting and members were asked to give what they felt they could afford toward our goal.

Early in the chapter's history there was a Fall Harvest Sale. Members brought homemade gifts and food and the items were auctioned off. Later, chances were sold on a gift box containing a surprise gift provided by a member. Another member would then take the box and put in another surprise and bring it to the next meeting. Chances were three for a dollar. When members were no longer able to make craft items and no longer baked, it was decided to assess each member $15 to be used in our general funds.

Founders' Day was always celebrated with our sisters in Chapters FA and X, taking turns with decorations, location and program. Decorations were always beautiful and the programs concerning our founding sisters were interesting and entertaining.

We have enjoyed so many interesting programs at our meetings, most of them presented by our members, following the president's chosen theme. Some of the themes were "Forever Friends," "Variety is the Spice of Life...Let P.E.O. Season Yours," "Hidden Treasures," and "Invest in the Future."

A Memorial Service was held for our last active charter member, Gladys Aldrich, in 2013. Her star and those of all our sisters in Chapter Eternal will forever shine brightly in our hearts.

Our chapter tried very hard to reinstate inactive members and to attract younger members. Sadly, due to the advancing age of so many of our members and the inability to find younger women, a unanimous vote was passed to disband Chapter GY. We were able to celebrate our 40th anniversary with cake and punch and enjoyed a program presented by our last active charter member Gladys Aldrich on the history of Chapter GY. Gladys passed into Chapter Eternal a few short weeks later. At the 2013 state convention, the disbandment of Chapter GY was accepted. The money left in our treasury was donated to Cottey College for the "Defining Moment Campaign," thus making it possible to fulfill our obligation to this project.

Members continue to "get together" for coffee at a local restaurant on the third Monday of each month and plan to continue with a Christmas luncheon. We feel so blessed to have been a part of such a wonderful chapter and will continue to nurture one another. We have an open invitation to transfer to Chapters FA and X. Both chapters have been very supportive and understanding of our decision to disband.

Chapter GY started as a "dream" in 1973 and enriched the lives of so many wonderful women who will remain sisters and friends forever.

TOTAL ENROLLMENT 118

Chapter GZ Hastings
Organized June 2, 1973
by Doris Cunningham, proxy organizer

Chapter GZ was organized on June 2, 1973, at Fuhr Hall Auditorium on the Hastings College campus. Doris Cunningham, second vice president of Nebraska State Chapter, served as the proxy organizer.

Honored guests were the following state officers who served on the initiatory team: Janet Atkins, BO, state president; Lois Ann Hansen, G, state recording secretary; Ellen Ann Qualsett, CT, first vice president; Vera Koefoot, GP, state organizer and Barbara Cobb, CL, state corresponding secretary. Charlotte Welch of Chapter G, Joyce Ohlsen of GK, Jane Johnson of G, Mary Northrop of DA, Berdina Strayer of GK, and Vera Moorhead of FH also assisted.

Charter members initiated were Katherine Asbury, Eunice Langvardt, Patricia E. Miller, Katherine O'Donnell, Hazel Ralph, and Shirley Sandstedt. Dimitting charter members were Bonnalee Asbury, Vera Clouse, Mildred Decker, Marcia Hayes, Luella Holthaus, Cynthia Kunz, Doris Laird, Mary Lou Neumann, Ethel Ochsner, Bessie Pauley, Elizabeth Ray, Cheryl Thompson, Inez Underhill, Katherine Wood, Mary Wood and Earlene Witt.

Chapter GZ, pictured above, hosted a Victorian Tea in honor of newly installed state president Cindy Biehl in 2009.

Since the inception of Chapter GZ, we have seen many changes. We are aware that change is inevitable, and that is true in P.E.O. Many of our new initiates have been involved with careers outside of the home. Because of these diversified interests, we have formed a reading group, a culinary group, and impromptu coffee get-togethers.

Chapter GZ has been extremely blessed with talented people. We have sisters who have been involved with many outside charitable organizations such as: YWCA, Literacy Program, S.A.S.A., Hastings symphony, Nebraska State Nursing Association, and many various church programs. Our local YWCA honors women yearly who have made outstanding contributions to their community. Chapter members who received this honor were Barbara Peck, Judy Reimer, Kathy Haverly and Judy Sandeen. Also, Judy Reimer received the "Outstanding Nursing Award" from the Nebraska Nursing Association and Judy Sandeen received the "Shining Star Award" given by AIDS Project for efforts in HIV/AIDS work.

One of Chapter GZ's proudest moments was the 2009 installation of Cindy Biehl as president of Nebraska State Chapter. A lovely Victorian tea was hosted by Chapter GZ in Cindy's honor. At the conclusion of her year, Chapter GZ proudly contributed to the P.E.O. STAR Scholarship in her honor.

Past State President Pam Kregg, Nebraska State and International Past President Joyce Goff, and honoree Cindy Biehl at the Chapter GZ tea.

Vicki Rouse served as chairman of the Nebraska State Finance and Budget Committee in 2009-2010.

In order for Chapter GZ to continue the tradition of supporting each P.E.O. project, the members have joined together in their yearly fundraising project which consists of a June Birthday Luncheon. Due to GZ's efforts and generosity, we have been able to sponsor five women for the P.E.O. Program for Continuing Education and one candidate who received the P.E.O. Educational Loan Fund. We have had several fundraising activities to help support "The Defining Moment Campaign."

It was 2011 when our president started sending a quarterly newsletter—via the internet—to all active and nonparticipating members to keep them informed of our various activities.

Tradition strengthens our ties when Chapter Eternal sisters are remembered with the P.E.O. Memorial Service. Those sisters who have been memorialized in the last twenty years are: Vivian Phelps, Christine Halloran, Elinor Bartholomew,

Marvella Burmester, Inez Underhill, Mary Searl, Doris Laird, Sally Whitcomb, Corinne Stickels, Pauline (Blue) Boyd, Katherine O'Donnell and Eunice Langvardt.

Chapter GZ continues to exemplify the true spirit of P.E.O. We share the joy of sisterhood, but foremost is the opportunity to help women further their education and reach the high ideals of our Sisterhood.

CHAPTER GZ'S MEMBERSHIP IS 68; TOTAL ENROLLMENT IS 152

★

CHAPTER HA COLUMBUS
ORGANIZED OCTOBER 23, 1973
BY VERA KOEFOOT

Chapter HA was organized October 23, 1973, by Vera Koefoot. Ten charter members of Chapter HA dimitted from Chapter FJ, Columbus: Barbara Ferguson, president; Berdean L. Miller, vice president; Sally L. Rice; Vee A. Hockenberger; Betty Jane McCarthy, chaplain; Lorayne Schacht, corresponding secretary; Sharon I. Hull; Ann Haugen Bernstein, guard; Shirley Wilken, recording secretary; Patsy Novicki, treasurer. Elda Powley, dimitted from GS, Norfolk. Initiates were: Arlis M. Klug, Mary Kay Peck, Helen I. Christensen, Phyllis L. Selig, Marilyn A. Gangel, Eleanor Heiser and Mary B. O'Donnell.

In its forty years, Chapter HA has grown and thrived, having initiated 115 women into the Sisterhood. The present active membership is fifty-two. At one point, Chapter HA had two families of three generations who were members at the same time.

Chapter anniversaries have played an important part of HA's history, having been observed with birthday cakes, luncheons, and appropriate programs. Celebrating our fortieth anniversary in October of 2013 was especially memorable. It was a luncheon with festive decorations and Lisa Helmick, recording secretary of Nebraska State Chapter, was in attendance. The highlight of the celebration was surprising Barbara Ferguson, the first president of Chapter HA, by reading her first president's letter.

Throughout the year we host luncheons, a brunch in the summer, and brown bag lunches. Recipes from the luncheons are printed and sold to the sisters as one of the means of fundraising for the all-important P.E.O. projects. Our main source of annual funding for the P.E.O. projects is the BIL supper and auction often hosted in a member's backyard. Members donate items such as tickets to Nebraska sporting events, gardening basket, BBQ basket, and many other creative items.

Chapter HA is always enthusiastic in their support of the P.E.O. projects and proud to submit names to our educational loans and scholarships. In 2005, we were proud to nominate Christine Labenz Zink for the P.E.O. Scholar Award for the 2005-2006 academic year, which she received. Chapter HA always enjoys visiting the Nebraska P.E.O. Home in Beatrice. Every few years, the chapter tries to schedule a meeting at the Home and members look forward to the journey to Beatrice.

In the spirit of reciprocity, HA participates in a city-wide social with the three Columbus chapters in September. This is always a dinner with a wonderful program and is a superb way to become better acquainted with sisters from the other city chapters.

Members of HA are all busy with family, career, church work, community service and personal improvement pursuits. Chapter HA has had seven members chosen Queen Isabella in recognition of community service and volunteerism.

As we proudly look back and reflect on the past forty years, we also look forward with enthusiasm and anticipation that the years ahead will be rewarding and fulfilling.

CHAPTER HA'S ACTIVE MEMBERSHIP IS 52; TOTAL ENROLLMENT IS 147

★

CHAPTER HB KEARNEY
ORGANIZED DECEMBER 7, 1974
BY BARBARA COBB

Chapter HB was organized at the First United Methodist Church in Kearney on December 7, 1974, by Barbara Cobb. The charter list, selected by Kathleen Gosch, was comprised of fourteen dimitting members: Kathleen Gosch, president; Miriam Frerichs, treasurer; Barbara Bancroft, recording secretary; Gaylene Aden; Carol Bacon, chaplain; Jane Smith, vice president; Mary Scott; corresponding secretary; Marian Payne, Karen Osentowski, Jolene Nachtigal, Mobie Chappell, guard; Jeanne Routh, Carla Brooke, and Barbara Hines.

Nebraska State Chapter President Ellen Ann Qualsett installed the officers and counseled the new chapter. Doris Cunningham, state chapter's first vice president, acted as secretary for the day. Also present were state officers Lois Ann Hansen, serving as corresponding secretary, Mary Ruth Wilson, treasurer; and Past State Presidents Helen Magill and Jean Johnson. After brunch, Chapter HB met with Mrs. Cobb.

Many of HB's members have been active in state and International P.E.O. positions. Cindy Hardekopf served as state chairman of the P.E.O. Program for Continuing Education for three years. Jane Smith served five years on the executive committee for the 1991 Convention of International Chapter in Omaha. She also served on the Nebraska P.E.O Home Board of Directors. Kathy Gosch was chairman of decorations for the Convention of International Chapter in 1991 and was chairman of the 1992 Nebraska State Convention in Kearney. At that time, Kathy was elected treasurer of the executive board of Nebraska State Chapter and ultimately served as president in 1998-99. Sharon Hammar has served on the Board of Directors of the Nebraska P.E.O. Home for nine years and publishes their newsletter.

The chapter enthusiastically supports the P.E.O. projects, with annual contributions to ELF, Cottey College, the Nebraska P.E.O. Home, Nebraska Cottey Scholarships, IPS, the P.E.O. Scholar Award, PCE, and the P.E.O. STAR Scholarship. Chapter HB has sponsored recipients for ELF loans and grants for PCE. We have sponsored two young women at Cottey College. The chapter initiated the idea of a "Van Fund" for the Nebraska P.E.O. Home. We award a scholarship to a daughter of an HB member each year.

Chapter HB activities include our annual Christmas auction as a FUN and FUNDRAISER. The silent auction accompanies a cocktail party at a member's home. Every other year we make this a progressive event, with hors d'oeuvres at one or two members' homes, followed by dessert and the silent auction at another member's home. In 2013 our summer social was a Wine and Cheese

Spa Social held at a local salon. Members were pampered and demonstrations were given. We are working at establishing smaller groups within our chapter with members taking bridge lessons together, forming a movie group, etc. We meet on Tuesday mornings and have many working members, so we have added lunch at a local restaurant following the meeting, so that our working sisters can meet us for food and socializing. For the same reason, we also change our meeting time to evening occasionally, especially for our social activities. Chapter HB has hosted summer reciprocity coffees, Founders' Day brunches, Reciprocity Group XIV luncheons and two state conventions.

Chapter HB is a very diverse group of women with the busy work and family schedules faced by so many women today. We work diligently to make HB a flexible and supportive home that allows members to meet family and work obligations and still be a valued and included member of our chapter.

Chapter HB celebrated its 40th birthday in December of 2014. This is a wonderful group of women who continue to make Chapter HB a STAR ATTRACTION among Nebraska P.E.O. groups.

CHAPTER HB'S ACTIVE MEMBERSHIP IS 77; TOTAL ENROLLMENT IS 167

★

Chapter HC Bellevue
Organized April 12, 1975
by Barbara Cobb

The organizational meeting of Chapter HC was held on April 12, 1975, at Fontanelle Hills Country Club. Ruth Knight of Chapter M, Omaha, was the charter head of the chapter. Nebraska State Chapter Organizer Barbara Cobb, CL, presided at the organization.

Dimitting charter members were Ruth I. Knight, Lynn Gebera, Patricia Crabtree, Mina Dawson, Margaret Vestal, Emalie Kay Castner, Carolyn Thompson, Carole Davick, Clairanne Hann, Marjorie Sargent, Bonnie Campbell, Donna Johannes, Carol French, Bettye McCracken, Janet S. Fidler, Dorothy Shuman, Dorothy Boileson, and Paula Mitchell. New initiates were Ethel O. Bishop, Nancy B. Worm, and Jan E. Knight. The charter members ranged in age from eighteen to eighty-seven. Dimitting members to Chapter HC came from Arizona, Iowa, North and South Dakota, Missouri, Virginia, and Nebraska.

The chapter has been fortunate to have as members military wives who brought ideas from other parts of the country and the world, and "Snowbirds" who bring ideas from chapters they visit while wintering in the southern United States.

Chapter HC is a day chapter and meetings are held in members' homes and also in the fellowship rooms of Bellevue First Presbyterian Church where several of our P.E.O.s are members. A Chapter HC Directory with a photo and information about each of the members helps newcomers to recognize other members of the chapter.

Chapter HC is a Happy Chapter for many reasons, but one is that since its organization, it has successfully sponsored twenty applicants for loans from the P.E.O. Educational Loan Fund. All have repaid their loans. The chapter has sponsored women for grants from the P.E.O. Program for Continuing Education and several girls have also received scholarships to Cottey College due to the chapter's sponsorship.

The chapter supports the Nebraska P.E.O. Home including visits to the ladies who live in the Home.

Within Chapter HC we care for each other by sending greeting cards and taking meals to those who are sick, as well as to those who have an illness or death in their families. We also have three lap quilts made by chapter members and taken to those who have an illness that keeps them house bound.

In addition to chapter socials we have small groups of members with similar interests that meet once a month and usually visit a place that speaks to their interests, followed by going out for lunch.

Due to increases in size, two new chapters have split off from Chapter HC: Chapter IR, with evening meetings, and Chapter IT, with daytime meetings.

CHAPTER HC'S ACTIVE MEMBERSHIP IS 60; TOTAL ENROLLMENT IS 206

★

CHAPTER HD LINCOLN
ORGANIZED MAY 17, 1975
BY BARBARA COBB

The unaffiliated P.E.O. sisters who became the original members of Chapter HD, the twenty-fifth P.E.O. chapter in Lincoln, were brought together through the efforts of Phyllis Blanke, Nelsine Scofield, Helen Curtiss, Doris Cunningham, and Betty Poague, as well as other "movers and shakers" active in Nebraska state P.E.O. Charter members were Jane Jelinek Basoco, corresponding secretary; Kim Bowers; Carole Curry; Sue Davis; Becky Samuelson Dietle, recording secretary; Dona Giles, vice president; Marty Gollner; Shirley Ingham, president; Cindy Kaliff; Patty Kampfe, guard; Karen Lupomech; Patti MacLean Conway; Mary Peterson; Mary Beth Rutledge; Marla Marrs Stahl; and Erna Todd, chaplain. Charter initiates were Bobbie Ingham Jones, Mary Martin, and Mary Oestmann Goldberg. Joan Earnhart was unable to attend the organizational meeting and became our first dimit. Since then, four sisters have passed on to Chapter Eternal.

When Chapter HD was organized, one of the charter members was a Cottey College graduate. Over the years, more Cottey graduates joined our chapter, and their enthusiasm has continued to make Cottey a very real place for us. We became a Cottey Golden Anniversary chapter, and in 1983 HD was the 38th chapter in Nebraska to contribute $50 per member to the Cottey 50th Anniversary Endowment Fund. We have sponsored several young women on the Cottey College Bus Trip to give them the opportunity to see the campus and visit with students. Several HD sisters have served as Cottey Area Chairmen.

In 1984, four sisters composed and copyrighted the *Golden Star Ceremony* to commemorate fifty or more years of membership in P.E.O. In 1985, the chapter was authorized to advertise the ceremony in The Record and sell it nationally, and twenty-seven years later, several hundred have been purchased by chapters all over the country. We have used the ceremony ourselves three times to honor our own Golden Star sisters, Shirley Ingham, Marcia Wythers, and Wynn Nuckolls.

Our oldest and most popular Ways and Means project is the auction held every other October. Starting in our first year, the auctions have continued throughout the life of our chapter. At first bids were oral and members acted as auctioneers, but the increasing number of attendees and enthusiastic bidding made them last too long, so the format was changed to silent bids. The variety of crafts, foods, and other delights contributed has been truly astounding. In 2006, a sister who is an experienced beader designed a P.E.O. bracelet made of clear and yellow crystals, silver beads, and a daisy charm and has sold them through The Record, on the Nebraska P.E.O. website, and at Lincoln Reciprocity Roundtable meetings. And since 2007, a bottle of wine is raffled for $1 a chance at every meeting with the winner providing the wine for the next meeting.

A potluck dinner before our September meeting provides members time to catch up on all the late summer news while enjoying a wide variety of delicious fare and has been a "just for fun" tradition since 1978. Another enjoyable activity is the Past Presidents' Luncheon that began in 1985 as an opportunity for all our previous presidents to relax and enjoy themselves without having to conduct a meeting! Now held in the summer at the Roca Country Inn, a bed and breakfast owned by a former sister's in-laws, it is a wonderful place to slow down, have a fabulous meal, and visit for several hours.

Several HD sisters have appeared in convention project skits. Mary Martin and Nancy Youngman took part in *P.E.O. in Bloom*, which was originally performed at the 1983 state convention and then videotaped and offered for rental as a fundraiser for Lincoln Reciprocity Roundtable. Cindy Lloyd helped stage and appeared in *Avenue of P.E.O. Dreams* at the 1990 state convention and the 1991 Convention of International Chapter in Omaha. She also took part in the Period of Instruction at the 2008 Nebraska State Convention in Omaha.

THE ACTIVE MEMBERSHIP OF CHAPTER HD IS 67; TOTAL ENROLLMENT IS 164

★

CHAPTER HE LINCOLN
ORGANIZED JANUARY 24, 1976
BY LOIS ANN HANSEN

On January 14, 1976, Chapter HE was organized in Lincoln by Lois Ann Hansen. The charter list of Chapter HE consisted of a group of unaffiliated sisters, many of whom had met as students at the P.E.O. College Group. The charter members were Chris Abernathy, Sue Anderson, Rennie Austin, Cynthia Bose (initiate), Dori Bush (initiate), Jennifer Coolen, Jo Daniel, Lucille Elliot, Mavis Ezersky, Barbara Haith, Judy Hempel (initiate), Lynne Holz, Lynelle Huck, Barbara Miller, Delores Otte, JoAnne Pool, Sidney Shadley, Marian Schmid, Nancy Steinkruger (initate), Doris Vetter, and Mary Lynn Walkington. Nine charter members remain in the chapter. Jo Daniel and Mavis Ezersky are in Chapter Eternal. In 1998 Lucille Elliot was recognized for thirty-five years in P.E.O., while Dee Otte and Lynelle Huck were recognized for thirty years. Barbara Haith was honored as a 50-year member in 2013.

We have had initiations of a sister, six daughters (one of whom is a fourth generation P.E.O.), two daughters-in-law, and a niece. Through the years, four sisters were active and their grandmother lived at the Nebraska P.E.O. Home, three generations of another family were active, and a member's mother-in-law was the Nebraska P.E.O. Home administrator.

The chapter has visited and held meetings at the Nebraska P.E.O. Home, including the 100th birthday celebration of Nebraska State Chapter. HE continues supplying "wish list" items to residents. When Nelsine Scofield moved to the P.E.O. Home, the chapter was as supportive of her as she was of Chapter HE in our early years.

Mary Lynn Schaffer served as Lincoln Reciprocity Roundtable President in 1998. Three others served as officers and more have been on committees. Chapter HE has hosted numerous times, co-hosting Founders' Day in 1992. The chapter has also provided numerous programs.

Mary Lynn Schaffer, Pam Carrier, and Karen Hand have been delegates to Conventions of International Chapter. When International Convention was held in Nebraska, eleven members served on the Courtesy Committee.

At state conventions, Jennifer Koolen, Lynelle Huck, Pam Carrier, and Marian Schmid served as guards. We provided decorations several different years. In 2012, Maggie Stuckey (a fourth generation P.E.O.) was the youngest delegate.

Chapter HE has sponsored a number of women for PCE grants. Kama Bedient received a grant. Chapter HE has also sponsored women receiving ELF Loans, including Kama Bedient and daughters of Anne Dietrich, Nancy Stuckey, and Catherine Roberts. We sponsored five women for P.E.O. Program for Continuing Education grants, resulting in a scholarship for one. HE has sponsored two IPS students. Several women were proposed for P.E.O. Scholar Awards, and Joy Currie was a recipient. The chapter has also sponsored applicants for the P.E.O. STAR Scholarship.

Chapter HE has provided the Lincoln College Group with dinners, gifts, and hosted them at the P.E.O. Home. We have also provided meals to interested students on bus trips to Cottey College and sponsored young women who attained scholarships. Daughters of Susan Ptacek and Judy Hempel attended Cottey, as did HE past president Carol Tillotson. We have supported Nebraska students there with remembrances. Chapter HE also purchased an engraved brick for the Cottey Walkway.

Successful and various FUNdraising has allowed the chapter to support all P.E.O. projects and International projects, as well as the Nebraska P.E.O. Home, Cottey College, and community projects.

The annual Christmas party is a favorite with P.E.O. sisters and guests; in addition, other socialization with BILs and families is significant. Abundant love and support between sisters is evident in times of life's joys and celebrations, sorrows and challenges.

Chapter HE actively seeks involvement of its membership by keeping in touch with nonresidents, non attending and inactive members. We also welcome unaffiliated members and visitors.

CHAPTER HE's ACTIVE MEMBERSHIP IS 60; TOTAL ENROLLMENT IS 157

*The great thing in the world
is not so much where we are,
but in what direction
we are moving.*

-Oliver Wendell Holmes

Chapter HF Omaha
Organized April 10, 1976
by Lois Ann Hansen

Due to a growing need for an evening chapter among Omaha's working women, Chapter HF—nicknamed "Happiness Forever"—was organized on April 10, 1976, as the 35th chapter in Omaha and the 207th chapter in Nebraska. Organized by Nebraska State Chapter Organizer Lois Ann Hansen, G, and Nancy Sutherland, M, charter head, nineteen unaffiliated members dimitted from chapters in Nebraska, Kansas, Iowa, Missouri, Illinois, South Dakota, and Colorado: Christina Anderson, Margaret Christiansen, Sara Lee Ferraro, Janell Toon Foote, Beth Ellen Hansen, Nancy S. Ksiazek, Beverly Elledge Montgomery, Teresa Sue Montgomery, Mary Elaine Polley, Marilyn A. Rowe, Jane Ann Sahly, Jamie J. Snyder, Jan Steggs, Jeanne M. Taylor, Marianna Tuttle, Linda Van Marter, Linda Ann Welburn, Barbara Anne Wharton, and Patricia Ann Zender. Three charter members were fourth-generation P.E.Os.

Handwritten invitations were distributed for the organizational meeting, which was held at the Ramada Inn West in Omaha, followed by a formal luncheon. Over eighty-five people attended, including a number of mothers, grandmothers, and sisters of members. Attractive table decorations, little planters made by a chapter member, were presented to those who assisted with the chapter's organization. Following the luncheon, the chapter's first official meeting was held, where Janell Toon Foote was installed as the first chapter president and began her duties under the first year's theme, "*In the Beginning*."

Thirty-some odd years later, our chapter has grown exponentially, but we continue our evening meeting tradition. We are a mix of members—old and new—including many multi-generational members, which makes for a diverse, fun, and supportive group of women.

In 2011, we celebrated our chapter's 35th anniversary with a birthday party! We had a wonderful luncheon at a fabulous local restaurant with cupcakes for dessert. We had a gift exchange which gave our party a real "birthday feel!"

Support of the P.E.O. projects is the top priority of our treasury. Past successful fundraising activities have included selling custom-made cookbooks full of yummy chapter recipes, holiday greenery and spring plant sales, tote bag sales, bake sales and "No Bake" sales, a BIL shrimp boil, and a Valentine's Day silent auction. Chapter HF sisters are always ready to volunteer their time and talents wherever and whenever needed!

We also have several social meetings and membership events throughout the year. During our recent BIL Road Rally social, we "raced" to locations while gathering information and answering questions. P.E.O. trivia was included! It was a great night that brought out our competitive spirits while also promoting sisterhood. We also enjoy any event that showcases our members' talents. For several years we have gathered together to create our own greeting cards with the help of one of our talented sisters. Other past social meetings and membership events have included family picnics, indoor golf, cocktail hour, crafting and art projects, a brewery visit, May Day flower baskets, and a holiday cookie exchange and recipe sale.

Chapter HF's active membership is 64; total enrollment is 159

Chapter HG Schuyler
Organized February 5, 1977
by Frances Key

The first meeting of Schuyler P.E.O.s to consider the formation of a new chapter was held on January 15, 1976. Approval for organization was received on February 3, 1976. One year later, on February 5, 1977, Chapter HG was organized. The new membership included sisters from Chapter BQ, David City, Chapter CT, North Bend, and new initiates from the Schuyler area.

Charter members of HG were Libbie Novotny, Ellen Ann Qualsett (past state president, Nebraska State Chapter, 1975), Margaret Quick, Delores Sucha, Della Cunningham, Claire Ehernberger, Heidi Ehernberger, Jane Eilers, Jo Ann Hruban, Joan Murr, Sherilyn Balak, Eunice Beran, Alma Blazek, Karen Breuer, Dona Jean Chalquist, Marianne Folda, Pamela Karel, Nancy Kehrli, Dorothy Krejci, Evelyn Krejci, Shirley Krejci, Editha Otradovsky, Margaret Pospisil, Marie Reinmiller and Maxine Johnston.

Since 1977, sixty additional sisters have committed to membership. How Great! Chapter HG membership represents a blend of ages, interests, lifestyles, religions, hobbies, and occupations. Members are a collection of women in medical professions, educators, government employees, and homemakers. Members volunteer in the community, serve on boards, and participate in other civic affairs. Members of Chapter HG have been recipients of many awards including the Sertoma Service to Mankind Award, GFWC Woman's Club Achievement Award, and Chamber of Commerce Outstanding Teacher and Para-educator of the Year. Chapter HG has also celebrated Founders' Day soup suppers, high teas, progressive dinners, along with social gatherings at members' cabins and homes.

In 2001, Chapter HG began selling afghans to support its local scholarship. The afghan's design features local historical sites in Schuyler and Colfax County. The local Chapter HG scholarship is awarded to a Schuyler Central High School graduating senior. Other fundraising projects have included an annual Christmas basket auction, rummage sales, and cookbook sales. The chapter has donated to the Schuyler Public Library, Schuyler Golf Club, and the local hospital. Members support the Nebraska P.E.O. Home in Beatrice, and have enjoyed visiting residents at the Home. In addition to annual contributions to the P.E.O. projects, Chapter HG has contributed to special fundraising projects for Nebraska State Chapter, Cottey College and P.E.O. International.

The chapter is honored to have sponsored four ELF loan recipients, one Nebraska Cottey Scholarship recipient, and three PCE grant recipients. Chapter HG has members who have celebrated 50- and 60-year memberships.

Chapter HG remembers its eleven members who have joined Chapter Eternal: Eunice Beran, Barbara Bieber, Dona Jean Chalquist, Marianne Folda, Evelyn Krejci, Libbie Novotny, Editha Otradovsky, Margaret Pospishil, Margaret Quick, Ellen Ann Qualsett, and Delores Sucha. Their stars will forever shine brightly in HG's P.E.O. history.

Being a member of Chapter HG of the P.E.O. Sisterhood has provided many opportunities for members to grow and learn. The history of Chapter HG began in 1977, and the chapter continues to support the P.E.O. mission: celebrate the advancement of women; educate women; and motivate women to achieve their highest aspirations.

CHAPTER HG'S ACTIVE MEMBERSHIP IS 28; TOTAL ENROLLMENT IS 85

★

CHAPTER HH YORK
ORGANIZED APRIL 30, 1977
BY VERA KOEFOOT, PROXY ORGANIZER

Chapter HH's birth included moments of joy, apprehension, laughter, anxiety, and plain hard work. Fourteen members dimitted from Chapter A, and two daughters were initiated. Officers were: Corinne Kidder, president; Ruth Robson, vice president; Donna Loschen, recording secretary; Susan Cox, corresponding secretary; Jane Thompson, treasurer; Eleanor Moore, chaplain; and Louise Wiley, guard. Other dimitting members were Lois Birt, Margaret Brink, Judi Jacobsen, Beth Lucas, Jennie Romohr, Kristie Scheele, and Jan Welch. New initiates were Julie Romohr and Jacque Kidder.

Nebraska State Chapter President Vera Koefoot installed the officers and acted as organizer, due to the illness of Organizer Frances Key, who had guided the chapter in preparation for the day. Ruth Robson, charter head, shared the original history of Chapter HH. A luncheon at the York Country Club followed the organizational meeting, which was held at the First United Methodist Church.

Chapter HH's enthusiasm and desire to support the projects of other special P.E.O. endeavors have resulted in generous contributions during the past 36 years.

In 1982, Chapter HH celebrated becoming a Cottey Golden Anniversary Chapter, thanks to the sales of its famous P.E.O. bean soup. In honor of HH's tenth anniversary, it presented a large screen television to the Nebraska P.E.O. Home. In 1999, it received a certificate for donating $1,000 to the Cottey College Academic Building Fund.

Chapter traditions include a special Christmas dinner meeting, and a P.E.O. Courtesy Committee, which provides meals for members during an illness or loss of a loved one. Chapter members share and celebrate their joys at each meeting with a "Star Brag Box," to which members donate $1 for each brag they make. Annual BIL parties are held, featuring themes such as the Kentucky Derby, the Great Gatsby, Husker Tailgate Party, a Mexican Fiesta, and a Shrimp Boil.

Philanthropic fundraisers include a chapter cookbook ("*In Good Taste*"); "Bling's the Thing," with the "Luck of the Draw" for a Kate Spade purse and a York County Afghan; and a silent auction, featuring items of members' special talents.

Chapter HH has proudly sponsored two women for loans from the P.E.O. Educational Loan Fund, and one woman for a grant from the P.E.O. Program for Continuing Education.

CHAPTER HH'S ACTIVE MEMBERSHIP IS 73; TOTAL ENROLLMENT IS 170

Every day the choices you make are writing your story.
—Coach Mike Riley, Nebraska Huskers

Chapter HI Ogallala
Organized January 21, 1978
by Mary Ruth Wilson

Chapter HI received its charter at the Nebraska State Chapter Convention in Grand Island on May 3, 1978, with Barbara Cobb serving as state president. This evening chapter was made up of thirteen dimits, all from Chapter CL, Ogallala, except for Beth Brandes of AB, Central City. Charter members were: Bonnie Harrington, Hattie (Bette) Padley, Patricia Harding, Carol Baldwin, Joan Dudden, Marbara Kuhlman, Lela Mae Thompson, Linda Lund, Carolyn Lowitz, Rhoda Larson, Beth Brandes, Lucille Adams, Marion Cole, Kathy Collura, Jennifer Kuhlman, Julie Kuhlman, Oleta Higgins, and Joanne Ervin. Six charter members have entered Chapter Eternal. Gail Brisson and Jill Harrington were the first dimits into the chapter.

HI continues to support higher education for women with multiple ELF loan recipients and an awarded PCE grant plus yearly donations to our projects. In September of 2001, Chapter HI welcomed Panhandle sisters to "*A Sand Hills Celebration of P.E.O. Spirit*" as they hosted Reciprocity at the historic Haythorn ranch near Arthur. April 2003 brought the 25th anniversary for Chapter HI and a farewell to charter member and this chapter's first president Bonnie Harrington, when she moved to Washington State. Three charter members attended from out of town. This chapter was honored at state convention in 2010 to receive an "Above and Beyond" P.E.O. Challenge Award.

Our own members have been honored for their contributions to their community, church, careers and to P.E.O. Chapter HI's roster includes a "Woman of Distinction," a former Nebraska P.E.O. Home Board of Directors member, reciprocity president, a convention guard and state and International delegates. Our current membership has a combined total of over 300 years of educating our youth as teachers with many receiving honors for their achievements.

Chapter HI Ogalalla quilt. Barb Meismer and President Mona Radcliffe with completed quilt. Mona sewed a quilt block for each of her meetings, and then stitched them into a quilt at the end of her year. A lucky Chapter HI sister got to take it home.

Funds were raised in traditional ways until 2010 when Chapter HI began assessing a fee for each member. Each December a philanthropy is chosen and a donation is taken at the holiday social. The food pantry, needy families, the local school Back Pack Program, Royal Family Kid's Camp and area volunteer fire departments have been some of the recipients.

Chapter HI Social Meeting. Front row: Peg Thalken, Pam Spurgin, Pam Abbott, Mary Kay Foy, Sally Harrington, Darlene Peterson, Mona Radcliffe, Maggie Abbott, Barb Jeffres. Middle row: Maggie Cutkosky, Karen Odstrcil, Marlene Kosmicki, Carol Dietz, Mary Cumming, Rose Holechek, Patty Meismer, Nancy Hollmann, Roberta Rager. Back row: Cherry Schreiner, Shirlee Knispel, Dorothy Glenn, Mary Bazata, Pam Walker, Barb Meismer, Loree Cain, Judi Adkins, Wanda Peters, Barb Engdahl.

The Bette Padley Memorial Award, first given to a member that HI chose to honor for being an especially loving P.E.O. sister, is now a monetary donation to the past president's favorite P.E.O. project. Founders' Day is celebrated each year in January. Beginning in 1999 we began sharing this event with the other Ogallala Chapter CL, as we alternate with the program and serving brunch.

Our meetings are now held monthly at 5:30 PM with social time before. Attendance has increased with the earlier meeting time and our bylaws were amended to reflect this change in June of 2013. Additional meetings are held in March, June and September.

This chapter accomplishes the mission of P.E.O. with a dedicated casualness and loves to socialize! This is achieved with a different committee for each social. There have been BIL backyard cookouts and festive holiday gatherings, wine tastings, summer wiener roasts at the lake with kayaking, salad suppers and shared social times with the gals from CL, Ogallala, and neighboring Chapter FU, Grant.

Our chapter letters "HI" exemplify the cornerstone of P.E.O. which is friendship. We support each sister with loving concern and care.

CHAPTER HI's ACTIVE MEMBERSHIP IS 54; TOTAL ENROLLMENT IS 140

I believe in the sun even if it isn't shining.
I believe in love even when I am alone.
I believe in God even when He is silent.

-World War II refugee

CHAPTER HJ GRAND ISLAND
ORGANIZED APRIL 1, 1978
BY MARY RUTH WILSON

Chapter HJ (Happy Joy) was organized at the Grand Island Women's Club. Charter members were Doris Carpenter, president; Candace Edwards, vice president; Mary Stuckey, recording secretary; Linda Placzek, corresponding secretary; Vera Reddish, treasurer, Mary Kay Tuma, chaplain; Susan Jacobs, guard; Susan Ribble, Linda K. Clabaugh, Katherine Rinder, Mary Ann Richards, Jeanne Ann Going and Linda Flaherty.

At this joyous occasion were Nebraska State officers President Barbara Cobb, First Vice President Lois Ann Hansen, Second Vice President Frances Key, Organizer Mary Ruth Wilson, Recording Secretary Helen Curtiss, Treasurer Julia McDougal, and Past State Presidents Vera Koefoot, Ellen Ann Qualsett, Harriet Lumbard, and Dorothy Smithberger.

A luncheon in Vera Koefoot's home was followed by the first meeting there. The dimit of Christine Brown was accepted at that meeting. We are especially indebted to Vera "Bobbie" Koefoot for helping Chapter HJ in our early years.

In 1982, HJ became a Cottey Golden Anniversary Chapter and added joy "adopting" Frances Weller of the Nebraska P.E.O. Home. We remembered her monthly with a note, card, or small gift until her death eight years later. We currently remember Mildred Thompson.

HJ traditions include a quarterly letter sent to all sisters keeping everyone up on happenings in their sisters' lives, BIL picnics, ice cream socials, caroling, a hayrack ride, a dinner theater and wine tasting. We've had many potluck and salad dinners, a potato bar, and summer coffees in the park with our children. We continue giving a gift for the firstborn or adopted child of a sister.

Chapter HJ member Joyce Victor, left, President of Nebraska State Chapter in 2011-2012, and member of the International P.E.O. Educational Loan Fund Board of Trustees; Joyce Goff, Past President of Nebraska State Chapter and Past President of International Chapter (middle); Mary Kay Tuma, right, served for seven years as Nebraska State Chapter's paid assistant.

Programs have explored issues, enjoyed trips, exercised and belly danced besides helping us learn more about our projects and how we can help women through them. Between 1994 and 2013, we sponsored five ELF recipients: Diana Wing and Monika Peters in 2002, Becky A. Oeltjenbruns in 2004, Sarah J. Selle in 2008 and Elizabeth A. Meyer in 2010.

We rejoiced at our 10th and 25th anniversaries celebrated at Trinity United Methodist Church and the 20th at the home of Vickie Davolt, and re-Joyced as our Joyce Goff presided at the 2005 Convention of International Chapter in Vancouver, British Columbia. Joyce Goff also served on the P.E.O. International Study and Research Committee (see page 460).

Joyce Goff ably led Nebraska State Convention as president in 1988, and Joyce Victor served as state president in 2012. Joyce Victor currently serves on the P.E.O. Educational Loan Fund Board of Trustees.

Other Nebraska State P.E.O. movers have been Paid Assistant Mary Kay Tuma, Amendment and Recommendations Committee sisters Ruth Steinkruger and Renita Wichert, and Assistant State Historian Linda Flaherty.

Chapter HJ presented the P.E.O. projects program for the 1991 Nebraska State Convention in Grand Island; that work and enjoyment drew sisters closer.

Some money-making projects include a Christmas silent auction, making available for sale a roster of sisters in all six Grand Island chapters, assessing a birthday donation of ten cents times your age, and baking cookies for our Christmas cookie trays.

CHAPTER HJ'S ACTIVE MEMBERSHIP IS 36; TOTAL ENROLLMENT IS 123

★

CHAPTER HK FREMONT
ORGANIZED SEPTEMBER 23, 1978
BY BERNICE ZAJICEK

"Love One Another" was the one thought two Fremont women, Barbara Johnson and Nancy Mead, had in mind when they realized the need for a new P.E.O. chapter in Fremont. Encouraged by the number of women interested in forming a new chapter, the group formally began meeting in January 1978. Chapter HK was organized by Bernice Zajicek on September 23, 1978. The twenty-four charter members, sixteen by lateral dimits and eight initiates were: Carole Bean, Carol Cooper, Paulette Cordes, Beverly A. Draemel, Joan Draemel, Jane A. Eberspacher, Jean Gausman, Marilyn Keyes Gordon, Jeanne Howery, Barbara Eberspacher Johnson, Gwen Knigge, Jacqueline Koolen, Joyce LaFond, Alberta Lamme, Virginia Laughridge, Marlene McClean, Nancy Mead, Sarah Mead, Ann Paulson, Sally Sheppard, Kathryn Swanson, Libby Vance, Mary Ellen Wieland, and Janet Yanike. It seemed that every meeting coincided with every hindrance Mother Nature could create. The organizer had to counsel by phone because a blizzard prevented her from traveling to Fremont. This "weather problem" continued over the years; an early fundraiser for the new chapter was interrupted by another blizzard. Tornado sirens disrupted a meeting at Midland College; members retreated to a basement boiler room where the president continued with the meeting.

One of our early traditions was a tablecloth with embroidered signatures of members that is displayed at Christmas meetings. A recipe shower is given for HK brides-to-be and a silver baby spoon is given to new HK mothers. A Founders' Day Brunch is held with Fremont chapters AJ, EX and GH. A luncheon is held in March honoring membership years and attendance. In December, a Holiday Open House is held in a member's home.

Fundraising methods have changed and grown over the years. Silent auctions used to be our main fundraiser; now we have an annual garage sale; we sell Younkers coupon books; we participate in a P.E.O. bridge marathon every year with Chapters EX and GH; and we "brag" about family for a price at the end of each meeting. The money from these various fundraisers helps support the P.E.O. projects. HK has sponsored many women who were awarded loans or grants from these projects to help them continue their education

One of our chapter's most memorable moments happened at the 1998 state convention in South Sioux City. Our sister, Anne Baumhover, began her seven years of service on the Nebraska State Chapter Executive Board. When Anne chose "*Stepping Out in P.E.O.*" as her theme, our chapter "Stepped Out" and hosted a tea for her at the May Museum in Fremont. Anne presided over the 2005 state convention held in Grand Island. Anne's commitment, dedication, enthusiasm, and devotion to P.E.O. are inspirations for all of us. She now serves on the Board of Directors of the Nebraska P.E.O. Home in Beatrice, where her mother is a resident.

The 2012 P.E.O. state convention was held in Fremont at Midland University. Chapter HK was in charge of registration. Marilyn Gordon, one of our chapter's charter members, served as convention treasurer.

Chapter HK has celebrated together, cried together, laughed together, worked together, and grown together. It is the goal of the Hugs and Kisses chapter to maintain that vibrant theme of 1978 — "Love One Another."

CHAPTER HK'S ACTIVE MEMBERSHIP IS 71; TOTAL ENROLLMENT IS 162

★

CHAPTER HL BLAIR
ORGANIZED SEPTEMBER 24, 1978
BY BERNICE ZAJICEK

P.E.O. Chapter HL was organized on September 24, 1978, at Dana College. Gail Jensen, president of Chapter EQ, Blair, served as their charter head. Chapter EQ officers assisted with the initiation ceremony. Charter members were Penny Buffalo, Nancy Lehl Chapman, Jesse Christopher, Nancy Dodd, Carol Fanoele, Kathleen Flynn, Robley Garrigan, Margaret Hansen, Carol Lady, Gaye Moseman, Paula O'Hanlon, LaVonne Patterson, Ann Sedlacek, Judy Sick, Edith Solomon, Kay Neef Spidle, Candy Suverkrubbe, and Wilma Wolfe. Six are still active members. Nancy Lehl Chapman served as HL's gracious and capable first president.

From the original eighteen, membership grew to forty-seven active members by the time of the publication of *Spirit of the Prairie*. Then it plummeted to a low of thirty-five, which led to a concerted effort to find new and often younger members. Active membership has held steady in the mid-40's over the past fifteen years—but it has not been static. Chapter IF disbanded in 2000 and HL was fortunate to welcome four of its members by dimit. There have been forty-three initiations, eight of whom were daughters. Twenty years ago, when

Chapter HL was young, only one member had entered Chapter Eternal; now sixteen have joined her. They are remembered during the May meeting and with garden flowers on Memorial Day and P.E.O. grave markers.

In recent years, Chapter HL has successfully sponsored Lindsey Wittry and Emily Kramer for P.E.O. STAR Scholarships, Sarah Rolland and Mary Down for PCE grants, and Jennifer Wittry for the P.E.O. Scholar Award. Two other applicants are awaiting decisions from projects.

Several members deserve special recognition. Robley Garrigan, a third generation P E.O., has worked indefatigably for P.E.O. She was on the Nebraska State Chapter Executive Board for seven years; chair of the 1984 state convention; state president in 1991; and served on the Board of Directors of the Nebraska P.E.O. Home in Beatrice for six years during the renovation of the Home and its licensing as an assisted living facility. Robley was editor of *Spirit of the Prairie*. She is now serving Chapter HL in her second stint as president, after having been the corresponding secretary for fifteen years.

In 2003, Edith Solomon, a 50-year P.E.O., was named Washington County Volunteer of the Year, chiefly for her tireless dedication to the library of Ott Middle School and costumer extraordinaire for school plays. Nancy Chapman has faithfully headed the Yearbook Committee for many years and her unique design has earned kudos at the state convention. She also posts a newsletter online within a day after every meeting to keep absentees up to date on chapter news. Betty Megrue has saved the chapter countless dollars by making get-well, sympathy, and birthday cards on her computer; she has never missed a special occasion.

In 1979, Edith Solomon served as a delegate to the Convention of International Chapter in Anaheim, California. In 1993, Chapter HL elected Nancy Chapman to serve as a delegate at the Convention of International Chapter in Atlanta, Georgia. In 1984, Blair hosted the Nebraska State Chapter Convention at Dana College. Chapter HL member Marilyn Gentry served as Chairman of Arrangement and Properties. When Nebraska hosted the International Convention in Omaha in 1991, HL member Ann Sedlacek and EQ member, Fran Aman, co-chaired the V.I.P. Courtesy Committee. Chapter HL, along with Blair sister chapters EQ and IF, made lovely quilted baskets to hold Nebraska favors for the International Chapter officers. Chapter poetess Margaret Hansen has had her poetry published in The P.E.O. Record.

Chapter HL hosted Reciprocity Group VI at a dessert buffet at Dana College in 2003. Its duties at state conventions were chair banners at Sioux City in 1998 and meals committee at the Fremont convention in 2012.

Members of Chapter HL use their talents and make the P.E.O. presence known in the community by serving on the Hospital Auxiliary Board, the Library Board, providing food for the Habitat volunteer builders and the Bloodmobile visits, serving cookies and ice cream after Spring and Christmas Blair Community Band concerts (founded by BIL Joe Chapman), and mentoring in Teammates, as well as a variety of committee and volunteer activities in their respective churches.

Most of the meetings are held in homes with two co-hostesses serving refreshments at 7:00 PM; the meeting starts at 7:30. Attendance ranged from fifteen on a stormy summer night with sirens blowing, to thirty, averaging twenty-two. Only two or three programs per year feature guest speakers; the rest of the programs are presented by multi-talented members to showcase the theme for the year chosen by the president.

Traditions that have endured since its founding include an anniversary dinner with reminiscences; a calling tree to remind members of meetings and convey other news; spontaneous help in times of challenges and sorrows; a brag bag to raise money while sharing family news of births, marriages, graduations, promotions—whatever joys sisters want to share. Chapter Eternal members are remembered during the May meeting and with garden flowers on Memorial Day and with P.E.O. grave markers. A brunch meeting is held jointly with Chapter EQ every January to honor the seven Founders of the Sisterhood.

Today, Chapter HL is a revitalized and vibrant group of diverse ages dedicated to upholding the ideals of P.E.O., promoting and supporting the projects and sharing a loving concern for each sister.

CHAPTER HL'S ACTIVE MEMBERSHIP IS 33; TOTAL ENROLLMENT IS 112

★

CHAPTER HM HOLDREGE
ORGANIZED SEPTEMBER 8, 1979
BY HELEN CURTISS

On December 5, 1978, several members of Chapter H, Holdrege, expressed their desire to form an additional chapter that would meet in the evenings. These members were unable to participate in chapter activities during the day, and wished to be more active in the Sisterhood. On December 19, Chapter H was asked to give consent to select a charter list for a new evening chapter.

Chapter H granted permission to Helen Magill of Holdrege and past president of Nebraska State Chapter, to select a charter list on January 16, 1979. On April 11, 1979, Chapter HM began as the little sister of Chapter H with ten sisters interested in making a lateral transfer to the new chapter.

Finally, on April 24, 1979, ten transferring members of Chapter H and seven initiates signed a petition for the new chapter. Chapter H graciously gave the charter fee which was sent in with the petition. Nebraska State Chapter granted permission, and Chapter HM was born.

Charter Members of Chapter HM were: Sandra Bishop, Lillis Brown, Kathy Bryan, Kathryn Deck, Sue Engler, Alice Erickson, Deborah Erickson, Patricia Hild, Pamela Hudson, Cheryl Linden, Leslie McClymont, Ruth Meyers, Dorothy Patrick, Demaris Sawyer, Harriett Silvey, Rebecca Williams, and Joan Yentes. Chapter HM was organized September 8, 1979, in the Holdrege Presbyterian Church. On February 5, 1980, Mary Louise Hoffman, AD, Trenton, Missouri, the mother of Alice Erickson, gave Chapter HM their white gavel. Kathryn Deck donated the portable podium on May 3, 1983, and it is still used today.

The first yearbook theme was, appropriately, "We've Only Just Begun." This marked the beginning of new growth and love for the energized young Sisterhood. The new members, delighted at being able to participate in their chapter, wasted no time in promoting the growth and love of P.E.O.

After thirty-five years, Chapter HM continues to grow with members of all ages, occupations and life phases. New initiates have included twenty-one daughters and four daughters-in-law of members. Over the years, HM sisters have shared the many joys of weddings, graduations, births, and retirements. Sadly, the chapter had to say goodbye to five beloved sisters who have joined Chapter Eternal.

Chapter HM members have established several traditions. The yearly auction, the primary fundraiser for P.E.O. projects, is held every November. Members are encouraged to bring a guest to bid on the many crafts and baked goods supplied by members. There is also an annual salad supper, and occasional BIL parties. Of special significance was the 25th anniversary of the chapter. This was celebrated in September 2004 with a meal at the Country Club with members escorted by their BILs

Every year, Chapter H and Chapter HM share in the celebration of Christmas with an inspirational music program given by "The Group." Every other year, both chapters share in the celebration and responsibilities of the P.E.O. Founders' Day.

Chapter HM has shared secret sisters, a "wise old owl bank," special sisters, goodie baskets, and a "Cheers and Tears" basket, where members donate $1 to share a personal message. One member, Gwen Harden, has spent many years creating beautiful, original birthday cards for each member's birthday. Any new baby born to a P.E.O. sister is presented with a hand painted china bootie.

Sister Lynn Sundquist was an ELF recipient in 1987, and four other names have been submitted for the P.E.O. Scholar Award and P.E.O. STAR Scholarship. In 1999, the chapter began a local scholarship of $200 to be given to a qualified young woman. A special project of Chapter HM is the Nebraska P.E.O. Home in Beatrice. The chapter has adopted residents, sent gift packages, and supplied them with bingo prizes.

The chapter has also been generous with other donations, including: a seat at the Tassel Performing Arts Center, Phelps Co. Paint-A-Thon, a color copier for the Holdrege library, the Red Cross for 9/11, and dictionaries to third grade students. Members have also picked up litter and planted trees for the community. "Let all that ye do, be done in love" is truly embraced by the sisters of HM.

The importance of their history and anticipation of the future has bound the sisters of Chapter HM through the years. "These things will someday be pleasant to remember" -Homer, was the quotation that Lillis Brown chose to begin the history book of the chapter.

CHAPTER HM'S ACTIVE MEMBERSHIP IS 55; TOTAL ENROLLMENT IS 120

★

CHAPTER HN SCOTTSBLUFF
ORGANIZED OCTOBER 17, 1979 BY HELEN CURTISS

As this history of Chapter HN was being written in the summer of 2013, we were preparing to initiate our eighty-fifth sister.

Our chapter, now thirty-four years of age, came into being on October 16, 1979, with an organization ceremony at the Episcopal Church in Scottsbluff. The seventeen charter members were initiates Marlene Boston and Sharon Englebart, joined by the following who came by dimit: Shirley Berger, Eleanor Borders, Glenda Cook, Barbara Coppom, Carolyn Fitts, Kathy Graham, Judy Hall, Pat Haiston, Marlene Hancock, Helen Henderson, Ruthanne Hooper, Barbara Ropp, Carol Sill, Betty VanNewkirk and Carol Windhorst.

Our early history is documented in poem form in *The Spirit of the Prairie* by Ruth Hopkins. We are the "youngest" chapter in our area, but now have reached our "middle age" in the Legacy of P.E.O.

Chapter HN initiation of our 85th sister, Michelle Powell, September 11, 2013. Left to right: Janet Gardner, Cindy Bowker, Jan Curtright, Michelle, Diane Hartwig, Barbara Ropp, Harriett Aden, Nancy Sloan.

September 11, 2013, Chapter HN meeting. Back row: Janet Gardner, Marilyn Kennedy, Donna Eckland, Nancy Hall, Ruthanne Hooper, Cindy Bowker, Judy Freouf, Barbara Kaes, Diane Hartwig, Nancy Sloan, Harriett Aden, Myrt Bacon. Front row: Jan Curtright, Barbara Ropp, Missi Iasillo, Michelle Powell.

We now have one 50-year member, have initiated ninety sisters and greeted fourteen others by dimit. Nineteen sisters are now in Chapter Eternal.

One highlight before 1995 was a trip by several to Lincoln on May 2, 1992, to help in organizing Chapter IL. Chapter HN conducted the initiation ceremony. Among the initiates in Chapter IL was Peggy Kent, daughter of Louise Kent of HN. The Legacy continues.

Twenty-six of our sisters have served as president, many serving more than one term. Each, with the help of all sisters, has left a lasting legacy for P.E.O. and Chapter HN. Among the memories and traditions that we observe are a chapter quilt made and signed by our sisters. We gather for lunch at Christmas, officer installation and after initiations. Mystery lunches help us become better acquainted with our sisters. We include our BILs in an annual summer picnic and an omelet brunch in the fall. We send birthday cards to each sister and our courtesy committee keeps up with the "health" of our chapter. We have had fun working together on fundraising events such as garage sales, chapter auctions, selling Butterbraids, bunco parties and participating in Community Days at a local department store. Our fundraising activities help support the P.E.O. projects as well as Cottey College and the Nebraska P.E.O. Home.

Since 1995 we have had two P.E.O. Scholar Award recipients, Karla Kent Jensen and Christine Hancock Dempsey; seven ELF recipients, Steffan Stacy, Kristin Luehrs, Kimberly Taylor, Jodi Hall, Leanna Booth, Misty Clawson and Alisa Stuckert. Kris Perez has received a PCE grant.

We also support our community by having a garden spot at our zoo, donating to the library and Casa, and by adopting a local family at Christmas.

Our programs have included such topics as doll making, trips around the world, painting a group Marguerite picture and making scarves from t-shirts.

Chapter HN has helped with two state conventions in 1996 and 2009. Janet Gardner was Convention Chair in 2009. We hosted a Reciprocity Group III and X area meeting in 2002 with a "Margueritaville" theme. Judy Hall served as Group III and X president in 2005, and currently Judy Meter will be III and X president in 2014. We participate in Founders' Day each year, where we learn of our P.E.O. legacy and share fellowship with other chapters.

We are proud to be a part of the P.E.O. Legacy and look forward to the future.

CHAPTER HN'S ACTIVE MEMBERSHIP IS 45; TOTAL ENROLLMENT IS 125

Chapter HO North Platte
Organized November 10, 1979
by Helen Curtiss

Chapter HO was organized in November 1979 as Nebraska's 234th chapter and the fourth chapter in North Platte. We started as an afternoon chapter but, because of members entering the daytime work force, became an evening chapter in 1987.

The original twenty dimitting members were: Maris Schad, president; Linda Nelson, vice president; Dori Bush, recording secretary; Patty Birch, corresponding secretary; Susan Christensen, treasurer; Barb Conley, chaplain; Margene Phares, guard; Sandy Fritz, Linda Gale, Nancy Gardner, Phyllis Krotz, Carol Overholt, Lynda Perry, Mattie Rumery, Bev Sallee, Carol Scoggins, Evelyn Smith, Christie Stafford, Jean States, Nancy Whitaker, and the two initiates were Jackie Lashley and Lynn Wilkinson. June Windrum and Erna Todd joined Chapter HO by dimit immediately afterward. The white cloth used in the initiation of the original two initiates plus all initiations since that day was donated by charter member Christie Stafford, and the names of all original members and the two initiates were embroidered on this cloth by charter initiate Jackie Lashley.

Eleven of these members are still active members, and eight have served as president of our chapter. In our thirty-four years of existence, we regretfully have had eight members enter Chapter Eternal.

Our meetings are held on the first Tuesday of each month as well as the third Tuesday in March and October and monthly email updates are sent to all members. Throughout the year, we have two dinner meetings, an annual Christmas party, BIL parties with initiations into the "Misterhood of the Sisterhood," monthly luncheons at local restaurants, we participate in our annual Founders' Day, and a monthly book club. Each year we "adopt" a Nebraska P.E.O. Home resident as well as a student at Cottey College.

Chapter HO has had two members graduate from Cottey. We have had four sets of three-generation mother-daughter-grandmother members and celebrated when four members became 50-year P.E.O.s.

Seventeen women have been sponsored for the P.E.O. Program for Continuing Education and ten for the P.E.O. Educational Loan Fund; several girls have been sponsored for Cottey College scholarships; and we have joined the other North Platte chapters in sponsoring an IPS student. One member's daughter was recipient of the P.E.O. Scholar Award. In conjunction with the other four North Platte chapters, we have hosted our Reciprocity Group I and the Nebraska State Convention. We host or give the program at Founders' Day every five years. Over the past thirty-four years, we have proudly donated to our P.E.O. projects with proceeds from garage sales, silent auctions, and ingenious ideas such as selling RADA knives, a Joy Box at our meetings, a traveling food basket, creating a cookbook and having a daily calendar with a suggested donation for various items in our homes.

CHAPTER HO'S ACTIVE MEMBERSHIP IS 55; TOTAL ENROLLMENT IS 142

★

CHAPTER HP OMAHA
ORGANIZED JANUARY 24, 1980
BY HELEN CURTISS

Chapter HP was organized at the First United Methodist Church by Helen Curtiss, who was assisted by Chapter FZ, Omaha. The charter list of eight dimits and seven initiates consisted of Sue Quast, president; Willa Smith, vice president; Kathy Lewis, recording secretary; Donna Sattem, treasurer; Nev Fredrickson, corresponding secretary; Roxanne Bliss, chaplain; Betty Cook Gerner, guard; Jean Bressman, Trill Engdahl, Barb Fredrickson, Carol Glasford, Lindsay Huurman, Gloria Schlichtemier, Lori Schlichtemier Loseth, and Peg Sorensen.

Honored guests included Past President of Supreme Chapter Irene Van Brunt; Dorothy Yeager, Catherine Anderson, and Frances Key, all past presidents of Nebraska State Chapter; and Mary Ruth Wilson, Bernice Zajicek, Helen Curtiss, June Steggs, Julia McDougal, and Marion Larmon, Nebraska State Chapter executive board members, to help this new daytime chapter get off to a great start.

As a new and enthusiastic chapter, we were eager to begin growing in charity and have donated to all of the projects every year since our inception. Our fundraisers have been as simple as collecting "Happy Bucks" for members sharing "happy news," to annual auctions of wonderful gift items, including a "mystery item" enclosed in a pretty box. In addition, we have sponsored a young lady for the P.E.O. scholarship, sent gifts to the students at Cottey College, and donated holiday gifts to the Nebraska P.E.O. Home in Beatrice. We also participated in the recent fundraiser "race" to raise funds for Cottey College's Defining Moment Campaign.

Chapter HP was very involved with the Convention of International Chapter held in Omaha in 1991. Jan Stolp, Joan McMillan and Barb Fredrickson were involved with the decorations committee, with Barb serving as secretary. Many HP members met delegates at the airport, staffed booths and worked at the hotels.

We look forward to each meeting and growing in knowledge. Our programs have been both varied and informative. Community professionals have brought programs on the transplant program at UNMC, the Make a Wish Foundation, and the Gerald Ford birthplace. Our members have also given programs such as a travelogue of Poland, the Semester at Sea, and team-building exercises to "Get to Know Your Sister."

As we reflect over the past years, we see countless instances of our members growing in community involvement. The generous donation of their time and commitment has benefitted such organizations as the Omaha Symphony, the Durham Museum, the Henry Doorly Zoo, the Salvation Army, Aksarben, and the Arthritis Foundation, as well as many hospital auxiliaries. We bring talents of teachers, nurses, interior designers, and business professionals, as many have served as our officers multiple times.

In a recent survey of our members, when asked "How would you describe our chapter?" three words came up repeatedly—"welcoming, supportive, and fun-loving." It is sometimes impossible for a new member to distinguish a member of 30+ years from a member of three months. Over the years, our BILs have become close friends as well, renewing their friendships at our annual country club holiday party.

"Life is a journey," and as we travel the road, we are so grateful we found these "sisters" to laugh with us, to mourn with us, to share our joys, to solve our problems, and to make our journey more meaningful, filled with love for each other.

CHAPTER HP'S ACTIVE MEMBERSHIP IS 33; TOTAL ENROLLMENT IS 82

★

CHAPTER HQ NORTH PLATTE
ORGANIZED MAY 31, 1980
BY JULIA MCDOUGAL

Chapter HQ, High Quality, was organized May 31, 1980, by Julia McDougal. Chapter HQ's original eighteen charter members were Dixie Colson, Vikki Kershner, Janet Shepherd, Denise Johnston, Sara Sup, Sandee Werblow, Pat Ball, Margo Hirshfeld, Jane Langvardt, Lindy Luers, Candy Myers, Diana Spearow, Jean Spiker, Ardys Stadler, Gen Evans, Barb Mohrman, Jo Wolf and Jamie Wright. Of the eighteen, only two remain members in HQ. We now have a membership of twenty-three and have enjoyed initiating new members.

Among our members we boast of one Cottey College graduate, and another member's granddaughter who also graduated from Cottey in 2013. We are a quite diverse chapter; we have a State Appeals Court Judge and an author with two published books, teachers, retired teachers, business women, retirees, and college students. Chapter HQ is proud of our record of supporting all of the P.E.O. projects each year. We had a member that utilized the P.E.O. Program for Continuing Education grant to receive her doctorate degree in physical therapy.

We no longer have a Bed and Breakfast Program for our fundraiser. We still have our annual garage sale in the summer, and have had several inventive fundraisers such as a "goodie basket" auction, a purse auction, bowling ball (painted like lady-bugs) sales, painting "ORIGINAL ART," and we participated with all five North Platte Chapters in a dinner theater, dividing the proceeds.

We continue to support delegates to state conventions and our Local Chapter Officer Workshops to bring about better understanding of P.E.O.

Chapter HQ's active membership is 23; total enrollment is 94

★

Chapter HR Gibbon
Organized August 2, 1980
by Julia McDougal

Chapter HR, Gibbon, was organized August 2, 1980, at Faith United Methodist Church in Gibbon, Nebraska. Catherine Dwiggins was given consent to select a charter list for Chapter HR by Chapter BI, Shelton. The nine members dimitting from Chapter BI were K. Kay Reed, Anita Ross, Jeannetta Bycroft, H. Jean Godberson, Doris Ganz, Nancy Power, Susan Reiber, Berenice Mercer, and Catherine Dwiggins. There were eight initiates: Linda Brodine, Gwen Wilkie, Judith Niemack, Lucile Walker, Mavis Bailey, Ilene Carter, Shirley Kozisek, and Janell Godberson. Members of Chapter BI served as assistants to Nebraska State Chapter Organizer Julia McDougal. Past President of Nebraska State Chapter Lois Ann Hansen installed the new officers: Catherine Dwiggins, president; Berenice Mercer, vice president; Doris Ganz, recording secretary; Nancy Power, corresponding secretary; H. Jean Godberson, treasurer; Anita Ross, chaplain; and K. Kay Reed, guard. Past state presidents in attendance were: Helen Magill, H, Holdrege; Janet Atkins, GQ, Lincoln; Vera Koefoot, GP, Grand Island; Lois Ann Hansen, G, Hastings. Nebraska State Chapter executive board members present were: Mary Ruth Wilson, president; June Steggs, corresponding secretary; Susan Harr, treasurer; and Julia McDougal, organizer.

Chapter HR assisted with Nebraska State Conventions and sent delegates to Conventions of International Chapter as well as participating in Reciprocity Group XIV.

Much has changed in the last thirty-five years, including the demographics of our chapter as more retire and younger women join our group, but our chapter's vitality remains strong. Members contributed as career women from many fields: education, healthcare, business, finance, leadership, philanthropy, and religion. Sisters have shared their knowledge and expertise in addition to full time commitment to family and career. Our programs are rich with tradition, but fresh with new ideas. In 2013 we moved our meetings to the local library to better accommodate our working women with young families. In 1995 Chapter HR had twenty-five members and thirteen nonresidents. In 2015 we have forty active members, ten of them nonresident.

Chapter HR actively promotes the P.E.O. projects with fundraisers: concession stands at the local mud drag races and estate auctions, bake auctions, Brag Bag ($1/brag to celebrate the successes of each other and our beloveds), traveling gift basket, and selling coupon books for a local retailer. In addition to the established projects, ten years ago the chapter launched and faithfully funded a local scholarship that has helped twenty-six young women to date. In the last eighteen years Chapter HR has given generously to women's education. This doesn't include countless donations to IPS students, funeral dinners, help for needy local students, and mittens for the school's reserve. Chapter HR is generous and joyful in its giving!

Perhaps the chapter's most enduring gift was the long-term support for a young sister, Marcy Weismann, during her long bout with cancer. P.E.O. sisters provided ongoing meals for her young family of four, paid for a housekeeper, babysat, and maintained her household for several months. We put on one amazing Christmas for them, complete with tree, gifts, and visit from Santa. In the end stages of Marcy's life, her sisters lovingly provided nursing care in her home. This loving service blessed us all.

Helen Keller wrote, "I long to accomplish great and noble tasks, but it is my chief duty to accomplish humble tasks as though they were great and noble. The world is moved along, not only by the mighty shoves of its heroes, but also by the aggregate of the tiny pushes of each honest worker." And so it is that our collective, powerful "tiny" pushes are changing the world around us.

CHAPTER HR'S ACTIVE MEMBERSHIP IS 40; TOTAL ENROLLMENT IS 82

★

CHAPTER HS ALLIANCE
ORGANIZED NOVEMBER 29, 1980
BY JULIA MCDOUGAL

A request from Gretchen Garwood, Chapter GC, Alliance, was received by state officers requesting the organization of a new P.E.O. chapter in Alliance due to the number of exceptional local women who were potential P.E.O.s. On November 29, 1980, Chapter HS was organized by Julia McDougal with ten dimitting members from Chapter GC, three from Chapter AH and four initiates. Charter officers were Gretchen Garwood, president; Leah Koester, vice president; Millie Kuncl, recording secretary; Maryetta Lyman, corresponding secretary; Sharon Hitchcock, treasurer; Sarah Fairbanks, chaplain; Charlotte Moravek, guard; and members Nadine Schlichtemeier, Linda Ocken, Sherrie Curtiss, Sue Fairbanks, Jolene McGinnis, and Eileen West. New initiates were Jerri Tomlin, Darlene Kenzy, Bette Cram and Nancy Fairbanks. Chapter GC served a lovely coffee before the organizational meeting and Chapter AH followed the meeting with a salad bar luncheon.

In September of 2003, Chapter IS in Hemingford, a small town nineteen miles from Alliance, was organized. One of our members, Robyn Prochazka, was responsible for requesting the charter for the new chapter. Seventeen members of Chapter HS were present to witness the organizational meeting and hold a salad luncheon for our new sisters. Our chapter helped organize an annual P.E.O. bridge marathon with proceeds going to Cottey Math and Science Camps, bus trips to Cottey and local scholarships. We have successfully sponsored one of our daughters for an ELF loan, nominated a P.E.O. STAR Scholarship recipient, sponsored a P.E.O. Program for Continuing Education grant for a local nursing student and gave additional financial help to IPS recipient Anne Gatobu for her continued studies. Our local chapters recently erected a highway sign entering Alliance in an effort to promote the P.E.O. Sisterhood. We kept in touch with our college girls by sending them holiday boxes. We have four members who have attended Cottey College.

2005 was the year of our 25th anniversary. A celebration was held at Pryors Heritage House. A cake with a photo of our charter members on top, candles everywhere, and yellow and white flowers and napkins adorned the tables. Six charter members were present and the special guest speaker was Joyce Goff, who since has served as president of International Chapter. The program included a fun skit and memories by all of the attending past presidents of Chapter HS.

To help fund our P.E.O. project donations, we have had Spring auctions of Easter breads and crafty bunnies donated by members. The Friendship Basket project involved one member placing an item in a basket and delivering it to the next sister on the list. That sister put a donation in the envelope for that item, put a new item in the basket and then took it to the next sister. This was a great way to involve ALL sisters in the chapter and gave us a chance to visit with each other. We raise funds through garage sales also, and have our brag box at the end of each meeting which allows us to share in the joys and concerns of our sisters. Each year at the Christmas meeting we have an ornament exchange. We have supported our local toy drive by donating gifts for underprivileged girls at Christmas. Our Daisy Chain has been a great way to keep members up-to-date if they have missed a meeting or two. Emails after each meeting have taken the place of letters in the mail which makes the news more timely.

We hold paper showers for all of our brides-to-be. It's amazing to see how creative each gift is since it can be "paper only." We give a gift to all new babies and a rose bowl to members who are ill. We give donations to a project of the sister's choice when a family member has passed away. Birthday cards are sent to each member, and the Nebraska P.E.O. Home Committee sends birthday cards to all Home residents. We send care packages to our college students on various holidays. We have held a number of BIL gatherings including Big Red parties, bunco parties, trips to the theater and patio parties.

We provided decorations for the BIL banquet at the 1995 state convention in Scottsbluff and provided the information boards for each of the state officers at the 2009 state convention. We helped sponsor the Cottey College presentation at the Alliance High College Night, organized Founders' Day every third year for Chapters AH, GC and HS, and more recently, the newly organized Chapter IS in nearby Hemingford. Our programs have ranged from "C3P.E.O." to "Sister Act" (of Whoopie Goldberg fame), providing a tea with treats made from recipies from the time of our Founders, always including the display of drawings of our Founders done by the daughter of our 50-year member.

2013 marked the twentieth year that our sister Dorothy Carnine and her BIL have served as Bed and Breakfast hosts. Sisters and BILs who found themselves hosted by Chapter HS found more than a bed and breakfast at the Carnine ranch in the beautiful Sandhills of Nebraska. All proceeds were donated to our projects.

Millie Kuncl, a charter member, is our 50-year member. Pat Taylor held each of the Reciprocity offices, most recently as president. Chapter HS is proud of its membership of talented women. Whether it involves giving a program, organizing a Founders' Day program for the four local chapters in Box Butte County, planning a fun BIL party or holding a chapter office, they do it with grace. We have a master gardener, a number of extraordinary artists, amazing home decorators, gourmet cooks, musicians, loving teachers, Chamber presidents and fair queens, just to name a few. Each of us, in our own way, has been encouraged to "reach for the stars" to become all we can be. Oh yes, we also have a member who was a contestant on "Who Wants To Be A Millionaire!"

CHAPTER HS'S ACTIVE MEMBERSHIP IS 48; TOTAL ENROLLMENT IS 117

Chapter HT Hastings
Organized September 3, 1981
by June Steggs

Organized September 3, 1981, Chapter HT became the 220th P.E.O. chapter in Nebraska. A spirit of generosity, laughter, and care has characterized Chapter HT since its inception, and dedication to our philanthropic projects has helped us instill those characteristics in countless other women throughout the first three decades of our existence.

In her February 1982 president's letter, Chapter HT's first president, Doris Kovar, expressed her gratitude to those special sisters who helped HT gain its charter: Nebraska State President Bernice Zajicek (BF) "for the rich counseling you provided on our organizational day"; Organizer June Steggs, "who displayed proficiency in her first new-chapter organization"; Advisor Julia McDougal (DA), "our mother-adviser"; and Donna Jane Fink (DA), "who diligently served as our charter head." The twenty-one members of the charter list included four initiates. Charter members were Elizabeth Collins (DA), Octavia Cramer (DA), Harriette Davis (DA), Mary Golgert, Louise Hanne (FS), Irma Hansen (DA), Esther Hill (DA), Clara Jean Horsham (DA), Mary Hutson (DA), Doris Kovar (DA), Celeste Kreifels, Alice Marvel (DA), Marilynn Miller (AS, Kansas), Mary Northrop (DA), Mildred Ott (DA), Alta Robbins (DA), Mary Robison, Hazel Seberg (DA), Jean Spiker (HQ), Jeanne Sulley (DA), and Barbara Zaroban. The dimit of Flora Mills (DA) was accepted at the first meeting on organization day.

The twenty-two members of Chapter HT in 1981 ranged in age from twenty-seven to eighty-nine, and this multi-generational strength continues to characterize Chapter HT today. Our oldest sister and first president, Doris Kovar Morhart, was 105 when she joined Chapter Eternal in 2013, and our youngest HT sister was twenty-six that year. In addition to multi-generational sisters "in heart and spirit," family legacies have also strengthened our chapter from its inception. Golda Collins, the mother of charter member Clara Jean Horsham, dimitted to Chapter HT during its first year. Irma Hansen and her daughter Alice Marvel were both charter members, and Alice's twin daughters dimitted to Chapter HT during its second year. Throughout our first three decades, mothers, daughters, daughters-in-law, granddaughters, and sisters have continued to invigorate Chapter HT; eighteen of our present Chapter HT sisters are also relatives, and many more daughters and granddaughters of HT sisters are members of P.E.O. chapters across the United States.

During its first decade Chapter HT concentrated on nurturing membership, and we enjoyed programs that created a strong sense of sisterhood. In addition to programs on our Founders and our philanthropic projects, charter members Barbara Zaroban, Marilynn Miller, Mary Golgert, and Doris Kovar shared their love of music and fostered in us all a delight in piano, violin, song, dance—and jingles. Charter member Alice Marvel consistently piqued our interest in literature and art, while new initiates added their talents in music, painting, weaving, crocheting, and fabric design. During these early years, singing, poetry reading, dramatic interpretation, caroling, dance, and art all solidified our sense of fun and sisterhood. Chapter HT continues to value the arts and has even shared some of its chapter talent with our local Greater Hastings P.E.O. Group, including a dramatic celebration of our Seven Founders, "The Oprah Wintry Show," starring comedienne charter member Marilynn Miller as Oprah and the irrepressible Georgene Allen as ad-woman. We also shared with our Greater Hastings P.E.O. sisters a musical tribute to P.E.O., *"From the Hills to the Heartlands,"* starring Penny Pratt soloist, charter member Mary Plock pianist, and a six-woman nearly silent chorus.

When HT had doubled its enrollment by welcoming new sisters who brought to the chapter their unique talents, concerns, and passions, we reached for the stars. We began to actively seek project recipients while also concentrating on our responsibilities to both Group XI Reciprocity sisters and Nebraska State P.E.O. By the time we tripled our original enrollment we had experienced the joy of sponsoring and supporting six P.E.O. Educational Loan Fund recipients and six young women who received P.E.O. Program for Continuing Education grants. Cottey College also became a special project for us: Doris Kovar Morhart and her husband Frank established the Mabel Morhart Scholarship at Cottey in 1994, and HT sponsored the first recipient of that scholarship, Amy Alonso. HT members have also enjoyed serving as Cottey Area Chairmen for Reciprocity Group XI, and we were honored when one of our HT sisters served three years on the Nebraska State Cottey Scholarships Committee. In addition to contributing as a chapter to the highly successful Defining Moment Campaign, individual HT sisters have consistently supported the Mabel Morhart Scholarship and earlier Cottey building projects throughout the years. The Nebraska P.E.O. Home also remains a special project for us.

Nineteen of our dear sisters have joined Chapter Eternal, including eleven charter members, but we continue to initiate new sisters whose intelligence, dedication to service, thoughtfulness, and humor invigorate our chapter. As we all work to balance the demands of complex personal and professional lives, and as we strive to be sensitive to the changing needs of our HT sisters and our International P.E.O. organization, we also continue to honor our traditions. Guided by charter member Mary Northrop, we limit our refreshments at regular meetings to beverages and cookies, we enjoy a luncheon once a year prior to March installation of officers, we maintain and value our chapter scrapbooks, we design creative fundraising projects, we invite our BILs to join us periodically at the symphony or for dinner, and most importantly, we continue to share a spirit of generosity, laughter, and care. Celebrating each other's successes, mourning each other's losses, sharing a good laugh or a good cry, and striving to be loving and loyal, Chapter HT members continue to work together to embody the true meaning of sisterhood.

CHAPTER HT'S ACTIVE MEMBERSHIP IS 56; TOTAL ENROLLMENT IS 112

*Life is like playing a violin in public
and learning the instrument as one goes on.*

-Samuel Butler

Chapter HU Norfolk
Organized November 29, 1981
by June Steggs

To meet the diverse needs of young women, an additional chapter in Norfolk, Nebraska, was organized by Nebraska State Chapter Organizer June Steggs on November 29, 1981. Charter members of Chapter HU were Donna Bleich, Patricia Bliss, Carol Cross, Bernice Davis, Teresa Ellwood, Carolyn Ely, Jean Engel, Kathryn Fishwood, Su Ellyne Holland, Leanne Johnson, Sharon Johnson, Diane Mackender, Dene Nedrow, Linda Pohlman, Debra Sabers and Joan Settles. Chapter HU was started with sixteen members—fifteen by dimit and one charter iniate, Diane Mackander. Dues were $18.50 per year in 1981.

The chapter has grown and adapted with the needs of the women throughout the years. Five years after inception the chapter had twenty-eight members and dues had increased to $20. In 1989 the chapter had forty resident members and two nonresident members. With the help of the fundraiser in November and Linda Pohlman dressed as "Fanny Annie of Nathans Auction House" the chapter purchased new initiation robes in 1990. The next year the chapter helped host Convention of International Chapter. Chapter HU made the table decorations for lunch and dinners and also supplied granola bars for the hospitality room. Carol Cross served as guard at International Convention.

Chapter HU has always supported the P.E.O. projects. Money is sent to each project every year at Christmastime. Chapter HU fulfilled a $1,000 commitment to the Nebraska P.E.O. Home in just two years in 1996. Chapter HU has also sewn napkins and placemats for the P.E.O. Home. Kathy Balsiger, Carol Cross, Carolyn Edy and Gladys Maxwell volunteered their talents for this project.

Again, to meet the needs of P.E.O. sisters, the meetings became year around for the first time in 1995. In 1998 the nightly meetings were changed from Wednesday nights to Monday nights at 7:30 PM. The starting time changed to 7:00 PM in 2001.

To promote and support strong women, applications have been sent in for the ELF loan and PCE grant. A high school senior is also nominated for the P.E.O. STAR Scholarship each year. In 2007 Chapter HU, along with the two other Norfolk chapters, started the Ninth Grade Leadership Award. This award is given to a ninth grade girl who has shown good character in school and in the community.

A special woman in Chapter HU that needs to be mentioned is 60-year member Nancy Rice. There are three 50-year members, Su Ellyne Hopkins, Bernice Davis and Carolyn Brower. Members who are in Chapter Eternal are Bernice Davis, Cindy Gail (Vogel) Froelich, Lynell Jensen Hajek and Carol Keating.

To keep Chapter HU fun and supportive of each sister, at the end of each meeting there are "Did you knows...." This helps each sister learn more about each other. This way each sister can be supported or share in the joys of each other. Birthday cards are mailed to each sister, visits are made to sisters who are hospitalized or in care centers and meals are brought in to homes of sisters who need some extra help. Every year since 1996 there is a spring formal dinner party at Kathy Balsiger's home. The fellowship time is enjoyed by each sister. There are two social meetings, one in July and another in October. Ideas for these have ranged from BIL parties, to dinner and a movie, to a destination meeting at an herb garden and lastly a wine tasting event. There have also been gatherings at the local coffee house on Saturday mornings "just for fun."

Chapter HU is a chapter that cares about each other. The members of HU support not only each other but support helping all women grow in charity and knowledge. May the characteristics of Faith, Love, Purity, Justice and Truth continue to enhance Chapter HU.

CHAPTER HU'S ACTIVE MEMBERSHIP IS 44; TOTAL ENROLLMENT IS 106

★

CHAPTER HV LEXINGTON
ORGANIZED APRIL 24, 1982
BY JUNE STEGGS

Chapter HV, Lexington, Nebraska, was organized on April 24, 1982. It has been our aim to exemplify the virtues written in the P.E.O. Creed by Effie Hoffman Rogers. This new link was added to the P.E.O. Sisterhood when Jean King suggested to Chapter FS on March 16, 1981, that a new chapter be organized in Lexington. Consent to select a charter list was granted by Chapter FS on May 19, 1981, with the first organizational meeting for the new chapter held on October 28, 1981. Permission was granted for a total of twenty-four charter members (twenty-two by dimit and two by initiation). Chapter HV was officially organized as a morning chapter on April 24, 1982, with June Steggs as organizer.

Charter members by dimit included Donna Trueblood, president; Gladys Salisbury, vice president; Barbara Knapple, recording secretary; Jean King, corresponding secretary; Nancy Pepper, treasurer; Marian Berke, chaplain; Betty Rowe, guard; Joan Stuckey, Francelene Skinner, Peggy Skinner, Wilma Orthmann, Marjorie Grafton, Helen Barrett, Mary Sarnes, Elsie Barrett, Fern Bieck, Eloise Batie, Eileen Biehl, Judy Zauha, Betsy Menke Larkins, Joan Huet, Berdena Bossung and charter initiates Jean Ford and Marcia Stoll.

Our chapter celebrated its 30th year of active, vibrant sisterhood in 2012 with four of our original charter members still active in the chapter. Although our chapter does not have a large membership, our average attendance is 65 percent of our total membership. We enjoy each other, love learning about each other and our projects through the programs which sisters present at each meeting. The programs are given from the heart, as we share ourselves in relation to the president's theme for each year. We enjoy chatting before meetings over coffee or at lunch following our meetings. We also share a Fall Luncheon, Christmas Luncheon and BIL parties. We have traveled to the Nebraska P.E.O. Home in Beatrice three different times over the years and we remember the sisters at the Home with birthday greetings. We also support Cottey College in the "adopt a student" program. HV sister Judy Zauha served on the Nebraska Cottey Scholarships Committee from 1989 to 1991.

In order to keep sisters who are unable to attend meetings up to date, we send a newsletter after each meeting. Chapter HV also shares Founders' Day and state convention reports each year with the Lexington Reciprocity consisting of all four chapters in Lexington. Our creative Ways and Means Committee presents fun ways to raise money to support the P.E.O. projects through auctions, tea parties, style shows, the sale of handmade garden ornaments, yearbook covers and Puffin Pastries.

Our chapter has been active in sponsoring area young women for projects. Over the years, we have successfully sponsored three P.E.O. Program for Continuing Education candidates, two P.E.O. Educational Loan Fund applicants, one P.E.O. STAR Scholarship candidate and applications for many more.

The long standing traditions of P.E.O. are important to Chapter HV. We like the rich heritage of memorizing the initiation ceremony, allowing us to focus on the candidate and the meaning of the ceremony words. Our chapter is filled with wonderful, loving, helpful and giving women, who very seldom say no and who care for and support each other, both in good times and in bad.

CHAPTER HV'S ACTIVE MEMBERSHIP IS 39; TOTAL ENROLLMENT IS 103

★

Chapter HW Lincoln
Organized March 26, 1983
by Marion Larmon

Chapter HW was organized on March 26, 1983, with Marion Larmon serving as organizer. The chapter was organized with twenty-two members on the charter list; five still are on the roll. State officers Jeanne Johnson and Phyllis Blanke assisted with the organization process.

Despite Mother Nature covering the ground with several inches of heavy snow, the excitement of organizing a new P.E.O. chapter was not tempered. It was a time of great excitement and anticipation for the twenty-two P.E.O. members and the culmination of several months of planning and fundraising. Chapter HW's charter membership included: Amy Ree Barnes Angelos, Margaret Calhoon, Janet Domeier, Jamie Fassnacht, Kristine Gist Madsen, Susan Grasmick, Marilyn Hoffman, Patricia Imig-Kauffman, Cynthia Martinez, Jane McReynolds, Claudia Neary, Sheri Paden, Deni Papke Hill, Laurie Prohaska, Peggy Sellon, Marcia Shanahan, Karen Swan, Joyce Victor, Diane Vigna, Angela Wilke Hendricks, Juanita Wilke, and Lori Willett.

Chapter HW developed fun and interesting fundraising projects and traditions that demonstrated a strong commitment to the P.E.O. projects. The annual fundraiser started as a craft and foods silent auction and has now evolved into a true Christmas auction. Another HW tradition is a "brag and whine box" where members can brag or whine about special happenings in their lives. At each meeting, another fun activity is raffling items that members have brought from some of their travels. Other fundraisers included making and selling cross-stitched pin holders, bookmarks, ceramic refrigerator magnets, aprons, bird houses, bracelets, decorated flower pots as well as holding garage sales.

Chapter HW celebrated several anniversaries these past years; our 10th, 20th, 25th, and 30th. At each celebration, programs were presented sharing the many memories and accomplishments of our chapter and its members. Through the thirty years, our chapter held several fun BIL gatherings. Some of these included picnics, miniature golf, attending Saltdogs baseball games, progressive dinners, bowling, and wine and beer tasting. Through the years, many of our sisters also gathered informally at the Farmer's Market, casinos, coffee shops, and for special lunches and dinners in various locations.

Our chapter has been well represented in the Lincoln reciprocity group, Lincoln Reciprocity Roundtable. Several members have served as officers with our own Janet Domeier serving as president in 1996-97. Several members have participated in state chapter convention choirs and programs. Our members also served in many capacities in helping Omaha host the P.E.O. Convention of International Chapter in 1991. These ranged from serving as guards, helping as greeters and hosts, and performing in the projects program *"Avenue of P.E.O. Dreams."* Our chapter also provided a delegate to the Convention of International Chapter in 1991 and 2013. The chapter also assisted with hosting the Lincoln Founders' Day in many capacities from greeting, registering guests, providing decorations, to even presenting the program.

Chapter HW has a strong commitment to education and to the many P.E.O. projects. In the past thirty years, we have sponsored loans for three P.E.O. Educational Loan Fund candidates and an IPS scholar. Our chapter also recommended two P.E.O. Scholar Award candidates and nominated two P.E.O. STAR Scholarship candidates. Giving to all the projects has always been the major emphasis of our fundraising. In the chapter's thirty-year history, we have visited and hosted a meeting at the Nebraska P.E.O. Home several times—always bringing gifts to the residents.

Although a relatively young chapter, we have lost two members to Chapter Eternal—Laura Huffman and Melinda Wilson. Chapter HW is still a group of Happy Women and always Hard Working! As sisters, we have helped each other celebrate the many successes at work and with our families, always remaining sisters and friends.

CHAPTER HW'S ACTIVE MEMBERSHIP IS 48; TOTAL ENROLLMENT IS 118

★

CHAPTER HX OMAHA
ORGANIZED APRIL 23, 1983
BY MARION LARMON

To meet the diverse needs of young women, an additional evening chapter in Omaha, Nebraska, was organized by Marion Larmon on April 23, 1983. Charter members and initiates had varied backgrounds which were reflected in their careers: law, medicine, architecture, teaching, business, banking, and homemaking. Charter members were: Sharon Agnew, Kim Bowers, Claire Evans, Denise Fischer, Raetha Smith, Arlene Stoney, Nancy Hicks, Deborah Hysack, Nancy Jones, Karen Loibl, Suzan Rohrig, Cynda Fontenello, Carol Taylor, Nancy TeKolste Velardi, Martha Wenstrand, Jennifer Holz, Lynne Holz, Cindy Wrenn, Carol Neth Shaw, Cathy Greenwald, and Kay Grammell.

From the birth of our chapter, we have incorporated many fun traditions that keep our members engaged! In the early years, pre-meeting dinners were organized at restaurants close to the meeting site. Those social events provided monthly opportunities for members to relax, catch up on news, and provide listening ears to those members needing advice. Annual BIL parties were important to the charter members as they strengthened their sisterly bonds and provided their spouses or significant others a chance to become familiar with their newly found sisters. We continue the traditions of Saturday morning coffees to meet prospective members and the annual Holiday Auction. We maintain a strong tradition of contributing significant donations to all P.E.O. projects on a yearly basis.

Many of our annual programs have been added to our list of traditions. Each year we have programs by Patti Leamen (Book Woman), Jody Siedelmann (Game Woman), our annual Chapter HX Birthday Bash program, and our July Potluck Dinner. These programs are fun, informative, and provide opportunities for members to invite and reconnect with members who have been unable to attend monthly meetings.

The technology age has been fully embraced by Chapter HX! We were one of the first chapters to have our own website that allowed us the ability to send meeting reminders and messages when members needed our love and attention during family/personal crises. We have archived presidents' letters, chapter programs, and handouts provided during meeting programs. Chapter officers are also able to reach our members who do not attend as frequently through the use of our website. It also has the flavor of social media, which allows members to create their own section using photographs and autobiographies. Members have been able to read their sisters' website pages to become more acquainted with family and personal interests. Technological advances will continue to provide unique opportunities for our chapter in future years.

Chapter HX members continue to involve themselves in the community in addition to their P.E.O. involvement. Chapter members are involved in such organizations as the American Heart Association, Boy Scouts of America, Girl Scouts of America, and various church committees, as well as participating in International Dental Mission trips to serve those who would not otherwise get dental care. No matter how busy Chapter HX members are through all of their endeavors, they always are quick to volunteer to help a sister when the need arises.

Chapter HX continues its strong tradition of participating at the Nebraska State P.E.O. level. Over the years, members have participated in the planning of Nebraska State Chapter Conventions in Omaha. Members volunteered their talents to create skits, design and make banners, and serve as Technical Director at the Convention of International Chapter in Omaha, 1991. Suzan Rohrig has shared her many talents by being the associate architect for the Nebraska P.E.O. Home kitchen and dining room addition. In addition to those duties, Suzan served as the 1991 Omaha Convention of International Chapter Luncheon Chairman, and 1993 Convention of International Chapter delegate in Atlanta, Unaffiliate Chairman of the Omaha Reciprocity, and along with Cathy Greenwald, Jody Siedelmann, and Beth Ann Placek, was a workshop leader during the 1991 Nebraska State Chapter Convention. At the 2013 state convention, chapter members Ginny Allumbaugh, Jill Champley, Trasy Sparr, and Heidi Winters served as workshop leaders. Our chapter continues to support relatives who have risen through the ranks of Nebraska State chapter officers. Chapter HX supported Sara Mitchell's sister, Kathleen Gosch, while she served as state president. A monetary gift was presented to her to honor her as state chapter president. Suzan Rohrig's mother, Beverley Karrer, was installed as Nebraska State Chapter president in 1993 and Chapter HX was there to support her as one of our "honorary members."

On a different level of P.E.O., Chapter HX is excited to facilitate the growth of P.E.O. in the Omaha area by serving as the sponsoring chapter to a developing chapter. Trasy Sparr is working with the new group in anticipation of the new chapter being formed in 2014 or 2015. Throughout our history, Chapter HX has provided officers to Omaha P.E.O. Reciprocity Association, including Arlene Stoney, Deb Hysack, Karen Blair, and Ginny Allumbaugh.

Chapter HX anxiously awaited a very special event that took place at the 2014 Nebraska State Convention... our own Karen Blair was installed as the 2014-15 Nebraska State Chapter president! Members busily prepared for this event and supported her in any way possible! Our chapter has been so proud of her tireless contributions to all aspects of P.E.O.! We would not be the chapter we are today without her love and guidance.

CHAPTER HX'S ACTIVE MEMBERSHIP IS 63; TOTAL ENROLLMENT IS 134

★

CHAPTER HY OMAHA
ORGANIZED JUNE 7, 1983
BY SUSAN HARR

Chapter HY was organized at First Methodist Church in Omaha on June 7, 1983. Susan Harr was the organizer and she was assisted by state officers Julia McDougal, president, Joyce Goff, June Steggs, and June Brunmeier. There were sixteen charter members. Seven members dimitted from Chapters M, EC, and DY to form the new chapter. Charter dimitting members were Cleo Pardee, president; Harriet Moore, vice president; Olivia Thompson, corresponding secretary; Inez Weltmer, Peggy Payne; Julie Bond, treasurer; and Katherine Angemeier, chaplain. Charter initiates were Sharon Gathmann; Jean Wilson, guard; Joan Gayle Chapin, Judy Gaylor, Julie Madsen, Mary Delle Bradley, Gail Parsonage, Julie Moore and Dian Moore.

When the chapter was formed, meetings were held during the daytime. As more members joined it was decided to become an evening chapter. Several traditional events for Chapter HY include a Christmas gift exchange, salad supper, and two BIL events each year. Members have also added three social meetings to our calendar.

Fundraising activities have kept chapter members busy. We have had projects that included "Bean Bag Soup" sales, Christmas candy sales, Pleasure Pak sales, garage sales, a Surprise Package raffle at each meeting, and one of our favorite events, the Chapter Auction. We also have a traveling library that members contribute to when they wish to borrow a book. We currently offer packages of P.E.O. note cards that were designed by one of our members and assembled by chapter members, to help add to our funds.

Chapter HY offered their assistance when the Convention of International Chapter was held in Omaha in 1991 and several members have served as guards during state conventions in Omaha. Each year at least one member attends state convention as our delegate and often several members attend to meet sisters from other chapters in the state. We have been privileged to have members serve as delegates to the Convention of International Chapter. Members have also been officers for the Omaha Reciprocity Group.

Two members have shared their quilting talents with sisters in the chapter to design and make a "Caring Quilt" which is delivered to each sister to use when she needs to be surrounded with our prayers of caring or for healing.

We have learned about our sisters' talents through our programs. One evening we had a garden walk and noted all of the different flowers in one member's gardens. We have had members share books they have read, had fun looking at baby pictures of our members, photos of our mothers and fun facts about each. Members have shared photo journals of trips they have taken and demonstrated how to prepare foods they love to cook. One fun program was when members brought items from their collections and told us how they started collecting each item. We have also had speakers from the community visit us and tell about their programs.

Each new baby born to a sister is given a silver spoon from the chapter and we hope that when the daughters are ready they will become members of our chapter.

We currently have four of our charter members—Joan Gayle Chapin, Sharon Gathmann, Judy Gaylor and Olivia Thompson—who are still active in Chapter HY after thirty years. Chapter HY is alive and well.

CHAPTER HY'S ACTIVE MEMBERSHIP IS 34; TOTAL ENROLLMENT IS 77

★

CHAPTER HZ HARTINGTON
ORGANIZED NOVEMBER 19, 1983
BY SUSAN HARR

Chapter HZ was organized at the instigation of Twila Anderson, who dimitted from Chapter EA, Randolph, and Julie Hulls, who dimitted from Chapter F, Illinois. There were fourteen charter members; Twila Anderson, president; Julie Hulls, vice president; Jennifer Pierce, recording secretary; Patricia Dykeman, corresponding secretary; Gloria Graham, treasurer; Helen Anderson, chaplain; Bernice Miller, guard; Ann Shumway, Laura Lou Marsh, Laura Stolpe, Doris Orwig, Anna Louise Parker, Vida Hunter and Ardys Schwartzenbach. Chapter HZ received their charter at the 95th Convention of Nebraska State Chapter at Dana College in Blair on June 7, 1984.

November 2013, Chapter HZ celebrated thirty years of being an organized chapter. There have been some changes through the years but the primary bond of sisterhood continues.

Patricia Dykeman is the last charter member who continues to be a nonresident member living in Sioux Falls.

Monthly meetings and socials continue as before. International has streamlined meetings but initiations continue to honor the original ceremony. Our presidents still present a theme for the year that each month's program is based on. Each month we have a raffle prize for everyone to enter or we "split the pot." The Courtesy Committee uses this for a variety of needs according to the need of the sister; illness, hospitalization, death in family, new baby, wedding or any special need. Another yearly highlight is our winter book club where we all read and then discuss a variety of books.

Projects continue to be the binding objective to the chapter. We have provided fifty-four area high school girls with scholarships and five recipients for the

P.E.O. Program for Continuing Education. Raising money and spreading the word of P.E.O. is a constant, but fun, endeavor. Some favorite memories include a holiday brunch we served and each sister set a table with her favorite dishes. The community really enjoyed this, as well as, "Nuns on the Run." This was a women's comedy act that we hired and had a great turn out. We have coordinated a "picture with Santa" for families to bring their children to a local gingerbread house to have a picture taken with Santa and Mrs. Claus.

But not everything we do is about money. For many years our chapter coordinated the local Toys for Tots program receiving, wrapping and distributing gifts to the needy throughout our county. HZ recently enjoyed a wine and canvas event. Members enjoyed wine and appetizers while painting a marguerite.

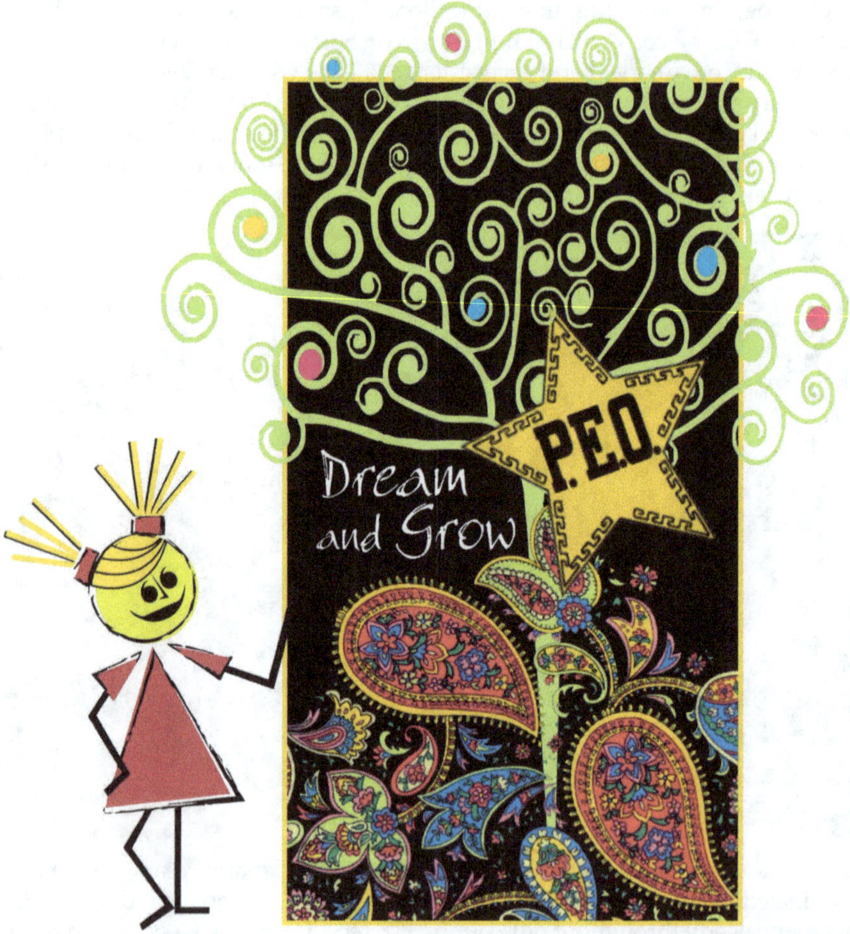
P.E.O.
Dream and Grow

WELCOME
P.E.O. SISTERHOO

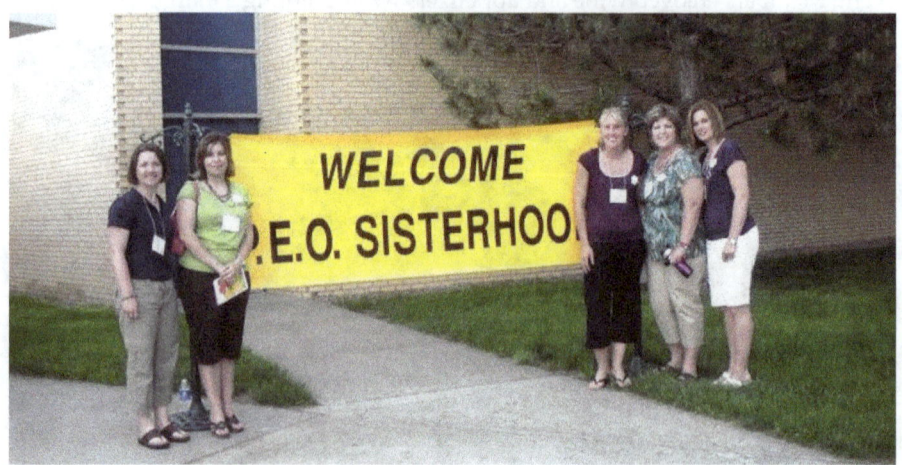

Of course, every November is a special anniversary social. Our 25th anniversary was celebrated over dinner, including etched ornaments and a champagne toast to celebrate the success of Chapter HZ. There have been many trips throughout Northeast Nebraska that we have experienced together as sisters.

Outside of monthly meetings, members continue to participate in the annual P.E.O. State Convention, Reciprocity Group IV and PACK (Pierce, Antelope, Cedar and Knox) picnics and Convention of International Chapter. Brenda Steiner was a Nebraska delegate at the Convention of International Chapter in Oklahoma City in 2003. We have had the privilege of helping host state convention in Norfolk in 2010 where we were responsible for decorations. We featured raised cake plates etched with *"Dream and Grow,"* which was the convention theme, and Kathy Fink sewed paisley themed placemats. We hosted Reciprocity in Hartington in 2009 and PACK picnic here in 2010. At many of these events we continue to sell our P.E.O. garden stake to help raise money for projects.

Chapter HZ's active membership is 27; total enrollment is 71

Above left, Chapter HZ garden stake fundraiser. Right, Team P.E.O. HZ. Below, HZ gathering.

Faith is putting all your eggs in God's basket, then counting your blessings before they hatch.

-Ramona C. Carroll

Chapter IA Lincoln
Organized November 3, 1984
by Joyce Goff
Merged with Chapter FF March 27, 2011

Chapter IA, Lincoln, was organized November 3, 1984, with eighteen charter dimits and one initiate. Nebraska State Chapter Organizer Joyce Goff presided at the chapter's organizing meeting. On March 27, 2011, Chapter IA merged with Chapter FF, and continues as Chapter FF-IA. Of the nineteen charter members of Chapter IA, nine are members of Chapter FF-IA.

Charter members of IA were: Shirley Marsh, Jean Sheffield, Ann Holm, Pamela Vuchetich, Cheryl Crueber, Carolyn Cramer, Pam Rosenau Fleury, Patricia Jones, Barbara Newcomer, Barbara Gaither, Jeanne Reesman, Stephanie Sintek, Mary Holm, Barbara Armbruster Bartle, Carla Dingman, Robyn Reesman, Donna Ficken, Karen Post Burns and Susan Watson. Over the years, the chapter has grown with new initiates and dimits.

IA met as a Monday evening chapter, first with an 8:00PM gavel, and later moving to 7:00PM in an effort to accommodate members who wished to not be out so late in the evening. Initially, the chapter met twice monthly with a summer hiatus, but eventually changed to a year-round schedule.

Chapter IA successfully sponsored several women for the P.E.O. Program for Continuing Education grants and P.E.O. Educational Loan Fund loans.

Among Chapter IA's traditions were a May Basket Exchange, a potluck salad meeting in June for the state convention report and a Christmas Ornament Exchange during December. The chapter also sponsored garage sales, raffled a hand-made quilt, and raffled chances for a catered dinner. Chapter IA held silent auctions and a book sale to raise funds for P.E.O. philanthropies. The handmade quilt was created by Janet Lepard, who during her year as president in 1991-92 made a quilt block for each meeting of her term. Raffle tickets were sold and the winner was announced at the 1992 Founders' Day celebration of Lincoln Reciprocity Roundtable. To everyone's surprise and delight, Jan's mother, Edna Chamberlain, a member of Chapter FW, Lincoln, won the quilt.

Several members of Chapter IA have been Roundtable officers or served as state project chairs. Shirley Mac Marsh, who received permission to create a charter list to start Chapter IA, was a Nebraska State Senator. She was initiated into P.E.O. in 1943 and is Chapter IA's member with the most years as a P.E.O.

Total enrollment prior to merger - 86
Chapter IA proudly continues its legacy as Chapter FF-IA

I can remember walking as a child. It was not customary to say you were fatigued. It was customary to complete the goal of the expedition.

-Katharine Hepburn

Chapter IB Cozad
Organized August 27, 1985
by Catherine Hutton

The vision that there was a need for a second chapter in Cozad was held by two IB sisters, Leila Brownfield, a P.E.O. for forty-four years and Elsie Faught, a P.E.O. for fifty-eight years. Charter members were: Beverly Brownfield, Gayle Brownfield, Mary Jeanne Hart, Jan Yeutter, Gwen Smith, Leila Brownfield, Jacqueline Neill, Mildred Atchison, Beverly Krushenisky, Doris Andersen, Elsie Faught, JoDean Rupp, Valerie Geiger, Frances Davis, Hazel Pharris, Jeanette Rosenau, Sara Eggleston, Ann Nelsen Rodhouse, and Geraldene Berryman.

Chapter IB has been faithful in supporting the P.E.O. projects, in observing Founders' Day, and has successfully sponsored four ELF recipients, eighteen PCE grants, one P.E.O. Scholar Award, and one P.E.O. STAR Scholarship. Chapter IB oversees the application and selection process for a local scholarship in memory of Saralyn Parish. The Saralyn Parish P.E.O. Chapter IB Memorial Scholarship has been awarded annually since 2003 to a senior girl to help further her education.

In 2010, Chapter IB was honored to be selected by the Nebraska State Chapter as the only chapter in the state to participate in the pilot program, *Learn and Grow in P.E.O.*, designed by the International Chapter Special Committee for Membership Advancement. This provided great opportunity to know our sisters better and to grow as a chapter. The chapter was recognized for its participation at the 2010 Nebraska State Convention in Norfolk.

Various fundraisers have been held to raise money for the projects. Some of the more recent endeavors have been a garage sale, the sale of pancake mix produced locally and provided by one of our members, the sale of invisi-belts, and a $20 drawing for items donated by members.

Our chapter found it difficult to find officers as many members are working and not always available to attend meetings. All members worked together with ideas for a meeting time. The schedule we came up with was to meet at six o'clock for a light lunch and to begin the meeting at six-thirty. This allows young mothers to be home early and has been very successful. Emails seem to work well as a valuable way of sharing news of meetings, and cares and concerns. In addition to the required meetings, we hold three social meetings each year, one with another local chapter, Chapter CO. We have also hosted Reciprocity Group I twice.

At the present time, our active membership consists of fifty-seven remarkable women who come together with the thought of sharing time and talents to support other women, remembering that sisterly love is one of our main objectives.

Chapter IB's active membership is 57; total enrollment is 96

Tomorrow is the mysterious, unknown guest.

-Henry Wadsworth Longellow

Chapter IC South Sioux City
Organized September 6, 1986
by June Brunmeier

Chapter IC of the P.E.O. Sisterhood was organized on September 6, 1986, at the Presbyterian Church in South Sioux City, fulfilling a desire of the ten dimitting members from other South Sioux City Chapters DE and GX for an afternoon chapter. Five new members were initiated that day bringing our initial membership to sixteen.

The organization for the new chapter IC was conducted by Nebraska State Chapter Organizer June Brunmeier. She was assisted by members of Chapter DE and GX. Other officers of Nebraska State Chapter who were present were: Susan Harr, president; Joyce Goff, first vice president; Catherine Hutton, second vice president; Robley Garrigan, corresponding secretary; and Mary Ann Eberspacher, recording secretary.

Guests were present from P.E.O. chapters in Ponca, Wakefield, Oakland and North Bend. Also, some Iowa chapters were represented. Charter members dimitting from DE and GX were Dorothy Stinger, president; Jan Robertson, vice president; Diana Kincaid, recording secretary; Nancy James, corresponding secretary; Goldie Krumwiede, treasurer; Lois Remer, chaplain; and Orpha Rapp, guard. Other dimitting charter members were Marion Shrader, Susan Smith and Robin Bird. The organizer had obtained a signed consent form and letters of recommendation for the following initiates: Lola Thomson, Peggy Pearson, Marcia Stinger, Helen Rohde and Jaye Loge.

Business meetings were initially held in members' homes, but in 1998 we began holding our business meetings in the Masonic Lodge in South Sioux City, and then in 2006 we moved our meetings to the St. Paul Methodist Church Hall, where we continue to hold meetings.

Sharing of members' talents and socialization has always been a continuing theme for our chapter. Our yearly themes have focused on involving members in programs, by wearing of Halloween costumes, or special hats, teaching members to play dominoes, to crochet scarfs and to make jewelry.

Social meetings annually involve our BILs, during which several have been initiated. Another social meeting that our chapter frequently attends is the Sioux City, Iowa, annual Reciprocity meeting. Chapter members have gathered in other non-meeting occasions together touring quilt displays, having tea parties, and in 2013 Chapter GX began hosting a coffee once a month for P.E.O. members from the area to gather.

Our membership has fluctuated during our twenty-seven years. There were five years where we did not initiate a new member. In 1988 and 2003 we had five new members each year, with at least one new member per year in other years. In 2013 we held a membership luncheon at which invited women were told about our organization and our chapter.

Chapter IC has been active in the state chapter. Marion Shrader, a charter member of our chapter, served on the State Centennial Committee and had an original verse used in the program at the centennial observance at Nebraska State Chapter's Centennial Convention in 1990. We have also assisted the state chapter in hosting state convention with one of those having been held in South Sioux City.

When the Convention of International Chapter was held in Omaha, several members assisted with welcoming and registering delegates. Two of our members have attended Convention of International Chapter as delegates. These conventions were held in Denver and in San Diego.

We have served as host for Reciprocity Group VI annual meetings.

Chapter IC has supported all P.E.O. projects each year. A special project is sending birthday cards to the Nebraska P.E.O Home residents. We have had two project recipients—one for the P.E.O. Educational Loan Fund, and the other for the P.E.O. STAR Scholarship.

On Founders' Day in the Centennial year, a joint meeting with Chapters DE and GX was held. This association continued for several years, and in 2012 Chapter DE resumed this joint meeting, with a social meeting of the three South Sioux City chapters. In January 2014, the three chapters renewed the practice of a joint Founders' Day celebration.

This short verse explains IC's motto as they enjoy their relationship with others. *"I Can because I Can to try my best to be a loving sister, friend: My Chapter is IC."*

CHAPTER IC'S ACTIVE MEMBERSHIP IS 19; TOTAL ENROLLMENT IS 64

★

CHAPTER ID WAYNE
ORGANIZED SEPTEMBER 27, 1986
BY JUNE BRUNMEIER

Chapter ID was organized to meet the needs of the working women in Wayne who could not attend the afternoon meetings of Chapter AZ. Members of AZ gave guidance and assisted in the chapter organization. We meet monthly, alternating Monday or Thursday, and complete the meeting requirements with scheduled social events.

At the time of organization, Chapter ID was composed of eleven dimits from other chapters, including nine from AZ, and seven charter initiates. Charter officers were Karen Marra, president; Jane O'Leary, vice president; Kay Cattle, recording secretary; Cindy Ridings, corresponding secretary; Kathryn Ley, treasurer; Jennifer Phelps, chaplain; Kay Marsh, guard. Dimitting members were Karen Christensen Marra, Kathryn Christensen Ley, Laura Lindner, Kathleen Tooker, Lois E. Youngerman, Kay Cattle, Jennifer Carmer Phelps, Paula Pfleuger, Cynthia Gregory Ridings, Kathy Manske and Sue Davis. Charter initiates were Ann Blanche Wells, Judith K. Schafer, Jane O'Leary, Kathleen Conway, Kay Marsh, Nicki Tiedtke and Claudia Koeber. Of the charter members, six are still active members of Chapter ID.

Education is a primary focus of Chapter ID. Six area women have received grants from the P.E.O. Program for Continuing Education and three have received loans from the P.E.O. Educational Loan Fund. We have sponsored three P.E.O. STAR Scholarship applicants, however unsuccessfully. In 1991 we began awarding scholarships to senior girls from Wayne High School, which promotes our organization locally.

Our fundraising efforts to support the projects are varied. Our annual holiday silent auction is a main fundraiser. We have expanded with magazine subscription sales, catered barbeque for golf league, sock-it-to-em (loose change in a sock), "Treasures" garage sale, and the "braggin 'n draggin box" we pass each meeting to share our sisters' accomplishments and concerns. We continue to seek new fundraising ideas to keep our chapter vibrant. Chapter ID is proud that we have increased our project giving five fold since 1986.

September 2011 was our 25th anniversary and we held an open house luncheon, inviting neighboring chapters. Each January, a Founders' Day meeting and program is planned with Chapter AZ. BIL and family socials are planned throughout the year.

Chapter ID is proud to include Lois Youngerman and Marian Clark as 50-year members, and we currently have eleven 20-plus year members. Anna Blanche Wells and Sandra Metz have entered Chapter Eternal.

CHAPTER ID'S ACTIVE MEMBERSHIP IS 47; TOTAL ENROLLMENT IS 124

★

Chapter IE Omaha
Organized February 21, 1987
by June Brunmeier

In February 1987, Chapter IE was organized by June Brunmeier. Charter members were: Sarah Blake, Marcia Steinkruger Wragge, Patricia Scarborough, Ann Girard Noodell, Lori Clark, Martha Haeberle Lawton, Erin Whitlock Schnoor, Michelle Barta TeKolste, Michele Francis Stine, Georgia Walter, Kathleen Willey, Kathy Wischow, Wendy Harris Moore, Kathryn Gardner, Delni McKibben Rasmussen, and Lisa Perrone.

Our first initiate was expecting a baby, and as thrilling as this was, it became a theme for our young, career minded members. During the next twenty years, we collectively gave birth to more than thirty-five children. Despite our best efforts, we were consistently unable to diversify the ages of members, which was almost our undoing. Nationally, group membership had fallen to an all time low.

By 2006, after years of meetings failing to make quorum, we talked with state officers about merging with another chapter. Since we had a small group of mostly charter members who were very dedicated to IE, we were discouraged from rushing to merging as the answer. (Dedicated to where we joked about cleaning the basement in case a tornado drove the P.E.O.s into the storm shelter during a meeting.) A creative option was proposed by the state officers called "Sisters On Loan." The concept involved two well established sisters from another chapter being "loaned" into the struggling chapter. These sisters assumed leadership roles to relieve other members from excessive leadership fatigue. After a year, the sisters on loan could stay in the new chapter or return to their previous chapter. Well, it worked! Through members increasing attendance and proposing women for initiation whose careers were at different phases, we were able to save Chapter IE!

In revitalization, even tragedy can strengthen women's resolve. In our twenty-seven years as a chapter, we have only lost one member to Chapter Eternal. Charter member Erin Schnoor passed very unexpectedly at a young age. Again, we were asked to look inside ourselves and find what our chapter and our sisters mean to us. For us, part of this answer lies in beginning to initiate daughters.

Melissa Brendel was the first daughter to be initiated. Ellie Wragge was the first daughter of a charter member to be initiated. Ellie is a 5th generation P.E.O. To us, our strength and determination are the true story of Chapter IE.

Ours is a story of survival.

CHAPTER IE'S ACTIVE MEMBERSHIP IS 26; TOTAL ENROLLMENT IS 63

★

CHAPTER IF BLAIR
ORGANIZED SEPTEMBER 12, 1987
BY ROBLEY GARRIGAN
DISBANDED JUNE 5, 1999

Chapter IF was formed when Fran Aman, who had served as an officer of EQ for the past twelve years, was granted permission in April 1987 to select a charter list in order to form the third chapter of P.E.O. in Blair. This permission was granted after a survey of each P.E.O. in Blair indicated a need for a second evening chapter. It was hoped that IF, with evening meetings on a different day than HL, would offer another alternative to the working woman who desired a P.E.O. home. After five months of preparation, Chapter IF was ready to organize.

Chapter IF held its organizational ceremony on September 12, 1987. Nebraska State Chapter Organizer Robley Garrigan presided. Members of Chapter HL and EQ assisted with the ceremony. Eight members dimitted from Chapter EQ: Fran Aman, Lorrie Samson, Linda Wardell, Karen Hunt, Gail Jensen, Charlotte Karpisek, Merri Vinton and Jennifer Jensen. Ten initiates were: Virginia Jensen, Mary Weckmuller, JoLynn Wolff, Judy Hardy, Alice Swihel, Virginia Bauer, Mary Beth Hunt, Delores Jensen, Janay Michael and Carolyn Brenneis.

Chapter IF meetings were held the second Tuesday evening of each month with additional meetings in January, February and June. The extra meetings usually involved Saturday brunches or luncheons.

Chapter IF grew with the initiation of ten new members and two dimits. The chapter was touched with sadness in 1989 when Virginia Bauer entered Chapter Eternal and again in 1990 with the death of Virginia Jensen.

Many IF sisters worked outside the home and many had small children. Members did, therefore, choose to raise money for projects by working within the chapter. One of the ongoing fundraisers was a "love basket." Each meeting, the love basket was raffled for fifty cents a chance. The sister who won the basket was responsible for filling and returning it at the next meeting. It was interesting and fun each month to see what would be in the basket. Another method of raising money involved a fine for not wearing the pin. At least once a year, Chapter IF held a major fundraising project. Each year, the Philanthropic Committee was challenged to design a fun project that would raise money. Some of the projects were: a white elephant sale, where each sister brought a wrapped white elephant and it was sold for $10, $12, or $15; a Phantom Halloween Ball when each sister paid for her ticket and enjoyed the "Ball" by staying home with her family; a chain Christmas Card signed by each member with a donation tucked inside.

Chapter IF was proud to have Fran Aman serve as co-chairman of the V.I.P. Courtesy Committee at Convention of International Chapter in Omaha in 1991. Gail Jensen served as a teller at that convention.

Memorial Day 1993 was the first Memorial Day service for all three P.E.O. Chapters in Blair. A brunch was followed by a brief memorial service to remember the sisters in Chapter Eternal. Following the service, those wishing to decorate graves proceeded to the cemetery. IF looked forward to this becoming an annual tradition.

IF was a small chapter, with hard-working, loving members. They felt sure they would continue to grow. They tried hard to keep the meetings short, to-the-point and relaxed. They gave generously to selected projects and in 1993, nominated the daughter of an IF sister for the P.E.O. Scholar Award.

Chapter IF disbanded in June of 1999.

TOTAL ENROLLMENT 37

★

CHAPTER IG IMPERIAL
ORGANIZED APRIL 30, 1988
BY ROBLEY GARRIGAN

Chapter IG of Imperial recently celebrated their 25th Anniversary. The idea originated through the dream of six P.E.O. sisters who wanted a chapter in their own community. Joan Osler wrote to Chapter FU in Grant for permission to select a charter list. Permission was granted on September 21, 1987. It all began on April 30th, 1988, when Nebraska State President W. Joyce Goff bestowed a dispensation to an eager group of ladies. The charter was granted by the 99th Convention of Nebraska State Chapter on June 3rd, 1988, in Kimball.

Prospective members were invited to meet with Nebraska State Chapter President Joyce Goff at the home of Betty Walts for an introduction to P.E.O. First officers were Joan Osler, president; Katherine Hoover, vice president; Sharon Walgren, recording secretary; Dianna Steggs, corresponding secretary; Marilyn Hain, treasurer; Linda Mollendor, chaplain; and Jane Lenners, guard. Other charter members were Patsy Beran, Shari Beran, Mary Jane Cooley, Carrie Creveling, Debbie Fuehrer, Teri Harris, Kathy Kuenning, Mary Luhrs, Margaret Mequire, Johnna Mollendor, Amy Osler, Wanda Shopp, Peg Walgren, and Betty Walts. Garneta Bauerle and Elna Johnson were unable to attend organization, but were initiated in July, making the chapter membership twenty-three the first year.

The chapter has been active in supporting the P.E.O. projects the past twenty-five years. It has sponsored nine ELF recipients, one PCE student and co-sponsored a designated IPS Scholar. During their efforts in fundraising, the sisters enjoyed recognition in The P.E.O. Record for their "Ralphie" project, which was a traveling wooden yard ornament. Other successful fundraisers included homemade candy; bake-less bake sale, Santa letters, white elephant raffles, yard sale and a Christmas silent auction.

Our members are a diverse representation of our community and work in fields such as education, health care, homemaking, agriculture, mass communication, real estate and those who are retired enjoy spending time with family and travel. Membership has been as high as forty-three in 2007 and is now at twenty-three.

The members have had fun entertaining many different themes throughout the years: *Getting to know you; A pattern for Living; Peace; Celebrations; School Days: Readin', Writin', and 'Rithmetic; What's Cookin; Songs from Musicals; The Art of....; Joy; Songs of the Decades; New Beginnings; Following the Star; America the Beautiful;*

Taking Time for Others; With a Song in my Heart; Gathering a Bouquet; P.E.O. Around the World; Celebrate; Life is the Canvas, You are the Artist.

Chapter IG has had the pleasure of hosting Reciprocity Group I in 1997 and 2012.

Although times seem to be hectic, sisters remember each other on their special days, provide a smile or a hug when needed, and provide assistance to those who may be struggling. "Sisterhood is the essence of all the wisdom of the ages, distilled into a single word. You cannot see sisterhood, neither can you hear it nor taste it. But you can feel it a hundred times a day. It is a pat on the back, a smile of encouragement. It's someone to share with, to celebrate your achievements." Anonymous

CHAPTER IG'S ACTIVE MEMBERSHIP IS 23; TOTAL ENROLLMENT IS 87

★

CHAPTER IH ELKHORN
ORGANIZED APRIL 1, 1989
BY MARY ANN EBERSPACHER

On April 1, 1989, Chapter IH, Elkhorn was organized. Charter members of Chapter IH were: Sheri Binder, Linda Bunnell, Joanie Evans, Nancy Hanson, Annette Stanley, Kathy McConnell, Penny Overmann, Sylvia Sample, Gail Stanley, Lisa Tollefsen and Marilyn Yeager. Charter initiates were: Chris Bunnell, Debra Ritter and Ann Winans. These eleven dimits and three initiates, led by Charter Head Penny Overmann, were organized in a special ceremony in which the Nebraska State Chapter officers served as initiatory officers. The chapter was honored to have a past International president in attendance, as well as many other past Nebraska State Chapter presidents as guests.

At this event State President Kathryn Hutton of Norfolk dubbed IH as the "Incredibly Helpful" chapter. Since those words were spoken, over twenty years have passed and Chapter IH continues to live up to that legacy.

First, we have been Incredibly Helpful to the P.E.O. Sisterhood by giving generous contributions to the projects annually. From 1996-2009 member Virginia Barnes hand painted porcelain pin boxes, which were sold in The P.E.O. Record. Her beautiful boxes traveled to forty-six different states plus three Canadian provinces. During this time, Virginia hand painted approximately 2,016 individualized pin boxes that generated an astonishing profit. Through her gifts and talents Chapter IH was able to contribute generously to the P.E.O. projects.

Secondly, over the past twenty years our chapter has been Incredibly Helpful to young women pursuing their educational goals. We have sponsored six women who received PCE grants and three women who received ELF loans.

Thirdly, we continue to be Incredibly Helpful to the community. We have given financial support to local scholarships; have donated clothes and gifts for families in need during the Christmas season, and given monetary gifts to our local library and community theater.

We have also been incredibly helpful to our own sisters. In 1999 the chapter sponsored a dessert/auction to help raise money for the remodel project for one of our past presidents, Sherri Binder. Her home needed to become wheelchair accessible, and through the loving concern of her sisters and the community the project was completed. We also provide meals, cards, and visit our sisters who are in need.

Chapter IH 50-year member Linda Hurt, left, with daughter Allison Hurt. The Hurt family is a five-generation P.E.O. family.

Four generations of P.E.O. - Kay Reed (HR Gibbon), Jessica Nordlund, Sarah Nordlund, Samantha Nordland (all of IH) and Amy Williams (CT North Bend).

Our chapter enjoys being incredibly helpful to the Nebraska P.E.O. Home in Beatrice. In 1996 our loving sister Virginia Barnes painted a beautiful china teapot for the Home. She and several Chapter IH sisters drove to Beatrice and presented the gift, then enjoyed having a tea party with the residents. In 2007 several Chapter IH sisters brought the residents May Baskets and had dessert. A tour of the Home was given and everyone had a fun day!

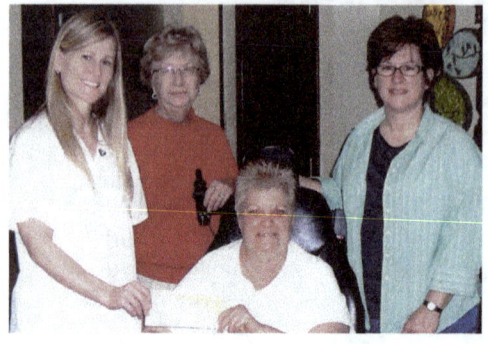

Chapter IH PCE recipient Jennifer Moseley (at left). Jennifer served as a caregiver to IH past president Sherri Binder (seated).

Virgina Barnes holds the hand-painted teapot she made for the P.E.O. Home.

Chapter IH is also incredibly generous. We have a very creative group of sisters who serve on our Ways & Means Committee. Some of our most successful project fundraisers include: silent auctions (in late October which included holiday items for Halloween, Thanksgiving, or Christmas); "Sock it to the Projects"—we collected coins and then filled up our socks. Another successful fundraiser was our "Run for Cottey College Derby Event" where we wore our best bonnets (an award was given to best hat!) and were served a delicious "derby" dinner. Prior to the event we filled up our "feed bags" with monetary donations.

A "gold" party proved to be successful, as well. At this event members brought old jewelry, coins, flatware and cashed them in for money; or had the option to weigh a purse and pay $2 per pound. Social gatherings are some of our favorite activities throughout the year! In 2009 we celebrated our 20th birthday party with a bedazzling BIL bash. We also have enjoyed trips to local restaurants, dinner theaters, and lakeside gatherings with our husbands and prospective new members.

The best part of our chapter is that we truly enjoy getting to know each sister. We try to include a "get acquainted" activity at several meetings so that we can grow in a bond of sisterly fellowship. Some examples: Take one item out of your purse that tells about who you are. Tell one truth and one "fib" and let us figure out which is true or false. Bring a special dress and tell us at what occasion you wore it.

Chapter IH is made up of women ranging in age from twenty to ninety years old. We are a diverse group of women who come together in a bond of sisterly love and who truly enjoy helping others. Our chapter is made up of mothers, artists, teachers, nurses, college students, businesswomen, and retirees who come from all parts of the Elkhorn Valley.

Our membership has grown over the years due to the diligence of our Membership Committee. They do a great job of calling unaffiliated members, attending Reciprocity Group II meetings, hosting guest events, inviting daughters to join, and extending invitations to women of noble character.

"We have a quorum" — One of Chapter IH's most memorable programs - their BILs version of a P.E.O. meeting. "It was hilarious."

P.E.O. Home residents investigate May baskets from Chapter IH in 2009

We are a thriving, fun, energetic and of course Incredibly Helpful chapter. Chapter Eternal includes two members: Nancy Peck Hanson (1996) and Janet Morris (2003).

CHAPTER IH'S ACTIVE MEMBERSHIP IS 37; TOTAL ENROLLMENT IS 90

Chapter II Grand Island
Organized April 28, 1990
by Mary Owens

Like a kaleidoscope that mirrors a variety of beautiful colors, Chapter II's charter list was composed of a varied, yet compatible combination of members. The charter members included Irene Abernethy, Dori Bush, Jeanne Cadwallader, Miriam Dokken, Delores Doran, Debra Glade, Marlene Goa, Sally Husen, Jane Jossi, Chery Lorraine, Cynthia Mohr, Debra Mason Phinney, Charlene Snyder, Pam Swanson, Kay Wall, Marlene Wallace, and Jamie Hardisty Wright. These colorful members came together on April 28, 1990, to organize Chapter II under the lovingly capable support of Nebraska State Organizer Mary Owens.

Chapter II celebrated its 20th anniversary in April 2010. The special event welcomed sisters from out-of-town for fellowship, memories and fun.

Cottey College's recruiting efforts in Nebraska have been enhanced by Chapter II member Dori Bush. Dori served on the Nebraska Cottey Committee for three years and on the Nebraska Cottey Scholarships Committee for an additional three years. (See 'A BIL's Gift of Love' on page 651 for more on the Bush family scholarships.)

Chapter II member Nancy Bishop served as an officer of Reciprocity Group XIII for three years.

Special chapter traditions include salad suppers in May and December, the annual city-wide Founders' Day Brunch, and BIL suppers and picnics. Our BILs have even experienced their own initiation!

Chapter II continues to contribute to each of our projects annually and has sponsored two women for PCE grants and five women for ELF loans. Chapter II also sponsored an IPS Designated Scholar from Japan. The Nebraska Cottey Bus Trip is supported annually by II and members and daughters have traveled along on the weekend adventure.

Chapter II

At each meeting sisters deposit "Pennies for our Projects" in a pink piggy bank. This fundraiser started as a way to enhance our giving to Cottey's Defining Moment Campaign. Chapter II continues sharing their "change" for all of our Sisterhood's projects. Though a small chapter, our 2012 gifts to International and state philanthropies amounted to a remarkably robust figure per active member.

Chapter II members continue to participate in worthwhile community activities, continue to grow with the challenges and responsibilities of being a P.E.O, and, more than anything, continue to appreciate the love and support of their sisters. We hope to continue to find and initiate women who share our lofty and worthy goals.

The camaraderie found in Chapter II is evident. We are a small but mighty chapter, including women from many walks of life who come together for meetings and experience laughter and light-hearted feelings. Our hearts come together whenever we gather and our conversations remind us of our common P.E.O. values.

Since our organization in 1990, three members have entered Chapter Eternal.

Chapter II's active membership is 35; total enrollment is 78

★

Chapter IJ Papillion
Organized April 13, 1991
by Beverley Karrer

Chapter IJ was organized because of a need for an evening chapter in the Papillion/Bellevue area and was sponsored by Chapter BX, Omaha. Nebraska State Chapter President Robley Garrigan pointed out at IJ's organizational meeting that thirteen must be the chapter's lucky number. They were organized on the thirteenth day of the month with thirteen charter members, which surely must mean good fortune for the chapter!

Chapter IJ's charter members by dimit were Marcia Brownlee, Linda Faulkner, Tacy Greiss, Mary Anne Knapple, Connie O'Hanlon, Amy Schmid, Lisa Strohmyer, Debra Volk, Lori Watson and Janet Winter. Charter initiates were Cyndi Brown, Terri Greenwood and Joye McLeod.

Chapter IJ Christmas 2010

As a young chapter, both in its age and the age of its membership, Chapter IJ developed a casual, friendly, generous, and fun-loving personality as it grew. Its membership soon included sisters from not only Papillion and Bellevue, but also LaVista, Ralston, and the Millard area of Omaha. Because of population mobility in the area, Chapter IJ has been lucky to welcome many wonderful members by dimit/transfer, yet sad to have to say goodbye to sisters when they move. Chapter IJ has been active and successful bringing many daughters and friends into the Sisterhood.

Chapter IJ PCE recipient
Erin Kumetat - 2013

Below:
Chapter IJ bingo

Chapter IJ embraced the change to twelve business meetings (second Thursday evening each month) with three social meetings each year. In fact, often Chapter IJ members find more reasons to assemble. Small interest groups which meet monthly include a Saturday morning coffee, book club, game night, and a periodic "Diners & Dives" restaurant group.

Chapter IJ has provided accommodations for traveling P.E.O.s in its Bed and

Breakfast Program, with four members alternating as hostesses.

Chapter IJ has sponsored three ELF recipients and one PCE recipient. Some of its most successful fundraising efforts have included a virtual cruise aboard the "IJ Marguerite" cruise ship, a virtual world tour, selling coupon booklets for Younker's Community Days, and theme basket auctions.

One of Chapter IJ's cherished traditions is the passing of the gavel during "For the Good of the Chapter" at the end of each business meeting. As each member or visitor holds the gavel, she fills her sisters in on what is happening in her life, her family's "brags," or her concerns. This time of sharing has helped to weave strong connections among Chapter IJ members.

CHAPTER IJ'S ACTIVE MEMBERSHIP IS 32; TOTAL ENROLLMENT IS 95

★

CHAPTER IK OMAHA
ORGANIZED MAY 18, 1991
BY BEVERLEY KARRER
MERGED WITH CHAPTER FI ON SEPTEMBER 10, 2006

Nebraska Chapter IK was organized on May 18, 1991, under the careful guidance of Sydney Winstrom, of Chapter FD. This day of organization was most memorable as a host of Nebraska State Chapter officers, both past and present, and numerous P.E.O. sisters witnessed the reception of fourteen members by dimit and seven through initiation who became the new Chapter IK. Charter members were: Kristin Hamborg, Tami Day, Michelle Millard, Cyndi Ferguson, Ann Huxtable Scates, Colleen Wilcox, Jolynn Whealy, Joan Flinspach, Nancy Kopecky, Lori King, Susan Nelson, Mary Swanson, Tammi Miller, Patricia Fellers, Elaine Hill, Barbara Pate, Beverly DeBoer, Cynthia Duell, Susan Hansen, Suzanne Raabe, and Barbara Pfeiffer. These new sisters soon began regular meetings on the second and fourth Tuesdays of the month.

The program theme for the first year, "New Beginnings," was a true inspiration as members of Chapter IK began to forge strong bonds of friendship. Programs regarding the many aspects of P.E.O. broadened members' vision and contributed to personal development during this important first year.

The sisters of Chapter IK reached out to others by selecting the Nebraska P.E.O. Home as a special project. Residents were "adopted" by members who provided special remembrances on holidays and special occasions.

Chapter IK's second year was a time of growth both for members individually and for the chapter as a whole. Eight new members were welcomed to Chapter IK — four by initiation and four by dimit. Programs included in the "Kaleidoscope of P.E.O." ranged from the deeply inspirational to the practical.

Two successful fundraisers enabled Chapter IK to offer support to the P.E.O. Educational Loan Fund, P.E.O. Program for Continuing Education, P.E.O. International Peace Scholarship, the P.E.O. Scholar Award and the Nebraska P.E.O. Home. Members nominated an applicant for the P.E.O. Scholar Award.

Chapter IK steadily increased its average attendance at meetings. Several members shared their unique talents and perspectives by contributing to programs under the theme of "The Patchwork Quilt of P.E.O." Increasingly successful fundraisers added to the stability of the chapter, as well as allowed continued support of important P.E.O. projects. Again, the Nebraska P.E.O. Home remained a special project of Chapter IK.

Although Chapter IK has had a relatively short history, the sisters shared many special memories since that first meeting in the spring of 1991. Chapter IK sisters shared the excitement as wedding days approached, showered congratulations upon the birth of children and comforted and supported each other during times of sadness. In just a few short years, Chapter IK became a strong and loving arm of P.E.O.—providing a special place for each of its members.

Chapter IK merged with Chapter FI to form FI-IK in 2006.

TOTAL ENROLLMENT 70

★

CHAPTER IL LINCOLN
ORGANIZED MAY 2, 1992
BY ROSELLA MEHLING

Chapter IL was organized May 2, 1992, by Rosella Mehling, with Chapter DL acting as the sponsoring chapter and Susan Ballew serving as charter head. Our charter members were: Susan Ballew, Marie Beatty, Janice Brown, Bobbi Clinch, Helen Curtiss, Joann Curtiss, Lorrie Davis, Shirley Deyke, Betty Fox, Linda Hartman, Peggy Kent, Naomi Marrs, Kay Matheson, Molly McGuire, Jane Nelson, Lynn Nelson, Margie O'Meara, Ruth Randall, Linda Stacey, Kim Windhorst, Stephanie Wright and Gail Yeager. The spirit and enthusiasm for P.E.O. that was evident among the twenty-two charter members that day in May is still very much alive in Chapter IL. Since our organization our chapter membership has continued to grow as we have welcomed many new initiates and transfers to our chapter. We are proud that one of our members, Helen Curtiss, was a past Nebraska state president. We were all saddened by her passing early in the spring of 2013. Our Loretta Metcalf has been a P.E.O. for over 65 years and is a Chapter IL "Shining Star." She maintains her active membership but no longer holds an office or serves as a hostess.

Everyone arrives thirty minutes before our regular business meetings to enjoy coffee time and goodies provided by the hostesses. During the months of July and August we have two luncheons for members and guests so that we remain in contact over the summer months and have the opportunity to meet prospective new members. Our social meetings and summer luncheons are special events filled with laughter and visiting. In all of our activities, getting to know each other is a high priority. Our programs showcase the interests of members and also include games and personal histories. We have a newsletter which shares special events in the lives of IL sisters and their families. Our yearbook includes pictures of all members. Even in our business meetings we take time to share news, especially from sisters who are unable to attend meetings.

Chapter IL has always been very supportive of our P.E.O. projects. We are especially proud to have been able to increase the amount of our giving to the projects each year since our organization, as well as meeting any special fundraising requests that have come to us through P.E.O. For several years one of our fundraising efforts for the projects has involved working at a Lincoln Optimist Club concession stand. Many of our BILs have helped us work this event, which lightens the work and brings fun into it as well! Our Brag Bag encourages sisters to share their joys and also helps our treasury to grow. At the annual Christmas Brunch we also mix fundraising with the fun of getting together.

Chapter IL - Halloween 2010

Chapter IL program

We were excited to sponsor the daughter of one of our members when she attended Cottey College. We also sponsored the granddaughter of one of our sisters as a candidate for the P.E.O. STAR Scholarship. It is important to give back to our community and we have made generous donations of classroom supplies and warm winter clothing to the kindergarten class of one member who teaches at a low income school.

Lincoln has an active reciprocity group and two sisters from IL—Betsy Sheets (2001) and Diana Frank (2013)—have served as president of that group. Another member has served as Cottey College Area Chairman. We are active in supporting, attending, and working for the spring Lincoln Reciprocity Roundtable luncheon and have also supported and worked at the three state conventions that have been held in Lincoln since our organization.

As our membership numbers have increased it has become easier for the Nominating Committee to recruit members to hold office. We all have different talents that lend themselves to the different offices. One charter member, Margie O'Meara, is the first recipient of the title of "Incredibly Loyal Sister" for serving in each of the seven offices in Chapter IL. This title of honor is one that we hope will be given to many other members as they hold the offices in our chapter. Everyone who holds an office discovers what a personal growth experience it is and also develops a better understanding and appreciation of P.E.O.

The strength of our chapter comes from the forty-eight women who are its members. They are generous in heart and spirit with each other and the women we bring into our chapter. All of us are grateful for the encouragement and love that surrounds us in Chapter IL.

CHAPTER IL'S ACTIVE MEMBERSHIP IS 51; TOTAL ENROLLMENT IS 91

Chapter IM Omaha
Organized May 14, 1994
by Phyllis Blanke

The first meeting for the prospective new chapter in Omaha was held at the home of Nebraska State Chapter President Beverley Karrer on November 22, 1992. Future members attending were Donna Callender, Kirstin Woodbury, Carol Perkins, Rita Petersen, and Cynthia Sponsler. Mary Ann Knappenberger acted as charter head and her chapter, GF, was the sponsoring chapter. Judy Keating, president of Omaha Reciprocity Association, and Unaffiliate Chairman Linda Sims provided additional help for the new chapter.

The organizational meeting was held at the Omaha First Presbyterian Church. The charter list of twenty-four consisted of eighteen dimits and six initiates. Charter members were: Sherie Agent, Donna Callender, Pam Edwards, Kathy Gray, Gretchen Harvey, Marjorie Hatch, Shirley Jones, Janet Kabourek, Annette Lyman, Sarah McDougal, Kaci Ogg, Carol Perkins, Kathryn Phillips, Kathryn Raasch, Cynthia Sponsler, Judith Sweet, Nancy Wedberg, Kirsten Woodbury, Kelley Baldwin, Marilou Greene, Beth Kowalski, Jill Mountford, Rita Pederson, and Jennifer Walet.

At the writing of the history for *Spirit of the Prairie* the membership for IM was listed as twenty-four active members and a total enrollment of twenty-five. The next three years found the new chapter struggling to maintain an active membership and membership dwindling. The active members were trying many social gatherings, brunches, and calling on unaffiliated members from the Omaha Reciprocity. Membership reached a new low of seven in 1998, when Trish Robertson, organizer of Nebraska State Chapter, convinced four unaffiliated members—strangers to each other—to join forces and try to revitalize the chapter.

It grew from seven to fifteen in that year with a focus on the driving force and essence of P.E.O.: Participation, Enthusiasm, and Optimism.

The women of Chapter IM continue to find new, incredibly talented initiates. The chapter has grown stronger because IM nurtures deep friendships. Although our lives are widely diverse, we offer strong emotional ties for each other on this journey called life—be it weddings, divorces, graduations, births, or family deaths.

Chapter IM adapts to overcome challenges. Amazingly, we have no difficulty in filling our officer positions. We do not require an officer to progress through all offices. However, with a large percentage of the membership less than forty years old and having no prior experience as P.E.O. officers, a plan was devised to maintain at least three or four of the same women in office each year. This enhanced transference of protocol for each of the officer positions.

Chapter IM has had phenomenal success in a time when national membership is a concern. We thoughtfully adapt, in a manner that perpetuates the ideals of P.E.O. and still allows our meetings to interweave with busy schedules. We are focusing continued growth toward the projects and increasing our support. Chapter IM has proudly sponsored scholarship candidates and will continue this effort, hoping that by the next history book we will have a recipient to record.

We are proud of past chapter presidents who have served as Omaha Reciprocity Association officers: Annette Lyman as treasurer and Tammy Davis as recording secretary. Another past president, Melissa Rewinkel Taylor, moved to Washington, D.C., where she served three years on the Executive Board of Washington, D.C., state chapter.

January 2012 closed with thirty-three active members and one nonresident member. We are now a strong chapter, proud to be P.E.O. women on a mission to improve our world via quiet ways of support and compassion.

CHAPTER IM'S ACTIVE MEMBERSHIP IS 28; TOTAL ENROLLMENT IS 78

★

CHAPTER IN PLATTSMOUTH
ORGANIZED MAY 20, 1995
BY ALICE FISHER

Lois Meeske (Chapter F) felt incomplete without her P.E.O. sisters because she was unable to attend daytime meetings. Along with her mother, Mildred Livingston (Chapter F), and the president of Chapter F, Charlotte Mars, Lois investigated the possibility of an evening chapter in Plattsmouth. Nebraska State Chapter Organizer Alice Fisher was notified and Chapter IN was proposed.

Lois' enthusiasm was infectious. Other Chapter F sisters were equally intrigued with the possibility of an evening chapter and a list of prospective initiates was added to the growing charter membership.

Chapter IN, Plattsmouth, with members coming from the communities of Murray, Nehawka and Plattsmouth, began meeting in January 1995. With Alice Fisher's invaluable assistance, a small group of intrepid sisters continued to meet twice a month, intent on the founding of a new P.E.O. chapter. Finally, on May 20, 1995, the organizational meeting of Chapter IN was held at the United Methodist Church in Plattsmouth.

Dimitting members from Chapter F, Plattsmouth, included Maris Gregg, Judy

McKulsky, Lois Meeske, and Nancy Nichols. Courtney Bird (Chapter A, York) and Catherine Hagge (Chapter O, Geneva) were also dimitting members. Initiates were Carol Anderson, Doris Hirz, Rosemary Miller, Linda Rice, Susan Rice, Carla Schneider, Cheryl Schneider, Christina Tritsch, Carol Uhe, and Kari Wehrbein.

At the writing of this informative brief, Chapter IN is eighteen years young, but our members' family histories run five generations deep with P.E.O. tradition. Lois Meeske, who was so instrumental in the organization of our chapter, has since served as committee chairman of the Nebraska State Chapter's Finance and Budget Committee. Chapter IN sisters were chairmen of the guards at both the 2000 and 2014 State Conventions and our "in group" hosted eighty-eight individuals for the 2008 Reciprocity Group VIII Luncheon. Our annual delegates' reports from both International and state Conventions have infused our members with new ideas for programs and fundraising and, in turn, inspired the growth of our chapter.

Chapter IN proudly invests in the future by providing two high school scholarships for deserving young women in our community. Our sponsored P.E.O. Educational Loan Fund recipient was also grateful for our support and assistance during her academic career.

Since its inception, Chapter IN has continued to serve the needs of its Sisterhood with evening meetings. We have fun, insightful programs. We share our various interests and talents. We indulge in fabulous desserts. We stay involved and in-touch with Salad Socials and BIL evenings. Basket Auctions/Raffles, Soup Auctions/Suppers, a Blessings Box, and surveys provide us with income for P.E.O. projects.

During our chapter's journey, some members have retired, while others are just beginning their careers outside the home. We have mourned the passing of three sisters and have rejoiced in the birth of new daughters. Indeed, we are a blessed group of industrious, intelligent women who are forever intertwined by the faith and support of sisterhood.

Total enrollment for this incredible chapter is 51.

CHAPTER IN'S ACTIVE MEMBERSHIP IS 37; TOTAL ENROLLMENT IS 51

★

CHAPTER IO YORK
ORGANIZED MARCH 23, 1996
BY KATHLEEN GOSCH

The seed of Chapter IO was planted one hot July afternoon by Toni Hess and Kristi Scheele having a Coke at the local Dairy Queen. The conversation had gotten around to P.E.O. and the challenge to start a new chapter. That started the ball rolling and in August we met with Nebraska State Chapter Organizer Kathy Gosch and made plans for organizing a third chapter in York. Kathy informed us of the proper procedure and Kristi Scheele volunteered to be charter head. Kristi then asked Chapter HH for permission to select a charter list. From there we had informational meetings at Chances R Restaurant and soon had a group of twelve sisters from Chapter HH and two sisters from Chapter A for our new chapter. The eight required meetings were held and Chapter IO was organized on Saturday March 23, 1996, at the East Avenue United Methodist Church. A luncheon was held afterward at Chances R.

Representing 245 years of P.E.O. membership are the charter members: Kristi

Harris Scheele, Beth Ann Lucas, Judy Davis Hannon, Ann Salzman Romohr, Bonnalyn Henderson, Darcy Ann McBride, Paulette J. Cordes, Elizabeth A. Cosgrove, Dawn M. Nannen, Courtney Bell Nixon, Audrey Gotschall Samuelson, Toni G. Hess, Janet F. Hedrick and Barbara A. Nielsen. Charter initiates were all daughters: Karla Scheele, Denise Cosgrove, Brenda Cosgrove, Jennifer K. Lucas and Gina M. Witwer.

From the beginning we decided that the most important thing was to be together so our meetings are held at the Chances R Restaurant at 9AM on the second Saturday of each month with coffee at 9AM and our meeting at 9:15. The three other meetings are also at Chances R on the 4th Thursday of February, March and September. We have dinner at 5:30PM and our meeting at 6:15PM. A member hosts our Christmas meetings, initiations, and visiting officers.

Giving to the P.E.O. projects is a high priority of Chapter IO. And over the years we have generously supported the International projects as well as the Nebraska P.E.O. Home, The P.E.O. Home Daisy (van) Fund, The Nebraska Cottey Scholarship Fund, and Joyce Goff's Scholarship Fund. Also, we have given to the Cottey Defining Moment campaign as well as the York Roundtable Scholarship. In 2011 we established a scholarship which is given to a local high school senior girl. At our Christmas meeting we collect food for the local food bank.

Our money-making projects include a raffle at each meeting, which we started at the very beginning to generate capital for our new chapter, as well as garage sales, selling cookies and flowers at member Leslie Wood's student Dance Recital, the Blessing Box, Premier Jewelry Parties, and the "Goodie" Basket which was passed from member to member. All were lots of fun and enabled us to give generously to the P.E.O. projects.

Chapter IO is proud to have sponsored nine girls for the ELF loan, one for the PCE grant, one for the P.E.O. Scholar Award and two for the P.E.O. STAR Scholarship.

Our courtesy committee arranges meals for members after surgery, or illness, a death in the family or taking the "Loving Concern basket" to a member to brighten her day. Our basket was even featured in The P.E.O. Record! The Courtesy Committee also sends wedding and baby gifts to our sisters.

We have had several BIL parties which included dinner at the Country Club and cards, cosmic bowling, Super Bowl party, bunco, and an afternoon at the lake. Social meetings have included trips to the Nebraska P.E.O. Home in Beatrice, shopping and lunch and making outdoor Christmas decorations.

In 1999 York hosted the Convention of Nebraska State Chapter with Kristi Scheele serving as convention chairman. Toni Hess and Paulette Cordes were in charge of the music and humor plus all members helped in one way or another. It was great fun and we hear wonderful comments about our York convention to this day. Kristi Scheele represented Chapter IO on the Reciprocity Group VII board, serving as president in 2009. She also was our delegate to Convention of International Chapter in 1999 and 2011. Kristi has served as state chair for Cottey College, Nebraska Cottey Scholarships and PCE.

Members of Chapter IO feel very blessed to be a part of such a special group of women with almost a spiritual connection. Whatever the occasion or whatever the need, we can always count on our sisters to be there for us.

CHAPTER IO'S ACTIVE MEMBERSHIP IS 32; TOTAL ENROLLMENT IS 47

Chapter IP Fairbury
Organized April 13, 1997
by Anita Kitt

The arrangements were made and the invitations sent for the organization of a new chapter in Fairbury, Nebraska, on April 12, 1997, when an early spring blizzard caused us to postpone the event until the next day.

Chapter IP was organized with seven dimitting members from Chapter AO, Fairbury, and six new initiates. The thirteen charter members of Chapter IP were Alana Harness, president; Marjorie Mooberry, vice president; Wynn Nuckolls, recording secretary; Julie Ondrak, corresponding secretary; Deborah McAllister, guard; Alberta Smith, chaplain and Maria Burkley, treasurer. Other charter members were Dorothy Stewart, Kellie Stang, Darla Kirwan, Kristin Jenkins, Janet Krumme and Marilyn Wrigley. Within a few months we had grown from our original thirteen members to sixteen by initiating Sandy Martin, Tracy Salava and Linda Barger.

Every January we observe Founders' Day with our sister chapter, AO. Members of both chapters meet for a lovely dinner and program to celebrate Founders' Day. We alternate years with one chapter serving as host chapter, and the other chapter providing the program. After a fun time together we split into our separate chapters to hold our business meetings.

The 2000 state convention was held in Beatrice and Chapter IP was asked to assist the courtesy committee with transportation. We were particularly proud to have Alana Harness designated ELF State Chairman as Chapter IP had only been in existence for three years.

At our October 2002 meeting Cristy McAllister was initiated into our Sisterhood. Her mother, Deb McAllister, was our chapter president at the time and her grandmother, Shirley McAllister, traveled from Chapter DC in Tekamah to witness the initiation. Cristy's great grandmother, Maude Ellenberger, was one of the original members of Chapter DC. Cristy is the first fourth generation P.E.O. to be initiated into Chapter IP.

In lieu of fundraising projects we pass a "blessing" bag at the conclusion of each business meeting. Each member donates to the bag and shares something that has happened in their lives since the last meeting. The blessing bag provides a great way to stay connected and to raise money for P.E.O. project donations.

In 2005 Chapter IP president Alana Harness journeyed to Vancouver, British Columbia, as a delegate to the Convention of International Chapter. Alana thoroughly enjoyed the Convention and had the chance to relive those exciting days each time she visited neighboring chapters to give her Convention report.

Through the years, Chapter IP has donated annually to the P.E.O. projects. Chapter IP hosted Reciprocity Group VIII in Fairbury in September 2008. Deb McAllister was installed as a Reciprocity officer. Five members presented a fun skit entitled "A Little Bit of Fairbury."

The beautiful Nebraska P.E.O. Home in Beatrice is one of our favorite projects as it is only thirty miles from Fairbury. We have joined residents of the P.E.O. Home for after-dinner dessert. Past State President Nelsine Scofield gave us a brief history of the Home and then we were given a tour of this lovely facility. We take

Christmas gifts to the Home each year, and have adopted a P.E.O. Home resident. We remember her each holiday with a card and honor her with small gifts or flowers for her birthday and Christmas. Chapter IP sister Eunice Stuart currently serves on the Board of Directors for the Nebraska P.E.O. Home.

We have also adopted a Cottey College student. We remembered her with greetings and sent her a care package. Our chapter tries to keep current with happenings involving Cottey College.

Some of our activities to benefit the local community include collecting toys and donating them to the Hope Crisis Center. The toys are to be distributed to the children of mothers who are victims of domestic violence. We have volunteered at the local library to rejuvenate the flower bed and planter boxes in the library courtyard. An on-going project is collecting non-perishable food for the local food pantry.

Chapter IP membership is made up of a wide variety of ages and careers. This makes for some very interesting programs and entertainment. We have a very loving chapter that reflects the true meaning of P.E.O.

CHAPTER IP'S ACTIVE MEMBERSHIP IS 28; TOTAL ENROLLMENT IS 40

★

CHAPTER IQ HEBRON
ORGANIZED APRIL 25, 1998
BY PATRICIA ROBERTSON

Hebron has been blessed with a rich heritage of P.E.O. The early Chapter AE even hosted the Grand Chapter Convention in 1913.

A feeling arose that more women might be included in the Sisterhood if a new chapter was organized. Chapter AE, along with State Organizer Patricia Robertson, gave Betty Crowder permission to select a charter list. Thirteen dimits and five new initiates adopted a theme of "New Beginnings," and organized on April 25, 1998. The meeting took place in the Presbyterian Church, the very site of sessions held during the 1913 convention.

Six state officers presided over charter members: Lorri Bantam, Joann Bruning, Betty Crowder, Diane Currey, Teresa Desmond, Laurie Fischer, Bonnie Head, Sandra Hoins, Carlece Kenner, Kathryn Kirchoff, Mary McKernan, Lynne Mesloh, Mary Lee Miller, A. Kathryn Peithmann, Mary Rozmajzl, Patricia Stewart, Phyllis Traudt, and Deb Vorderstrasse.

A time of 5:30PM on the third Monday of the month was chosen for the meetings. Because of the early meeting hour, the members look forward to a light meal and dessert before departing. Many of the meetings are still held in homes with two ladies serving as co-hostesses. We like to highlight community participation as well as P.E.O. projects for our programs. Each April, a special birthday party is enjoyed with Chapter AE. The chapters take turns for these occasions.

Chapter IQ has been proud to sponsor several women for various programs, along with donating to all projects.

We belong to Reciprocity Group XI, and it was our turn to host the meeting in October 2013. Many new initiates have been enrolled in our "teen-age" chapter, with the hope of P.E.O. becoming the special bond the seven Founders had in the beginning.

Chapter IQ's active membership is 40; TOTAL ENROLLMENT IS 63

CHAPTER IR BELLEVUE
ORGANIZED AUGUST 9, 2003
BY JOAN FINK

Chapter IR was officially organized on August 9, 2003, at the Offutt Air Force Base Officers' Club. Nebraska State Organizer Joan Fink presided at the organization. Mary Linn Sonnemaker of Chapter HC, Bellevue, was the charter head of the chapter.

There were seventeen charter members. Transferring members to Chapter IR were Mary Linn Sonnemaker, Theresa Hartwiger, Sharra Smith, Marilyn Scahill, Shelli Dart, Joyce Kamrath, Martha Zink, Louise Hamilton, Teresa Casart, Dana Nielsen, Judy Schmidt, and Joanna Hike. New initiates to Chapter IR were Allison Scahill, Mary Reding, Glenna McVey, Linda Hayton, and Paula Groff. Four members, Susan Hobbs, Amy Griffin, Vesta Serefko, and Linda Henjum, were a part of the petition and pre-organizational meetings, but were not able to attend the organization. They are considered our "unofficial" charter members. Most of the transferring members came from Chapter HC, Bellevue, and the rest were from other Nebraska chapters. The charter member list was comprised of educators, business women, a realtor, a medical professional, a college student, and a social worker—all of them leading the complex, busy lives of today's women.

The organization was attended by many members of Chapter HC, Bellevue, as well as P.E.O. members from all over Nebraska. Past Nebraska state presidents in attendance were International Chapter 1st Vice President Joyce Goff, Trish Robertson, Susan Harr, and Jeanne Reigle. Anne Phillips, Chapter HC, directed the choral group, HC Harmonizers. A luncheon was held following the organization.

Chapter IR is an evening chapter and thus is able to continue to appeal to those busy women who are multifaceted and are involved with work, community activities, and family obligations. Although several of Chapter IR's charter members have moved on to other chapters through transfer, Chapter IR has also gained new members through transfer. Chapter IR welcomes the enthusiasm and energy of our younger, "new to P.E.O." members as well as the wisdom and experience of our "long-time, seasoned" P.E.O. members.

Chapter IR is proud to have recommended and sponsored two recipients of the P.E.O. Program for Continuing Education and one recipient for the P.E.O. Educational Loan Fund. We have also recommended a young woman who received a Nebraska Cottey Scholarship. We are continually on the lookout for deserving women who will benefit from one of the P.E.O. projects.

The members of Chapter IR have enjoyed social outings where we ate with our BILs along the Missouri River, listened to live music and sipped wine at "Soaring Wings Winery," enjoyed coffee and tea at "Morning, Noon, and Night," let our creativity be seen at Canvas and Cabernet, and walked together in the Race for a Cure.

One of our charter members, Shelli Dart, was the impetus behind compiling a cookbook very soon after our organization. The name of the cookbook is "IR A Cookbook" which is a bit quirky, but lends itself to our chapter motto which is "IR A Chapter." Sometimes we are a bit unconventional, but we are members of P.E.O. and proud of it!

CHAPTER IR'S ACTIVE MEMBERSHIP IS 20; TOTAL ENROLLMENT IS 42

CHAPTER IS HEMINGFORD
ORGANIZED SEPTEMBER 28, 2003
BY JOAN FINK

In the beginning there was one. Amy Petersen, FO, contacted Robyn Prochazka, HS, April E. Casey, AX, and Kristy A. Hanks, FO, encouraging them to charter a chapter in Hemingford. When dedicated P.E.O. sisters put their heads together something wonderful usually happens. And so it was on February 16, 2002, the three along with Caryn Ziettlow, FP, and Susan E. Shaver, AH, met with Nebraska State President Jacci Irwin and four members of Chapter FO, Hay Springs, to discuss the requirements needed to obtain a charter. All agreed to undertake the project at this, our first meeting. Robyn Prochazka, HS, wrote her chapter asking for Consent to select a Charter List and it was granted on March 4, 2002.

Our quest began for "seven wonderful women." The search was long and all were busy fulfilling the requirements necessary to become a chapter. The goal was reached on July 7, 2003. On September 28, 2003, our petition was presented and dispensation was granted to organize Chapter IS. It was a beautiful fall day when state officers and sisters from neighboring chapters came to witness the birth of Chapter IS. President of International Chapter W. Joyce Goff appeared unannounced and offered her congratulations. Charter members were April E. Casey, president; Caryn Ziettlow, vice president; Robyn Prochazka, recording secretary; Kim Haas, corresponding secretary; Kristy Hanks, chaplain; Cindy Lanik, treasurer; Kelly Thompson, guard; Sally Engelhaupt, Deborah E. Mundt, Marilyn L. Hucke, Susan E. Shaver, and Pam Huddle. WHAT A WONDERFUL DAY! We're on our way!!

We began to "Grow in P.E.O." through meetings, Founders' Day programs hosted by our Alliance sister chapters, as well as Reciprocity Group III and state conventions. Our enthusiasm grew as "Little IS" hosted Founders' Day, assembled convention kits for the 2009 State Convention and watched with pride as Deb Mundt served on the Convention Planning Committee and her daughter, Katrina, served as guard.

Our programs are an eclectic mix ranging from inspirational messages to the decoration of a museum charity Christmas tree. Throughout it all we shared laughter and good cheer.

Humor also extended to our fundraising projects when our "P.E.O. Potty" appeared. For a small fee our tastefully decorated toilet was placed around town. For a small fee it was also removed. Our "Potty" raised a generous amount, and, combined with our brag box and monthly "Surprise Bag" raffle, we have made annual contributions to new chapters, the projects, the Nebraska P.E.O Home, our annual Cottey College student, our own college student sisters, the local volunteer fire department and an award to a Hemingford senior girl. Thanks to enthusiastic sisters, we reached out to bring Christmas to a local family in need, and sponsored our first PCE recipient, helping her get a much-needed computer to continue her nursing education.

Since our organization we have initiated eleven, granted four dimits out, welcomed two dimits in, and hold two inactive members close in our hearts. Our 60-year member graciously hosts our "Post Playhouse" meeting each summer, and we were blessed when our youngest member was initiated at her home, making a three-generation family in our chapter. As we look forward to our next ten years, we still aim to "Grow in P.E.O." while each of us continue to express a loving concern for each sister and uphold the traditions of Faith, Love, Purity, Justice and Truth.

CHAPTER IS's ACTIVE MEMBERSHIP IS 20; TOTAL ENROLLMENT IS 27

★

CHAPTER IT BELLEVUE
ORGANIZED APRIL 8, 2006
BY LEANN DRULLINGER

Chapter IT, Bellevue, was organized on April 8, 2006. All the Nebraska state officers were present for the initial meeting. The chapter began with nineteen members, several from Chapter FI, HC and DZ as well as four new members. Chapter IT has grown to twenty-nine with no transfers out and only two inactive members. The organization of Chapter IT was spearheaded by beloved member, Trudy Carlton, who went on to serve as chapter president for two years. Sadly, Trudy has gone to Chapter Eternal and her loss is still mourned.

Chapter IT is made up of a warm, caring group who enjoy socializing. One social that has become an annual event is bunco. The sisters meet for an afternoon of laughter, food and fun, and bringing guests is encouraged. Several other socials were a visit and tour of Lauritzen Gardens (Omaha's beautiful botanical garden), a "sundae on Sunday" at an ice cream parlor, Christmas caroling at local assisted living homes, Veteran's Home and homebound sisters followed by lunch, and eating out on several occasions at local popular restaurants. The chapter sisters look forward to spending time in social settings getting to know each other better.

Over the years, fundraising efforts have included auctioning items donated by members, tissue box cover sales, sale of Chapter IT cookbooks, tie purse sales and a successful craft fair held jointly with Chapter HC. As a result of these efforts, Chapter IT has budgeted and contributed increased amounts to the P.E.O. projects nearly every year and they are proud of these fundraising successes.

In addition to supporting the projects financially, Chapter IT has sponsored two ELF recipients, has sponsored three candidates for the P.E.O. STAR Scholarship, and, proudly, one P.E.O. STAR Scholarship recipient. The process of finding and proposing candidates has been a good learning experience and Chapter IT will continue to look for promising candidates in future years.

As Chapter IT reflects on its relatively short history, they are pleased to have grown in membership. The chapter members are thankful for the support they receive from one another and the time they share at the twelve regular meetings and three annual socials.

CHAPTER IT's ACTIVE MEMBERSHIP IS 30; TOTAL ENROLLMENT IS 34

*No one has ever achieved anything
from the smallest to the greatest
unless the dream was dreamed first.*
-Laura Ingalls Wilder

Chapter IU Waverly
Organized January 28, 2007
by Cindy Biehl

The idea of a chapter in Waverly was sparked when two P.E.O.s who lived on opposite ends of the block met at an auction. The casual question was asked, "What do you think about a chapter in Waverly?" In December 2005, sisters Cathy Evans, Jeanene Cordes, Leigh Ann Ochsner, Jean Danley, Cara Piper, Chris Roffers, and Teresa Greve began the journey to begin a new P.E.O. chapter in Waverly. Calls were made, lists gathered, and with the consent and love from Chapter HW on February 6, 2006, the ball was in motion. From that point on it was a whirlwind of activities and gatherings consisting of a Fiesta, a card making party, BIL dinner with silent auction and meetings, each event bringing more women together to learn about P.E.O. and if the Sisterhood was something they might be interested in. By July the group had enough signatures on the petition to move forward, making the dream a reality.

Chapter IU and Nebraska State Executive Board celebrate the chapter's organization

On January 28, 2007, Chapter IU was granted dispensation with Cathy Evans, president; Jeanene Cordes, vice president; Jean Danley, recording secretary; Leigh Ann Ochsner, corresponding secretary; Teresa Greve, treasurer; Cara Piper, chaplain; Chris Roffers, guard; Christin Sutter, Camie Bremer, Toni Cordes, Becky Schroeder, Bridget Bogle, Christi Etheridge, Lona Benes, Pam Davis, and Allison

Franzen as charter members. The new group consisted of nine dimits from six different chapters, seven new initiates, two of which are a daughter or daughter-in-law of a P.E.O., one mother, daughters, and daughter-in-law group. Chapter IU has seven 2nd generation P.E.O.s and one 3rd generation P.E.O. Three are past chapter presidents and eleven in the group work in education. In June 2007, Chapter IU was given its official charter by Nebraska State Chapter.

Chapter IU has been active in supporting not only the P.E.O. projects every year but also engaging in philanthropic activities within the local community. The sisters accepted the challenge to adopt a shelter for battered women and children for an entire year, bringing much needed items to monthly meetings to then donate to the shelter. They have volunteered for Special Olympics as part of the torch run ceremony in Waverly. An early morning walk on a beautiful fall day and then pancakes and good conversation helped raise funds to support the Back Pack food program for a local school where one of the members works.

Many activities and events have supported and allowed the chapter to support the P.E.O. projects. Chapter IU celebrates its birthday each January with a grand party. These celebrations have included BILs for a potluck dinner, silent auction, and games for entertainment. The sisters have also used the Birthday celebration to host a lady's night out inviting women from around the community to spend a fun evening together. The lady's night out brought a large crowd together and introduced several prospective members to P.E.O. for the first time. Chapter IU has sold coffee cakes, P.E.O. tote bags and Kaywos cloths as fundraisers over the years.

The sisters of IU enjoy spending time together, sharing laughs and conversation during socials such as attending ball games with their families, visiting local wineries, attending drama and music events together, and celebrating special events and milestones together. The chapter adopted the slogan of "I ♥ You" as that is what members first thought of as they became Chapter IU. It is this love and concern for others that has bound the group together as it has celebrated the births of many new children, anniversaries and birthdays and expressed warmth and care for members in need with thoughts, prayers and always food.

CHAPTER IU'S ACTIVE MEMBERSHIP IS 31; TOTAL ENROLLMENT IS 34

★

CHAPTER IV HICKMAN
ORGANIZED APRIL 20, 2008
BY JAN LOFTIN

"P.E.O. Continues to Grow! A new star is born!" These were the words scribed on the announcement for our new chapter, Chapter IV in Hickman. Our journey to becoming a chapter began at the home of charter member Diane Snook. Diane had a vision of creating a chapter in Hickman for several years. So, on January 26, 2007, she invited a number of ladies over to her home to discuss the P.E.O. Sisterhood and the possibility of starting our own chapter in the Hickman community.

The meeting was attended by a group of women in their 20s, 30s, 40s, 50s, 60s and 70s. What was meant to be a brief informational meeting quickly turned, by choice, into an enjoyable evening of visiting and getting to know one another. Time flew by, and before we knew it, we had overstayed our intended time by several hours! Diane knew her dream of having a solid P.E.O. group in

Hickman was a strong possibility. And so our journey to becoming an official chapter began!

Chapter IV charter members

Chapter IV charter initiates
Shelley Jasa, Traci Parde, Becky O'Connor, Evey Lesoing, and Julie Brandt

Charter president Diane Snook (center) with Organizer Jan Loftin (left) and State President Pam Kregg (right).

Chapter GJ in Lincoln was our sponsoring chapter, and member Martha Brown was key in helping support us in our early days. State Organizer Jan Loftin quickly became our friend and cheerleader as our chapter formed. On April 20, 2008, at the Hickman Presbyterian Church in Hickman, Nebraska, Chapter IV was formally organized. We appropriately used ivy to help decorate our special day. Fifteen members began as charter members of Chapter IV—ten dimitting to the chapter and five new initiates!

Chapter IV charter officers

Front row: Margaret Devine, guard; Nancy Brandt, recording secretary; Diane Snook, president; Cheryl Scott, treasurer. Back row: Denise Haag, corresponding secretary; Betty Mason, vice president; Sarah Ideus, chaplain.

Our first officers were Diane Snook, president; Betty Mason, vice president; Nancy Brandt, recording secretary; Denise Haag, corresponding secretary; Cheryl Scott, treasurer; Sarah Ideus, chaplain; and Margaret Devine, guard. Other charter members included Julie Brandt, Janelle Coady, Shelley Jasa, Evey Loesing, Sharon Mills, Becky O'Connor, Traci Parde, and Stacey Troxel.

As our first five years have passed, it is safe to say we have grown together as a chapter and as sisters. We have learned and are still learning how to run an official meeting. We have perfected how to have fun at our socials and continue to think of fun ways to get together with family and friends. We have attended road races, breakfasts, movies and theatrical performances. We've had family picnics and silent auction parties. We've promoted our chapter with a booth at a local community event and have adopted flower beds to care for along the town's walking trail. We continue to support the P.E.O. projects and we've recommended local students for the P.E.O. STAR Scholarship. Being close to Beatrice, we've been to the Nebraska P.E.O. Home for a couple of meetings, too. We are very much enjoying the sisterhood aspect of the chapter, and have laughed with and supported each other countless times in our young chapter's life.

CHAPTER IV'S ACTIVE MEMBERSHIP IS 23; TOTAL ENROLLMENT IS 29

Every great dream begins with a dreamer.
Always remember, you have within you the strength,
the patience, and the passion to reach for the stars
to change the world.   -Harriet Tubman

Chapter IW Lincoln
Organized March 15, 2009
by Joyce Victor

Chapter IW was organized on March 15, 2009, by State Organizer Joyce Victor. With encouragement from former organizer Jan Loftin, charter head Tessa Breneman, had begun to envision Chapter IW as a group geared toward young, career-oriented women. Charter members included nine transfers: Heather Baksys, Andrea Belgum, Tessa Breneman, Jennie Korth, Tricia Mason, Libby Nutzman, Julie Rogers, Kristen Sedlacek and Becky Unterseher. It also included seven new initiates: Sara Farhnbruch, Susan Kirchmann, Timoree Klingler, Kay Krivolavek, Ashley Kumpula, Lori Thomas, and Kendra Virgil. Many of our charter members are second, third and even fourth-generation P.E.O.s, so many family members were able to attend and participate in the chapter's organization ceremony.

The chapter's initial fundraisers were Daisy Bread and P.E.O. window decals. The Daisy Bread was a packaged mix that individuals could buy and mix in their favorite carbonated beverage before baking. The window decal was designed by member Ashley Kumpula. Both were successful, but with many of our members busy with their careers and becoming new moms the chapter opted to discontinue both and focus efforts on a single fundraiser that would be both efficient and successful.

Chapter IW organization meeting March 15, 2009

In 2012 two of our members, Tessa Breneman and Lori Thomas, spearheaded the first fundraiser that would combine efforts from 21 of the 28 Lincoln Reciprocity Roundtable Chapters. The fundraiser was called the P.E.O. Cake Ball Gala. It was held at the Country Club of Lincoln. Cake entries were sponsored by chapters, sampled by attendees and judged based on appearance and taste. Attendees paid $35 per ticket to attend. The event also included a silent auction. Total proceeds exceeding every expectation went to the P.E.O. projects. January 2014 marked the successful recreation of this "all-city" P.E.O. project.

Chapter IW's active enrollment is 35; total enrollment is 44

This beautiful cake was made and decorated by Lori Thomas, charter member of Chapter IW. It graced the celebratory table on IW's organization day, and may very well have been the inspiration for the innovative Cake Ball Gala fundraising event hosted by several Lincoln chapters.

This cake is representative of the inspired offerings to the Cake Ball by local bakers. It says, most appropriately, "Reach for the stars, and even if you fall, you'll land among the clouds."

Chapter IX Kearney
Organized April 25, 2009
by Joyce Victor

Chapter IX was organized April 25, 2009, by State Organizer Joyce Victor at Cash-Wa Distributing in Kearney. Charter members included ten transfers: Elizabeth A. Duncan, Amy Fahnholz, Mary E. Henning, Susan Jasnoch, Kim M. Lowe, Cindy A. VanMeter Pickel, Kim Roberts, Karen S. Sorenson, Lois Wiens, and Renae L. Zimmer and eight new initiates: Julie Bray, Dorothy DeLaet, Michelle Harter, Becky Hilsabeck, Nelta L. Melton, Jayne Meyer, Kathryne Welty, and Debra A. Young. Mary Henning was charter head and also the first president of Chapter IX.

Nebraska State Chapter officers who were present were Leann Drullinger, Cindy Biehl, Jo Victor, Terri Ridgway, Merikay Gengenbach, and Karen Blair. Past state presidents Kathy Gosch and Pam Kregg were also present.

Chapter IX is the sixth P.E.O. chapter in Kearney. When we were told our chapter would be named IX, we knew it was fate—
- IX is the Roman numeral for the number 9
- Kearney is in #9, Buffalo County
- The idea of forming a new chapter in Kearney happened in September of 2008, the 9th month of the year
- 9 new initiates joined when we organized on April 25, 2009
- 10 P.E.O. Transfers brought our membership to 19
- We received our charter at the State P.E.O. Convention in 2009

Chapter IX meets at noon on the second Wednesday of the month. Twice a year we have an evening meeting, usually April and October.

Three of our members have moved to other communities, but with transfers and new initiates, our current membership has grown to twenty-nine.

In the past six years, we have accomplished much. We not only support all of the P.E.O. projects, but have many projects of our own. We "adopted" a family from Elm Creek, providing gifts and food for the holidays and paid for summer programs for the children; we help with Habitat for Humanity every year by providing a lunch and devotions for the workers; every year we send gifts to the Nebraska P.E.O. Home in Beatrice; our chapter has presented names for the P.E.O. STAR Scholarship three years in a row; we nominated a PCE candidate, Joene Crocker, who was awarded a grant; Chapter IX purchased clothing for a young girl in Kearney. Every year we donate money to the local Christmas Goodfellows Drive—many sisters help deliver the boxes. In 2013 we helped a burn victim write her "thank you" notes because her hands were severely burned. Every year IX sisters donate pajamas and socks to the Family Advocacy Network, and we helped make food bags for "Feed the Starving Children."

We are a very active and highly motivated group of women who find great satisfaction in helping others.

Chapter IX has an active social calendar as well. Our BILs are very important to us, so we include them in some fun activities. Every year we go Christmas caroling and have a soup supper afterwards at one of our members' homes. We had a supper at a member's cabin on the Platte River, and had a barbecue supper at another cabin near the river. Touring the Classic Car Museum with our BILs was delightful and we are on tap to tour the New World Theatre in downtown Kearney. We have had ornament exchanges and enjoyed a "Julie, Julia" party at a member's cabin.

Although at this writing we are only in our sixth year, we strive to be the best group of ladies P.E.O. would have as members. Most importantly, we are Chapter IX sisters and friends. P.E.O. has brought us together and we share a wonderful lifelong bond.

Chapter IX's active membership is 29; total enrollment is 33

★

Chapter IY Lincoln
Organized March 16, 2013
by Karen Blair

During the summer of 2012, Judi Adams (Chapter GJ), looked in the mirror and saw herself as a frustrated P.E.O. member and decided that she had three choices: a lateral transfer to a daytime chapter, go inactive or try to start a new daytime chapter. She called GJ president Cheryl Petrig and told her about her dilemma. Cheryl encouraged her to inquire about starting a new daytime chapter. She called Karen Blair, the state organizer, and they set a time for lunch with Cheryl and Jan Loftin, a past state president. They decided to organize what is today Chapter IY.

On September 15, 2012, Judi asked Chapter GJ for permission to form a charter list. They voted to grant Judi that permission on October 1, 2012.

Our charter members include: Judith Adams, Shirley Armold, Gloria Aron, Phyllis Busch, Jane Crouch, Mary Derscheid, Patricia Fritz, Rita Gelsheimer, Caroline Hobbs, Terri Huss, Ranell Johnson, Connie Madson, Nancy Mawson, Carolyn McCall, Vickie McDonald, Diane Mollring, Marylin Nunn, Marge Petersan, Cheryl Petrig, Sharon Richardson, Carolyn Schneider, Marilyn Smith, and Marilyn Watson.

IY has members from six chapters, from Lincoln, Gering, O'Neill, Iowa Falls and Hastings. Two inactive members decided to become active and join IY. We also have initiated three new members. Chapter IY has twenty-seven active members, with one a nonresident member.

Our group is made up of bankers, real estate agents, a medical technologist, a former state legislator, a photographer, a pianist and many former teachers. We have two 50-year members. The newest has been a P.E.O. for two years and we have initiated two new members. Many of our members have been in P.E.O. thirty or forty years. Some of us come with deep roots in the Sisterhood. There are three members who are fourth generation P.E.O.s, one member has three generations and six more members have two generations.

Chapter IY members' interests are varied and include: reading, golfing, knitting, bridge playing, shopping, traveling, cooking, grandchildren, church and lots more! We truly are a fun and diverse group of women.

Although we have only been a chapter since March of 2013, we have enjoyed many interesting programs and fun socials. We look forward to our future as a P.E.O. chapter while upholding the qualities of Faith, Love, Purity, Justice and Truth and expressing a loving concern for each sister.

Chapter IY's active membership is 27; total enrollment is 28

Rely on your own strength of body and soul. Take for your star self-reliance, faith, honesty and industry. Don't take too much advice — keep at the helm and steer your own ship, and remember that the great art of commanding is to take a fair share of the work. Fire above the mark you intend to hit. Energy, invincible determination with the right motive, are the levers that move the world.

–Noah Porter

Section Four
Pioneers and Visionaries
GALLERY OF PAST STATE PRESIDENTS
NEBRASKA STATE CHAPTER
P.E.O. SISTERHOOD
1890-2015

Alice Cary Brooks Briggs
NEBRASKA GRAND CHAPTER PRESIDENT
1890-1891

★ SUPREME GRAND CHAPTER PRESIDENT
1893-1895

Alice Cary Brooks was born near Bloomfield, Iowa, December 29, 1848. She received her education at Iowa Wesleyan College, but left in 1867 to be married to A.J. Briggs, brother of one of the original seven Founders, Hattie Briggs. Alice and A.J. moved to Nebraska where Mrs. Briggs was initiated into P.E.O. at Superior in 1889. A few years later, the family moved to Chicago, where she was active in Chapter A, serving as its president. From there, the Briggs family moved to Elkhart, Indiana. During her last years, she lived in California.

She was the first P.E.O. to hold the office of a state president, having been elected as Nebraska Grand Chapter's first president. At the close of her term of office, Alice was elected to the presidency of Supreme Chapter. She had a large part in establishing P.E.O.s present system of government. She went to the Grand Chapter Convention and asked for the establishing of state chapters. After being refused, she smiled and went again the next year with the same request and smile.

Alice Cary Brooks Briggs was an attractive woman, a talented musician, and one who made friends easily. She always will be special to Nebraska P.E.O.s as the president of P.E.O.'s first state chapter—Nebraska Grand Chapter.

Alice Cary Brooks Briggs organized Chapter H (Originally AR) in Holdrege, Nebraska. She died in Los Angeles on March 14, 1922.

Lulu Ballard Patrick

NEBRASKA GRAND CHAPTER PRESIDENT
1891-1893

Lulu Ballard Patrick was the second president of Nebraska Grand Chapter. She was born in Nevada, Iowa, but her girlhood years were spent in Washington, Iowa. Her family moved to Hastings, Nebraska, when she was a teenager. She was educated at the Washington, Iowa, Academy and the University of Nebraska. In 1884, she moved to Holdrege and assumed the duties of County Clerk of Phelps County.

On April 13, 1887, she was married to J. R. Patrick at Hastings. They lived in Holdrege where Mr. Patrick was an attorney.

Lulu Patrick became a prominent figure in the social and club life in Holdrege. A particular love for her was introducing youngsters to literature. For two years in the 1890s, she headed a charity organization which assisted families affected by a severe drought.

Chapter H, Holdrege, was organized in her home on December 14, 1889, and she served in all of the local chapter offices. She was elected as a delegate to the first Nebraska Grand Chapter Convention held in Omaha on April 2, 1890. There she was elected corresponding secretary. In 1891, she became the second president of Nebraska Grand Chapter and served two terms. In 1896, the Patrick family moved to Seattle and later to Everett, Washington. Lulu Ballard Patrick organized Chapter L, Harvard; and Chapter N, Minden. She died in Everett, Washington, on October 29, 1920.

Jennie Holtzinger Bryant

NEBRASKA GRAND CHAPTER PRESIDENT
1893-1895

Jennie Holtzinger Bryant was born in Mount Pleasant, Iowa, in 1855, the daughter of a Methodist minister. She graduated as valedictorian from Iowa Wesleyan University. She moved to Omaha in 1875, and soon after, married F.B. Bryant, a close relative of William Cullen Bryant, the poet. One of her four sons was given his name.

She was considered thoroughly domestic, retiring and dignified but she gave her time to P.E.O., the Methodist Church and other cultural and civic societies. She was recognized for her executive abilities.

Chapter E, Omaha, was organized in her home on June 1, 1889, and she was initiated as a charter member. On April 2, 1890, the Nebraska Grand Chapter was organized in her home. She was elected state recording secretary and later served as corresponding secretary. She became Nebraska's third state president in 1893. While still serving as Nebraska president, she became the first vice president of Supreme Grand Chapter. She was very involved in preparing for "P.E.O. Day" at the Omaha Exposition in 1898.

Jennie Bryant maintained her P.E.O. membership in Nebraska throughout her lifetime. She died October 18, 1936.

Carrie Flint McNaughton
NEBRASKA GRAND CHAPTER PRESIDENT
1895-1896

Carrie Flint McNaughton was born in Michigan in 1858. Twenty-one years later she moved to Nebraska. Before her move to Nebraska, she had graduated, at age eighteen, from the Michigan Female Seminary at Kalamazoo. She completed her education at Nyack-on-the-Hudson where she cultivated her talent for painting. She was considered cheerful, generous and loyal.

Soon after her marriage, the family moved to Nelson, Nebraska, later to Superior, and then on to Villisca, Iowa. She was the mother of three children, Fred, Florence and Malcolm.

Mrs. McNaughton was initiated as a charter member of Chapter D, Superior, in 1889. She served Nebraska Grand Chapter as recording secretary for one year and was elected to the presidency in 1895, serving as Nebraska Grand Chapter's fourth president. She was considered an efficient officer, accomplishing much for the Sisterhood in Nebraska. About her work for P.E.O. she wrote, "True it is, nothing of real worth can be achieved without courageous working." Although her move to Iowa necessitated the vacancy of her presidency in February, she had planned her convention well. She returned to Nebraska to preside at the convention in Holdrege. Carrie Flint McNaughton organized Chapter P, Bloomington. She died in Oskaloosa, Iowa, on July 22, 1934.

Not to go back is somewhat to advance.
And men must walk, at least, before they dance.
-Alexander Pope

Clara A. Smith Crawford West
NEBRASKA GRAND CHAPTER PRESIDENT
1896-1898

Clara A. Smith was born in Columbus, Ohio, on February 2, 1855. She attended Tilden Seminary in New Hampshire and college at Quincy, Illinois. At the age of fifteen, she taught music at the Seminary in Morgantown, West Virginia. Clara married William B. Crawford of Staunton, Virginia, when she was seventeen. In 1880, they moved from Quincy to Nelson, Nebraska. There she became a pioneer leader in the social, intellectual and church life of the community. In 1891, Chapter J, Nelson, was organized and Clara A. Smith Crawford became its first president.

Some years after Mr. Crawford's death, she married Dr. Benjamin West and moved to Lincoln. There she organized Chapter K, Lincoln, on March 28, 1893, where she served as its first president. She served for two terms as the fifth president of Nebraska Grand Chapter and both of her administrations were marked by growth and increased strength for the Sisterhood in Nebraska.

A talented musician, Clara Smith West served as a choir soloist for twenty-three years. For many years, she spent her summers in Bay View, Michigan, where she established the custom of having P.E.O. Days at the Bay View Assembly. This custom did much to make P.E.O. known and to encourage its spread into new areas.

When Dr. West retired, the family returned to Nelson and Clara was reunited with Chapter J. After Dr. West's death, Clara moved to Omaha to be near her daughter, Mary Crawford Follmer, and her granddaughter, Marcia. There she dimitted to Chapter BX. Clara A. Smith Crawford West organized three chapters in Nebraska, Chapter K, Lincoln; Chapter Q, Wymore; and Chapter R, Crete (disbanded). Clara died in Lincoln on January 26, 1927.

The dream was always running ahead of me.
To catch up, to live for a moment in unison
with it, that was the miracle.

-Anais Nin

Mary Spaulding Munro
NEBRASKA GRAND CHAPTER PRESIDENT
OCTOBER 5, 1898-MARCH 5, 1899

Mary Spaulding was born in Crown Point, New York, a descendant of the Essex County pioneers. Her great-grandfather served with Ethan Allen at Ticonderoga in 1775. *Spaulding's History of Crown Point* was written by her grandfather. Her mother was a direct descendant of Sir Ellice Hicks, knighted at Agincourt by Henvy V. Captain. Simeon Hicks, who served with distinction under General Stark at Bennington, was her other great-grandfather.

At age fourteen, she entered the academy at Port Henry, New York, and graduated with special honors as valedictorian. The following year she moved with her parents to northern Nebraska where she became a public school teacher. During the blizzard of 1888, she kept every child in the building and was recognized as one of the heroines of the famous blizzard.

In January 1889, she was appointed principal of South Omaha High School and held this position until her marriage to Alexander A. Munro in 1891. Mary devoted much of her time to art and public speaking. As a result of completing courses in elocution, oratory and the philosophy of expression, she became popular as a reader.

In 1894, her three-month old baby boy died suddenly. At this time, she became a member of Chapter M, South Omaha. She served the chapter in three offices, including president. A second son was born to the Munros during this time.

In 1898, she was elected by South Omaha to serve on the Board of Lady Managers and the Bureau of Education at the Trans-Mississippi Exposition, one of only two women to serve in that position.

Chapter M hosted the Nebraska Grand Chapter Convention October 4 and 5, 1898. Mary was elected the sixth president of Nebraska Grand Chapter at that convention. A day later, she served as president of the Women's Congress of the Exposition in Omaha. That was a great day for P.E.O. At a reception held at P.E.O. Headquarters in the Nebraska Building, loyal P.E.O.s from distant states, visitors and friends gathered there to learn more about this "Peculiarly Exclusive Order." Representatives from the executive boards of Supreme Grand Chapter, Nebraska Grand Chapter and Founder Alice Bird Babb attended this reception.

Mr. Munro resigned his position as superintendent of South Omaha Schools and moved to New York. Mary and her young son remained in Nebraska for a few months to finish P.E.O. business. On February 1, 1899, Mary Spaulding Munro resigned her presidency of Nebraska Grand Chapter.

Alberta Corbett Fox

NEBRASKA GRAND CHAPTER PRESIDENT
March-June 1899

Alberta Corbett Fox was a charter member of Chapter J, Nelson. She was known formally as Ellen Alberta Corbett but she preferred her middle name. She was educated at the public schools in Nelson and at Hastings College. She taught school in Nelson, where she met and married Henry Fox. They had three children—Henry, Virginia and Mary Elizabeth.

Her daughters, mother and three sisters were all P.E.O. members. A sister, Virginia Corbett, was the first president of the Colorado State Chapter and also served as the chairman of the 1919-1921 revision of the P.E.O. Ritual.

The unexpected duties of president of Nebraska Grand Chapter fell upon Alberta after the resignation of her predecessor, Mary Munro. Alberta Corbett Fox had served Nebraska Grand Chapter as treasurer, first vice president and upon the sudden departure of Mary Munro, was elevated to the position of its seventh president. The plans for the 1899 convention held in Nelson fell upon Alberta. Nebraska records indicate that "the convention was a very pleasant and profitable one with an unusually large amount of business being disposed of." Although Alberta Corbett Fox was reelected, she declined because of duties at home. However, the convention elected her as the first delegate to the Supreme Grand Chapter Convention in Chicago in 1899.

Alberta was particularly interested in the growth of P.E.O. in Nebraska. Although only one chapter—Q, Wymore—was organized in Nebraska during her term on the board, she selected the charter list for Chapter BM, Lincoln, Illinois, where she lived before moving to Kansas City.

Alberta Fox was an active member of the Presbyterian Church. She held P.E.O. dear to her heart her entire life. She died in Kansas City, Kansas, on July 29, 1927. At that time, she was president of Chapter EG, Kansas City, Missouri.

Grace is not an event. It is an experience.
A river that can't be dammed. A sun that
can't go dark. A mountain with no peak.

-unknown

Carrie Russell Hapeman

**NEBRASKA GRAND CHAPTER PRESIDENT
1899-1901**

★ **SUPREME GRAND CHAPTER PRESIDENT
1901-1903**

Carrie Russell was born on October 14, 1860, in Wyoming, New York, the daughter of Baptist minister, Reverend A.A. Russell. Carrie enjoyed exceptional educational and social advantages in her youth. Her girlhood was spent in Polo, Illinois, where she taught in the public schools. She married Dr. Harry Hapeman in October 1883. She lived in Minden where she was a member of the Presbyterian Church.

Carrie was a charter member of Chapter N, Minden. Her life and education suited her perfectly for the work of P.E.O. She served the Sisterhood in many capacities, from local chapter treasurer through the various offices of Nebraska Grand Chapter to the presidency of Supreme Grand Chapter in six years. She was Nebraska Grand Chapter's eighth president. At the Holdrege convention, she was appointed by Clara A. West to design an installation ceremony. It was taken to Supreme Grand Chapter Convention at Newton, Iowa, and later adopted by Supreme Chapter at the Chicago convention of 1899.

A chapter member, Julia M. Klinck, said of Carrie, "She was of a progressive spirit, of broad and liberal views, of just and generous impulses, delighting to give of her time and talents to any public enterprise or philanthropic work which she believed would tend toward improvement of the little city of her adoption. She was a disciple of the Master; constant in church, Sunday School, and mission work, finding the P.E.O. Sisterhood another branch of His service in which she lived to labor."

Carrie Russell Hapeman died on April 24, 1915, in Minden.

*My life has been a tapestry of rich and royal hue,
An everlasting vision of the ever-changing view.
A wondrous woven magic in bits of blue and gold,
A tapestry to feel and see, impossible to hold*

-"Tapestry" by Carole King

Mary Johnson Axtell

NEBRASKA GRAND CHAPTER PRESIDENT
1901-1902

Mary Johnson was born near Cincinnati, Iowa, on April 14, 1868, the daughter of Walter S. and Sarah B. Johnson. Her only sister was Ida Johnson, Chapter K, Lincoln, the originator of the star ceremony. When she was two, her family moved to Centerville, Iowa. She was educated in the public schools there and at Hastings College. At the close of her college days, her family moved to Lincoln.

Mary was initiated into P.E.O. in Centerville, Iowa, and later dimitted to Chapter K, Lincoln, as a charter member. There she served her chapter continuously for thirty-three years. She married Oren Irwood Axtell on January 4, 1899, and assumed the care of his two daughters, Evelyn and Marie.

Mary Johnson Axtell presided at the thirteenth annual convention of Nebraska Grand Chapter. She was Nebraska Grand Chapter's ninth president. Also, Mary served as the recording secretary of Supreme Grand Chapter for two terms.

Mary led the Nebraska delegation to Supreme Grand Chapter in Des Moines in 1901. Carrie Russell Hapeman from Minden was elected Supreme Grand Chapter president at this convention and Mary Axtell extended an invitation from Chapter K for the 1903 Supreme Grand Chapter Convention to be held in Lincoln.

Flora W. Jones said of Mary, "Mrs. Axtell was a woman of unusual refinement, ever modest, yet strong and constant in her faith in God and her loyalty to her friends and the principles of P.E.O. Characteristic of her kindly thought was her recommendation in Nebraska State Convention in 1925 that all chapters place floral offerings on the graves of their departed members on Memorial Day."

Mary Johnson Axtell died in Lincoln on September 21, 1926.

Jennie Allen Burch

NEBRASKA GRAND CHAPTER PRESIDENT
1902-1903

Jennie Allen Burch was best known in the P.E.O. Sisterhood for her contribution in the organization of new chapters. In Nebraska alone, she organized ten chapters. She served as state organizer for two years and as organizer of Supreme Chapter for two years. Winona Evans Reeves, in a 1927 address, announced that Jennie had pioneered chapters in Nebraska, Oklahoma, and Minnesota. Considered a builder and a teacher, she was credited with creating ideals adopted by succeeding generations.

Jennie Allen was born in Maryville, Missouri. Her parents moved to Nebraska when she was only a year old. She began teaching at a young age and served as principal of one of the South Omaha schools for six years. She married Charles A. Burch on March 11, 1897. She became a P.E.O. in Chapter M, Omaha, on June 15, 1898. Attending her first Nebraska Grand Chapter Convention in 1900, she was elected state organizer. Two years later, Jennie was elected as the tenth president of Nebraska Grand Chapter at the convention in Geneva in June 1902, and presided at Wymore in 1903.

Jennie Allen Burch must have traveled continuously during her two years as organizer for she organized ten Nebraska chapters: Chapter U, Butte; Chapter V, University Place (later Lincoln); Chapter W, Blue Hill; Chapter X, McCook; Chapter Y, Red Cloud; Chapter Z, Beatrice; Chapter AA, Edgar; Chapter AB, Central City; Chapter AC, Aurora; and AD, Seward (disbanded).

In later years, the Burch family moved to Minneapolis, to Victoria, British Columbia; and finally to Seattle, Washington. Jennie Allen Burch died in Seattle on February 13, 1918.

Lillian Pollock Parmele

NEBRASKA GRAND CHAPTER PRESIDENT
1903-1904

Lillian Pollock was the daughter of Thomas and Mary Renick Kerr Pollock and was born in Madison, Indiana, on September 28, 1862. Her family moved to Plattsmouth where she grew up. On December 18, 1899, she married Charles Calvin Parmele, a banker. They had a daughter Hallie, and a son, Pollock.

Lillian was initiated into Chapter F, Plattsmouth, on March 1, 1890. She served her chapter three times as president, the Nebraska Grand Chapter as first vice president and as its eleventh president. Lillian also served as Supreme Grand Chapter recording secretary.

Lillian Pollock Parmele was the originator of the idea of the P.E.O. Educational Fund. Editor Winona Evans Reeves, in *The Story of P.E.O.*, speaks of Lillian: "To those P.E.O. members who have known the Educational Fund from its inception, there will always be associated with it the charming personality of the woman who first presented the plan. In carrying forward any project the personal element always enters largely into its success."

Lillian was a gentle woman of grace and fine manner but busy every waking hour. As well as originating the idea of the Educational Fund, she helped the chapters in the Sisterhood understand and realize this goal. With Supreme Grand Chapter President Carrie M. Peterson, she toured state conventions and introduced this new philanthropy. Unfortunately, she did not live to see the Educational Fund grow to the great proportions of later years. She served as the chairman of the first board of trustees of the Educational Fund and had the privilege of granting the first loan to a girl seeking funds for higher education.

Lillian Pollock Parmele organized Chapter AI in Lincoln. She died on March 17, 1915.

Carrie M. Peterson

NEBRASKA GRAND CHAPTER PRESIDENT
1904-1906

★ SUPREME GRAND CHAPTER PRESIDENT
1907-1909

Carrie M. Kendall was born at DeKalb, Illinois, on June 28, 1860, the daughter of Charles and Jane Clark Kendall. Her family moved to Beloit, Wisconsin, where she was educated in the public schools and at Beloit College. She was married to Andrew G. Peterson, September 19, 1882, at Beloit and moved to Aurora, Nebraska, where Mr. Peterson became a banker and merchant. They had two children, Harry A. Peterson and Nell K. Peterson.

An active member of the Christian Church where she served for a number of years on the board of trustees, Carrie was a woman of broad sympathies and great charity. She served as state chairman of the Liberty and Victory Loan drive for World War I and served as a member of the Board of Control of Nebraska, being the first woman in the state and one of very few women in the entire United States to hold so important an administrative office. Carrie was also a member of the Woman's Committee of the State Council for Defense on which she served as treasurer. She served as president of the Nebraska Federation of Women's Clubs in 1913-1915 and as editor of the Nebraska Club Bulletin. She was vice president at large of the General Federation and later served as the Nebraska director.

Carrie M. Peterson served as the twelfth Nebraska Grand Chapter president, the last to serve two terms. She also served as the fifteenth president of Supreme Grand Chapter and presided at the 1909 convention held in Mount Pleasant, Iowa. She was the chairman of the committee which prepared the revised initiation ceremony adopted at the Brookfield Convention in 1907. Her devotion to P.E.O. was evident and the Sisterhood gained much from her service, at both the state and Supreme level.

Carrie M. Kendall Peterson died on November 15, 1921.

Hattie A. Little
NEBRASKA GRAND CHAPTER PRESIDENT
1906-1907

Hattie A. Little was born in Charles City, Iowa, May 8, 1869, the daughter of William Irving and Emeline Updike Little. She was a member of the Congregational Church and served for many years as Sunday School superintendent of the Geneva Congregational Church. She taught for two years in the public schools and worked for nine years as a secretary in a law office. She also served as clerk of the Fillmore County Court and for five years as the assistant postmaster of the Geneva Post Office. The Fillmore County Red Cross, the Geneva School Board and the Geneva Library also were beneficiaries of her dedication and talent.

Hattie became the thirteenth president of Nebraska Grand Chapter after holding the offices of treasurer and recording secretary. At the Supreme Grand Chapter conventions in 1909 and 1911, she was elected recording secretary. Records indicate that she was "a scribe of unusual perfection in accuracy."

The same attention to detail prevailed during her term of office as Nebraska state president. She possessed an ability for quickly perceiving and promptly improving opportunities for progress. When she died, Chapter O, Geneva, said of Hattie, "Her legacy to her sisters is the memory of a life of service to others. Wherever the stars of our Sisterhood are found gleaming, there will be found someone who knew and loved Hattie Little."

Hattie Little died in Geneva, Nebraska, on November 15, 1929.

Maude Chilcote Harrison
NEBRASKA GRAND CHAPTER PRESIDENT
1907-1908

Maude Chilcote was born in Washington, Iowa, the daughter of John H. and Sarah Simmons Chilcote. She was educated in the public schools of Washington and Knoxville, Iowa. When the family moved to York, Nebraska, she attended the Nebraska Methodist College at York. She was a member of Alpha Chapter, Nebraska, Pi Beta Phi, organized in York on June 26, 1884.

Maude married Harry Stephen Harrison of the Harrison Nursery Company of York on

March 16, 1892. Maude presided at the nineteenth Nebraska Grand Chapter convention in Red Cloud as the fourteenth president. At the 1905 state chapter convention, she was elected corresponding secretary; at the 1906 convention, first vice president; and at the 1907 convention, president.

In 1911, the Harrisons moved to California, but Maude's P.E.O. membership remained in Chapter A, York, from March 7, 1902, when she was initiated until September 15, 1939, when she dimitted to Chapter GT, Beverly Hills, California. She was a member of the Christian Science Church of Beverly Hills.

Maude Chilcote Harrison died in California on February 15, 1960.

Flora Wilson Jones

NEBRASKA GRAND CHAPTER PRESIDENT
1908-1909

Flora Wilson was born in Marietta, Ohio, the birthplace of her parents, Charles Louis and Mary Duff Hill Wilson. Her maternal great-grandparents were born in Maryland and her great-grandfather was a friend of General George Washington and a member of his staff. He served throughout the American Revolution. Her paternal grandparents were of Scotch-Irish descent from County Down, Ireland.

The Wilson family moved to Berlin, Wisconsin, at the close of the Civil War; Flora grew up and received her education there. Although she had prepared to become a teacher, her plans were changed when she married Lucius Orville Jones. They established their first home in Beatrice, Nebraska, where Mr. Jones was engaged in the mercantile business. Later they moved to Lincoln. They had four daughters and two sons.

Flora Jones became a member of Chapter K, Lincoln, September 1, 1894. She served Chapter K for three years as president and the Nebraska Grand Chapter as treasurer, first vice president and president. She was Nebraska State Chapter's fifteenth president. Flora served both the state and Supreme chapters many times on committees, often as chairman. She was always interested in higher education for women and an ardent worker for the P.E.O. Educational Fund. She was a member of the Methodist Church and was instrumental in organizing the Women's Wesleyan Educational Council.

Flora Jones died in Lincoln, Nebraska, on November 28, 1942.

*Progress is the sum of small victories
won by individual human beings*

-Bruce Catton

Myra Lynn Grimes
NEBRASKA GRAND CHAPTER PRESIDENT
1909-1910

Myra Eva Lynn was born in Lockport, Illinois, on July 13, 1857. She came to Hastings to live with her sister, Louise Lynn Hoover. Later the Hoover family moved to Blue Hill and Myra took a position as the first teacher in the Blue Hill school. She taught there until her marriage to John F. Grimes. She had a daughter and three sons. Myra was initiated into Chapter W, Blue Hill, on May 17, 1904. She later dimitted to Chapter G, Hastings, on February 9, 1916.

Myra Lynn Grimes became the sixteenth president of the Nebraska Grand Chapter, after having served as organizer and first vice president. During her term on the Executive Board of Nebraska Grand Chapter, Myra organized six P.E.O. Chapters in Nebraska. At the time of her death, she had given thirty-four years of active service to the P.E.O. Sisterhood. After her husband's death in 1913, Mrs. Grimes and her daughter returned to Hastings to live.

Myra Lynn Grimes organized Chapter AS, Kearney; Chapter AT, Tecumseh; Chapter AU, Peru; Chapter AV, Pawnee City; Chapter AW, Gothenburg; and Chapter AX, Crawford. She died on November 20, 1938.

Clara M. Wilson
NEBRASKA GRAND CHAPTER PRESIDENT
1910-1911

Clara Margaret Winegar was born in Lima, New York. Her parents, Daniel and Charlotte Winegar, moved their family to Ann Arbor, Michigan, and Clara received her education there. In 1883, she married Dr. Frank Duane Wilson, first cousin of Woodrow Wilson. After their marriage, they moved to Omaha where she became a member of Chapter E. The Wilsons had three sons: Robert D., Carl C., and Leo R.

Clara was active in YWCA work and in a number of other local charitable institutions. She was an active member of the First Methodist Church of Omaha and served as president of the Ladies Aid Society continuously over a period of thirteen years.

Clara gave of her time and talent to promote the growth and prosperity of the P.E.O. Sisterhood. She served Nebraska Grand Chapter as second vice president, organizer, and as the seventeenth president. At the Supreme Chapter Convention in St. Louis in 1911, she served on the Dispensation Committee. She is given credit for designing and making the first "artistic" Question Box, a huge ball of popcorn, indicative of the most important product of the convention site, Ord.

Clara Margaret Winegar Wilson organized three chapters in Nebraska: Chapter AY, Auburn (disbanded); Chapter AZ, Wayne; and Chapter BA, Sidney. She died on October 7, 1959.

Helen M. Drake

NEBRASKA GRAND CHAPTER PRESIDENT
1911-1912

★**SUPREME CHAPTER PRESIDENT**
1915-1917

Helen Marr Bradley was born in Cuba, New York, the daughter of James S. and Elizabeth Anglim Bradley. Her father was descended from the Van Valkenbergs, early settlers on the Hudson River. In New York, she received an academic and normal school education, supplemented by a course in music and by extensive reading and travel.

On June 11, 1884, she was married to Ellet Grand Drake of Bradford, Pennsylvania. Later the family moved to Beatrice, Nebraska, where Mr. Drake was a successful business man. There she joined Chapter Z. The Drakes had three children: Ellet Bradley, Helen and Elizabeth.

Helen was a member of the Methodist Episcopal Church and was prominent in the Daughters of the American Revolution. She served as state regent of Nebraska and vice president general of the National D.A.R. She was active in local clubs and for six years was a member of the Beatrice school board. She was one of four women appointed from the state of Nebraska as a member of the National Central Committee of the Republican Party.

Helen came to the Nebraska GrandChapter presidency through the offices of treasurer and first vice president. She served as the eighteenth president of Nebraska Grand Chapter. She was president of Supreme Chapter in 1915-1917 and also served as organizer of Supreme Chapter.

Mary Allen Stafford, one of the Founders, was an honored guest at Helen's convention in Omaha in 1917. Unfortunately, Helen was unable to preside at that convention because of a serious illness. However, she followed the work of the convention closely and at the close of every meeting, her executive board met with her to keep her informed and solicit her opinions and guidance.

Helen had great administrative and organizational ability. She devoted much time to increasing the efficiency of all departments of the Sisterhood, especially the P.E.O. Supply Department and The P.E.O. Record.

Helen Marr Bradley Drake died on July 15, 1939, in Detroit, Michigan.

Ida B. Johnson Lewellen
NEBRASKA GRAND CHAPTER PRESIDENT
1912-1913

Ida B. Johnson was born in Centerville, Iowa, the daughter of Walter Samuel and Sarah B. Gibson Johnson. Her father was an attorney and a veteran of the Civil War. Her sister, Mary Johnson Axtell, was president of Nebraska Grand Chapter in 1901-1902. The Johnson family moved to Nebraska shortly after Ida graduated from high school. She attended the Lincoln Normal University, Hastings College, the University of Nebraska, and the National Kindergarten College in Chicago, Illinois. For years she was a kindergarten teacher in the Lincoln public schools. She served as president of the Kindergarten Section of the Nebraska State Teachers' Association. Ida was a member of the Methodist Church. She traveled widely over America and Europe.

After serving as treasurer and first vice president, Ida B. Johnson served as the nineteenth president of the Nebraska Grand Chapter in 1912-1913. She was a charter member of Chapter K, Lincoln. Ida served Nebraska State Chapter many times as a delegate to Supreme Chapter conventions. She served as chairman of the board of trustees of The P.E.O. Record in 1913-1915 and chaired the committee which prepared the 1919 revision of the P.E.O. Constitution. It was Ida who created and introduced the star ceremony adopted in the Convention of Supreme Grand Chapter in Chicago in 1899. She was a member of the committee which issued the first P.E.O. History in 1903.

In December 1921, Ida was married to Parker Lewellen of Thedford, Nebraska. After an illness of several months, she died in Hastings, Nebraska, on April 7, 1923.

Flaming enthusiasm,
backed up by horse sense and persistence,
is the quality that most frequently
makes for success.

-Dale Carnegie

Bertha Clark Hughes

NEBRASKA GRAND CHAPTER PRESIDENT
1913-1914

★ **SUPREME CHAPTER PRESIDENT**
1921-1923

Bertha Estella Clark was born July 3, 1880, in Bethany, Illinois, the daughter of Zedock Hudson and Emma Josephine Scheer Clark. Later, her family moved to Omaha where she completed school. She was graduated from Northwestern University in 1901 with a degree from the School of Speech. She taught English, dramatics and public speaking in Omaha for six years. On February 28, 1903, Bertha was initiated into Chapter M, South Omaha. Three times she served as chapter president.

On June 5, 1907, she married John Rutherford Hughes, a graduate of the Law School in Ann Arbor, Michigan. They had one daughter, Mary Jane Hughes Joy. The Hughes family lived in Omaha their entire lives.

Bertha was a member of many civic and cultural organizations. She was a registered parliamentarian and served as president of the National Association of Parliamentarians from 1945-47. Five times she served as a Nebraska presidential elector and in 1952, she was the first woman to serve as parliamentarian for the National Republican Convention.

Bertha Clark Hughes was known to many of her contemporaries as "Mrs. P.E.O. in Nebraska" and was one of the state's most capable and colorful personalities. Before becoming president of Nebraska Grand Chapter, she had served as organizer and first vice president. Nebraska's twentieth president, Bertha presided at the twenty-fifth convention in Lincoln and she was elected president of Supreme Chapter at the twenty-fifth convention in Kansas City, Missouri. She presided at the Supreme Chapter Convention in Seattle, Washington, in 1923. At that time, the Executive Board of Supreme Chapter presented her with a colorful ostrich feather fan of a rosy hue. From that time on, she became known to her P.E.O. sisters all over the world as "the Lady of the Fan." At every Nebraska or Supreme Chapter Convention banquet, a dramatic moment was reached when Bertha was presented and she would gracefully open and wave her precious fan.

Bertha served her local, state and Supreme chapters well. In 1932, she was appointed by Bernice Tillett to serve on a history committee with Rose M. Owens and Helen M. Drake. In 1935 she was appointed chairman of the committee. Until her death she served as historian and chairman of the committee. She gave long and loving service to gathering and compiling material for P.E.O.'s history.

Bertha served as a member of the committee that drafted the first laws governing the Educational Fund adopted in 1909, at Mount Pleasant, Iowa. This convention marked her first attendance at a Supreme Chapter Convention. She went on to set a record as the only member of the Sisterhood to attend Conventions of Supreme Chapter consecutively from 1909 to 1965. As treasurer of the Educational Fund, Bertha headed the drive for $100,000 which was realized at the Anniversary P.E.O. Jubilee in 1919 in Denver, Colorado.

Bertha claimed she was a link between the past and the present. She had known three of the Founders very well: Mary Allen Stafford, Alice Bird Babb and Franc Roads Elliott.

Bertha Clark Hughes organized six Nebraska P.E.O. chapters: Chapter BB, Ord; BC, Cambridge; BD, Ashland; BE, Pierce; BF, Wilber; and BG, Franklin.

The graceful motion of the rosy fan was stilled when Bertha Clark Hughes died on October 27, 1967. However, the gentle zephyr from the one who waved it so well will forever caress her sisters with the memories of her profound influence on P.E.O.

Rose M. Owens
NEBRASKA GRAND CHAPTER PRESIDENT
1914-1915

Rose M. Owens was born on a farm near Mosherville, Michigan, the only daughter of James F. and Nellie Welsh Owens. She received her education in the Fenton Normal School; upon completing the course, she became secretary of that institution. Thus began her secretarial career. Later, Rose moved with her parents to Bloomington, Nebraska, where she became a charter member of Chapter P, Bloomington, which was organized on November 30, 1895.

The story is told that the organizing group was hard pressed to raise enough money for the charter fee. Without any hesitation, Rose sold her most cherished possession, a beautiful side saddle, and paid the fee. This selfless act was typical of her life-long philosophy. She was completely unselfish and put the interests of others above her own. Rose served Chapter P as president and served the Nebraska Grand Chapter as corresponding secretary for three administrations, in 1910, 1911, and 1912. In 1913, she became first vice president, and in 1914, she became the twenty-first president.

Supreme Chapter will be forever grateful for her skill in helping organize and coordinate the work of the executive office and her ability in setting up the Supply Department. For six years, she served as chairman of the board of trustees of the Supply Department. She was first appointed to that position by Bertha Clark Hughes, who as president of Supreme Chapter, moved the executive offices from Chicago to Omaha. In 1935, Rose was elected treasurer of Supreme Chapter. Because she felt that she could best further the work of the Sisterhood by serving in that office, she remained as treasurer for twelve years, from 1935 to 1947. At that time, ill health forced her to resign.

Rose died at the P.E.O. Home in Beatrice, Nebraska, on November 4, 1955.

Abbie C. Burns

NEBRASKA GRAND CHAPTER PRESIDENT
1915-1916

Abbie C. Burns of Chapter V, University Place, was elected president of the Nebraska Grand Chapter in the convention at Fullerton in 1915. For three years she had performed the duties of recording secretary. Abbie served as the twenty-second president of Nebraska Grand Chapter.

Abbie Burns loved P.E.O. To an unusual degree, she realized the possibilities of the organization. No labors were too arduous; no personal sacrifice too great. Having no sisters of her own, her affection seemed to be directed to her sisters in P.E.O.

Abbie Burns was a teacher. For over twenty years she was the head of the Department of German at Nebraska Wesleyan University. She also served as assistant in the Department of Spanish. Her home was open to all Wesleyan students and her many heart-to-heart talks with them sent each one away happier and stronger.

On July 11, 1920, after a very brief illness, Abbie Burns died.

Lue R. Spencer

NEBRASKA GRAND CHAPTER PRESIDENT
1916-1917

Lue Reynolds was born at Prophetstown, Illinois, May 27, 1871, the daughter of Phineas Bates and Elizabeth Gardner May Reynolds. Her father was a descendant of Colonial and Revolutionary families. She was married to Charles F. Spencer at Holyoke, Colorado, on October 26, 1892. They had three children.

For many years Lue Spencer taught high school. She identified with church, patriotic, civic, philanthropic and social activities. She was interested in genealogy and amassed the Lue Spencer Library, a traveling genealogical library of over a thousand volumes. She served as Register General of the National Society of the Daughters of the American Revolution, 1935-1938. She also served as Genealogical Editor of the D.A.R. Magazine. She appealed to President Roosevelt and obtained favorable action by the government in restoration and preservation of the early Census Records of the United States. After having served as treasurer for two years and as first vice president for one year, Lue R. Spencer became the twenty-third president of Nebraska Grand Chapter. For five years she had served her chapter, AN, Lexington, as president before dimitting to North Platte Chapter AK. To Lue Spencer goes the honor of bringing to the floor of Convention of Supreme Grand Chapter in Brookfield, Missouri, in 1907, the motion to amend the amendment that the "then called" Memorial Fund be loaned for educational purposes. In that same convention, by motion of Mrs. Reeves, the fund became known as the Educational Fund.

Lue R. Spencer died at her home in Washington, D.C., on July 28, 1947.

Sara D. Reuling
NEBRASKA GRAND CHAPTER PRESIDENT
1917-1918

Sara Deemer was born at Atalissa, Iowa, the daughter of John A. and Elizabeth Deemer. She was reared and educated in West Liberty and Muscatine, Iowa. Sara married John A. Reuling on November 16, 1893. After the marriage, they went to Wymore, Nebraska, to live. Although born a Quaker, Mrs. Rueling was an active member of the Episcopal Church and the Order of the Eastern Star, in which she had served as a Grand Chapter officer. Her life was one of service, not only to P.E.O., but also to her community. She was instrumental in establishing the Wymore City Library and served as a member of the Library Board for many years.

Sara D. Reuling was elected the twenty-fourth president of Nebraska Grand Chapter, after serving as recording secretary, organizer and first vice president. She was a charter member of Chapter Q, Wymore, where she was active in its leadership.

Sara Deemer Reuling organized four chapters in Nebraska: Chapter BL, Chadron; Chapter BM, Ainsworth; Chapter BN, Omaha; and Chapter BO, Sidney. Her wise counsel and friendly tactfulness were invaluable in promoting the growth and prosperity of her own P.E.O. chapter, as well as those she organized.

Sara Reuling died on February 25, 1928.

Common sense is instinct. Enough of it is genius.
-George Bernard Shaw

Minnie M. Stuff
NEBRASKA GRAND CHAPTER PRESIDENT
1918-1919

Minnie Moore was born in Rushville, Illinois, the daughter of Thomas Whitfield and Emily Ann Bertholf Moore. She received her education in the public schools of Peoria, Illinois, and at the University of Nebraska. Her father had brought the family to Lincoln in 1885. On September 8, 1890, Minnie Julia Moore was married to Frederick Ames Stuff, for many years a member of the English Department at the University of Nebraska. The couple had four daughters, three of whom lived to adulthood.

Minnie Stuff was initiated into P.E.O. by Chapter V, University Place, in 1901. Later, she dimitted to Chapter K, Lincoln. When Chapter DX was organized in Lincoln with the special purpose of looking after the social and personal interests of the student members of P.E.O. who were in Lincoln, Minnie dimitted to that chapter.

Minnie Stuff was a member of the Methodist Church, the YWCA, the Daughters of the American Revolution, the Daughters of the Founders and Patriots of America, and the League of Women Voters.

After serving as corresponding secretary for three years, Minnie M. Stuff was elected the twenty-fifth president of Nebraska Grand Chapter—the last year before it became known as Nebraska State Chapter. She had also served as first vice president. She attended several conventions of Supreme Chapter and was a member of the committee for the revision of the ritual in 1921.

Minnie Moore Stuff died in Lincoln, Nebraska, on December 16, 1961.

Nora S. Killian
NEBRASKA STATE CHAPTER PRESIDENT
1919-1920

Nora Steen was born in Omaha on June 23, 1872, to John and Louise Hough Steen, both pioneer Nebraskans. Nora was reared in Wahoo and educated at Nebraska Wesleyan and Cornell College in Iowa. In 1894, Nora married Albert C. Killian. They had three daughters and one son.

Nora Killian was a member of the Methodist Church, the Order of the Eastern Star, the Federation of Women's Clubs, and the City Charity

Association of Kearney which she helped organize.

Nora presided at the Nebraska State Chapter Convention in Fairmont in 1920, as the twenty-sixth president. This was the first convention to enjoy singing songs and to present the memorial service then in use. Previously Nora had served as organizer, second and first vice presidents. She had been initiated into Chapter I, Wahoo, in March 1892. Her mother and her daughters also were P.E.O.s, making Nora a part of a three-generation P.E.O. family. Later she dimitted to Chapter AS, Kearney, but returned to her original chapter after the death of her husband. In 1949, she went to live with her daughter in New Brunswick, New Jersey. There she dimitted into Chapter I, New Jersey. She was keenly interested in her local chapter and held all the offices on the local level.

Nora was devoted to the Educational Fund and did what she could to encourage Nebraska to generously support that project. She also took great interest in the establishment of a Nebraska P.E.O. Home. She served as superintendent of the Home for a short time until her failing eyesight took her east to live with her two daughters.

Nora Steen Killian organized eight Nebraska chapters: Chapter BP, Omaha; Chapter BQ, David City; Chapter BR, Lincoln; Chapter BS, Omaha; Chapter BT, Weeping Water; Chapter BU, Atkinson; Chapter BV, Beaver City; and Chapter BW, Orleans.

Nora Steen Killian died in New Brunswick, New Jersey, on January 20, 1959.

Clara E. Waterhouse

NEBRASKA STATE CHAPTER PRESIDENT
1920-1921

Clara E. Waterhouse was born in Weeping Water, Nebraska, on July 5, 1874. She was reared and educated in Lincoln where she married Professor A.H. Waterhouse. They had two daughters and two sons. She was initiated into Chapter K, Lincoln, in 1897. Upon her move to Fremont, she dimitted to Chapter AJ, Fremont.

Clara's life centered around her church, her family and P.E.O. Her home was a meeting place for young people. She was a woman of charm with a smile that was the outward symbol of a happy, radiant life.

Clara E. Waterhouse served as the twenty-seventh president of Nebraska State Chapter in 1920-1921. She contributed much to the development of P.E.O. in the state. As well as serving as president, she served in the offices of corresponding secretary and first vice president. Clara also served Supreme Chapter as a member of the first Memorial Library Committee.

Clara Waterhouse died on August 16, 1935.

Elizabeth C. Robertson
NEBRASKA STATE CHAPTER PRESIDENT
1921-1922

Elizabeth Cleland was born in Beaver Centre, Pennsylvania, on March 6, 1870, the daughter of John and Janet Corbet Cleland, who were both born in Scotland. Elizabeth was educated in the public schools of Pennsylvania and was graduated from Edinboro Normal. She taught school before her marriage to Wallace Robertson on October 10, 1906. Mr. Robertson was president of the Beatrice National Bank. They had one daughter, Jane Elizabeth.

Both Elizabeth and Jane were members of Chapter Z, Beatrice. Elizabeth was initiated on February 18, 1903, in the first year after Chapter Z's organization. Elizabeth was elected treasurer of Nebraska State Chapter and served two terms in that office. Later she became corresponding secretary and first vice president. In 1937, she was appointed chairman of the building committee for the Nebraska P.E.O. Home in Beatrice. Due to illness, she was unable to preside over her convention in Fairbury in 1922, but the program was carried out as she had planned. At that convention, Bertha Clark Hughes served as Supreme Chapter's representative. During her term of office, Elizabeth Robertson signed seven dispensations for new chapters. She served as the twenty-eighth president of Nebraska State Chapter.

Because of the generous gift of Jane Elizabeth Robertson Layman, a magnificent dormitory at Cottey College bears the name of Elizabeth C. Robertson Hall. Jane Layman also was a major benefactress of the P.E.O. Home.

Elizabeth C. Robertson died on January 14, 1949.

Ona Tourtelot Baird
NEBRASKA STATE CHAPTER PRESIDENT
1922-1923

Ona Tourtelot was born in 1872 in Nemaha City, the daughter of David and Elizabeth Skeen Tourtelot. Her paternal ancestors came from France in colonial days. Her mother was descended from William Blevens, one of the "Long Hunters." In 1879 she was graduated from the Lincoln College of Oratory and in 1901 from the Nebraska Wesleyan School of Expression. In 1902, she married William Baird of Lincoln. The

Bairds had a son and a daughter.

Ona Baird was a member of the Methodist Episcopal Church of Plattsmouth where she served for fourteen years as the president of the Ladies Aid Society; she also was active in the Daughters of the American Revolution; the Order of the Eastern Star; and other civic and cultural organizations.

For twenty years, Ona Baird gave much time and effort to the P.E.O. Sisterhood. She was initiated into Chapter F, Plattsmouth, on December 1, 1911. She held office in her local chapter continuously until the time she was elected to the presidency of the state chapter in 1922. During World War I, she devoted much energy to war work. She had unusual literary talent and had articles published in The P.E.O. Record and other magazines.

Ona became the twenty-ninth president of Nebraska State Chapter after serving as recording secretary and first vice president. Because of the illness of Elizabeth Robertson, she presided at the 1922 convention in Fairbury, as well as the 1923 convention in Omaha.

Ona Tourtelot Baird died on December 10, 1945.

Lulu S. Wolford

Nebraska State Chapter President
1923-1924

Lulu S. Wolford claimed to be cosmopolitan, being Scotch-Irish, English and German. She was a native of Muscatine County, Iowa, but lived in Nebraska since early childhood. She received her education at Fremont College, Nebraska Wesleyan, and the University of Nebraska. She specialized in home economics and was a pioneer in vocational education, spending three years in the field in extension work. During that time, she was under the direction of the University of Nebraska and the State Department of Public Instruction and organized girls' domestic science clubs and boys' agricultural clubs. She also conducted and judged cooking and sewing contests. In her later years, she specialized in journalism. Lulu spent five years as county superintendent of schools for Pawnee County and six years as head of the Certification Department in the office of State Superintendent of Public Instruction. She was a member of the First Presbyterian Church of Lincoln and the Order of the Eastern Star.

Lulu Wolford was initiated into Chapter AV, Pawnee City. On March 17, 1916, she dimitted to become a charter member of Chapter BR, Lincoln. On May 10, 1927, she dimitted again to become a charter member of Chapter DL, Lincoln. While there, she helped publish a cookbook to raise funds for Cottey College.

Lulu Wolford served the state for two years as organizer and one year each as second and first vice president. As organizer, she gave special attention to establishing a definite and simple plan for keeping all books, securing uniformity in bylaws, and emphasizing the importance of perfect ritualistic work. She organized eight chapters in Nebraska. Lulu served as the thirtieth president of Nebraska State Chapter and presided at the 1924 convention in St. Paul. In 1935, she was appointed as a member of the committee for revision of the P.E.O. Constitution, by Supreme Chapter President Mabel D. Doud.

Lulu S. Wolford organized Chapter CD, Scottsbluff; Chapter CE, Arapahoe; Chapter CF, Nebraska City; Chapter CG, Curtis; Chapter CH, Columbus; Chapter CI, Chappell; Chapter CJ, Burwell; and Chapter CK, Grand Island.

Lulu left Nebraska to make her home in Colorado where she became a member of Chapter AO, Glenwood Springs. She died in Colorado on April 28, 1962.

Maude Mollyneaux Hendy
NEBRASKA STATE CHAPTER PRESIDENT
1924-1925

Maude Mollyneaux was born in Sutton and graduated from high school there. She attended the University of Nebraska for two years and graduated from Peru State Normal in 1906. For thirteen years she was a teacher in the public schools, seven of them in primary work in North Platte. In 1910, she spent a summer in Europe witnessing the Passion Play, one of the highlights of her life. She was married January 1, 1913, to William J. Hendy, an automobile dealer in North Platte. They had two sons, William and Fredrich and a daughter Katherine.

Maude was a member of the English Lutheran Church where she taught a boys' Bible class; the Women's Club and the Daughters of the American Revolution.

Maude was initiated into Chapter AK, North Platte, in 1911, and dimitted to Chapter EB, North Platte, on May 27, 1931. She served her local chapter as treasurer, corresponding secretary, and two years as president. She was appointed to the state board in 1920 to fill a vacated term as treasurer. She later served the state as corresponding secretary, first and second vice presidents. She was elected Nebraska State Chapter's thirty-first president in 1924.

In 1925, Maude was appointed by Alice Scott to the Educational Fund Board of Trustees and served as chairman in the 1929-1931 biennium. She possessed a spirit of understanding and a sympathetic attitude toward young people. Her perfection in the mechanics of granting loans was widely recognized.

Maude Mollyneaux Henry died March 18, 1978, at the P.E.O. Home in Beatrice, Nebraska.

Nelle Horner Grantham

NEBRASKA STATE CHAPTER PRESIDENT
1925-1926

Nelle Horner was born in Eau Galla, Wisconsin, September 21, 1880. Her family moved to Iowa and later to Nebraska where she received her education at Lexington High School and Kearney State Teacher's College. She taught school for several years and then engaged in real estate, abstracting and the insurance business with her brother of Kansas City. She married Henry Varley Grantham from Brantford, Ontario, Canada, on December 31, 1903. They had three daughters and three sons, including twins.

Nelle was a member of the Methodist Episcopal Church, the Order of the Eastern Star, and served for years on library and school boards. Nelle was initiated into Chapter AN, Lexington, in March 1911 and dimitted to Chapter AS, Kearney, in 1922.

Nelle presided at the Kearney convention in 1926 as Nebraska State Chapter's thirty-second president. In 1921, she had been appointed to fill a vacancy in the office of state recording secretary. She served as organizer for two years and set a record in P.E.O. history by organizing fourteen chapters. She also served in the offices of second vice president, first vice president and president.

Nelle Horner Grantham organized the following Nebraska chapters: Chapter CL, Ogallala; Chapter CM, Crete; Chapter CN, Osceola; Chapter CO, Cozad; Chapter CP, Omaha; Chapter CQ, Neligh; Chapter CR, Omaha; Chapter CS, Lincoln; Chapter CT, North Bend; Chapter CU, Norfolk; Chapter CV, Omaha; Chapter CW, Sargent; Chapter CX, Lyons; and Chapter CY, Falls City.

Nelle Homer Grantham died on July 26, 1957.

Harriette Gorsline Salter

NEBRASKA STATE CHAPTER PRESIDENT
MAY 19-AUGUST 16, 1926

Harriette Gorsline was born September 23, 1870, in Battle Creek, Michigan. She was the daughter of Samuel and Louisa Griswold Gorsline. Her early childhood was spent in Battle Creek and she was educated in the public schools there. She taught school in several central Nebraska towns and also served as principal and superintendent. On New Year's

Day, 1896, she married Dr. Frank Salter of Pierce. She was a member of the Congregational Church, Daughters of the American Revolution, the local school board, and served as County Chairman for Red Cross during World War I. The Salters had two children, Harold and Helen.

Harriette was initiated into Chapter BE, Pierce, and served through the various offices in her local chapter. She served the Nebraska State Chapter two years as treasurer, recording secretary, and first vice president. She organized three chapters in Nebraska. She was elected as Nebraska State Chapter's thirty-third president but served only three months before she died. Harriette Salter organized the following Nebraska chapters: Chapter CZ, Wakefield; Chapter DA, Hastings; and Chapter DB, Auburn.

Harriette Gorsline Salter died on August 16, 1926.

Viola Jennings Cameron
NEBRASKA STATE CHAPTER PRESIDENT
AUGUST 1926-MAY 1927

Viola Jennings, the daughter of Reverend and Mrs. Jesse Jennings, was born in South Bend, Indiana, on July 29, 1875. Her father was a Methodist minister in Nebraska for thirty years. He assembled a genealogy of the Jennings family now on file at Yale and many state university libraries. The ancient arms of the Jennings family commemorate a crusader who headed an expedition to the Holy Land.

Viola Jennings graduated from Norfolk High School in 1894, and attended Nebraska Wesleyan University for three years. In 1912, she received the honorary degree of Master of Letters from Wesleyan. On September 8, 1898, she married Melville DeLeal Cameron, a banker at Schuyler. They later moved to Omaha.

Viola was an active member of the First Methodist Episcopal Church in Omaha. It was said that she majored in church work. In 1928, she was appointed by the General Conference of the church as one of three women members of "The World Peace Commission." She served on that commission for eight years. Viola also served for eight years as the Republican National Committee Woman for Nebraska. She held offices in the YWCA, Omaha City Mission, Community Chest, Council of Social Agencies, Omaha Woman's Club, Nebraska Federation of Women's Club, General Federation of Women's Clubs, Fine Arts Society, Drama League, and League of Women Voters. Her name appears in *The Blue Book of Nebraska Women* by Winona Evans Reeves, in *Distinguished P.E.O.s* by Muriel Brown Chew, in *Who's Who in Omaha*, and in *American Women, Vol. 3, 1939-1940*, by Durward Howes.

Viola assumed the office of president upon the death of Harriette Salter and became Nebraska State Chapter's thirty-fourth president. She was initiated into

Chapter BK, Omaha, and served in various offices in her chapter. She served Nebraska State Chapter as corresponding and recording secretaries, second and first vice presidents, and president.

Viola Jennings Cameron died on December 26, 1951.

Mae Schadel Bond
NEBRASKA STATE CHAPTER PRESIDENT
1927-1928

Mae Schadel was born in Wisconsin, educated in the public schools there and graduated from the Milwaukee State Teachers College. She specialized in public school music and piano, majored in pipe organ and received private instruction in Chicago.

In 1904, Mae married Dr. J.H. Bond, a dentist from Fairbury. She became active in civic affairs, the Woman's Club, and musical circles. She served her Methodist Church twelve years as organist. The Bonds had one son, Jack, Jr.

Mae was initiated into Chapter AO, Fairbury, in 1911. She had filled every office in the local chapter when she was chosen state treasurer at the convention in 1922. She also served as corresponding and recording secretary, organizer and as president. She was Nebraska State Chapter's thirty-fifth president and presided over the convention in Beatrice. Nelle Grantham said of her, "Nebraska never had a more efficient, painstaking, and better loved woman in that high office." Mae was titled "the artist musician" by Nebraska State Chapter.

Mae Schadel Bond organized four chapters in Nebraska: Chapter DJ, Albion; Chapter DK, Lincoln; Chapter DL, Lincoln; and Chapter DM, Lincoln. She died at the P.E.O. Home in Beatrice, Nebraska, on November 13, 1972.

Elizabeth Warren Stephens
NEBRASKA STATE CHAPTER PRESIDENT
1928-1929

Elizabeth Warren was the daughter of Lucius A. and Jennie M. Warren and a native Nebraskan. She married Lamont L. Stephens, an attorney from Loup City. They had two children, Ruth and Norman. Elizabeth was a member of the Daughters of the American Revolution, the Order of the Eastern Star, and a trustee of the Presbyterian Church.

Elizabeth was initiated into P.E.O. in Chapter

AQ, Loup City, in 1916. She served in many offices of her local chapter. For Nebraska State Chapter, she served as organizer, second and first vice presidents, and president from May 1928 to June 1929. She was Nebraska State Chapter's thirty-sixth president. Although no great projects were launched during her year as president, she stressed at all times the spirit of the law rather than the letter. She especially urged the memorizing of the Objects and Aims.

She authorized the first loan ever granted from the Nebraska Welfare and Trust Fund on January 21, 1929, just sixty years to the day after the organization of the P.E.O. Sisterhood. Elizabeth presided over the fortieth annual convention of Nebraska State Chapter at Peru.

Elizabeth Warren Stephens organized four chapters in Nebraska: Chapter DF, Stanton; Chapter DG, Ponca; Chapter DH, Omaha; and Chapter DI, Humboldt.

Elizabeth Stephens died March 8, 1953.

Lulah T. Andrews
NEBRASKA STATE CHAPTER PRESIDENT
1929-1930

Lulah Trott was born near Shelbyville, Missouri, the daughter of Enoch Marvin and Mary Parker Trott. The family moved to southeastern Kansas where she received her earlier education, and later to Kearney. There she attended high school, normal training, and taught in the public schools. She attended business college in Omaha and became the first woman secretary of the Nebraska Republican State Committee. She resigned that position in 1901 to be married to Dr. James Alfred Andrews.

Mrs. Andrews was a member of the Presbyterian Church, Order of the Eastern Star, Omaha Woman's Club, and the Business and Professional Women's Club (where she served as president).

Lulah was initiated into Chapter H, Holdrege, on May 9, 1905. She was an active, devoted member of P.E.O. for forty-five years, having dimitted from Chapter H, Holdrege, to AS, Kearney, on March 15, 1916; to Chapter K, Lincoln, on November 15, 1919; and to Chapter BN, Omaha, on December 8, 1924. She was president of her chapter when appointed to the position of corresponding secretary of Nebraska State Chapter. She also later served as organizer, and second and first vice presidents. When Lulah was elected Nebraska State Chapter's thirty-seventh president in 1929, she had the distinction of seven years' service as a state officer. She also served Supreme Chapter for nearly seven years as executive secretary and treasurer of the Educational Fund. She had been appointed by Bertha Clark Hughes in 1921. During her original term on the state board, Lulah organized four chapters in Nebraska.

In 1915, Lulah had withdrawn from the Nebraska State Chapter board because of the serious illness of her husband. She later came back to the state board to continue her service to Nebraska State Chapter. After his death in 1917, she became involved with war work and served as the executive secretary of the Woman's Committee of Nebraska State Council of Defense for nearly a year. She was then appointed as the first woman named by the Nebraska Order of the Eastern Star War Relief Fund board to serve the Red Cross overseas. In January 1919, she was with the A.R.C. debarkation service in New York where she was appointed by Governor McKelvie as a member of the Nebraska welcoming committee.

Upon her return to Nebraska, Mrs. Andrews was appointed secretary and publicity director for the Republican State Central Committee. Later she was vice chairman of the Nebraska Republican State Central Committee for the election of President Herbert Hoover. In May 1929, she went to Washington, D.C. to serve as president of the United States Housing Corporation, the first woman to so serve. She also had the unique distinction of signing the first deed ever to have been executed by a woman on behalf of the United States Government. It was also at that time that Lulah served as president of Nebraska State Chapter.

Lulah T. Andrews organized Chapter BH, Sutton; Chapter BI, Shelton; Chapter BJ, Alma; and Chapter BK, Omaha.

Lulah T. Andrews died on December 14, 1950.

Emma C. Gilbert

NEBRASKA STATE CHAPTER PRESIDENT
1930-1931

Emma C. Gilbert was born in Colorado, July 18, 1879. She received her education in the public schools of Colorado, Nebraska, and Nebraska Wesleyan University. She was married January 8, 1902, to Marvin E. Gilbert, a Methodist minister. They had two sons, John Dawson and Lauren Edwin. When Dr. Gilbert joined Nebraska Wesleyan University, Emma was persuaded to serve as Dean of Women, a position she held for six years.

She was an active church woman, especially interested in missionary work. She was director of young people's work of Topeka Branch of Women's Foreign Missionary Society for three years, student secretary of Topeka Branch for two years.

Mrs. Gilbert was initiated into Chapter K, Lincoln. As the wife of a Methodist minister, she moved around a lot and held membership in several chapters. She belonged to AS, Kearney, where she served in all chapter offices; to DA, Hastings, where she selected the charter list for DA. In 1925, she affiliated with Chapter V, Lincoln.

Emma served Nebraska State Chapter as corresponding secretary, two years as recording secretary, as second and first vice presidents and as the thirty-eighth president.

After Dr. Gilbert's retirement, the family moved to California where Mrs. Gilbert became active in P.E.O. circles there. In 1945, she served for one year as president of EY, California. She also assisted in the organization of Chapter MX, South Gate, California. At the time of her death, she was a member of Chapter EY, Laguna Beach, California. In 1950, she was chosen to be Ralph Edward's honored guest on *This is Your Life*. Because of her deep interest in Cottey College, the college received three hundred plates, cups, saucers, glasses, and twenty-five hot plates for their dormitory suites.

Emma Gilbert died on October 20, 1968.

Bernice K. Tillett
NEBRASKA STATE CHAPTER PRESIDENT
1931-1932

Bernice Kridelbaugh was born near Corning, Iowa, the daughter of John and Lida Kridelbaugh. In her early childhood, the family moved to Holdrege where she attended school. She also attended the Black Hills College where she specialized in music. As a youngster in Holdrege, she was a student of Lulu B. Patrick, Nebraska Grand Chapter's second president. She received excellent instruction in P.E.O. ideals as well as parliamentary procedure. The family later moved to Alliance.

In 1914, she married Samuel Grant Tillett who was with the Burlington Railroad. They made their home at the Drake Hotel in Alliance. Bernice taught music and for twenty-five years, served as church organist. She was a member of the Episcopal Church there. She was initiated into P.E.O. in Chapter AH in 1903. At the 1953 state chapter convention in Scottsbluff, she was honored for her fifty years of service to P.E.O. Her mother, Lida Kridelbaugh, also had been honored for fifty years of service to Chapter H, Holdrege.

Bernice held every office in Chapter AH. She served the state as organizer, second and first presidents, and as the thirty-ninth president of Nebraska State Chapter. She organized eight chapters during her term of service. She also represented Nebraska in many sessions of Supreme Chapter. In the course of years, she talked to over a hundred chapters on the early history of P.E.O. In 1932, she appointed the first History Committee. She served that committee until 1943, when she was appointed Custodian of Articles of Historical Value, a post she held until her death.

Bernice Kridelbaugh Tillett organized Chapter DN, Lincoln; Chapter DO, Newman Grove; Chapter DP, Bridgeport; Chapter DQ, Friend; Chapter DR, Omaha; Chapter DS, Superior; Chapter DT, Kimball; and Chapter DU, Omaha.

Bernice Tillett died on February 4, 1972.

Dora Belle Wenner
NEBRASKA STATE CHAPTER PRESIDENT
1932-1933

Dora Belle Richardson was born near Novelty, Knox County, Missouri, on March 11, 1870, the daughter of Ole and Martha Nelson Richardson. She received her education in the public schools and Oaklawn College. After the death of her parents, she went to Minden, Nebraska, to teach school. There she married Richard H. Gilson, a business man in Minden. A daughter, Inez, and a son, Charles, were born to them. After her husband's death, she moved to Lexington. On December 29, 1915, she married George H. Wenner. They resided in Minden until 1918, when they moved to Kearney. Mr. Wenner died February 20, 1920. Dora was a member of the Methodist Church and a past matron of the Order of the Eastern Star.

Dora was initiated into Chapter N, Minden, but after moving to Kearney, she dimitted to Chapter AS, where she served as corresponding secretary, vice president, and president. She served as Nebraska State Chapter corresponding secretary for two years, as recording secretary for two years, and as first and second vice presidents. In 1932, she was elected as the fortieth president of Nebraska State Chapter and presided in Lincoln in 1933. At that convention, first steps were taken to secure the Nebraska P.E.O. Home.

Dora Belle Gilson Wenner died on August 12, 1938.

Josephine Gifford Waddell
NEBRASKA STATE CHAPTER PRESIDENT
1933-1934

Josephine Gifford was the daughter of William M. and Elizabeth Harlan Gifford, the seventh in a family of nine children. She was born, reared, and educated in Nebraska. Her early childhood was spent on a farm near Lewiston. Later, the family moved to Lincoln where she married James Clyde Waddell, who was then superintendent of schools in Pawnee County. They lived for several years in Pawnee City, then Lincoln and Omaha where Mr. Waddell completed his medical studies. Later, they moved back to Pawnee City, where they lived until 1920, when they moved to Beatrice.

Josephine was affiliated with the Presbyterian Church and actively engaged in the work of women's organizations. She was president of the Service Society for several years. She kept in close touch with the P.E.O. Home. She often expressed her gratitude to Helen M. Drake, past president of Supreme Chapter, for her help and inspiration for the ideals of P.E.O.

Josephine Gifford Waddell served Nebraska State Chapter as corresponding secretary, two years as organizer, second and first vice presidents, and president. She served as the forty-first president of Nebraska State Chapter. She organized eight chapters in Nebraska.

Josephine was initiated into Chapter AV, Pawnee City, in 1916, and dimitted to Chapter Z, Beatrice, in 1921. She served both chapters in various offices and was president of Chapter Z when Beatrice entertained state convention in May 1928.

Josephine Waddell organized Chapter DV, St. Edward; Chapter DW, Rushville; Chapter DX, Lincoln; Chapter DY, Omaha; Chapter DZ, Omaha; Chapter EA, Randolph; Chapter EB, North Platte; and Chapter EC, Omaha.

Josephine Waddell died November 6, 1962.

Ruth Courtright Kennedy
NEBRASKA STATE CHAPTER PRESIDENT
1934-1935

A native Nebraskan, Ruth Courtright was reared on a farm in Furnas County and was the daughter of Clarence and Emma Courtright. She was educated in Beaver City and graduated from Peru College. She taught several years in Nebraska and Montana. During World War I, she volunteered and served in a Red Cross Canteen in Nantes, France. She married Cassius Kennedy on July 28, 1920. They resided on a farm near Brownville for fifty-one years. The Kennedys had three children: Bond, Betty, and Clay.

Ruth served on her church board, as superintendent of Sunday School, as president of the Women's Society WSCS, and was a Gold Star Mother. In 1952, she was selected by the Peru Community as Woman of the Year, by the state of Nebraska as a Good Neighbor, by Governor McKelvie as an Admiral in the Nebraska Navy, and in 1969, as the Nebraska Mother of the Year.

Ruth came from a family of four sisters and one sister-in-law who were P.E.O.s. Ruth became a P.E.O. in Chapter AU, Peru, in 1922, and served as president when the chapter entertained convention in 1929.

At that time, she was elected state treasurer. She served for six years on the board and later accepted an appointment as corresponding secretary under Rebecca Lee. She later served as Nebraska State Chapter's forty-second president and presided at the 1935 state convention. In 1972, Ruth received her fifty-year P.E.O. pin. At the writing of *The Saga of Nebraska P.E.O.*, Ruth had attended forty-one state and seven Supreme Conventions.

Ruth Courtright Kennedy died on April 28, 1976.

Anna Loutzenheiser

NEBRASKA STATE CHAPTER PRESIDENT
1935-1936

Anna Wickland was born at Ogallala on February 25, 1889, the daughter of Swan and Carolyn Lindquist Wicklund. She was reared and educated in Nebraska. After entering civil service and working for the postal department for five years, she married Edwin J. Loutzenheiser, a Gothenberg banker, in 1910. They had five children—Bernice, Edwin, Carolyn, Thomas, and Marian.

Anna gave many years of service to the Methodist Church. She was on the Conference Board of the Woman's Society of Christian Service for six years and served as president for two. She was a delegate to the General Conference of the Methodist Church at Boston in 1948 and to the Ecumenical Conference at Springfield, Massachusetts. She was honored in 1948 by being selected Nebraska Mother of the Year.

Anna Loutzenheiser was initiated into Chapter AW, Gothenburg, in 1916. She served as president of her chapter for three years. She was elected to the Executive Board of Nebraska State Chapter in 1931 and served as recording secretary, organizer, second and first vice presidents, and president. She was Nebraska State Chapter's forty-third president.

From 1937, she served for many years on the Board of Trustees of the Nebraska P.E.O. Home and served as their secretary-treasurer for eleven years.

Anna died on January 20, 1973.

Isabelle B. Nelson

NEBRASKA STATE CHAPTER PRESIDENT
1936-1937

Isabelle McElhinney was born in Somonauk, Illinois, the daughter of T.J. and Jeanette McElhinney. She received her education in the Minden schools and Monmouth College, Monmouth, Illinois. In 1906, Isabelle was married in Washington, Iowa, to William M. Nelson. They had three children: Jeanette, Willabelle, and William M., Jr.

Isabelle was a member of the Presbyterian Church and active in the Bible School and the Home Missionary Society. She served as a member of the board of the Nebraska P.E.O. Home from 1937-1949. For many years, she was a House Mother at Hastings College.

Isabelle was initiated into Chapter H, Holdrege, in 1906, dimitted to Chapter G, Hastings, in 1918, and became a charter member of Chapter DA, Hastings, on February 21, 1924. She was elected state recording secretary at the Hastings convention in 1932, and served as the organizer, second and first vice presidents, and president. She was the forty-fourth president of Nebraska State Chapter. Isabelle presided at the 1937 convention which met in Omaha. That convention was a remarkable one because it was then that the Nebraska P.E.O. Home was established. Isabelle B. Nelson organized one chapter in Nebraska, Chapter ED, Omaha.

Isabelle Nelson died September 23, 1957.

Ada Hardy Mead

**NEBRASKA STATE CHAPTER PRESIDENT
1937-1938**

In 1915, Ada Hardy married Charles Wilbur Mead, a banker. The Meads had one son, Wilbur Marlow Mead.

Ada Hardy Mead was initiated into Chapter BN, Omaha, in 1919. She served as an officer in that chapter until she was elected to the Executive Board of Nebraska State Chapter in 1931. In 1937, she was elected the forty-fifth president of Nebraska State Chapter. In 1933, Nebraska State Chapter President Dora Wenner appointed Ada chairman of a committee to study the possibility of establishing a P.E.O. Home. The efforts of this committee made it possible for the state chapter to accept the generous gift of Mr. and Mrs. J. Stewart Elliott of their home in Beatrice. The Nebraska P.E.O. Home was dedicated on May 15, 1938. Ada served on the Home board from its beginning.

Ada served Supreme Chapter as head page, head guard, secretary of the Centennial Committee, and chairman of the Building and Furnishing Committee for the P.E.O. Centennial Center in Des Moines. She gave many keynote addresses for Supreme and state chapter conventions, devotional addresses and inspirational messages in Nebraska, Missouri, and Iowa, and in many local Nebraska P.E.O. chapters.

Ada was a member of the First United Methodist Church in Omaha. She served on the local level in women's work, youth work, church school, as an Administrative Board member, delegate to annual conference, and as chairman of the Administrative Board, being the first woman to hold that position.

On the state level of the Methodist Church, Ada served in many capacities: the first president of Nebraska Women's Society of Christian service, chairman of the Conference Board of Missions, and elected delegate to Jurisdictional and General Conferences. On the jurisdictional level, she served as chairman of the Board of Missions and spoke at many conference and jurisdictional meetings.

Ada served the national level of the Methodist Church as a member of the executive committee of the General Board of Missions and four of its divisions for sixteen years; chairman of the Wesleyan Service Guild for eight years, and member of the executive committee of the Board of Evangelism for eight years. She also served as president of the Board of Trustees of National College in Kansas City, Missouri; as a member of the Board of Trustees and Executive Committee of Saint Paul School of Theology; and as a member of the Executive Committee of the Board of Evangelism.

On the world level, Ada was a member of the Executive Committee of the World Methodist Council for five years. Ada's work within the Methodist Church earned her the nickname "Mrs. Methodist."

In Omaha, Ada served as president of the Omaha YWCA and the Omaha City Mission. She was a member of the boards of the Child Saving Institute; Fontenelle Boulevard Home, the Urban League, Community Chest (U.C.S.), and United Church Women.

Ada served on the board of Nebraska Wesleyan University and the National Council of Churches. Many well-deserved honors were bestowed upon Ada. She was the recipient of an honorary Doctor of Humane Letters degree from Nebraska Wesleyan University; was made an honorary member of Nebraska Delta Kappa Gamma and of the Omaha Altrusa Club.

While she was on the Executive Board of Nebraska State Chapter, Ada Mead organized three chapters: Chapter EE, Lincoln; Chapter EF, Omaha; and Chapter EG, Kearney.

Ada Hardy Mead died on May 20, 1983.

Hattie Button Engleman
NEBRASKA STATE CHAPTER PRESIDENT
1938-1939

Hattie Button was born at Doniphan, Nebraska, and was reared and educated in Nebraska. She taught school until her marriage in 1918, when she went to live in Des Moines, Iowa, to be near her husband, Edwin E. Engleman, who was stationed at Camp Fort Dodge. He was a Captain in World War I. Later the Engleman's lived in Sunrise, Wyoming, where he was superintendent of schools. They had two children, Hesper Lynette and Ivan Merle.

Hattie was active in all community affairs. She was a past Worthy Matron of the Order of the Eastern Star, a past regent of the Daughters of the American Revolution, was active in the Methodist Church, and a charter member of the Crawford Woman's Club. She also was active in the Auxiliary of the American Legion.

Hattie was initiated into Chapter AX, Crawford, in 1921, and held all the offices of her local chapter. In 1932, at the convention in Hastings, she was elected as treasurer of the executive board. She served through all of the state offices and became Nebraska State Chapter's forty-sixth president. Hattie organized two chapters in Nebraska: Chapter EH, Grand Island; and Chapter EI, Bayard.

Hattie Button Engleman died on November 21, 1968.

Marie Joseph Williams

NEBRASKA STATE CHAPTER PRESIDENT
1939-1940

Marie Joseph was born in Creston, Iowa, the daughter of Jonathan M. and Belinda Shur Joseph. She was educated in Iowa and Ohio and taught in both states. She resigned her position as principal to become the wife of Dr. B.F. Williams, a psychiatrist of Lincoln, Nebraska.

Marie was a member of the Methodist Church and active in religious, civic and social affairs. She was president of the city YWCA for several years, a member of the University Y.W. Board and of a committee of the National Board. She was a member of the first executive board for the Community Chest, a past president of the Nebraska State Medical Auxiliary, a member of Phi Mu sorority, a patroness of Sigma Alpha Iota and Nebraska Girl's State.

She was chosen from Nebraska to serve on the national advisory committee of women to participate in the New York World's Fair of 1939. She also was a member of A.A.U.W. and the American Legion Auxiliary. While her husband took special psychiatry training, he and Marie lived in Vienna, Austria, and London, England. After Dr. William's retirement, they made their home in Washington state.

In 1912, Marie Joseph Williams was initiated into Chapter K, Lincoln. In 1927, she dimitted to head the new chapter, DM. In 1933, she was elected to serve on the state board and she filled all of the offices. In 1939, Marie was elected as the forty-seventh president of Nebraska State Chapter. She presided at the 1940 convention in Lincoln.

While on the board, Marie organized two chapters in Nebraska: Chapter EJ, Creighton; and Chapter EK, Omaha

Marie Joseph Williams died on September 14, 1964.

The great thing in the world is not so much where we are, but in what direction we are moving.

-Oliver Wendell Holmes

Edna B. Casper

NEBRASKA STATE CHAPTER PRESIDENT
1940-1941

Edna Call was born in Stockham, Nebraska, the daughter of Delmar W. and Nettie McVey Call. A native Nebraskan, Edna was graduated from Aurora High School in 1911 and attended Nebraska Wesleyan University where she majored in music. While at Wesleyan, she was a member of the Willard Society.

In 1916, Edna married Dr. Robert W. Casper, a graduate of the University of Nebraska School of Dental Surgery. The Caspers had one daughter, Dorothy Jean.

Edna was active in club life and in the First Presbyterian Church where she taught Bible School for five years, served as president of the Ladies Association for three years, and worked with the choir and missionary society. She served as commissioner and vice commissioner of the Girl Scouts and the progress of the organization in her community is largely due to her efforts. She served for ten years on the Wayne Hospital Board and was chairman of the committee that organized the Hospital Auxiliary, sponsored by the Woman's Club. She enjoyed contact with the P.E.O. college girls at Wayne State College.

Edna was initiated into Chapter AZ, Wayne. She served her chapter as president in 1933-1935. In 1935, she was elected to the executive board of Nebraska State Chapter and she held every office on the board. In 1940, she was elected the forty-eighth president of Nebraska State Chapter and presided at the convention in 1941 in Fremont. Edna organized six chapters in Nebraska: Chapter EL, Oakland; Chapter EM, Bloomfield; Chapter EN, Pender; Chapter EO, West Point; Chapter EP. Wisner; and Chapter EQ, Blair.

Edna B. Casper died on December 30, 1977.

Mary Russell Koupal

NEBRASKA STATE CHAPTER PRESIDENT
1941-1942

Mary Russell Koupal was a native Nebraskan. She was born in Salem, the daughter of George H. and Ruth Biggerstaff Russell. The Russells were Missouri pioneers who originally came from Kentucky. In 1909, they moved to Ord, where in 1911, Mary was married to Anthony S. Koupal, who was engaged in the mercantile business.

A member of the Christian Church, Mary sang in the choir, taught Bible School and served as president of the missionary society.

Mary was initiated into Chapter BB, Ord, in 1914. One of her prized possessions was one of the over-sized, older P.E.O. pins and she wore it in testimony of her longtime membership in the Sisterhood. Mary was elected to office on the Nebraska State Chapter board in 1935 when Chapter BB was the last single chapter to serve as hostess for a state convention. She served as Nebraska State Chapter's forty-ninth president.

In 1938, the Koupal family moved to Lincoln. Upon the death of her husband, Mary moved to New York City to reside with her only child, Ruth Elizabeth. Ruth is a third generation P.E.O., having been initiated into Chapter BB as were her mother and grandmother. In New York, Mary served for twenty-seven years on the Staff of Student Activities at New York University on Washington Square.

While serving on the Executive Board of Nebraska State Chapter, Mary organized two chapters in Nebraska: Chapter ER, Benkelman; and Chapter ES, Lincoln. Mary Russell Koupal died on October 13, 1986.

Florence Wells Davis
NEBRASKA STATE CHAPTER PRESIDENT
1942-1943

Florence Wells was born in Schuyler, the daughter of George Hiram and Anna Albertson Wells. She was educated in Schuyler High School and the University of Nebraska where she received special training in library work. She was a member of Delta Gamma sorority and the Episcopal Church. For three years, she served as librarian in the public library of Fremont. In 1916, she married Clarence A. Davis, a graduate of Nebraska Wesleyan and the Harvard Law School. He was Nebraska's attorney general for several years and served as an Under Secretary of State under President Eisenhower. They had one son, Thomas M.

Florence was an active volunteer in many organizations: Maternal Health Board, State Presidents Pro America, YWCA, and full-time librarian at the Lincoln Air Base Hospital.

Florence Davis was initiated into Chapter K, Lincoln, in 1921. On June 19, 1923, she dimitted to Chapter H, Holdrege, and on December 8, 1944, to Chapter CS, Lincoln. After her return from Washington D.C., she dimitted back to Chapter H. She was elected to the state executive board at the Holdrege convention in 1936 and served through all the state offices. She presided at the 1943 convention at North Platte as the fiftieth president of Nebraska State Chapter. At the Supreme Chapter Convention in Washington, D.C. in 1961, she gave a beautiful tea at her apartment in honor of Bertha Clark Hughes. While she served on the board of

Nebraska State Chapter, Florence Wells Davis organized one Nebraska chapter: Chapter ET, Scottsbluff.

Florence Wells Davis died in Lincoln, Nebraska, on January 24, 1970.

Mary Craig McCulloch Nixon
NEBRASKA STATE CHAPTER PRESIDENT
1943-1944

Mary Craig McCulloch was born in Omaha, the daughter of Bruce and Adeline H. McCulloch. Her maternal grandfather was the first Congregational minister to settle west of the Mississippi River. Her father, a graduate of Monmouth College, Monmouth, Illinois, founded and for sixty years edited the Daily Journal Stockman. Her mother founded one of the earliest Federated Woman's Clubs and both she and her mother served as presidents. Her college education was at Knox College, Galesburg, Illinois, which four generations of her family have attended. She was a member of Pi Beta Phi sorority.

On June 20, 1917, Mary married John Alfred Nixon with whom she had started kindergarten. They had two children, John A., Jr. and Grace Adeline.

For ten years, Mary was superintendent of the junior and intermediate departments of Wheeler Memorial United Presbyterian Church, president of P.T.A., and president of South Omaha Woman's Clubs. She served for six years on the Educational Loan Board of the Federation of Woman's Clubs.

In 1924, Mary Nixon was initiated into Chapter CR, Omaha, where her mother was a charter member. Mary served her chapter as president, the Omaha P.E.O. Association as president and was elected to the Executive Board of Nebraska State Chapter at the 1935 convention in Omaha. Mary was the fifty-first president of Nebraska State Chapter and presided at the 1944 Omaha convention.

While Mary served on the Nebraska State Chapter board, she organized one chapter, Chapter EU, Mitchell.

Mary resided in Phoenix, Arizona, and died on November 24, 1980.

The things we fear most in organizations
—fluctuations, disturbances, imbalances—
are the primary sources of creativity.

-Margaret J. Wheatley

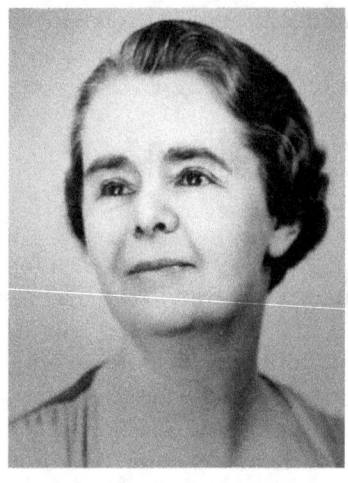

Marion Hart Crites

NEBRASKA STATE CHAPTER PRESIDENT
1944-1945

Marion Hart was born in Colwich, Kansas, the only child of Sherman E. and Carolyn S. Hart. When she was three, her parents moved to Kansas City, Missouri, where she lived until her marriage. She graduated from high school in Lincoln, Nebraska and received her B.A. degree from the University of Nebraska in 1909. She was a member of Alpha Omicron Pi sorority. When she married Frederick A. Crites in 1914, they went to live in Chadron where Mr. Crites practiced law until his death in 1941. They had three children: Wallace, Sherman and a daughter, Marion, who attended Cottey College for one year.

Marion was a member of the Congregational Church where she taught Sunday School for many years and was active in the Ladies Aid. She served as secretary of the Chadron Library Board, was a member of the Chadron Culture Club, the Audubon Society, Order of the Eastern Star, director of the Junior Hostess Corps of the USO and chairman of publicity for Dawes County during two United War Fund drives. She also served as Dawes County chairman for the American Red Cross.

Marion lived for many years on the Chadron State Teacher's College campus where she was a student of creative writing and painting, especially play, short story, and poetry writing. She was a member of Arts Poetica, Midwest Chaparral.

Marion Crites was initiated into Chapter BL, Chadron, in 1921. She served her chapter for two years as president. In 1937, she was elected to the state executive board at the convention in Chadron. She held every office of the state chapter and served as the fifty-second president of Nebraska State Chapter. She presided at the 1945 convention in Falls City.

Marion Crites died on June 23, 1983.

Love is the crowning grace of humanity,
the holiest right of the soul, the golden link
which binds us to duty and truth, the redeeming
principle that chiefly reconciles the heart to life,
and is prophetic of eternal good.

-Petrarch

Eva Huston Curtiss

NEBRASKA STATE CHAPTER PRESIDENT
1945-1946

Eva Huston was born in Geneva, the daughter of Mr. and Mrs. T.O. Huston. She was graduated from Geneva High School and Peru State Teachers College. For several years she taught in the public schools of Lincoln and Geneva. Eva married John E. Curtiss, district manager of the Consumers Public Power Company. They had one daughter, Ruth Ann.

Eva was an active public servant. She was a member of the Trinity Methodist Church and the Women's Society of Christian Service. She also served as Spiritual Life Chairman for the Lincoln Council of Church Women. Other organizations which benefited from her talents were the Red Cross Surgical Dressing Corps where she served as County Chairman and the advisory board of Cornhusker Girls' State. She was involved with Girls' State from its inception.

Eva Curtiss was initiated into Chapter BR, Lincoln, in 1926. Later she dimitted and became a charter member of Chapter DL, Lincoln. Every year after her initiation, she served P.E.O. in some official capacity, either on the local or state level or Lincoln Reciprocity Roundtable. Eva served as state treasurer, recording secretary, organizer, second and first vice president. She was elected the fifty-third president of Nebraska State Chapter and presided at the convention in 1946 in Fairbury. While on the executive board, Eva organized one chapter in Nebraska: Chapter EV, Gering.

Eva Huston Curtiss died in Lincoln, Nebraska, on July 1, 1956.

Rebecca Pierce Lee

NEBRASKA STATE CHAPTER PRESIDENT
1946-1947

Rebecca Pierce was born in Pennsylvania but in early childhood moved to Fremont with her parents Frederick and Bertha E. Pierce. She was educated in Fremont public schools, Midland College and Iowa State Teachers College in Cedar Falls, Iowa. She taught school for several years. In 1915, she married Earl J. Lee, son of a Nebraska pioneer family and a graduate of the University of Nebraska. He headed a law firm in Fremont and for many years served in the Nebraska Legislature. The Lees had two sons, Jackson F. and Robert E.

Rebecca was an active member of the First Congregational Church, the Order of the Eastern Star and many other civic organizations. She was initiated into P.E.O. on February 7, 1930, into Chapter AJ, Fremont. She shared membership in Chapter AJ with her mother and later her daughter-in-law.

Rebecca served the state chapter as corresponding and recording secretary, organizer, second and first vice presidents. In 1946, she was elected as the fifty-fourth president of Nebraska State Chapter and presided at the Lincoln convention in 1947. From 1948-1958, she was a member of the Board of Trustees of the Nebraska P.E.O. Home and served most of the time as treasurer. She worked untiringly to raise funds to build a wing to the Home. While she served on the Nebraska State Chapter board, Rebecca organized three chapters: Chapter EW, Genoa; Chapter EX, Fremont; and Chapter EY, Omaha.

Rebecca Pierce Lee died on August 14, 1989.

Florence Fay Stewart

NEBRASKA STATE CHAPTER PRESIDENT
1947-1948

Florence Fay was the daughter of pioneer parents, Stephen and Rosetta Fay. She grew to womanhood on her father's farm in Loup County. For seven years, she taught in the public schools of Loup and Custer counties. Twice she was elected Loup County Superintendent of Public Instruction. In 1909, she married Charles M. Stewart of Aurora. The Stewarts had four sons: Arthur G., Glen M., Fay A., and Keith W.

In Aurora, Florence served on the City Library Board, the Board of Education, as department head in the Woman's Club, and as superintendent of Sunday School in the Congregational Church. After the family moved to Grand Island, her activities included: service on the YWCA board, president of Federated Women's Club and chairman of its Public Speaking Department; president of the Fifth District of Nebraska Federated Women's Clubs, and for ten years, she was a teacher of an adult class in the Methodist Sunday School.

Florence Stewart was initiated into Chapter AC, Aurora, on January 18, 1926. She dimitted to Chapter CK, Grand Island, in 1929. She served as president of Chapter CK and in 1941, was elected to the Executive Board of Nebraska State Chapter. She presided at the Hastings Convention of 1948 as the fifty-fifth president of Nebraska State Chapter. She headed the Nebraska delegation to the Convention of Supreme Chapter in Los Angeles in 1947. During her term of service on the state board, Florence organized one chapter in Nebraska, Chapter EZ, Grand Island.

It was said of Florence that she was a grandmother who retained the enthusiasm of youth; a homemaker who loved to have her home filled with friends; a daughter of pioneers who was still looking for new horizons in education and in the P.E.O. Sisterhood. Florence Fay Stewart died in Grand Island on December 28, 1967.

Helen Copsey Riddell
NEBRASKA STATE CHAPTER PRESIDENT
1948-1949

Helen Copsey, daughter of Fay David and Edith Ely Copsey, was born on September 6, 1896, in York County near Henderson, an area named for her paternal great-grandparents. She received her education from York High School, attended York College and received a B.A. degree from the University of Nebraska in 1918. She was a member of Alpha Phi sorority.

In 1926, Helen married John L. Riddell, a lawyer in York. For many years she taught school. Many civic organizations were the beneficiaries of Helen's talents: York School Board; York Woman's Club (where she served as president); the Business and Professional Women's club; the David Bryant Chapter of the Daughters of the American Revolution; the Grace Chapter of the Order of the Eastern Star; Westminster Women of the Presbyterian Church where she served as president and as an elder of the church.

Helen Riddell was initiated into Chapter A, York, in November 1921. She served her chapter as corresponding and recording secretaries, vice president and president. At the York convention in 1942, she served as general chairman and was elected treasurer of Nebraska State Chapter. She held every state office and served as the fifty-sixth president of Nebraska State Chapter. She presided at the convention in Wayne in 1949. At that convention, she was elected to the Board of Trustees of the Nebraska P.E.O. Home. She served in that position for five years and as chairman in 1953 and 1954. In 1949, she was appointed by Laura Storm Knapp, president of Supreme Chapter, to the board of The P.E.O. Record. She served on that board for six years and as chairman in 1953-1955.

During her term of service to Nebraska State Chapter, Helen organized one chapter in Nebraska: Chapter FA, McCook.

Helen Copsey Riddell died on August 15, 1983.

Courage is grace under pressure.
-Ernest Hemingway

Bessie F. Buchanan

NEBRASKA STATE CHAPTER PRESIDENT
1949-1950

Bessie F. Salisbury was born near LaSalle, Illinois, the daughter of William N. and Lena L. Salisbury. When she was a child, the family moved to a ranch near North Platte and she attended school there. After high school, she was employed as a bookkeeper for a number of years in the Lincoln County Courthouse. Later she became secretary of the Mutual Building and Loan Association of North Platte. She held this position until the time of her marriage in 1924 to Frank N. Buchanan, president of the Mutual Building and Loan Association.

Bessie was a woman of good judgment and logical mind—a true perfectionist. She possessed quiet dignity, and was retiring almost to a point of shyness. But she had a warm and generous personality. She was a member of the Presbyterian Church, many local and civic organizations, and the Order of the Eastern Star.

Bessie Buchanan was initiated into Chapter AK, North Platte, in 1926. She served her chapter as treasurer, corresponding secretary and twice as president. She was elected treasurer of the state chapter at the convention in North Platte, which she had served as general chairman. She held every office on the state executive board and served as the fifty-seventh president of Nebraska State Chapter. She presided at the state convention in Grand Island in 1950. Under her experienced hands, the books of Nebraska State Chapter, in each progressive office, became models of perfection. While she was on the state board, Bessie organized two chapters, Chapter FB, Lincoln, and Chapter FC, Scottsbluff.

Bessie Salisbury Buchanan died in North Platte on May 13, 1965.

Trust yourself. Create the kind of self that you will be happy to live with all your life. Make the most of yourself by fanning the tiny, inner sparks of possibility into flames of achievement.

-Golda Meir

Irene Simpson Van Brunt

NEBRASKA STATE CHAPTER PRESIDENT
1950-1951

★ SUPREME CHAPTER PRESIDENT
1964-1965

Irene Simpson, like her mother and father before her, was born in Omaha. She was the only child of Dr. John Emerson Simpson and Anna Petersen Simpson. She was educated in the Omaha public schools, Wellesley College, and the University of Nebraska where she was a member of Kappa Kappa Gamma. She received a B.A. degree in 1924. On October 1, 1924, she married Winslow Matthews Van Brunt of Beatrice, a graduate of the University of Nebraska with a B.S. in Civil Engineering. The Van Brunts had three children, Alice Irene, Mary Elizabeth and Winslow Jr. (who preceded his mother in death).

Irene was a member of the Dundee Presbyterian Church where, for seven years, she served on the board of the Women's Association. She also served as president of the Omaha Wellesley Club; secretary of the Kappa Alumnae Association; secretary of the Friends of Children's Hospital; director of both the local and national University of Nebraska Alumni Association; member of the board of Joslyn Women's Association; and as past matron of Vesta Chapter, Order of the Eastern Star, and as a member of the Daughters of the Nile. In 1975, the University of Nebraska at Lincoln honored Irene with a National Accomplishment Award for her civic service and her work with the P.E.O. International Peace Scholarship.

Irene was initiated into Chapter DD in Omaha in February 1928. The initiation took place at her family home with her mother as president. Prior to her mother's death in 1956, Irene, her mother, and her two daughters both were members of Chapter DD. Irene served Chapter DD as treasurer, corresponding secretary, recording secretary (five years) and president (two years). At the state convention in Omaha in 1944, she served as general chairman and was elected treasurer of Nebraska State Chapter. She held every office on the executive board and presided at the 1951 convention in McCook as Nebraska State Chapter's fifty-eighth president. Her convention theme was *Progress, Enthusiasm and Opportunity*. Irene served as a member of several state chapter committees and was instrumental in setting up the basic laws governing Cottey Junior College Grants and the Cottey College Area Chairmen. At the end of the 1957 convention, she was appointed a member of the publication committee of the *History of P.E.O.* in Nebraska. She served as its chairman in 1968-1971. She also served as Historian for Nebraska State Chapter at that time. During her term of service to Nebraska State Chapter, Irene organized two chapters: Chapter FD, Omaha; and Chapter FE, Plainview.

At the Philadelphia Supreme Chapter Convention in 1951, Laura Storms Knapp appointed Irene to serve on a committee for the Collection of Historical Material. At the 1953 convention in Vancouver, B.C., Mabel Scurrah appointed her to the committee on Amendments and Recommendations. At the Indianapolis Convention in 1955, she was elected corresponding secretary of Supreme Chapter. She also served as organizer, third, second and first vice presidents and upon the death of Uretta Hinkhouse in 1964, was elevated to Supreme Chapter President. She presided at the Supreme Convention in Atlantic City in 1965 where her theme was *Communication with God, with Man and with Nature*.

Irene also served on the P.E.O. International Peace Scholarship Committee for four years, and in 1961-63, was its first chairman. From 1959-61, she was chairman of a special committee to investigate the proper placement of the invested funds of the P.E.O. Sisterhood for managerial and custodial service. From 1971-1973 she was chairman of the P.E.O. Foundation Board of Trustees. From 1966-1969, she served as a member of the Publication Committee for *Out of the Heart*.

Irene Simpson Van Brunt died on June 16, 1995.

Maude Hart Weaver

NEBRASKA STATE CHAPTER PRESIDENT
1951-1952

Maude Hart was born on a farm near Nottawa, Michigan, the sixth child of Benjamin F. and Harriet Eggleston Hart. She graduated from high school in White Pigeon in 1903. She was a graduate of Michigan State Teachers College, Ypsilanti, where she specialized in public school music and drawing. She also took graduate work at Northwestern. She was a supervisor of fine arts at Bellaire, Michigan, and later for one year at Falls City, Nebraska. She married Arthur J. Weaver in 1908 in Falls City. Mr. Weaver enjoyed a long career in public service, serving as governor of Nebraska in 1928-1929. The Weavers had six children: Maude Harriet, Dorothy, Arthur J., Ruth, Phillip H. and Josephine. In 1952, Maude was chosen Nebraska Mother of the Year. The committee selected her because "of her charming personality, ability and Christian character, but also as an outstanding citizen of Nebraska and an ideal mother of six children."

Maude took an active part in civic and cultural groups both in Falls City and in Lincoln. She served as president of the Falls City Woman's Club, Falls City Music Club; as a member of the Reavis Ashley Chapter of the Daughters of the American Revolution and of the Order of the Eastern Star.

Maude Weaver was initiated into P.E.O. in 1923, as a charter member of Chapter CY, Falls City. At the Falls City convention of 1945, she was elected treasurer of Nebraska State Chapter. She served through all of the state offices and presided at the 1952 convention in Omaha as Nebraska State Chapter's fifty-ninth president. While on the Nebraska State Chapter board, Maude organized three Nebraska chapters: Chapter FF, Lincoln; Chapter FG, Lincoln; and Chapter FH, Hastings. Maude Weaver died in Maryland on December 23, 1971.

Lucy Nuckolls Livingston
NEBRASKA STATE CHAPTER PRESIDENT
1952-1953

Lucy Nuckolls was born in Fluvanna County, Virginia. In her early childhood, she moved with her parents, Leighton Leigh and Alice Nuckolls, to Nebraska. She received her education in the public schools of Fairbury. After graduation from Fairbury High School, she taught for a year in the rural schools of Jefferson County. Later she graduated from Business College. On November 26, 1914, she married LeRoy Livingston, a merchant in Fairbury. They had one daughter, Alice Mae, who died on December 2, 1962.

Lucy was an active member of the Methodist Church, a dimitted member of the Order of the Eastern Star, and several other organizations.

Lucy Livingston was initiated into Chapter AO, Fairbury, in 1935. With the exception of guard and chaplain, she held every office. She was elected treasurer of the Nebraska State Chapter at the Fairbury convention in 1946. She held every office on the executive board and presided as Nebraska State Chapter's sixtieth president at the convention in Scottsbluff in 1953. In 1954, she was elected to a five-year term on the Board of Trustees of the Nebraska P.E.O. Home. As chairman of the board, she presided at the dedication ceremony of the addition to the Home on April 28, 1955. While she was on the state board, Lucy organized two chapters in Nebraska: Chapter FI, Omaha; and Chapter FJ, Columbus.

Lucy lived for a time in Redlands, California, and then became a resident of the P.E.O. Home, where she died on March 6, 1984.

Margaret Hager McVicker
NEBRASKA STATE CHAPTER PRESIDENT
1953-1954

Margaret Hager was the daughter of Jennie Harris and George Edward Hager. She called Nebraska her state because she was born and educated in Lincoln. In 1924, she graduated from the University of Nebraska with a major in dramatics. She was very active in student affairs and received many honors, climaxed with membership in Mortar Board. She served as province president for Alpha Chi Omega sorority. Soon after graduation, she married Dwight S. McVicker. For a period of ten years, they moved a lot.

The McVickers had two children, Shirley and Dwight S., Jr. Shirley McVicker Marsh was elected as a Nebraska state senator in 1972.

Margaret served as president of the Women's Society of Trinity Methodist Church, on the YWCA board, and on boards of many other civic organizations.

Margaret's P.E.O. career began when she was a University of Nebraska freshman. She was initiated into her mother's chapter, Chapter K, Lincoln, on April 18, 1921. She always managed close association with P.E.O. and held active membership in the following chapters: K, Lincoln; AE, Kansas City, Missouri; C and I, Arkansas; ED, Kansas; and DK, Lincoln.

She served as chairman of the 1947 convention in Lincoln and was elected treasurer of the state chapter. She held every state office and presided at the 1954 convention in Norfolk. In 1953, she led the Nebraska delegation to Supreme Chapter Convention in Vancouver, British Columbia. She was Nebraska State Chapter's sixty-first president. While she was on the executive board, she organized three chapters in Nebraska: Chapter FK, Omaha; Chapter FL, Omaha; and Chapter FM, Beatrice.

Margaret summed up her philosophy of life in a quotation from Henry Van Dyke, "Be glad of life because it gives you the chance to love, to play, and to look up at the stars." Margaret Hager McVicker died at her home in Lincoln, Nebraska, on July 18, 1955.

Ruth Gellatly

NEBRASKA STATE CHAPTER PRESIDENT
1954-1955

Ruth Gellatly was born in Beaver City, Nebraska, where she received her early education. Later she attended Temple High School in Lincoln and the University of Nebraska where she majored in music with a specialization in voice. There she met and married H. Chal Gellatly on December 31, 1914. They established their home in Red Cloud. The Gellatlys had three children: John Chalmers, Richard Murney and Joan Ruth.

Ruth served as president of the Women's Association of Westminster Presbyterian Church, Lincoln, and the First Presbyterian Church, Hastings; and president of the YWCA, Hastings. She also served as president of the Women's Guild and a member of the executive committee of the Fourth Presbyterian Church in Chicago.

Ruth was initiated into Chapter Y, Red Cloud. In 1936, she dimitted to Chapter

K, Lincoln. In 1944, she dimitted to G, Hastings, and later she became a charter member of Chapter GK, Hastings. At the time of her death, she was a member of Chapter A, Chicago, Illinois, where she resided with her daughter.

In 1948, Ruth served as chairman for the state convention in Hastings. She was elected treasurer of Nebraska State Chapter at that meeting. She held every office on the state board and presided at the 1955 convention in Lincoln. She was Nebraska State Chapter's sixty-second president. Ruth said at the time she served on the board that it had been "nip and tuck" for her three loves—family, the Presbyterian Church, and P.E.O.– with all three getting a fair portion of her daily allotted twenty-four hours. While Ruth served on the Executive Board of Nebraska State Chapter, she organized four Nebraska chapters: Chapter FN, Kearney; Chapter FO, Hay Springs; Chapter FP, Chadron; and Chapter FQ, Lincoln.

Ruth Gellatly died in Chicago on December 2, 1974. Her burial was in Hastings.

Dorothy Smithberger

NEBRASKA STATE CHAPTER PRESIDENT
1955-1956

Dorothy Pugh was born in Stanton, Nebraska, the daughter of George and Rosa Carroll Pugh, She received her education in the local schools and the University of Nebraska where she was affiliated with Gamma Phi Beta and Pi Lambda Theta. For a short time, she taught English and Latin. Her school years were shared with Louis Smithberger, whom she later married. The Smithbergers had four children: Dorothy Elaine, Wynn, Susan and Linda.

Dorothy is a member of the Methodist Church and she taught Sunday School, sponsored youth groups, and held W.S.C.S. offices on both the local and district level. She served on the County Centennial Committee, which included promoting community improvement for town and county. She helped organize the Stanton Historical Society and worked to update county history. She promoted organization of the Stanton Church Women United and became its first president. She is a past president of Stanton Federated Woman's Club, Historical Society and Methodist Women. Dorothy also wrote *The Stanton History*.

As a bride, Dorothy was initiated into Chapter DF, Stanton. She served her local chapter three times as president, the last time while serving as the treasurer of Nebraska State Chapter. She served as co-chairman of the state convention at Wayne in 1949, and also president of the model meeting. There she was elected to the state board and served through every office. Dorothy was elected as Nebraska State Chapter's sixty-third president in 1955, and she presided at the Fremont convention in 1956. The theme of her convention was *P.E.O. as a Pathfinder in the Way of Life*— very appropriate for the city named for pioneer pathfinder, John C. Fremont.

One of the highlights of Dorothy's P.E.O. career was seeing her daughter, Susan Smithberger Harr, serve all offices of the state executive board and preside as Nebraska State Chapter's ninety-fourth president at the convention in Omaha in 1987. The "Smithberger-Harr" combination is the first mother-daughter duo to serve Nebraska State Chapter as presidents.

In 1971, Helen Magill, president of Nebraska State Chapter, appointed Dorothy historian and editor of the Nebraska P.E.O. History. Some years before, Bertha Clark Hughes suggested to Dorothy that she become a writer. That challenge was met when Dorothy and her committee devoted countless hours researching the history of P.E.O. in Nebraska. In 1975, *The Saga of Nebraska P.E.O.* was published. It was a precious labor of love and Nebraska P.E.O.s are forever grateful to Dorothy for her talent and dedication.

Dorothy Smithberger died on April 28, 2003.

Flora M. Stevens
NEBRASKA STATE CHAPTER PRESIDENT
1956-1957

Flora M. Stevens lived her entire life in southwest Nebraska except for four years in Pawnee County. She was born in Hendley, the daughter of George and Eliza Ann Warner. She was graduated from Beaver City High School in 1915. She returned to teach English after graduating from Peru Normal. While in college, she was mezzo soprano soloist for Girls Glee Club and gave a vocal recital her senior year.

In 1920, Flora married Wade Stevens, a lawyer who had the designation of being the first business airplane pilot in the world. Wade had served as an overseas pilot in World War I. The Stevens had three children, Warner, Ann and Marilyn (now in Chapter Eternal.) Wade Stevens died in 1983. Flora's daughters, daughter-in-law, and three granddaughters all were privileged to become P.E.O.s. Flora and her family were active in the Memorial United Methodist Church, serving in various capacities there. She also was very involved in civic groups. Flora served as chairman for National Humanities.

On January 21, 1919, Flora was initiated into Chapter BV while she was teaching in Beaver City. She served her chapter there as treasurer and president.

The Stevens family moved to McCook in 1941, where Flora dimitted to Chapter X. She served as their president twice. For the 1951 convention in McCook, Flora served as convention chairman and was elected to the office of state treasurer. She served in six of the seven offices, missing the office of recording secretary. Flora was elected as the sixty-fourth president of Nebraska State Chapter and presided at the 1957 convention in Columbus. Her theme was *O Magnify the Lord With Me and Let Us Exalt His Name TOGETHER*. An entertaining feature of the convention was the "Singing Pages." Flora was a delegate to three Supreme Conventions—Los Angeles in 1947, Vancouver in 1953, and Denver in 1957. While she was on the board of Nebraska State Chapter, Flora organized two chapters: Chapter FR, Sidney; and Chapter FS, Lexington. In 1973, Flora also was instrumental in organizing Chapter GY in McCook, where she became a charter member. Flora Stevens died June 21, 2001.

Emma McLaughlin Sanderson
NEBRASKA STATE CHAPTER PRESIDENT
1957-1958

Emma McLaughlin, a native Nebraskan born in Edgar, was the daughter of Guy and Lulu Holmes Lake McLaughlin of Fairfield. She received a B.S. degree from the University of Nebraska where she was active in Alpha Delta Theta which later merged with Phi Mu. She also was involved with YWCA Big Sister Board; Tassels; and the University Dramatic Club. She did post graduate work at the University of Colorado.

She met and married Charles J. Sanderson. Together they taught school—he as superintendent and she as a classroom teacher. The Sandersons had a son, Charles, and a daughter, Frances Ann, who attended Cottey College.

Emma was active in community life, especially working with youth. She served with the Campfire Girls for fifteen years, with the Job's Daughters Council; as a 4-H leader; and with the Cub Scouts. She also held office in the W.S.C.S., both on the local and district level. Other organizations Emma participated in were Federated Woman's Club, Daughters of the American Revolution; and Eastern Star. Emma was a member of the Episcopal Church but also served on the board of trustees of the United Church of Christ. She also served as chairman of the Clay County Bloodmobile for the Red Cross and was a charter member of the Clay County Historical Society. She also was a past state president of Delta Kappa Gamma sorority. Her hobbies were outdoor sports and gourmet cooking.

Emma was initiated into Chapter T, Clay Center, on May 5, 1942. As her husband's business took them elsewhere, she dimitted to Chapters DP, Bridgeport, and EU, Mitchell. She eventually dimitted back to Chapter T, her original chapter. At the 1953 convention in Scottsbluff, she was elected recording secretary of the state chapter. She served five years on the state board and presided as Nebraska State Chapter's sixty-fifth president. While she served on the state board, Emma organized one chapter in Nebraska, Chapter FT, Omaha.

Emma Sanderson died in Clay Center, Nebraska, on January 22, 1991.

Marthena Peacock Stevens
NEBRASKA STATE CHAPTER PRESIDENT
1958-1959

Marthena Peacock was born in Superior, the daughter of William Harry and Mary Lawrence Peacock. When she was a young child, the family moved to Omaha. She graduated from Omaha Central High School and Business College. For ten years, she was a legal secretary for an Omaha law firm. On May 5, 1932, she married Harold F. Stevens, a building and loan executive. They had two children, Sandra and Keith H. The Stevens were members of the First Central Congregational Church. Marthena served as a member of the Women's Fellowship. For three years, she served as treasurer of the Omaha Council of Church Women and also as a board member for Uta Halee. For years, she served as a member of the election board. Marthena's interests centered around P.T.A., scouts, church and later, her grandchildren.

On March 17, 1919, at age eighteen, Marthena was initiated into Chapter BP, Omaha. Her mother was a charter member of BP, having dimitted from Chapter D, Superior. Marthena's mother was an active P.E.O. for over fifty-five years and Marthena was part of a three generation P.E.O. family. Her daughter was president of Chapter BC, Minnesota.

Marthena served her chapter in four offices. She also was general chairman for the Omaha Convention in 1952, where she was elected treasurer of the state chapter. She served through all the state offices and presided over the Omaha convention in 1959 as Nebraska State Chapter's sixty-sixth president. For eleven years, she served the state chapter on the Amendments and Recommendations Committee.

While serving on the state board, Marthena organized two chapters in Nebraska: Chapter FU, Grant, and Chapter FV, Nebraska City.

Marthena Stevens died April 20, 1979.

Harriet Taylor Lumbard
NEBRASKA STATE CHAPTER PRESIDENT
1959-1960

Harriet Taylor was born in St. Paul, Nebraska, the daughter of Charles E. and Vera I. Taylor. She was educated in St. Paul High School, Monticello College, and the University of Nebraska where she received a B.S. degree in Home Economics. She was a member of Alpha Chi Omega sorority. She taught Home Economics in Ord and Grand Island. On January 5, 1935, she married Carl

Lumbard, a Grand Island business man. They had two children: Jane L., a Cottey College graduate; and David T.

The Lumbards were members of the Presbyterian Church. Harriet served as president of the Auxiliary Presbyterian, president of the YWCA board, and as a member of the Grand Island planning commission.

Harriet was initiated into Chapter AP, St. Paul, on May 21, 1924. Her mother and her grandmother, Harriet E. Force, were members there. Her initiation was unique as she and her twin sister, Cathryn (now Mrs. George Armstrong) were initiated in the model meeting of the St. Paul convention. Harriet dimitted to Chapter CK, Grand Island and later she became a charter member of Chapter GP, Grand Island. She served through all the offices of her local chapter. At the Scottsbluff convention in 1953, she was elected state treasurer. She held every state office and presided at the convention in Nebraska City in 1960. She was Nebraska State Chapter's sixty-seventh president. While on the board of Nebraska State Chapter, Harriet organized two Nebraska chapters: Chapter FW, Lincoln; and FX, Lincoln.

Harriet Lumbard died on April 11, 1991, in Grand Island, Nebraska.

Mildred Wilson Robertson
Nebraska State Chapter President
1960-1961

Mildred Wilson was born in Delta County, Michigan, the daughter of Worship and Olive Wilson. She graduated from high school in Gladstone, Michigan, and from the American Conservatory of Music in Chicago, Illinois. She also attended the Chicago Art Institute. She taught music in the public schools of Madison, Nebraska. There she met and married James W. Robertson. They had one son, Durwood.

Music served a special interest in Mildred's life. She was a member of the First United Presbyterian Church, and in 1974 she was honored for forty-eight years as organist and choir director. She also was a Past Matron of the Order of the Eastern Star.

Mildred was initiated into Chapter AL, Madison, in 1934. She served her local chapter well. In 1954, she served as general chairman of the state convention in Norfolk where she was elected treasurer of the state chapter. She served in every office and was elected the sixty-eighth president of Nebraska State Chapter in 1960. She presided at the 1961 convention in Beatrice. While she was a member of the state board, Mildred organized Chapter FY, Omaha.

Mildred Robertson died on September 21, 1979.

A bird doesn't sing because it has an answer,
it sings because it has a song.

-Lou Holtz

Lois M. Newell

NEBRASKA STATE CHAPTER PRESIDENT
1961-1962

Lois Holmwood was born in Edison, Nebraska, the daughter of Charles and Edna B. Holmwood. Her mother was a pioneer in Kearney County. She was graduated from Hastings College with a B.S. degree and taught mathematics and Latin in Minden until her marriage to Dr. Laurence C. Newell, professor of agronomy at the University of Nebraska and research agronomist for the U.S.D.A. The Newells had three children: Warren, Bruce, and Carol.

Lois was a member of the United Presbyterian Church and served in many capacities there: as a member of session, a trustee, and president of the Woman's Association. She also served as president of the Nebraska City Presbyterial. She accompanied the Junior Choir and the Girls' Choir. Her hobbies were music, reading and her grandchildren.

Lois was initiated into Chapter N, Minden, in 1923. She later dimitted to Chapter BY, Lincoln. At the Lincoln convention in 1955, she served as general chairman and was elected treasurer of the state chapter. She served through all of the state offices and was elected Nebraska State Chapter's sixty-ninth president. She presided at the 1962 Lincoln convention. While she was a member of the state board, Lois organized Chapter FZ, Omaha.

Lois Newell died on September 26, 1986.

Marietta Jack

NEBRASKA STATE CHAPTER PRESIDENT
1962-1963

Marietta, like her husband Leroy C., lived all her life in Tekamah, Nebraska. She was the daughter of Fred Nathan and Blanche Miller Morehouse. She received her early education in the Tekamah public schools. She graduated from Christian College in Columbia, Missouri, and the University of Nebraska, where she received a B.A. degree. Marietta was a member of Kappa Kappa Gamma sorority.

Besides being a housewife and pursuing her hobbies of reading, gardening and bird-watching, she was for years the bookkeeper for the Jack Brothers Hardware. The Jacks had two sons, Leroy C. Jr. and Fred Gary.

Marietta was a member of the Presbyterian Church and sang in the choir and taught Sunday School. For three years, she served as clerk of the session and she was an honorary member of the Board of National Missions. She held all offices in the Tekamah Book Club and was president of the Tekamah unit of the National Parliamentarians.

On May 14, 1945, Marietta was initiated into Chapter DC, Tekamah. She served her chapter as treasurer, corresponding and recording secretary, vice president and president. In 1956, she served as chairman for the state convention in Fremont, where she was elected as treasurer of the state board. She served in every office and presided as Nebraska State Chapter's seventieth president. While on the state board, Marietta organized Chapter GA, Scottsbluff. She served as parliamentarian twice for the state chapter conventions.

Marietta died June 4, 2002, in Tekamah, Nebraska.

Dorothy D. Yeager

NEBRASKA STATE CHAPTER PRESIDENT
1963-1964

Born in Des Moines, Iowa, Dorothy Dawson was the daughter of Lester L. and Dora B. Dawson. The family moved to Lincoln where she received her education in the public schools and the University of Nebraska. She taught in the McCook and Lincoln schools before marrying George Yeager, an Omaha attorney, in 1930. The Yeagers had one daughter, Joanne.

Dorothy was an active member and held offices in the Omaha Branch of A.A.U.W. During World War II, she taught in an Omaha high school and also for the adult education department. For the War Bond drives, Dorothy was responsible for staffing twenty bond booths daily, working with thirty-two women's organizations.

Her activities also included being a member of the YWCA board and teaching adult education there. She also was a member of the Order of the Eastern Star. A member of the First United Methodist Church, Dorothy served as president of the Women's Society of Christian Service and as director of Parish Activities for eleven years. Radio station KOIL honored Dorothy as "Lady of the Day."

Dorothy was initiated into Chapter E, Omaha, in 1936. She served in all offices of her local chapter and was an officer of the Omaha P.E.O. Reciprocity Association. Dorothy served in five offices on the state board and presided over the seventy-fifth *Diamond Jubilee: 75 Years of Starshine* convention in Grand Island in 1964. She was Nebraska State Chapter's seventy-first president.

Dorothy served for ten years on the board of the Nebraska P.E.O. Home as president. While she was on the state board, Dorothy organized four chapters in Nebraska: Chapter GC, Alliance; Chapter GD, Lincoln; Chapter GE, Omaha; and Chapter GF, Omaha. Dorothy Yeager died on March 6, 1994.

Thelma Millen

NEBRASKA STATE CHAPTER PRESIDENT
1964-1965

Thelma Sexton was born near Savannah, Missouri, the daughter of Lawrence V. Sexton and Grace Harris Sexton Figgens. The family moved to Kansas where she was educated in the public schools and Kansas State College in Manhattan. She taught in the Kansas public schools. Nebraska became her home in 1927 when she married Herrold Millen, an area conservationist of the U.S. Soil Conservation Service. The Millens had two daughters, Clarice and Elaine.

Thelma was a member of the United Methodist Church and served on the administrative board. She taught Sunday School, was superintendent in the Youth department, and a charter member of W.S.C.S., where she held numerous offices in addition to the presidency. She also worked as an officer at the district level. She was president of the Albion Woman's Club and the Community Youth Council and served as sponsor of the Future Homemakers of America in the Albion schools. The state chapter of FHA honored her by naming her its first State Chapter Mother. Besides P.E.O., church and civic activities, Thelma's hobbies were needlepoint, rose gardening, history and "grandmothering." The Millens were ardent world-travelers.

Thelma was initiated into Chapter CQ, Neligh, in 1935. She dimitted to Chapter BT, Weeping Water, and later to DJ, Albion. Her mother and two daughters joined her in membership in Chapter DJ. She was elected to the state board at the Omaha convention in 1959 and held all offices except organizer.

She presided as Nebraska State Chapter's seventy-second president at the Holdrege convention in 1965. She served for five years on the Board of Trustees of the Nebraska P.E.O. Home.

Thelma Millen died on September 7, 1979.

The Lord your God is with you. He is mighty to save.
He will take great delight in you. He will quiet you
with His love. He will rejoice over you with singing.

-Zephaniah 3:17

Josephine B. Davis
NEBRASKA STATE CHAPTER PRESIDENT
1965-1966

Josephine Berggren Davis, daughter of Joseph and Elva Berggren, was born in Wahoo. After graduating from Wahoo High School as class valedictorian, she studied at the Oberlin Conservatory of Music in Ohio for one year. She graduated from the University of Nebraska in 1931 with a major in piano and a minor in education. There she was a member of Delta Omicron, Pi Lambda Theta and Alpha Phi. She served as zone director and vice president of the University of Nebraska Alumni Association.

While teaching music in the public schools of Nebraska City, Jo met and married Woolsey Davis, manager of an insurance company. The Davises had one son, William, and a daughter, Barbara Jo, who was recognized as one of the Outstanding Young Women of America.

The Davis family was active in Saint Mary's Episcopal Church where Jo served as choir director for several years. She also assisted in the organization of the Concert Association, Joslyn Guild, and the first Beta Sigma Phi chapter in the city.

Josephine was initiated into Chapter I, Wahoo, her mother's chapter, and later became a charter member and first president of Chapter FV, Nebraska City. She was chairman of the 1960 Nebraska City convention at which time she was elected treasurer. She served the state in every office except recording secretary. She presided at the Omaha convention in 1966 as Nebraska State Chapter's seventy-third president. For three years, she served on the Amendments and Recommendations Committee, as chairman of the Budget Committee that presented a new budget format at the South Sioux City convention in 1970 and was chairman of the Music Committee to select a state song at the Beatrice convention in 1961. At the Ogallala convention in 1972, she was elected to the P.E.O. Home Board of Trustees. She also served as president. While she served on the state board, Jo organized two Nebraska chapters: Chapter GG, Kearney; and Chapter GH, Fremont.

Josephine Davis died February 14, 2006, in Nebraska City.

Logic will get you from A to B.
Imagination will take you everywhere.

-Albert Einstein

Helen M. Noble
NEBRASKA STATE CHAPTER PRESIDENT
1966-1967

Helen M. Rhoads was born in Emerson, Iowa, the daughter of Clyde and Ethel M. Rhoads. In 1925, she graduated from the University of Nebraska. In 1926, she married Leslie Hugh Noble, an attorney who served for sixteen years as a Gage County judge. The Nobles had two sons, Leslie H. Jr. and John R. Helen's husband and two sons were also graduates of the University of Nebraska.

The Noble family belonged to the United Methodist Church where Helen was a charter member of the Women's Society. Her other activities included: lifetime membership in the P.T.A., the Order of the Eastern Star, Fortnightly Study Club, Naphis Temple of Daughters of the Nile, and Kappa Delta sorority. Her special interests included her grandchildren, knitting, sewing and swimming.

Helen was initiated into Chapter FF, Glenwood, Iowa, in 1925. Her mother was a charter member of the chapter. She dimitted to Chapter Z, Beatrice, after her marriage. On April 23, 1974, her granddaughter, Susan J. Noble, was initiated into Chapter ES, Lincoln. Susan's mother, Laraine Noble, was chaplain at the meeting. Helen served Chapter Z as guard, recording secretary, vice president and president. She was chairman for the state convention in Beatrice in 1961 and at that time was elected treasurer of the state chapter. She held every state office but that of corresponding secretary and presided at the Sidney convention in 1967 as Nebraska State Chapter's seventy-fourth president. She served on the state Amendments and Recommendations Committee 1967-1973. She also served on the History Committee. While on the state board, Helen organized Chapter GI, Gering.

Helen Noble moved to the P.E.O. Home in Beatrice and died September 11, 1996.

It is impossible to live without failing at something, unless you live so cautiously that you might as well not have lived at all – in which case, you fail by default.

-J.K. Rowling

Nelsine Shafer Scofield

NEBRASKA STATE CHAPTER PRESIDENT
1967-1968

Nelsine Shafer Scofield was born in Falls City. She attended Peru College and the Dickinson Secretarial School. Most of her adult years were spent as a secretary. For twenty-five years, Nelsine was secretary in the School of Health, Physical Education and Recreation at the University of Nebraska, Lincoln.

The year 1967-1968 was an eventful one for the Scofields. Nelsine and her husband, Gerry, celebrated their twenty-fifth wedding anniversary; Nelsine earned a B.A. degree from the College of Business Administration at the University of Nebraska in Lincoln; and she completed requirements for a Professional Standards Certificate from the National Association of Educational Secretaries. She was also elected president of the Nebraska State Chapter that year. Quite a year of achievements!

Nelsine's community interests placed her on the Board of Directors of the Volunteer Bureau of Lincoln; as president and director of the Women's Interclub Council; treasurer of Nebraska Chamber Orchestra Guild; and president of 40th and A Neighborhood Association. Her other volunteer interests included supporting all phases of her church life as a member of the Good Shepherd Presbyterian Church and serving as a member of A.A.U.W. Reading and her grandchildren were a high priority in Nelsine's life.

Nelsine was initiated into Chapter DN, Lincoln, on November 22, 1948. She served her chapter in most of the offices. Serving as general chairman for the Lincoln convention in 1961, Nelsine was elected recording secretary of the state board at that time. She served in every state office but that of treasurer and presided as Nebraska State Chapter's seventy-fifth president at the convention in Valentine in 1968. Nelsine held key positions on state committees and was enthusiastic as a sponsor to the P.E.O. College Group in Lincoln. Nelsine retired from the University in 1980, and at that time she assumed the responsibilities of assistant secretary-treasurer of Nebraska State Chapter. She served in this capacity for ten years, until 1990. When she was a member of the state board, Nelsine organized Chapter GJ, Lincoln.

Nelsine Scofield moved to the Nebraska P.E.O. Home in Beatrice in 1999. Soon after moving she found herself involved in Beatrice's civic life. Within three weeks of her move she was introduced at the library and on their volunteer roster. A short time later she signed up as a volunteer at the Main Street Beatrice office. In October 2001 Nelsine received honors from Main Street Nebraska, a state organization, for her volunteerism. In May 2002 she was recognized with honors from the Beatrice City Library for her contributions and activities as a volunteer. Nelsine loved living at the P.E.O. Home. She said, "I never dreamed that the latter part of my life would be spent surrounded by such beauty—inside and out—as I have found at the P.E.O. Home." After fourteen years as a resident, she died there on July 21, 2013.

Jean Alden Johnson
NEBRASKA STATE CHAPTER PRESIDENT
1968-1969

Jean Alden Johnson, daughter of Claude and Nellie Ludden Alden, was born June 12, 1913, at Kimball. She attended Kimball Schools where, in the second grade, she met her future husband. Jean was valedictorian of the high school class of 1930. In 1934 she graduated from the University of Nebraska, a member of Phi Beta Kappa, Alpha Chi Omega, Pi Lambda Theta and Mortar Board. Her civic activities included serving as president of the YWCA, treasurer of W.A.A. and manager of football stadium concessions and she was on the Junior-Senior Prom Committee.

For four years, Jean taught girls' physical education in Grand Island. In 1937, she became the second initiate of Chapter EH. In 1938, she married William Franklin Johnson in Kimball. Jean dimitted to Chapter DT where her mother had been a charter member and where she held every office except treasurer. She was the "middle member" of a three generation P.E.O. family group. Her two granddaughters, Kristy Mays of Greencastle, Indiana, and Valerie Payne of Kearney, are fourth generation P.E.O.s.

For years her hobby was serving as the girls' Sunday School teacher, Camp Fire leader and Guardian of Job's Daughters. She served a term on Job's Daughters Grand Council and as Grand Deputy. She was an A.F.S. mother to Italian daughter, Paola Redogliani, in 1968-1969.

Jean was elected to the P.E.O. state board in 1962 and held every office of Nebraska State Chapter. As organizer, she organized five chapters: Chapter GK, Hastings; Chapter GL, Omaha; Chapter GM, Omaha; Chapter GN, Kimball (where she initiated her daughter Marian); and Chapter GO, North Platte. She attended the first Presidents' and Organizers' Conference held in Des Moines. Always interested in youth and students, Jean organized College Groups for P.E.O. in Hastings, Kearney, University of Nebraska and Wesleyan University. Jean served as Nebraska State Chapter's seventy-sixth president and presided at the 1969 convention in Lincoln, celebrating "*A Century of Sisterhood.*" Some of her pages were her daughters Judy and Marian (who came from Germany) and life-long friend, Jean Long. Frances Key and Phyllis Blanke presented a delightful story of the founding of P.E.O. that in turn served as the basis of the skit *A Star in the Window* written by Frances and Phyllis for the 1969 Centennial

Convention of Supreme Chapter in Des Moines. Jean served as president in the skit and gave the no-longer-used signs and passes, as remembered by Bertha Clark Hughes and Bernice Tillett, past presidents of Nebraska State Chapter. In 1972 Jean, serving as proxy organizer, visited eleven chapters.

After the 1969 Supreme Convention in Des Moines, Jean and Bill flew to Germany to visit daughter Marian and son-in-law Charles Payne. Together they toured Germany, Austria, Switzerland and visited their Italian daughter Paola in Italy. During the next few years, they saw much of the world on a dozen tours, including the 1970 and 1980 Passion Plays at Oberammergau. In 1982, they bought a condo in Sun City West, Arizona, where they enjoyed the balmy winters, the Sundome programs, the Phoenix opera, church activities, as well as frequent bridge games with P.E.O.s and Alpha Chis. P.E.O. "Chatter Groups" took the place of chapter meetings and P.E.O. friendships were enjoyable. Sadly, these days ended when Bill developed colon cancer and died on November 6, 1988, just days after Jean and Bill had celebrated their golden wedding anniversary.

Jean later moved to Northfield Villa in Gering, where she joined Chapter EV. Jean joined Chapter Eternal April 24, 1996.

Sheila B. Shreck

**NEBRASKA STATE CHAPTER PRESIDENT
1969-1970**

Sheila B. Shreck was born in Nelson, the daughter of Harvey A. and Ruth Brubaker. She was educated in south central Nebraska. In 1938 she graduated summa cum laude with an A.B. degree from Hastings College. She was listed in Who's Who Among College Women, was May Queen, and was president of the College YWCA. Her major fields of study were English, history and economics. She married Dr. Horace W. Shreck. They had two sons, both third generation doctors.

For fifteen years Sheila lived the life of a wife of an army doctor; this included a tour in the Canal Zone. During World War II, while her husband was overseas, she was employed with the Department of Justice, Federal Bureau of Investigation in New York City.

Sheila's activities included the Presbyterian Church, Cub Scouts, Hastings College Alumni Board, Adams County Medical Auxiliary, Shrine Hospital Auxiliary, Mary Lanning Hospital Auxiliary, Heart Fund, Bloodmobile, Fortnightly Study Club, Order of the Eastern Star, Daughters of the Nile, and ladies golf association. The Shreck family were all ardent sports fans. Sheila's special interests were bridge, golf, books, roses and ocean travel.

Sheila was initiated into her mother's chapter, J, Nelson, in 1939. Sheila was a member of Chapter H, Holdrege; Chapter G, Hastings; and dimitted to Chapter AC, Youngtown, Arizona. She held offices in all of her local chapters. Sheila served as general chairman for the Hastings convention in 1963, at which time she was elected treasurer of the state chapter. She served through all offices of the state board and served as Nebraska State Chapter's seventy-seventh president, presiding at the South Sioux City convention in 1970. Sheila headed the Nebraska delegation to the Centennial Convention of Supreme Chapter in Des Moines. In that convention she had a part in the skit, *A Star in the Window*. At the Detroit Supreme Convention in 1971, she served on the Amendments and Recommendations Committee. While she was on the state board, Sheila organized three Nebraska chapters: Chapter GP, Grand Island; Chapter GQ, Lincoln; and Chapter GR, Lexington.

The Shrecks moved to Sun City, Arizona, where Dr. Shreck had a practice in ophthalmology. Sheila died January 27, 2005.

Kathryn K. White

NEBRASKA STATE CHAPTER PRESIDENT
1970-1971

Kathryn Kerr was born in Central City, the daughter of William and Pearl Kerr. She was educated at the University of Nebraska and Nebraska Central College. Prior to her marriage to Elgin O. White, publisher of a weekly newspaper, she taught kindergarten and primary grades. During World War II, Kathryn taught junior high English. When her brother died, the Whites took his two-year-old son and raised him as their own.

The Whites belonged to the Methodist Episcopal Church, where for over twenty years Kathryn served as organist. She was a charter member of Job's Daughters, serving as an officer. Kathryn was one of a select group of women who had a private pilot's license. A member of the women's pilots association, the 99s, Kathryn's life-long interest was flying. Although there have been others since, at the time of her service on the Nebraska State Chapter board, Kathryn was the only member to ever have been a pilot.

In 1924 Kathryn was initiated into P.E.O. in Chapter AB, Central City. She served through every office of her local chapter. She served as co-chairman of the Grand Island Convention of 1964 and it was there that she was elected treasurer of Nebraska State Chapter. She held every office on the state board and presided over the York Convention in 1971 as Nebraska State Chapter's seventy-eighth president.

While she was on the state board, Kathryn organized Chapter GS, Norfolk.

Kathryn Kerr White died in Central City, Nebraska, on January 26, 1993.

Helen Magill

**NEBRASKA STATE CHAPTER PRESIDENT
1971-1972**

Helen Emig was the oldest of seven children born to David Nelson and Elsie Lee Emig on July 19, 1901, in Fremont, Nebraska. She graduated from Fremont High School and Midland College with a B.S. degree. She was a teacher and administrator of schools in Leshara, Arthur and Benedict. She came to Holdrege in 1926 as an English teacher. On October 28, 1936, Helen married Roy Magill, a Goodyear Tire representative in Holdrege.

Helen's life was filled with service to others. Her activities included serving as local, district and state president of the Women's Club, on the General Federation Convention Committee, and with the Literature and Drama and International Affairs departments. Helen received a commemorative medal from the Treasury Department for organizing the Women's Clubs of the state to sell savings bonds and stamps through the schools during World War II. She served ten years as Phelps County Red Cross chairman during the war years.

Other community organizations which have benefited from Helen's service include the Presbyterian Church, Memorial Homes, the Phelps County Memorial Hospital, the Naamah Temple of the Daughters of the Nile (where she served as an officer), the Phelps County Museum, the Priscilla Club and the Holdrege Garden Club. Helen is a charter member and was secretary for thirty-two years for the Holdrege Community Concert Association. She served as director and as one of three instructors of the Leadership Training for Youth activities, a course that was set up and given at all colleges and universities in Nebraska. It was funded by the Phillips Foundation and sponsored by Mrs. R. L. Cochran and the National Camp Fire. Helen received the Wo Hc Lo award for this pilot program. Helen was chosen to be included in *Who's Who of American Women*, Volume 1, 1958-1959, and subsequent early volumes.

Helen was initiated into Chapter H, Holdrege, in 1953. For five years she served her local chapter as an officer. She served as general chairman of the Holdrege state convention in 1965 and at that time was elected state treasurer. She served in all offices of the state board and at the 1972 Ogallala convention Helen served as Nebraska State Chapter's seventy-ninth president. While she was on the state board, Helen organized Chapter GT, O'Neill.

The Magills were avid travelers and enjoyed a trip around the world. Their other travels took them to all fifty states, all seven continents, and many large islands in the Pacific, the Caribbean and the Mediterranean. Roy passed away January 23, 1989. Helen died February 3, 1998, in Council Bluffs, Iowa.

Catherine C. Andersen
NEBRASKA STATE CHAPTER PRESIDENT
1972-1973

Catherine Cook Andersen was born in Omaha, the daughter of Edith M. and Curtiss E. Cook. She graduated from Stephens College and the University of Nebraska with distinction and an A.B. degree in sociology. She married Edwin M. Andersen. For twelve years she worked for the commercial department of Northwestern Bell Telephone Company as an area instructor and as an assignee to prepare training materials. During World War II she spent a year and a half in the Panama Canal Zone as an employee of the U.S. Corps of Engineers.

Catherine was a member of the First Presbyterian Church where she served as an officer in the Women's Association. For many years, she served as organist at the Wheeler Memorial United Presbyterian Church. She belonged to the Omaha Chapter of the American Guild of Organists and also the Alpha Xi Delta alumnae organization.

Catherine was initiated into Chapter CR, Omaha, on December 13, 1940. Her mother was a charter initiate of CR. She held all chapter offices except guard and chaplain. She was general chairman of the Omaha convention in 1966, where she was elected treasurer of the state chapter. She held every state office and presided as Nebraska State Chapter's eightieth president in 1973. She was elected delegate to Supreme Chapter Conventions three times, in 1967, 1969, and 1973. She served on the program at Supreme Convention in 1973 as an accompanying organist. At the 1972 Presidents' and Organizers' Conference in Des Moines in 1972, she served as organist for the worship service. Catherine served until 1980 as Nebraska State Chapter's first assistant secretary-treasurer. While serving on the state board, Catherine organized Chapter GU, Omaha; and Chapter GV, Lincoln.

Catherine Andersen moved to the P.E.O. Home in Beatrice and died April 1, 1999.

Two turtles discussing ethics. The first one says, "Sometimes I'd like to ask God why he allows poverty, famine, and injustice when he could do something about it."

The other turtle says, "I'm afraid God might ask me the same question."

Janet Atkins

NEBRASKA STATE CHAPTER PRESIDENT
1973-1974

Janet was born in McCook, the daughter of Mary Bernice Rector and John Nissen Gaarde. She received her education in the McCook public schools and in McCook College. On June 20, 1942, she married Neal Willard Atkins. They had three children: Carolyn, Marilyn, and Thomas Neal. Mr. Atkins died February 1, 1963. Janet lived most of her life in Nebraska except for two years when she traveled the country with her husband during World War II.

Janet resided in Lincoln for a time where she served as assistant loan officer for the Cornhusker Bank. She was a member of the First United Methodist Church. She served the church for fifteen years in the Women's Society, six years on the church board, and four years on the worship commission. In Sidney, she organized the local P.T.A., served on the parent's advisory council at Sidney High School, and in both McCook and Sidney, she served as president of Beta Sigma Phi sorority. Janet was an accomplished musician. Her entire family played the piano, sang and some played other instruments. Janet enjoyed swimming, golf, tennis and bridge, especially duplicate.

Janet was initiated into Chapter BO, Sidney, in 1953. For six years she served her local chapter as recording secretary, vice president and president. At the state convention in Sidney in 1967, she served as general chairman and was elected to the state board as treasurer. She served through every office in the state chapter and presided at the 1974 convention in Peru as Nebraska State Chapter's eighty-first president. While she was on the state board, Janet organized Chapter GW, Lincoln.

Janet moved to Elk Grove, California, where she lived with her son Tom, a physician. She died February 27, 1998.

Ring the bells that still can ring.
Forget your perfect offering.
There is a crack in everything.
That's how the light gets in.

-Leonard Cohen

Ellen Ann Qualsett

NEBRASKA STATE CHAPTER PRESIDENT
1974-1975

Ellen Ann was born on January 8, 1919, at St. Paul, Nebraska, the daughter of Robert Armstrong and Elnora Christensen Armstrong. She attended elementary and secondary schools in St. Paul, Nebraska, and one year at Colorado Women's College. She completed her B.S. degree from the University of Nebraska at Lincoln in 1940. During her college years, Ellen Ann was employed by the Citizens National Bank which was managed by her father. After her college graduation, she taught science in the Tekamah Public Schools. In 1941 she married Harold Qualsett and she took a position as science teacher in the St. Paul schools. In 1943, she worked as an experimental chemist with Shell Oil in Long Beach, California, where Harold was stationed during his military service.

The Qualsetts had three sons: David, Richard and Robert. During their married life, the Qualsetts resided in St. Paul, Tekamah, and Clarkson. When they purchased the First National Bank in Schuyler, the family moved there. Upon Harold's death in 1972, Ellen Ann was elected president of the bank and she held that position until her death.

Ellen Ann was active in many community and civic organizations: She served as a member on the boards of the Nebraska Art Foundation, the Schuyler Public Library, the Colfax Foundation, Dana College Board of Regents, and Central Community College. She was also affiliated with the Nebraska Bankers Association, the Order of the Eastern Star, Nebraska Associated Artists, Schuyler Memorial Hospital Auxiliary and St. John's Lutheran Church. Ellen Ann was recognized statewide for her work with prison ministry and served on the board of the Prison Fellowship State Council. She also was recognized for a gift of $100,000 to the University of Nebraska at Lincoln for research grants, scholarships and fellowships. A similar gift to Dana College in Blair made possible an area in the Dana Classroom Center known as The Forum, an art exhibition and learning center. She made this gift in memory of her husband Harold, a Dana graduate.

Ellen Ann was initiated into P.E.O. in St. Paul, Chapter AP, where she grew up. She later dimitted to Chapter DC, Tekamah, and CT, North Bend. On February 5, 1977, she became a charter member of Chapter HG, Schuyler. Ellen Ann served as the eighty-second president of Nebraska State Chapter and presided at the 1975 convention in Crete. Her convention theme was *"Walk in the Light"* from a quotation from 1 John 1:7. While she was on the state board, Ellen organized Chapter GX, South Sioux City. She was appointed as a member of International Chapter's P.E.O. Foundation Committee and served for several years until her poor health forced her to resign.

Ellen Ann Qualsett died September 9, 1993, in Lincoln, Nebraska. Her burial was in Schuyler.

Doris Cunningham
NEBRASKA STATE CHAPTER PRESIDENT
1975-1976

Doris Cunningham was born and raised in a rural area of Otoe County. In 1941, she married her husband Roger who later became affiliated with the First National Bank of Lincoln. The Cunninghams had four children: Robert, John, Susan and Nancy. Both girls are P.E.O.s and served as pages at Doris's convention.

Doris was a Nebraska delegate to the National 4-H conference in Washington, D.C. in 1935. She attended Peru State College for two years, Merrill Palmer in Detroit for a semester, and the University of Nebraska, graduating in 1939 with a B.S. degree in Vocational Home Economics. She taught in Cambridge, Sidney, and Minden, and later did substitute teaching and adult classes in millinery and genealogy in Scottsbluff and Lincoln. For 15 years she was known as the "hat lady" in Lincoln.

On January 14, 1953, Doris was initiated into P.E.O. in Scottsbluff, in Chapter CD. In 1955 she dimitted to Chapter CS, Lincoln.

She was elected to the state board in 1971 and served Nebraska State Chapter for seven years, presiding at the 1976 convention in Lincoln as the eighty-third president. Doris chose as the theme for the Bicentennial year convention, "*The Spirit of P.E.O.—A Patchwork of Many Special Things.*" The convention was filled with special things. Centered on the stage was a special P.E.O. quilt lovingly developed by all 207 chapters in Nebraska under the skilled guidance of Bev Kimball of Chapter GG, Kearney. Since convention, the quilt has hung at the P.E.O. Home in Beatrice. Added interest on the stage was provided by antique quilts draped over old trunks, crockery, patchwork pillows and ferns. Guards and pages wore long colonial-style dresses with pinafore patchwork aprons and cottage bonnets. Throughout the convention, bouquets of yellow gingham marguerites, pots of calico flowers, gingham-tied box suppers, and bright patchwork tote bags emphasized the theme. Frances Key presented a special pageant, directed by Phyllis Blanke, entitled *Patchwork Pattern of P.E.O. Heritage*. Presented in pantomime and using colored slides, authentic costumes and coiffures, the pageant depicted the beginnings and high points of the achievements of P.E.O. Music was provided by the Lincoln Reciprocity Roundtable Singers. While Doris was on the state board, she organized Chapter GY, McCook, and served as proxy organizer for Chapter GZ, Hastings.

Following the death of her husband Roger, Doris moved to Wilsonville, Oregon, to be near her family. She died May 1, 2012.

Vera (Bobbie) Koefoot

NEBRASKA STATE CHAPTER PRESIDENT
1976-1977

★ **INTERNATIONAL OFFICER**
1987-1990

Vera (Bobbie) Koefoot was born in Jerome, Idaho, but she and her husband Bob were raised in Broken Bow, Nebraska. Bobbie attended the University of Nebraska where she received a B.S. in education. They were married during Bob's last year in medical school. In 1954, after his residency and military commitments, the Koefoots moved to Grand Island, Nebraska. Five children were born to the Koefoots: four daughters and a son—Bonnie, Ann, Adele, Carol and Robert Jr.

During the years her children were in school, Bobbie was involved in various activities which support youth. She provided leadership for their many activities. Bobbie was a member of the Presbyterian Church, Daughters of the Nile, Medical Auxiliary, a board member of the YWCA and a Red Cross volunteer. Her hobbies and special interests included family activities, reading and bridge.

Bobbie was initiated into Chapter EH, Grand Island, and she became a charter member of Chapter GP, Grand Island, in 1966. All four of her daughters were initiated into Chapter GP. She served six years on the board of Nebraska State Chapter, serving as their eighty-fourth president at the 1977 convention in Hastings. Her convention theme was *"Take My Hand—It's A Small World."* Bobbie served the state chapter in other capacities: in 1979-1981 as chairman of the Research Committee and as workshop leader from 1978 through 1987. While Bobbie served on the state board, she organized Chapter HA, Columbus, and served as proxy organizer for Chapter HH, York.

In 1981, Bobbie was appointed to the Finance Committee of International Chapter. She served six years on that committee and as chairman in the 1985-1987 biennium. At the 1987 Convention of International Chapter in Orlando, Florida, Bobbie was elected recording secretary of International Chapter. Shortly after that, because of a vacancy on the International Chapter board, she was appointed second vice president. At the following convention in Phoenix in 1989, Bobbie was elected first vice president of International Chapter. Nebraska State Chapter was so looking forward to celebrating with Bobbie her election as president of International Chapter in Omaha. Tragically, Bobbie died while serving as first vice president of International Chapter.

Vera (Bobbie) Koefoot died in Grand Island, Nebraska, on December 15, 1990.

Barbara Cobb

NEBRASKA STATE CHAPTER PRESIDENT
1977-1978

Barbara was born January 11, 1915, in Seattle, Washington, the daughter of Maude Booth and Clarence Benton Myers. When she was an infant, her family moved to Salina, Kansas, where she graduated from high school and Marymount College. On August 10, 1936, she married Ed Cobb, a realtor. They moved to Ogallala in 1945. There were two Cobb children, Diane England, also a realtor, and Dr. E. Benton Cobb, a professor of mathematics at Kansas University. There were three grandchildren.

Barbara was a noted Bible scholar, lecturer and leader in the United Methodist Church on the local, state and national levels for more than thirty years. For seventeen years, Barbara served as a nationally-accredited teacher for Methodist Schools of Christian Mission and taught in sixteen states. She was elected delegate to the quadrennial General Conference of the church four times from 1960 to 1972 and to consecutive multi-state Jurisdictional Conferences from 1960 to 1976. Barbara also served as a state officer of the United Methodist Women for thirteen years and as the state president from 1959 to 1961.

Barbara also served as trustee of the Iliff School of Theology in Denver and for the Nebraska Methodist Board of Diaconal Ministry. She served as dean of the Methodist Regional School of Mission in Fayetteville, Arkansas, from 1968 to 1970. The school trains about 400 church leaders a year.

Other honors were bestowed upon Barbara. She was named Nebraska Bicentennial Mother of the Year in 1976 and State Future Homemakers of America Mother of the Year in 1959. In 1967, she was named distinguished graduate of Marymount College, Salina, Kansas, from which she was a summa cum laude graduate. Barbara was the first woman ever named to the National Radio Commission which airs the Protestant Radio Hour over 500 stations. She also served on the Jurisdictional Television, Radio and Film Commission. Barbara is listed in *Who's Who in American Women*, and *Who's Who in the Midwest and International Biography*.

Barbara led four tours to the Holy Land and another to Switzerland and England. At the time of her death, she was organizing a trip to Europe to see the Passion Play in Germany. She conducted studies on the Middle East throughout the state and as a teacher for Schools of Christian Missions. She taught subjects ranging from Bible Studies and the "Role and Status of Women" to courses on other lands such as China, Africa, Japan and India.

Barbara was initiated into Chapter CL, Ogallala. She served on the Executive Board of Nebraska State Chapter for six years, serving as their eighty-fifth president. She presided at the 1978 convention in Grand Island. Her convention theme was "*Choose Life*." While she was on the state board, Barbara organized three chapters in Nebraska: Chapter HB, Kearney; Chapter HC, Bellevue; and Chapter HD, Lincoln.

Barbara Cobb died on June 1, 1980.

Lois Ann Hansen

NEBRASKA STATE CHAPTER PRESIDENT
1978-1979

Lois Ann Hansen was born in Chicago, Illinois, the daughter of Frances Corrigan and James Harold Roberts. She received a B. A. degree in speech and drama from Marymount College. On September 14, 1950, she married James Thomsen Hansen in Hastings, Nebraska. They had five children: David, Thomsen, Kristin, Mark and John.

Lois Ann was initiated into Chapter G, Hastings, in 1958 and served her second term as its president during its Centennial Year of 1989. She served as Nebraska State Chapter's eighty-sixth president at the 1979 convention in North Platte. Because North Platte was the home of Nebraskaland days, the hostess chapters chose a western motif for convention. Lois Ann's theme was *"Let Us Then Be Up and Doing."* While Lois Ann was on the board, she organized two chapters in Nebraska, Chapter HE, Lincoln; and Chapter HF, Omaha.

One of Lois Ann's favorite quotations that she used often during her chapter visitations was from John Janovy, Jr., in his Keith County Journal, "For I and those close to me have been the recipients of untold gifts, whose value increase daily. The donors have very often been people who did not realize at the time what they were giving. The gifts have been those of time, talents, visions, performances; but most of all, they have been the gifts of opportunity."

After her husband's death, Lois Ann moved to Englewood, Colorado. She dimitted to Chapter HB, Colorado, in 1993 then dimitted back to G Hastings in February 2009. Lois Ann went inactive in 2009 and now lives in Littleton, Colorado.

You are a child of God.
Your playing small does not serve the world.
There is nothing enlightened about shrinking.
    -Marianne Williamson

Frances Key

NEBRASKA STATE CHAPTER PRESIDENT
1979-1980

Frances Key was born in St. Paul, the daughter of Mr. and Mrs. J. C. McChesney. Frances found it difficult to distinguish between her profession and her hobby because they both revolved around the arts. A native Nebraskan, Frances was graduated from the University of Nebraska at Lincoln, where she was a member of Delta Delta Delta, Phi Lambda Theta, and Mortar Board. She received a Bachelor of Science degree in education with a major in dramatics, which led to a teaching career in English, public speaking, and drama in Lincoln and Omaha public high schools, Brownell Hall and the University of Nebraska at Omaha.

After her marriage to Dr. Walter Key, an oral surgeon, on December 25, 1943, she carried her same interest into the volunteer field, presenting programs, book reviews, and skits for civic or social clubs, churches and hospital benefits. She served for many years on the Board of Trustees of the Omaha Community Playhouse, two terms as its president, and received several awards for her work with the playhouse. She received the President's Award and two Fonda-McGuire Awards. Frances was co-founder of the Omaha Playhouse Guild. Her other activities included membership in Joslyn Museum Women's Auxiliary, board of Nebraska Arts Council, and Children's Theater, which she served both as a board member and at times, as director. She was also a member of the First Presbyterian Church, Mortar Board Alumnae, Mu Sigma Study Club, Midmonth Book Club, and the Nebraska Methodist Hospital Auxiliary.

Frances was initiated into Chapter M, Omaha, in 1949, and later dimitted to become a charter member of Chapter FK. Her mother also was a member of Chapter FK. Frances served as general chairman for the 1973 Omaha convention and was elected to the state board at that convention. Frances served six years on the state executive board. In 1980 at the Omaha convention, she presided as Nebraska State Chapter's eighty-seventh president. Her convention theme was *"Let the Star in the Window Light a Path in the World."* During her term on the state executive board, Frances organized Chapter HG, Schuyler.

Intrigued by the early history of P.E.O., Frances from time to time put it into dramatic form for local and state chapter programs. In 1969, she wrote the skit *A Star in the Window* which Nebraska presented for the Centennial Convention of Supreme Chapter. This delving into P.E.O. history brought a great appreciation for the way in which the rays of that star hold close the members of each chapter, yet how far they radiate to bring hope and happiness to others through P.E.O. projects.

Frances Key died December 21, 1996, in Omaha.

Mary Ruth Wilson

NEBRASKA STATE CHAPTER PRESIDENT
1980-1981

Mary Ruth Wilson was born in Dexter, Missouri, the daughter of Eva and George Coy. Mary Ruth and her husband Gilbert lived in Peru, Nebraska. He retired as director of musical activities at Peru State College. The Wilsons were a very musical family. Their daughter, Mary Ellen Oestmann, was a music teacher at Northeast High School in Lincoln. Mary Ellen was a member of Chapter HD, Lincoln. Their son Jim was a music teacher of stringed instruments, and daughter Janet Grush lived in Omaha and was a member of Chapter CY.

Mary Ruth was a member of the Presbyterian Church and served as director of music for several churches in the area. She served as branch president of A.A.U.W. and was a member of Delta Kappa Gamma. She served for years as Director of Continuing Education at Peru State College in Peru, Nebraska.

In 1954, Mary Ruth was initiated into Chapter AN in Galesburg, Illinois. She dimitted to Chapter AU, Peru, when the family moved to Nebraska. Mary Ruth served in all of the offices of the state chapter, and served as their eighty-eighth president, presiding at the 1981 convention in Chadron. Mary Ruth had the designation of being the first full-time employed president of the state chapter. While serving on the state board, Mary Ruth organized two Nebraska chapters: Chapter HI, Ogallala; and Chapter HJ, Grand Island.

The theme of the 1981 convention in Chadron was *"Walk in Beauty"* from a Navajo poem. One of the special memories of that convention was the gift each delegate was given—a Ponderosa pine seedling in a paper cup to be taken to their homes all over the state and planted. Mary Ruth's tree is growing strong and beautiful. The convention committee cleverly decorated with old shoes and cutout footprints in keeping with the *"Walk in Beauty"* theme. One of the most interesting parts of convention was Mary Ruth's pageant written and presented as a take-off on William Shakespeare's various well-known lines in his plays. The narrator was played by Mary Ruth. Shylock, from *The Merchant of Venice*, was aghast at the way P.E.O. handled their projects. He was sure that much more profit could be realized if they just handled it "his way." At that convention, the delegation voted to give $1 per member to the Cottey Golden Anniversary Fund. This amounted to a donation of over $12,000.

After serving as P.E.O. state president, Mary Ruth retired as Director of Continuing Education at Peru State College. Her retirement activities included resuming piano teaching, and accepting the position of Director of Music at Peru Community Church, where she was organist and chancel choir director.

She also became very involved in the Peru Chamber of Commerce by helping to establish two major projects—a community newsletter called *Peru Printout* and the Peru Historical Foundation which was restoring a building for use as a museum. Mary Ruth served as president of the foundation. She also took leadership in restoring the 1912 fifteen-rank Barckhoff pipe organ in the Peru Community Church. The completion of its restoration depended upon an extensive fundraising campaign.

In 1988, Mary Ruth received the Citizen of the Year Award and at the 1991 Convention of International Chapter in Omaha performed a two-piano selection with another Nebraska State Chapter president, Bernice Zajicek.

Mary Ruth and Gil Wilson lived in Peru, Nebraska, where Mary Ruth died October 28, 2003.

Bernice Greer Zajicek
Nebraska State Chapter President
1981-1982

Bernice Greer Zajicek, salutatorian of the Class of 1943, received a Bachelor of Music in Education degree in 1948, and a Master of Music degree from the University of Nebraska at Lincoln in 1975. She and classmate Glenn Zajicek were married in Washington, D.C., in 1944 and had three sons. Bill was a mortician with Glenn and lived in Wilber with his wife Jeanette. Son Tom, a Certified Public Accountant, died in 1994; Rick, a Doctor of Optometry, lived in Chicago with his wife Debra. The Zajicek's enjoyed their many grandchildren: Ginger, Wendy, Nicole, Molly, and Abby; a step-grandson and granddaughter Matt Kunc and Tammy Packer and two great-granddaughters, Chrissy Kunc and Samantha Colgate and two great-grandsons, Michael Colgate and Bobby Packer.

Bernice was very active in community organizations and also held state offices in the American Legion Auxiliary as music chairman, Girls' State counselor and president, Grand Organist of the Eastern Star, and as a member of the Board of Directors of the Masonic-Eastern Star Home for Children in Fremont. She also served as organist of the First Lutheran Church in Wilber for over forty years and as choir director, vacation Bible school director and music leader. She also chaired the committee to secure a lovely Baldwin organ for the church. In 1989, she wrote the centennial hymn, *The Church Lives On* for the church's 100-year celebration. She retired after serving as piano accompanist for the junior and senior choirs in the Wilber-Clatonia schools for twenty years.

In 1992 Bernice was selected as Lady of the Year by local chapters of Beta Sigma Phi, national business women's sorority. She was a private piano teacher and helped to develop the musical abilities of many students, including six Miss Nebraska Czech Queens, over a span of fifty years. Bernice and Glenn were very active in the 'Nebraska Czechs of Wilber', promoting the community and its heritage. They made generous donations to the swimming pool and Wilber Nursing Home. They contributed many hours to restoring Hotel Wilber and donated a room in memory of their parents.

Bernice was initiated into Chapter BF, Wilber, in 1963. She served in four offices of her local chapter, including president. She served as a Cottey College Area Chairman and as general chairman of the state convention in 1975 at Doane College in Crete. There she was elected as treasurer of the state board. She served in the seven offices of the executive board and in 1982 she presided as Nebraska State Chapter's eighty-ninth president at Wayne. Her convention theme was "*P.E.O. — Our Melody of Love.*" To her, "P.E.O. love is an extension of the steadfast love we receive from God, sung to our families, our friends, and to our P.E.O. sisters, a beautiful consonant sound created in the beginning of time, continuing to grow, and becoming the ethereal music of the future." While she was on the state board, Bernice organized two chapters in Nebraska, Chapter HK, Fremont; and Chapter HL, Blair. After serving as state president, Bernice served for three years on the Amendments and Recommendations Committee.

On June 24, 1994, Bernice and Glenn celebrated their fiftieth wedding anniversary in Wilber where they were life-long residents. Bernice died November 16, 2004.

Helen Curtiss

NEBRASKA STATE CHAPTER PRESIDENT
1982-1983

Helen Curtiss lived in Nebraska all of her life. Her college education included Nebraska Wesleyan, Lindenwood in Missouri, and the University of Nebraska, where she met her husband Art, a Lincoln attorney. The major part of her education was raising four sons! John lived in Denver, Jim in Washington D.C. and Alan and David in Lincoln.

Years of Helen's volunteer work were "boy-oriented," including serving as Cub Scout den-mother, as a Sunday school teacher, soap box derby enthusiast, pink lady and many years in the P.T.A. She received honorary life membership in Nebraska P.T.A. as well as national life membership. Another challenge and also a joy were her nine granddaughters. Helen was a member of the Trinity Methodist Church and served on the Board of Trustees. She also served as president of the Lincoln Attorneys Wives.

Helen's hobbies were gardening, sewing, reading, volleyball, handicrafts and playing bridge.

Helen was initiated into Chapter ES, Lincoln, in 1957. She held all offices in her chapter and the Lincoln Round Table. At the 1976 Lincoln convention, Helen was general chairman and elected to serve as treasurer for the state board. After serving all seven offices on the board, she presided at the 1983 Lincoln convention as Nebraska State Chapter's ninetieth president. While serving on the state board, Helen organized four chapters in Nebraska: Chapter HM, Holdrege; Chapter HN, Scottsbluff; Chapter HO, North Platte; and Chapter HP, Omaha.

Helen's theme for the 1983 convention was "*P.E.O.—A Garden Where Love Grows.*" The highlight of the convention was the project skit, *P.E.O. in Bloom*, which was skillfully produced and directed by Jean Patoka and Phyllis Blanke. P.E.O.s from all over Lincoln sang and danced their way through a story of the P.E.O. projects. The guards wore denim jumpers appliqued with a red clay pot with a yellow tulip and they wore yellow blouses. The Guard's March was the music of Willa Foster Jones. Helen relates the meaning of her theme: "Many years ago the Founders planted a seed and we have seen the strong roots of those seven: we have seen the budding and beautiful blossoms and the many shades and hues of the blooms in our P.E.O. garden of love. We must cultivate our own special gift of P.E.O. and continue to plant strong seeds and help them to blossom and bloom."

Helen dimitted as a charter member to Chapter IL, Lincoln, on May 2, 1992. Helen and Art lived in Lincoln. Helen died March 23, 2013.

Julia A. McDougal

NEBRASKA STATE CHAPTER PRESIDENT
1983-1984

Julia A. McDougal was born in Nemaha County, Kansas, the daughter of Jay L. and Mary Beamer Crom. She was educated in the Pawnee County, Nebraska, schools, graduating from Pawnee City High School in 1942. She graduated from the University of Nebraska in 1946 with a major in home economics. She taught school for several years and also was on the staff of the University of Nebraska extension service.

Following her marriage in February 1952, she and her husband, O.J. McDougal, Jr., spent three years living in Banes, Oriente, Cuba, where he was employed as a research agronomist for the United Fruit Sugar Company. They have lived in Hastings, Nebraska, since 1957 when he joined the staff of City National Bank. He retired as Chairman of the Board. Julia has served as deacon and elder in the Presbyterian Church.

Three daughters and one son were born to this family. Their son, Owen James III, died in 1987. Daughters Ann Koozer, Susan May, and Sarah, all are active in the leadership of their respective P.E.O. chapters. Julia's husband, Jim, died in 2008.

Julia was initiated into Chapter DA, Hastings, on March 17, 1961. She served as chairman of the state convention in 1977, when Vera Koefoot was state president. She served all offices on the state board and in 1984 presided as Nebraska State Chapter's ninety-first president. Julia organized three chapters in Nebraska while she was on the state board: Chapter HQ, North Platte; Chapter HR, Gibbon; and

Chapter HS, Alliance. She also has served as the Historian and Custodian of Articles of Historical Value for Nebraska State Chapter. She and her husband Jim served as chairmen of BIL activities for the 1991 Omaha Convention of International Chapter.

For her convention theme in 1984, Julia chose *"To Seek Growth"* as a reflection of her belief in the possibility of personal growth as members relate to one another as caring sisters. She was particularly pleased that her sister, Virginia Metzger, AV, and her three daughters served as pages during the convention at Dana College in Blair. Chapters HY, Omaha, and HZ, Hartington, were presented with their charters at this convention. Julia remembers fondly the talk given by Past President of Supreme Chapter Irene Van Brunt in a final appearance on the Nebraska State Chapter Convention program and also the final presentation given by Past State President Dorothy Smithberger to a state convention. Dorothy served the state chapter well as historian and editor of the "green" history, *Saga of Nebraska P.E.O.*

Julia McDougal lives in Hastings.

June Steggs
NEBRASKA STATE CHAPTER PRESIDENT
1984-1985

June is a native Nebraskan. Having been born in Hyannis, her childhood years were spent in the Sandhills region of Nebraska. She attended high school in Alliance. Her college years were spent at Stephens College in Columbia, Missouri, where she graduated with a major in business administration and a minor in home economics.

June's husband Jerry is deceased. She and Jerry had two married children. A son Jeff resides in Imperial, Nebraska, with his wife Dianna. A daughter, Jan Steggs Leckway, resides in Highlands Ranch, Colorado, with her husband Chip and young daughter Eliza. Jerry was self-employed in many phases of aviation for many years.

June is a member of St. Patrick's Catholic Church in Imperial. She also is a member of the Ft. Kearney NSDAR and enjoys doing genealogy research. Other interests which fill June's spare moments are reading, crocheting, cross stitching and enjoying "Big Red" football games.

June received the gift of P.E.O. in 1965 when she was initiated into Chapter S, Broken Bow, Nebraska. Through the years, June has been very dedicated to serving P.E.O., as it has been a very enriching part of her life. She served in all seven offices of the state board and presided as Nebraska State Chapter's ninety-second president at the convention in Columbus in 1985. While she served on the state board she organized three chapters in the state of Nebraska: Chapter HT, Hastings; Chapter HU, Norfolk; and Chapter HV, Lexington. Following her presidency June was elected to the Nebraska P.E.O. Home Board of Trustees for a five-year term, serving as president for four years. She currently is serving her chapter as chaplain, an office she did not hold in earlier years.

June wrote a poem from which she used the last phrase as her convention theme:
'Ere deep within the heart let dwell
Love's soft warm glow.
This is the dream our Founders founded,
"Lovingly in P.E.O."

June's theme for the 1985 state convention was "Lovingly in P.E.O." Reciprocity Group VII was the hostess group under the leadership of Shirley Deyke, convention chairman. The guards and pages wore aprons like those of the Founders over yellow jumpers and white blouses. Joan Bradshaw, second vice president of International Chapter, was the representative from Ohio. For June, her theme is the essence of P.E.O.

June Steggs lives in Imperial, Nebraska.

Marion Larmon

**NEBRASKA STATE CHAPTER PRESIDENT
1985-1986**

Marion L. Larmon was born in Lincoln, Nebraska, the daughter of William R. and LaVerne Harrison Patton. She was educated in Lincoln and attended the University of Nebraska where she was a member of Alpha Phi sorority. While at the university, she met Harold Larmon, an Alpha Tau Omega from McCook. Upon Harold's graduation from the university and his completion of Officer's Candidate School, U.S. Marine Corps, they were married on October 10, 1942. Following the war they returned to McCook where they lived for 60 years until his death, at which time Marion moved to Lincoln to be near family. The Larmons have two children, Courtney and Craig, three grandchildren and five great grandchildren.

Marion was initiated into Chapter X, McCook, in January 1948. She was a member of Chapter FD, Omaha, in 1950 and 1951, and a member of Chapter DA, Hastings, in 1951-1953. Marion always has been active in P.E.O. She served as a Cottey Area Chairman and on other state committees. She served in every office of her local chapter and participated in many state conventions as guard, soloist and committee member. She completed all of the state offices and in 1986 presided as Nebraska State Chapter's ninety-third president in Peru. She has attended eight Supreme and International Conventions. Marion organized Chapter HW, Lincoln, and Chapter HX, Omaha.

Marion's convention theme was "New Horizons," appropriate as the 1986 convention was the first to be held on a weekend. Another innovation at the convention included holding the honors recognition at a luncheon rather than at night so more honorees could attend. Both innovations proved to be successful and well received by the delegates.

Especially meaningful to Marion was having her daughter, Courtney Townsend, Chapter CG, Lubbock, Texas (a fifth-generation P.E.O.) as her page, along with Courtney's former Cottey suitemate, Beth Kaiser Flynn of Chapter HG, Schuyler. During Marion's year as president, she was in charge of the delegation attending the Convention of International Chapter at Winnipeg, Canada.

A beautiful set of china was given to the P.E.O. Home in Beatrice in Marion's honor representing monetary gifts from family and friends.

New horizons aptly describe Marion's philosophy that there is always something to learn. She developed an interest in aviation, and although she was not the first state president to have a pilot's license, she went further to earn a commercial rating and also a glider license.

Both Marion and Harold Larmon shared state and community interests, having served on many boards and foundations, and both were active in music activities. They enjoyed traveling, home and family. Marion is now living in Lincoln and is a member of Chapter DL.

Susan Harr

NEBRASKA STATE CHAPTER PRESIDENT
1986-1987

Susan Harr began her P.E.O. experience at the knee of her mother, Dorothy Smithberger, who was serving as an officer of Nebraska State Chapter. Susan was only twelve when Dorothy was president. They are the only mother-daughter combination to serve as presidents of Nebraska State Chapter.

Susan was raised in Stanton, Nebraska, where her father Louis was in the cattle and grain business. She loved hours spent with her father in the Sandhills and for years helped him in his business while she was living in Omaha. The two-hour drive back and forth gave her time to organize and to plan for her P.E.O. and family activities.

With her husband Larry, she raised four children. Larry was counsel for Mutual of Omaha for twenty-four years, and retired from there as Senior Executive Vice President. He became a partner of Lamson, Dugan and Murray Law firm. Daughter Sharyl is married to Steve Baca. They live in Omaha and have six children (Zachary, Brianna, Eileen, Susan, Keenan, and Maura) who make regular treks through two backyards to Grandma's house. Steven has a medical degree but has spent several years working on Wall Street. He and his wife Allison (Oaks) have two children, Carolina and Jackson. Twins Brian and Burke both practice law in Omaha. Brian and his wife Sarah (Stuckey) have two sons, Leo and Sam. Burke and his wife Jennifer (Peterson) have three children, Rita, Augusta and Ambrose. Burke serves as a state senator.

Susan graduated from the University of Nebraska at Lincoln in 1965 with a degree in journalism and home economics. She is a member of Kappa Kappa Gamma sorority, was editor of The Daily Nebraskan, and was an Ak-Sar-Ben countess. Her son Brian informed her that before he asked his bride out on a second date he found out she was both a Kappa and a P.E.O. so he thought it would be alright.

Susan was on the Nebraska State Executive Board during child-raising years so was on the sidelines of soccer, basketball, baseball, debate, speech and 4-H dog shows. She was active in school parent groups, and was a leader in Girl Scouts, Cub Scouts and 4-H.

As a young person, Susan was a reporter for the Omaha World-Herald. Years later, as an empty-nester, she became a realtor, from which she retired in 2013. She is active in Assistance League of Omaha, and Prayer Shawl group at her church.

Susan was initiated into Chapter DF, Stanton, and was a charter member of Chapter GM, Omaha. When the family moved to the Chicago area, she dimitted to Chapter EP, Palatine, Illinois. Upon their return to Omaha, she joined Chapter BP where she is now proudly a member. Susan was elected treasurer of the state board at the 1980 Omaha convention. She served in all offices of the state board and in 1987 presided as Nebraska State Chapter's ninety-fourth president. While she was on the board, Susan organized two Nebraska chapters, HY, Omaha, and HZ, Hartington.

When the Executive Board of Nebraska State Chapter issued an invitation to entertain Convention of International Chapter in 1991, Susan was serving her first year on the state board. As a board member she continued to be involved in the initial plans for convention, and in 1987 became assistant chairman for the Executive Planning Board of Convention. She also served on the Finance and Budget Committee, the Chapter Groupings Committee, and the Nominating Committee for Nebraska State Chapter. She is currently serving as Historian and Custodian of Historical Articles.

"The horse is here today,
but the automobile is only a novelty - a fad."
— *President of Michigan Savings Bank*
advising against investing in the Ford Motor Company

"Video won't be able to hold on to any market it captures
after the first six months. People will soon get tired of
staring at a plywood box every night."
— *Daryl F. Zanuck, 20th Century Fox, commenting on television in 1946*

W. Joyce Goff

NEBRASKA STATE CHAPTER PRESIDENT
1987-1988

★ INTERNATIONAL CHAPTER PRESIDENT
2003-2005

Willa Joyce Goff was born in Ord, Nebraska, the daughter of Ernest and Bessie Achen. She attended school at Ord, Hastings College and Nebraska Wesleyan University. Joyce was valedictorian of her high school class and because of achievements in high school was made an honorary Admiral in the Nebraska Navy. Joyce was a member of Phi Kappa Phi scholastic honorary society at Wesleyan. She graduated from college in 1951. In the years that followed, Joyce taught school in Sidney, Ord, and Alliance in Nebraska and at Ramey Air Force Base in Puerto Rico. She also operated and taught a private preschool for ten years. In August of 1951, Joyce was married to Wayne A. Goff of Ord. Wayne is a graduate of the University of Nebraska. Wayne and Joyce have two children, Allen and Jane. Allen is married to Shelley Hoover of Lincoln and Jane is married to Scott Nelsen of Norfolk. The Goffs have three grandchildren: Jay Nelsen and Ashley and Spencer Goff.

Joyce is a professional registered parliamentarian. She has served as president of the Grand Island unit and has held several offices in the Nebraska State Association of Parliamentarians.

Joyce served as church librarian for a total of thirty years in Alliance and Grand Island United Methodist churches. She served as president of Trinity United Methodist Women in Grand Island and for several years served as conference parliamentarian. Joyce was initiated into P.E.O. by Chapter GC in Alliance, Nebraska, in December of 1965. She served in every office except treasurer in Chapter GC.

In 1981, Joyce was elected to serve on the Nebraska State Chapter Executive Board. She held every office on that board and in 1988 presided as Nebraska State Chapter's ninety-fifth president at the convention in Kimball. The theme of Joyce's term as president was, "*P.E.O....small as a daisy, great as a star.*" The guest of honor at that convention was Jean Boswell, past president of New Mexico, who served on the International Study and Research Committee and later served on the International executive board. Another special guest was Helen Washburn, then president of Cottey College.

In 1985, the Goffs moved to Grand Island, Nebraska, and Joyce dimitted to Chapter HJ. Joyce has enjoyed many wonderful opportunities to grow in P.E.O. In Orlando, Florida, in 1987, she issued the first invitation to Convention of International Chapter which was to be held in Omaha in 1991. In 1988, Joyce was the guest speaker at the President's and Organizer's Conference in Des Moines. At the Convention of International Chapter in 1989, Joyce issued an amusing invitation to hold the next International Convention in Omaha, Nebraska. When the meeting adjourned Joyce trembled as she saw Past State President of Nebraska Irene Van Brunt walking down the aisle toward her. Joyce was sure she was about to be scolded for the way she had given the invitation. Instead, Irene amazed her by complimenting her presentation! In 1990, Joyce accepted a five-year appointment to the Study and Research Committee of International Chapter. She served as chairman of that committee during the 1993-95 biennium. In 1991, she served as chairman of and speaker at the "Hour of Remembrance" at the Convention of International Chapter in Omaha. In 1995, Joyce was elected recording secretary of the Executive Board of International Chapter at the Convention in Denver. In 2003, Joyce was elected president of International Chapter in Oklahoma City, Oklahoma. Her theme during her biennium as president was, "P.E.O....small as a daisy, great as a star!."

Joyce's work on the Study and Research Committee and later on the International Executive Board included many, many trips to Des Moines and to numerous state conventions. Joyce's first assignment was to the Texas State Convention where there was a great debate going on about a proposed amendment. Some of the state officers met in Joyce's room until after midnight discussing the situation. The next day, the amendment was defeated and Joyce received a lot of the credit. She never figured out what she had said that they appreciated so much!

Whether she was aware of it or not, Joyce has always been a gifted communicator. This gift is made evident in articles she penned for The P.E.O. Record, which can be read on page 512.

During her years on the Study and Research Committee and the Executive Board of International Chapter, Joyce visited a total of forty-four state chapter conventions. She also visited Canadian chapters several times and Alaskan chapters on three different trips. One of the most interesting chapters in Alaska performed the Ceremony of Initiation with the officers dressed in appropriate Eskimo clothing. In Hawaii, Joyce visited chapters on the islands of Oahu, Maui and Kauai.

Joyce presided as president of International Convention in Vancouver, Canada, in 2005. During convention, Joyce and Wayne were impressed to learn that they were staying in the same rooms where Queen Elizabeth and Prince Phillip had stayed.

Wayne once figured that Joyce had traveled over 44,000 miles for P.E.O. and visited state conventions in all but four states.

Joyce has always enjoyed reading, giving book reviews, public speaking and her stamp collection.

In 2010, Joyce and Wayne Goff moved from Nebraska to Sun City, Arizona. Joyce dimitted to Chapter CC in Sun City where she took the office of guard.

Creativity is not the finding of a thing,
but the making something out of it
after it is found.
— James Russell Lowell (1819-1891)

Catherine Hutton

NEBRASKA STATE CHAPTER PRESIDENT
1988-1989

Catherine was a native Cornhusker. Her father was a professor of educational psychology at the University of Nebraska in Lincoln. Her mother was involved with many groups, P.E.O. being her first priority. It was while in high school that Catherine became Cay to her family and friends.

To Cay, P.E.O. day was "Hat Day." In those days, no lady went anywhere without a hat. However, since hats are not worn at P.E.O. meetings, they had to be removed. After school on P.E.O. day, Cay was cautioned to come in the back door and to go to her room and be quiet until the ladies left. She followed instructions—almost. Instead of going directly to her room, she would go to her mother's room and have a wonderful time trying on all of the hats. She was careful to return each to its place on the bed so no one would know! In retrospect, she imagines that those P.E.O.s knew exactly what she was doing!

It was many years later when Cay arrived home one afternoon to find her mother quietly excited, holding a Special Delivery letter addressed to Cay. It was an invitation to become a P.E.O. On May 29, 1949, Cay was initiated into Chapter BY.

Cay was graduated with distinction from the University of Nebraska in Lincoln with a B.S. in education on June 5, 1950. That evening she married Lynn D. Hutton, Jr. As she put it, "One day I was out of one institution, and into another." She taught one year in Lincoln while Lynn finished his law degree. They moved to Norfolk where Lynn entered the law profession and Cay dimitted to Chapter CU. Cay was also a charter member of Chapter GS, which was organized on January 27, 1968. This wonderful chapter initiated both of Cay's daughters, Ann and Laura. It also paid her the honor of proposing her name as convention chairman for the 1982 state convention and as nominee for the state board of Nebraska State Chapter. It was then that Cay fully realized how important that sustaining faith of her sisters was to her. Cay served in all offices of the state board and at the 1989 convention in Hastings, she presided as Nebraska State Chapter's ninety-sixth president. While she was on the state board, Cay organized Chapter IB, Cozad.

"Light a Candle of Faith and Reach for our Star" was the theme Cay chose for her convention. P.E.O. sisters seem to be able to recognize qualities a sister has been unaware of or has deprecated. To acknowledge their faith in an ability or talent one has not recognized in oneself and then to act on that faith, reaching for one's very best is a way we can grow through P.E.O. It can be and often is, a scary thing to do. Cay concluded her president's closing remarks this way, "Accept the faith that is offered you. With it, you will be surprised at what you can do. I did... and I know it is true."

Special highlights of Cay's convention were several: There was 100 percent attendance of chapter delegates. The 1989 convention was a bridge from the first 100 years to the second 100 years of the first state chapter. Three chapters also celebrated their centennials, and displays of chapter memorabilia along with that of state chapter formed a fascinating look into P.E.O.'s past history. Having Cay's two daughters serve as pages was "icing on the cake."

Cay participated in a variety of activities. She was a member of her church choir and directed the Junior Choir. She was a member of a book review club for fifty years. She was named Outstanding Mrs. Jaycee of Nebraska in 1956. She worked in ceramics, did pastel portraits, wrote and illustrated three children's books, designed and acted as contractor for the two homes the Huttons built. She was an income tax consultant for many years. Cay was a private pilot and enjoyed sewing, counted cross stitch, gardening and travel.

Cay died January 14, 2002.

*To be a great leader
and so always master of the situation,
one must of necessity have been
a great thinker in action.*

An eagle was never yet hatched from a goose's egg.

-James Thomas

June Brunmeier

NEBRASKA STATE CHAPTER PRESIDENT
1989-1990

June Ayers was born an identical twin on July 4, 1932. June married Dr. Richard Brunmeier, a dentist in Lincoln. June was initiated into Chapter I, Wahoo, on January 16, 1951. June's twin sister, Janet Ayers Lindley, also was initiated that same evening. Their mother, June Winter Ayers, served as chaplain.

June comes from a family with deep P.E.O. roots. Her great grandmother, Ella J. Collins, lived in Mount Pleasant, Iowa, and knew the seven Founders of P.E.O. Three of the Founders were her good friends. When P.E.O. was organized in Wahoo, Ella served as the first president of Chapter I. June's grandmother, Ethel Collins Winter, her mother, and her twin sister all have served as presidents of Chapter I. Patricia June Lindley Ahlers and Ann Elizabeth Lindley, daughters of June's sister Janet, are fifth generation P.E.O.s. June's daughter, Christine Thurlow, is a member of Chapter II, Kansas.

June dimitted into Chapter FB, Lincoln, on April 28, 1959. She held offices in Chapter FB for sixteen years, repeating the offices of guard and chaplain.

June served as convention chairman for the 1983 convention in Lincoln and at that time was elected as treasurer of the state board. She served in all offices of the state board and in 1990 presided at the Centennial Convention of Nebraska State Chapter as its ninety-seventh president. During her term on the state board, June organized three chapters in Nebraska: Chapter IC, South Sioux City; Chapter ID, Wayne; and Chapter IE, Omaha. June's presidential year, 1989-1990, was dedicated to helping P.E.O.s achieve a higher level of satisfaction which comes from commitment to the P.E.O. ideals and principles.

June and her husband Dick had three children: a daughter Christie who married Todd Thurlow, a son Dr. Richard A. Brunmeier (wife Sherri), and a son Ronald Brunmeier. They had three grandchildren: Stephanie June Brunmeier, Richard Wayne Brunmeier, and Sarah Beth Thurlow.

The Centennial Convention of Nebraska State Chapter at which June presided was entitled *"A Century of Sisterly Love."* It was a success in every way and thanks go to Phyllis Blanke, convention chairman, and all the P.E.O. sisters in Lincoln who gave of their time and talents to produce a successful convention. Honored guests were International Chapter President Mary Louise Remy and Second Vice President Nancy Hall. The projects program, *Avenue of P.E.O. Dreams*, was a highlight. Also present was Dr. Helen Washburn of Cottey College. The memory of the Centennial Convention will remain as one of June's most special joys in life.

June lives in Lincoln, Nebraska.

Robley Garrigan
NEBRASKA STATE CHAPTER PRESIDENT
1990-1991

A Nebraska native, Robley was born on October 4, 1948, the daughter of Robert Cheney Hunt and Jeanette Hedelund Hunt. She has resided in Blair for most of her life, except for living away during college. Robley does however consider herself part Minnesotan as she spent every summer from age three to eighteen with her grandparents on Potato Lake in Park Rapids, Minnesota. She earned her A.A. degree from Christian College in Columbia Missouri and a B.A. degree in English and history from the University of Tampa in Tampa, Florida. After graduation she worked in urban planning at the Tampa Metropolitan Development Agency.

Robley met her husband Tim in Florida and they were married in Blair on July 1, 1972. They returned to Jacksonville for two years where Tim worked as a division manager at a manufacturing company and Robley worked in marketing for a wholesale paper distributor. They returned to Blair in January 1974 to join the family telecommunications business, Great Plains Communications. Tim retired in 2010.

The Garrigans have two sons, Riley and Casey. Both sons work in the family business, Great Plains Communications. Casey is married to Valerie Naranjo of Denver and they have three sons: Liam, Aiden and Declan. Riley is single. Both sons live in Omaha.

Robley's volunteer activities have included serving on the board of directors of a hospital in Omaha and the Omaha Area Youth Orchestra. She is a member of the Methodist Church, the National Association of Parliamentarians and has served as treasurer of the Omaha Beta Unit. For five years, she fostered her love of writing as editor of *The Lieder*, a quarterly publication of the University of Nebraska Performing Arts Center Guild. She served as editor of *The Spirit of the Prairie, a History of P.E.O. in Nebraska*. She currently serves on the board of directors of the family business Great Plains Communications and on the board of Unit 241 of the American Contract Bridge League.

Leisure time activities for Robley include duplicate bridge, genealogy, reading and writing. She has achieved the rank of Bronze Life Master with the ACBL. Her favorite pastimes include spoiling the grandchildren and the family cats.

Robley's first memory of P.E.O. dates back to 1955 when she was only seven. Her grandmother Vera Hunt made Robley sing "Who's Sorry Now" for her P.E.O. chapter. That was in the days when every P.E.O. meeting had musical numbers. A few years later when she was about twelve Robley was coerced into donning a grass skirt to dance the hula for the chapter. She remembers that as the height of embarrassment but one didn't deny a grandmother's request. In spite of her dubious musical talents, Chapter EQ, Blair, initiated Robley in September 1967. In 1978 Robley dimitted to become a charter member of Blair's first evening chapter, Chapter HL.

Prior to serving as 1984 state convention chairman, Robley served for two years as a Cottey Area Chairman. After serving as chairman of convention in 1984, Robley was elected to the state board as treasurer. She served in all of the state offices and presided as Nebraska State Chapter's ninety-eighth president. While serving on the state board, Robley organized Chapter IF, Blair, and Chapter IG, Imperial. At the 1991 Convention of International Chapter in Omaha, Robley gave the orientation programs. She served as parliamentarian for two state conventions.

Robley presided at the 1991 state convention in Grand Island. The convention theme was *"Joy Be With Us as We Soar On The Winds of Destiny."* The guards were attired in shirtwaist dresses of either hot pink or emerald green and wore muslin vests on which were silk screened the convention logo of three sand hill cranes in flight. The pages' dresses were purple and included aprons which also featured the sand hill crane logo. Robley's pages were her sister Gail Jensen from Blair, her niece Abby Jensen from Texas and friends Jane Gilbert from Omaha and Judy Sick from Blair, Minday Schriner from Colorado (her children's first and long-time babysitter) Ann Carroll from Elk City, Oklahoma, and Eunice Hummel from Lincoln. A highlight of convention was a cello performance by Jill Rausch, an ELF loan recipient sponsored by Robley's chapter.

Robley explains her convention theme and logo in this way: "Today P.E.O.s are facing tough challenges through increasing demands in work and family. But P.E.O.'s foundation is strong and unfailing. The magnificent sand hill crane, the convention symbol, has defied odds and survived threats of extinction. So has P.E.O. endured societal upheavals to emerge as a premiere women's organization. As P.E.O. looks to a new millennium, let us rejoice as we build upon the foundation forged for us by the Founders years ago. Like the graceful and powerful sand hill crane, may we soar on the winds of destiny as we continue to thrive. May joy be with us on our journey."

Robley and Tim Garrigan reside in Blair.

Anyone can look for fashion in a boutique or history in a museum. The creative explorer looks for history in a hardware store and fashion in an airport.

-Robert Wieder

Mary Ann Eberspacher

NEBRASKA STATE CHAPTER PRESIDENT
1991-1992

Mary Ann Eberspacher's home town is Sutherland, Nebraska, where she lived with her parents, Mike and Mary Holmstedt, her brother Jim and sister Connie. She attended Nebraska Wesleyan University, majoring in English and business. There she was a member of Alpha Gamma Delta sorority.

Fine arts play an important role in Mary Ann's life, as she is a pianist, organist, and speaker for church and community events. She was a member of the Seward Methodist Bell Choir and a patron of the Lied Center for Performing Arts in Lincoln. Her favorite pastimes are reading, visiting art galleries, playing bridge, attending plays and concerts, and cheering at Cornhusker football games.

As owner of the Travel Port, Mary Ann's dreams of faraway places have become tours to Europe, Australia, Egypt, Israel, Turkey, Mexico, Hawaii, and the Caribbean. Her favorite itinerary is taking her grandchildren, Dustin and Ashley Norberg, to Disney World.

Mary Ann's family includes daughters Suzie Norberg (EK, Corvallis, Oregon) and C.K. Duryea (CC, Seward); her mother, Mary Holmstedt (AK, North Platte); and her sister, Connie Witt (FB, Lincoln).

Mary Ann is a member of Chapter CC, Seward, where she was initiated in 1976. Mary Ann was elected treasurer of the Executive Board of Nebraska State Chapter in 1985 and served in all seven offices of the board. While serving on the board, she assisted with the travel arrangements for the Nebraska delegation to Conventions of International Chapter in Winnipeg, Orlando, Phoenix, and Omaha. Mary Ann presided as Nebraska State Chapter's ninety-ninth president at the 1992 convention in Kearney. Her theme *"Celebrate P.E.O. with Arts, Music and Drama"* reflected the cultural aspects of P.E.O.'s heritage. While on the board, Mary Ann organized Chapter IH, Elkhorn. At the International Convention in 1991, Mary Ann took part in the parade of state presidents for the opening ceremonies, bearing the flag of Nebraska.

In 2000 Mary Ann retired to Naples, Florida, where she attends the P.E.O. Group meetings. Her many travels now include granddaughters Simone and Camille Duryea. When in Omaha, Mary Ann volunteers for Omaha Performing Arts and enjoys Nebraska P.E.O. events.

Mary Owens
NEBRASKA STATE CHAPTER PRESIDENT
1992-1993

As Mary repeated the Objects and Aims at the beginning of each P.E.O. meeting, she was struck with the realization that the entire message was stated in the very first sentence: all the rest was elaboration. The goal of general improvement was first envisioned by the seven Founders and remains the challenge for each member of P.E.O. Mary expressed the many ways of striving for positive action in a poem entitled *"The Plus of P.E.O."* This poem later became the theme for the one hundred fourth convention held in McCook. Mary presided as Nebraska State Chapter's one hundredth president during that convention on June 18 to June 20, 1993.

During the year of her presidency, Mary had requested that individual members send examples of the "P.E.O. Plus," and these accounts were featured on pluses mounted on the walls of the school. The convention colors of red, navy, and metallic gold were exhibited in the stage setting, flowers, and the costumes of the guards and pages. Navy dresses for the guards and red dresses for Mary's two pages, her daughter and daughter-in-law, were accented with silk-screened scarves featuring stylized stars and pluses. Mabel Otis, second vice president of International Chapter, gave an inspiring keynote address entitled "A Starlit Journey." Project recipients spoke eloquently during the opening meeting which was followed by "Summing Up the Projects Exposition" held in the high school gymnasium.

Mary was initiated into Chapter AQ, Loup City, in 1958, and served as an officer until her family moved in 1963. At that time, she dimitted to Chapter BT, Weeping Water, her current chapter. In addition to serving as chapter president, she was a Cottey Area Chairman, president of Reciprocity Group VIII, a guard during the 1974 state convention in Peru, and convention chairman for the 1986 convention at the same site. Mary co-authored a manual to be used for the Local Chapter Officer's Workshops first held during her term as state president. While she was on the board, she organized Chapter II, Grand Island.

The daughter of Frank and Mildred Domingo, Mary was born in Weeping Water in 1935 where she completed high school. Attending the University of Nebraska in Lincoln, Mary received a B.S. in business education in 1956 when she was honored as the recipient of the Boucher Award for the senior with the highest cumulative average. A member of Kappa Chapter of Delta Gamma, she served as president.

Mary's family includes husband Jim, who worked in the family-owned

Keystone Lumber Yard in Loup City and the Nebraska State Bank in Weeping Water. In addition, she has a daughter Cynthia Owens Moss Naughton, who is a music and drama teacher at Smith College Campus School in Northampton, Massachusetts, and a son, Timothy Owens, an electrical engineer with NPPD in Columbus, Nebraska. Her grandchildren are Rebecca and Matthew Owens, Geoffrey and Robert Moss, and Thomas and Jonathan Naughton.

Volunteer activities for Mary have included the local school board, P.T.A., Junior Women's Club, the Lofte Community Theatre, and many roles in the First Congregational Church, U.C.C. of Weeping Water. Following their move to Lincoln in 1991, Jim and Mary became active members of Vine Congregational Church. Her interests include music, drama and cooking.

Beverley Karrer
NEBRASKA STATE CHAPTER PRESIDENT
1993-1994

Beverley Karrer is a third generation P.E.O. Her grandmother Elsie Bush of Chapter Y, Red Cloud, and her mother Ilah Bush of Chapter FA, McCook, instilled in her a deep love for P.E.O. At least twenty-one members of her family are P.E.O.s.

Beverley was initiated into Chapter FD, Omaha. She served as Omaha Reciprocity Association president, was on the P.E.O. Home Board of Trustees for fourteen years, and served for seven years on the Executive Board of Nebraska State Chapter. She presided as Nebraska State Chapter's one hundred first state president at the Omaha convention in 1994. Her mother-in-law, Elinor Karrer, FA, McCook, was an honorary page. While she served on the state board, Bev organized two chapters in Nebraska: Chapter IJ, Papillion, and Chapter IK, Omaha.

Bev's immediate family consists of her husband Bill, who is an oncologist/ surgeon. Her daughter Suzan Rohrig, Chapter HX, is an architect AIA, and her husband is Brad Rohrig of Parker Plastics. They have two girls: Courtney Rohrig Molettiere (Matthew) and Ashley Rohrig Snowdon (Ryan), both in Chapter HX Omaha. Her son Dr. Fritz Karrer is a pediatric transplant surgeon and chairs the surgery of the University of Colorado Children's Hospital. His wife Debbie is a member of Chapter BF, Colorado. They have two boys, Michael and Thomas.

Bev taught at an elementary school while her husband attended medical school. She then became involved with volunteering, and many community and civic organizations benefited from her devotion. She served as president of both the Nebraska Medical Auxiliary and the Omaha Alpha Phi Alumnae and was founder of the Brownville Fine Arts Association. She has been active in and president of the Museum of Nebraska Art in Kearney since 1978 and is now honored as emeriti. Bev has served locally on the boards of Junior Theater, Lied Center for Performing

Arts, Nebraska Heart Association, Joslyn Art Museum, Omaha Symphony, D.A.R. and the Methodist, Clarkson University and Immanuel Hospital Auxiliaries. She started the "Garden Walk" for Meyer Therapy in Omaha.

Bev and her husband received the Nebraska State "Court of Honor" Aksarben Award. Her husband's recognition was for his profession. Her recognition stemmed from her starting the Aksarben Buyers Club for the 4H auctions and for her historic book "Aksarben Memories."

Bev's favorite thing is enjoying her home at "Whipoorwill Farm." She enjoys sculpting in her studio and tending twenty-five garden beds. Her great grandchildren constantly share her week!

For the 1994 state convention, Bev's theme was *"P.E.O. Like A Kaleidoscope Reflects Change and Reveals Beauty."* Her personal belief concerning P.E.O. is reflected in this theme: "I look to the coming generation of P.E.O. women and I see lifestyle changes. In the past generations of P.E.O., I see the beauty of traditions that have upheld us. With over half of the women working in the U.S., P.E.O. should address the changing needs of its chapter members. A kaleidoscope is colorful, harmonious, symmetrical and beautiful. Certainly we want all of these same characteristics to thrive within our chapters. Each chapter can be likened to a kaleidoscope with a colorful blending of sisters, the harmonious love within them and an appreciation of the symmetrical procedures symbolized by our ritual that reveal an internal beauty radiated by all."

Rosella Mehling

NEBRASKA STATE CHAPTER PRESIDENT
1994-1995

Like the beauty of the sun reflecting through a stained glass window, the beauty of P.E.O. is reflected through its members. Each chapter is a reflection of the interest and energy expended by its members. *"Reflections from a Star"* is the theme Rosella chose for her convention in Scottsbluff in 1995. Because of her love of creating stained glass art, she sees a similarity to the growth and development of P.E.O. Each item of stained glass is created by fitting one tiny piece after another and bonding them together with lead until the project is completed. P.E.O., in a like manner, has been created by adding member by member, chapter after chapter, until there is a wonderful Sisterhood of nearly 250,000 sisters all bonded together with the love and values set forth by the Founders more than one hundred twenty-five years ago.

Rosella Mehling grew up in Walthill, Nebraska, a small town in northeastern Nebraska. She was unfamiliar with P.E.O. until she moved to Sidney. In 1966, Chapter FR gave the gift of P.E.O. to Rosella and later to both of her daughters. Rosella went on the state board as treasurer at the 1988 convention in Kimball.

She served all offices on the state board and presided as Nebraska State Chapter's one hundred second president at the convention in June 1995, in Scottsbluff. While she was on the state board, Rosella organized Chapter IL, Lincoln.

Rosella was valedictorian of her Walthill class and attended Wayne State College. After marrying Lew Mehling, Rosella moved several times before settling in Sidney. While raising four children, she was involved with all the customary community activities such as Brownies, Girl Scouts, Cub Scouts, Band Auxiliary, and P.T.A. She also was active in the "Panhandle Players" theatre group in Sidney. She still helps with Meals on Wheels. Rosella has taught stained glass classes for the community college in Sidney. The Mehlings are members of Holy Trinity Lutheran Church. Lew was in the banking business for over forty-two years before retiring. When their children were nearly grown, Rosella went to work in the medical records department of their community hospital. She was supervisor and Accredited Records Technician (A.R.T.) for nine years. She retired from Medical Records the same month her youngest graduated from the University of Nebraska.

Rosella and Lew have four children. Lynn Nelson is a home health nurse in Denver. She has two children, Chadd and Brooke, and two grandchildren, Tyler and Madysen. Bill Mehling is Senior Vice President of the First National Bank in Goodland, Kansas. His wife Janet is a member of Chapter ID, Goodland. They have two children, Scott and Crystal, and four grandchildren: twins, Kailee and Kaiden, and Blaize and Neely. Claire and her husband Dave live in Southlake, Texas. They have four children, Katie, Kristy, Tom and Craig, and five grandchildren, Jase, Mack, Caleb, McKenna and Collin. Claire is a member of Chapter GK, Bedford, Texas. Claire has been a recovery room nurse for many years. Rosella's youngest son Charles (Chuck) was a CLU agent with Northwestern Mutual Life Insurance Company for over twenty years and is now in business for himself in Spring, Texas. He and his wife Cheryl have one daughter, Taylor, who is a student at Texas A&M.

Besides having a love for her stained glass accomplishments, Rosella's hobbies include collecting cook books, making counted cross stitch items, playing bridge and being grandmother to her growing (both in size and number) grandchildren and great-grandchildren.

Rosella and Lew Mehling live in Sidney.

The very least you can do in your life is figure out what you hope for. And the most you can do is live inside that hope. Not admire it from a distance but live right in it, under its roof.

-Barbara Kingsolver, an American novelist

Mary Lainson Olsen
Nebraska State Chapter President
1995-1996

A fourth generation P.E.O. and native Nebraskan, Mary Lainson Olsen was initiated into Chapter G, Hastings, in 1966, where she is still an active member. She served in all chapter offices. Her mother, Gretchen Hollman Lainson, is a 74-year member of Chapter G. Other members of her family who belong to Chapter G include her daughter, sister, nieces, cousins, late grandmothers, late mother-in-law, and late aunt. Her maternal grandmother was a member of Chapter N in Minden and her paternal great grandmother was a charter member of Chapter AW in Gothenburg. P.E.O. has been a very important part of her family's history since the early 1900's.

Mary presided over the one hundred seventh Nebraska State Convention held in Norfolk, Nebraska, in 1996, at the Johnny Carson Theatre. *"The Gifts of P.E.O."* was the theme of the convention which emphasized many gifts that P.E.O. has given to each sister, beginning with the gift of membership. For Mary, P.E.O. is a loving way of life, guided by our Objects and Aims, a foundation that helps us to become stronger women. It reaches out not only to us but to the women we support through our International projects. Each sister plays a small part but together we accomplish so much, as shown by the success of our organization.

Mary attended Lindenwood College in St. Charles, Missouri, and graduated from Hastings College, Hastings, Nebraska, with a Bachelor of Arts degree, majoring in English. After graduation, she attended the Katherine Gibbs School of Business in New York City. She worked in Omaha at the Omaha National Bank as an administrative assistant and in Hastings at her family's business, Dutton-Lainson Company. She was the assistant corporate secretary for the firm until she retired.

On April 26, 1975, Mary married Jorn C. Olsen in Hastings, Nebraska, at her parent's home. They resided in Nashville, Tennessee, while he was in graduate school. After Jorn's graduation, they moved back to Hastings where he went into the family business. Mary and Jorn have two children and a daughter-in-law, Christopher and Allison Olsen and Erica Olsen.

Mary has been active in community and state volunteer work, serving on boards of the YWCA, United Way, Hastings Public Library and Foundation, the Salvation Army, the Friends of Lied, Nebraska Art Collection Foundation, otherwise known as MONA, Hastings College Alumni, Hastings Symphony Orchestra, Hastings Community Arts Council, and the executive board of the Nebraska Republican Party. She is an elder in First Presbyterian Church of Hastings, has served on many committees and has sung in the choir.

Mary enjoys traveling with her husband who is not only a business executive but also a fine art landscape photographer. When not traveling, visiting her children, or volunteering, Mary enjoys reading, jigsaw puzzles, music and playing with her cat, Quigley.

Phyllis Blanke
NEBRASKA STATE CHAPTER PRESIDENT
1996-1997

Phyllis Chard Blanke was initiated into P.E.O. Chapter DS in Superior, Nebraska, in December of 1953 while at home during Christmas break from Cottey College.

Actually, Phyllis has always been surrounded by P.E.O. Phyllis's great-grandmother, two great-aunts, her mother (Lila King Chard), two aunts, and a cousin were all members of P.E.O., Chapter AA, Edgar, Nebraska. Additionally, Phyllis's daughter, Annette Hinrichs and Phyllis's daughter-in-law are also P.E.O.s.

Both Phyllis and her daughter are graduates of Cottey College; Phyllis in 1955, Annette in 1984.

In 1963-64 Phyllis assisted in organizing P.E.O. Chapter GJ in Lincoln, Nebraska, and served as the first president of that chapter. In 1974-75 Phyllis served as president of Lincoln P.E.O. Reciprocity Roundtable. Phyllis worked on and assisted with numerous state P.E.O. conventions and attended five International P.E.O. conventions.

Phyllis was elected as an officer of the Nebraska State P.E.O. Executive Board in 1992 and served as state president in 1996-97. The theme for her year was *"Celebrate the Future of P.E.O."* Her term as president was interrupted in March of 1997 when she suffered a nearly fatal brain aneurysm, was in a coma for more than two months and was still hospitalized at the time of the 1997 Nebraska State P.E.O. convention. Because of these conditions, Nebraska State First Vice President Alice Fisher presided at the state convention. While she was on the state board, Phyllis organized Chapter IM, Omaha.

Phyllis was born in Norfolk, Nebraska, started school in Beatrice, and because of her father's work the family was forced to move frequently. Thus she also attended elementary schools in Crete, Davenport and Des Moines, Iowa, and in Lincoln. In 1949 the family moved to Superior, Nebraska, where Phyllis's father, Edgar Chard, a pharmacist, purchased a local pharmacy. Phyllis completed junior high and high school in Superior as class valedictorian in 1953.

After earning her A.A. at Cottey College, Phyllis enrolled at the University of Nebraska, Lincoln, and earned her B.A. degree majoring in English, Theatre Arts, and Education in May of 1957. On June 30th of that year Phyllis married Henry H. Blanke, Jr., and together they completed their master's degrees in 1958 at the University of Nebraska. Phyllis began her teaching career at the

University and next taught at Tarkio College in Tarkio, Missouri. After the birth of her two children, Gregory in 1961 and Annette in 1964, Phyllis began teaching at Nebraska Wesleyan University, teaching speech, and designing and constructing costumes for theatre productions. Phyllis was also responsible for developing and categorizing the Wesleyan costume collection of some 40,000 costume items. After working and teaching at Nebraska Wesleyan for some 35 plus years, Phyllis's aneurysm forced her retirement in 1997.

In 1967, Phyllis and Henry founded the Brownville Village Theatre, Nebraska's oldest Resident Repertory Summer Theatre. Together they received the Nebraska Governor's Arts Award in 1970 and the Lincoln Mayor Arts Award in 2001. Together they have acted in over thirty plays. In 1998 Phyllis was the recipient of the Madonna Rehabilitation Hospital Goal Award.

Although Phyllis's teaching and theatre work consumed much of her time and energy, she always made time for and loved P.E.O. Phyllis and Henry live in Lincoln, Nebraska.

Alice Jennings Fisher

Nebraska State Chapter President
1997-1998

Alice Jennings Fisher graduated from the University of Nebraska with a bachelor's degree in elementary education. While at the university, she became a member of Alpha Chi Omega Sorority. She married Dan Fisher, who was a second lieutenant in the Marine Corps, and they lived in Orange, California, while Dan continued as a helicopter pilot in the Marines and Alice taught grade school. Dan then finished his degree at the University of Nebraska, and Alice taught second grade in Lincoln. They moved to Crawford, Nebraska, where Dan was an employee and part owner of Crawford State Bank.

Alice was initiated into Chapter AX, Crawford, in 1964. A move was made to Grand Island, Nebraska, in 1981. Alice felt the benefits of P.E.O. hospitality and love and soon dimitted to Chapter GP. A few years later Alice's mother, Mary Jennings, was initiated into Chapter GP when she moved to Grand Island from Davenport, Nebraska.

The Fishers have three children. Dan Jennings Fisher is a computer draftsman for Corning Fiber-Optics in Wilmington, North Carolina. Catie Limbach lives in Crawford with husband John and daughters Whitney and Jocelyn. Catie is a member of Chapter AX and teaches in the same kindergarten room where her mother taught. Amy is a member of Chapter GP, Nebraska. She and husband Joel King reside in Kansas City. Amy received a master's degree in social work from the University of Kansas.

Alice has been active in community involvements in both Crawford and Grand Island. She served on the Crawford School Board and the Crawford City Council and was president of the Crawford Chamber of Commerce. While in Crawford, she taught school a short time and then opened a boutique she appropriately named "The Daisy."

In Grand Island, Alice volunteered for the YWCA, Friends of the Library, Stuhr Museum and the St. Francis Hospital. She has served as an elder in the First Presbyterian Church where she and Dan were members.

Alice and Dan spent four interesting and educational years in Lincoln, Nebraska, while Dan served a four-year term as state senator representing the Grand Island district. Alice said the two P's, Politics and P.E.O., left little time for much else. Alice especially enjoys her family, travel, reading, bridge, golf, politics, and P.E.O.

Alice served on the Executive Board of Nebraska State Chapter from 1991 to 1998. She presided at the 1997 state convention in Lincoln when Phyllis Blanke suffered a stroke. She also presided at her own convention at the Marina Inn in South Sioux City, Nebraska, in 1998. Her theme was *"One Shining Star, Many Loving Hearts."* While on the state board Alice organized Chapter IN, Plattsmouth. Following her term on the state board, Alice was chosen to serve on the Finance Committee of International Chapter. She now resides in Bend, Oregon.

Kathleen Gosch
NEBRASKA STATE CHAPTER PRESIDENT
1998-1999

As a second generation P.E.O., Kathleen learned the impact of this woman's organization from her Mother, Lorayne Wrenn, a charter member of Chapter GP, Grand Island. Her family of sisters include her daughter, sisters, and nieces. Her immediate family includes her husband, Gene, a retired hospital pharmacist, and children, Phil and his wife Allie Gosch of Denver and Alyssa White of Omaha. Grandsons are Hayden and Harrison White and Brandon and Spencer Gosch.

Kathy was initiated into Chapter CK, Grand Island, while in nursing school. Upon marriage and moving to Kearney, she became active in Chapter AS, serving many offices as well as president. She was the charter head for the organization of Chapter IID, Kearney, serving as president for two terms. She also served as president of Reciprocity Group XIV. When it was announced Nebraska State Chapter would host the 1991 Convention of International Chapter, Kathy served as chair of the decorations committee. Times were spent gathering prairie grasses and making cornhusk flowers for bouquets with the help of her Nebraska sisters. As organizer of Nebraska State Chapter, one of Kathy's greatest joys was realized with the organization of Chapter IO, York.

The theme of the 1998-1999 Convention of Nebraska State Chapter held in York was, *"A P.E.O. Garden—Planted In Faith, Nurtured With Love."* Kathy's sister, Sara Mitchell, Chapter HX, Omaha, provided one of the convention highlights by playing a flute solo, *"His Eye is on the Sparrow."* Her sisters Linda Pohlman, HU, Norfolk, and Jane Gangwish, BI, Shelton, daughter Alyssa White, HB, Kearney, and niece Erin Gangwish, BI, Shelton, served as pages. The pale yellow dresses worn by the guards included vests on which Kathy had painted flowers. Members of Reciprocity Group VII both capably and lovingly brought their resources and talents in preparing for a convention that met the needs of the state and the opportunity to learn and grow in P.E.O.

Kathy's professional career of nursing grew from teaching for the Licensed Practical Nursing Program in Kearney to school health. She served thirty years as school nurse for many area rural schools, having her own business while serving as school health coordinator at ESU 10. After presiding as president of the Nebraska School Nurses Association, she also served as state director and secretary-treasurer of the National Association of School Nurses. Kathy also has been very active in her church, serving on the administrative council and other committees. It was her passion for her faith and her nursing knowledge that led to her becoming a Faith Community Nurse (Parish Nurse). After several years of working a health ministry grant for Good Samaritan Hospital, her "encore career" is in Telehealth.

Upon retirement, Kathy and Gene look forward to more time with the grandsons, travel, more time with friends and family and more time serving her faith community. Her "ever-present" flower garden awaits.

Anita Kitt

NEBRASKA STATE CHAPTER PRESIDENT
1999-2000

Anita Kitt was initiated into Chapter ER Benkelman, Nebraska, in 1969. She and her husband Larry live on a farm/ranch approximately twenty-six miles northwest of Benkelman. The Kitts have two children—Allison and Van. Allison is a member of Chapter FA McCook.

From 1971 to 1973 Anita lived at the Karamursel Common Defense Installation in Turkey, where she was a Red Cross volunteer at the well baby clinic provided by the base dispensary. After returning to the Benkelman area, she served as a 4-H leader and council member in the early 1980's. In the late 1980's she was a member of the Crisis Intervention team at the local high school, then served on the board at the Sarah Ann Hester Home for five years, acting as chairman for four of those years.

The Kitts volunteer in several areas through their county and community.

Anita says, "Much like many rural areas, we are experiencing a general decline in population and services, and without volunteers to take up the slack, our theater, county fair activities and golf course would never be able to operate."

Born and raised in Benkelman, Anita is a member of the Benkelman United Methodist Church. Although not "gainfully employed," in her words she describes herself as the "chief gofer" for her husband, spending quite a bit of time on the road and keeping the financial records for their operation.

In her spare time, Anita enjoys reading, golfing, walking, traveling, and playing bridge.

Anita served on the state Executive Board of Nebraska State Chapter from 1994–2000. Her state convention, following her theme of *"Star Gazing, Star Raising, Star Amazing,"* was held in Beatrice, Nebraska. While she was on the state board, Anita organized Chapter IP, Fairbury.

Anita's Chapter ER, Benkelman, relinquished its charter on June 6, 2009, and she is now a member of Chapter FA, McCook. Anita and her husband continue to maintain their ranch in McCook.

Patricia Parsons Robertson
NEBRASKA STATE CHAPTER PRESIDENT
2000-2001

Born in and spending all but twenty years of her life in Omaha, Trish is part of a three generation family in P.E.O. Her grandmother Minnie Parsons was a member in Red Oak, Iowa, and mother Dixie Parsons, of Chapter BX, Omaha. Trish was initiated into BX four days before her marriage and her sister Vicki Parsons eight years thereafter. She and her mother are still the only mother and daughter to be presidents of the chapter.

Trish attended the University of Nebraska where she was a member of Gamma Phi Beta. She married Richard Robertson in 1957 and they had one son, Scott, who presented them with two grandchildren, Christian and Skylar. Because Dick's career with Ralston Purina Company required quite a bit of relocation, Trish dimitted five times, the last move ironically and happily bringing her back to her original BX in Omaha.

Travels to new places offered the opportunity to meet many wonderful P.E.O.s and observe the different interpretations of procedures. She became a legal secretary and gained invaluable experience taking notes under pressure! The final move took them back to Omaha where she joined with Dick and ran the Omaha office of his business AGRI-associates, an agricultural recruiting business with offices throughout the states and internationally.

During her second tenure with BX, she became active in convention planning; serving as secretary for Beverly Karrer's state convention committee, secretary for the planning committee for Convention of International Chapter when it was held in Omaha in 1991 and finally chairman of the convention committee before she went on the board in 1994. Trish's theme for the 2001 convention was "*I Wish for You a Star to Cast All Your Dreams Upon*." She was delighted to have her sister Vicki and three past state presidents who also share close birthdays and friendships with her to serve as pages. While serving on the state board, Trish organized Chapter IQ Hebron and worked hard to save several other chapters from disbandment. She served all seven offices while on the state board and continues to serve offices in her local chapter and committees for Nebraska State Chapter. She was also privileged to serve on the first Nominating Committee for the state and was tremendously gratified to see how many extremely well qualified P.E.O.s there are in the state of Nebraska to carry on the torch for future board members. She considers serving on the 1991 International planning committee and helping International President Mary Louise Remy present her convention an honor that will always be very precious to her. The experiences gained and friendships made can never be replaced.

After fifty-four years of marriage, Trish is now a widow, but continues to live in Omaha.

Jacqueline J. Irwin
NEBRASKA STATE CHAPTER PRESIDENT
2001-2002

Jacqueline has lived in the Alliance, Nebraska, area all her life, with the exception of one school year spent in Ft. Collins, Colorado, while her husband Jim completed his senior year at Colorado State University. Jacci was educated at Nebraska State Teachers College, now Chadron State College, where she received a bachelor's degree in 1968 and a master's degree in 1972, both in elementary education.

Initiated into her current chapter, AH Alliance, in 1981, Jacqueline was the first member in her family to become a P.E.O. She initiated her mother, Dorothy Stull, into that same chapter in 1986 while serving as president for the first time. Jacqueline has three brothers and sisters-in-law – Don and Harriett Stull; David and Marilyn Stull; and Dick and Dot Stull. She also has two sisters – Marian Dalton and Cheryl Spurrier. Twenty nieces and nephews and thirty-five great-nieces and nephews complete the family!

Before they retired, Jacqueline was completely involved with Jim as owner and operator of 600 irrigated acres of corn, dry edible beans, sugar beets and wheat, as well as 600 acres of dry land wheat/summer fallow. She was a volunteer on the advisory board for the Carnegie Arts Center and a member of the National Association of Parliamentarians. She is also an active member of First Presbyterian Church, singing in the choir and serving on the coordinating team and as a circle leader for Presbyterian Women. An ordained elder of her church, she served on many committees at the local and presbytery levels. For Presbyterian Women, she served at the local presbytery and synod levels. In addition, she was moderator of convening convention of the Box Butte and Boulder Presbyteries when they joined to become Plains and Peaks Presbytery.

For six years, Jacqueline was on the Carnegie Arts Center board of directors and was involved with fund raising, renovations and the opening of the center from the old Carnegie Library. She also taught elementary school for seventeen years. In her spare time, Jacci enjoys quilting, reading, traveling, bowling, gardening and doing yard work.

After serving in all the offices Jacci presided over the 2002 state Convention of Nebraska State Chapter as the one hundred ninth state president. Her theme was *"The Patchwork of P.E.O. – A Unique Pattern of Love."*

Jeanne M. Reigle

NEBRASKA STATE CHAPTER PRESIDENT
2002-2003

Jeanne was given the gift of P.E.O. in 1989 into Chapter AL, Madison, Nebraska. This invitation began an important journey for her. "I was surrounded by women I had only seen in passing and who were now including me as part of their family." She was so inspired by the impact of our organization that in 1995 she accepted her Reciprocity group's request that she serve at the state level. She was instrumental in creating the state Membership Committee during her presidency.

Jeanne presided at the Nebraska State Convention in Hastings in 2003. Her theme was *"P.E.O. – A Legacy of Love."* Jeanne feels that these years serving the Sisterhood inspired her to continue her leadership roles in her home town. To date, she has served in leadership roles in city government, the local chamber of commerce, arts center, medical clinic, and her church.

Jeanne has been married to her BIL John for thirty-two years and still resides in Madison. They have four children and seven grandchildren.

Life isn't about waiting for the storm to pass,
it's about learning to dance in the rain.

-Mary Ann Radmacher

Dee Anne Weyeneth
Nebraska State Chapter President
2003-2004

Dee was initiated into Chapter K, Lincoln, Nebraska, in 1986. Her sister, Cay Tiernan, is also a member. Dee has two sons, Len and Phillip. Len's wife, Sara, is a member of HW. Dee has three grandsons and one granddaughter.

Born in Kansas City, Missouri, Dee was raised in Lincoln. In 1958 she moved to Minnesota where she graduated from Anoka High School and attended the University of Minnesota.

Volunteering in her sons' schools and serving as chairman for the Arts in General for Lincoln General Hospital were just some of the activities that kept Dee busy. Currently she is active at First Plymouth Church, where she organized funeral luncheons for several years, chaired the reception desk volunteers, and served on the Abendmusik Board as president, the Board of Christian Outreach, the Women's Ministries Board, and the Diaconate Board. Currently she serves as family liaison for Roper and Sons Mortuary.

Dee was elected to the Nebraska State Executive Board in 1996 and presided at the 2004 state convention in Lincoln. Her theme, *"Let's Go and Get the Others,"* exemplified Dee's enthusiasm for P.E.O.

"The big thrill of my service on the state board came back to me at the 2013 state convention in Columbus. On the first night of the 2004 convention when I was presiding officer, I talked with two young members representing their chapter. It was their first convention and they were excited to be there. They had questions and I talked with them for quite a lengthy time on Friday night. During the following years, I often remembered the exchange with them and wondered where P.E.O had taken them. In Columbus I met Kris Ferguson, outgoing state IPS chairman. She asked if I remembered talking with two young women at the 2004 convention. She was one of them and I was thrilled to reconnect with her, and to see how she had grown in P.E.O. That is really what P.E.O. is to me. The relationships that you form and how these continue the growth of our Sisterhood.

"I always feel a great deal of responsibility when I attend International Convention. Seeing the full delegation, listening to reports, and voting always moves me. This reminds me we are a powerful group of women who come together for the good of the Sisterhood.

"I am very excited as P.E.O moves forward addressing the needs of our Sisterhood for today's society, the role it plays in our lives, and the continuing growth of our projects. P.E.O.s are powerful women."

Dee lives in Lincoln, Nebraska.

Anne Baumhover

Nebraska State Chapter President
2004-2005

Anne Baumhover was initiated into Chapter HK in Fremont in 1987. A very dear friend who is now in Chapter Eternal gave her the gift of P.E.O. The gift led to serving on the state board, where Anne's love for shoes prompted her to choose *"Stepping Out in P.E.O."* as her theme. She encouraged chapters and members to step out of their box and give something new to P.E.O. During her year as president Anne's board made changes in the financial organization, giving them the advantage of having the same person to work with year after year. Following her term on the state board, Anne served on the P.E.O. Home Board of Directors for nine years, serving as president for six of those years.

Anne Baumhover grew up on a farm in southwest Iowa near Shenandoah. She knew about P.E.O. because she had two aunts that belonged to a chapter, but she always thought her mother couldn't belong because she was a farm wife. Her mother later became a P.E.O. member when the family moved to town. Anne was initiated into Chapter HK when she moved to Fremont. Her two sisters and her daughter became members as a result of Anne sending FR forms to chapters where they lived.

Anne graduated from Shenandoah High School and attended Iowa State College for one year. She worked as a secretary for Carpenter Paper Company where she met her husband Ray. They were married in 1963 and lived all their married life in Fremont. They had two children Cynthia and Gregory. Cynthia became a school counselor in Phoenix and Gregory is married to Susan and has Anne's only grandchild Megan. Gregory is employed in the computer field.

Anne finished her college education with a Bachelor of Education from Midland College and a Master's in Literacy from the University of Nebraska – Omaha. She taught first graders for fifteen years and then taught in Boys Town High School for five years, finishing out her career as a consultant and workshop presenter for Boys Town.

Anne's husband passed away a week before she became state president. Although she was hoping he could see her installed as president, she knew he was there in spirit. Anne presided at the 2004 state convention in Grand Island.

Anne loves to play tennis, read, and likes to do some form of exercise at least five times a week. She has traveled to many overseas countries and likes to take cruises as well as travel within the good old USA.

Anne resides in Fremont, Nebraska.

Cynthia Jarecke
NEBRASKA STATE CHAPTER PRESIDENT
2005-2006

A third generation P.E.O., Cynthia (Cyndi) Jarecke shares the bond of sisterhood with four great aunts; her mother, Roberta Uhlmann; sister, Cathy Evans; and aunt Jeanne Johnson. She began her P.E.O. journey in 1979, joining Chapter CH, Columbus, Nebraska. Cyndi served in various offices in Chapter CH and was president in 1992–1993. She served Reciprocity Group VII as an officer and president 1997–1998.

Cyndi is an alumna of Cottey College and the University of Nebraska and now works as a floral manager for a regional grocery store chain in Columbus. An active member in her community, she volunteers for the Columbus Area Chamber of Commerce, most actively as a commodore, the good will arm of the Chamber. She has also been retail services chairman, was on the mayor's downtown improvement committee, and was Taste of Columbus decoration chairman. She has been a Festival of Trees exhibitor for more than twenty-five years. In the past, she has been the United Way Duck Derby chairman, Rotary president, and a board member and president of the Columbus Area Arts Council. She has also been active in the Columbus Community Hospital Extravaganza, Big Pals/Little Pals, and Relay for Life, and she taught floral design classes through Central Community College.

Statewide she has served on the Friends of Lied board, Lied Tables of Inspiration Exhibitor, Lied Legends, and Board of Directors of the Nebraska Florist's Society. Cyndi and her husband served as co-chairmen for the Scotus Central Catholic Gala. Cyndi is married to Jerry and enjoys spending her free time reading, playing bridge, and painting. Cyndi and Jerry are members of the Federated Church and St. Bonaventure Church. Since graduating from Cottey Cyndi influenced hundreds of children by teaching them swimming lessons.

Cyndi presided at the 2006 convention in Kearney hosted by Reciprocity Group XIV, where her theme was *"May We All Be Stars among Women and Angels among Our Sisters."* Highlights of her term were helping with the organization of two chapters and leading the Nebraska delegation to the 2005 Convention of International Chapter in Vancouver, BC.

Serving as president of Nebraska State Chapter was one of the most rewarding experiences of her life. The Sisterhood is truly a wonderful organization made up of many amazing women that she has had the privilege of knowing.

P.E.O....Peculiarly Exclusive Order

Joan Fink

**NEBRASKA STATE CHAPTER PRESIDENT
2006-2007**

A Nebraska native, Joan was the daughter of Leonard A. and Belva Borden Rinne. She spent her childhood on a Pawnee County farm that her great grandparents homesteaded in 1869. Joan attended Pawnee City High School and graduated in 1957 as valedictorian of her class. She attended the University of Nebraska at Lincoln for two years, where she was a member of Delta Gamma Sorority. She married Jon Fink on February 1, 1959. For the first five of their 55+ years of married life, Joan and husband Jon lived in Georgia, Texas, Alabama and Kansas while Jon served as a helicopter pilot in the Army. Their family consists of sons JD and Jeff, daughters-in-law Tami and Jana and nine grandchildren, which includes two sets of multiples, twin granddaughters and triplet grandsons.

Joan clerked in their family business, Tecumseh Livestock Market, for twenty-eight years. When they sold the business in 1990, she returned to college, graduating with honors from Peru State College in 1994 with a Bachelor of Fine Arts in History.

Joan was initiated into Chapter AT, Tecumseh, in 1971. She served as 2000 state convention chairman and was elected to the Executive Board of Nebraska State Chapter in 2000. Joan was privileged to organize two new P.E.O. chapters, Chapter IR, Bellevue, and Chapter IS, Hemingford. Her convention theme for the 2007 state convention in North Platte at which she presided was *"Reaching for a Hand, Touching a Heart."* She served on numerous state committees, including three years on the Membership Committee and as lead editor of the *"Legacy of Nebraska P.E.O."* in 2015.

For Joan, P.E.O. has been a wonderful gift which has helped her to grow as a person. She has learned leadership skills and how to work with others. Serving on the Executive Board of Nebraska State Chapter gave her the opportunity to meet the wonderful women in Nebraska P.E.O. and to travel to all corners of this great state. She treasures the close friendships that she has made through P.E.O.

A dedicated volunteer, Joan has been a member of Tecumseh United Methodist Church for 50+ years, serving on all church committees. She was a teacher for adult basic education and has served on the Tecumseh Library Improvement Foundation and the Johnson County Hospital Task Force. She also served as a judge for History Day at Peru State College for twenty years and on the executive board of Friends of Lied Performance Center for six years. She is a member of Friends of Lied Legends and Delta Gamma Legends. Joan helped found the Tecumseh Area Arts Council and currently serves as treasurer. For over fifty years, she has been a member of Friends in Council, a book club founded in 1895. Joan enjoys playing bridge, reading, doing needlepoint, and working in her flower garden, and most of all, spending time with her nine grandchildren. Jon and Joan Fink reside in Tecumseh.

Pam Kregg

**NEBRASKA STATE PRESIDENT
2007-2008**

Pam Kregg is a third generation P.E.O. She was initiated into her mother's chapter, ER, Arlington Heights, Illinois, in 1975. Her other chapters are HS, Hinsdale, Illinois; DH, Omaha, Nebraska; DO, Hudson, Ohio; ET, Hudson, which she helped organize; and her current chapter, GM, Omaha.

Born in Camp LeJeune, North Carolina, Pam was raised in Arlington Heights, Illinois, and attended Eastern Illinois University in Charleston, Illinois. Pam met her husband Geoff at a wedding of mutual friends and they were married June 7, 1975. They lived in Hinsdale, Illinois, for one year before Geoff's career as a chemical engineer took them to Omaha. Their son Brad was born in Omaha. It was in Chapter DH that Pam held her first office in P.E.O. as recording secretary. She remembers taking minutes as chapter members took turns holding baby Brad.

In 1978 a career opportunity for Geoff took the family to Hudson, Ohio. Pam was a stay at home mom and active volunteer in both the Hudson community and the local schools. She served as president of the Welcome Wagon, P.T.O. and League for Service. Pam also enjoyed singing in a women's ensemble called "The Encores" which sang for various organizations around northeast Ohio and even sang at an Ohio P.E.O. convention. While in Hudson, Pam was a member of Chapter DO and received permission to organize Chapter ET. Pam also served on the Amendments and Recommendations committee of Ohio State Chapter.

Pam, Geoff, and Brad moved back to Omaha in 1995 and Pam served as secretary for the planning committee of the 2001 Convention of Nebraska State Chapter. She went on the state board that same year in the office of treasurer. Prior to 1995, Pam served on the state Finance and Budget committee. She presided at the 2008 state convention selecting "*P.E.O. — Imagine the Possibilities*" as her theme. Pam said her favorite part of serving on the state board was getting to travel the state as she visited local chapters.

After her term on the state board, Pam served on the state Membership and Nominating Committees as well as serving on the Nebraska P.E.O. Home Board. She also served four years on the Special Committee for Membership Advancement for International Chapter reviewing membership policies, designing, implementing and then evaluating a series of twelve programs that chapters could use to provide a balanced year of programs for their chapter, and developing several workshops for use at state conventions.

Pam continues to be an active member of Countryside Community Church where she served as moderator, sings in the choir and serves on various committees. She loves cooking, attending musical theater productions, traveling, reading, and spending quality time with friends and family.

Leann Drullinger
NEBRASKA STATE CHAPTER PRESIDENT
2008-2009

Leann was born in Rock Rapids, Iowa, the oldest child of Gerald and Joanne Elbers, and spent most of her growing up years in Sioux Falls, South Dakota. She graduated from the University of Sioux Falls in 1977 with a degree in medical technology, following her year of clinical training at Lincoln General Hospital in Lincoln. She worked at Kearney Clinic and Children's Memorial Hospital in Omaha before moving to North Platte in 1979. She began working at Great Plains Health and continues to work there on a part-time basis. Working primarily in microbiology, she obtained her specialist registry in microbiology in 1984 and was department supervisor for ten years while still working full-time. Leann currently also serves as the site coordinator for the UNMC clinical laboratory scientist students that train at GPH.

Darrell, a Chadron native, and Leann met while in college in South Dakota and were married in August of 1979. After teaching for thirty-three years in the North Platte Public Schools, Darrell retired from teaching and now works as the sales and catering manager at a local hotel. He also serves as the webmaster for the Nebraska P.E.O. website. They have three children: son Shea, and daughter Brittany and her husband, Sam, all live in North Platte. Brittany is a member of Chapter AK and the mother of their grandson, Allen. Their youngest son, Kalen, lives in Lincoln.

While the kids were in school, much of Darrell and Leann's spare time was involved with them and their activities—sports, marching band, music, speech and drama. They are active members of First Baptist Church and have served in various leadership roles in the church over the years. Both are also active volunteers for the Miss Nebraska scholarship pageant and the North Platte Community Playhouse. Most of Leann's hobbies revolve around crafting of some kind, especially scrapbooking, quilting and sewing. She is a member of the National Association of Parliamentarians and is active on the state level in the Nebraska State Association of Parliamentarians.

Leann's P.E.O. journey began in 1992 when she was initiated into Chapter AK, North Platte, where she remains a member. Her P.E.O. "spark" really began when she attended her first state convention in 1998 and she learned that her reciprocity group would be hosting convention in 2002. She served as chairman of the 2002 convention in North Platte and was elected to the state Executive Board as treasurer at that convention. She served seven years on the board, presiding at the 2009 Convention of Nebraska State Chapter held in Gering. The theme of the convention was *"Perceive, Believe, Achieve."* Highlights of her years of board service include the organization of Chapter IT, Bellevue, the many cherished lifelong friendships made and the memories of board meetings where much P.E.O. business was carried out and laughter was found in abundance. Being organizer of Nebraska State Chapter in 2005 when Joyce Goff presided at the Vancouver convention was a special experience for Leann.

At the Convention of International Chapter in 2009, Leann was appointed to a six-year term on the International Study and Research Committee by President of International Chapter Elizabeth Garrels. She served as chairman of the committee for the 2013-2015 biennium.

Cindy Biehl

NEBRASKA STATE CHAPTER PRESIDENT 2009-2010

Cynthia K. Biehl is the daughter of Willard E. and Dolores L. Zavodny. Cindy was born in Fairbanks, Alaska, on June 13, 1952. Her childhood years were spent near Brainard, Nebraska, in Pueblo, Colorado, and Cozad, Nebraska. During high school in Cozad, Cindy met her husband-to-be, Dave Biehl from Lexington. Dave and Cindy were married on August 11, 1972. They moved to Manhattan, Kansas, where Dave attended Kansas State University's School of Veterinary Medicine, graduating with a DVM in 1976. Upon his graduation they moved to Hastings. Cindy graduated from Hastings College with a Bachelor of Arts degree in Business Administration in 1992. The Biehls have three children, Bradley, Elizabeth and Benjamin. Brad is married to Leslie Pritkin. Liz is married to Nathan Farmer. Ben is married to Katy Zahn. Dave and Cindy have three grandchildren, Rocco and Lyla Biehl, and Liam Farmer.

Cindy was initiated into Chapter GZ, Hastings, in 1980. She served as president, vice president and corresponding secretary in her chapter. Cindy served the Hastings Reciprocity Group in all offices and Reciprocity Group XI in all offices before being elected to the Executive Board at Convention of Nebraska State Chapter held in Hastings in June 2003. This convention was held at Hastings College and is remembered as being cool and rainy. She completed every state chapter office and in 2010 presided as Nebraska State Chapter's one hundred twenty-first president in Norfolk. Convention that year was held at the Johnny Carson Theatre at Norfolk High School. The 2009-2010 year was the final year P.E.O. state chapters had seven state officers. During her time on the board, Cindy organized Chapter IU, Waverly, and helped to merge Chapters FI and IK, Omaha. In September of 2009 she led the Nebraska delegation to Convention of International Chapter in San Diego, California. Following her time on the state board, Cindy served on the Nebraska Membership Development Committee and on a special committee under the direction of the organizer of International Chapter, Beth Ledbetter. This committee was charged with writing updates to the Procedure for Merged Chapters. She also served as a supporting editor on the committee responsible for publishing the *Legacy of Nebraska P.E.O.*, the third in the sequence of history books of Nebraska P.E.O.

Cindy's convention theme was "*Dream and Grow in P.E.O.*" Four hanging textile quilts representing trees of the four seasons hung as the stage decoration at the Johnny Carson Theater in Norfolk. These quilts were designed and made by Kathy Haverly, a Chapter GZ sister and long-time friend. Especially meaningful to Cindy was having her daughter, Liz Biehl, Chapter ES (later HX), as one of her pages, along with sister-in-law, Carol Sandau, Chapter HQ; niece, Lindsey Sandau-Tomlin, Chapter HQ (later HX) and niece, Amy Biehl-Owens, Chapter HV. Lindsey also served as the speaker for the P.E.O. Educational Loan Fund during the Projects Program following the Saturday night banquet. It was an honor and pleasure to have Past President of International Chapter Joyce Goff give devotions at the final meeting of convention on Sunday morning. Cindy ended her years on the state board on a rainy June 13, 2010, which happened to be her 58th birthday.

Cindy explains her passion for P.E.O. this way, "This Sisterhood of loving women has helped me to become a better woman, wife, mother and friend. For me, the best things about P.E.O. are my lifelong relationships with wonderful women."

Dave and Cindy live in Hastings.

Jan Loftin

Nebraska State President
2010-2011

Jan was the third child of Nina and Eugene Morrison. Born and raised in north central Kansas, Jan became a third generation P.E.O. when she was initiated into her mother's chapter in Concordia, Kansas. She was a college student at the time, so didn't start attending P.E.O. meetings until she moved to Lincoln, Nebraska, where she was asked to dimit to Chapter ES Lincoln. She has held most of the offices in her local chapter, and has also been treasurer, vice president and president of the Lincoln Reciprocity Roundtable.

She has two children, a son Terry and a daughter Juli. Juli is a fourth generation P.E.O. and is a respiratory therapist living in Lincoln. Terry and his wife Kimberly live in Ft. Collins, Colorado, and both are computer programmers.

Jan earned her BS degree in Microbiology at the University of Nebraska Lincoln and served as Supervisor of Microbiology at the V. A. Medical Center in Lincoln for twenty-two years. She retired from the VA and later worked part time as a microbiologist in the laboratory at Bryan Medical Center in Lincoln for almost fifteen years.

Jan's love of the outdoors and travel has led her on many adventures with her

BIL and family, including playing golf, canoeing, scuba diving, skiing, biking, and hiking in the mountains. She also loves to organize events. First it was golf tournaments, and now she co-chairs an annual regional duplicate bridge tournament that attracts professional and amateur bridge players from all over the world. Jan has served as president of the Lincoln Women's Golf Association and was chairman of the Women's City Golf Tournament in 2003. The following year she went on the state board of P.E.O. and golf had to take a back seat.

After serving in every office, Jan presided as president at the one hundred twenty-second Convention of Nebraska State Chapter in Lincoln June 11-13, 2011. Her theme was *"P.E.O. – A Network of Love."* As she visited chapters and attended state and International Conventions during her years on the board, Jan came to realize what a really powerful network P.E.O. is. Everywhere you go in P.E.O. there is that connection to your P.E.O. sisters and the love we have for each other. While serving on the state board, Jan had the privilege of organizing Chapter IV, Hickman.

Following her time on the board, Jan has served on the state Membership Development Committee, Nominating Committee, Groupings Committee, Unaffiliate Committee, and the History Committee that is responsible for publishing this book, *Legacy of Nebraska P.E.O.* She enjoyed participating in the first "infomercials" introduced to Nebraska State Convention in 2013. Her passion for P.E.O. has led to many beautiful lifelong friendships and richly rewarding experiences.

Besides P.E.O., Jan's life is filled with traveling with her family and friends, reading, golf, duplicate bridge, playing the piano and many forms of exercise.

In 2015, Jan accepted a six-year appointment by the president of International Chapter to serve as a Regional Membership Representative (RMR), beginning July 1, 2015, and terminating June 30, 2021.

Joyce Victor

NEBRASKA STATE CHAPTER PRESIDENT
2011-2012

Joyce Yates was born in Des Moines, Iowa, to Reginald and Patricia Yates. Her family soon moved to Ashland, Nebraska, where she spent her entire life until she was married. She was the oldest of three children with a brother, Jim, and a sister, Janet. Her Dad was a computer programmer for Western Electric in Omaha. Her mother worked as the sales person at the local plumbing shop. Joyce (Jo) met her husband, Tim Victor, while working at her summer job at a truck stop in Omaha. Tim is the owner of Computer Concepts, a computer retail store in Grand Island, Nebraska. After working as a medical technologist for a number of years Joyce now works in the family business. Jo and Tim have one daughter, Katie, who is married to Matt Green, and they have one grandchild, Marissa Jo.

Jo was initiated into Chapter BD in Ashland, Nebraska, in 1974. She remained an active member during her years of college. Jo's mother was also an active member in Chapter BD and entered Chapter Eternal in 1993. P.E.O. continues in Jo's family as her sister, sister-in-law, niece and daughter are all P.E.O.s. Joyce transferred to Chapter K in Lincoln after getting married and was a charter member of Chapter HW in Lincoln. After her move to Grand Island she transferred to Chapter HJ where she is currently an active member.

In 1991 Joyce was selected as a teller for the Convention of International Chapter that was held in Omaha, Nebraska. That was truly an experience she will always cherish. In 1996 Jo was asked by the Nebraska state board to assist in the development of a Nebraska standing committee for unaffiliated members. She served as Chairman of Unaffiliated Members from its inception in 1996 until 2003. In 2002 she served as a part of the ad hoc committee that reviewed the guidelines, goals, and purposes of a state membership committee. That committee recommended the formation of the Nebraska state Membership Committee which was started in 2003. In 2004 Joyce served as Nebraska State Convention chairman and in 2005 she was elected treasurer of the Nebraska State Chapter executive board on which she served for seven years. Joyce presided at the 2012 state convention in Fremont, Nebraska, where her theme was *"Playing the Keys of P.E.O."* While serving on the state board, Joyce organized Chapter IW Lincoln and IX Kearney. Following her time on the executive board, Joyce was appointed to a four year term on the state Membership Development Committee.

Joyce also served as a personal page for Susan Sellers at the Convention of International Chapter in Vancouver, British Columbia, in 2005. She has been blessed to be a close friend of Past International President Joyce Goff for many years, and they were members of the same chapter in Grand Island where Joyce Goff lived until she retired in Arizona. In October 2012 Jo accepted a five year term on the P.E.O. Educational Loan Fund Board of Trustees, which she has found to be very interesting and inspiring. Joyce enjoys the friendships she is making as a part of the International Leadership Team and looks forward to sharing more about ELF on the state and local level.

In her free time Jo loves to play the piano, do needlework, read and travel. She has accompanied the church choirs for a number of years. Tim and Jo have participated in Worldwide Marriage Encounter and Engaged Encounter weekends since 1981. Joyce looks forward to retirement days with Tim so they can do even more traveling. In the meantime she is happy doing lots of P.E.O. work, working in the family business and spoiling their precious granddaughter.

Reach high, for stars lie hidden in your soul.
Dream deep, for every dream precedes the goal.

-Pamela Vaull Starr

Terri Ridgway
NEBRASKA STATE CHAPTER PRESIDENT
2012-2013

Until 2013 Terri Ridgway lived in the great state of Nebraska all of her life. She was initiated into her mother's chapter, Chapter T, Clay Center, Nebraska, in 1972 as a high school senior. She was an active member of Chapter T for many years, serving as guard, chaplain, corresponding secretary and treasurer. Chapter EG, Kearney, invited Terri to join them in 1998, where she has served as both president and vice president.

Terri's post high school education was at the Medical Institute of Minnesota, Minneapolis, where she trained as a clinical laboratory technician. She worked in the laboratory at Mary Lanning Memorial Hospital in Hastings for many years and later at the Kearney Clinic in Kearney.

Terri and her BIL Ron were married in 1996 and lived in Kearney with their blended family. Ron's three daughters Lolly, Bianca, and Tara and their four grandchildren live in Colorado. Terri was blessed with two daughters but lost her dear Jessica in 1996 at the age of 16. Her daughter Angela and family live in Kearney where Grandma Terri has enjoyed many wonderful hours with her three grandchildren Alexis, Genevieve and Rome.

Terri was elected to the Executive Board of Nebraska State Chapter at the 2006 state convention in Kearney. After serving seven years on the board, she presided at the 2013 state convention in Columbus, celebrating her theme of *"When You Wish Upon a Star."*

In the summer of 2013 Terri and Ron moved to Camano Island, Washington.

In her spare time Terri enjoys movies, sewing, crossword puzzles, and crafts of all kinds.

Merikay Berg
NEBRASKA STATE CHAPTER PRESIDENT
2013-2014

Merikay Theresa Berg grew up in Bismarck, North Dakota. She was taught to love and respect her fellow man, animals, history and the land.

Merikay was thrilled to become a P.E.O. member in 1975. Chapter CE, Arapahoe, shared their joy of P.E.O. with her. She later moved to Lexington, and was joyfully welcomed into Chapter FS. Her daughter Laura Barber and granddaughter Annastasia Barber are also members of Chapter FS.

Merikay is a graduate of three Nebraska Schools: Central Community College, LPN, University of Nebraska Medical Center, College of Nursing, BSN, and University of Nebraska at Kearney, BSBA Business Comprehensive. She had a dual career in farming/agribusiness and nursing for over thirty years. She is an oncology certified nurse and a wound care specialist. Merikay has retired from the farming enterprise and her position as a clinical nurse manager. She worked part time at Lexington Regional Health Center, but is now fully retired. Her greatest professional joy is helping people. Eppley Cancer Center, Cattle Men's Ball has recognized her twice with grants for her work in oncology and wound healing.

Merikay is an award winning quilter. She enjoys all types of needlework. She has served on several educational boards at the state level. Merikay has been a religion teacher and community volunteer. Lexington is an ethnically diverse community, and Merikay helps many immigrant families navigate the educational and health care systems.

Merikay has two children, Chad Neuens (wife, Julie) an attorney in Tulsa, Oklahoma, and a daughter, Laura Barber, a banker in Lexington. The best part of her life is her grandchildren.

Merikay always enjoys hearing and telling a good joke. She is an avid reader and enjoys walking her dogs. (They really walk her!) She is always ready to volunteer her skills. Summers find Merikay at the lake enjoying outdoor activities.

Merikay presided over the 2014 state convention held at Peru State College where her theme was "*Share the Joy.*" Following her term on the state board she served as a member of the state Membership Development Committee. Merikay resides in Lexington.

Karen Blair

**NEBRASKA STATE CHAPTER PRESIDENT
2014-2015**

Karen Blair was born in Lawrence, Kansas, and moved with her family to Emporia, Kansas, at the age of ten. Her first memory of P.E.O. was attending a mother-daughter tea, wearing a frilly spring dress and her Easter bonnet, at the age of five. She recalls seeing huge vases of daisies, and plates of delicious cookies.

Karen received her Associate of Arts degree from Cottey College (1974), Bachelor of Arts from the University of Kansas (1976) and Masters in Business Administration from the University of Kansas (1982).

Karen is a third generation P.E.O. and was initiated into Chapter ES, Emporia, Kansas, in 1976. She shortly relocated to the Kansas City area as a college graduate. Chapter GW, Overland Park, Kansas, provided Karen with her first opportunity to serve as a chapter officer and to develop close ties with women of all ages.

A career change prompted Karen to relocate to Omaha in 1982. After two years of extensive travel as a Union Pacific corporate auditor, she accepted a position with Union Pacific Railroad and established permanent roots in Omaha. Karen transferred her membership in 1985 to chapter HX in Omaha, which had been organized less than two years before. Together, the chapter members learned not only about each other, but about the important work that P.E.O. does.

In August 2014 Karen retired from a 30 year career with Union Pacific Railroad, which had included accounting and customer service functions. Outside of P.E.O. Karen enjoys traveling, reading, needlepoint and Sudoku puzzles.

Karen's mother, Alice Blair, served as president of Kansas State Chapter in 1983-84. From observing her mother, Karen saw that service to P.E.O. at the local chapter, reciprocity, and state chapter level was a growth opportunity which she wanted to experience. Karen served as a Cottey Area Chairman, Cottey state chairman, president of the Omaha P.E.O. Reciprocity Association and 2008 state convention chairman. Karen was elected to the Executive Board of Nebraska State Chapter in 2008 and served seven years with the completion of her year as state president in June 2015. While serving on the state board, Karen organized Chapter IY, Lincoln.

As a tribute to her mother, Karen selected the same theme for her year as state president, *"P.E.O. – A Pattern for Living."* It reflects Karen's love of needlepoint, and her belief that the principles of Faith, Love, Purity, Justice and Truth provide a structure by which we each can pattern our lives.

Some of Karen's favorite P.E.O. memories involve state and International conventions. As a Cottey graduate, Karen knows firsthand the impact that P.E.O.'s financial support and personal acts of kindness can make in the life of a project recipient.

Karen presided over the 2015 state convention in La Vista and currently resides in Omaha.

★

Over and over in these biographical sketches we see the hallmarks of love, the giving graces that our Founders hoped would underpin their beloved Sisterhood. These Presidents have been true to the Seven who gave us this legacy, this passion to reach always for the star and pin it with loving hearts upon every effort made in behalf of Nebraska P.E.O. We cheer for those who are yet to come, honor those who continue to work alongside us, and remember those who have passed to Chapter Eternal...those who have gone before us...gone to paint the stars.

She's Gone to Paint the Stars

Her Chapter Eternal began that day, the stars her home would be
This Sister whom we love so much has slipped away — she's free.
Some lucky angels got to come and teach her this new part
They were surprised when they found out she knew it all by heart.
She memorized a little bit each day she walked this earth.
So she'd be ready for this time — this joyous angel birth.
Her God was close beside her as He whispered each dear word.
Remembering her smiling face we've no doubt that she heard.
We miss her voice, her quiet touch, her kind and clever ways.
We miss her like a melody that perked up gloomy days.
Now late at night we search the skies toward Jupiter and Mars,
Because we know she's on the job —She's gone to paint the stars.

~written for Catherine Trenchard Potter, BC, Nebraska, DC, Texas
by her Nebraska daughter Mary Schwaner, AI

Past State Presidents don '50s getup for 2012 State Convention in Fremont

Nebraska State Chapter
Past Presidents Club

BY *JULIA MCDOUGAL AND CYNTHIA BIEHL*
PAST PRESIDENTS OF NEBRASKA STATE CHAPTER

Past presidents of Nebraska State Chapter meet together each year at convention time. They meet to renew the warm ties of friendship that characterize their group and to maintain their common, deep interest in P.E.O. concerns. From its beginning in 1919, this organization continuously has provided a time of fellowship for its members. Mary Johnson Axtell, a past state president from Lincoln, invited other past presidents to meet prior to the 1919 convention to consider organization with the following note:

> "The Past Presidents of Nebraska Grand Chapter residing here have been talking and are quite of the opinion that we should organize a 'Past Presidents Club'. We will therefore be pleased to arrange (providing it meets with the approval of the others) for a breakfast at eleven-thirty at one of our hotels on the morning of Tuesday, June seventeenth, the day Nebraska Convention opens here in Lincoln. We are extremely anxious to have at least all past presidents residing in Nebraska with us in convention this year and trust you will plan to come. If you favor the organization of this N.P.P. club and wish a plate reserved for you at this breakfast (which may cost from one dollar to one twenty-five) please advise me."

Eleven "pasters" met in response to her invitation and were joined by Winona E. Reeves, Editor of The P.E.O. Record, and Grace R. Parks, past president of Supreme Chapter. The vote to organize was unanimous and Mary Axtell was chosen the first president. Mrs. Parks initiated members present.

They adopted a simple constitution and appointed committees to choose a name and emblem and to set the amount of annual dues. Dues have ranged from fifty cents to five dollars by 2015, with assessments if needed. The president, vice president and secretary-treasurer are elected and installed at the annual meeting of the "pasters." These officers are decided according to a rotation so everyone has a turn and no one is left out.

The past presidents of Nebraska State Chapter wear an emblem encircled by seven marguerites which is presented by the State Chapter. This pin was designed by Mrs. Cornelia J. Sawyer of Iowa and was presented to representatives of Past State Presidents Clubs in 1925 at the convention of the Supreme Chapter. Many states use this pin, although its use is optional.

Initiations for a new member of this group were not always used. In 1939, Helen M. Drake gave a charge to the new member. In 1949, Eva Curtiss again used this ceremony and Irene Van Brunt moved that it be regularly used. The motion carried. Since this time, a formal initiation or charge is not always used when a new member is welcomed to the group. Initiation of the newest member to the "pasters" consists of a fun welcome, sometimes a P.E.O. quiz or simple poem.

The newest member is presented with a daisy or Nebraska guard for her past state president's pin. This guard is purchased with group funds.

Throughout the years, officers of the group have made every effort to maintain communication with all living past presidents. Greeting cards are circulated to members present to sign for those unable to attend the annual meeting. The president notifies all members of the death of a past state president and relays any other message deemed important to the group.

In the early days, the group sent flowers to the service for a deceased member. At present, a monetary gift to the Nebraska P.E.O. Home is given in memory of a deceased past president.

Another important task of this group is to keep a record of burial sites for all Nebraska past state presidents. By 2015 all but eight sites are recorded and kept with the officers. It is the responsibility of the president of the group to send all changes of address, telephone numbers and email addresses to the state secretary for inclusion in the state proceedings. During the odd number years, this group decides which past state presidents will be entitled to Convention of International Chapter. This, too, is on a rotation. The group prepares a roster of members each year that is given out at the annual meeting and mailed to those not present. This group also makes sure that copies of The P.E.O. Record are placed in the Nebraska P.E.O. archives. The International Representative attending state convention is invited to the annual luncheon. She is considered a guest of honor and brings greetings from her home state and from International Chapter.

"Think where one's glory most begins and ends,
And say my glory was I had such friends."
-W. B. Yeats

Gallery of Nebraska State Executive Boards

1992-1993 STATE OFFICERS
Seated: Rosella Mehling, President Mary Owens (BT Weeping Water), Beverley Karrer
Standing: Alice Jennings Fisher, Kathleen Gosch, Mary Lainson Olsen, Phyllis Blanke

1993-1994 STATE OFFICERS
Kathleen Gosch, Alice Jennings Fisher, Anita Kitt, Phyllis Blanke,
President Beverley Karrer (FD Omaha), Rosella Mehling, Mary Lainson Olsen

1994-1995 STATE OFFICERS
Starting in left foreground clockwise: President Rosella Mehling (FR Sidney),
Anita Kitt, Phyllis Blanke, Mary Lainson Olsen, Trish Robertson,
Alice Jennings Fisher, Kathleen "Kathy" Gosch

1995-1996 STATE OFFICERS
Seated: Phyllis Blanke, President Mary Lainson Olsen (G Hastings),
Alice Jennings Fisher, Kathleen Gosch
Standing: Trish Robertson, Jacqueline J. Irwin, Anita Kitt

1996-1997 STATE OFFICERS
Seated: Alice Jennings Fisher, President Phyllis Blanke (GJ Lincoln), Kathleen Gosch
Standing: Trish Robertson, Jeanne Reigle, Jacqueline J. Irwin, Anita Kitt

1997-1998 STATE OFFICERS
Jacqueline J. Irwin, Trish Robertson, Dee Anne Weyeneth, President Alice Jennings Fisher (GP Grand Island), Jeanne Reigle, Anita Kitt, Kathleen Gosch

1998-1999 STATE OFFICERS
Seated: Trish Robertson, President Kathleen Gosch (HB Kearney), Anita Kitt
Standing: Jeanne Reigle, Jacqueline J. Irwin, Dee Anne Weyeneth, Anne Baumhover

"'Who am I to be brilliant, gorgeous, talented, fabulous?' Actually, who are you not to be? You are a child of God. Your playing small does not serve the world. There is nothing enlightened about shrinking so that other people won't feel insecure around you. We are all meant to shine, as children do. We were born to make manifest the glory of God that is within us. It's not just in some of us; it's in everyone. And as we let our own light shine, we unconsciously give other people permission to do the same."

~ Marianne Williamson, A Return to Love:
Reflections on the Principles of "A Course in Miracles"

1999-2000 STATE OFFICERS
Seated: Trish Robertson, President Anita Kitt (ER Benkelman), Jacqueline J. Irwin.
Standing: Jeanne Reigle, Cynthia Jarecke, Dee Anne Weyeneth and Anne Baumhover

2000-2001 STATE OFFICERS
Front: Jeanne Reigle, President Patricia Robertson (BX Omaha), Jacci Irwin.
Back: Anne Baumhover, Cynthia Jarecke, Dee Anne Weyeneth and Joan Fink

2001-2002 STATE OFFICERS
Front: Dee Anne Weyeneth, President Jacci Irwin (AH Alliance), Jeanne Reigle
Back: Pam Kregg, Cynthia Jarecke, Joan Fink, and Anne Baumhover

2002-2003 STATE OFFICERS
Front: Anne Baumhover, Dee Anne Weyeneth. Back: Joan Fink, Pam Kregg, seated center back, President Jeanne Reigle (AL Madison); Cyndi Jarecke and Leann Drullinger

2003-2004 STATE OFFICERS
Front: Anne Baumhover, Joan Fink, Pam Kregg. Back: Cynthia Jarecke, President Dee Anne Weyeneth (K Lincoln), Leann Drullinger, Cindy Biehl

2004-2005 STATE OFFICERS
Front: Cynthia Jarecke, President Anne Baumhover (HK Fremont), Joan Fink. Middle: Pam Kregg, Leann Drullinger. Back: Jan Loftin, Cindy Biehl

2005-2006 STATE OFFICERS
Seated: Pam Kregg, President Cynthia Jarecke (CH Columbus), Joan Fink
Standing: Leann Drullinger, Joyce Victor, Cindy Biehl, Jan Loftin

2006-2007 STATE OFFICERS
Front: Joyce Victor, Pam Kregg, President Joan Fink (AT Tecumseh), Leann Drullinger
Terri Ridgway. Back: Jan Loftin, Cindy Biehl.

2007-2008 STATE OFFICERS
From left leaning forward: Jan Loftin, Leann Drullinger, President Pam Kregg (GM Omaha), Cindy Biehl. Back row: Merikay Berg, Joyce Victor, Terri Ridgway

2008-2009 STATE OFFICERS
Seated: Cindy Biehl, President Leann Drullinger (AK North Platte), Jan Loftin
Standing: Terri Ridgway, Joyce Victor, Karen Blair, Merikay Berg

2009-2010 STATE OFFICERS
Seated: Jan Loftin, President Cindy Biehl (GZ Hastings), Joyce Victor
Standing: Patti Cowher, Merikay Berg, Terri Ridgway, Karen Blair

2010-2011 STATE OFFICERS
Seated: Joyce Victor, President Jan Loftin (ES Lincoln), Patti Cowher
Standing: Terri Ridgway, Merikay Berg, Karen Blair

Amendments adopted at Convention of International Chapter in 2009 removed the office of state corresponding secretary in 2010-2011 and the office of first vice president in 2011-2012. During 2010-2011, Nebraska had six state officers. During 2011-2012, Nebraska had five state officers for the first time.

2011-2012 STATE OFFICERS
Patti Cowher, Karen Blair, Merikay Berg, Terri Ridgway,
President Joyce Victor (HJ Grand Island)

2012-2013 STATE OFFICERS
Nicole Berner, Patti Cowher, Karen Blair, Merikay Berg,
President Terri Ridgway (EG Kearney)

2013-2014 STATE OFFICERS
President Merikay Berg (FS Lexington), Karen Blair, Patti Cowher, Nicole Berner, Lisa Helmick

2014-2015 STATE OFFICERS
Seated in front: President Karen Blair (HX Omaha), Patti Cowher
In back: Lisa Helmick, Nicole Berner, Nancy Wheeler

reaching for a hand

...touching a heart

P.E.O. Jewelry

Take a look at your sister's P.E.O. pin. It might just tell you a lot about her!

If she wears a star encircled by daisies, she's sure to be a past state president. If the daisies encircle a star with the letters NEBR on the face, it's a treasured old pin passed along from previous generations.

Is hers a gold daisy crossed by a gavel? She has served her Reciprocity Group as president.

That gold circlet pin? It's the badge of a Nebraska delegate to International Convention, proudly worn by sisters who have had the privilege of attending P.E.O.'s biennial gathering.

And if she happens to sport a lovely gold pendant on a necklace chain, you can be sure that she or someone close to her purchased it to celebrate the 100th anniversary of Nebraska State Chapter.

So never apologize for staring at your sister's P.E.O. jewelry. There may or may not be a story behind that pin, but there's guaranteed to be a smiling sister.

Articles by Joyce Goff

Come on Along!

by Joyce Goff

Published in the September-October 2003 P.E.O. Record while Joyce was President of International Chapter

I am starting a great adventure as president of this wonderful Sisterhood of ours. I invite each of you to join me as we learn more about P.E.O. and strive to do the best we can—no matter what our position is in our local chapter, in our state, or on the International level. Every assignment is important, and every member is an essential part of the whole.

...Let's examine this great organization that we embrace. P.E.O. can be very, very small! As small as a daisy! Success in P.E.O. is taking one step at a time; it is a note of encouragement, a phone call, a smile. It is sitting beside a new member and making her feel welcome. It is new friends who accept you and old friends who still love you even when you move away. Cultivate the little things! P.E.O. is trying, and making mistakes, and learning. All of these things that happen are like daisies. Taken one at a time they are not so much, but bunched together, they can be glorious!

A long time ago, my husband and I were privileged to host our graddaughter's first birthday party. Of course, she got too many presents! Her five-year-old cousin was helping her open them, and she was going too slow to suit him. Finally, in exasperation Ryan said, "Ashley, if you don't open the present, you will never know the surprise!" Well, they finally got everything unwrapped, and Ashley spent the rest of the day pushing around an empty box while Ryan played with the birthday toys.

I learned something from Ryan that day! If you don't open the gift, you will never know the surprise! Each of you has been given a gift—P.E.O. Open the gift; don't keep it forever unused! Accept an office, propose a name, look for a project recipient—all little things, but put together they make the gift of P.E.O. very large.

Now, not only must you accept the little things, you must pass them on. As a P.E.O., you learn tolerance. One of your biggest surprises may be that your Sisterhood is not perfect, and neither are any of your sisters—including your officers! But they are all very, very good! Learn to love the goodness!

Now that I told you that P.E.O. can be very small, P.E.O. can also be very great! As great as a star! It is this greatness that makes my job such a challenge.

Some of you ask me, "Is it worthwhile? The hundreds of hours you work, the thousands of miles you travel, is it worthwhile?" And I answer, "Yes, it is worth every bit of the time and effort I spend." By contributing to the work of this great Sisterhood, my little life can make a difference, and that is exactly why whatever you do for P.E.O. is worth it! It's worth it to do your work and do it well. So open the gift, enjoy the surprises!

I thank each of you for giving me the courage to accept the gavel as president of this great organization. I invite you to come along as we explore my theme for the biennium: *P.E.O. small as a daisy, great as a star!*   -Joyce

P.E.O. Pockets

BY JOYCE GOFF

PUBLISHED IN THE NOVEMBER-DECEMBER 2003 P.E.O. RECORD
WHILE JOYCE WAS PRESIDENT OF INTERNATIONAL CHAPTER

Thank you for the faith you have shown in me by electing me to the high office of president of International Chapter. I shall do my best to earn your confidence in my ability to guide this great organization. I believe I can succeed because I have four fine officers on my board, I have a great chief administrative officer, and about thirty-five other people in Des Moines who will help me when I flounder. Most of all, there are a quarter of a million P.E.O.s who believe we can do it!

A minister stood before his congregation and said, "I have good news and bad news. The good news is, we have enough money to pay for our new building program. The bad news is, it's still out there in your pockets!"

I stand before you today with some good news and some bad news. The good news is that we have enough membership to continue our history of being a vital, effective Sisterhood. The good news is what we saw at the projects program at Convention of International Chapter—P.E.O. *is* helping women! I love to give the figures for the money we have given when I am speaking at BIL banquets because when I do, all the BILS wake up and start listening! The good news is that our Cottey College has just received the highest evaluation by the Northeast Accreditation Association with no requirements for further evaluation for ten years. The good news is that all across the United States and Canada, a quarter of a million women are enjoying the unique comfort of P.E.O.

Well, then, what's the bad news? The bad news is that for many members, P.E.O. is still in their pockets! They have been initiated but they aren't living the lives of P.E.O.s. The bad news is the competition we face in this modern world of ours. The bad news is that every year we lose hundreds of active members because, unless we work hard, two years from now our enrollment will surely be down. If we want to continue the benefits of our Sisterhood, we are going to have to get our enthusiasm for P.E.O. out of our pockets and build our membership.

We who attend conventions of International Chapter know the immense scope of P.E.O. I believe if we could get every P.E.O. to attend even one International Convention, our Sisterhood would prosper beyond our wildest dreams. If we could get them to visit our beautiful headquarters in Des Moines or to tour the campus at Cottey College, it would almost certainly change their concept of this great organization to which they belong.

The bad news is that thousands of members really don't know much about their Sisterhood, and this biennium I want you to get your enthusiasm out of your pockets and teach them!

Here's something that might interest you. We have no law that says only delegates and hostess chapters may attend a state convention. I have visited chapters where that *would* be news! Take that message seriously. Next spring, let's invite and offer rides to lots of visitors to our state conventions and teach them what we are about. What fun it would be for all the members of a newly organized chapter to attend their first convention together!

Here's another thing some of you apparently don't know about chapter meetings—there is nothing in our Constitution that says you *must* sit beside the person you rode with! The next time you go to a chapter meeting, I challenge you to sit beside someone you don't know very well and make her happy she came!

Under the leadership of Nancy Hoium, this has been a biennium of great achievement. The new executive board looks forward to the challenges of a new biennium. We have plans for progress and plans for helping the Sisterhood adapt to the changes inherent in this century. We will continue to accommodate our faithful older members who know the methods of the past, and we will offer all our members easier ways to accomplish their work in this age of advanced technology. There is room for all of us and there is strength in our union.

We want our membership to grow, but whether it declines or grows, we will enjoy what it offers us. We who love P.E.O. know that when we finally empty our P.E.O. pockets, we will find them filled with the joy of happy memories and dear friendships. In good times and bad we are sustained, and nothing is better than that.

-Joyce

★

The 2003-2005
Executive Board of International Chapter

W. Joyce Goff, president

Ann H. Fields, first vice president

Barbara Andes, second vice president

Elizabeth E. Garrels, organizer

Susan Reese Sellers, recording secretary

Others Who Served Nebraska State Chapter
P.E.O. Sisterhood
1890-2015

Executive Board Members

Members of the executive board of Nebraska State Chapter did not always progress from one office to another. There were many dedicated women who served less than seven years but, nonetheless, played an important part in the history of Nebraska State Chapter.

Dora Budenz, C, Norfolk - first vice president, 1890 and 1891

Minnie Dutton, G, Hastings - second vice president, 1890 and 1891

Carrie Z. Smith, A, York - treasurer, 1890 and 1891

Winifred F. Smith, A, York - second vice president, 1891-1893

Anna Wykoff, I, Wahoo - recording secretary, 1891-1893

Elizabeth D. Jones, G, Hastings - corresponding secretary, 1891-1892

Dora McNaul, H, Holdrege - treasurer, 1891-1892

Ida Wagner, F, Plattsmouth - recording secretary, 1892-1893; 1895-1896

Alma Waterman, F, Plattsmouth - treasurer, 1892-1894

Clara C. Crawford, J, Nelson - chaplain, 1892-1893, chaplain and second vice president, 1893-1894

Celia A. Gorby, J, Nelson - recording secretary, 1893-1894

Ella J. Collins, I, Wahoo - corresponding secretary, 1893-1894

Kittie Dutton, G, Hastings - second vice president and chaplain, 1894-1895, first vice president, 1895-1896

Dorothy Higby, A, York - corresponding secretary, 1894-1896

Virginia Corbett, K, Lincoln - second vice president, 1895-1896

Cora G. Little, H, Holdrege - first organizer, 1895-1896

Carrie Norburg, H, Holdrege - second vice president, 1896-1898

Ella Allen, E, Omaha - corresponding secretary, 1896-1897

Laura Allen, D, Superior - organizer, 1896-1897

Adde Sexton, O, Geneva - recording secretary, 1897-1898

Grace Kipp, G, Hastings - corresponding secretary, 1897-1899

May Frush, I, Wahoo - treasurer, 1897-1900

Kate M. Barbour, L, Harvard - organizer, 1898-1900, first vice president, 1900-1902

Mary R. Patterson, P, Bloomington - second vice president, 1898-1899, first vice president, 1899-1900

Hulda Miller, H, Holdrege - second vice president, 1899-1900

Barbara Stryker, M, Omaha - recording secretary, 1899-1900

Laura M. L. Vance, Q, Wymore - second vice president, 1900-1902

Edith Youngstedt, I, Wahoo - corresponding secretary, 1900-03, second vice president, 1903-1904

Candace Black, P, Bloomington - treasurer, 1900-1902

Louie Diffenbacher, A, York - recording secretary, 1901-1903, first vice president, 1903-1904

Ella J. Brown, G, Hastings - second vice president, 1902-1903 and 1906-1907, treasurer, 1904-1906

Cora G. McMullen, Q, Wymore - corresponding secretary, 1903-1905, second vice president, 1905-1906

H. Grace Thomas, J, Nelson - organizer, 1902-1904, second vice president, 1904-1905

Martha A. Hunter, S, Broken Bow - first vice president, 1904-1905

Eva A. Wagner, E, Omaha - organizer 1904-1906

Elizabeth H. Clark, T, Clay Center - first vice president, 1905-1906

Laura V. Donisthorpe, O, Geneva - recording secretary, 1906-1907

Ann E. Kyd, Z, Beatrice - corresponding secretary, 1906-1908

Ellington C. Britt, X, McCook - recording secretary, 1907-1909, first vice president 1909-1910

Harriet M. Clearman, N, Minden - treasurer, 1907-1909, second vice president, 1909-1910

Gertrude M. Thomas, AD, Seward - corresponding secretary, 1908-1909

Helen Koehler, G, Hastings - recording secretary, 1909-1910

Nina King, AA, Edgar - second vice president, 1910-1911

Bessie B. Hartigan, G, Hastings - recording secretary, 1909-1910

Martha B. Quein, Z, Beatrice - second vice president, 1911-1912

Amber B. Hartquest, AC, Aurora - recording secretary, 1911-1912

Addie E. Schiller, AB, Central City - treasurer, 1911-1913

Anna E. Y. Morgan, AE, Hebron - second vice president, 1912-1914

Elizabeth H. Travis, F, Plattsmouth - corresponding secretary, 1913-1914, second vice president, 1914-1915

Rose E. Shedd, G, Hastings - second vice president, 1915-1916

Ellinor O. Kemp, AG, Fullerton - treasurer, 1915-1917; organizer, 1917-1919

Hester B. Copper, M, Omaha - recording secretary, 1917-1918

Hattie Rincker, AK, North Platte - second vice president, 1918-1919

Marie Johnson, BI, Shelton - second vice president, 1919-1920

Grace Funkhouser, E, Omaha - treasurer, 1923-1924; 1926-1927

Eloine C. Gettys, BY, Lincoln - organizer, 1924-1925

Grace Leftwich, AP, St. Paul - treasurer, 1924-1926

Gertrude G. Dafoe, AT, Tecumseh - treasurer, 1927-1929, corresponding secretary, 1929-1930; recording secretary, 1930-1931

Julia Lowry, AV, Pawnee City - treasurer, 1930-1931, corresponding secretary, 1931-1932

Floy Roper, DK, Lincoln, treasurer, 1931-1932

Harriett Charlton, CU, Norfolk - treasurer, 1939-1940

Edith Melville, S, Broken Bow - treasurer, 1950-1951, corresponding secretary, 1951-1952

Laura Miller, CH, Columbus - treasurer, 1957-1958, corresponding secretary, 1958-1959

Dorothy Kain, AN, Lexington - treasurer, recording secretary, organizer, second vice president, 1958-1962

Verna Drayton, CA, Valentine - treasurer, 1968-1969, corresponding secretary, 1969-1971

Margie Martin, FF, Lincoln - treasurer, 1969-1970

Penny Dinklage, EP, Wisner - recording secretary, 1970-1971

Muriel Clarke, A, York - corresponding secretary, 1971-1972

Nebraska's Assistant Secretary-Treasurer/ Paid Assistant

Catherine Anderson, Chapter CR, PSP, 1972-1973 was the first Assistant Secretary-Treasurer and served from 1973 to 1980.

Nelsine Scofield, Chapter DN, PSP, served from 1980 to 1990.

Julia Peetz, BO, served from 1990 until 2006.

Mary Kay Tuma, HJ, served from 2006 until 2013.

The title Assistant Secretary-Treasurer changed to Paid Assistant in 2008.

Sheri Rasmussen, BG, became Nebraska's Paid Assistant in 2013.

Since 1995, the responsibilities of the Nebraska paid assistant have fluctuated little and her main job was always to support the work of the state chapter. The assistant secretary-treasurer processed all receipts and disbursements of Nebraska State Chapter. Gift envelopes were used by local chapters to facilitate sending and processing contributions. Computerized receipts and acknowledgements were mailed to chapters for gifts received. Monthly and annual financial reports were prepared and sent to the state officers. Annual reports were sent to International Chapter. All chapter contributions were sent to International Chapter on a monthly basis. The books were audited by a CPA. The H-I-J Forms were posted to the Nebraska State Chapter Enrollment Book and summaries were sent to the executive office in Des Moines. Notices of dues for members of disbanded chapters were mailed in January. The assistant secretary-treasurer mailed the annual reports of membership to each Nebraska chapter by February 1st and prepared the annual report for International Chapter by April 1st.

Because of the numerous questions from local chapters and members, Nebraska State Chapter added an 800 phone line for the assistant secretary-treasurer. The assistant secretary-treasurer attended the annual Finance and Budget Committee meeting and reported to the executive board at board meetings when required. She prepared bulk mailing for the president, convention chairmen and for the state Proceedings. She also kept the memorial roll and gifts list for state conventions. In 1999, the assistant secretary-treasurer installed and implemented membership and accounting software purchased from International Chapter. Some years the assistant secretary-treasurer gave a workshop at state conventions. She had the opportunity to attend International Conventions with the Nebraska delegation and at times there were workshops provided for her. She often served on the Credentials Committee or the Committee to Approve the Minutes and helped with registration during state conventions.

By the early 2000s, the assistant secretary-treasurer used a computer for most of her accounting and membership work and worked more closely with International Chapter to keep records electronically. Membership information from the H-I-J forms was put into membership software summaries and sent electronically to Des Moines. She continued to mail a copy of proposed amendments to local chapters. In 2006, the assistant secretary-treasurer was trained on the new iMIS State Membership System in Des Moines. This system connected directly with the membership records at International in Des Moines. She in turn trained the executive board about using iMIS. She used email for corresponding with the executive board, local chapters and members. Gift envelopes were no longer used for chapter or individual contributions. A contribution form was available on the Nebraska P.E.O. website. Following the 2009 Convention of International Chapter, there were changes to the way the paid assistant sent, received and processed annual reports from local chapters. During this time the paid assistant prepared welcome letters to new initiates in Nebraska Chapters.

In 2013 the accounting system was converted to the new accounting system of P.E.O., QBE State Accounting. This accounting system is housed in a secure system and backup is done by Alliance Technologies in Iowa.

Over the years, the Nebraska P.E.O.s who have served as assistant secretary-treasurers and paid assistants have been an integral part of the success of Nebraska State Chapter. Each past state president appreciates their hard work and dedication to the Sisterhood.

In 2008, the title Assistant Secretary-Treasurer was officially changed to Paid Assistant.

Gallery of Nebraska's International Presidents

Past Presidents of Nebraska State Chapter
who served P.E.O. as Supreme Grand/Supreme/International President
1890-2015

Alice Cary Brooks Briggs
Nebraska 1890-1991
Supreme Grand 1893-1895

Carrie Russell Hapeman
Nebraska 1899-1901
Supreme Grand 1901-1903

Carrie M. Peterson
Nebraska 1904-1906
Supreme Grand 1907-1909

Helen M. Drake
Nebraska 1911-1912
Supreme Chapter 1915-1917

Bertha Clark Hughes
Nebraska 1913-1914
Supreme Chapter 1921-1923

Irene Simpson Van Brunt
Nebraska 1950-1951
Supreme Chapter 1964-1965

W. Joyce Goff
Nebraska 1987-1988
International Chapter 2003-2005

Section Five
Nebraska P.E.O.s Who Have Led the Sisterhood
1893-2015

Nebraskans can be proud of their contribution to P.E.O. From the very beginning, their authority and determination predominated in many areas of the Sisterhood. Words from Winona Evans Reeves' note written in 1950 to Bertha Clark Hughes elaborate on Nebraska's influence:

> "Nebraska's contribution to the general organization of P.E.O. itself was a notable one. As the first state chapter to be formed, she set the pattern for our form of government, that of a republic. In all the history of P.E.O. there is no more interesting and dramatic incident than that night in the Savery Hotel in Des Moines, Iowa, when a small group of delegates from Nebraska stood their ground against all comers, for the right to be the first state chapter; that Iowa should form a state chapter and that the two of them should be on a parity with over-all jurisdiction."

Nebraska is proud to have seven members who were presidents of Supreme or International Chapter. All of them were past presidents of Nebraska State Chapter and their biographies are found in Section Four of this book.

Alice Cary Briggs, 1893-1895, was an officer of grace, dignity and efficiency. She brought knowledge and experience to the presidency, although she had been initiated as late as 1889. She had pleaded successfully for forming the first state grand chapter in Nebraska, had been its first president, and had been on a committee to draw up a form for its state charter. She had urged formation of a supreme power for the Sisterhood, and was on the committee to draft a constitution and bylaws for Supreme Grand Chapter. As president, she urged formation of state grand chapters where practicable, installing the officers for Iowa State Grand Chapter. Missouri State Grand Chapter was organized during her presidency, as well as five local chapters widespread from the Midwest to California.

Carrie Russell Hapeman, 1901-1903, was a clear-thinking person of excellent judgment, wit and good humor. Her leadership ability and zeal for P.E.O. led to her rise from initiation in Minden in 1895 to the presidency of Supreme Chapter in 1901. She wrote an installation ceremony, was on the committee promoting the star ceremony, and helped to write a proposed member form used in chapters. She presided at Supreme Chapter Convention in 1903 at Lincoln. During her administration, the Sisterhood grew rapidly in membership and in state and local chapters. Colorado, Illinois and Kansas State Grand Chapters all were organized in 1903. She lived to be only fifty-five, but life and accomplishments had moved rapidly for her.

Carrie M. Peterson, 1907-1909, was prominent in a broad spectrum of activities in church, Federated Women's Clubs, in patriotic drives and on the Nebraska Board of Control. She was a member of Chapter AC, Aurora. She presided at the 1909 Supreme Chapter Convention in Mount Pleasant, Iowa. A woman of administrative and business ability, she also demonstrated personal charm and modesty. She was chairman of the committee which revised and distributed the initiation ceremony adopted in Brookfield, Missouri, in 1907.

Helen M. Drake, 1915-1917, had unusual administrative ability as president of Supreme Chapter. She had knowledge of the strong and weak points of P.E.O. procedure and worked tirelessly to increase efficiency. Unfortunately, following her devotion to P.E.O. responsibilities, she became ill and was confined to her room at the Fontenelle Hotel at the convention in Omaha. Delegates were grieved and disappointed, but her planning and guidance were felt constantly, as she kept in close touch with the meeting.

Bertha Clark Hughes, 1921-1923, became president of Supreme Chapter at the age of 41, bringing youth and enthusiasm for perfection in every area of P.E.O. The Executive Office was moved to Omaha from Chicago, and she closely supervised every department. The working capital of the Educational Fund was increased to $204,163. The revised ritual was distributed to all chapters. Mary Allen Stafford was guest of honor at the large Seattle convention over which Bertha presided in 1923.

Irene Simpson Van Brunt, June 1964-October 1965, was elected to the executive board of Supreme Chapter in 1955 and unexpectedly acceded from the first vice presidency to the presidency of Supreme Chapter in 1964. She presided at a beautiful and inspiring convention in Atlantic City, New Jersey, October 4-7, 1965. After her term as president ended, she continued to serve Supreme Chapter on the publication committee for the Centennial History, *Out of the Heart,* and was chairman of the P.E.O. Foundation Board of Trustees. She devoted many hours to the publication of Nebraska State Chapter's first history, *The Saga of Nebraska P.E.O.* Irene's capabilities, her energy and her faithful devotion to P.E.O. were hallmarks of her service to the Sisterhood.

W. Joyce Goff, 2003-2005, was installed as recording secretary on the International Executive Board in 1995 and completed service in all five offices. She presided in Vancouver, Canada, October 6-8, 2005. Joyce graduated from Nebraska Wesleyan University in Lincoln, Nebraska, in 1951. She is a teacher and professional registered parliamentarian. Joyce held several offices in both the local and state bodies of the Nebraska State Association of Parliamentarians. She served on the International Study and Research Committee from 1990 to 1995. During her fifteen years of service to International Chapter, Joyce visited 44 state chapter conventions and several Canadian, Alaskan and Hawaiian chapters. She estimated her travels for P.E.O. amounted to nearly 44,000 miles. Joyce's reputation as a beloved speaker with an uncanny to-the-point humor preceeded her whenever she was invited to a P.E.O. convention or meeting. If you have been fortunate enough to have met Joyce, you know what a P.E.O. is. One of her favorite quotes is *"Sooner or later we are all asked the question, 'What is a P.E.O.?' I have the perfect answer. You say, 'I am!' If you have lived your life as a P.E.O. should, that is all the answer they will need."* This book, the third history of Nebraska P.E.O., is dedicated to Joyce, the seventh president of International Chapter from Nebraska.

Vera "Bobbie" Koefoot, 1987-1990. It should be noted that Vera (Bobbie) Koefoot, GP, Grand Island, served through the offices in International and would have been elected president in Omaha in 1991 had cancer not claimed her a few months earlier.

Others Who Have Served International Chapter

Executive Secretary

Lulah T. Andrews of Chapter H, Holdrege, later K, Lincoln, and BN, Omaha, was Executive Secretary of Supreme Chapter nearly seven years from January 1922 to October 1928. She assisted in moving the office from Chicago to Omaha. When the Memorial Library in Mount Pleasant was finished she helped to move the office there and remained for a year. In 1929, she represented Nebraska State Chapter in presenting the portrait of Franc Roads Elliott to the Memorial Library.

Deborah Cowan who was initiated into Chapter CM, Crete, served as Chief Administrative Officer of International Chapter for five years, from 1988 to 1993. Before she moved to Des Moines to accept that position, Deborah and her husband lived in South Dakota. Deborah also served as International Convention Coordinator for both the Phoenix and Omaha International Conventions in 1989 and 1991, respectively.

MEMBERS OF INTERNATIONAL BOARDS OF TRUSTEES

Ida B. Johnson (Lewellen) was chairman of the first Board of Trustees of The P.E.O. Record, 1913-1915.

Bertha Clark Hughes was chairman of the Board of Trustees of The P.E.O. Record.

Rose Owens served as chairman of the Board of Trustees of the P.E.O. Supply Department.

Maude Hendy was appointed by Alice Scott to the Board of Trustees of the P.E.O. Educational Fund in 1925 and was chairman from 1929 to 1931.

Helen Riddell was appointed in 1949 by Laura S. Knapp to the Board of Trustees of The P.E.O. Record. She served six years, the last two as chairman from 1953 to 1955.

Ellen Ann Qualsett served on the Board of Trustees of the P.E.O. Foundation. She served for four years from 1985 to 1989. Ill health forced her to resign before completing her term.

Dr. C. H. Oldfather, of the University of Nebraska, Lincoln; *Dr. D. L. Crawford,* of Doane College and *Dr. Milo Bail,* of the University of Nebraska at Omaha, served on the Board of Trustees of Cottey College.

Joyce Victor, HJ, Grand Island, was appointed to the Board of Trustees of the P.E.O. Educational Loan Fund in 2012 for a five-year term.

COMMITTEES AND OTHER SERVICES

Ida B. Johnson was on the committee which compiled the first history of the P.E.O. Sisterhood—the 1903 *White History*—which is now out of print.

Bertha Clark Hughes was a member of the committee drafting the first laws governing the P.E.O. Educational Fund, adopted in 1909 in Mount Pleasant. She also was the fund treasurer in 1917-1919, a parliamentarian, and was known for her sincere, powerful prayers.

Clara A. Waterhouse, AJ, Fremont, was appointed to the first committee for promotion of a memorial library, 1921-1923.

Minnie M. Stuff, K, Lincoln, was a member of the Committee for Revision of the Ritual, including the Burial Ritual in 1921.

Helen M. Drake was chairman of the finance committee for erection of the Memorial Library in Mount Pleasant, Iowa, honoring the seven Founders. At the dedication service it was announced that the library was completely free of debt and Mrs. Drake was commended for her work.

Ada H. Mead served as secretary of the Centennial Commission and then became chairman of the P.E.O. Centennial Center Building Committee where she gave magnificent service to Supreme Chapter. Through The P.E.O. Record and elsewhere, she explained the idea and the plans and promoted the building of the Center. In addition to working with the architects, she was responsible for much of the planning and supervision of furnishings and worked closely with the decorators in Omaha. To quote from the Centennial issue of The P.E.O. Record, "*Extreme admiration for the work of the P.E.O. Centennial Building Committee was often voiced. Those who knew the chairman, Ada Mead, could see her fine hand in making the building a representative structure of P.E.O., a building which she wishes to elevate those who would visit in years to come.*" Ada presided at the dedication ceremonies during the 1969 Des Moines convention, accepting the keys from the architect and in turn presenting them to Ethel Gardiner, Supreme Chapter President. Ada was well-known in Supreme Chapter for her inspirational addresses and devotional messages. She served as head page and head guard for many Supreme Conventions.

Vera Koefoot was appointed to the Finance Committee of International Chapter in 1981. She served six years on the committee and as chairman from 1985 to 1987.

Joyce Goff, HJ, Grand Island, was appointed to the International Study and Research Committee in 1990 and served five years. She was the chairman from 1993 to 1995.

Alice Jennings Fisher, GP, Grand Island, was appointed to the Finance Committee in 2003 and served until 2005.

Pamela Kregg, GM, Omaha, was appointed to the Special Committee for Membership Advancement in 2008 and served until 2011.

Leann Drullinger, AK, North Platte, was appointed to the Study and Research Committee in 2009 and served a six-year term. She served as chairman from 2013 to 2015.

Joyce Goff was appointed to the International Study and Research Committee in 1990 and served five years. She was the chairman from 1993 to 1995.

This treasured Nebraska daughter was elected to the Executive Board of International Chapter in 1995, and served for eight years before her installation as President of International Chapter in 2003.

She completed her tenure on the Board in 2005 at the International Convention in Vancouver over which she presided.

Section Six

Nebraskans Who Have Influenced P.E.O.

In addition to standing and special committees, many other Nebraska P.E.O.s have served Supreme and International Chapter or Supreme and International conventions in various capacities. Nebraska State Chapter is pleased with the many members who were initiated in the state and who have served as presidents of other state chapters. Although there is risk of omission, they deserve mention.

Hulda S. Miller, N, Minden, served on a 1901 Supreme Grand Chapter Auditing Committee, and after moving to Los Angeles, she held Supreme Grand Chapter offices of second vice president from 1905 to 1907 and corresponding secretary from 1907 to 1911.

Olga Iddic, initiate of Chapter G, Hastings, served Missouri State Chapter, was first vice president of Supreme Chapter from 1911 to 1913 and organizer from 1915 to 1917.

Hallie Newell, initiated into Chapter F, Plattsmouth, served Illinois and Missouri State Chapters and served as president of Supreme Chapter from 1935 to 1937.

Irene Kerr, born in Central City, was president of Supreme Chapter from 1969 to 1971.

Alice Provost, initiate of Chapter DF, Stanton, served as treasurer of Mississippi State Chapter from 1974 to 1975.

Lilas Brandhorst, initiate of Chapter DF, Stanton, served Missouri State Chapter, the Centennial Commission, and as president of International Chapter from 1981 to 1983.

Mary Owens, BT, Weeping Water, served as chairman of the Credentials Committee during the 2005 Convention of International Chapter.

Jacqueline J. Irwin, AH, Alliance, served as chairman of the Committee to Approve the Minutes for the 2005 Convention of International Chapter.

Nebraska P.E.O.s Who Have Served As President Of Other State Chapters

Adele Reed, EE, Lincoln, president of Washington D. C. District Chapter, 1972-73.
  A Time to Every Purpose

Jane Knox, CS, Lincoln, president of Maryland State Chapter, 1984.
  Finding the Joy

Grace Loewenstein, BR, Lincoln, president of New Jersey State Chapter, 1976-77.
  P.E.O., a Trail of Stardust

Helen Davis, EN, Pender, president of Iowa State Chapter.

Margaret Waddell, Z, Beatrice, president of Georgia State Chapter.

Eliza Sams, DX, Lincoln, president of Louisiana State Chapter 1993-94.

Priscilla Moller Drayton, CZ, Wakefield, president of North Dakota State Chapter.

Helen Swanson Gale, T, Clay Center, president of Idaho State Chapter

Jan Goodsell, BB, Ord, president of Tennessee State Chapter in 2009.

Irene Mortensen Church, CB, Ravenna, president of Colorado State Chapter in 1980-81

Alice Greenslit Provost, DF, Stanton, president of Mississippi State Chapter in 1982-83.

Lilas Brandhorst, DF, Stanton, served as president of Missouri State Chapter in 1961-62, and as President of Supreme Chapter in 1981-83.

Mary Bowen, GM, Omaha, served as president of New Mexico State Chapter and as secretary of Supreme Chapter

It is interesting to note the number of presidents of California State Chapter with Nebraska origin, including the following:

Ella J. Brown, G, Hastings.

Ollie P. Cramer, AC, Aurora.

Leah S. Shirey, CN, Osceola. Later serving Supreme Chapter as corresponding secretary and organizer from 1947 to 1951.

Ethel Desparias, BE, Pierce.

Mabel R. Jessup, T, Clay Center.

Mary Davis Garvin, AL, Madison.

Doubtless, many others with roots in Nebraska have made valuable contributions to the P.E.O. Sisterhood in other places. Although Nebraska P.E.O.s do not boast of their transplanted talents, they can feel quiet pride in their continued love for P.E.O. ideals and their gifts of themselves.

Gifts Of Love

Star Ceremony — In the 1903 *White History of P.E.O.*, the following words by Julia M. Klinck are found: *"The impress of a beautiful mind and heart has been stamped indelibly upon P.E.O. by the gift to our Order of the Star ceremony...."* A modest teacher, Miss Ida B. Johnson, K, Lincoln, originated the ceremony for initiation, and Joanna Van Boskirk, K, contributed her hand work in making the beribboned gold star. Chapter K exemplified the ceremony in 1897 at the Convention of Grand Chapter in Wahoo, where it received cordial approval. It was again exemplified in 1899 at the Convention of Supreme Grand Chapter by Chapter A, Chicago. The Convention enthusiastically adopted it and a committee was appointed to promote uniform use in all chapters. It soon became a well-loved part of the ceremony.

Size of the Pin — After the size of the official P.E.O. emblem was reduced in 1915, there was much nostalgia expressed in The P.E.O. Record and among longtime members for the older, larger pin. A wise and thoughtful observation by Nebraskan Lue R. Spencer, AK, North Platte, said in essence, "It's not the size of the pin which counts, but the size of the woman who wears it." Widely quoted, this remark seemed to quiet the matter. Over the years, the official P.E.O. emblem has been made by different jewelers. In 2011, the size of the emblem was once again changed. It is slightly larger than earlier emblems.

For the Record — In 1919, the P.E.O. Sisterhood observed its Golden Anniversary. To quote *Out of the Heart:* "One outstanding commemorative feature used throughout the anniversary year was the lovely golden cover used on The P.E.O. Record. It appeared first on the February issue, then on all others throughout the year. The cover plate was designed by Sylvia Holmstrom, then an instructor of art in the public schools of Havelock (now Lincoln), Nebraska, and one of the charter members of Chapter AI. The classic, stylized design uses P.E.O. symbolism effectively. Seven marguerites representing the seven Founders form the base of the design. Tall burning torchieres suggest light and a star at the top center symbolizes the P.E.O. emblem." (See cover art page 657.)

Elizabeth C. Robertson Hall — A most generous contribution of $100,000 to Cottey College was made by Jane Robertson Layman, Z, Beatrice, in memory of her mother, Elizabeth C. Robertson. This gift stimulated the building of the beautiful dormitory named after Jane's mother. It was completed in 1962.

A Century of Sisterhood — When the P.E.O. Sisterhood celebrated its one hundredth birthday in 1969, chapters throughout the state incorporated the observance into programs. Response to Supreme Chapter's funding suggestions for the Centennial Center began early. Nebraska State Chapter presented $2,000 to the Building and Furnishing Fund. This gift was translated into the twelve beautiful ceiling chandeliers in the Great Hall and was given to honor Ada H. Mead, chairman of the Centennial Building Committee and past president of Nebraska State Chapter, the six past presidents of Supreme Chapter from Nebraska, and Rose M. Owens, treasurer of Supreme Chapter for twelve years. The Nebraska past presidents' club honored Ada Mead with a $100 gift. A total of $9,011.62 was given by May 15, 1968, with 85 percent of the chapters participating. By the 1969 convention, 93.8 percent of the chapters had responded, the major portion honoring members with $100 gifts. Chapter gifts by then amounted to $12,837.77 and individual gifts totaled $1,118. Gifts from Nebraska then totaled $16,055.77. Later individual gifts added $1,382, making the centennial gift of love from Nebraska State Chapter $17,437.77.

A Star in the Window — A memorable and gratifying occasion for Nebraska P.E.O.s was experienced when they were accorded the privilege of presenting *"A Star in the Window"* for the 1969 Centennial Convention of Supreme Chapter in Des Moines. The play was written and narrated by Frances Key, FK, Omaha, assisted by Phyllis Blanke, Julie Anwyl and Dorothy Johnson. It was a presentation of a turn-of-the-century P.E.O. meeting, using historic articles from the collection of Bernice Tillett. The talented author combined detailed knowledge of P.E.O. history and respect for early customs, with humor, love and dignity. Dramatic effects were achieved with period costumes, effective lighting, background music and scenery. The presentation was entertaining and instructive of early customs, yet left no doubt in the minds of the audience of the sincerity and dedication of early members. Despite change in customs and ceremonies, one sensed and was comforted by the indestructibility of the foundation principles of deep friendship and character symbolized by *"A Star in the Window."*

Nebraska State Chapter Centennial Gift — Nebraska State Chapter celebrated its centennial at the May convention in 1990. The centennial celebration had been kicked off at the 1989 convention in Hastings. The festivities continued all year long and climaxed at the convention in Lincoln culminating the year-long celebration of Nebraska State Chapter's one hundred years. On April 2, 1990, exactly one hundred years from the date of the organization, June Brunmeier, the president of Nebraska State Chapter along with the other members of the executive board of Nebraska State Chapter traveled to Des Moines to present a gift to International Chapter. This gift of $12,305 represented one dollar for every active member of Nebraska State Chapter as of March 1, 1990. Also present to receive the gift in behalf of International Chapter was Bobbie Koefoot, first vice president of International Chapter. The gift was earmarked for a climate-controlled archive to display the early P.E.O. historical items which Nebraska State Chapter has permanently loaned to International Chapter. Bobbie was instrumental in urging Nebraska to push for construction of the archives.

Koefoot's Cache — When Vera "Bobbie" Koefoot was elected as recording secretary of International Chapter in 1987, Nebraska State Chapter started accumulating funds and pledges from chapters and individuals to present as an honorarium at the culmination of her year as president of International Chapter. Sadly, this honorarium became a memorial as Bobbie died less than a year before being elected and installed as president of International Chapter. At the 1991 International Convention in Omaha, president of Nebraska State Chapter Mary Ann Eberspacher presented International Chapter with the Koefoot's Cache funds which were subsequently placed in a Vera G. (Bobbie) Koefoot Memorial

Fund within the P.E.O. Foundation. Two hundred twenty Nebraska chapters had contributed $38,000 to "Koefoot's Cache." With interest, the total amount of the gift presented to International Chapter was $40,624. The interest from this gift and others presented to International Chapter as memorials for Bobbie was allocated to the P.E.O. Scholar Award. The Vera G. Koefoot Endowed Award will be given every other year.

Goff's Goal — When Willa Joyce Goff was appointed to the Executive Board of International Chapter in 1995, Nebraska chapters started a plan to honor her service to the Sisterhood. Goff's Goal was a fund intended to include all local chapters in Nebraska and would be presented to Joyce in 2005 when she completed her term as president. It was suggested to local chapters that they contribute $1 per active member each year to this fund. On April 1, 1999, the fund amount was $13,137 and by March 31, 2005, the amount was $77,393. Nebraska State Chapter held these funds in a restricted fund. At Convention of International Chapter in Oklahoma City, Oklahoma, in 2003, $5,000 from Goff's Goal fund was presented to Joyce as an honorarium upon her installation as president. She asked that this $5,000 be given to a Nebraska woman attending Cottey. In 2005, at Convention in Vancouver, Canada, the final amount was presented to her in honor of her service to the Sisterhood. At the 2006 state convention an amendment to the Nebraska bylaws was adopted by the members of convention to establish the W. Joyce Goff Nebraska Cottey Scholarship Endowment Fund in the P.E.O. Foundation, and to establish the Goff Cottey Scholarship. The Nebraska Cottey Scholarship Committee will assist the P.E.O. Foundation in the administration of the scholarship to deserving Nebraska women attending Cottey.

Bucks for Beds at Cottey College — During a trip to Cottey College Seminar in the summer of 2008, state recording secretary Merikay (Gengenbach) Berg was made aware of the deteriorating condition of the bedroom furniture in the Nebraska Suite. After discussion at the next meeting of the executive board, it was decided to begin an investigation about what it would cost to replace the ten beds, ten dressers, ten desks and ten chairs. With the help of Cottey College, it was determined that the amount of $15,000 was necessary to buy the new bedroom furniture for the Nebraska Suite. The executive board made the decision to start a state-wide campaign in 2009 and to call it "Bucks for Beds." Each chapter was asked to pledge to contribute at least $1 per active member. As of March 1, 2009, Nebraska had 11,295 active members. The paid assistant collected pledges and payments from the 241 local chapters. As of March 31, 2009, the campaign raised $22,718. There was a display of a bed at the 2009 state convention thanking chapters for their generous contributions to "Bucks for Beds." $15,000 was sent to Cottey College in time for delivery of the furniture for the 2009 fall semester. In 2010, the extra $7,718.00 was sent to Cottey College for addition to the Nebraska Suite Endowment Fund. The total campaign including individual P.E.O., reciprocity group, and corporate matching contributions sent directly to Cottey totaled over $25,000.

Section Seven
Changes Grace the Sisterhood
"It's Not Your Mother's P.E.O."
1995-2015

by Joan Fink, Lead Editor and Past State President

Today's P.E.O. is not your mother's P.E.O. The years between 1995 and 2015 brought more changes to P.E.O. policy and procedures than at any other time in our history. As an organization, P.E.O. has never been afraid of change, always seeking to make a more inclusive and more welcoming Sisterhood that adapts to changes in our society. Each biennium, Convention of International Chapter debates and decides the fate of amendments to our constitution. Amendments that emerge from these sessions change our business meetings and our rituals. The Sisterhood decides the direction that our organization will travel.

P.E.O. membership numbers peaked in 1997-1998. In 1999, after years of continuing growth, the Sisterhood experienced a loss of 800 members. Thus began a small but steady decline in membership that continued with the ensuing years. It was a wake-up call for P.E.O. The Executive Board of International Chapter immediately formed ad hoc committees to begin researching ways to stop declining membership.

P.E.O. was not alone in this phenomenon. Many volunteer organizations, civic clubs and religious groups saw similar declines in membership. For many years, women formed the majority of their close friendships through social contacts in community and church. As society neared the new millennium, women began to form networks and friendships with individuals with whom they worked. With the growth of technology, social networking became popular through the advent of Facebook and Twitter. Email and tweets began to replace face to face communication and sharing ideas through organizations. Organizations which depended on close personal communication to promote their programs saw their membership slowly slip away.

Today's working women value their free time, and seek altruistic organizations that accomplish their goals in short and to-the-point meetings. In order to attract and keep these women in our Sisterhood, the procedures for business meetings were simplified and streamlined. Policies concerning membership were relaxed and ritual memorization began to fade into the past. P.E.O. values remained the same, but the structure of our meetings changed.

International Chapter led the way into the new millennium by adopting technology as a fast and economical means of communicating within the Sisterhood. Computers enabled organizations to store and retrieve vast amounts of information, and International Chapter began to track membership by these means. The official

P.E.O. website—www.peointernational.org—was unveiled. P.E.O.s on the state and local level could now access the site and keep up to date with the latest information. States soon followed the example with their own websites. Today, chapters have their own websites, and many sisters maintain contact by Facebook. In 2014, International Chapter opened a page on Facebook, and announced that P.E.O. International would soon be on Twitter. Every chapter has a technology contact who receives the latest information from state officers via an email newsletter or bulletin. She then passes this information on to her local chapter.

Advances in technology during this time period brought about changes in the way state chapters communicated with fellow officers. Email was a quick and economical way to communicate with each other and with local chapters. Technology helped bring about more streamlined executive board meetings. State officers with busy schedules and limited time appreciated shorter business meetings.

Local chapters were quick to adapt the pattern set by state and International chapter. Most women have access to personal computers, ipads, and cell phones. They check their emails, text messages, and Facebook on a daily basis. Chapters no longer depend solely on post cards or telephone committees to remind members of upcoming meetings or changes in meeting places or programs. Chapter technology chairmen send out group emails to pass along information and stay in constant contact with members. Those sisters without access to email still receive a phone call or note. Personal contact is still important and always appreciated. Our P.E.O. values have not changed.

Here are some changes that have occurred in the Sisterhood since 1995.

1995: P.E.O.s sponsored new members by written ballot for membership. **Nebraska's Past State President Joyce Goff was elected Recording Secretary of International Chapter.**

1996: International Chapter joined the technology wave that was sweeping the country. The staff in Des Moines began tracking membership via computers.

1997: Nebraska Past State President Joyce Goff was elected Organizer of International Chapter. Delegates to Convention of International Chapter listened to concerns of members that they didn't have time to memorize the lengthy chaplain's prayer. An amendment passed that would allow the chaplain's prayer to be read. International Chapter created the official P.E.O. website—www.peointernational.org—and the website was officially launched in 1998.

1998: Chapters began to use a written ballot for visually impaired.

1999: Nebraska Past State President Joyce Goff was elected Second Vice President of International Chapter.

2001: Delegates to Convention of International Chapter voted to allow proxy officers for the purpose of initiation. Cottey Junior College officially changed its name to Cottey College. **Nebraska Past State President Joyce Goff was elected First Vice President of International Chapter.**

2002: Membership numbers continued the downward spiral, and International Chapter responded by creating a *"MEmbership Begins with Me"* task force to study membership issues, and to assist state and local chapters with membership growth, structure and process. The official website—www.peointernational.org—was updated and made more interactive.

2003: The Directory of Presidents went online and eventually ceased to be published in hard copy. Nebraska State Chapter created one of the first state websites—www.nebraskapeo.org.—**W. Joyce Goff was elected President of International Chapter. Nebraska Past State President Alice Fisher was appointed to the Finance Committee of International Chapter.**

2005: **Joyce Goff, president of International Chapter,** unveiled a new campaign entitled *"It's OK to Talk about P.E.O."* at Convention of International Chapter in Vancouver, BC. This campaign grew out of a study about who we are and where we are going. P.E.O.s were encouraged to promote the Sisterhood, and we learned about elevator speeches, tag lines, and our new mission statement. Fifteen meetings were still required in each chapter's year, but now chapters had a choice of scheduling either business or social meetings for three regular meetings. Struggling chapters were encouraged to go through the reorganization process or to merge with another chapter. Declining interest rates and an economic downturn prompted a dues increase.

2006: The first chapter merger in Nebraska took place between two Omaha chapters. Chapters FI and IK officially merged September 10, 2006, to become Chapter FI-IK.

2007: At the Convention of International Chapter in Minneapolis, a special ad hoc committee was appointed to study P.E.O. ceremonies and meeting procedures and how to streamline the work of state chapter and local chapters. This was the first convention to use electronic voting devices, thus eliminating the need for paper ballots. A Special Committee for the Advancement of Membership was formed, and **Nebraska State President Pam Kregg** was appointed to this committee.

In 2007 the search began for answers to the problem of why members become inactive, and what changes were needed to be made in the Sisterhood to stop this trend. Members were encouraged to take the *Noel-Levitz Survey* which was offered online or by hard copy in The P.E.O. Record. Over fourteen thousand P.E.O. members responded to the survey. A new initiative was unveiled—"OK, Let's Grow ." We were encouraged to reach out and help more women.

2008: Information from the *Noel-Levitz Survey* provided the impetus to create a new philanthropy that would reach a new group of young women. The P.E.O. STAR Scholarship was born. Logos for our philanthropies were updated to a more contemporary look.

2009: A year of change. The P.E.O. STAR Scholarship officially became the sixth P.E.O. philanthropy. This project, with a $2,500 award, was open to young high school women who were leaders in their community and who wished to pursue a college degree. The word 'dimit' was dropped in favor of the term 'transfer', and 'vouch' was dropped in favor of the word 'sponsor'. The ballot box was eliminated. Our emblem changed. The star was now gold-plated brass, but larger in size, and available with a button back. Chapters could now initiate three new members at a time. Chapters campaigned for years to be able to read the initiation ceremony, and this amendment finally passed. Reading the initiation part is now allowed at the discretion of each chapter. The number of state executive board officers was reduced from seven to five. The P.E.O. Program for Continuing Education began to offer online applications for this philanthropy.

The Ad Hoc Committee to Streamline the Work of Local Chapters recommended changes that consolidated meeting procedures and reduced the number of reports and paperwork.

The emphasis on increasing membership continued, and four regional membership representatives were appointed by International Chapter. A Special Committee to Study P.E.O. Ceremonies and Meeting Procedures was appointed to study and address member needs. **Nebraska Past State President Leann Drullinger was appointed to the Study and Research Committee of International Chapter.**

2010: Online training for local chapter officers was implemented to help with changes in meeting procedures.

2011: Cottey College received approval to offer three Bachelor of Arts degrees. Local chapter officers could access online tutorials for annual reports. An amendment passed permitting two unfavorable ballots for membership. An all-member survey concerning meeting procedures and policy was offered online. Delegates at Convention of International Chapter approved a dues increase.

2012: Chapters may now submit online applications for The P.E.O. STAR Scholarship. **Nebraska Past State President Joyce Victor was appointed to the Board of Trustees of the P.E.O. Educational Loan Fund.** Wooden ballot boxes were retired.

2013: Membership surveys indicated that women want simplicity in attire as well as meeting procedures. Black pants or skirts and white blouses became an option for initiating officers.

2014: International Chapter of the P.E.O. Sisterhood joined the trend towards social media and officially opened a page on Facebook. A new section in The P.E.O. Record, "Tech Tips," walked members through the procedure on how to access the page and gave suggestions on what to post on the site. The interest rate of the P.E.O. Educational Loan Fund was lowered to 2 percent.

The P.E.O. Record announced that P.E.O. International would soon be on Twitter. The latest Tweets can be found @PEOSisterhood.

During this time period we also saw many changes in the format of The P.E.O. Record. The official publication of the Sisterhood was redesigned so that it was more reader friendly, and it reflected the changes in our society and our Sisterhood. Today, local chapters share pictures, fundraising ideas, membership successes, and personal stories with *Record* readers.

This listing is not complete. These were the noteworthy changes that affected the Sisterhood on the state and local levels. It has been said that change is good. We need to change in order to move forward. Our Sisterhood *is* moving forward. We continue to attract talented women with similar values who strive to make the world a better place.

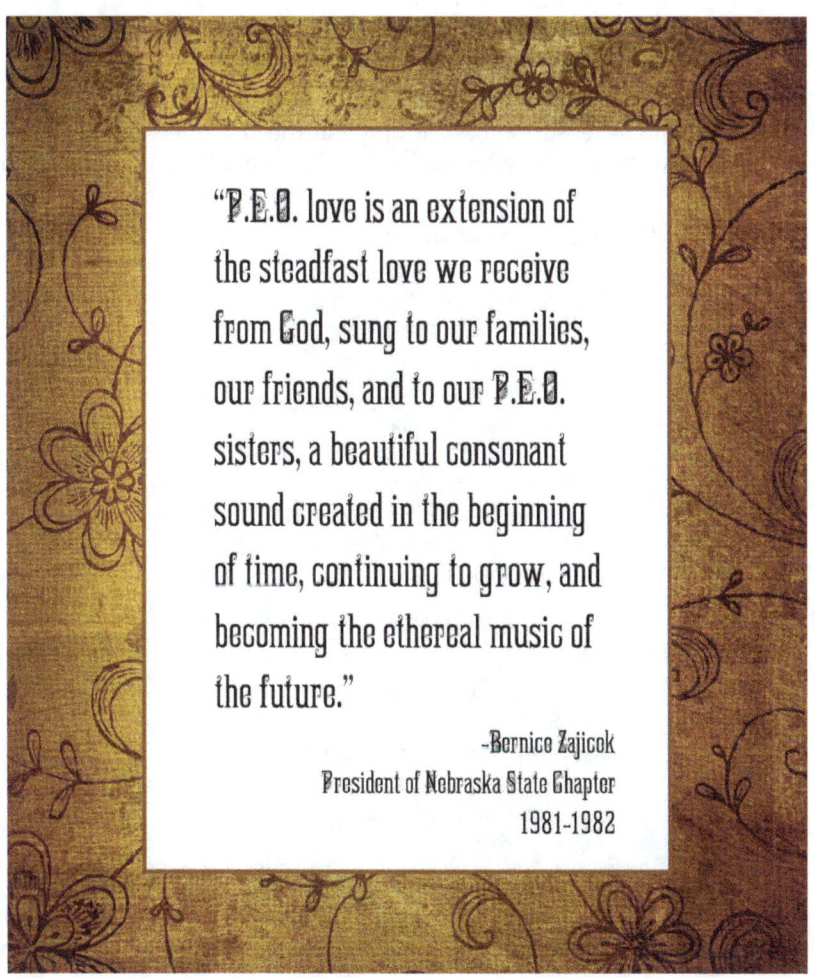

"P.E.O. love is an extension of the steadfast love we receive from God, sung to our families, our friends, and to our P.E.O. sisters, a beautiful consonant sound created in the beginning of time, continuing to grow, and becoming the ethereal music of the future."

-Bernice Zajicek
President of Nebraska State Chapter
1981-1982

We who are Sisters...
History of the Opening Ode
By Ruth Krebill, Past President Iowa State Chapter

Times and tunes have changed, but since P.E.O.'s first days, when the Founders sang "Blest Be The Tie That Binds," a spiritually suggestive ode has been used to open its meetings.

The November 1913 P.E.O. Record contained *"An Ode to the P.E.O. Star"* written by Alice Casady to the tune of *"Blest Be The Tie That Binds"*:

> *"Blest be the tie that binds*
> *Our hearts in Unity,*
> *In Justice, Faith and sweetest Love*
> *In Truth and Purity.*
> *This bond of golden links*
> *Forms an enduring chain*
> *That holds our hearts in thralldom dear*
> *Until we meet again."*

The first officially acted-upon ode, adopted at the 1893 meeting of Nebraska Grand Chapter, was written by Jennie Moore. The melody is not recorded, but the words are meaningful:

> *"We meet again our sisters dear*
> *O, may no discord here appear;*
> *And as our tasks we now pursue*
> *May each to each in thought be true.*
> *May we protect in word and deed*
> *Our sisters all, and strive to lead*
> *Whoever to our care may fall*
> *To Him whose love surrounds us all.*
> *Our Father's care we humbly ask*
> *And pray for strength for every task.*
> *We know that He our guide must be,*
> *That all may work in unity."*

The February 1922 P.E.O. Record recognized another *"P.E.O. Ode,"* this one by Elizabeth Green, sung to the tune of *"Come Thou Fount"*:

> *"Grant thy blessings, oh, our Father,*
> *On this Sisterhood so dear.*
> *Fill our hearts with loving kindness,*
> *Fill our lives with heavenly cheer.*
> *Help us share with those about us;*
> *Help us ever to be true;*
> *Help us keep the vows we've taken,*
> *Vows we here again renew."*

The words of today's Opening Ode—"which filled a long-felt need" for uniformity—

were written by Caroline Kettle, Chapter G, Colorado, transposed into music by Howard S. Reynolds, Colorado Conservatory of Music, and were adopted at the 1921 Convention of Supreme Chapter. "Mr. Reynolds held the copyright until 1950 and received a five percent royalty annually. It amounted to only a few dollars per year, but placed the Sisterhood in correct relationship with the author." In 1957, Fred Wright, husband of Chellie Stevens Wright, past president of Supreme Chapter, transposed this tune to a lower key.

Many melodies for the Opening Ode were submitted to the executive board of Supreme Chapter throughout the years, and at the beginning of the P.E.O. Centennial year celebration, Ethel O. Gardner, then president of Supreme Chapter, appointed a Wyoming P.E.O. to review all music received for the purpose of selecting an alternate melody for the Opening Ode. This second "optional" tune, introduced at the Centennial Convention in 1969, was written by Goodsell Slocum of Albuquerque. Mr. Slocum was a college instructor, composer of religious music and a BIL "in tune" with P.E.O. through his wife, mother, and two sisters.

Twenty years later [1989], P.E.O.s attending the International Convention in Phoenix listened to, loved, sang and adopted a third alternative tune composed by Roberta Lindly, president of Chapter EM, Texas.

First, second, third—We who are sisters in heart and spirit give thanks for the Star and its message, its melodies. Blest be this tie that binds!

We who are Sisters in heart and spirit give thanks for the Star and its message. May Purity, Justice, Faith, Truth and Love make glad and holy the secret places of our hearts. Amen.

...in heart and spirit

The words of today's Opening Ode were written by Caroline Kettle, Chapter G, Colorado, transposed into music by Howard S. Reynolds, Colorado Conservatory of Music, and adopted at the 1921 Convention of Supreme Chapter...in 1957, the husband of a past president of Supreme Chapter transposed it to a lower key.

Section Eight
Seven Lovely Ladies... One Shining Star

Alice Bird Babb
May 8, 1850 - November 21, 1926

Ella Stewart
May 8, 1848 - December 12, 1894

Hattie Briggs Bousquet
October 10, 1849 - June 22, 1877

Mary Allen Stafford
December 30, 1848-July 10, 1927

Suela Pearson Penfield

August 24, 1851 - September 20, 1920

The work begun by these visionary women grew... and grew...and chapters sprang up one by one, in the most unexpected places.

In 1881, the Village of Norfolk was organized when a three-train caravan of prairie schooners carrying forty-four German families arrived and were attracted by the rich land open for settlement.

Seven years later, it boasted a P.E.O. chapter.

Just ten years after the first log cabin was built in Superior, Nebraska, Chapter D organized in April 1889, and was extremely active and rigorous in its twenty years of existence. It was promoted by Alice Carey Briggs, sister-in-law of Hattie Briggs, one of the P.E.O. Founders. Alice became Nebraska's first state president.

INITIATION
by Selma Malm

There's a tapestry hangs by a window
In memory's sacred hall,
Where I trace old fashions and fancies
That have colored its mottled wall.

There are moments of solace and sorrow
Woven close in a network of pain;
And passions, and love scenes, and gladness
Mounting high on ecstacy's plane.

Some outlines are blurry and faded;
Some hold but a thread-worn space;
But down in the foreground, the Master
Placed a scene that not blight can efface.

Its peak is the arch of the heavens;
Its base is a garden below;
And it centers around the portals
That open to P.E.O.

I can see, where I stood at the doorway,
Its pillars entwined with bloom
From a garden, tended and guarded,
Back of its entry room.

I can see, as I crossed o'er the threshold To the
whispering words of a prayer.
Faith solemnly open her window
And point to the blossoms there.

I can see Truth stand like a statue,
Holding the torchlight high.
And Purity, kneeling and watchful,
Plucking a weed nearby.

I can see where the clean path of Justice
Leads straight to the beckoning glow
Of an emblem — a search light gleaming —
The star of the P.E.O.

I can see a dim outline of faces
Rise out of the aeons of time;
And as they draw nearer and greet me,
From out those reaches sublime,

I can see Love stirring among them,
And weaving an intricate band
That merges with each smiling welcome,
And with each firm clasp of my hand.

I can see how the garden is nurtured—
How each fair bloom that is grown
Is a joy to those in communion,
And a staff when one walks alone.

I can see how the graces embellished
The lowliest things that grow,
When the Sisterhood called me a Sister,
In the garden of P.E.O.

Section Nine
The Legacy Preserved

Nebraska State Chapter's Articles of Historical Value

BY JULIA McDOUGAL
PAST STATE PRESIDENT
AND FORMER NEBRASKA STATE CHAPTER HISTORIAN

Early Nebraska chapters, like those in other states, were creative and imaginative in designing items for chapter activities that characterized their life and times. The early years before 1900 found resourceful P.E.O.s' handiwork on items ranging from fancy embroidery to beautifully hand-written minutes of the first conventions. We now call the work of these early members our P.E.O. memorabilia.

Bernice Tillett recognized the value of preserving these items as a part of the heritage of Nebraska P.E.O. As state president in 1932, she appointed the first history committee and later became a member of that committee. In 1942, the committee was divided, with Bertha Clark Hughes serving as Historian for many years and Bernice Tillett serving as Custodian of the Articles of Historical Value for the next thirty years. From the beginning of her collection of a few choice articles, she added many items donated by early chapters. As she spoke with the chapters, her winsome personality prompted Nebraska P.E.O.s to search attics and trunks for unique P.E.O. artifacts. Her display rooms at conventions were popular stops for delegates and her enthusiastic talks to Convention drew great interest. From Bernice's Centennial Convention presentation in 1969, one learns something of her philosophy underlying the collection of "things," which to her were visible "stand-ins" for all that early P.E.O. meant.

> "There's always a good reason when something survives and attains greatness... the reason for our remembering them and their heritage to us is their ideals!... they built a foundation that was to last... sincerity, love in thought and action, not only for today, but for the yesterdays and the tomorrows..."

From Bernice's death in 1972, her friend and assistant Ruth Knight, also of Chapter AH, Alliance, took over this work. She soon urged Nebraska's leadership to consider permanent archives to provide safe storage for the fragile, irreplaceable items. The executive board initiated correspondence with Supreme Chapter officers concerning the possibility of transferring these articles to the Centennial Center in

Des Moines for preservation and for a display which would be available to the entire Sisterhood.

After some period of discussion and thoughtful consideration, the state board asked the 1974 convention to approve a motion to send an agreed list of articles to the Centennial Center of Supreme Chapter, with the understanding that they "be held in perpetuity at the headquarters in Des Moines, Iowa, or returned to Nebraska State Chapter. Because of the policy of rotating displays, objects not being shown will be carefully stored under proper conditions." The Convention approved the motion. In October 1974, Barbara Kennedy, AU, Peru, who had succeeded Ruth Knight as custodian, delivered the designated items to the Centennial Center.

Description of Articles of Historical Value in Des Moines

Three old emblems from Minden, Wymore, and Wahoo, and an embroidered pillowcase from Broken Bow

Three floor stars

Lillian Pollock Parmele's dress

Old handwritten initiatory service from Lexington and P.E.O. Creed

Convention badges belonging to Bertha Clark Hughes mounted in notebook

Ballot Bag

Question Box Bag

Wooden door star

Wooden display box built to display articles

Envelope with special dimit card

Old tin box for president's materials. It now contains: mourning rosette and pin; one large banner and a string of many small banners; bell to call meeting to order; wooden plaque of P.E.O. Founders sitting on the fence; picture of Mary Allen Stafford

Special Dimit Card

Return Dimit Card

Nelson emblem

Alliance Star and White Satin Cloth

Wooden Star

Question Box

There followed several years of confusion concerning jurisdiction as well as proper storage of the articles from Nebraska. This confusion was caused primarily because of new personnel in the office in Des Moines, as well as the natural progression of state and Supreme officers. In 1981, Vera "Bobbie" Koefoot was named to the International Finance Committee and became a frequent visitor to the Centennial Center. She soon urged Nebraska P.E.O.s to take a leadership role in providing funds for the special kind of storage needed to preserve these items of historical significance. In 1990, Nebraska State Chapter, as part of its Centennial celebration, presented a gift of $12,305 to International Chapter to spearhead funds needed to provide the special storage.

In 1996, a letter from Chief Administrative Officer Anne S. Pettygrove to Nebraska Historian Julia McDougal speaks of International Chapter's appreciation. The letter, in part, follows:

> "As you know, the archives room was constructed following Nebraska's generous gift toward such an area, and special items from Nebraska were among the first to be located there.
>
> This year, we are planning to expand the area! We are preparing to construct an enlarged public viewing museum area which will be adjacent to the locked storage area. Both rooms will be equipped with humidity and temperature controls to ensure proper archival storage and display. Display cases will be constructed and proper lighting installed to show items to their best advantage.
>
> This new area, in addition to providing added space, will provide an improved traffic flow for our visitors. The area to be used is adjacent to Great Hall in the Centennial Center.
>
> It is wonderful to have a proper place to store and display the precious pieces of P.E.O. History that we have, and we are continuing to receive additional items as people know that we have the proper resources for preservation. Much credit goes to our Nebraska sisters for having the foresight and generosity to get this project underway. An area such as this allows all of our P.E.O. visitors to share—and see the history of P.E.O."

Nebraska State Chapter "smiles" with quiet satisfaction at this culmination of the vision that began with Bernice Tillett. She realized the need for action to save the precious treasures that our sisters in the early chapters had created. Much credit is due to many Nebraska P.E.O. leaders who carefully planned and carried out the venture to provide the best care possible for our Articles of Historical Value. The archive room will carry—in Nebraska P.E.O. hearts—a warm and lasting memory of the leadership of Bobbie Koefoot whose persistent and loving nudges urged the state chapter to act.

The Nebraska Articles of Historical Value have been viewed by those in attendance at three Supreme (1969) and later International Conventions (1981, 1991). Frances Key, FK, Omaha, was asked to write a short play for the Supreme Centennial Convention in 1969 and she included many historical items as she traced the story of P.E.O. through its early years. She enlisted Nebraska P.E.O.s as players in her most interesting account of the beginning of the Sisterhood. *A Star in the Window* has been much loved by P.E.O.s across the Sisterhood. Frances was an accomplished dramatist and actress and she wrote several plays for P.E.O. She served as Nebraska State Chapter President in 1979-1980. In 1981, International Chapter (as it was called by then) asked if they might again present her play at their convention in Kansas City. Many of the same players repeated their roles in the second presentation. The third appearance of the articles came as Nebraska past state presidents hosted a display room at the Omaha Convention of International Chapter in 1991. Again, it was Vera Koefoot who was instrumental in furthering the idea to make this display a reality by obtaining permission from International Chapter to add the display to the pre-convention roster of events. Many delegates and P.E.O. visitors toured the display with great interest. Bobbie's untimely death in 1990 cast the only shadow across this very meaningful event in the history of Nebraska State Chapter.

In 1988, Nebraska asked permission to return a large part of their historical items to Nebraska for display during conventions prior to and during the Nebraska Centennial Year of 1990. Executive Secretary Rosemary Wood wrote that permission had been granted and that she had decided that the time had come for an accurate inventory to be taken of all items ever given to the Center from Nebraska. She assembled the complete list and clarified the confusion which had surrounded the articles since their arrival in Iowa, drawing up an agreement for an official sign-out by the Nebraska historian. Their stay in Nebraska was appreciated by a new generation of P.E.O.s who had their first glimpse of these creative and imaginative items from the distant past. Later, permission was granted for their stay to be lengthened to include the 1991 International Convention in Omaha. An interesting sidelight relating to P.E.O. history at the Omaha convention involved the tellers' boxes which were exact replicas of the voting bag from the early days of Chapter M, Omaha. The articles were returned to Des Moines in October 1991, following the International Convention at Ak-Sar-Ben in Omaha.

Nebraska State Chapter continues to maintain a collection of other items of interest and historical value, some of which come from the papers of longtime Nebraska Historian, Bertha Clark Hughes. Recent additions have included items that the state chapter sold during the centennial celebration. These included a lovely china plate, jewelry and note cards, all distinguished by original designs created by Nebraska P.E.O.s. All articles of interest from the 1991 International Convention have been preserved so that future members may look back on the exciting year when Nebraska P.E.O.s entertained their sisters from across the United States and Canada. It is an exciting day for the historian when a member contacts her about a possible addition to the collection, recently found, or made available.

Articles of Historical Value Committee

The committees of Nebraska State Historian and Custodian of Articles of Historical Value have not always been one and the same. After much reading and investigating and with the help of Susan Harr, who at present is Historian and Custodian of Articles of Historical Value, the following is how the history of Nebraska P.E.O. has been maintained.

State Historian

Bernice Tillett, AH, Alliance, served Nebraska State Chapter as president in 1931-1932. In 1932, Bernice appointed Bertha Clark Hughes, Chapter M, Omaha, as the first History Committee, thus the state Historian. Bertha Clark Hughes served as president of Nebraska State Chapter in 1913-1914 and as president of International Chapter in 1923. Bertha saved everything about P.E.O. and planned to someday write a history of Nebraska P.E.O. She served as Historian and chairman of the committee until her death in 1967.

In 1968 a History Committee with a rotating chairman was established. Ada Mead, Chapter BN, Omaha, president of Nebraska State Chapter from 1937-1938, served as chairman in 1968. Helen Riddell, Chapter Z, Beatrice, president of Nebraska State Chapter from 1948-1949, served as chairman in 1969. Irene Van Brunt, Chapter DD, Omaha, president of Nebraska State Chapter from 1950-1951, served as chairman in 1970. Dorothy Smithberger, Chapter DF, Stanton, president of Nebraska State Chapter in 1955-1956, served as the History Committee from 1971 until 1984. Dorothy was asked to follow up with Bertha Clark Hughes' planned history book and served as one of the editors of the "*Saga of Nebraska P.E.O.*" published in 1975. In 1977, Dorothy Smithberger became the Historian and the Custodian of Articles of Historical Value. The committees have remained combined since then.

In 1984, Catherine Anderson, Chapter CR, Omaha, president of Nebraska State Chapter in 1972-1973, became the Historian and Custodian of Historical Articles. She was assisted by Francis Key, FK, Omaha, president of Nebraska State Chapter in 1979-1980. Together they served until 1987. Francis had a keen interest in history and a great writing ability. She wrote at least three highly regarded presentations on P.E.O. One of her most acclaimed, "*A Star in the Window*," was presented at state and International conventions.

In 1987, Julia McDougal, Chapter DA, Hastings, president of Nebraska State Chapter in 1983-1984, was appointed as Historian and remained until 1997. Julia was the Historian to prepare the display of our historical items at Convention of International Chapter in 1991 in Omaha.

Susan Harr, BP, Omaha, (shown above right) president of Nebraska State Chapter in 1986-1987, has served as Historian and Custodian of Articles of Historical Value from 1997 until the present. Her sister Linda Flaherty, HJ, Grand Island, (above left) has served as her assistant. Susan and Linda are daughters of Dorothy Smithberger, past state president.

Susan's annual oral history reports during state convention (see a collection of these reports beginning on page 559) are much anticipated because of her love of P.E.O history and her lively and informative presentations.

Custodian of Articles of Historical Value

In 1943 Bernice Tillett, AH, Alliance, became Custodian of the Articles of Historical Value, a post she held until her death in 1972. Ruth Knight, Chapter AH, of Alliance followed Bernice from 1972 until 1974, continuing her work as Custodian and completing a thorough inventory of all the items Bernice and Bertha collected and held so closely. In 1974, Barbara Kennedy, AU, Peru, became Custodian of Historical Articles (note the name change) and delivered several historical items to the Centennial Center in Des Moines to be held in perpetuity and under proper conditions.

. . . .

For many years, a wood carving identical to this was presented to each outgoing president of Chapter ES, Lincoln. It was hand carved and finished by "Mac" McCarty, husband of past chapter president Bea McCarty. It depicts Hattie Briggs and Franc Roads as they sat on a stile in the southeast corner of Iowa Wesleyan University in December of 1868 and first imagined the Sisterhood which would become P.E.O. In less than two months they were organized, had a constitution, a pin, a secret oath, and introduced themselves to the campus...and to the world.

Reminiscences from Bertha Clark Hughes

The following excerpts are from *The Saga of Nebraska P.E.O.*, Nebraska's history published in 1975. Bertha Clark Hughes recalled many stories about her P.E.O. experiences during her service to the Sisterhood. As Historian of Nebraska State Chapter, she often told amusing stories and jokes to the convention delegation. A few of her treasured ones are listed here.

1956 report—"My rendezvous with conventions included many amusing incidents. The two most outstanding conventions, of course, were in Lincoln in 1914, at St. Paul's Methodist Church where I presided over the 25th Nebraska State Chapter Convention—called our Silver Anniversary—and decorations all white and silver. There are many here who shared my Seattle convention, October 1-5, 1923, when my pathway led me to my pink plume fan, the gift of the Board of Supreme Chapter."

"Did you ever hear of a Houseparty? We used to have them. Once at Minden twenty P.E.O. sisters were entertained for a whole week at the home of Hattie Clearman and Carrie Hapeman. I came across a card not long ago which revealed the fact that I had collected 15 cents from each guest to buy two silver trays for the two hostesses. (Fifteen cents was equal to one dollar now, believe me.)"

"I recall how proudly I rode down Farnam Street once with Viola Cameron in her Electric (at twenty miles an hour). We were going to the station to meet Carrie Peterson, the president of Supreme Chapter. The time I forgot to get off the train at my station enroute to Chapter U, Butte, when I was organizer; the time my hat blew out the train window, (not a Pullman, an old railroad coach with open windows and smoke and cinders). Did I get my hat back? No, it went on to Kansas; the time Mrs. Winona Evans Reeves was our honor guest at a North Platte convention, and on the return trip home some P.E.O. sister took the wrong suitcase off at her station and at Omaha no suitcase was available for Mrs. Reeves. That was Nebraska's most embarrassing moment."

1957 report —"This is a true story. It happened to two P.E.O. girls returning from the 1955 Supreme Chapter Convention in Indianapolis via the P.E.O. special train west. One of the girls was from Colorado and one was from Nebraska. They were seated in the dining car for lunch across from two men, one a young man and the other an elderly gentleman. Both had boarded the train at Aurora, Illinois. True to form, the men inquired "Who, What, When, Where, Why" all the women were on the train? In an ecstasy of joy, these young, enthusiastic P.E.O. members told of the achievements and possessions of the Sisterhood. Just fresh from Supreme Chapter convention and bubbling over with knowledge, they told of the College, of the P.E.O. Educational Loan Fund, of the International Peace Scholarship and of the six P.E.O. Homes owned and operated by six state chapters.

"As the luncheon neared the end, the young man casually said, 'You left out the Founders.' The girls were sunk. It was their most embarrassing moment, but it lasted for a moment only, because the young man said, 'May I present my friend, the Honorable Miles T. Babb, son of your Founder Alice Bird Babb.'

Hark ye! These modern girls rose to the occasion and invited the men to return with them to the Colorado-Nebraska coach where they got a thrill of a lifetime introducing Mr. Babb to their P.E.O. sisters."

1959 convention—"Time or space will not permit my telling you...of Mrs. Carrie Peterson who presided in 1909 in Mount Pleasant, Iowa, at my first Convention of Supreme Chapter; of Alice Bird Babb who took me arm in arm to see the old music room. Winona Evans Reeves was elected president there in 1909 and yours truly served on the committee that framed the rules to govern the Educational Fund."

1964—"1907...I was married, and 1908 found me at Red Cloud convention, where I recall trunks carried the finery and petticoats for the stylish ladies of 1908 at Red Cloud, where we met Willa Cather and her sisters, both P.E.O.s. I recall I coveted a lovely white plume fan owned by Lillian Pollock Parmele."

1965—"I remember how P.E.O. guarded secrecy. When I became a P.E.O., I was deeply impressed by the way I was instructed to preserve secrecy. Newspaper publicity, as of today, was unheard of. It would have shocked a P.E.O. sister to read that some chapter would hold Exemplification of the Ritual at the next regular meeting. I remember that we opened our meetings joyously by singing 'Blessed Be The Tie That Binds' and closing by solemnly singing 'God Be With You 'Till We Meet Again.' It was the custom in the early days to kneel for prayer, and the Chaplain had time to offer a few meditations on her scripture readings. We had time for study programs and we had an ambition to improve ourselves. That was before radio, TV, and all the available outside entertainment. My chapter took the Bay View course for several years, a real study course."

"I remember stories of P.E.O. conventions, having attended every Supreme Chapter since 1909. At my age of 84 years, my goal is 1965 Supreme Chapter at Atlantic City, when my dear friend and neighbor and P.E.O. sister, Irene Van Brunt, will preside." (Bertha did attend and gave the invocation at this, her last convention of Supreme Chapter.)

Bertha attended the Cumnock School of Oratory, Northwestern University. She often gave readings in local chapters and in conventions. "Mercedes" and "The Old Red Cradle" were two favorites. Her training made effective her many addresses, powerful prayers and invocations in conventions of state and Supreme Chapters. And how she loved to tell jokes! She often entertained guests at the P.E.O. Home with them while she lived there the last five years of her life.

This article was reproduced from *The Saga Of Nebraska P.E.O.*
with gratitude to Julia McDougal for preserving this valued legacy

*Painting is easy when you don't know how,
but very difficult when you do.* -Edgar Degas

A Legacy of Historian Reports

The reports that follow are representative of those recorded in the Proceedings of Convention of Nebraska State Chapters

From the Historian Reports
of Julia McDougal, DA, Hastings, and Susan Harr, BP, Omaha

1991 Report:

One hundred years ago this week Alice Briggs presided over the first convention of Nebraska State Chapter, hosted by Alice's chapter, D, Superior. Sixteen delegates from eight chapters—all but B, Fairfield—were in attendance. The record shows that all were talented in some artistic ability and participated by sharing writings, singing or playing of music, or recitations. The delegates were determined to make a success of this new venture in P.E.O.

In 1981 the Executive Board of Nebraska State Chapter, with Bernice Zajicek president, voted to extend an invitation to International Chapter to meet in Nebraska in 1989 to kick off a centennial celebration of P.E.O. life and growth in Nebraska. The 1982 convention confirmed this, except that the date had been changed to 1991, since an Arizona bid for 1989 had already been accepted. Hosting of International Chapter was to wind down the centennial instead. One hundred years later finds Nebraska P.E.O.s very busy indeed. 1991 is the first Convention of International Chapter hosted by Nebraska State Chapter. The previous three were hosted by Chapter E, Chapter K, and the Omaha chapters.

Actually the 1991 state convention is listed as the 102nd. Past President and Parliamentarian Joyce Goff has explained that the 1890 meeting should have been called a convocation instead of a convention.

Nebraska State Chapter, under President June Brunmeier and Chairman Carol Baldwin, celebrated in 1990 in appropriate style. The convention was blessed with the attendance of International President Mary Louise Remy, First Vice President Vera Koefoot, and Second Vice President Nancy Hall.

International Chapter honored Nebraska with an invitation to include a history room at the Omaha convention where Nebraska State Chapter will have on display its articles of historical value. Past President Lois Ann Hansen was chairman of this event.

The cast (made up of twenty-five Lincoln P.E.O.s) of the original musical production "Avenue of P.E.O. Dreams" presented as the convention's projects program was invited to recreate their performance at the 1991 Convention of International Chapter.

Nebraska State Chapter was honored when your historian was invited by International President Mary Louise Remy to speak to the meeting of Presidents and Organizers, together with the International Board at their meeting in Des Moines in July 1990, to relate the history of the beginnings of Nebraska State Chapter.

-Julia McDougal

See the Historian's report of Nebraska Chapters hosting the 1991 Convention of International Chapter in Omaha on page 577

1993 Report:

The 1990's have been busy and exciting years for Nebraska P.E.O.s. One reason is the celebration of our centennial of the state chapter. That helps us to realize that the 1890's were exciting and challenging ones for early P.E.O.s as the organization had to be thoughtfully and carefully planned if it was to succeed.

Nebraska State Chapter was blessed with two strong leaders who not only led our state group, but also were instrumental in surmounting the confusion that arose as P.E.O. sought to change its structure to achieve a chapter that would provide guidance and leadership to all state chapters that would follow. Alice Briggs, D, Superior, and Lulu Patrick, H, Holdrege, were the two with the vision and the extraordinary ability to plan in a way that the envisioned goal was achieved. They worked with women from Iowa and other states to bring into being the Supreme Grand Chapter, the needed instrument to lead the P.E.O. structure. Nebraska had called a preconvention meeting before the Grand Chapter meeting in Des Moines in the fall of 1892. The new Nebraska State Chapter had been organized, but it had yet to be worked out how this group related to the original Grand Chapter which had included all chapters. *Out of the Heart* notes that no one knew quite what to do with this strange child.

The Des Moines meeting cleared the air and the sisterly harmony prevailed that was needed to begin the plans for the new Supreme Grand Chapter. Alice Briggs worked on the committee with Founder Alice Bird Babb to set up the constitution in the form that we now know, with local, state and Supreme sections.

In 1893 the organizing meeting of Supreme Grand Chapter met in Waterloo, Iowa. Most of the time and energy was spent reviewing and voting on this constitution. Alice Babb read it aloud, section by section, and debate followed until the convention agreed on the new structure and ordered it to be printed. They also voted to begin biennial conventions, chose the marguerite as the society flower, and approved the petition to form Iowa Grand Chapter.

Nebraska in 1893 added three chapters to bring its total to eleven. Chapter J, Nelson, had been added in 1891, but Chapter B, Fairfield, had not been able to send a delegate to any state gathering and obviously was not strong enough to continue. It was disbanded in 1893, having been preceded in this step by Chapter C, Norfolk, in 1892. Chapter K, L, and M were to be strong chapters and ushered in a time when interest in P.E.O. in Nebraska became widespread and the fledgling state chapter was off and running.

This important part of our early heritage set the stage for the attitudes and actions that have characterized Nebraska P.E.O. We salute these women with the vision and the courage that marked their ways and especially for the grace that was found in them that enabled sisterly harmony to prevail. We cherish the heritage that is ours.

-Julia McDougal

1997 Report:

As we gather here in Lincoln at Nebraska Wesleyan University, it only seems appropriate to turn our minds a few hundred miles to the east, a few hundred plus years ago to Iowa Wesleyan and the seven young girls who donned the now-famous aprons and paraded into chapel to mark the beginning of our P.E.O. Sisterhood.

Who among us is not familiar with the story of the two young women at the stile deciding to form a society in response to the I.C. Sorosis Society. But there was something different about this group of young women. It was not their intention that P.E.O. stay on the college campus. Rather, they immediately took it beyond by initiating Cassie Allen Fink as one of its first new members. Cassie was the sister of Founder Mary Allen Stafford. She was also a college graduate. She has written: "Two of the seven came to our home, just two blocks from the college, one morning and said the seven had just organized a society and wanted me to join. I had graduated in June of the year before and seemed still to belong over there and was a sort of sister-in-law, since my sister Mary was one of the seven. And so I was initiated at our own home the day they asked me to join."

Perhaps the reason they planned to extend beyond college life had something to do with the fact that five of the seven were about to graduate at the time P.E.O. was conceived. In fact, plans for P.E.O. were laid in January, 1869, and classwork for these five ended only two months later, in March, although commencement was not held until June. Alice Bird Babb was to write many years later, "At the time, we little dreamed of the great outcome, and yet we were earnest and even then desired something broad and substantial. We did not for one moment wish it to be a mere college fraternity, we wished a society of more lasting name and reputation."

Those first few months — indeed the first few years — were cloaked in great secrecy, and will always remain so, as there were few written records made and later recollections by those involved were sketchy. These young women must have had great fun skirting around town in order to avoid being detected. No member went directly from her home to the meeting place. Customarily, she would start in the opposite direction, or make stops along the way, eventually arriving at the designated place. Even revealing an officer's name was an offense worthy of expulsion. They did not keep minutes, so no record of initiation dates exists. They did have a constitution, written that very first day, but no exact copy of it remains today.

The early years seemed to set certain patterns that exist still today. Secrecy was certainly one, although it was much more important then than now. The desire for specific basic principles and orders of organization is another.

Within six years of the beginning of P.E.O., the first convention was held, with the six existing chapters in attendance. Entertainment, reports from each chapter, and the creation of a new constitution were the main concerns. During the first 12 years, a constitution did evolve. Some of the provisions of that early work still apply today:

- that no one shall be initiated without the willing consent of all members,
- that a name shall be proposed at one meeting and voted upon at the next,
- that meetings shall be held every two weeks,
- that a chaplain will begin the meeting with a prayer - if she is present,
- that initiation shall be conferred on only one member at a time.
- Other provisions have been dropped over the years:
- that this society shall be composed principally of young ladies attending school, but shall not exclude the alumnae of any institution or young ladies of excellent standing not in school attendance,

- that the star, although worn at other places, will find its properly acknowledged place on the left shoulder and when in that place may be touched at times as a signal of distress.
- that officers shall be elected every six months
- that a fine of 10 cents shall be affixed to any member who absents herself from any regular meeting except in case of sickness or absence from the city. A written excuse was submitted and voted upon by the chapter.

In 1881, a new constitution was written and adopted. In records of subsequent conventions, further revisions or total rewritings seem to be a constant.

Only one other topic of discussion was more prevalent, the writing of a burial service. Committees were appointed, they reported and then were sent back to do more work — year after year. Incorporation of music composed by P.E.O.s was desired to include in the ritual, but none was found that was deemed suitable. Another consideration was changing the meaning of the letters P.E.O. Some favored using several meanings, some wished a Latin interpretation. Later an idea to change the letters to German was defeated. Several proposals were made to join P.E.O. with other organizations — Greek organizations, Federated Women's Club and others.

In 1887, the desire for uniformity among chapters was very strong. Local constitutions were compared and no two were found to be alike. A uniform constitution was adopted and distributed to all chapters. All old ceremonies and constitutions were ordered sent in and were destroyed. Much valuable history was lost at this time, so much so that one frustrated historian referred to the event as "this holocaust." In order to make sure that all complied, a similar great effort was made again in 1888 to have all old ceremonies, differing local constitutions, bylaws and sundry papers sent in for destruction with a view to unifying the work. Chapter A was granted a dispensation from this order and allowed to retain its old papers. However, by the time of the publication of the first P.E.O. history, these papers had all been lost. As a result, much of our early history was compiled from remembrances written by early P.E.O.s some years after the fact.

Prior to 1882, there was no written initiation. New members subscribed to a series of oaths presented to them. However, in 1882, an initiation was adopted that contains many of the same phrases that we use today. It was around that time that a Nebraska chapter designed a floor star and brought it to convention. It was never formally adopted, but many chapters took the idea home and made their own. A small table was placed over the star, covered with a white tablecloth. A large Bible and a satin pillow with the pin on it were placed on the table. Officers stood between the points of the star. It included a secret handshake and instructions on four signs known by every early P.E.O.

That original initiation did not include the star ceremony as we know it today. A member of Chapter K, Lincoln, wrote the star ceremony to be inserted into the initiation. The design for the table star also came from that chapter. They were submitted to the 1887 convention and adopted. Again, chapters returned home to their sewing machines to design a star. It was not until after the turn of the century that a uniform star became available.

Lincoln hostess chapters may well empathize with one of these remembrances, written in 1904 concerning the 1884 convention:

> "We were more careful of our secret leaking out in those days than now, as the sessions were held in Odd Fellows hall, in the third story, and I think we kept the windows down and the blinds closed. The social side was very much the same then as now. We spent several months in talking it over and making preparations, and at the last there was the same rushing to and fro of frantic committees, to see about dishes and spoons, invitations and salads and to see how your best dress was going to fit. But at last all was ready, and a happy smiling committee met all the trains and brought the delegates to our homes. Just think what ancient history—that was before we had society colors or flowers. How we ever had a convention without yellow and white drapery is almost past understanding."
>
> -Susan Harr

1998 REPORT:

We have had a rare treat during this convention, an opportunity to sit in on a meeting from the past, to feel what it was like to be in the room with the early P.E.O.s. [This refers to a performance of Frances Key's P.E.O. play, "*A Star in the Window*," which re-created an early P.E.O. meeting complete with period costumes and original props.] P.E.O. owes a great debt to Frances Key, Chapter FK, for preserving these moments for us and for our daughters. Frances was always generous in giving to P.E.O. her time and talents. An accomplished actress, she was president of Nebraska State Chapter in 1979-1980. At the time of the centennial of Nebraska State Chapter, she wrote and produced a pageant depicting the day of organization of our state chapter. She had a fantastic ability to breathe life into her characters, adding wit, humor and interest. She is one of the giants in Nebraska P.E.O. history.

Another giant was a young kindergarten teacher in Lincoln. Ida Johnson was a member of Chapter K when she wrote the Star Ceremony used in our initiations. Another chapter member, Joanna VanBoskirk, provided her handiwork and Chapter K first exemplified the ceremony at Supreme Grand Chapter in 1897. It was adopted in 1899. A little later version exists in our history files. I hope that you had an opportunity to see it in the History Room. Ida also was a member of the committee that issued the first P.E.O. history, the famous *White History*, in 1903. She went on to serve as president of Nebraska State Chapter in 1912-1913 and as chairman of the Board of Trustees of The P.E.O. Record in 1913-1915. In 1919, P.E.O. undertook an extensive revision of the Constitution. Right in the middle, there was Ida, lending her expertise to the committee. Ida was also active in education circles in Lincoln and in Nebraska. In 1921, at the age of 46, she married Parker Lewellen of Thedford. After an illness of several months, she died in 1923.

I would like to take this opportunity to point to one other item of special historic interest this year. The Centennial of the Trans-Mississippi Exposition has been celebrated this year in Omaha, with a culmination last weekend. P.E.O., as we all know, was cloaked in great secrecy in its infancy. But a departure from this was the organization's participation in shows and fairs such as this one. P.E.O.s maintained a booth at the Trans-Mississippi Exposition, lavishing attendees with treats and hospitality and enhancing the reputation of our Sisterhood. It was similar participation in the St. Louis World's Fair that led to the creation of the P.E.O. Educational Loan Fund, adopted in 1907.

We are fortunate in Nebraska that a record of our history has long been held to be important and that efforts have been taken to preserve many historical items. It is important that we continue to do this. Most of our historic items stem from the early part of this century, up through the 1920's. Items and events later than that have not been preserved, probably because they have been deemed as too recent. NOW is the time to preserve these items, before it is too late. Many concessions were made to the times during the Depression, but yet P.E.O. persevered. There was much involvement in the war effort during World War II, with every chapter participating in some way. Do you know what your chapter did during that time? Do you have the old stories of the contacts made with overseas needy? NOW is the time for you in your chapters to glean this information from your older members. Would you consider a program where you ask older members to share their memories? And would you then consider sharing this information with us? Our history files are too important to allow them to lapse.

-Susan Harr

2002 Report:

We are all so proud of our International officer Joyce Goff, who adds so much love, warmth and spice to our meetings. But do we really realize how rare a commodity she is? Since 1890, there have only been six Nebraskans who have served as president of International Chapter (previously called Grand, Grand Supreme, and Supreme). They are Alice C. Briggs, disbanded Chapter D, Superior; Carrie Hapeman, N, Minden; Carrie M. Peterson, AC, Aurora; Helen M. Drake, Z, Beatrice; Bertha Clark Hughes, disbanded Chapter M, Omaha; and Irene Simpson VanBrunt, disbanded Chapter DD, Omaha. Irene presided in Atlanta in 1965—47 years ago. It should be noted that Vera (Bobbie) Koefoot, GP, Grand Island, served through the offices in International and would have been elected president in Omaha in 1991 had cancer not claimed her a few months earlier.

A discovery earlier this month leads me to focus on one of these distinguished ladies, Bertha Clark Hughes. Bertha served as president of Nebraska State Chapter in 1913-14 and of Supreme in 1923. The stories about Bertha are numerous. Many are told in *"The Spirit of the Prairie,"* Nebraska's latest [at the time this report was written] P.E.O. history book. She served as president of the National Association of Parliamentarians and was the first woman to serve as a parliamentarian for the National Republican Convention. She held many offices in the United Methodist Church. She was also an inveterate collector and saver. It is to her that we owe our thanks for many of the items in our history displays. She worked for years to gather information to publish a Nebraska P.E.O. history, but it was left to others to finally accomplish that task. P.E.O.s seem to have portions of her collections in several locations, because every once in a while someone contributes a stack, a box or a sack full of her items. Many of the items are various unrelated clippings, from which she drew ideas and content for her many talks. There may be a scrap of a napkin on which is scribbled a quote from some speaker. Bits about parliamentary procedure, the Republican Party or current events, Bible quotations and various other tidbits are interspersed with P.E.O thoughts and papers.

The stack I examined this month contained a motherlode of information. There was an entire file of correspondence with Winona Reeves, editor of The P.E.O. Record, all written within a few months' timespan. Every note is handwritten and thoughtfully phrased, bringing a renewed appreciation for the time taken for all the work of these P.E.O.s. Bertha was a frequent contributor to The Record. The letters reflect a great deal of admiration between these two women who worked so closely. One letter brings a smile, as we sit here in the lovely self-contained Quality Inn, where everything is held within the building:

> "Dear Bertha:
> Thank you for your letter and for its enclosure, the interesting interview you gave as it appears in The Omaha World-Herald.
> The convention was grand, I thought. It may be many years, but an all-hotel convention, that is to hold the meetings inside a hotel as well as live there, does save time and strength. Of course, Supreme Convention — and state conventions, too—have gotten too big and too popular for that. Both size and popularity being all to the good as indicators.
>   With love to you, Child. Winona E. Reeves"

Another letter spoke of the trunk Mrs. Lillian Parmele brought to convention, full of gorgeous clothes. Lillian was from Chapter F, Plattsmouth. Another spoke of May DeMoney, who had a trunk just for her hats.

The true gem, however, is a handwritten President's Book from 1907. It was written and certified to be a correct copy by Mary Johnson Axtell, recording secretary of Supreme Grand Chapter. Mary was initiated into Chapter D, Iowa, and became charter head of Chapter K, Lincoln, organized March 28, 1893. She was president of Nebraska State Chapter in 1901-02. At the convention of Supreme Grand Chapter in 1901, when her chapter was only eight years old, she extended an invitation for the convention to come to Lincoln in 1903. At that time, there was only one other chapter in Lincoln, Chapter V. Mary served as recording secretary of Supreme Grand Chapter for several terms and must have copied many of these books. Incidentally, the star ceremony initiation included there was written by her sister, Ida Johnson.

We are so fortunate to have these items from early P.E.O. days. But we do not build an accurate history by including only the early days. Each chapter is asked to check its items to see if there are historical items from later years— the 30s, 40s, 50s, and on. Many chapters contributed to the war effort in World War II. Do you have records you could share with us? They would be greatly appreciated, and lovingly cared for.

-Susan Harr

2003 Report:

As we make a special effort to recognize and appreciate the legacies of P.E.O. this year, it seems appropriate to look back to the first days of P.E.O. in Nebraska.

P.E.O. made its first appearance in Omaha in 1874, but this group only lasted a few years. Etta Hurford (or Hereford), who had been initiated at Mount Pleasant, Iowa, brought with her only the concept of P.E.O. She had lost her pin and had no constitution. Early records show that representatives from that chapter did attend a Grand Chapter Convention in Iowa. A letter referring to this read: "The Omaha girls read their constitution. It was not ours, but they were considered P.E.O.s and a copy of our Constitution given them. They are to have their pins sold, and get like ours. Their pins had very long points and P.E.O. engraved on them; they had no pins for a pattern, so just had one made..." So secretive were the members of that the chapter that after a few years the chapter vanished from sight and memory, leaving behind only Etta's name.

By the 1890s, Nebraska was ready for P.E.O. to begin in earnest. The first chapter, Chapter A, was organized in York on February 14, 1885. (see photo page 20) The account of this organization is charming:

> "In the summer of 1884 a petite, yellow-haired girl, whose home was in York, Nebraska, packed her trunk, and with many happy anticipations journeyed to Mount Pleasant, Iowa, to spend the summer with relatives. Nebraska trees were not so numerous or well grown in those days; roses did not bloom in York gardens and homes in the little Nebraska town were less commodious. Mount Pleasant boasted of an older civilization and there were many charms lurking in the shaded streets for a girl from further west...
>
> "During that happy summer, Lily Smith was initiated into the mother chapter of P.E.O. She came home in early autumn, wearing a golden star which excited many questions from her friends..."

On February 14, 1885, a new chapter was organized.

> "Seven girls quietly slipped into my (Lily's) home. They did not all come at once, but one by one, so that no one would suspect a secret meeting. Very reverently each girl took the vows, and all were sorry they could not don their stars at once and wear them to the Valentine social given by the college students in a downtown hall that night. In time the stars arrived and there was great glee in watching the whispering of those who were in 'outer darkness', and lots of fun in replying to the guesses at the meaning of our mystical letters. But we tried to impress on the curious public that we were 'Pretty Every One' and let it go at that."

By 1890, chapters had been organized in Fairfield, Norfolk, Superior, Omaha, Plattsmouth, Hastings, Holdrege, and Wahoo. Although not all these chapters survived, P.E.O. had taken root and gained a firm stronghold in Nebraska.

With the addition of the eighth and ninth chapters, Nebraska had met the qualifications which had earlier been set, at Nebraska's insistence, for forming its own state chapter.

Nebraska State Chapter was organized on April 2, 1890, at the spacious home of Jennie Bryant, 530 South 25th Avenue, Omaha—the very first state chapter. Since all chapters at that time served under Iowa, Nebraska delegates began immediate plans for some sort of an organization which would serve over all states. Thus came about Supreme Grand Chapter, later to be called Supreme Chapter, and then changed in 1979 to International Chapter.

And so P.E.O. in Nebraska was off and running. Many, many contributions have been made by its outstanding leaders—a topic for a sequel to this report.

-Susan Harr

P.E.O....Pretty Every One

2007 Report:

The bright and shining star that each of us wears so proudly is the same star suggested and planned at the very beginning by Founder Alice Coffin and agreed to by the other Founders.

They immediately contacted a jeweler, Mr. Hervey Crane, who crafted the ones worn by the Founders as they paraded into chapel. Through many years after, Mr. Crane obtained pins, but from various manufacturers, and kept a supply in his store to be engraved as needed. It was our pin which occasioned the first initiation fee. In October 1870, after a troublesome debt had built with Mr. Crane because some of the initiates were slow in paying their $3.00 for the pin, a bylaw was put into effect requiring an initiation fee of $3, the society then to furnish the pin. That bylaw remains in effect today, although the amounts have varied through the years.

The original pin was much larger than ours—almost an inch across. One of the original pins is on display in the history room. Special permission was given by International many years ago for us to keep this pin rather than send it in. Another old pin has been worn by our state president during her time to preside. However, a ruling by International stated that only the International President may wear this size of pin, so this practice has been discontinued. That pin originally belonged to Mary Esther (Antonides) Lannin, who was initiated into Chapter AK, here in North Platte in November 1914.

A replica of this pin, with a beautiful diamond added, is given to the President of International as she is installed. She continues to wear it as a past president. Check out our dear Joyce Goff, as she will be wearing hers.

When Founder Ella Stewart was in her forties, she wrote:

> "Our Star, as a badge, what could be more significant?...The stars of heaven are bright because they are reflected upon. Likewise should our lives be made radiant by the reflection of God's love upon our hearts, giving us light and wisdom...."

What beautiful, inspiring words.

However, it must be reported that not quite all were so inspired. Rules were made but often they were difficult to enforce. Many of the early minutes recorded something relative to pins. The young college girls insisted on lending their pins to the gentlemen in their lives. According to *Out of the Heart*, a P.E.O. history published in 1968 by International Chapter: "Periodically, all Chapter A pins were collected or called in and deposited, temporarily with a designated officer. This was done in an effort to repossess the pins that were in the hands of the gentlemen. It was against the rules for anyone except P.E.O.s to wear the pin, even though members of other societies exchanged theirs. Naturally, this created problems for P.E.Os on the campus. If caught lending their pins, they were fined $1.00.

> "At Belden's Female Seminary pins were once collected for a different reason. It was during the time in the seventies when the second chapter of P.E.O. and the third chapter of I.C. Sorosis (the competing sorority) were active on campus. Rivalry became so acute that Mr. Belden ordered both groups to deposit their pins with him. He placed them in the bank vault until the girls could get along peaceably."
>
> *Out of the Heart*, page 182

There were no suggestions at that time as to how the pin was to be worn. It might appear in a sister's hair, or on a cuff. The most popular place was high on the left shoulder. This made it easy to touch the pin with her left hand, a signal of distress sent to another sister—distress such as might be found at a dance, "this fine young man is a fine big bore. Please rescue me."

There were rules on the uniformity of the pins and all were to be ordered through Chapter A and their jeweler. However, the first chapter in Nebraska was probably unaware of this rule and created their own. In 1873, Etta Hurford (of Herford) an initiate at Belden's Seminary in Mount Pleasant, returned to her Omaha home and began a new chapter. The chapter lasted only a few years and was so secretive that it vanished from sight and memory with few details. Etta had remembered only bits and pieces about the P.E.O. chapter to which she had belonged. A letter from an Iowa member wrote to another P.E.O. friend:

> "The Omaha girls read their constitution. It was not like ours, but they were considered P.E.O.s and a copy of our Constitution given them. They are to have their pins sold and get like ours. Their pins had very long points and P.E.O. engraved on them; but they had no pins for a pattern so they just had one made..."
>
> Saga of Nebraska P.E.O. page 3

Through the years the pins did change slightly, mainly due to the use of several different jewelers. Some were quite flat, some had plain points. The biggest change was in 1915 when the pin was made smaller, reflecting the current size. Note that Mary Esther Lannin's pin, given in November 1914, would have been one of the last of the larger pins. There was quite a controversy over this change in size for a long period of time. Finally a thoughtful, widely quoted statement by Mrs. Lue R. Spencer of Nebraska carried the day. "It is not the size of the star, but the size of the P.E.O. who wears the star that is the utmost importance," she said.

Nebraska past presidents used to wear a past president's ring, an example of which is found in the history display. These became unavailable for a while. Chapter K, Lincoln, donated to Nebraska State Chapter one of these rings, which had at one time belonged to a member. That ring is now worn by the Nebraska State President. The ring may frequently be found advertised in The P.E.O. Record.

Take a look at the past state president's pin (see page 511) now being worn and you will be able to tell a little about its age—and authenticity. Before there was an official pin, Nebraskans adopted a pin with the shape and abbreviation of the State of Nebraska inside a ring of daisies (see page 511). Some of our past presidents wear these older pins, which have been passed down. Others wear the very similar official past state president's pin, a ring of seven daisies with the words "P.E.O." in the middle. This was adopted by International.

Ella Stewart, in a continuation of her remarks, concluded:

> "...Let it (the star) shed over our hearts and lives a golden splendor and point us ever to God who guides us with his love. Our lives should be affected by our emblem in that we are pure minded, truthful, faithful and loving in character, wearing upon our hearts the zeal of our Master's love."
>
> -Susan Harr

A History of P.E.O. in Nebraska   569

2008 Report:

As a member of an Omaha chapter, I am so glad to wish you a hearty welcome to our proud city. We are thrilled to share this historic area with you. But perhaps you might want to know a little about it. We are sitting in what was known during the late nineteenth and early twentieth centuries as the "Burnt District," an area "where sin held full sway and Satan reigned supreme." It ranged from Douglas to Cass Streets, the Missouri River west to Sixteenth Street—and we are sitting smack dab in the middle of it. Saloons, restaurants serving rowdy crowds and the infamous "Cribs," where prostitutes plied their wares, filled the area. No respectable lady would be found dead anywhere nearby. The P.E.O.s of the past must be shaking their heads in dismay. Remember, at that time, walking past a saloon, without first crossing the street, was a deed worthy of having to relinquish your pin.

But just a few blocks south and west, P.E.O. history was made that would change the way P.E.O. is organized. It was at 850 South 25th Avenue, at the home of Jennie Bryant, that the first state chapter, Nebraska State Chapter, was organized. The idea had first come from Ella Stewart, one of our Founders, in the 1887 Convention of Grand Chapter, held in Iowa.

In 1889, four delegates represented the seven chapters – Alice C. Briggs of Superior, Mary M. Houseworth of Plattsmouth, Jennie Bryant of Omaha, and Florence Wightman of York. And were they ever eager to pursue this idea of a state chapter. On motion of Alice Briggs, it was voted that as soon as Nebraska had eight chapters, permission would be granted "to organize a state chapter of its own. It will still be under the jurisdiction of the present Grand Chapter which will now grant all charters," the motion said.

Can't you just hear those girls on the train on the way home. "Whom do you know in another Nebraska town?" "Do you know anyone in Grand Island or Beatrice or Nebraska City?" It's fun to look at the seven "gutsy" chapters that raised all this stir.

But first, it's necessary to know a little about those times in Iowa and Nebraska. Iowa began being settled in 1833, and, although prairie life was hard at first, settlers found fertile soil and support from each other. By 1860, it was almost completely settled.

Settlement in Nebraska, on the other hand, was not allowed until the Kansas-Nebraska Act of 1856.

So it is easy to understand why in 1884 a petite yellow-haired girl, whose home was in York, Nebraska, would pack her trunk and journey to Mount Pleasant, Iowa, to spend the summer with relatives. Nebraska trees were not so numerous, roses did not flourish in York gardens and Nebraska homes were less commodious. Mount Pleasant boasted of an older civilization and there were many charms lurking in the shaded streets for the young Lily Smith. Among those charms was P.E.O. and when she returned, she introduced it to her friends in York, organizing the first Nebraska chapter in 1885. York at that time was not yet fifteen years old, but it was bustling. Located on the Nebraska City cut-off of the Oregon Trail, it had been an early stopping place for many early-day travelers. Incidentally, the young ladies in that brand new chapter decided that in their chapter married women could not be initiated. But they conceded that marriage after initiation would be permitted.

In 1886, the small town of Fairfield organized a second chapter. Fairfield was a tiny town then, and has grown only to 467 today. Unfortunately, this chapter disbanded after only seven years.

In 1881, the Village of Norfolk was organized when a three-train caravan of prairie schooners carrying forty-four German families arrived and were attracted by the rich land open for settlement. Seven years later, it boasted a P.E.O. chapter.

P.E.O. had grown slowly and carefully during its first twenty years. There were fewer than twenty-five chapters in 1887 anywhere. So it had to be a bit of a shock when five new chapters were formed in Nebraska alone in 1889.

Just ten years after the first log cabin was built in Superior, Nebraska, Chapter D organized in April 1889, and was extremely active and rigorous in its twenty years of existence. It was promoted by Alice Carey Briggs, sister-in-law of Hattie Briggs, one of the P.E.O. Founders. Alice became Nebraska's first state president.

In June of 1889, an Omaha chapter joined the group. Jenny Bryant had moved to Omaha from Mount Pleasant where she had known the original seven Founders and was familiar with P.E.O. She and a neighbor spoke frequently about P.E.O. and then decided to organize a chapter.

By September 7, 1889, a chapter was organized in one of Nebraska's oldest settlements, Plattsmouth, located on the Missouri River, just a few miles south of the mouth of the Platte River. The new chapter was asked to send a delegate to the P.E.O. Grand Convention in October. Finances were a problem. Mrs. Houseworth was chosen because her husband was a railroad man and she could travel on a pass.

Hastings joined the group on October 2, 1889, shortly before the convention. The City of Hastings began in 1871 when George Wilkes was drawn by a railroad advertisement. It wasn't quite what he had envisioned, but he said: "We couldn't walk back, so there was nothing to do but stay." He was also said to have commented: "No more honest men as a class ever lived than our early settlers." Railroad lines ensured its existence, and by the time P.E.O. arrived, there was already a small college.

Shortly thereafter, the delegates made their merry way to convention. I am continually awestruck by the fact that these early sodbusters donned their finest gowns and made their way across the open prairie to gather to speak for the creation of a state chapter. This morning, Susan Sellers, our International officer, said: "If you don't know where you're going, any road will take you there." These ladies knew exactly where they were going, they just didn't have many dusty roads from which to choose. It was at this convention where they received the challenge to have eight chapters before they could organize a state chapter. And they more than satisfied it.

Immediately came Holdrege on December 14, 1889. Early settlers, primarily of Swedish descent, had given birth to the "Magic City of the Plains" in 1883. The Burlington & Missouri Railroad helped determine its survival through its placement of a railroad line. It was only six years later that six married ladies and one spinster gathered to form the "magic chapter of P.E.O." that met the requirement for a state chapter.

Jennie Bryant, through a college classmate named Ella Collins, lent her enthusiasm to organize a chapter in Wahoo. Mrs. Collins became a charter member. This was the last organization before Nebraska State Chapter was born. Incidentally, its first money-making project was a mouse party, where a prize was given to the one who made the best mouse out of chewing gum. It was welcomed into a community that had begun its existence in 1890 as "Leesville," and changed its name to Wahoo after a bush which grew along a nearby creek and was used by Otoe Indians for medicinal purposes. It was actually spelled Wauhoo, but the 'u' was dropped. Good thing, or David Letterman might not have chosen this city for his mythical post office.

And so the scene was set. A State Chapter was to be formed. There's much more to tell—a flu epidemic, a merry rush through muddy streets looking for the organizer from Iowa, a battle over the creation of a Grand Chapter, the precursor of what is today called International. But those are stories for another day, another convention. So stay tuned. You don't know what you might miss.

David L. Bristow, *A Dirty, Wicked Town*, Tales of 19th Century Omaha
Saga of Nebraska P.E.O., a History
Spirit of the Prairie
Harry B. Otis with Donald H. Erickson, *E Pluribus Omaha, Immigrants All*
Websites by each of the cities named.

-Susan Harr

2009 REPORT:

It is no secret that our country is faced with multiple and unmanageable challenges that seem to discourage us. Many comparisons have been drawn between this time and the Thirties and Forties—economic instability, loss of savings, loss of jobs, wars on multiple fronts. Drought and insects made that period extra hard. Global unrest and terrorism add to our current woes.

So it seems a good time to look back at how P.E.O.s faced these challenges in the past. A glance through chapter histories in the *Saga of Nebraska P.E.O.* and the *Spirit of the Prairie* reveals much support of the "newly-needy:" library cards and graduation dresses provided to students, tons of coal, food and clothing, help to a destitute family to become self-supporting, a sousaphone for a school. You know the drill. They saw a need and they addressed it.

But it was during the war that the drive, organization and hard work combined with direction from Supreme (now called International) that P.E.O. really came to the forefront. Immediately, Supreme Convention was cut back from 150 delegates to 50 to save use of valuable fuel.

The P.E.O. United Victory Fund was begun. It supported the Red Cross by helping provide more portable X-ray machines, mobile hospital units, plasma processing machines, mobile blood donor units, ambulances and equipment of every type. It furnished recovery rooms on hospital ships. The Sisterhood owned a club-mobile, dubbed "The P.E.O. Truck," which followed behind troops as they went into battle. It transported food, extra comfort items, distributed coffee and doughnuts—and an extra toothbrush. The Red Cross, which manned the vehicle, said that the fact that people back home recognized that the GIs were normal young men who were not living in normal circumstances meant more to them than the actual articles. Many of the boys had P.E.O. mothers or sisters at home and felt especially touched.

Monies for food parcels for prisoners of war were sent and became indispensable to the lads. One prisoner sent instructions to his parents to withdraw money from his own account to send to this worthy effort.

So how did this happen? By enormous support from local chapters. Every single chapter joined in the war effort in some way. Chapters raised funds and individuals made contributions. Bonds were bought, fundraisers were held.

In addition, members knitted, sewed and wrapped bandages. Often sewing was done after meetings. They learned and practiced first aid—to the delight of the young children who became the pretend patients being treated by setting a pretend broken bone or dressing a pretend wound. Many giggles and cherished memories came from those learning sessions. One chapter, Chapter DB, Auburn, noted that the absence of an accompanying package or report of work done meant embarrassment at roll call.

Railway station work was done in several Nebraska cities—Omaha, Kearney, Lincoln and North Platte. Much has been written of the welcome center in North Platte where over 6 million members of the Armed Forces eagerly wolfed down sandwiches, cookies, cakes and cases of hard-boiled eggs. They joined in dancing, accompanied by popular area bands. Those sandwiches and cakes and other goodies came from, among others, the kitchens of P.E.O. members. Every troop train between Christmas 1941 and April 1, 1946, was met by volunteers. Soldiers said it was the first time anyone had met their train.

There were similar happenings at the canteen at Union Station in Omaha. In addition, boxes were sent to servicemen and support was given to their families at home.

Social events and entertaining were cut back in chapters. Luncheons and BIL parties were not held. Chapter DR, Omaha, lightheartedly acknowledged these sacrifices to the war effort. During war rationing, a patriotic motion to dispense with refreshments passed, but not unanimously. At the next meeting came the aroma of coffee, but paper cups were passed sans coffee and paper plates had pictures of luscious cakes.

Post-war planning came early. A 1943 P.E.O. Record carried proposals for that period, emphasizing the need for educational opportunities throughout Europe and the Far East. Huge bags of nylon hosiery were sent to Japan and clothing to Germany and once again P.E.O. rallied—this time to rebuild that which had been destroyed.

It is good today to remember what was done and to reflect upon the possibility that we could better support our troops and their families today.

~~~~~~

It would seem remiss to stand at a podium in Western Nebraska and not mention Bernice Tillett, AH, Alliance. She served Nebraska State Chapter as president in 1931-32, organizing eight chapters. She was a true P.E.O. legend. She loved P.E.O. history and spoke to over 100 chapters on the early days of P.E.O. In 1932 she was appointed the first History Committee. In 1943, she became Custodian of Articles of Historical Value, a post she held until her death. And she was a fierce lion in that position. At that time Nebraska was in possession of several precious and secret items. Supreme Chapter repeatedly requested that these items be sent to Des Moines, as they are the early history for all P.E.O.s—floor stars upon which officers stood for initiation, a star which was placed in the window to alert would-be visitors that P.E.O. was in session. These and other items remained in Nebraska until her death.

This writer got to know Bernice in the 1960's at a Hastings convention. For several years we exchanged letters and hers were wonderful specimens of a time gone by—full of encouragement, inspiration and beautiful flourishes. This warm and loving side of Bernice was the side her friends and P.E.O. sisters saw daily. She and her husband lived in the Drake Hotel and they spent many evenings sitting on the porch greeting passers-by.

-Susan Harr

2010 Report:

I would like to take a look back at some of the early traditions of P.E.O. and how they came about.

Nebraska is so very fortunate that our history was well preserved through the years. This is due primarily to two women: Bertha Clarke Hughes of M, Omaha, and Bernice K. Tillett, AH, Alliance. Bertha was absolutely adamant that a written history be kept. She worked for years gathering information for a book. Although she never completed the book, the information she gathered was a starting place for the committee that later wrote the *Saga of Nebraska P.E.O.* Bernice was more interested in collecting the artifacts of the early chapters. Supreme Chapter was interested in having some of these early examples of history. But Bernice held on with an iron hand. It was not until after her death that some of this collection was delivered to Des Moines for safekeeping and preservation. They have been in Des Moines since 1974, but can be brought back to Nebraska for visits if we wish. Several have been displayed from time to time.

Bernice spoke at great length at the state convention in Lincoln in 1969, explaining some of these pieces. She showed a small black rosette. At one time the bylaws stated that upon the death of a sister, your pin would be draped for twenty-one days. In Nebraska, it was also required that members abstain from places of frivolous amusement during those days.

P.E.O. pins were originally made by local jewelers before there was a supply department in Des Moines. Much discussion took place at Nebraska's first convention about the jeweler. A jeweler in Omaha had been making them for $1.75, but a jeweler in Norfolk agreed to make them for $1.50. The cheaper price was chosen. At one time, pins were much larger. There is an example of one of these in the History Room. For a time after adoption of the smaller pin, either pin was acceptable. Of course, upon the death of a member, her pin is either buried with her or returned to Des Moines, so there are not any of the large ones being worn any longer. Except by our own illustrious Joyce Goff. The pin worn by the International president and past presidents is larger than others. And it just happens to have a diamond to set it off. Nebraska's History Committee does have one of the old, larger pins for you to see. And have you seen the new pins just released? They aren't quite as large as the old ones, but they are close. And they have the shiny finish as do the old ones.

Bernice related that her mother told her that in the younger days they didn't have ballot boxes. They simply wrote pro or con on a piece of paper and put it in a basket. Chapters were very small at that time, probably nine or ten members, and when the guard collected those little white papers with pros and cons, she was particularly interested in how each person voted.

So they went to white bags which the guard either passed or hung on a chair.

Inside were black and white buttons. The member chose her button and placed it in a small pocket on the side. There is an original of one of these bags, which had been located in the attic of a member of Chapter M. It is currently housed in Des Moines. But it was brought back to Nebraska to be copied and used as teller bags in 1991, when International Convention was held in Omaha. Members of Chapter CC, Seward, made enough of these bags for each teller to have one. There is an example of one of these in the history room

Of course, this was followed by placing balls in a ballot box, which was followed by placing ballots in the ballot box, and now we have returned to white ballots placed in a basket. But, of course, the desired vote is just circled so privacy is protected.

Ballot boxes and gavels just weren't available to women in the early days of P.E.O. So they made do; they used bells instead of a gavel, or borrowed the little hammer from the pantry, or used a spoon.

There is so much more to tell from Bernice's report but I promise to stop after one more. There were not printed invitations for prospective members. If you had a member who was chosen to become a P.E.O., you called on her yourself and told her the good news. Many times she accepted on the spot, but sometimes she had to think it over or consult with her husband. Carrie Hapeman of Minden was a prominent leader. She was president of Supreme in 1901-1903. She wrote the installation ceremony, was on the committee to promote the star ceremony and led P.E.O. through a time of rapid growth. A very good friend of Carrie's was invited into P.E.O. and wrote a very nice acceptance note, but added a P.S. "And old, dear friend Carrie, please provide an old steady goat for my initiation." That was just too much for Carrie, who thought everything about P.E.O. should be taken seriously. And so an elaborate printed invitation was devised.

I can't tell stories of old traditions without retelling my personal favorite. The early initiations included a secret handshake and instructions on four signs known by every early P.E.O.:

1. A touch upon the star worn on the left shoulder signaled *distress*.

2. Two fingers of the right hand on the right temple, with the thumb on the right cheek asked: *"Are you a P.E.O.?"*

3. A touch of the left shoulder with the middle finger of the left hand replied: *"I am."*

4. Placement of the forefinger of the right hand on the right temple was the appropriate acknowledgement: *"We are sisters."*

In closing, I just want to remind you of one thing. We know this history because chapters saved their history and donated it to the state. Each year we receive something from a chapter in Nebraska. Remember, what is not old today, will become old tomorrow, so please help us preserve historic items for our future sisters by donating them to the History Collection. They will be well loved and cared for.

-Susan Harr

Our Star, as a badge, what could be more significant?...
The stars of heaven are bright because they are reflected upon.
Likewise should our lives be made radiant by the reflection of
God's love upon our hearts, giving us light and wisdom.

-P.E.O. Founder Ella Stewart

PRAIRIE FLOWERS BY GEORGE LUNDEEN

2011 Report:
1991 International Convention Remembered

To gain a great respect for the P.E.O. Sisterhood, take a look back and learn our wonderful heritage while at the same time plotting our journey into the future. But today it seemed fitting to look back only a little ways—20 years ago, to one of the proud moments in Nebraska history, to 1991 when Nebraska hosted Convention of International Chapter. It seemed especially appropriate this year before those who worked on it are gone—or can't remember what we did.

This fall, our delegates will go to the St. Louis Convention. This historian has been to the Phoenix Convention, the Orlando Convention, the Vancouver Convention, etc. But there was no Omaha Convention in 1991. It was truly a state-wide *Nebraska* Convention in 1991. When the Convention Committee sent out a feeler almost three years in advance to see who might be interested in helping, almost 125 chapters responded immediately. Others volunteered later.

And these were workers. The Convention Executive Committee came from all parts of the state—Lincoln, Randolph, Kearney, North Platte, Kimball, Humboldt, Weeping Water and Omaha. Past State President Helen Curtiss of Lincoln suggested the theme of the Convention, *"Spirit of the Prairie,"* inspired by a mural of the same name in the Law Library of the State Capitol Building in Lincoln. A line drawing of the mural was used on convention programs, bags, The P.E.O. Record and convention paraphernalia. It depicted a pioneer woman with her children, standing on a windy hill looking into the distance.

Jane Smith, Kearney, contacted well-known artist George Lundeen to design a medal for the convention. He also brought his sculptures to anchor the stage décor and to create a sculpture garden in the lobby. Jane also was instrumental in obtaining the slides of scenes over the Platte River that were projected on the stage during business meetings.

Jean Patoka of Lincoln created the invitational skit which was presented in Phoenix in 1989. It was an intricate, humorous performance that captivated the audience. At the end, Pat Beebe, CT, North Bend, narrated a slide show highlighting the scenic and historic sights of Nebraska. The presentation was enthralling and brought tears to the eyes of many of the delegates who responded with a long standing ovation. Nebraska delegates handed out written invitations wrapped around ears of miniature Indian corn. The corn had been specially grown and carefully stored the year before. But that didn't deter the mice who broke into the stash and destroyed it entirely. Much scurrying was done to find replacements.

The Design Committee, chaired by Omahans Sally Kampfe and Norma Hinchcliff, was charged with making the large Ak-Sar-Ben Coliseum look like a conventional convention center. They borrowed over 100 handmade quilts from

Omahans and surrounding communities. Cherry pickers were used to hang them from the ceiling, giving a warm, charming feeling. And afterwards, they got every quilt back to every rightful owner.

Jan Mardis, DH, Omaha, spent a whole summer creating an enormous 30-feet by 50-feet quilt to be used as a stage backdrop. The pattern was the Nebraska Windmill. She noted that the quilt was half the size of a wall in Solomon's temple.

Stage backdrop quilted by Jan Mardis, DH, Omaha

Prairie vegetation, a euphemism for weeds, was gathered from road sides, around lakes, and in Nebraska pastures. When a county sheriff pointed out that it is illegal to pull weeds along roadsides, Nebraska P.E.O.s quickly moved elsewhere. The vegetation was used in large, five-foot-in-diameter barbed wire wreaths, joining harness and quilted stars to make an attractive décor down the long halls.

The "prairie vegetation" was also used by the Centerpiece Committee, headed by Kathy Gosch and Mary Scott of Kearney. They filled intricately painted crocks used for a luncheon decoration. Members of Chapter HB, Kearney, shocked, dried and baled wheat a year in advance to add to the crocks.

And then there were the cornhusk flower arrangements. Chapter HB held a slumber party and made flowers into the wee hours. On other occasions, P.E.Os from all over central Nebraska gathered to continue the process of making 12,000 flowers.

Two hundred thirty-four chapters sent creative quilted pot holders which were hung over small easels for breakfast decorations. A Scottsbluff chapter made the miniature easels. Another morning, carousel ponies decorated the breakfast tables, painted by the PACK chapters (chapters in Pierce, Antelope, Cedar and Knox counties).

A moving van was hired to bring all the decorations to Omaha, where they were stored on one level and used on another in the coliseum. No escalator has ever been prettier than the ones that were lined with hundreds of decorations marching in line from one floor to another!

Robley Garrigan of Blair found a gentleman in Arizona who agreed to make beveled-glass candleholders for the BIL banquet. He did a beautiful job at a low cost. South Sioux City chapters made 3,250 napkin rings to complement the candleholders.

Anita Kitt of Parks headed the Sales Committee which offered all the decorations and several momentos for sale.

Darlene Ladehoff of Fremont and Pat Beebe headed the Tours Committee. At other convention cities, the tours are pre-packaged and pre-priced, but that was not available in Omaha. So Pat and Darlene created their own. No detail was overlooked. Tour buses took participants to "Worship on the Prairie" at a little country church and then on to the Elkhorn Valley Railroad train for lunch. Along the way many P.E.O.s were in their yards waving quilts or holding welcome signs.

A tour to a Big Red football game with Utah State included a first-ever evacuation of the stadium and a 20-minute delay for a severe thunder storm and tornado warning. No sweat for Darlene and Pat.

There were so many, many others, but time is running short so I must be quick. Julia and Jim McDougal and Mary and Frank Northrup, all of Hastings, kept the BILs entertained; Jean Cuda and Joyce Bumsted, Lincoln, provided Courtesy to the delegates in all NINE hotels; Fremont P.E.O.s Ann Paulson and Libby Vance and their committee arranged for and stuffed 1,800 kits for delegates. Joyce Goff, Grand Island and Chapter AV, Pawnee City, presented a moving Memorial Hour. Bernadine Wherry, Pawnee City, Mary Ruth Wilson, Peru, and Gloria Dunbar, Omaha, assembled an unbelievable cadre of musicians who kept the attendees enthralled.

Twenty-five members from Lincoln chapters sang and danced through the projects program written and directed by Mary Schwaner, AI. Their *Avenue of P.E.O. Dreams* carried us into a musical escapade as Cinderella, sung by Anne Moore, and Foggy, her fairy godmother played by Joyce Bumsted, GQ, sought to rectify the girl's sad situation. Maryland Past State President Janie Knox made her debut as a delightfully ugly stepsister, and Cottey President Dr. Helen Washburn made a cameo appearance. Together they discovered the P.E.O. educational projects, each time singing the refrain *"and then...and then...and guess what happened then? Then P.E.O. went marching out into the fray, offering a scholarship and carrying the day! Hark! The blood is pounding in our ears. Jubilation! We can hear our grateful sisters' cheers!"*

And did I mention the cookies and other treats? They were everywhere! Fifteen thousand cookies from every corner of the state, 72 gallons of cider, 20 bushels of apples and NOWHERE to store them. P.E.O. was using every room in the coliseum. So they were stashed in offices, and corners, and every other nook and cranny. Chairmen Margaret Norton, Osceola, Barbara Sprague, Red Cloud, and Kristi Scheele, York, did an unbelievable job of remembering where they were and cheerfully serving them in the Hospitality Room. A recipe book was compiled and placed in delegate kits. Included was a moving introduction by Jean Hylton, York.

Delegates were housed in nine hotels around the city. This meant nine Lost and Found booths, nine courtesy committees, nine worker committees, nine sets of directional signs, nine breakfast sites for placement of breakfast decorations. To say nothing of all the workers needed at Ak-Sar-Ben. And each one wore a costume—white blouse, dark skirt, and a convention collar. Mary Ann Knappenberger of Omaha and her committee cut out over 675 collars and sent them all over the state to be constructed. During convention, workers "checked out" the collars for use during their shift. Keeping track of all that coming and going was Vida Schworm of Omaha.

And there were other seamstresses. Donna Lin of Kimball made ten of the dresses I am wearing, one for each member of the Executive Committee. She also made ten of a "working" costume. A bit earlier today we sang "Catch a Falling Star and Put It In Your Pocket." This historian has to recommend not putting it in your pocket, as that is where her lost P.E.O. pin has resided for the last 20 years until she put on this costume to model it today. What a thrill to find!

Chapter CC Seward made hand embroidered bags used by the tellers to collect ballots, replicas of early bags used in some chapters for voting.

Lexington's Dottie Anderson and her company Custom Creations handmade costumes for guards, pages, tellers, and ushers—all those tiny pieces in the quilt squares in each skirt and collar!

And so it came to a close, this gathering of P.E.O.s from all over the nation, this "P.E.O. Party on the Prairie." A Convention guest was heard to say that the 1991 Convention was "one against which all others will be measured—beyond compare." It was the largest convention ever held in Omaha up to that time. It was a grand party!

The Spirit of the Prairie, a History of P.E.O. in Nebraska, pp. 492-519
Susan Harr, BP, Past State President and Historian

2012 Report:

This afternoon I am going to talk about the history of our history—or more precisely, the preservation of Nebraska's history. High school students say that history is boring. But the history of history? Goodness, I hope I don't bore you.

We are so fortunate in the state of Nebraska to have this collection of facts and artifacts, and it is mostly due to two women—Bernice Tillett, who lived in Alliance, and Bertha Clark Hughes, who lived in Omaha—opposite ends of the state. Bernice cared for the items and Bertha collected the facts.

Omaha's Bertha served as president of Nebraska State Chapter from 1913-1914; and as president of Supreme Chapter (now International Chapter) in 1923. She had a great sense of the importance of what P.E. O. was doing and what it was accomplishing. And so she saved.

She was president of the National Association of Parliamentarians and was the first woman to serve as a parliamentarian for the National Republican Convention. She was also a leader in the Methodist Church. She had unusual administrative and legislative ability.

And she had an unusual ability to save—a saying, a snipit from the newspaper, a thought. These were frequently taped to the back of leftover stationery from the office of her husband, John, an attorney. What she didn't do was separate her interests, so for several years your history committee received boxes from here or there with various pieces of paper concerning her various interests. It was an adventure into the mind of a curious, lively and intelligent woman to meander through those writings.

In 1932 she was appointed by Bernice to serve on a history committee, of which she later became chairman. "She gave long and loving service to gathering and compiling material for this history." But she was never to publish the history book for which she aimed. This was left to other hands after her death in 1967.

Western Nebraska's Bernice was state president in 1931-32, and became a member of that history committee she created during her presidency. "As a girl she attended a music class in Holdrege directed by Lulu B. Patrick, second president of Nebraska State Chapter" and from whom she received "excellent instruction in P.E.O. ideals as well as parliamentary procedure."

Bernice became Custodian of Articles of Historical Value in 1943 and cared for those articles well. "In the course of the years she talked to over a hundred chapters on the early history of P.E.O."

At that time Nebraska had some items of rare value to P.E.O. In the very early days, floor stars were used for initiation instead of the current table stars. Nebraska had three. Nebraska also had an early ballot bag which used buttons as ballots (there is a replica in the history room), and a window star placed in the window when there was a P.E.O. meeting to indicate to others that the hostess was busy and not to be bothered, and many other items. These were items that were of value to the entire Sisterhood and Supreme Chapter did not have such examples. Supreme asked that they be placed in the P.E.O. headquarters in Des Moines.

Bernice would have none of that.

The fiery Nebraskan and her husband Samuel lived in the Drake Hotel in Alliance and frequently greeted P.E.O.s from there. This historian has no idea where Bernice stored the trove of P.E.O. items, but she was always gracious to share them with Nebraska P.E.O.s at conventions or other meetings. And she was known for her graciousness and generosity. But Supreme was not to have those items! They remained in her custody until her death in 1972.

Many historians have followed. Ruth Knight of Alliance was the first. She was the one who did know where Bernice kept everything and meticulously created a complete inventory of all of the items. Barbara Kennedy was the one who, following the instructions of the Executive Board of the Nebraska State Chapter, transported those items to Des Moines, who has always been willing to lend them back to us when we ask. In 1971, Dorothy Smithberger of Stanton was appointed historian and one of the editors of Bertha's planned book, *Saga of Nebraska P.E.O.*, which was published in 1975. I personally can tell you where she stored the remaining items, because I helped carry them to the car many times.

Julie McDougal, Hastings, prepared a display of our items and presented them at Convention of International Chapter when it was held in Omaha. Nebraskans can take great pride in the many compliments received from delegates from other states at that time.

And then Linda and I became the history committee. Where do I keep them? In a closet, of course. And under a bed. And the most precious ones in a safe deposit box. Some are frequently pulled out for programs to chapters, and most of them come here to convention.

With all of this saving and storing done in the past, it is important that we all remember to continue to contribute.

We are tomorrow's history.

Our chapters made many concessions during the Depression. There was much involvement during World War II. If we don't collect those facts now, they will soon be gone. What has happened lately? Has a member excelled in some way? Did you do anything during a natural disaster, a tornado, a hurricane? Many chapters helped other individuals chapters. Be sure you are collecting this history for your scrapbooks.

And would you consider sharing it with us, so that we can fill up more closets, carry more boxes to cars and give the P.E.O.s of the future a glimpse of the wonderful and loving things that still go on in our P.E.O. chapters.

Saga of Nebraska P.E.O., pages 195 and 207
Susan Harr, BP, Past State President and Historian

2013 REPORT:

It is always a concern of this historian to come up with a report each year that will be of interest to you. So when I found a note to myself that the 1905 P.E.O. Records have some interesting material, I quickly dug into them.

They give a view of P.E.O. just after the turn of the century that in many ways is similar to today, but its small size gave it a familiarity that is not possible now.

P.E.O. was founded in 1869. In 1905, it was 36 years old. It had grown in size and scope, but there had not been much organizational change. There was not even a uniform initiation ceremony until 1907. In 1903, the Constitution was amended for only the third time. This set the tone for much that was done at the 1905 Convention. The November issue of The P.E.O. Record was devoted almost entirely to a report on the 17th Supreme Convention. There were 82 delegates in attendance, from 7 state chapters and one subordinate chapter, Indiana. Kansas State Chapter was not represented because its president was detained in the hospital. One of the topics of business on the agenda was response to the amendments to the Constitution made at the 1903 Convention. We today are used to multiple amendments at each convention. This fall's Convention will consider over 30 amendments. In 1903, they considered a similar number (just under 30) but remember that this was only the third time that amendments had been proposed.

Some of the adopted amendments stand today. "The Supreme Grand Chapter Convention shall hold its regular meetings bi-ennially," "at death the pin shall be buried with deceased sister or returned to the chapter." The Robert's Rules of Order was adopted, replacing the *Women's Manual of Parliamentary Law*. One of the proposed amendments that lost provided that "a member shall be termed inactive upon failure to pay dues by March 1st." This obviously was adopted at a later time.

At the 1905 Convention, a firm for printing and binding the new Constitutions was chosen. Said the author of the report: "The immense amount of labor and expense incurred by this revision is beyond explaining and we trust it will be many years before our laws will again require so complete a reconstruction; also, that members of Convention will give serious thought before voting so cheerfully for amendments that may be proposed. Rather let us use our time and energy for the development of our higher ideals, and the expense necessary in assisting the smaller state grand and the subordinate chapters in the work of extending their interests."

And of course this required a revision of the bylaws, which was done.

The Convention adopted a plan for state organizers to exemplify the inspection of a chapter at each state convention. This eventually evolved into the Period of Instruction still used today. One proposal was to become involved with the saving of Niagara Falls from destruction before it was too late. It seemed that it may be adopted, but there was no practical plan proposed and the matter was dropped.

A lengthy report was made on the P.E.O. Day at the World's Fair in St. Louis. Much discussion was held on what to do with the unexpected $658.13 that remained at the close of P.E.O. Day. The money was set aside as a memorial fund until a special need arose. This of course became the seed money for the P.E.O. Educational Loan Fund.

So let us be done with Convention and take a look at The P.E.O. Records from the rest of the year. The monthly Records are a contrast in the formality of many serious papers and the informality of chapter letters reporting goings-on in each town. In the December 1905 issue, Chapter AL, Madison, laments the departure of two members, including the president. They were preparing a reception for some possible new members. Chapter U, Butte, had just celebrated its anniversary at the home of Mrs. Warner. In addition to a social time, a sewing contest was held for the neatest French hemming. Mrs. Dereg won the prize. The chapter had spent some time contemplating a P.E.O. flag, and even had several designs in mind. Members recommended to Supreme that such a flag be adopted.

In October, Chapter S, Broken Bow, gave a report on all its activities and programs; Chapter K, Lincoln, had helped the YWCA increase the size of its building fund. It also reported on the summer locations of all its members—Green Lake, Wisconsin, Minneapolis, Pueblo, Denver, Estes Park, South Dakota, California, Iowa, Canada, Chicago, New York, Ohiowa, Nebraska. There's notification of a pin lost at Yellowstone Park,

Chapter I, Wahoo, reported that Tuesday evening March 21st was a red letter day in the life of Chapter I. Every member of the chapter was present, also Mrs. Miller of Chapter K, Lincoln. Four ladies were initiated. Chapter E, Omaha, reported that it had taken upon itself the endowment of a room to be called P.E.O. Room in the new Methodist Hospital which was to be completed in the fall. "This is, indeed, an undertaking," they reported, "and will take the combined efforts of every member of the chapter to accomplish this end, but we feel ourselves equal to the task."

In contrast was a treatise that asked: *Does Higher Education Fit Men and Women for Practical Life?* Another: *Our Star and Its Meaning*. Other titles were *Sincerity and Plain Dealing; Love and Service, the True Source of Happiness*, and more.

Many advertisements were sold to support The P.E.O. Record. "P.E.O. Members can buy watches at fifty per cent less," touted one. A True P.E.O. Spoon was a frequent offering as well as hotels in tourist spots, courses from the Columbia College of Expression, sale of a P.E.O. History.

All local chapter officers were listed annually in one of the months.

The main lesson that can be taken from these early Records—that our organization was built on and has maintained a solid base, always exemplifying progress, but more especially exemplifying a true love of each individual sister. Can we ask for more?

2014 Report:

It is wonderful to be in Peru this weekend, with all its history, warm people and cool shade—and the maker of the best watermelon pickles ever. It is also the home of a true pioneer and inspiration for today's P.E.O.s—Mary Ruth Wilson. Mary Ruth, Chapter AU, was one the first full-time employed Nebraskans to go through the seven years of the executive board and to serve as Nebraska State president. She set a fine example for others to follow.

Mary Ruth was Director of Continuing Education at Peru State College. She was also a fine musician and writer, a mother and grandmother, and wife to Gil, who was director of musical activities at Peru State College, and whose physical disabilities required extra care from Mary Ruth. She was tiny in stature but mighty in good works. It is a privilege to pay tribute to her today.

Nebraska's P.E.O. history is full of leaders who have led the organization on its wise path. I would like to talk today about those who had such influence on the Educational Loan Fund. Its beginnings came about in discussion of what to do with funds left over from the P.E.O. Day at the St. Louis Louisiana Purchase Exposition. Three ideas were presented at the 1907 Convention of Supreme Chapter: a home for P.E.O.s to be located in Colorado, a printing plant, and scholarships for worthy young women. This last was presented by Nebraska Past State President Lillian Pollock Parmele of Chapter F, Plattsmouth. When a motion was made that the fund be used for establishment of a P.E.O. Home, Lillian moved to amend by substituting the word "scholarship" for "Home." In spite of a little flurry at the change of intent (we have always been very intent on correct parliamentary procedure), the amendment was ruled in order. Lue R. Spencer, AN,Lexington, moved to amend the amendment (are we having fun yet?) by substituting for "scholarship" the words "educational purposes." Both motions passed and the fund was to be called The Educational Fund. Grand President Carrie M. Peterson, Nebraska AC, Aurora, appointed Lillian, along with 27-year-old Bertha Clark Hughes, M, Omaha, to serve on a committee to organize the work.

Actually, the idea of a scholarship had been promoted by Lillian for some time prior to all this hullabaloo. She and Carrie had traveled from chapter to chapter to promote the idea. Once it was adopted, the two of them again took to the road at their own expense to travel from state convention to state convention to promote the fund.

Are you getting the Nebraska connection? It was almost a collusion.

Now it is fourteen years down the road. It is 1919, the fund has been growing and monies have been given out. There is over $112,000 in the fund, with only the interest being awarded. Our young Bertha Clark Hughes has been Nebraska State President and has just been elected first vice president of Supreme, slated to become president in 1921. She has been instrumental in raising the "Bucks for Bertha" to get it to the $112,000. In Nebraska the slogan had been "Give your dollar or Bertha will holler." Bertha walked through the delegation gathering more dollars as delegates waved them in the air. She tucked them in her pocket, up her sleeves and down her bosom. What a wonderfully enthusiastic and humorous spectacle she must have been. No wonder she was so successful.

But now she would like to see that amount doubled again by 1923. And, in addition, an ambitious board of directors would like to see a million dollar endowment created. This was thought to allow $40,000 to be awarded each year and would give the fund financial stability. The board suggested that, although it might mean temporary sacrifice for some, each chapter was to raise ten dollars for each member for each of the next three years. Oh, the uproar both for and against. One supporter was President of Nebraska State Chapter Ona Tourtelot Baird, Chapter F, Plattsmouth. She favored the idea of an endowment fund and did not object if others wished to give ten dollars per year for three years, but she did not favor making members feel thus obligated.

Even the Founders weighed in. Bertha received handwritten letters from Franc Roads Elliott and Alice Bird Babb. The originals of these letters are on display in our history room. Franc wrote to recommend a scholarship recipient and to support Bertha. Alice, who said her eyes and health were failing, regretted doing what her father told her never to do—write a letter in pencil. She expressed concern for the member to whom this created a hardship. "I am sure," she wrote, "that among our 30,000 members are 20,000 who cannot pay out from their family fund more than annual dues…Mrs. Reeves said that I gave money to it and did not buy a fur collar! Why, bless your hearts, I had a fur collar, and if I had had none, maybe I would have used the money to buy one, for I believe P.E.O.s should be as well-dressed as possible." And on it went. Eventually the fund was doubled as Bertha had wished, but that pesky endowment? Well, it was voted down.

It is gratifying that Nebraska women have continued to provide time and talent and leadership to P.E.O. in their chapters, their state and beyond. Thank you for your attention.

Susan Harr, BP, Past State President and Historian

Early handshake and signs of the Sisterhood

A touch upon the star worn on the left shoulder signaled distress.

Two fingers of the right hand on the right temple, with the thumb on the right cheek asked: "Are you a P.E.O.?"

A touch of the left shoulder with the middle finger of the left hand replied: "I am."

Placement of the forefinger of the right hand on the right temple was the appropriate acknowledgement: "We are sisters."

This Royal Doulton plate was commissioned in honor of Nebraska State Chapter's centennial and was made available for purchase at the celebratory conventions in 1989 and 1990.

Section Ten
Nebraska State Chapter Centennial

BY CAROL BALDWIN, CENTENNIAL COMMITTEE CHAIRMAN

"I thought P.E.O. started in Iowa!" And so it did, in 1869, on the January date that we celebrate every year as "Founders' Day." However, P.E.O. was an idea whose time had come, and by the late 1880s, new chapters had been organized wherever its members chanced to rove. The neighboring central states of Illinois, Indiana, Michigan, Missouri, Nebraska and Kansas, as well as far away California and Washington, D.C., each had at least one P.E.O. chapter by the close of the year 1890. Women of foresight were concerned that such far-flung chapters might drift away from the cherished precepts set forth by our Founders without proper oversight. Concerns were voiced at convention time in Iowa, and The P.E.O. Record carried letters expressing possible solutions to the problem. The dialogue in The Record even became somewhat heated, but the concern was genuine.

In Nebraska, P.E.O. was represented by three chapters in York, Fairfield, and Norfolk, organized in 1885, 1886, and 1887. A fourth chapter in Superior was organized April 10, 1889. A very active member of that chapter was Alice Cary Brooks Briggs, a sister-in-law of Founder Hattie Briggs. Alice Cary Brooks had married Hattie's brother and left Mount Pleasant a little over a year before the organization of P.E.O., but her two sisters became active members in Mount Pleasant. And so, when P.E.O. came to Superior, Alice embraced it immediately and took up the task of expansion. Chapters E, Omaha, F, Plattsmouth, and G, Hastings, were all organized prior to the Mount Pleasant convention of 1889. Alice Cary Brooks led the Nebraska delegation and carried to that meeting a request for a Nebraska Grand Chapter. The convention "voted to require eight chapters in a state before a State Grand Chapter may be organized." Then, on her motion, Nebraska was granted permission for a "Grand Chapter of its own. It will still be under the jurisdiction of the present Grand Chapter which will now grant all charters."

Alice then returned to Nebraska, organized Chapter H, Holdrege, in mid-December 1889, (the eighth chapter), while Clara Mason organized Chapter I, Wahoo, in January 1890. Nebraska was now ready to become a state chapter. Mrs. Nannie Torrence Stockman, president of Grand Chapter, journeyed to Omaha and organized Nebraska Grand Chapter on April 2, 1890. It wasn't quite that simple. The story of that organizational meeting was tragically funny, but it was "mission accomplished." Among women of good will, solutions were found to all problems and following the close of the 1893 convention, the Iowa State Chapter was organized. And in 1894, Missouri State Chapter came into being. The state chapter concept was fully accepted. Grand Chapter, which carried the burden of P.E.O. oversight since 1883, ordered a complete revision of the constitution and bylaws in 1892. Founder Alice Bird Babb, who had written the first P.E.O. Constitution, was appointed to head the committee that included Alice Briggs and Ida Mathews.

The 1893 convention considered thoughtfully each provision of the new constitution and accepted the restructuring of the organization into three parts, Supreme Chapter, State Chapters, and Local Chapters. The seven officers elected to serve Supreme Chapter were from six states (Nebraska, Michigan, California, Iowa, Missouri, and Illinois). Mrs. Alice C. Briggs, president, and Mrs. Winnie Durland, organizer, became the first women from the state of Nebraska to be Supreme Chapter officers.

In April 1987, women from the fourteen Nebraska reciprocity groups received letters from June Brunmeier (an initiate of Chapter I, Wahoo), organizer of Nebraska State Chapter, asking them to serve on a Centennial Committee to coordinate the celebration of Nebraska State Chapter's 100th year. At Nebraska State Chapter Convention in Omaha in May 1987, June gave a report on the purpose and makeup of the committee. In August of that year, the first meeting was held in the home of Nebraska State Chapter President Joyce Goff. The meeting was productive, but it was soon discovered that a review of Nebraska P.E.O. history was a first priority. Other than the members of the few chapters who had just celebrated their first 100 years, or were preparing to celebrate, the members of the remaining 223 chapters in the state were, for the most part, unaware of Nebraska's unique "claim to fame." As planning progressed, the startled statement, "I thought P.E.O. started in Iowa!" was frequently heard by the members of the committee. Fortunately, Frances Key, FK, Omaha, a past president of Nebraska State Chapter, was a committee member. Frances was the author of *"A Star in the Window,"* an historical skit presented at Centennial Convention of Supreme Chapter in 1969, and presented again at the first Convention of International Chapter in Missouri in 1981. Frances was an excellent choice to write some skits that would be informative and fun to produce in local chapters.

Jean Patoka, DX, Lincoln, was asked to compose a centennial melody that would put a little pep into the celebration. (See music page 592). In addition, she proved to be a tireless accompanist who would fill in whenever needed.

Ideas discussed at that first meeting included some commemorative items and possibly a contest to garner designs that could be used in various ways throughout the year. The contest also would be a way of eliciting local chapter interest.

The Executive Board of Nebraska State Chapter allowed one mailing to the local chapters, a generous offer when the committee realized that included the costs of postage, photocopying, and envelopes for 231 chapters. Our sisters are ever mindful that our projects deserve all that we can give them, and so expense moneys are evaluated carefully. After this initial mailing, the committee was granted a paragraph in each president's letter to keep the local chapters informed. The letter asked for a Centennial V.I.P. to be appointed in each chapter who would serve throughout the three years or so of planning as a liaison from reciprocity meetings in order to carry sales and plans to her chapter. A ruling of International Chapter had banned any sales at state conventions other than sales by the hostess chapters to help recoup costs of convention. The validity of this ruling was recognized and affirmed. Each member of the committee became responsible for sales in her reciprocity group.

The commemorative items discussed that received the most interest were a collector's plate, a charm or a pin, and note paper. Past State President Julia McDougal, DA, Hastings, and Helen Easterbrook, AS, Kearney, were appointed to investigate costs of note paper. Mary Ann Knappenberger, GF, Omaha, was asked to check on plate manufacture. Opal Saum, GC, Alliance, accepted appointment as committee secretary. The first meeting adjourned with a feeling of accomplishment and a determination by most of the members to check the President's Box for copies of *Out of the Heart* and *The Saga of Nebraska P.E.O.*

At the September Convention of International Chapter, the members of the Nebraska State Chapter executive board and past presidents of Nebraska State Chapter met informally and expressed a sense of urgency. Centennial planning had begun none too soon. June Brunmeier realized that her duties as state officer would not leave enough time for the details of the Centennial Committee. She became advisor to the committee and appointed Carol Baldwin, HI, Ogallala, as chairman.

In early November the committee met again in the Grand Island home of Vera Koefoot, newly-elected recording secretary of International Chapter. The remaining committee assignments had been made: Janet Lindley, I, Wahoo; Marion Schrader, IC, South Sioux City; and later Peggy Kaufman, BQ, David City, joined Frances Key on the program committee. Marjorie Ann Porter, AZ, Wayne, and Nancy Shafer, BY, Beaver City, joined Mary Ann Knappenberger on the plate committee. Helen Hayes, CS, Lincoln, went to work with Julia McDougal and Helen Easterbrook on the stationery committee. June Steggs, S, Broken Bow, past president of Nebraska State Chapter, and her committee for the charm, Jana Puls, BT, Weeping Water, and Jeannette Rosenau, IB, Cozad, began researching suppliers. Opal Saum accepted the additional duty of committee treasurer. Jean Patoka gave a run-through of her *"Centennial Melody"* (see page 592). Marion Shrader shared some centennial lyrics written for a chapter meeting to the tune of *"Marching Along Together."*

The letter to local chapters including the contest rules for centennial designs was postmarked November 12, 1987, and the contest deadline was January 20, 1988. During a busy holiday season this did not allow a great deal of time for P.E.O. artists to respond, but the designs were essential to obtain manufacturing quotations.

Thirty-three artists responded to the call with sixty-nine designs of wonderful variety. Judges were: Mary Wherry Kellner, AT, Tecumseh, chairman; Lavona Smith Lemons, GA, Scottsbluff; and Adele Koefoot Swihart, GP, Grand Island. They met to evaluate the designs and then award Most Outstanding Design to Barbara J. A. Vondras, AN, Lexington; and Outstanding Designs to Donna Beck, N, Minden, and Gretchen Olberding, CJ, Burwell. Six Special Mention Awards went to Lois Messinger, CY, Falls City; Nancy S. Wilkins, O, Geneva; Nicki Tiedtke, ID, Wayne; Dorothy Groesser, BT, Weeping Water; Lois E. Stevens, CY, Falls City; and Suzan Rohrig, HX, Omaha. All of the designs were showcased at the Kimball convention of Nebraska State Chapter in 1988. Each artist received a grateful letter from the Centennial Committee for her contribution.

The committees for commemorative items immediately went to work to determine which of the designs were best adapted to manufacture. The design by Barbara Vondras was chosen for the centennial charm and pin. The designs by artists Vondras, Beck and Olberding were reproduced, each with an appropriate choice of inks and paper, for the note cards. And the design by Gretchen Olberding was deemed most appropriate for the commemorative plate. Members of the committee became specialists in manufacture in short order!

The first commemorative items (note cards, charms and pins) were ready for sales in time for reciprocity meetings in the fall of 1988, and were met with delight. Instructions for advance plate sales went home with V.I.P.s. Other designs were used by hostess chapters of both conventions during the centennial year on program covers, favors, and note cards, etc.

Convention 1989 at Hastings began the year of celebration with the theme *"Light a Candle of Faith and Reach for Our Star."* Catherine Hutton presided. The first rendition of the *"Centennial Melody"* came at the BIL banquet. It was sung by Ruth Stephenson, FB, Lincoln, accompanied by Jean Patoka. The guards made their entrances and exits to the *"Melody"* and soon everyone was humming it.

The blue and white Centennial plate by Royal Doulton was on display at the banquet for the first time; and following the close of convention, nearly 800 advance sale plates were picked up by homeward-bound delegates in less than twenty minutes. Plates purchased in Omaha were distributed there at a later date, and a very few remained for mail purchase at an increased price.

Two of the hostess chapters, J, Nelson, and DS, Superior, gave a charming evening presentation of the two skits written by Frances Key. Announcement was made of Nebraska State Chapter's gift of $1,000 to endow a chair in the new performing arts building at Cottey. On the closing morning of convention, a gift kit was presented to each delegate for her local chapter. It included printed copies of the *"Centennial Melody"* and copies of the two skits with a cover letter from the committee asking that they be performed at chapter meetings during the year, and requesting that each member give silent honor on the day of April 2, 1990, by wearing her emblem throughout the day.

On the second day of April 1990, the Nebraska State Chapter Executive Board traveled to the P.E.O. Executive Office in Des Moines, taking with them First Vice President of International Chapter Bobbie Koefoot. The board presented a check to the P.E.O. Sisterhood for a designated repository to house and display P.E.O. memorabilia and special papers. The check in the amount of $12,305 represented $1.00 for each active member of Nebraska State Chapter. Deborah Cowan, Chief Administrative Officer, brought in a beautiful cake decorated in yellow and white in honor of the occasion. Deborah was initiated into Chapter CM, Crete.

In May 1990, Nebraska State Chapter celebrated *"A Century of Sisterly Love."* June Brunmeier presided at the Centennial Convention in Lincoln which was held on May 23, 24, and 25, 1990. Nebraska State Chapter was honored by several special guests who joined the celebration: President of International Chapter Mary Louise Remy; Second Vice President of International Chapter Nancy Hall; Member of Honor Vera "Bobbie" Koefoot, First Vice President of International Chapter; from the Iowa State Board, Second Vice President Mary Jane Huntington, and Organizer Pam Holub; and Cottey College President Dr. Helen Washburn.

The guards were attired in slate blue, long dresses with quaint crocheted collars, reminiscent of the clothing of our sisters a hundred years ago. The pages' dresses were similar but of a darker blue color. The guards marched in to Jean Patoka's *"Centennial Melody,"* the song which had been given to all Nebraska chapters at the previous convention and which they had been encouraged to sing and use during the Centennial year.

Special events at the convention included a Centennial Choir directed by Jane Knox and accompanied by Jean Patoka. Wednesday evening ceremonies were climaxed with a clever and entertaining project presentation entitled, *"My Fair Cinderella or The Avenue of P.E.O. Dreams."* This skit was written and directed by Mary Schwaner, AI, Lincoln (photo page 579). The BIL Banquet, *"Hitch Your Wagon To A Star,"* was hosted by Nebraska State Chapter First Vice President Robley Garrigan. The entertainment was provided by Roger Welsch, Nebraska author and humorist, who entertained with a talk on *"Laughter on the Prairie."* Mary Louise Remy delivered a snappy tribute to the BILs, and George Washburn, BIL of Cottey College President Helen Washburn, responded.

Historian Julia McDougal enriched the experience of every delegate and visitor by setting up beautiful Nebraska history displays at every convention of Nebraska State Chapter from 1987 through 1991, and again at Convention of International Chapter in Omaha in 1991. She placed samples of each of the commemorative items and programs of both centennial conventions with these history materials.

Assistant Secretary-Treasurer Nelsine Scofield, DN, Lincoln, and Committee Treasurer Opal Saum put in countless hours taking care of sales records of commemorative items. And, indeed, nearly every member of the committee stated that they had never envisioned the amount of work involved in such a celebration, but that it was ultimately satisfying.

At the close of the 1990 convention, the Lincoln hostess chapters honored the delegates with a special Centennial Luncheon. Hostess chapters in 1989 and 1990 entered into the centennial spirit wholeheartedly with their costumes, table decorations, project presentations, and music to give the delegates and convention visitors a lovely experience to remember and a special beginning for the second century of P.E.O. in Nebraska.

Section Eleven

The Big Picture of P.E.O.

State Convention Highlights
1995-2015

Cindy Biehl, Past State President

Why do so many of us attend state convention year after year? What exactly is so appealing? What prompts us to look forward to these days together? There are many answers to these questions. The following synopses of convention highlights from 1995 to 2015 may explain why conventions are important to so many Nebraska P.E.O. sisters.

Annual conventions are held in each state or district in the United States and each province in Canada from April to June. Nebraska's bylaws state June as the month of preference. But from time to time because of the way the calendar falls or because of the availability of the venue, we've come together as early as May 30th and ended convention as late as June 13th. Meetings begin on Friday and end on Sunday, early enough for sisters to make their way home before it gets too late. There has been discussion about shortening convention days from three to two, but because of the size of our state and the time it takes to travel, the three day convention schedule has remained. International Chapter requires certain business to take place at convention and we absolutely won't give up our time to enjoy each other as sisters, to share good ideas and to have fun.

During the last twenty years we welcomed twelve new chapters; Chapters IN through IY. We saw the merger of six of our chapters into three new chapters: FI-IK, Omaha, CR-DZ, Omaha and FF-IA, Lincoln. Much to our sadness, we accepted the disbandment of thirteen chapters: Chapters L, M, U, CR-DZ, DB, DD, DH, DO, DR, ER, GD, GY and IF.

Even though each Nebraska chapter is allowed only one voting delegate during convention, hundreds of sisters attend convention as visitors. Many chapters encourage all their members to attend the Saturday meetings of convention. The Saturday Honors luncheon is a favorite event and is the largest meal of convention. Many years there are 500 or more in attendance. Chapters celebrating 125, 100, 75 and 50 year birthdays are honored. These chapters come out in force. Often times they wear matching scarves, shirts or hats and sit together at the front of the banquet hall. Each chapter's history is written in a commemorative booklet. In 2011, Nebraska's first chapter, Chapter A, celebrated 125 years during the Honors Luncheon. All 50 and 50-year-plus members in attendance are recognized as well. Some of these sisters we see each year, and honoring up to 75-year members is not unusual.

Over the past twenty years, state conventions have been held in high school auditoriums or theatres, college campuses and larger city hotels. We've gathered together all over the state from Scottsbluff/Gering to Norfolk and South Sioux City to Beatrice and Peru. We've met in Omaha and Lincoln several times and enjoyed our times in Central Nebraska, too, in the cities of North Platte, York, Hastings, Kearney, Grand Island, Fremont and Columbus. In 2016 and 2017 we're trying something new. Convention will be held in the central location of Kearney at the Younes Convention Center.

Just as P.E.O. has changed over the years, so has state convention. In 1996, rule number eight of convention read, "No hats are worn in the meetings of convention and are optional for the Memorial Hour." The next year this rule no longer appeared and hasn't been included in convention rules since. There have been times since when hats have been worn for a presentation, skit or workshop. Actors in the presentation of *"A Star in the Window"* wore hats at the 1998 convention. In 2004, the executive board wore hats as they were "Stepping Out in P.E.O." during the convention procession. P.E.O.s appearing as the seven Founders wore hats during the Honors program in 2006.

These were the early years of changes in technology in P.E.O. We see that again in the rules of convention. By 1999, rule 13 asked that we turn off cellular phones during meetings of convention. Later, pagers were included in this rule. In the early 2000s, all kinds of technology came to conventions with our sisters. By 2010 camera phones and laptops were prohibited during meetings. Only the Committee to Approve the Minutes was allowed to use laptops. Many of our workshops are now on Power Point so non P.E.O. technicians are allowed to be in attendance at meetings of conventions.

These were the years when chapters no longer brought several yearbooks to convention. One yearbook and several Yearbook Information Forms were required. The "YIF" as it was called—and later the CIF, Chapter Information Form— listed the meeting dates, officers, members, addresses, phone numbers and email . Later on, chapters brought one yearbook to convention and the "YIF" was emailed to the executive board for distribution. By 2011, chapters started doing a self-evaluation form of their yearbook which is brought to convention.

The biggest changes to Nebraska State Chapter and therefore state convention took place following the Convention of International Chapter in 2009. P.E.O. approved our sixth philanthropy, the P.E.O. STAR Scholarship. And the number of state officers decreased from seven to five. Eventually there would no longer be a recording secretary or a corresponding secretary on the state board. This set in motion an array of changes for P.E.O. from procedure to policy. It took two years to accomplish this transition and by 2012 those attending convention were greeted by five state officers.

State committees changed, also. The International Transportation Committee was approved to assist in travel arrangements to Conventions of International Chapter. The state Research Committee was eliminated as a standing committee. The president is allowed to appoint an ad hoc committee if the need arises. The Chairman of Unaffiliate Members became the Unaffiliate Committee and changed from one to two members and then was eliminated and then reinstated with three members. A state Membership Committee was approved and later the name changed to the state Membership Development Committee. The Ad Hoc

Convention Steering Committee was appointed each year starting in 2011.

For many years the philanthropies program was presented during Friday evening of convention. Project speakers were introduced to the Convention and enlightened us with their stories of educational success largely because of P.E.O. Later on, the philanthropies program was incorporated into the Saturday evening banquet. Eventually convention workshops and buzz sessions were held on Friday night following dinner and the welcome to convention.

The Time of Remembrance hour continued to be an important time to memorialize our sisters who have entered into Chapter Eternal. Over the years this special time has generally been presented on Sunday morning prior to the final meeting of convention. Technology has allowed us to not only hear the names of our sisters who have entered Chapter Eternal, but also to see their images. This has become a powerful reminder of these sisters who during their time with us, gave so much.

The report of the Historian and Custodian of Historical Articles is a much anticipated part of convention. Since Susan Harr, past state president, has taken this position, she has been an inspiration to attendees. Susan tells stories of P.E.O. history with humor and always with devotion to this post she has held since 1997.

Convention guards and pages continue to be an integral part of state convention. Over the years they assumed more of the work of the logistics of convention. Guards and pages helped with everything from registration to hospitality to meals. They reported early, left late from convention hall and always had smiles on their faces. Guards continue to dress for convention according to the state president's wishes, often wearing matching vests, aprons or dresses. The pages, too, enjoyed wearing the convention theme colors selected by the president.

Convention committees and convention hostess chapters continue to serve on a rotation basis among Nebraska's reciprocity groups. For many years different colored polo shirts were worn by the hostess chapters during convention. This practice was started to make a distinction between the different convention committees. Usually the convention theme was incorporated into the artwork on the polo.

The following changes came about because of convenience or finances.

Copies of the state convention Proceedings were no longer mailed to each chapter following convention. The Proceedings was available on the Nebraska website. Chapters and individual P.E.O.s could order and pay for a hard copy to be mailed to them. For most of these years a receiving line for greeting new state officers was held after the recessional at the close of convention or on Sunday morning prior to the Time of Remembrance. For a few years around 2010, convention hosted a P.E.O. Market where local chapters could display their fund-raising items to convention attendees. Sales did not take place during convention but orders were taken for delivery at a later date.

During these years everything became more expensive, including P.E.O. The annual dues of Nebraska State Chapter increased from $25 in 1995 to $40.50 by 2012. This was largely due to increases in International dues from $12.50 to $26. During this same time, state convention registration fees for chapter delegates increased from $10 to $30.

From 2011 to 2014, three to six new initiates to Nebraska P.E.O. chapters were invited to convention as guests of the executive board and the state chapter. They were seated in the front row and introduced to the members. In 2013, the

Nebraska P.E.O. Home celebrated its 75th anniversary at convention.

Nebraska has been fortunate to have Joyce Goff, past president of Nebraska State Chapter and past president of International Chapter, in attendance at several of our state conventions over the past twenty years. Starting in 1996 when Joyce was serving as recording secretary of International Chapter until 2005 when Joyce was serving as president of International Chapter and many times since then, she has attended as a most Honored Member of Convention. Joyce gave numerous devotions, invocations and workshops over the past twenty years. She continues to be an inspiration to all Nebraska P.E.O.s.

The new acquaintances made and old friendships renewed during state conventions continue to be an inspiration for Nebraska P.E.O.s. These ties bind us together for a lifetime. The celebration of state convention is more than business at hand; that is but only a part of it. The celebration of state convention is the renewal of spirit and the love for one another and for P.E.O. All of these things make the anticipation of another state convention so compelling to so many sisters.

Convention Highlights 1890-1974

BY ROBLEY GARRIGAN WITH EXCERPTS FROM THE SAGA OF P.E.O.

Throughout the years, Nebraska Grand/State Chapter Conventions have been glorious events. Lavish receptions, teas and banquets have been enjoyed since the very first conventions. Only the war years saw a decrease in the extravagant entertaining. The ingenuity and decorative talents of hostess chapters were without limits and an abundance of flowers was everywhere, especially in the early years. Records indicate that in 1910, bushels of daisies were sent from fields near Kearney. Other convention records tell of three thousand paper marguerites being made by hand; a thousand tulips coming from California in 1947; and orchids being flown in from Hawaii. P.E.O.s always have been known for their elegant and gracious entertaining and conventions were no exception! Bertha Clark Hughes, past president of both Nebraska and Supreme Chapters, called conventions "Festivals of Friendship." And so they are!

From the origin of P.E.O., proper parliamentary procedure was followed. The general procedure which is followed today (including a memorial service) was established at the very beginning and has changed little. P.E.O.'s goal of self-improvement through personal growth was evident and exemplified at those early conventions through readings, papers and symposiums.

The performances of the early days have given way to summaries of president's letters, P.E.O. project reports, workshops, and periods of instruction. One tradition which lasted until recently was the "model meeting." A chapter was chosen to present the initiatory ceremony for the convention delegation to exemplify perfect P.E.O. procedure. Occasionally, real candidates were initiated at conventions. Today the organizer's Period of Instruction has increased in scope and only occasionally is a model meeting presented. Clever staging, acting, and innovative ideas have contributed to P.E.O. instruction that has taken on pizzazz and flair. Parodies of game shows, television shows, movies, and short plays and songs have replaced the serious with the imaginative. In the very earliest conventions, the delegates, themselves, were expected to perform. At the very first convention, all sixteen delegates contributed artistic talent! Quite a requirement for representation! What would today's delegate say if she were required to sing, dance or read a paper as well as represent her chapter in convention?

Delegates were formerly entertained in the homes of local P.E.O.s. Since the size of the delegation has increased dramatically, it is no longer possible to house everyone in homes; hotels or dormitories are now used. This expanded need for housing has initiated a significant change in the convention venues. No longer are the small towns able to host convention as they did in the past, as most do not have adequate hotel or motel space available. Unless a town has a college available where dormitories can provide lodging, the convention must be held in cities large enough to have quite a few motels or hotels available. Until 1936, only one chapter was responsible for the entertainment of convention. At that time the geographic groupings were designated, allowing for multiple chapters to act as hostesses. As the Sisterhood grew, the number of delegates allowed representation changed. In 1943, chapters were limited to one instead of two delegates.

Early records contain little of the greatest value of a convention—the uplifting addresses, the inspiring devotions, the lovely music—the intangible things which delegates carry home with them in their hearts and memories. It was not until 1940 that convention themes were used, creating a continuity which linked all the convention entertainment and presentations.

The very first convention was the organization of Nebraska Grand Chapter on April 2, 1890. This was held at the home of Jennie Bryant in Omaha and Alice Briggs was installed as the first president. Beset by calamity, the convention delegates carried on bravely in spite of adversity and Nebraska State Chapter was born.

The second convention of Nebraska P.E.O.s was held at Superior in 1891. At that time chapter re-lettering was completed. The Question Box was used, a tradition which has continued today. At the third convention, a constitution and bylaws were adopted and the entire state membership of P.E.O. was reported at 172. The fourth convention saw adoption of an Opening Ode, written by Jennie S. Moore of Holdrege.

At the sixth convention in 1895, the office of state organizer was created. The next year the convention allowed $50 for a chapter to entertain convention and devised an alphabetical rotation system for designating hostesses. (A convention footnote indicated that the Holdrege gentlemen extended an invitation for a drive in carriages drawn by the finest horses in the city!) In the subsequent year, dues were raised to twenty-five cents! Conventions always included instruction in proper procedure and at the ninth convention in Omaha in 1898, drills were conducted in the P.E.O. signs. The TransMississippi Exposition followed the next day and P.E.O. had a booth where many came to learn more about this "Peculiarly Exclusive Order."

Conventions the next few years were similar in nature and content. Proper procedures were stressed, especially for the offices of president and secretary. Reminders of the requirements for chapter inspection were recurring features.

One receives the impression from reading early convention accounts that the organizer arrived for "inspection" with a stern look, a magnifying glass and white gloves. In 1900, visits by the organizer every other year were approved. No doubt, a sigh of relief could be heard among the local chapters.

At the 1901 convention in Minden, the state membership was reported at 721, showing phenomenal growth in ten years. At that convention, the delegation voted that no chapter shall be organized in a town of 1,000 or less. It was only recently that this requirement was dropped. It was reported that the state corresponding secretary had purchased a membership book similar to that of Supreme Chapter and a "perfected" list of members had been entered into it. By 1995, ninety-five years later, this book had now grown to two enormous volumes and they contained the names of over 40,000 women who have held membership in Nebraska P.E.O. These records were lovingly referred to as "The Big Books," as they weigh about forty pounds. Every state chapter had such books, although Nebraska's and Iowa's undoubtedly were the largest. The name of every woman ever initiated or dimitted into Nebraska State Chapter was hand-entered into these books, as well as the names of dimits out of the state and deaths. Susan Harr, when she was state president, had instructed her boys that in case of a tornado siren, to grab the "Big Book" before going to the basement. Oh, if that corresponding secretary of 1901 could see the "Big Books" now!

Five years later in 1906, Nebraska State Chapter President Carrie Peterson recommended that each local president send an annual letter by January 1 to the state president describing the work done by the local chapter the previous year. This tradition continues today and it is one of the highlights for the state president to receive and read these chapter treasures.

The next few years of convention minutes speak often of the new P.E.O. project, the "memorial fund." Nebraska's Lillian Parmele, F, Plattsmouth, suggested that scholarships from the "memorial fund" be recommended to Supreme Chapter. Thus was born the Educational Fund. The convention recommended that a day each year be designated as "Educational Day" for the pursuit of educational subjects and for receiving gifts to the new P.E.O. project.

Convention reports of the next few years were unremarkable. Enthusiasm grew for the Educational Fund and conventions regularly voted $100 as contributions from the state chapter—an enormous amount at that time. Individual chapters also donated generously to the project—$673.05 in 1913.

Pennants to identify delegates' chairs came into use in 1915. The hostess chapter AG, Fullerton, provided lovely fabric chair markers. A year later, the convention voted to divide the Nebraska chapters into four groups for representation at Supreme Chapter Convention. This system continues today, although there are seven groups instead of four.

During the following few years, conventions reported many World War I activities. Red Cross work was highlighted. In 1918, President Sara Reuling reported that "in spite of the relief work and strain of war, P.E.O. interests were not neglected." Educational Loan Fund gifts were reduced due to war work and the president gently reminded the delegates that "this fund should be of first interest."

At the 1919 convention in Lincoln, the title "Nebraska Grand Chapter" was used for the last time. Supreme Chapter had changed the designation to "State Chapter." It was reported that most chapters had held only one or two meetings before all gatherings were banned due to a severe influenza epidemic. In spite of the lack of meetings, state membership had increased to 2,118.

At the next convention in 1920, a "Pep Meeting" included short talks by delegates on P.E.O. questions. Was this the beginning of our "Buzz Sessions" which are so popular today? The following year, the convention voted a memorial fund in memory of two past state presidents to be used for Near East relief and $175 for the children of Central Europe. P.E.O. continued to display extraordinary concern for others.

The 1924 convention was memorable for two items in the records: President Lulu Wolford admonished the members to memorize the Objects and Aims. The president also reported that only one chapter in Nebraska favored the proposal of the Board of Trustees of the Educational Fund to raise a million dollar endowment fund. The proposal was lost.

The P.E.O. memorial markers which grace the graves of so many of our beloved sisters in Chapter Eternal were approved by the Convention in 1926. These markers were designed by Mary Johnson Axtell as a memorial to her sister Ida Johnson Lewelleyn.

Nebraska's ever-changing and unpredictable weather played a part in the 1929 convention. It was reported that, "due to intense rain, the auto drive to Brownville was canceled." Undoubtedly, the smooth, paved highways we have today were yet far in the future back then.

Three interesting items were reported in the minutes of the 1930 convention. The revised convention rules permitted no gifts except flowers be presented during a session. One wonders what gifts could have prompted that ruling! During that convention, a resolution was passed endorsing the 18th Amendment to the Constitution of the United States. (The 18th Amendment was passed on January 29, 1919, and it stated that the manufacture, sale or transportation of intoxicating liquors within the United States and all its territories for beverage purposes was prohibited.) It was voted that a chapter unable to entertain convention was released from the obligation by a payment of $200 and the next chapter in rotation was to assume responsibility.

Financial conditions worsened as the country plunged deep into economic depression. In 1933, it was reported that three chapters about to be organized could not complete plans due to bank failures and the moratorium. Also at that convention, a motion for a biennial convention was lost.

At the 1934 convention in Wayne, the first new chapter in three years received its charter. It was reported that due to the economic situation, many chapters had reduced their dues. Report of a questionnaire concerning interest in a P.E.O. Home in Nebraska indicated that most chapters agreed with the need and concept of a retirement home for P.E.O.s.

In 1935, requirements for yearbooks were adopted and yearbooks were displayed at convention for the first time. Two years later, the P.E.O. Home became a reality through the generous gifts of the J. Stewart Elliotts of Beatrice. Chapters enthusiastically made pledges to the Home fund.

The Lincoln convention of 1940 saw a theme instituted for the first time. It was *"Our Projects"* and each received "due emphasis."

During the next few years, World War II work was emphasized in convention reports. Wartime conventions were streamlined with no open sessions and few social functions. It was reported that thousands of letters had been sent to servicemen and all war efforts increased. Due to travel restrictions, members of the executive board were designated to represent and report to chapters entitled to be delegates to Supreme Chapter Conventions. Peace and patriotic themes were popular during those years.

At the 1949 convention in Wayne, wind, rain and flood appeared and caused the members of a group performing a musical program to travel one hundred extra miles to detour around the flooded roads. It was reported that "the presiding officer was never quite sure that the announced number was in the wings." Nebraska weather intervened again at the 1950 convention when rain and a blizzard greeted guests at the May 4-6 convention in Grand Island!

Cottey College became a popular program at the next few conventions and gifts to the college increased. In 1954, Nebraska Chief Justice of the Supreme Court Robert Simmons addressed the Convention on international understanding, a fitting topic in the post-war years. At the convention the next year, Nebraska IPS students from India and Formosa spoke at the Educational Hour.

During the 1957 convention in Columbus, three pages wore aprons like those worn in chapel when the Founders first introduced P.E.O. The guards and pages at the 1985 convention, also in Columbus, wore aprons which were exact replicas of the same Founders' aprons.

Convention themes during the first two decades of their existence were varied and original. Several followed religious themes using biblical quotations. Others stressed "Progress," "Building for Tomorrow," "Look to this Day," or specific P.E.O. themes, such as "Gift of P.E.O." and variations on the star themes. A complete list of the convention venue, presiding officer, her theme and date is located at the end of this chapter (page 606).

At the 1964 convention in Grand Island, Nebraska State Chapter celebrated its seventy-five years as a state chapter with the theme "Diamond Jubilee." In its seventy-five years, membership had grown to 8,261 in 184 chapters. At that convention, a "gift march" for the projects was instituted. This practice was discontinued some years later.

Five years later in 1969, the convention celebrated one hundred years of P.E.O. with the theme "A Century of Sisterhood." Members of convention wore 1869 costumes the first day and for the "sidereal soiree." Frances Key authored and Phyllis Blanke directed "Centennial Memories." This magnificent play featured fifteen scene changes and beautiful, authentically-designed costumes.

In 1972, Nebraska State Chapter President Helen Magill challenged the membership to "change with the times." This charge led to varied business items and bylaw changes. The following year, in 1973, the convention delegates took Helen's advice to heart when they authorized the appointment of an assistant secretary-treasurer for Nebraska State Chapter. This was a giant step forward for Nebraska P.E.O. in terms of record-keeping and continuity of records—a sign of changing with the times!

In 1974, an agreement with Supreme Chapter was accepted for the preservation of Nebraska's historical articles at the Des Moines headquarters.

The first eighty-five years of Nebraska State Chapter's history saw monumental changes for the Sisterhood. Nebraska State Chapter convention attendance went from the second one with sixteen delegates, to the eighty-fifth with two hundred

A HISTORY OF P.E.O. IN NEBRASKA 605

thirty-four delegates. The unfailing support and love of their sisters guided P.E.O. members through difficult years of wars, depression, bank failures, drought, crop failures, blizzards, floods and a flu epidemic. It is remarkable that every convention was held and that the delegates faithfully supported P.E.O. and its projects with their unfailing presence and their gifts. Their dedication to the Sisterhood was exemplified through loyalty, devotion, strength, determination, and love—a perfect example of "the spirit of the prairie" in action.

. . . .

Jacci Irwin presides at 2002 Convention in North Platte

The Patchwork of P.E.O.
—A Unique Pattern of Love

Conventions of Nebraska Grand and Nebraska State Chapter
1890 - 2015

Nebraska Grand Chapter's first "convening" occurred on April 2, 1890, in Omaha at the home of Jennie Bryant. Alice C. Briggs was installed as the first president of Nebraska Grand Chapter. This event marked the organization of Nebraska as the first state grand chapter in P.E.O. Nebraska, ever the trail blazer, paved the way for state chapters and others soon followed their lead. Conventions have followed every year and each has been special in its own way. The convention venues, presiding officer, date and theme (where applicable) follow.

2nd Annual Convention
 Alice Briggs presided at Superior on June 9-12, 1891

3rd Annual Convention
 Lulu B. Patrick presided at York on June 8-10, 1892

4th Annual Convention
 Lulu B. Patrick presided at Plattsmouth on April 5-7, 1893

5th Annual Convention
 Jennie Bryant presided at Hastings on May 9-11, 1894

6th Annual Convention
 Jennie Bryant presided at the Senate Chamber in Lincoln on May 28-30, 1895

7th Annual Convention
 Carrie F. McNaughton presided at Holdrege on May 6-8, 1896

8th Annual Convention
 Clara A. West presided at Wahoo on October 6-8, 1897

9th Annual Convention
 Clara W. West presided at South Omaha on October 4-5, 1898

10th Annual Convention
 Alberta C. Fox presided at Nelson on June 13-15, 1899

11th Annual Convention
 Carrie R. Hapeman presided at Harvard on June 5-7, 1900

12th Annual Convention
 Carrie R. Hapeman presided at Minden on June 12-14, 1901

13th Annual Convention
 Mary J. Axtell presided at Geneva on June 17-19, 1902

14th Annual Convention
 Jennie Burch presided at Wymore on June 9-11, 1903

15th Annual Convention
Lillian P. Parmele presided at Broken Bow on June 8-9, 1904

16th Annual Convention
Carrie M. Peterson presided at Clay Center on June 21-22, 1905

17th Annual Convention
Carrie M. Peterson presided at Blue Hill on June 20-21, 1906

18th Annual Convention
Hattie A. Little presided at McCook on June 19-20, 1907

19th Annual Convention
Maud C. Harrison presided at Red Cloud on June 17-18, 1908

20th Annual Convention
Flora W. Jones presided at Beatrice on June 15-17, 1909

21st Annual Convention
Myra L. Grimes presided at Edgar on June 14-16, 1910

22nd Annual Convention
Clara M. Wilson presided at Central City on June 13-15, 1911

23rd Annual Conventon
Helen M. Drake presided at Aurora on June 17-19, 1912

24th Annual Convention
Ida B. Johnson presided at Hebron on June 18-20, 1913

25th Annual Convention
Bertha Clark Hughes presided at Lincoln on June 17-19, 1914

26th Annual Convention
Rose M. Owens presided at Fullerton on June 16-18, 1915

27th Annual Convention
Abbie B. Burns presided at Alliance on June 14-16, 1916

28th Annual Convention
Lue R. Spencer presided at Fremont on June 20-22, 1917

29th Annual Convention
Sara Reuling presided at North Platte on June 19-21, 1918

30th Annual Convention
Minnie Stuff presided at Lincoln on June 17-19, 1919

31st Annual Convention
Nora Killian presided at Fairmont on June 15-16, 1920

32nd Annual Convention
Clara Waterhouse presided at Lexington on June 14-16, 1921

33rd Annual Convention
Elizabeth Robertson president. Due to the illness of the president, first vice president, Ona T. Baird, presided at Fairbury on May 23-25, 1922

34th Annual Convention
Ona T. Baird presided at Omaha on May 15-17, 1923

35th Annual Convention
Lulu Wolford presided at St. Paul on May 20-22, 1924

36th Annual Convention
Maude M. Hendy presided at Loup City on May 19-21, 1925

37th Annual Convention
Nelle Grantham presided at Kearney on May 18-20, 1926

38th Annual Convention
Viola J. Cameron presided at Tecumseh on May 17-19, 1927

39th Annual Convention
Mae Bond presided at Beatrice on May 15-17, 1928

40th Annual Convention
Elizabeth Stephens presided at Peru on June 4-6, 1929

41st Annual Convention
Lulah T. Andrews presided at Pawnee City on May 14-16, 1930

42nd Annual Convention
Emma Gilbert presided at Gothenburg on June 9-11, 1931

43rd Annual Convention
Bernice Tillett presided at Hastings on June 1-3, 1932

44th Annual Convention
Dora Wenner presided at Lincoln on May 4-6, 1933

45th Annual Convention
Josephine Waddell presided at Wayne on May 30-June 1, 1934

46th Annual Convention
Ruth Kennedy presided at Ord on May 6-8, 1935

47th Annual Convention
Anna Loutzenheiser presided at Holdrege on April 29-May 1, 1936

48th Annual Convention
Isabelle Nelson presided at Omaha on April 27-29, 1937

49th Annual Convention
Ada H. Mead presided at Chadron on May 31-June 2, 1938

50th Annual Convention
Hattie Engleman presided at Norfolk on May 31-June 2, 1939

51st Annual Convention
Marie Williams presided at Lincoln on April 18-20, 1940
Convention theme: *Our Projects*

52nd Annual Convention
Edna Casper presided at Fremont on April 23-25, 1941
Convention theme: *Friendship*

53rd Annual Convention
Mary Koupal presided at York on April 27-29, 1942
Convention theme: *The Five Points of the Star*

54th Annual Convention
Florence Davis presided at North Platte on April 28-30, 1943
Convention theme: a patriotic theme without name

55th Annual Convention
Mary Nixon presided at Omaha on April 18-20, 1944
Convention theme: *Faith in Tomorrow's Peace*

56th Annual Convention
Marion H. Crites presided at Falls City on April 25-26, 1945
Convention theme: *Ye Shall Know the Truth and the Truth Shall Make You Free*

57th Annual Convention
Eva M. Curtiss presided at Fairbury on April 23-25, 1946
Convention Theme: *Let All That Ye Do Be Done in Love*

58th Annual Convention
Rebecca P. Lee presided at Lincoln on April 22-24, 1947
Convention Theme: *Ideals in Practice*

59th Annual Convention
Florence Stewart presided at Hastings on April 22-24, 1948
Convention Theme: *To Seek Growth*

60th Annual Convention
Helen Riddell presided at Wayne on June 1-3, 1949
Convention Theme: No specific theme. Banquet was *the gold rush of '49*

61st Annual Convention
Bessie Buchanan presided at Grand Island on May 4-6, 1950
Convention Theme: No theme specified

62nd Annual Convention
Irene Van Brunt presided at McCook on April 26-28, 1951
Convention Theme: *Progress, Enthusiasm, Opportunity*

63rd Annual Convention
Maude Weaver presided at Omaha on May 6-8, 1952
Convention Theme: *The Spirit of the Sower*

64th Annual Convention
Lucy Livingston presided at Scottsbluff on May 26-28, 1953
Convention Theme: *As You Give So Shall You Receive*

65th Annual Convention
Margaret McVicker presided at Norfolk on April 27-29, 1954
Convention Theme: *Count Every Star*

66th Annual Convention
Ruth Gellatly presided at Lincoln on April 26-28, 1955
Convention Theme: *Building Today for Tomorrow*

67th Annual Convention
Dorothy Smithberger presided at Fremont on April 25-27, 1956
Convention Theme: *P.E.O. as a Pathfinder in the Way of Life*

68th Annual Convention
Flora Stevens presided at Columbus on April 30, May 1-2, 1957
Convention Theme: *O Magnify the Lord with Me and Magnify His Name TOGETHER*

69th Annual Convention
Emma Sanderson presided at Kearney on April 22-24, 1958
Convention Theme: *The Gift of P.E.O.*

70th Annual Convention
Marthena Stevens presided at Omaha on May 5-7, 1959
Convention Theme: *The Star as our Guiding Light*

71st Annual Convention
Harriet Lumbard presided at Nebraska City on May 3-5, 1960
Convention Theme: *Light is the Symbol of Truth*

72nd Annual Convention
Mildred Robertson presided at Beatrice on April 25-27, 1961
Convention Theme: *Faith in the Power of Prayer*

73rd Annual Convention
Lois Newell presided at Lincoln on May 15-17, 1962
Convention Theme: *Look to This Day*

74th Annual Convention
Marietta Jack presided at Hastings on June 4-6, 1963
Convention Theme: *Great Possessions*

75th Annual Convention
Dorothy Yeager presided at Grand Island on May 19-21, 1964
Convention Theme: *Diamond Jubilee*

76th Annual Convention
Thelma Millen presided at Holdrege on May 4-6, 1965
Convention Theme: *The Magic Power of P.E.O.*

77th Annual Convention
Josephine Davis presided at Omaha on April 26-28, 1966
Convention Theme: *Symphony of P.E.O.*

78th Annual Convention
Helen Noble presided at Sidney on April 25-26, 1967
Convention Theme: *The Light of Understanding*

79th Annual Convention
Nelsine Scofield presided at Valentine on May 22-23, 1968
Convention Theme: *Fruits of the Spirit*

80th Annual Convention
Jean Johnson presided at Lincoln on June 3-5, 1969
Convention Theme: *A Century of Sisterhood*

81st Annual Convention
Sheila Shreck presided at South Sioux City on May 5-7, 1970
Convention Theme: *LOOK TO YOURSELVES, that we lose not those things which we have wrought.* II John 1:8

82nd Annual Convention
Kathryn White presided at York on June 1-3, 1971
Convention Theme: *Look to the Stars*

83rd Annual Convention
Helen Magill presided at Ogallala on May 2-4, 1972
Convention Theme: *Follow Your Star*

84th Annual Convention
Catherine Andersen presided at Omaha on May 22-24, 1973
Convention Theme: *Creating Your Own Starlight Right Where You Are*

85th Annual Convention
Janet Atkins presided at Peru on May 27-29, 1974
Convention Theme: *Love Makes The World Go 'Round*

86th Annual Convention
Ellen Ann Qualsett presided at Crete on June 3-5, 1975
Convention Theme: *Walking in the Light*

87th Annual Convention
Doris Cunningham presided at Lincoln on May 25-27, 1976
Convention Theme: *The Spirit of P.E.O—A Patchwork of Many Special Things*

88th Annual Convention
Vera Koefoot presided at Hastings on June 7-9, 1977
Convention Theme: *Take My Hand—It'a A Small, Small World*

89th Annual Convention
Barbara Cobb presided at Grand Island on May 3-4, 1978
Convention Theme: *Choose Life*

90th Annual Convention
Lois Ann Hansen presided at North Platte on May 1-2, 1979
Convention Theme: *Let Us Then Be Up and Doing*

91st Annual Convention
Frances Key presided at Omaha on May 6-8, 1980
Convention Theme: *Let the Star in the Window Light a Path in the World*

92nd Annual Convention
Mary Ruth Wilson presided at Chadron on May 26-28, 1981
Convention Theme: *Walk in Beauty*

93rd Annual Convention
Bernice Zajicek presided at Wayne on May 26-27, 1982
Convention Theme: *P.E.O. Our Melody of Love*

94th Annual Convention
Helen Curtiss presided at Lincoln on May 24-26, 1983
Convention Theme: *P.E.O.—A Garden Where Love Grows*

95th Annual Convention
Julia McDougal presided at Blair on June 6-8, 1984
Convention Theme: *To Seek Growth*

96th Annual Convention
June Steggs presided at Columbus on May 21-23, 1985
Convention Theme: *Lovingly in P.E.O.*

97th Annual Convention
Marion Larmon presided at Peru on May 30- June 1, 1986
Convention Theme: *New Horizons*

98th Annual Convention
Susan Harr presided at Omaha on May 17-19, 1987
Convention Theme: *Let us Stir Up One Another to Love and Good Works*

99th Annual Convention
Joyce Goff presided at Kimball on June 2-4, 1988
Convention Theme: *P.E.O. - Small as a Daisy, Great as a Star*

100th Annual Convention
Catherine Hutton presided at Hastings on June 3-4, 1989
Convention Theme: *Light a Candle of Faith and Reach for Our Star*

101st Annual Convention
June Brunmeier presided at Lincoln on May 23-25, 1990
Convention Theme: *A Century of Sisterly Love*

102nd Annual Convention
Robley Garrigan presided at Grand Island on June 7-9, 1991
Convention Theme: *Joy Be With Us As We Soar On The Winds Of Destiny*

103rd Annual Convention
Mary Ann Eberspacher presided at Kearney on June 5-7, 1992
Convention Theme: *Celebrate P.E.O. with Art, Music, and Drama*

104th Annual Convention
Mary Owens presided at McCook on June 18-20, 1993
Convention Theme: *The Plus of P.E.O.*

105th Annual Convention
Beverley Karrer presided at Omaha on June 10-12, 1994
Convention Theme: *P.E.O. Like a Kaleidoscope Reflects Change and Reveals Beauty*

A History of P.E.O. in Nebraska

106th Annual Convention
Rosella Mehling presided at Scottsbluff on June 9-11, 1995
Convention Theme: *Reflections from a Star*

107th Annual Convention
Mary Lainson Olsen presided at Norfolk on June 7-9, 1996
Convention Theme: *The Gifts of P.E.O.*

108th Annual Convention
Alice Jennings Fisher presided for Phyllis Blanke at Lincoln on May 30-June 1, 1997
Convention Theme: *Celebrate the Future of P.E.O.*

109th Annual Convention
Alice Jennings Fisher presided at South Sioux City on June 5-7, 1998
Convention Theme: *One Shining Star, Many Loving Hearts*

110th Annual Convention
Kathleen Gosch presided at York on June 4-6, 1999
Convention Theme: *A P.E.O. Garden, Planted in Faith, Nurtured With Love*

111th Annual Convention
Anita Kitt presided at Beatrice on June 2-4, 2000
Convention Theme: *Star Gazing, Star Raising, Star Amazing*

112th Annual Convention
Patricia Robertson presided at Omaha on June 1-3, 2001
Convention Theme: *I Wish For You a Star to Cast all Your Dreams Upon*

113th Annual Convention
Jaqueline J. Irwin presided at North Platte on May 31-June 2, 2002
Convention Theme: *The Patchwork of P.E.O.—A Unique Pattern of Love*

114th Annual Convention
Jeanne M. Reigle presided at Hastings on June 6-8, 2003
Convention Theme: *A Legacy of Love*

115th Annual Convention
Dee Anne Weyeneth presided at Lincoln on June 4-6, 2004
Convention Theme: *Let's Go and Get the Others*

116th Annual Convention
Anne Baumhover presided at Grand Island on June 3-5, 2005
Convention Theme: *Stepping Out In P.E.O.*

117th Annual Convention
Cynthia Jarecke presided at Kearney on June 9-11, 2006
Convention Theme: *May We All Be Stars Among Women and Angels Among Our Sisters*

118th Annual Convention
Joan Fink presided at North Platte on June 1-3, 2007
Convention Theme: *Reaching for a Hand, Touching a Heart*

119th Annual Convention
Pamela Kregg presided at Omaha on June 6-8, 2008
Convention Theme: *Imagine the Possibilities*

120th Annual Convention
Leann Drullinger presided at Gering on June 5-7, 2009
Convention Theme: *Perceive, Believe, Achieve*

121st Annual Convention
Cynthia Biehl presided at Norfolk on June 11-13, 2010
Convention Theme: *Dream and Grow in P.E.O.*

122nd Annual Convention
Jan Loftin presided at Lincoln on June 3-5, 2011
Convention Theme: *P.E.O... A Network of Love*

123rd Annual Convention
Joyce Victor presided at Fremont on June 8-10, 2012
Convention Theme: *Playing the Keys of P.E.O.*

124th Annual Convention
Terri Ridgway presided at Columbus on June 7-9, 2013
Convention Theme: *When You Wish Upon A Star*

125th Annual Convention
Merikay Berg presided at Peru on June 6-8, 2014
Convention Theme: *Share the Joy*

126th Annual Convention
Karen Blair presided at LaVista on June 5-7, 2015
Convention Theme: *P.E.O... A Pattern for Living*

At the 2010 Convention of Nebraska State Chapter it was decided that candidates for the executive board may be recommended by an active Nebraska P.E.O. or Nebraska chapter, and a Nominating Committee would be responsible for this nomination process.

Conventions of International Chapter
1995-2013

Convention of International Chapter is held every biennium in order to conduct the business of the Sisterhood. It is the big picture of what our Sisterhood is about and a wonderful opportunity to expand our knowledge of P.E.O. For the approximately forty Nebraska delegates who attend, it is also a time to widen our circle of friends both within the Nebraska delegation and P.E.O. sisters in other states. Fifty states, provinces and districts send delegates, and 1,500-3,000 women attend. It is a huge event, and to Nebraska P.E.O.s during the years between 1995–2013, it was a time to remember.

We watched on the sidelines as Nebraska's own Past State President Joyce Goff served as an officer on the Executive Board of International Chapter, and Past State Presidents Alice Fisher, Pam Kregg, Leann Drulinger, and Joyce Victor served on International committees or as trustees of our projects. We were so proud of these sisters, and we enjoyed the small perks that come with following great leaders.

During the Joyce Goff terms as an officer of International Chapter, 1995–2005, Nebraska delegates had prime seating in the front of the convention halls, near the stage. We stayed in lovely hotels across the street from the convention sites. The Nebraska delegation loved it, and we had a bit of an attitude. Most of all, we loved being there to support Joyce during her years of serving International Chapter. When Joyce's term was completed, Nebraska delegates found themselves seated in the back of the auditorium. Our moment of fame was over.

Nebraska P.E.O.s who attended Convention of International Chapter during the years 1995 through 2013 were proud to support Nebraska State Chapter past state presidents serving on International committees. Alice Fisher served on the Finance Committee (2003-2005); Pam Kregg served on the Special Committee for Membership Advancement (2007-2011); Leann Drulinger served on the Study and Research Committee (2009-2015); and Joyce Victor served on the Board of Trustees of the P.E.O. Educational Loan Fund (2013-2017). Nebraska P.E.O.s are not afraid of leadership roles.

The president of the Executive Board of the Nebraska State Chapter during the uneven years is privileged to lead the delegation. She makes the travel arrangements, organizes housing and meals and a ton of other small details for the International trip. This challenging task is not for the faint of heart. Things do not always go as planned. Real life sometimes gets in the way. The air conditioning on the bus breaks down, the 9-11 tragedy just days before the Convention makes the delegation uneasy about the flights to Milwaukee; travel to Vancouver requires passports or proof of citizenship for all delegates, and table decorations are held up in Canadian customs.

Enjoy these stories about the Nebraska delegations' experiences at Convention of International Chapter during 1995–2013.

JOAN FINK, PAST STATE PRESIDENT, LEAD EDITOR *LEGACY OF NEBRASKA P.E.O.*

1995
Convention of International Chapter
Denver, Colorado—September 28-30, 1995

The Nebraska Delegation to the Convention of International Chapter in 1995 was led by Mary Lainson Olsen, president of Nebraska State Chapter. The thirty-seven members traveled by bus on Tuesday, September 26th, beginning in Omaha at 6:30 AM, traveling across I-80, stopping eight times, and arriving in Denver at 6:30 PM. There was great hilarity, visiting, ordering delegates to return to the bus promptly at each stop (sometimes with luck), the opportunity to make new friends, and of course, eating. There was much excitement because our very special Joyce Goff was going onto the International Executive Board.

We were housed in the Denver Marriott City Center which was located very close to the convention site, as well as to the other convention hotels. The convention center located in the heart of Denver was huge and spectacular, a perfect setting for our Convention.

Kathy Gosch and I were proud to represent Nebraska during the Opening Ceremonies' parade of flags. Wilma Turner emceed the thrilling projects program entitled "To Lose Sight of the Shore." Convention opened on Friday with Jean Boswell, president, presiding. Joyce Goff gave the devotions as only she can. When elections came and Joyce was nominated to the Executive Board, we Nebraskans erupted singing a special song. It was loud and proud, and we showed off that Nebraska pride wearing white sweatshirts with a large gold "N" in the middle surrounded by large gold stars and of course, each of us wearing our "ReJoyce" buttons.

Another special moment was when the great-granddaughter of Hattie Briggs Bousquet was introduced. That truly brought the reality of our Founders into the Convention.

Newly elected International board member Joyce Goff (right) visits with Nebraska Past State Presidents Mary Owens and Phyllis Blanke

Saturday began with Time of Remembrance where tribute was given to Nebraska's Irene Van Brunt, past president of International Chapter. The keynote speaker was the former treasurer of the United States, Francine Neff, who spoke of the importance of the influence her mother had on her life. Mabel Otis was installed as the new president and her theme was *"Dream and Grow in P.E.O."* What a wonderful and inspiring convention.

At left, Nebraska Past State President Mary Olsen celebrates in Denver with Joyce Goff

Right, Joyce Goff poses amid the copious balloons and flowers she received upon her election to the Executive Board of International Chapter

One funny event was during the luncheon on Saturday. A group of Nebraska delegates were eating with a group from Washington State and it just happened that the Nebraska Cornhuskers were playing the Washington Huskies in football that day! It was a very lively lunch.

Our bus trip back was as delightful as the one coming. The delegates presented me with a gold star—sheriff's badge—because I did such a good job of keeping them in line with a smile! It was a trip I shall never forget, or the wonderful sisters who shared those many hours together.

MARY LAINSON OLSEN, PAST STATE PRESIDENT

1997
Convention of International Chapter
Seattle, Washington — September 12-14, 1997

The 63rd Convention of International Chapter of the P.E.O. Sisterhood was held in Seattle, Washington, September 12-14. International President Mabel Otis presided. Her theme *"Dream and Grow in P.E.O."* was carried out throughout the Convention. Our own Joyce Goff advanced to the office of recording secretary of International Chapter at this Convention.

The Nebraska delegation wore bright red cardigans, held signs saying "Nebraska P.E.O.s ReJoyce!" and gave ten Letterman-type reasons why Joyce Goff was a good choice for the International Executive Board.

A Star in the Window performed at International Convention in Seattle: From left, Mary Olsen, Gretchen Treadway, Jane Knox, Anita Kitt, Kathy Gosch, Alice Fisher, Robley Garrigan, Jeanne Reigle, Jacci Irwin, June Brunmeier and Trish Robertson.

Quoting from the November-December 1997 P.E.O. Record, "The highlight of Sunday morning's business meeting was the presentation by Nebraska P.E.O.s of the historic dramatization, *"A Star In The Window,"* a composite picture of a P.E.O. meeting at the turn of the century. Written by Nebraska P.E.O. Frances Key for the Centennial Convention of International Chapter, it was first performed there on October 2, 1969. Beautifully costumed in period dresses, the actors drew many chuckles as they illustrated some of the customs which long since have been discarded. Of special interest were the large cloth star placed on the floor under the table for initiation, with officers standing between the points, and the ballot bag with white and black buttons for voting. Having no gavel, the president used her large knitting needle to call the meeting to order. Following the business meeting, the literary portion of the meeting was held, "a chance to continue their pursuit of knowledge" and a foretaste of our present chapter programs. However, this portion of their meeting had to be limited to two hours! Near the end of their meeting came a precursor of our "For the Good of the Chapter." Various reprimands and suggestions had been placed in the "Chip Basket" to be read by the recording secretary, such as "A sister was heard to use slang expressions," and "A sister behaved in a flirtatious way in front of the hotel: one should never talk to traveling salesmen!" They were reassured that these suggestions "were meant in a most kindly spirit."

Mary Owens, past president of Nebraska State Chapter, (pictured above left with her cast of *A Star in the Window*) did a wonderful job of directing and narrating this effort, and all who participated were much congratulated on its success. Unfortunately, the dramatization is not available for use by chapters or individuals, as it was the author's intent for it to remain with International Chapter.

1999

Convention of International Chapter P.E.O.
Baltimore, Maryland — September 9-11, 1999

The 1999 Convention of International Chapter was held in Baltimore, Maryland, September 9-11. The Convention was a huge undertaking for the Maryland P.E.O.s and their surrounding neighbors, the District of Columbia and Virginia. The steering committee chose a patriotic theme of *A Star Spangled Celebration of P.E.O.*

Wilma Leonard Turner, Missouri, presided at the meetings. Nebraska had been fortunate at past state conventions to have had Wilma Turner as our International representative. Wilma had a wonderful sense of humor and a ready smile. I think that it is safe to say that Wilma was a P.E.O. extraordinaire. Missouri's then First Lady, Jean Carpenter Carnahan, gave the keynote address entitled "Chapter Y2K." Her opinion that "Education is the best gift that we can give" has stuck with me and I have used her words to inspire others.

Nebraska's delegation and visitors wore red polo shirts to show our support of Joyce Goff. Our delegation and visitors in their red had a bit of a high profile, which we all enjoyed. We serenaded Joyce with a customized song when she was elected second vice president of International Chapter for 1999-2001. We were so very proud of Joyce. Nebraska's state officers and some of its past state presidents assisted Joyce with her Period of Instruction for presidents of subordinate territories. Past State President Kathy Gosch organized this effort. Being a state delegation which had a sister on the International Board, we sat right in front and across the aisle from Wilma Turner's Missouri delegation.

As the state president, it was my obligation to make travel arrangements for the entire delegation. All of the airline tickets were paperless for the first time which kind of threw a curve ball for some of the delegates. I think that everything went smoothly. The convention site was right on the Chesapeake Bay and it was a bit of a novelty to take a water taxi to a destination. A big neon Domino sugar the size of a three story building illuminated our evening rides along the bay.

Anita Kitt, Past State President

2001
Convention of International Chapter
Milwaukee, Wisconsin — September 20-22, 2001

The 2001 Convention of International chapter met in Milwaukee, Wisconsin, at the Midwest Express Center, September 20-22—just nine days after the destruction of the World Trade Center in New York City on 9-11. The theme for the convention was *"Illuminating the 21st Century"* with Jane Burtis Smith, past president of Florida State Chapter, presiding.

The Nebraska delegation stayed at the Hilton Hotel, which was just across the street from the convention center. The Nebraska get-together and dinner were planned by First Vice President Jeanne Reigle, who enlisted the help of the other state officers to carry table decorations in their suitcases. Nebraska delegates wore red polo shirts with a daisy motif on the left pocket area with Nebraska spelled out below the daisies. Nebraska delegates were seated right behind the Florida delegation which sat front and center.

Recording Secretary of International Chapter W. Joyce Goff hosted the philanthropies program *"Celebrate Our P.E.O. Projects."* Joyce was elected to serve as first vice president of International Chapter and the Nebraska delegation serenaded her with a song, with words written especially for her at the time of her election.

As president, it was my assignment to register all delegates and past presidents attending Convention and make all travel arrangements for the delegates. Groups were assigned to fly out of Lincoln, Omaha and Denver. The number of delegates flying out of Denver was not enough to get a group rate, so I contacted Carol Wackerlin, president of Wyoming State Chapter, and together we had enough to get the group rate. After 9-11 all passengers were told to arrive at the airport two hours in advance of flight time to check in for outgoing flights. We all arrived and got into line, but the airlines had not been told, so we had an hour to get well acquainted with our Wyoming sisters. Omaha sisters provided housing the night before departure for delegates who had to travel long distances. When the Nebraska delegation arrived at the convention center we found a sense of comfort being with sisters who were loving and supportive.

It was stated and mentioned many times by the Milwaukee convention participants and hotel employees that they thought the Convention would be less than successful, but very few delegates did not attend and it was business as usual for the 2001 Convention of International chapter, P.E.O. Sisterhood.

JACQUELINE J. IRWIN, PAST STATE PRESIDENT PRESIDENT

2003
CONVENTION OF INTERNATIONAL CHAPTER
OKLAHOMA CITY, OKLAHOMA—SEPTEMBER 18-20, 2003

The road to Oklahoma City began in 1995 when the Nebraska delegation boarded a bus for the International Convention in Denver. Our own Joyce Goff was elected to the International Executive Board at that Colorado gathering. We were all so proud. Little did I know how this would affect Nebraska sisters and me personally. Two months later I was chosen to chair the 1997 state convention which led to being elected to the state executive board.

Nebraska State Organizer Joan Fink accompanies State President Dee Weyeneth in the traditional presentation of the flags

At a board meeting in 1997 the state board began planning what we wanted to do to help Joyce on her journey. With the plans made, each year brought us closer to Oklahoma. Two buses carried the delegation and visitors as many sisters wanted to be there for Joyce. Because Joyce served on the executive board, the Nebraska delegation was housed in the official hotel across the street from the convention center and we were placed upfront for the meetings of Convention.

All of our planning came to fruition when Joyce was installed as president of International Chapter in Oklahoma City. We hosted an ice cream social for the executive family after her election. We cheered her on wearing our red polos emblazoned with "REJOYCE"! Can you believe our Oklahoma sisters were in red polos, too!

After Joyce accepted the gavel, I went on stage to present her with a monetary gift for all the incidentals that she would incur during her term as president.

It was a very exciting time for Nebraska sisters and we were so proud to be there to "REJOYCE" with Joyce.

DEE WEYENETH, PAST STATE PRESIDENT

2005
CONVENTION OF INTERNATIONAL CHAPTER
VANCOUVER, BRITISH COLUMBIA—SEPTEMBER 6-8, 2005

The 67th Convention of International Chapter took place in Vancouver, British Columbia, September 6-8, 2005, with 3,400 delegates, volunteers and visitors. The theme of the convention was *"Fall for Vancouver"* and hostesses were the thirty-seven chapters of British Columbia. President of International Chapter, Past State President of Nebraska State Chapter W. Joyce Goff presided. Joyce's theme was *"P.E.O...Small as a Daisy, Great as a Star."* This was the same theme that Joyce selected for her state convention. The backdrop of the stage featured pictures of British Columbia, daisies and red maple leaves. On opening night of Convention, bagpipes and drums from The Simon Fraser University Pipe Band ushered members into the convention center. Wayne Goff announced state presidents and organizers, and Nebraska State Chapter President Cyndi Jarecke and Organizer Leann Drullinger proudly carried the Nebraska flag wearing the bright red fleece jackets that the entire Nebraska delegation wore.

Mabel Otis, Past President of International chapter (1995-1997) gave the keynote address "Proud to Be a P.E.O." Mabel spoke about women who were leaders, and women who made major contributions to the advancement of women and what they had in common with the P.E.O. Founders.

The "It's OK" campaign was unveiled. The first clue that "something was up" came with the hotel key that proclaimed that "It's OK." Badges, bookmarks, candy, fans, brochures, notepads and a clever video proclaimed that "It's OK to Talk About P.E.O." We were encouraged to talk about P.E.O. and to publicize what we do. We also learned about our mission statement, tagline, and elevator speech.

President W. Joyce Goff's pages were her daughter Jane Nelsen, past president of Chapter DM, Litchfield Park, Arizona; niece Andrea Stubbendick, FV, Nebraska City; three past presidents of Joyce's Chapter HJ, Grand Island: Joyce Victor, Renita Wichert and Sandra Meyer; and Robley Garrigan, Chapter HL, past state president of Nebraska State Chapter. The pages wore brown corduroy jumpers with white long-sleeved turtle necks.

Julia Peetz, BO, assistant secretary-treasurer, with Nebraska executive board members

International President Joyce Goff presides at Vancouver convention

The Nebraska delegation gathered at the Fairmont Watermark on Thursday evening for an elegant dinner honoring Joyce. It was a lovely affair but the table decorations, which had been shipped to the hotel in advance of our arrival, were held up in customs. We never could figure out why, and we never saw them again.

After Joyce gave her closing remarks, the Nebraska delegation serenaded her with the Nebraska fight song using words written to proudly reflect our pride in Joyce.

At left, Leann Drullinger and Cynthia Jarecke, members of the Executive Board of Nebraska State Chapter, prepare to introduce the Nebraska flag at International Convention in Vancouver, 2005.

You couldn't miss the Nebraska delegation with their red fleece jackets and dark pants or skirts. We were highly visible and greatly admired. The delegates were housed in the Fairmont Watermark Hotel adjacent to the Vancouver Convention and Exhibition Center. The hotel overlooked the Vancouver Bay, and we enjoyed watching all the activity on the water and cruise ships arriving and departing. The hotel and convention center were only a short walk from the Gas Town tourist area, and many delegates used free time to explore the shops and restaurants. Many new and lasting friendships were formed during social hour at a local pub.

Joyce Goff and her husband Wayne enjoy a banquet break during her convention

Pictured above, the Nebraska delegation with International President Joyce Goff on the steps of the convention hall.

Above left, Cyndi Jarecke, president of Nebraska State Chapter 2005-2006, displays the sign used to designate seating for the Nebraska delegation. No, NB is not our state abbreviation. It stands for New Brunswick, but we'll never tell! In photo above right, Nebraska P.E.O.s enjoy getting acquainted at a Gas Town establishment.

In the eyes of the Nebraska delegation the 2005 Convention of International Chapter in Vancouver was the ultimate International Convention. What a privilege to have attended this moment in history for Nebraska P.E.O.

JOAN FINK, PAST STATE PRESIDENT

2007
Convention of International Chapter
Minneapolis, Minnesota—September 13-15, 2007

The sixty-eighth Convention of International Chapter of the P.E.O. Sisterhood was held in Minneapolis, Minnesota, September 13-15, 2007. A delegation of forty-seven Nebraska P.E.O.s (and BIL Henry Blanke) boarded a bus EARLY on Wednesday morning September 12th to begin the journey northward to where we would hear *"Minnesota Calling."* The delegation was led by President Pam Kregg and Organizer Jan Loftin. In true P.E.O. fashion, the bus was full of laughter, comments on the various movies watched on the trip, and the ever-present challenge of making sure all the sisters were back on the bus after "rest" stops! Entering Minneapolis as the rush hour began proved exciting and Jan Loftin assisted the bus driver in navigating the bus to our hotel, the Hyatt, in downtown Minneapolis.

This was the first International Convention Nebraska had attended in ten years without Joyce Goff gracing the dais. Joyce also became ill and was unable to attend this first Convention after becoming a past International president. We missed her smiling face and ever-present sense of humor. Joyce wrote the invocation for the opening ceremonies and it was read by Jane B. Smith, past president, International Chapter.

The meetings and workshops of Convention were held at the convention center which was only a few blocks from the hotel and accessible by overhead enclosed walkways so there were no worries about hair being blown or getting wet from the rain. Several sisters did "take to the streets" to visit one of the few multi-storied Target stores in the U.S. as well as have their pictures taken by the Mary Tyler Moore statue which were both only a few blocks from the hotel.

Nebraska delegates continued the tradition of wearing matching attire in the form of blue chambray shirts with a daisy logo. The long sleeved shirts proved to be a necessity in the very cold convention hall. It was such fun spotting those shirts all over Minneapolis!

One memory of the Convention (besides sitting in the back for the first time in ten years!), was the use of electronic voting pads. It proved to be a challenge as the delegation navigated learning how to use the pads, exchanging pads which did not work for those which did, when to enter their vote, and patience in waiting for the results. "Left section cast your votes now" became a familiar line to the Nebraska P.E.O.s as well as not leaving the convention hall without handing their voting pads to Pam or Jan who had to account for all the pads at the end of each session.

Nebraska State Officers Jan Loftin and Pam Kregg (holding flag) present the Nebraska colors at the International Convention in Minneapolis

As always, Convention proved to be not only an opportunity to learn more about P.E.O. from the various workshops, but also an opportunity to see sisters from across the U.S. and Canada. And last but not least… what fun to see some Minnesota sisters flapping their wings, dressed as loons, cavorting throughout the various Convention activities. That only happens with sisters!

Pam Kregg
Past State President

2007 was the first International Convention after Joyce Goff's term on the International executive board was completed.

2009
Convention of International Chapter
San Diego, California—September 9-11, 2009
"Eureka! P.E.O.!"

The 69th Convention of International Chapter of the P.E.O. Sisterhood was held from Wednesday, September 9th through Friday, September 11th at the San Diego Convention Center. President of International Chapter Barbara Andes presided. President of Nebraska State Chapter, Cindy Biehl led the delegation. Those representing Nebraska consisted of the seven state officers, Paid Assistant Mary Kay Tuma; thirty-four elected chapter delegates and thirteen past state presidents, including Past President of International Chapter Joyce Goff. Entitled members included the state president, state organizer, elected chapter delegates and three past state presidents: Leann Drullinger, Alice Fisher and Kathleen Gosch. Convention registration was available on the International P.E.O. website and in The P.E.O. Record.

Those entitled by Nebraska bylaws and policies were allowed up to $300 each to apply toward traveling expenses. Each entitled member made her airline reservation and submitted the expense to the Nebraska Executive Board for reimbursement. The cost of housing and meals for entitled members was paid by International Chapter. For the first time, a Delegation Booklet was made containing pictures and contact information of the Executive Board, chapter delegates, past state presidents and visitors attending Convention.

The Nebraska State Dinner was held on the evening of Tuesday, September 8th. All entitled members and several visitors were present and enjoyed a delicious meal at the Athens Market not far from Convention Center. Several BILs joined us at the Nebraska Dinner.

2009 Nebraska State Chapter Executive Board with Joyce Goff at International Convention in San Diego. L to R, Merikay Berg, Karen Blair, Joyce Victor, Joyce Goff, Cindy Biehl, Jan Loftin, Terri Ridgway, Patti Cowher. This was the final year to have seven state officers.

At left, Nebraska State President Cindy Biehl prepares to present the Nebraska flag with Organizer Terri Ridgway.

Required Seminars and Learning Labs were held on September 9th. The delegation wore the Nebraska red neck scarf (first worn during Convention of International Chapter in 2007) with our First State Chapter pin. Together these were considered the Nebraska Badge. The scarf with pin was worn over white or black blouses. White one day and black the next. The pin was designed by Nebraska State Chapter President Cindy Biehl. It was a silvertone circle around the goldtone shape of Nebraska with the words, "P.E.O. First State Chapter 1890". Seven red jewels represented the seven Founders. Each Nebraska P.E.O. attending Convention purchased a scarf and pin. That evening the delegation attended the Opening Night Ceremonies and Project Night. Cindy Biehl and Nebraska State Organizer Terri Ridgway presented the Nebraska flag.

The business meetings of Convention began on September 10th. There were 91 proposed amendments presented at this Convention. This was the second time the voting members used handheld electronic voting devices. Numerous changes to P.E.O. came about at this Convention. Amendments were adopted to gradually change from seven to five state officers; to use the word transfer instead of dimit and change the transfer process; to allow chapters to initiate lineal descendants regardless of residence; to sponsor instead of vouch for new members; to require three signatures not five to propose a name for membership; to increase the initiation and reinstatement fees to $35; to allow the Ceremony of Initiation to be read from official booklets and to be conferred upon up to three candidates at a time; to officially established the P.E.O. STAR Scholarship; to dispense with the ballot box and to re-order the local chapter meeting order of business.

Anne Baumhover, '05, Joan Fink, '07, Jeanne Reigle, '03, Anita Kitt, 2000 — Past State Presidents participate in San Diego 2009 International Convention

The proudest moment of Convention for the Nebraska delegation was the announcement that our very own Past State President Leann Drullinger had been appointed to the International Study and Research Committee for a six-year term. Leann served as chairman of this committee from 2013 to 2015.

Prior to the end of Convention, Judy Rogers, president of Cottey College, announced to the Convention that Cottey was embarking on its first ever comprehensive five-year fundraising campaign, to be called "A Defining Moment."

Past State President Leann Drullinger is tapped for a 6-year term on the International Study and Research Committee.

Voting members of Convention participated in one of the most important and decisive International Conventions in recent history. Sixty-nine of the 91 proposed amendments were adopted and the P.E.O. Sisterhood was ready to embark upon our future.

Cindy Biehl, Past State President

2011

Convention of International Chapter

St. Louis, Missouri — September 29-October 1, 2011

The 70th Convention of International Chapter of the P.E.O. Sisterhood was held September 29 through October 1, 2011, at the America's Center Convention Complex in St. Louis, Missouri.

Nebraska was entitled to 34 voting delegates and four past state presidents. As is the case with many International Conventions, Nebraska had some guests that chose to attend Convention also.

Nebraska traveled to Convention via bus. The bus left North Platte, Nebraska, at 5:30AM on Wednesday, September 28th, and made stops in Grand Island, Lincoln and Omaha. By the time the bus headed for St. Louis there were forty P.E.O.s on board and one P.E.O. from Hawaii.

Thirteen hours later we arrived in St. Louis. It had taken longer than expected, leaving no time to change clothes before attending the Nebraska state dinner that evening. It was held at Lombardo's Trattoria. The food was delicious and we all received last minute details about Convention.

Nebraska State Officers with International Officer Maria Baseggio

While in St. Louis, the Nebraska delegation was housed at the Hilton. This was about ten or twelve blocks from the convention center, so the delegation used buses to travel back and forth.

The Nebraska delegation could be spotted easily in Convention. We wore red scarves that had the state of Nebraska on the back. They were pinned in the front with our "Nebraska first state chapter pins." These were worn with black slacks and white tops. We looked sharp and could be recognized in the crowd. We received many compliments about our Convention attire.

Delegate Kristi Scheele joins Nebraska State Officers Joyce Victor, Cindy Biehl and Jan Loftin to capture a moment with International Officer Maria Baseggio. Nebraska P.E.O.s will remember Maria's charming warmth and capable leadership from her visit to the 2011 state convention.

Past State President Leann Drullinger, AK, North Platte, was a member of the Study and Research Committee for International during this biennium. She assisted in the workshop on the amendments prior to the start of convention.

The parade of flags was part of the opening ceremony. President Joyce Victor and Organizer Merikay Berg participated in that event

A highlight of our bus trip to St. Louis was a side trip we made on the way home to Mount Pleasant, Iowa. Here we were given a walking tour of Old Main and we had the opportunity to see the music room and take a picture of those on the bus standing at the stile where our Founding sisters had stood. It was a special time for everyone.

The bus completed its round trip on Sunday around 9:30 PM in North Platte. We had met new sisters and had become great friends. We had talked and laughed and had a great time. It was an event that will be remembered for years to come.

JOYCE VICTOR, PAST STATE PRESIDENT

2013
CONVENTION OF INTERNATIONAL CHAPTER
DALLAS, TEXAS—SEPTEMBER 26-28, 2013

Eagerness and anticipation were in the air when delegates, past state presidents, executive board members and visitors boarded the bus in York, Nebraska, early in the morning on September 26, 2013, to attend the Convention of International Chapter in Dallas. The Nebraska delegation spent a fun day traveling via motor coach. Most of the travelers brought along treats to share with others. State Organizer Patti Cowher was in charge of the festivities. Those on the bus played several games and won prizes. It helped sisters get to know each other better and shorten the long bus ride. Upon arriving in Dallas, the Nebraska delegation attended a special state dinner arranged by Vice President Karen Blair. The delegation was housed at the Hilton Anatole.

The Nebraska delegation received many compliments on their smart attire. All Nebraska sisters wore red Nebraska scarves with Nebraska first state chapter pins holding the scarves in front. Black pants and white shirts completed the outfits. A group photograph was taken.

Nebraska was proud to have Past State President Leann Drullinger, AK, North Platte, serving on the Study and Research Committee and Past State President Joyce Victor, HJ, Grand Island, serving on the Educational Loan Fund Board Of Trustees for this biennium of International.

Merikay Berg, Nebraska state president, and Karen Blair, vice president, presented the Nebraska flag in the opening ceremony.

Convention attendees were able to attend a variety of self-enrichment workshops and seminars prior to the convention business meetings.

International Chapter President Susan Sellers presided over the 2013 Convention of International Chapter. The convention theme was, "Deep in the Heart". Nebraska P.E.O.s were proud to know Susan, as she had been the International representative to the 2008 Nebraska State Convention held in Omaha. The Nebraska delegates focused on the business of International Chapter by attending all the sessions and voting when required.

Six project recipients inspired attendees with their stories of achieving educational success with the help of P.E.O. Saturday night entertainment was a highlight as we enjoyed a very lively concert by the "Texas Tenors".

Delegates came home enthused about the mission of P.E.O. and eager to share their convention experiences with their chapters.

MERIKAY BERG, PAST STATE PRESIDENT

2013 Delegation

When she visited the 1969 Convention of Nebraska State Chapter on the eve of their Centennial kick-off, Wilma Turner, who would later serve as President of International Chapter, remarked about Nebraska's rich P.E.O. heritage and the focus of the centennial celebration.

She offered sage advice.

"Remember," she admonished, "the past is prologue."

And so it is.

Section Twelve
P.E.O. Projects in Nebraska

Love in Action

P.E.O. Educational Loan Fund

When a small pebble is dropped into a still pond, ripples begin that eventually reach to the far shore. In 1907, a P.E.O. pebble of love and concern started a ripple that has since reached far and wide, benefiting the lives of tens of thousands of women and their families. From those first yearnings for a philanthropic but distinctly P.E.O. work, the P.E.O. Educational Loan Fund was established. ELF celebrated its 90th birthday during the 1997 Seattle Convention of International Chapter. During these ninety years, the P.E.O. Educational Loan Fund grew to more than $20 million. Since money is returned to the fund as loans are repaid, the fund has been able to loan more than $58 million. Called the "Loan Fund with a Heart," an exciting announcement of a raise in the maximum amount of a loan to $7,000 was made at this Convention with the interest on the loan remaining at the low four percent. It is amazing that even in our competitive society money can be lent safely with no collateral except the integrity of character. Default rates are less than 1 percent.

Effective on October 1, 2000, the new maximum loan amount was raised to $9,000 with 4 percent interest, the same as it was when the first loan was issued in 1908. The chapter votes on the loan request at a regular or special meeting, including the amount, now using a voice vote rather than the previously used written ballot. From the initial amount of $2,000 in 1907, the fund now exceeded $26,000,000 (including loans outstanding, investments and money available for loans). Outstanding loans totaled more than $16,000,000 and almost $9,000,000 was available to be loaned. Over ninety-three years, the P.E.O. Educational Loan Fund loaned over $69,000,000, assisting more than 35,000 women in the U.S. and Canada. It was the goal of the ELF board of trustees to increase the usage of those available funds to seventy-five percent. The only way this goal would be met was if local chapters increased their participation in the loan process. Chapters were challenged with this motto; **TEAM**—Together **E**LF **A**chieves **M**agic.

In 2004, the maximum loan amount remained at $9,000 but the interest rate was lowered to two percent. As the world of technology surrounded us, the ELF Chapter Recommendations Form was provided on the P.E.O. website for use by chapters. The completed Recommendation Form and chapter letter were mailed to the P.E.O. Executive Office. In 2004 there were funds available for more ELF loans. Our wise and encouraging ELF board of trustees chose a new theme, "Help us Trim our Fat," challenging each local chapter to sponsor at least one ELF recipient in the 2003-2005 biennium to attain full utilization of our loan fund. By 2006 chapters had sponsored loan applicants in record numbers. During the 2005-2006 fiscal year alone 1,091 loans totaling $9,042,900 were approved. The trustees approved another 356 loans amounting to $3,044,500 from March to July 2006. During ELF's first century, more than $110,000,000 was loaned to more than 40,000 women. That is an impressive legacy!

The P.E.O. Educational Loan Fund celebrated its 100th birthday in 2007. Our loan fund was nearly 100 percent utilized due to the diligent search for applicants by our chapters and our very attractive two percent interest rate. The "Trim the Fat" challenge had been successfully met. At the 100th birthday all were glad to announce "ELF is now Slim and Trim!"

During ELF's lifetime we have seen many changes in our society and in women's roles within that society. The P.E.O. Educational Loan Fund assisted thousands of women with their educational goals during the first 100 years because its policies are regularly rewritten to address the needs of contemporary students. As ELF entered its second century it continued this tradition which has become the hallmark of its success. Honoring ELF's past is important. It is our foundation. But securing ELF's future is vital. It will become our legacy!

In 2007 we fondly remembered a "Very Special Number" associated with P.E.O.'s very first project! "656.88." This number represents the amount where "The Educational Fund" began. Following the 2007 International Convention, when P.E.O. celebrated ELF's 100th birthday, $656.88 again has the potential to make a special impact on ELF. Once again a challenge was delivered to chapters to consider what a difference would be made to the fund's ability to serve women if every chapter sent a special $656.88 birthday gift to ELF. As contemporary P.E.O.s we could secure ELF's future by making that very special gift of $656.88 to honor ELF's past and support the efforts of past generations of P.E.O.s. As our P.E.O. Educational Loan Fund ended its 100th year, it awarded 40,495 loans totaling nearly $112 million to women students of all ages. We are all so very proud to cherish the memory of the 1907 delegates who voted to establish a loan fund. By doing so they made a difference to generations of women students.

In the early months of 2008, many observers believed that a U.S. recession had begun. Our loan fund, though still strong and offering loans up to $9,000, found it necessary to increase the interest rate to four percent. That updated interest rate of four percent was extremely competitive in the 2008 financial market. Comparisons of federal government student loans showed a rate of approximately eight percent. However, since ELF is need-based, it became evident that many students may be having a difficult time making the annual interest payments on the loan before their graduation dates when they would most likely be starting their careers. In response to that, the ELF trustees proposed that beginning July 1, 2008, all interest would be waived until the recipient reached her stated graduation date. This meant that the recipients whose loans were approved on or after July 1, 2008, would make no payments at all until after their originally stated graduation. The final installment to pay off the loan would still be due six years from the date the student receives the money, but the student would essentially have use of the money without any fees or repayment until after graduation. Beginning July 1, 2008, ELF also began accepting payments using Visa and MasterCard from U. S. recipients.

Due to the sluggish national economy still looming in 2009 and rising costs of college tuition rates, the ELF loan amount increased from $9,000 to $10,000 effective with Chapter Recommendation Forms received in the Des Moines office on or after October 1, 2009. The interest rate remained at the same affordable four percent. The women who established the P.E.O. Educational Loan Fund were indeed forward thinking. Not only did they provide a means for women to obtain money for education but they also extended the use of the donations by establishing a loan fund rather that a grant or scholarship. As loans are repaid the fund is replenished and made available to other women. In 2009 the loan fund was strong and ready to help qualified women who need financial assistance to fulfill their educational goals. When the job market flounders, employees realize a golden opportunity to return to school in order to upgrade skills or change the focus of their careers. ELF is ready to assist those qualified women who need help to retool, revamp or redirect their life's path as well as those who are just beginning their education. This can only be done with the help of local chapters who find, sponsor and support applicants.

The board of trustees, always diligent to meet the best needs of our borrowers, announced the ELF loan interest rate would be reduced from four percent to three percent for all loans issued after April 15, 2010. Also, as of May 1, 2010, individuals living at the same address may be cosigners for a loan applicant. This means that both parents may be considered as cosigners on a loan application. ELF's loan maximum remained at $10,000 as announced in San Diego at the 2009 Convention of International Chapter.

As of April 1, 2012, the P.E.O. Educational Loan Fund announced new and considerably higher maximum loan amounts. Qualified women could apply for loans up to $12,000 for all programs of study and up to $20,000 for doctoral degrees at only 3 percent interest. In 2012, more than ever, women were in need of financial help for educational purposes. Popular fields of study for recipients were health, education, business and law. Almost ninety percent of recipients were pursuing either a bachelor's or advanced degree. Educational costs are rising rapidly and ELF is pleased to make additional funds available to qualified women. "Invest in ELF—Reap Dividends!" becomes our updated motto! During the 2011-2013 biennium, 1,205 women received loans totaling $13,914,200 from the P.E.O. Educational Loan Fund.

Once again keeping up in our technological world, as of May 1, 2014, the P.E.O. Educational Loan Fund's recommendation and application process is now online. This simplified process included online submission of the Chapter Recommendation Form and the chapter letter. Chapters will find it even easier to invest in ELF and help women reach their educational goals. With an all online loan process students will appreciate time-saving steps in completing an application and uploading transcripts. The ELF office no longer accepts paper submissions of chapter recommendations or student applications. ELF has money to lend. P.E.O. Chapters were thanked for an enthusiastic response to the debut of ELF Online! "Interest Rates are falling" was more good news from the ELF board in September 2014! Students whose Chapter Recommendation Forms were received on or after October 1, 2014, qualified for the new two percent interest rate for loans up to

$12,000 for all programs of study and up to $20,000 for doctoral degrees.

P.E.O.s are reminded that ELF loan recipients should become much sought after candidates to become P.E.O. sisters! There is no better advocate for P.E.O. than a woman whose life was touched through one of our philanthropies. These are sisters who are eager to pay it forward. What a wonderful way to invest in the future of P.E.O.

Nebraska is not only served by the International Chapter's appointed board of trustees and the ELF staff at the administrative offices in Des Moines, Iowa, but also by the Nebraska ELF chairman who is an active member of a Nebraska chapter and is appointed to serve a two-year term. Since 1988 the following sisters have served as Nebraska ELF Chairmen.

Carol Sandau, HQ, North Platte	2014-2016
Cathy Fagot, GR, Lexington	2012-2014
Kay Mader, ID, Wayne	2010-2012
Sharrel Arterburn, CL, Ogallala	2008-2010
Kris York, EK, Omaha	2006-2008
Shari L. Brosz, GT, O'Neill	2004-2006
Judy Mischke, HU, Norfolk	2002-2004
Alana Harness, IP, Fairbury	2000-2002
Ellen Campbell, AB, Central City	1998-2000
Suzanne Shaw, O, Geneva	1996-1998
Stanley Jean Rediger, GW, Lincoln	1994-1996
Breta Hurst, BS, Omaha	1992-1994
Chalice Harvey, CT, North Bend	1990-1992
Millie Howe, DN, Lincoln	1989-1990
First ELF Chairman, Margaret McGill, EJ, Creighton	1988-1989

The primary duty as the Nebraska P.E.O. Educational Loan Fund chairman is to promote the ELF philanthropy so that chapters continue to support the fund both financially and through the recommendation of qualified women applicants.

In October 2008 the Board of Trustees of the Education Loan Fund increased from three to five members because of the workload, but all agree they have been glad to perform their duties and have found joy in the service. In addition to the administration of ELF, promoting ELF has always been a primary duty of the trustees. Members of the ELF board of trustees are appointed by the president of International Chapter and serve a five-year term. Each year on October 1st a new member is appointed and the fifth year member, the chairman, retires. Trustees constantly review all policies and procedures, forms and material pertaining to ELF. The application process continues to be "a work in progress." All loan applications are reviewed and approved or denied by the trustees. Nebraska P.E.O.s are proud of Nebraska Past State President Joyce Victor who was appointed to the P.E.O. Educational Loan Fund Board of Trustees of International Chapter on October 1, 2012. She will serve until 2017.

Following are the statistics for
Nebraska ELF Program from 2000 through 2014.

YEAR	NUMBER OF LOANS	AMOUNT OF LOANS	CONTRIBUTIONS
2000	28	186,600	17,303
2001	34	248,500	22,312
2002	35	293,500	20,017
2003	28	222,500	25,773
2004	15	117,000	23,378
2005	32	259,500	22,678
2006	45	369,000	18,709
2007	27	219,000	22,890
2008	26	223,900	38,142
2009	26	198,650	27,772
2010	24	215,500	25,837
2011	16	154,000	26,879
2012	16	155,000	27,095
2013	16	199,000	29,807
2014	30	384,000	29,447

The following listing shows the total number of loans, the dollar amount of loans approved as well as total number of contributions and bequests received on a cumulative basis for the period 1907 through 2014 for Nebraska.

Number Approved	Amount Approved	Contributions & Bequests
2,528	$6,445,868	$716,375

Our P.E.O. Educational Loan Fund, established 107 years ago, has loaned $152,646,659 to 46,359 women. Contributions and bequests totaling $29,011,559 have been received since 1907. P.E.O.s' generous gifts are truly a legacy in memory of our Founders. Nebraska P.E.O.s remain proud of our state's legacy to ELF. Be attuned to women seeking financial help to finish their educations. ELF cannot function without our active participation. Always remember who we are as P.E.O.s: *Women helping Women Reach for the Stars.*

CATHY FAGOT, GR, LEXINGTON

P.E.O. PROGRAM FOR CONTINUING EDUCATION

The P.E.O. Program for Continuing Education (PCE) was created to fill a different need than the P.E.O. Educational Loan Fund (ELF). At the 1973 Supreme Chapter Convention, the plan of grants was proposed and adopted. These grants were to go to recipients, sponsored by a local chapter, who needed to re-enter the workplace due to economic or family needs. The grant of $500 could go to a recipient of any age or interest who did not qualify for an educational loan and might not be able to attend school full time. From this small beginning, PCE has grown and evolved. While the purpose to provide financial assistance to women remains the same, the wording has been clarified to reflect that the applicant's education must have been interrupted and a need exist to resume studies due to the changing demands in her life. A financial need must also be demonstrated. From 1973 until 2004, the applicant needed to demonstrate a twelve-month hiatus in schooling in addition to being within twenty-four months of her educational goal. As of 2005, the period required as a non-student was extended to twenty-four (24) consecutive months. May 1, 1994, the amount of the one-time maximum grant increased to $1,500. By 2005 the grant maximum amount was increased to $2,000 and in 2009 was increased to $3,000. The money is a grant, not a loan, and may be used for any necessary educational expenses. It is interesting to see how Nebraska has supported this project through grant money given to PCE recipients through the years.

1974-75	$ 855	1994-95	44,268
1975-76	2,186	1995-96	26,660
1976-77	3,266	1996-97	39,333
1977-78	3,397	1997-98	49,953
1978-79	4,033	1998-99	47,600
1979-80	4,538	1999-2000	38,046
1980-81	5,907	2000-01	50,804
1981-82	5,877	2001-02	38,244
1982-83	6,041	2002-03	40,168
1983-84	7,541	2003-04	28,600
1984-85	6,982	2004-05	37,700
1985-86	7,501	2005-06	57,476
1986-87	14,743	2006-07	56,000
1987-88	10,121	2007-08	56,000
1988-89	11,428	2008-09	61,240
1989-90	11,837	2009-10	47,900
1990-91	11,421	2010-11	61,900
1991-92	11,649	2011-12	74,400
1992-93	15,116	2012-13	43,050
1993-94	14,123	2013-14	45,250

The total of these gifts is $1,103,154, surpassing the one-million dollar mark! The fund is totally distributed each year and therefore must be replenished yearly. This need is met because P.E.O.s are so generous.

Not included here are all the extras that many sponsoring chapters give "their" women. This includes small gifts, stamps, gift cards, extras limited only by the imagination and interest of the chapter.

Goals differ widely. From Dental Assistant to Master of Science Education in Instructional Technology, from business degree to R.N., the desire for the education and the financial need is the same. The recipient's gratitude is also the same. Comments such as these make it all worthwhile. *"The grant was heaven sent..."* and *"...This is a wonderful program and your group should be highly praised for their work."* One recipient later donated the amount of her grant back to the fund. She did this not just one year, but several—a non P.E.O. making an opportunity for others, as opportunity had been given her.

Praise is nice, but any P.E.O. will tell you that is not why she contributes and supports this program. In the years from 1981 to 2014, over 800 chapters have sponsored just over one thousand PCE grants. It is impossible to know how many lives have been helped by making these grants available.

Changes are necessary for the times. In 1998 a new logo was unveiled and the PCE Named Grant was established. The PCE Named Grant began as a $2,000 donation to PCE from an individual, chapter, group of chapters or state/provincial/district chapter. The PCE Named Grant donation total has since been increased to $3,000. 1998 was also the year project information could be found on the website. September of 2011 was the start date for the directive that all applications be submitted electronically online.

Originally, the chairman of this committee was the state treasurer. In 1983, the responsibility was moved to the recording secretary. Then in 1988, the state chapter bylaws were changed and a separate committee was established. Under the new guidelines, Cindy Hardekopf, HB, Kearney, was the first chairman. There have been many chairmen chosen from around the state since, typically serving in this role for two years. The chairman's job is to keep track of the grant women within Nebraska, extending help and information to chapters as requested and keeping chapters up to date with information from International. Their efforts and dedication are appreciated.

FROM SPIRIT OF THE PRAIRIE UPDATED BY JOAN ALLEN, E, OMAHA

P.E.O. INTERNATIONAL PEACE SCHOLARSHIP

During World War II, P.E.O. had a special fund called the United Victory Fund and Peace Participation Committee. After generously providing thousands of dollars toward club mobiles at the "front," comfort for the wounded, food and relief work, P.E.O.s began to look to the future. A Post War Planning Committee, appointed in 1943, ventured suggestions as to improving world understanding through use of the Educational Loan Fund for foreign students, through considering attendance of foreign students at Cottey College, or through provision of scholarships by state chapters.

Local chapters were requested to give twelve dollars annually for the biennium 1947-1949. In 1949, over $31,000 was given to CARE and to veterans' services. Three thousand dollars was allocated for the first two scholarships—$15,000 each to Kirsti Jaantila of Finland and Margretta Alder of Switzerland. The 1949 Convention of Supreme Chapter voted to ask local chapters to contribute at least three dollars a year for international scholarships. In 1959, in addition to post-war work, the Victory Fund provided fifty scholarships to students from sixteen countries. In 1955, it was voted that the United Victory Fund be used exclusively for international scholarships. In 1959, the program became the P.E.O. International Peace Scholarship Fund, and in 1961 it was placed on an equal basis with other projects with a rotating board of trustees. Irene S. Van Brunt, past president of Nebraska State Chapter, was then second vice president of Supreme Chapter and became the board's first chairman. Beginning in 1960-1961, scholarships were granted only to graduate students, except those attending Cottey College.

For the first biennium, the office for the IPS Fund was in the homes of board members—in car trunks, closets or wherever there was room for files and supplies. Those early trustees worked at home and carried their typewriters with them even on vacation trips. The volume of operation increased tremendously, making it difficult to do all the necessary work from home. If Irene's experience was typical, her home was converted into an office. With her working a regular eight-hour day, her social life was limited to after dinner. In 1963, a permanent office was established at the P.E.O. Executive Office and a secretary was hired for the routine work of the project. The administration of the fund is still under the direction of the trustees.

The essence of P.E.O. success with international scholarships is found in the hearts of sisters who care—not just with financial aid but also in giving continuing friendship, helping with problems, entertaining in homes, sharing affection. Nebraska chapters in university and college towns have had the wonderful opportunity to meet and get to know these women. However, even those from other areas have found ways to show their IPS students P.E.O. love.

An example of the essence of the IPS program is in the story of Hiroko Mori, the designated scholar of Chapter CR, Omaha. A letter in which Hiroko introduced herself was written, duplicated and sent to Nebraska chapters, who wrote, sent gifts, and generally showed their loving concern. Over 120 chapters responded at Christmastime alone. Caring was made tangible in every way from needed typing to fruit baskets, warm meals, stamps, money and showers of small gifts. Hiroko constantly expressed her gratitude for all that was done for her. She stated that when she returned to Tokyo Woman's College, she would like to put in place a similar support system for the women from other countries who came to study there. She felt it had helped her that much. Hiroko was selected to represent all IPS students and speak at the 1985 Convention of International Chapter in Winnipeg. In 1988, Hiroko Mori wrote a Christmas letter to Nebraska P.E.O.s in which she said, "I often remember the support and warm regards from the P.E.O. members in Nebraska. Peace and joy be with you, P.E.O. members in Nebraska!"

In 2013, the Partners in Peace Program was established. For a special contribution of $500 a chapter or group of chapters is paired with an IPS recipient. It offers an opportunity for an IPS recipient to experience the warmth of P.E.O. and learn more about our culture, and for P.E.O.s to learn, not only about the recipient and her studies, but about her homeland as well. A special bond often develops with the student who may become a better ambassador for peace upon returning to her country.

IPS contributions from Nebraska chapters to this effort grew from $264 in 1951-52 to $22,627 in 2005-06. By the end of 2014 the IPS project has awarded $33.3 million to over 7,000 women from around the world.

From Spirit of the Prairie with update by Jackie Nelson, HX
and Past State President Jan Loftin

P.E.O. Scholar Award

As of this writing, the P.E.O. Scholar Award (PSA) theme is "Supporting Women...Changing the World." Our fifth project was established in 1991 at International Convention in Omaha after a feasibility study in 1990. The award recognizes and encourages academic excellence and achievement by women who have the potential to make significant contributions in their fields of endeavor; it has become an extremely competitive award. To date, Nebraska has had thirty-seven Scholars (one woman has received the award twice).

Up until 2006, those seeking masters degrees, doctorates, and post-doctorate degrees were all eligible for an award. Throughout the years, the eligibility requirements have changed; currently, only those pursuing a doctorate level degree at an accredited college or university are eligible for the award. There were 441 nominations during the first full year of the award; the number of nominees has been as high as 695 with 623 in the most recent class. The table on page 648 illustrates the growth and changes that have occurred over the years since the PSA was established.

Our Nebraska Scholars are exceptional, displaying a variety of talents. Many still live and work in Nebraska while others have spread their gifts across the country in Iowa, Oklahoma, Oregon, South Dakota, Illinois and Washington, to name a few states. We are even represented in Paris, France. Their professions include college/university professors, music, law, medicine/dentistry and politics. Unfortunately, at least two have been called Home.

Recognizing that not all chapters have the opportunity to nominate a woman for a Scholar Award, the P.E.O. Scholar Awards Laureate Chapter Program was first announced at the 2011 International Convention in St. Louis. This program was created to help all local chapters feel the pride of ownership in the Scholar Awards project.

There are currently two ways to become a Laureate Chapter: 1) A chapter that has nominated a successful Scholar will automatically be designated as a Laureate Chapter for the year of selection; 2) A chapter that makes a lump sum contribution of $500 or more through their normal process during the chapter fiscal year (March 1 – February 28) will be designated as a Laureate Chapter. Individuals who wish to make a contribution of $500 or more with credit going to their local chapter may submit the contribution directly to the Scholar Awards office, identifying their chapter in the submission. To date, sixteen Nebraska chapters have the distinction of being Laureate Chapters.

Another way to "own" a piece of the PSA program is to make a contribution to the Vera G. (Bobbie) Koefoot Memorial Fund. This fund is held and administered by the P.E.O. Foundation. The inception date for the fund was 1988 for $2,000. The fund source was gifts in honor of Vera (Bobbie) G. Koefoot. In 1987, Bobbie, Chapter GP, Grand Island, was elected recording secretary of International Chapter. Nebraska State Chapter established "Koefoot's Cache" to which Nebraska chapters could donate monies in her honor. The money was to have been presented to Bobbie when she was elected president of International Chapter. Unfortunately, Bobbie joined Chapter Eternal in 1990 when she was first vice president, and the $40,624 that had been collected was given to her family. They, in turn, donated the money to the memorial fund.

Originally, it was intended that the interest from the fund was to be transferred to the PSA fund every two years to be given to a designated PSA scholar. However, the financial climate and the increase in the amount of each PSA award have impacted the frequency of this distribution. The PSA award has been increased over time (from $5,000 at its inception to $15,000 in 2008), thus the fund's interest income must grow over a longer time period before that interest can be transferred and an award in Bobbie's name can be presented. To date, seven awards have been given totaling $59,000. Nebraska Chapters are encouraged to donate their PSA allotments to this fund in honor of our Nebraska sister.

Let's continue to spotlight our extraordinary Nebraska women by nominating them for a Scholar Award. What a wonderful gift of P. E. O.

Year/Notes	# of Awards	$$ Awarded	NE Scholars
1990-Pilot Project Established			
1991-Project Approved	30	$5,000	1
1992	45	$5,000	4
1993	75	$5,000	3
1994-Amount Increased	75	$6,000	5
1995	80	$6,000	1
1996	80	$6,000	1
1997-Amount Increased	75	$7,000	3
1998	80	$7,000	0
1999	85	$7,000	3
2000	85	$7,000	2
2001-Amount Increased	85	$8,000	3
2002	85	$8,000	0
2003	85	$8,000	0
2004-Amount Increased	85	$10,000	3
2005	85	$10,000	1
2006-Non-terminal Masters Degree Category Eliminated	85	$10,000	2
2007	85	$10,000	2
2008-Amount Increased, All Masters Degrees Eliminated	85	$15,000	0
2009	85	$15,000	3
2010	85	$15,000	0
2011	85	$15,000	0
2012	85	$15,000	0
2013-Post-Doctoral Degrees Eliminated	85	$15,000	0
2014	85	$15,000	1

BARB FRISKOPP, FN, P.E.O. SCHOLAR AWARD CHAIRMAN

P.E.O. STAR Scholarship

A STAR was officially born at the 2009 Convention of International Chapter and became the sixth P.E.O. project. STAR stands for scholarship, talent, achievement and recognition. The scholarship provides $2,500 to high school senior women who will be attending a post-secondary educational institution in the United States or Canada after graduation. The applicant must be recommended by a P.E.O. chapter, have at least a 3.0 grade point average and exhibit excellence in leadership, extracurricular activities, volunteerism in community service, academics and potential for future success.

The P.E.O. STAR Scholarship has quickly become a very sought after and competitive scholarship. In 2009 during the pilot project year, 1,524 applications were submitted and reviewed with 151 selected as recipients. In 2014, just five years later, the trustees received and reviewed 1,049 applications with 350 women selected as recipients. Eighty-four applications were from Nebraska with eleven scholarships awarded. A total of 528 applications have been received from Nebraska with forty-nine scholarships awarded since its inception in 2009. The amount of funds donated annually determines the number of scholarships available for that year.

The recipients of this scholarship and their recommending chapter are listed on the International website under the projects and P.E.O. STAR Scholarship page. The International website is used for online submission of applications for the scholarship. Also found on the website are instructions for submitting the forms for the recommending chapter and applicant. The chapter recommendations can only be submitted between September 1 and November 1.

Renee Piper, Chapter AK, P.E.O. STAR Scholarship chairman

Cottey College

The "Cottey Chapter Challenge" was approved in 1995 during Convention of International Chapter. Cottey was expanding due to an 8.9 million addition to the Rubie Burton Academic Center. Nebraska State Chapter pledged $10,000 in honor of Nebraska Past State President Phyllis Blanke, 1996-1997. Both Phyllis and her daughter Annette are Cottey graduates. In 1997, NSC presented $10,000 to the Chapter Challenge. To commemorate this contribution, a faculty office was named in Phyllis' honor. By 1999, over twenty-five Nebraska chapters contributed $1,000 or more to the Chapter Challenge. One wing of the Academic Center was named for Nelle Horner, past Nebraska state president, 1925-1926.

"Adopt-a-Cottey student" was a popular way of encouraging Nebraska students attending Cottey. Each Nebraska reciprocity group was assigned one or two Cottey girls to "adopt." These Cottey girls were either Nebraska girls or girls living in the Nebraska Suite. Each reciprocity group organized a rotation among their chapters to send notes, care packages and gift cards throughout the school year.

During the late 90's and into the early 2000's the Cottey "Share the Vision" campaign became the "Scholars and Dollars" campaign as chapters and individual P.E.O.s were encouraged to financially support Cottey. By 2007, thirteen percent of Nebraska chapters participated. In 2003, Cottey implemented the "Diamond Anniversary Scholarship Fund." This campaign combined different levels of chapter contribution including dollar giving and chapters helping with finding Cottey students. During 2006, chapters, reciprocity groups and individual P.E.O.s could purchase a "Cottey Brick" for $100. Bricks were purchased in honor of or in memory of P.E.O.s. This campaign was so successful that the college extended it until 2012.

At Convention of International Chapter in 2009, Dr. Judy Rogers, president of Cottey College, announced the "Defining Moment" campaign. This was a five-year, 35-million dollar campaign for Cottey. The information about the "Defining Moment" campaign "Chapter Challenge" was disclosed at the 2011 Convention of International Chapter in St. Louis.

"Bucks for Beds" was a Nebraska campaign started in early 2009 with a goal of $15,000. This amount was earmarked for ten new rooms of bedroom furniture in the Nebraska Suite. Each Nebraska chapter was asked to send one dollar per member. As of May 1, 2009, this goal was met and surpassed. The new furniture was ordered and installed prior to the beginning of the fall semester in 2009. The excess contributions totalling nearly $10,000 were added to the Nebraska Suite Endowment Fund at Cottey.

In Nebraska, each reciprocity group appoints a Cottey Area Chairman to facilitate activities within their group. The State Cottey Committee gives a workshop for the Cottey Area Chairmen during state convention. The Cottey Area Chairmen take this information back to their reciprocity groups. They stay busy meeting with high school counselors, attending college fairs around the state, attending their individual reciprocity meetings, hosting student gatherings and sponsoring the annual Cottey Bus Trip. The Cottey Committee encourages students in their sophomore year to take the Cottey Bus Trip. Cottey allows students sixteen years and older to come for a visit. It was believed that a spring Cottey Bus Trip would allow more students to attend, so Nebraska arranges to go to Cottey during the "C for yourself" weekend in April.

Applications to Cottey by Nebraska students declined from twenty-six in 2003 to seven in 2007. This may have been the result of the end of the Kimmel Foundation grants in 2004. In order to try to curb this decrease in applicants, the Cottey Committee implemented a new activity during area reciprocity meetings. The Cottey Area Chairmen presented workshops for the local chapter Cottey Chairmen.

During the summer in the even years Cottey College hosts the Cottey Seminar. All Cottey Committee members, Cottey Scholarship Committee members, Cottey Area Chairmen and members of the Nebraska executive board are invited to attend.

The new president of Cottey College, Dr. Judy Rogers, was a special guest at the 2005 Nebraska State Convention in Grand Island. Dr.Brenda Ross, Assistant Dean to the Faculty at Cottey, was a special speaker at state convention in 2009. At state convention time in 2011, the announcement was made about the three bachelor degree programs that would be offered to Cottey students beginning in the fall of 2011. These were Environmental Studies, International Relations and Business and English. In addition, by the fall of 2013, Cottey offered bachelor's degrees in Psychology, Business and Liberal Arts.

In 2014, President of Cottey College Dr. Judy Rogers resigned. She will be missed by everyone associated with Cottey and all P.E.O.s. In February 2015, the Presidential Search Committee announceed the appointment of Cottey's twelfth president, Dr. Jann Rudd Weitzel.

Dori Bush, II, Cottey Chairman

A BIL's Gift of Love

Dori Bush, II, Grand Island, was introduced to Cottey College at a young age. Her father, Gordon H. Sheffield, honored Cottey and Nebraska P.E.O. by starting three scholarships at Cottey College: Edna Z. Sheffield Scholarship (Dori's grandmother) – designated for second year students in the field of music; Dorothy M. Sheffield Scholarship (Dori's mother) – designated for second year students in the field of education; Dori Jeanne Bush Scholarship – designated for first year students from other countries.

Every year when she goes on the April bus trip, Dori makes the attempt to find each of the recipients and has experienced many, many hugs and frequent tears. She became especially close to two of her scholarship recipients, Dichen Lahm (below left) from Bhutan, and Rainatou Abdoulaye (below right) from France, but born in Niger. The year they received their associate degrees (2010), both asked her to cap them.

Gordon Sheffield loved P.E.O. Because Dori was a charter member of three different chapters (EH, HO and II) and her mother was a charter member of Chapter CH, Arizona, he suggested they just go around the country and organize chapters. He was one of our most outstanding BILs. Gordon passed away on July 4, 2012, at the age of 95.

Nebraska Cottey Scholarships

Until 2004, Nebraska students attending Cottey had the opportunity to apply for grants from the Richard P. Kimmel and Laurine Kimmel Charitable Foundation. These grants were for full tuition and room and board for one year. They were given in memory of Laurine Kimmel, a P.E.O. from Nebraska City. These grants were intended to end in 2003 but in order to fulfill obligations to second year students the grants continued through the 2003-2004 school year.

The Nebraska bylaws have established annual scholarships of $3,500 from the general fund. The annual contributions from chapters and individuals to the Nebraska Cottey Scholarships is given to Nebraska girls attending Cottey. The amount given per individual is determined by the Cottey Scholarship Committee. One scholarship is given annually in honor of Helen Houseman by the Bertha Clark Hughes Foundation. Another scholarship is given annually in honor of Bertha Clark Hughes from her foundation. Other Nebraska scholarships are the P.G. Richardson; the Chapter HD Shirley Bair and Cynthia Lloyd Scholarship and the Chapter V Doris Bair and Jo Anne Bair Scholarship.

In 1999, Reciprocity Groups III and X gave a one-time scholarship to a Nebraska Cottey student in the amount of $1,300 in honor of Rosella Mehling, past president of Nebraska State Chapter.

From 2000 to 2001, the Nebraska Cottey Scholarship Committee received gifts of stocks from Jan Nurnberger, Chapter FT, Omaha.

In 2001, a one-time award of $1,800 was available to an applicant from Reciprocity Group I in honor of Anita Kitt, past president of Nebraska State Chapter.

In 2002, a one-time award of $3,075 was available to applicants from Omaha Reciprocity Groups II and IX in honor of Patricia Robertson, past president of Nebraska State Chapter.

In 2003, a one-time award of $1,100 was available to applicants from Group III and X in honor of Jacci Irwin, past president of Nebraska State Chapter.

In 2004, a one-time award of $2,000 was awarded to an applicant from Group IV in honor of Jeanne Reigle, past president of Nebraska State Chapter.

In 2004, a one-time award of $5,000 was awarded in honor of Joyce Goff, past president of Nebraska State Chapter and past president of International Chapter.

Bylaws concerning the development of the W. Joyce Goff Nebraska Scholarship Endowment Fund were adopted at state convention in Kearney in 2006. This fund originated because of the contributions from Nebraska chapters during "Goff's Goal" in honor of Joyce Goff. This fund is managed through the P.E.O. Foundation by agreement with Nebraska State Chapter. The recipients of the scholarship are designated by the Nebraska Cottey Scholarship Committee.

The $6,000 W. Joyce Goff Scholarship was awarded for the first time in the 2009-2010 school year.

CINDY BIEHL, PAST STATE PRESIDENT

A DEFINING MOMENT: THE CAMPAIGN FOR COTTEY COLLEGE

Cottey College's Defining Moment Campaign, inaugurated to address the strategic goals of the Campus Master Plan, was announced at the 2009 Convention of International Chapter in San Diego. The campaign goal of $35 million was established to focus on five areas of excellence: Scholarship Endowment ($10 million); Faculty Chairs ($3 million); Fine Arts Instructional Building ($9 million); Library Endowment ($3 million), and Unrestricted Funding ($10 million). As Cottey was beginning to offer accredited baccalaureate degrees, increased financial support was required. At the conclusion of the Campaign (January 31, 2014), $40,420,737.58 had been received in pledges and financial contributions, exceeding the initial goal by more than $4 million!

To reach this goal, the Campaign was divided into phases, including solicitation of Cottey alumnae, special friends of the College, and the Chapter Challenge, which began in 2011. Any gifts received from chapters between January 2009 and the conclusion of the Campaign were credited to the donor's P.E.O. Chapter.

Pictured at left, Dori Bush, II, Grand Island, wears the Nebraska Defining Moment "Green Team" shirt

The Chapter Challenge goal was $16 million and involved a "horse race," pitting four geographical regions of the United States and Canada (Teams) against each other to see which region would reach the Winner's Circle. Nebraska was a member of the Green Team. A horse race was the visual depiction to gauge progress of Nebraska's efforts encouraged by our five Area Ambassadors. Each Area Ambassador was assigned about fifty chapters in Nebraska to inform, encourage, and motivate chapters to bring in as many dollars as possible to enable the Green Team "horses" to move forward on the race tracks. Nebraska's Area Ambassadors were Dori Bush (Chapter II, Grand Island, Green Team 19), Megan Ferris (Chapter HD, Lincoln, Team 20), Marilyn Smith (Chapter GI, Scottsbluff, Team 21), Sandy Wolfe (Chapter CU, Norfolk, Team 22), and Anne Yost (Chapter GF, Omaha, Team 23).

Each local chapter was asked to register one C-3 (Chapter Challenge Captain) Sister with the Campaign to be a liaison between Campaign Central, the Area Ambassadors, and local chapters. Nebraska was the first chapter to have 100 percent of our chapters with a registered C-3 Sister! Area Ambassadors used these C-3 Sisters to disseminate information about the progress of the Campaign as well as to suggest fundraising ideas.

At the 2013 Convention of Nebraska State Chapter in Columbus, a "Walk for Cottey" was held at the conclusion of the Saturday business meeting. Local chapters were encouraged to send their chapter's contribution to the Chapter Challenge with their convention delegate as the "entry fee" to walk in the "Walk." The combination of chapter contributions and extra monies donated by individuals attending the convention yielded a "Walk" total of $15,128.12 to be credited to the Chapter Challenge. As the Fine Arts Instructional Building portion of the Campaign designated focus area was lagging behind, it was decided that Nebraska's "Walk for Cottey" proceeds would be designated for the FAIB, which was later named the Judy and Glen Rogers Fine Arts Building, in honor of Cottey President Dr. Judy Rogers.

At the conclusion of the Campaign, 100 percent of Nebraska chapters had contributed over $250,000! Again, Nebraska P.E.O.s generously contributed to the betterment and advancement of women's education through their efforts and contributions to the Cottey Defining Moment Campaign.

DORI BUSH, CHAPTER II , GRAND ISLAND

International First VicePresident Joyce Goff (right) with the Executive Board (from left) Elizabeth Garrels, Ann Fields, Nancy Hoium, Barbara Andes and Joyce

State Membership Development Committee

In 2002, Jeanne Reigle, president of Nebraska State Chapter, appointed a special ad hoc committee of Kathleen Gosch, HB, Jacci Irwin, AH, Joyce Victor, HJ and (ex officio) Anne Baumhover, HK, to create operational guidelines and recommendations for proposed amendments to the Nebraska bylaws for the creation of a state membership committee. The committee recommended a rotating membership of three with one member to be a past state president and two to be past presidents of a local chapter. This committee would assist with the health concerns of local chapters and assist local chapters in the development of a local membership committee. The committee was not responsible for organizing new chapters or initiation of new members. The Membership Committee was officially created by a bylaw at state convention in 2003. At state convention in 2013, the name of the committee was officially changed to the Membership Development Committee.

Jeanne Reigle was the first chairman and served as chairman until 2007. During these years membership information was gathered together for reference. Chapters with membership concerns were visited by members of the committee and offered support and ideas. In 2007, the committee was changed to a rotation of three past state presidents, each serving for three years. Nebraska remains one of the few, if not the only state that requires the Membership Development Committee to be made up of three past state presidents. The committee started to correspond with all Nebraska chapters by writing Membership Moments for the Nebraska website each month. Membership references were made into a Membership Manual and made available on the Nebraska website, and guidelines were developed for membership committees in local chapters. In 2008, a membership workshop was added to the Local Chapter Officer Workshops. Membership workshops were presented by this committee at state conventions from 2010 through 2015.

In September 2010, this committee met with the Regional Membership Representative, Jane Attaway, to discuss recent membership initiatives and to plan workshops and a display for the 2011 state convention. Availability of membership resources on the Nebraska and International websites was increasing each year. Chapter visits, phone calls and emails were increased as the need increased for membership support in the local chapters. Committee members began mentoring relationships with chapters that lasted for years. Time was devoted during state convention to meet with chapter delegates representing chapters who have asked for membership support during the year.

In 2012 and 2014 the Membership Development Committee attended the Regional Membership Summit in Des Moines. The Nebraska committee gained knowledge and new ideas on how to help chapters enhance their membership. Following the summit, the idea of monthly "Nuggets" sent directly to chapter membership chairmen was pursued, and a mailing list was developed with the help of the state technology consultant, Leann Drullinger. The mailing list has been used to send monthly or bi-monthly communications directly to the local chapter membership chairmen, giving them membership ideas and links to helpful information on the International website.

This committee assists the state organizer by providing membership workshops and "infomercials" at state conventions. In February of 2015 the Membership Development Committee participated in International Chapter's "Phone Every One" event.

The committee continues to meet with chapters to help them work on self-revitalization programs or find solutions when their membership declines or enthusiasm lags. At this writing, Nebraska's total membership continues to decline as our population ages, and the goal of this committee is to turn that around.

Cindy Biehl, Past State President and Legacy Associate Editor

Unaffiliate Committee

In 1997, at the Nebraska State Convention in Lincoln, a new standing committee was added to the bylaws: Chairman of Unaffiliated Members. This committee of one was to maintain a file of all unaffiliated members of Nebraska State Chapter and unaffiliated members of other state chapters who were living in Nebraska. She was to send the names of all unaffiliated members to proper reciprocity contact persons and/or chapters, to communicate with all new unaffiliated members offering the interest and encouragement of Nebraska State Chapter, and to serve as contact person for P.E.O.s needing assistance in affiliating with a chapter.

Joyce Victor, Chapter HJ, was appointed as Chairman of Unaffiliated Members in 1997 and fulfilled her duties in that position with diligence and loving care until 2004. According to the state bylaws this was a three year appointment. In 2004 the bylaws were changed to provide for a second member of the committee, appointed in odd numbered years, who would serve as co-chairman the first year, sole chairman her second year, and chairman with a co-chairman her third year. This rotation continued until 2010.

During her time as Chairman of Unaffiliated Members, Joyce gathered 2,059 unaffiliate names from Nebraska's 1997-1998 yearbooks, FL Forms and lists from other states. She started keeping the names in a database on the computer. Over the next couple of years, unaffiliate lists were provided to the Nebraska executive board when they attended meetings in Des Moines. Unaffiliate lists were prepared for each chapter in Nebraska and were sent with the annual reports and given out during official visits by state officers. By 2003 Internet communication with reciprocity unaffiliate chairmen kept information accurate. The return response due to the member lists sent with annual reports also helped to keep the list of unaffiliate names up to date.

During state convention in 2010 the Chairman of Unaffiliated Members was removed from the state bylaws and the duties were moved to the Policy Manual of the Nebraska State Chapter under the paid assistant. This was done because the database had been lost in a computer crash and now the chairman had nothing to work with. However, the paid assistant could generate unaffiliate lists from the International database on the iMIS Membership System. She continued to provide unaffiliate lists for the executive board for official visits and for when chapters needed help in finding new members in their area.

In the summer of 2012 members of the state Membership Committee attended a Membership Summit Meeting in Des Moines. At that meeting state membership committees were instructed to start cleaning up their unaffiliate lists by making sure names were linked to the proper areas and identifying names that shouldn't be on the list. It was announced at that meeting that a state membership portal was being established that would be available to executive boards, chairmen of membership and unaffiliate committees, and reciprocity chairmen. That portal became available February 1, 2013, and was instrumental in the process of cleaning up the Nebraska unaffiliate lists in the iMIS Membership System on the International website.

It became clear that the unaffiliate duties for Nebraska had increased, and at state convention in 2014, newly installed President Karen Blair appointed an Ad-Hoc Unaffiliate Committee of two past state presidents, Jan Loftin, ES, and Cindy Biehl, GZ, and Renita Wichert, HJ. The committee eagerly started the process of connecting cities to the proper areas, identifying names of non-unaffiliates that came up on the list, and correcting any errors found. Updated lists of unaffiliates were mailed or emailed to the city reciprocity contacts as well as the presidents of local chapters not affiliated with a city reciprocity group.

January 2015 marked International's first comprehensive effort to contact every unaffiliate in the U.S. and Canada, called Phone Every One Day. Because of the magnitude of this undertaking, the Membership Development Committee combined efforts with the Unaffiliate Committee to achieve success. On and around January 21, 2015, Nebraska P.E.O. chapters attempted to contact each active unaffiliate in Nebraska. The goal was for 100 percent of our chapters to contact as many unaffiliates as possible and invite them to a local chapter activity. We didn't achieve 100 percent, but the result was nevertheless a resounding success. There were over ninety unaffiliated P.E.O.s in Nebraska who were contacted, some for the first time, and many of them have visited chapters and are transferring. The response from Nebraska chapters was heartwarming.

An amendment will be proposed at the 2015 Convention of Nebraska State Chapter in La Vista establishing an Unaffiliate Committee once again. The goal of this committee will be to assure that as many sisters as possible will be contacted and invited to meetings when they move into our state.

JAN LOFTIN, PAST STATE PRESIDENT/LEGACY ASSOCIATE EDITOR

"SPIRIT OF THE PRAIRIE" DISTRIBUTION COMMITTEE

For several years after the printing of Nebraska P.E.O.'s *Spirit of the Prairie* history book in 1995, Nebraska Past State President Rosella Mehling acted as a committee of one. Books were available each year at state convention or by mail. In 2000, chapters were given two more books each and asked to share one of them with their public library. Rosella held the remaining books, bringing some to state convention each year and mailing others when requested. By 2000, the remaining books were offered without charge except for a $5 shipping and handling fee when mailed.

In 2006 the final few books were given to the executive board for distribution to new chapters upon their organization.

CINDY BIEHL, PAST STATE PRESIDENT/LEGACY ASSOCIATE EDITOR

THE P.E.O. RECORD

In 1919, the P.E.O. Sisterhood observed its Golden Anniversary. To quote *Out of the Heart:* "One outstanding commemorative feature used throughout the anniversary year was the lovely golden cover used on The P.E.O. Record. It appeared first on the February issue, then on all others throughout the year. The cover plate was designed by Sylvia Holmstrom, then an instructor of art in the public schools of Havelock (now Lincoln), Nebraska, and one of the charter members of Chapter AI. The classic, stylized design uses P.E.O. symbolism effectively. Seven marguerites representing the seven Founders form the base of the design. Tall burning torchieres suggest light and a star at the top center symbolizes the P.E.O. emblem."

Section Thirteen
Reciprocity and Collegiate Groups
RECIPROCITY GROUPS

Fourteen reciprocity groups continue to provide important structure within the framework of P.E.O. in Nebraska. Omaha was the pioneer city in forming such groups. The first group was known as the P.E.O. Federation of Omaha. The name was changed to Omaha P.E.O. Association, and today is known as Omaha P.E.O. Reciprocity Association. It was an outgrowth of cooperation of seven Omaha chapters, E, M, BK, BN, BP, BS and BX in entertaining the 1917 Convention of Supreme Chapter. The first president was Bertha Clark Hughes. There are currently thirty-eight chapters in the Omaha area, including chapters in Bellevue, Elkhorn, and Papillion which comprise the state convention groups of II and IX. These chapters meet four times a year to introduce unaffiliated sisters to Omaha area chapters and to encourage interest in the philanthropies of the P.E.O. Sisterhood. Meeting dates and times can be found on the Omaha P.E.O. Reciprocity Association's website. This website can be accessed by a link on the state website: nebraskapeo.org.

In March 1922 the Lincoln P.E.O. Roundtable was formed with chapters K, BR, and BY. They were led by Lue R. Spencer, past president of Nebraska State Chapter. There are currently thirty chapters in the Lincoln area, including a chapter in Waverly. These chapters, which comprise the Reciprocity Groups of V and XII, meet three times a year in the months of May, October, and a Founders' Day brunch in March. In 2014, Roundtable established a website for communicating with Lincoln chapters. This site can be viewed at www.lincolnpeo.org, or by accessing a link on the Nebraska P.E.O. website. It shows chapter meeting days and times, helpful information about P.E.O., and on a private page makes names of local unaffiliates available for chapters.

Six Hasting chapters comprise the Greater Hastings Reciprocity Group. The group meets annually in the spring for a brunch, and the six chapters rotate providing officers for the group. A college group advisor and an unaffiliated chairman also function within the group. The six chapters also have a rotation system called The Reciprocity Program where each chapter gives a program and receives a program from one of the other chapters. Each year presidents of these six chapters meet in the fall and spring to plan the annual meetings.

Chapter AU, Peru, formed Reciprocity Group VIII for the southeast area of the state in 1932, and these eighteen chapters currently comprise the group. The sandhills chapters followed suit in 1936 with the organization of the Panhandle Reciprocity, under the original direction of Bernice Tillett of Alliance. There are currently twenty-eight chapters in this area that comprise Reciprocity Groups X and III.

Daisy-bedecked sisters from Lincoln Reciprocity Roundtable chapters decorate portraits of our Founders with daisy chains while 300 luncheon guests sing along.

Chapter ER members, with assistance from other chapters, perform "*A Star in the Window*" at a Reciprocity Group I luncheon - (standing, from left) Carol Peterson, Jean Matthews, Christy Tecker, Allison Sandman, FA, Julie Jones, Chris Schrader, Velda Wright, Jana Mintling, IG, Barbara Waters, Nichole Sis, and Past State President Anita Kitt.

At the present time there are fourteen reciprocity groups. Each is comprised of chapters grouped geographically, with approximately the same number of total members in each group. The two reciprocity groups in Omaha host state convention every seven years, as do the two reciprocity groups in Lincoln. The remaining ten reciprocity groups host state convention every fourteen years. Every fourteen years the Chapter Groupings Committee studies the composition of the groups and rearranges, if necessary, in order to keep a similar number of members in each group. The Chapter Groupings Committee places new chapters within existing reciprocity groups after organization, and also places them in rotation for representation at Convention of International Chapter. The vice president of Nebraska State Chapter acts as an advisor to the Reciprocity Groups and receives reports of elections, bylaws, and financial statements from every group each year.

Members of Omaha Reciprocity Group chapters join State President Cindy Biehl in a tribute to our Founders.

Chapter AT hosted Reciprocity Group VIII

Historically, reciprocity groups have promoted and financially aided many projects, including war work, the Victory Fund, hospital and other community endeavors. The main function of reciprocity groups is to act as a clearing house for new members moving into the area, especially in towns with more than one chapter. Representatives of the state board, the Nebraska P.E.O. Home, the philanthropy projects chairmen, and the Cottey Area Chairman attend these meetings to disseminate information to the individual chapter representatives.

Sometimes there are groups within a Group. In Scottsbluff several chapters worked together to sponsor an IPS student. In Omaha all the "F" chapters donated money to sponsor an IPS student. P.E.O.s in Pierce, Antelope, Cedar and Knox Counties within Reciprocity Group IV meet every summer for a very well attended P.A.C.K. Picnic.

Reciprocity groups provide opportunities for Nebraska P.E.O.s to meet new sisters in their areas and to develop new friendships. Chapters who host these annual reciprocity meetings discover that working together builds stronger relationships and stronger chapters. What better way to promote the goals of the P.E.O. Sisterhood?

JOAN FINK, PAST STATE PRESIDENT AND LEAD EDITOR

Joyce Goff entertained Lincoln Reciprocity Roundtable Founders' Day Luncheon guests in 2002 with her usual generosity and witty flare. At right is Judy Duff, EE, who presided at the event

P.E.O. College Contacts

In the 1960's Supreme Chapter authorized the formation of P.E.O. College Groups to meet the needs of P.E.O.s who could not assume full responsibilities of a chapter, and who retained membership in their respective chapters. P.E.O. College Groups were formed in Lincoln, Omaha, Kearney, Hastings, and Wayne. The University of Nebraska College Group was sponsored by Nelsine Scofield, DN and Ann Wherry, DX. The Nebraska Wesleyan Group was sponsored by Phyllis Blanke, GJ, and Lois Weyand, DN. These two groups eventually merged into one group under the sponsorship of the Lincoln Roundtable. This Lincoln College Group held regular meetings, enjoyed meals hosted by Lincoln P.E.O.s and was fairly active for several years. P.E.O. College Groups in other towns struggled to maintain a structure, and between the years 1960-2015 all of the college groups ceased to function. P.E.O. college students faced the demands of maintaining scholastic levels, participating in college activities and holding down part time jobs.

P.E.O.s in college towns across Nebraska remained committed to the philosophy of nurturing these new P.E.O. college students, and a program known as Nebraska P.E.O. College Contacts evolved. The College Contact program is a voluntary effort to assist P.E.O.s attending college in Nebraska communities, and thus facilitate continued membership and interest in P.E.O. Eight Nebraska communities participate in this effort, but are dependent upon local chapters to inform them of chapter members attending college at that location. The College Contact form is available on the Nebraska P.E.O. website, and chapters can complete this form and mail it to the college contact person who is listed in the Nebraska State Chapter Convention Proceedings and on the Nebraska website. When the college contact receives this form, she can reach out and assist the student as the student wishes.

P.E.O. College Contacts are active in the following towns: Chadron, Crete, Hastings, Kearney, Lincoln, Omaha, Peru, and Wayne. The vice president of the Executive Board of Nebraska State Chapter is the liaison for the P.E.O. College Contacts.

Karen Blair, HX, President
Nebraska State Chapter

Joan Fink, AT
Past State President
Nebraska State Chapter

Perhaps Virginia Alice Cottey Stockard presented P.E.O. with its greatest challenge when, in 1927, she placed her college within its keeping. For any woman to establish and develop a college in the late nineteenth century was a tremendous accomplishment. Then to give it, debt free, to a large organization of women was almost too fantastic an idea to be credible.

-Out of the Heart page 235

P.E.O. Trivet

Section Fourteen
"The Home that Love Built"

Nebraska P.E.O. Home

You have to visit to inhale the wonderful smells of freshly baked bread and ladies who wear lavender.

This article was written in large part by Nebraska State Chapter Historian Julia McDougal. Contributions to the history of the past twenty years were gathered from the annual reports lovingly prepared by Home Board presidents, including Sue Fisher, EF, Omaha; Chalice Harvey, CT, Fremont; Debra J. Hanlon, EY, Omaha; Kathryn Olson, EE, Lincoln; Anne Baumhover, HK, Fremont, and Pam Kregg, GM, Omaha.

Nebraska P.E.O.'s devoted historian Julia McDougal describes beautifully the early days when the idea of a P.E.O. Home in Nebraska was little more than a dream. In the paragraphs below, she captures for you the essence of an idea as can only be birthed in the heart of a Sisterhood. Here, in Julia's precise retelling, and with updates from a succession of Home Board presidents, is how it happened.

The Nebraska P.E.O. Home sits quietly on the west side of tree-shaded Fifth Street in Beatrice, its tranquil dignity unchanged since the day in October 1936, when the committee from Nebraska State Chapter first drove to Beatrice to tour this home belonging to the J. Stewart Elliotts. They had come at the invitation of Elizabeth Robertson, member of the committee who belonged to Chapter Z, Beatrice. She had written to them to say "very gently" that the Elliotts were interested in giving their home to the P.E.O. Sisterhood.

Chairman Ada Mead, BN, Omaha, gave the report to the 1937 Convention of Nebraska State Chapter, in part, as follows:

> "So long as I remember anything I shall never forget the joy that filled my heart when I saw that home. Seldom in my life have I seen so beautiful a setting; lovely lawns, beautifully landscaped, a fine brick home with wide verandahs and a tiled roof set on spacious grounds so rarely seen anywhere these days....."

The reality had exceeded their fondest dreams.

The history of how Nebraska P.E.O.s responded from that day in October 1936, through the succeeding three-quarters of a century is a story of extraordinary women responding to an idea—the idea that a gracious and loving home be available to Nebraska members at whatever price a sister can afford to pay. It should be a retirement home for members in need of congenial companionship. The story of how the beautiful house given by the Elliott family in 1937 was transformed so smoothly from a seven-bedroom home with shared bathrooms to its present [1995] capacity of twenty-four residents, each with her private bedroom and bath, is a story of inspired vision followed by unending commitment.

The story features many persons in starring roles. In a sense, all Nebraska P.E.O.s are stars, but most have served in supporting roles. The Home is a success because Nebraska chapters and members have taken the Home and its family to their hearts. Their financial gifts have made the physical plant what it is today, an extremely beautiful building, stately and dignified, making sure that changes made were done without loss of architectural unity and charm. In addition to the dollars given, chapters have poured lavish amounts of concern so that a spirit of love flowed from chapter members to the Home family, bringing reciprocal warmth and appreciation from the residents and the staff. The P.E.O. Home Board of Trustees provided, through its leadership, the opportunity for this chemistry to happen and to develop. Nebraskans have fondly called this project "The Home That Love Built." And so it is.

Chapter communication with the Home has been and continues to be vital to the success of the Home. Newsletters from the Home to Nebraska chapters began after Nettie Brown became superintendent in 1947 and have continued in some format since that time. However, chapter and individual visits have personalized the relationship. Such visits, of course, have been most convenient for those chapters within a distance of about a hundred miles. Occasionally, chapters located in towns much farther away plan for a time when they also may have the privilege of visiting the Home. In addition, delegates to state convention have combined a trip to convention with a Home visit. The Ada Mead Suite on the lower level provides a room in which a chapter may convene for a meeting with some of the Home family as guests. Chapters schedule visits with the Home administrator and enjoy bringing dessert and perhaps a program as special treats for Home residents.

In addition to chapter visits, individual P.E.O.s living nearby often make personal visits to the Home. These visits provide opportunities for Home residents to join them for drives to see the beauty of the flowers and fields, or perhaps to see the magic of the Christmas lights. As a celebration of the Home's 50th anniversary, Nebraska P.E.O.s provided for the restoration of the lovely antique piano and the purchase of a twelve-passenger Chevrolet sports van, lovingly referred to as "Daisy." During her tenure, Administrator Jeanne DeVore served as chauffeur for drives or for transportation to events in southeastern Nebraska. Beatrice community organizations and local pastors also bring programs of inspiration and enjoyment to the Home.

The daily schedule of the Home provides for a variety of activities. Exercise programs are adapted to each resident's need. Bible study, bingo, and bridge are regular activities. Once a month, "theme" parties bring seasonal or "just fun" decorations, followed perhaps by a movie on the big screen TV. Springtime finds the large screened-in porch ready for the relaxed tempo of some outdoor hours when residents gather to visit over a glass of lemonade or iced tea. The local library brings books that may be enjoyed on the porch on pleasant days or in a cozy room inside when the weather turns cooler. Personal visits are encouraged and guest privileges and fees were set up soon after the Home was opened. In 1938, the first trustees of the Home established that a visitor could stay overnight for fifty cents. Meal rates for guests began at twenty cents for breakfast, thirty-five cents for dinner and twenty-five cents for supper.

More than 200 members have called this special place their home since 1938. Residential stays have ranged from a few months to over twenty-five years. Happily, the list of residents includes some who labored long for its success. Two of the best known residents served earlier as administrators of long tenure. Nettie Brown, DX, Lincoln, became a resident in 1960 after thirteen years of dedicated service; and Helen Wallace, also of DX, retired to become a resident in 1980, following sixteen years of energetic activity as superintendent. Two esteemed officers of Supreme Chapter were residents: Rose Owens, BN, Omaha, long time treasurer of Supreme Chapter; and the inimitable Bertha Clark Hughes, M, Omaha, President of Supreme Chapter from 1921 to 1923. Two members of the Home Board have called it home: Ada Mead, BN, Omaha, who had worked for thirty-eight years to benefit the Home and Lucy Livingston, AO, Fairbury, a five-year resident. These four were past presidents of Nebraska State Chapter, as were Mae Bond, AO, Fairbury; Maude Hendy, EB, North Platte; Catherine Andersen, CR, Omaha, and Nelsine Scofield, DN, Lincoln.

By now, the Home had been a much-loved institution among Nebraska P.E.O.s for seven decades, and few recalled its inception. The idea of a retirement home took root in Nebraska in the early thirties. Iowa had opened its Home in 1930 and California was preparing to open its Chapter House. Each of these state chapters had received gifts of large residences that could be transformed into retirement homes with sufficient room for a number of persons to live with privacy and dignity. In Nebraska, Chapter K, Lincoln, had brought to Convention several times the suggestion that the need for a retirement home be studied. At the 44th convention in Lincoln in May 1933, Ada Mead, BN, moved that a committee be appointed to investigate such a need and to report back to the Convention in 1934. The motion carried. State President Dora Wenner, AS, Kearney, named the following to serve as a standing committee: Ada Mead, BN, Omaha, chairman; Floy

Roper, DK, Lincoln; Grace Julian, G, Hastings; Gertrude Dafoe, AT, Tecumseh; and Mary Jane Hughes, DY, Omaha. The committee's task was to enter into discussion with Nebraska chapters to ascertain the amount of interest and support available for this project.

Mrs. Mead reported to the Wayne Convention in 1934 that chapters had indicated interest. Sixty-two chapters were in favor and thirty-six were opposed "at the present time." The opposition undoubtedly was due to the depressed economy in Nebraska. During those years, banks were closing and many families were losing all that they owned. The "thirties" became known as an era of depression, drought, dust storms, grasshoppers, and bread lines, so the caution was understandable. However, Mrs. Mead pointed out that these same economic factors made the need for a Home even more urgent, and State President Josephine Waddell asked the previous committee to serve for the coming year.

P.E.O. Home private room awaits the personal touch of a new resident

The following convention in 1935 found the delegates ready to respond to the committee's request for a transfer of $5,000 from the General Fund to serve as a nucleus in establishing the P.E.O. Home Fund. They voted favorably to this request and also for the setting aside of four percent of the state dues to be added to this fund, beginning March 1, 1936.

The committee personnel changed in 1936, with Elizabeth Robertson, Z, replacing Gertrude Dafoe and Nina King, G, succeeding Grace Julian. Ada Mead reported widespread interest and growing enthusiasm among the chapters and a balance of $5,315.69 in the Fund. The spark of hope in this dream becoming reality burned brighter, but even the redoubtable Ada Mead might have had a pang of misgiving about the long road ahead. Then on a day in late summer, the letter to her from Elizabeth Robertson arrived telling her "very gently" (she said later) that the Elliott home in Beatrice might be available to Nebraska P.E.O.s if they wanted it.

Her hasty reply, assuring Elizabeth of their interest, led to the day in October when the committee members were joined by State President Isabelle Nelson to have lunch with her before meeting Mr. and Mrs. J. Stewart Elliott. The P.E.O.s were delighted with the Elliotts and with their beautiful home, which they were offering debt free, with taxes paid and in good repair, to Nebraska State Chapter for the sum of one dollar.

The committee voted to accept the generous offer and to forward it to the Nebraska State Chapter executive board. That board, after a satisfying tour of the residence in late October, voted to accept the house as the P.E.O. Home, pending approval of the 1937 convention.

When the 1937 convention met in Omaha, Mrs. Mead made the report of the offer of the Elliott family to the delegation and moved its acceptance. Then, Elizabeth Robertson, speaking to Convention, described the city of Beatrice and gave the history of the Elliott home.

In 1873, J.E. Smith, a financier from New York, purchased the lot on Fifth Street between High and Grant from Daniel Freeman, the "No. 1 Homesteader." The original house, built in 1880 for $62,000, had a steeple and was three stories. The property included a barn and the lawn was a block deep. Smith lost the house in the financial crisis of 1893, and it was purchased by R.J. Kilpatrick in 1903. R.J. remodeled it extensively—removing the steeple, increasing the rooms to seventeen, adding electricity with a private generating plant, an elevator, formal gardens and a wrought iron fence surrounding it. Mr. Kilpatrick was a close friend of Stewart Elliott's father, and following the untimely death of the father, young Stewart made his home with the Kilpatricks. R.J. Kilpatrick bequeathed his palatial residence and furnishings to his foster son, J. Stewart Elliot. Elliot and his wife lived there for eight years and then, since their sons were grown, decided to move to smaller quarters and donate their home to a charitable organization. Since Mrs. Elliott was a member of Chapter Z, Beatrice, Elizabeth Robertson presented her with the idea of a gift to P.E.O. Her response was favorable and the rest, as they say, is history. [Reference: *It's in the Blood, The Story of the Kilpatrick Brothers* by Chris Millspaugh and Jean Swartling].

As Mrs. Robertson finished the background material, Mr. Elliott was escorted to the platform of the state convention and was introduced to the delegates. He then graciously presented the Elliott residence to the Nebraska State Chapter of the P.E.O. Sisterhood. The Convention voted its approval and gratitude with a standing ovation.

The executive board recommended that the administration of the Home be delegated to four committees:

BUILDING: Elizabeth Robertson, Z; Carrie Spellman, Z; and Louise Moore, M.
ADMISSION: Anna Loutzenheiser, AW; Gladys Titus, H; Vera Ann Rodman, DT.
RULES AND REGULATIONS: Isabelle Nelson, DA; Margaret Clearman, N; and
    Florence Stewart, CK.
FURNISHINGS: Floy Roper, DK; Amy Grubb, K; and Betty Gass, CC.

The Convention voted that fifty cents of the state dues of each member be added to the P.E.O. Home Fund.

At the 1938 convention, Ada Mead, serving as Nebraska State Chapter president, had the privilege of receiving the report dear to her heart—the successful completion of plans to establish the P.E.O. Home. The committees appointed to convert the Elliott house into an attractive retirement home reported that Nebraska chapters had responded generously to the project. Bedrooms were furnished by K, DW, DA, E, BK, AS, EG, and CS. Gifts of money, furniture, china, silver and linens came in abundance from chapters all over the state.

The dedication of the Home was held on Sunday, May 15, 1938, with 2,500 persons in attendance. The dedication address was given by Rose Owens, BN, treasurer of Supreme Chapter. Elizabeth Robertson, chairman of the Building Committee, presented the Home to Nebraska State Chapter. Mr. and Mrs. J. Stewart Elliott were honored guests and welcomed as the warm friends they had become. They continued to be strong supporters as Nebraska P.E.O.s' dream became reality.

The P.E.O. Home quickly touched the hearts of P.E.O.s who had the opportunity to see it on its dedication day or in the weeks that followed. Certainly, the heart of the attraction was the charm of the lovely brick home. The half-block setting of green lawns, trees, and shrubs complemented the house itself. In summer, the air was filled with the scent of many flowers, especially the beautiful roses. It was a warm and inviting home to those first few who shared in the venture of this special Nebraska P.E.O. project. A visitor entering the house found a spacious hall with a stately stairway leading to the second floor. A large living room lay to the left where the south windows overlooked the lawn, carefully tended through those dry and dusty years to keep it an inviting area. The dining room graced the rear of the house with the kitchen on its right. An elevator in the hallway provided easy access to the second floor of seven large bedrooms, five single rooms plus five bathrooms.

The committee oversaw the work that summer to complete a new heating system, wiring and fixtures plus necessary painting and cleaning to ensure inviting and comfortable surroundings.

Opening day, September 1, 1938, found Superintendent Gertrude Brown, CM, Crete, and three would-be residents ready to move in. Gertrude, a woman of efficiency and culture, had accepted the offer of $35 per month salary to guide the opening of the Home. She worked to establish a warm and caring atmosphere for those first Home family residents. She remained at the Home until December 1941, serving with commitment and dedication.

The 1939 state convention approved a recommendation that a Home Board of Trustees should govern the Home and be made up of five members, each serving five years. No limit was suggested on the number of terms a member could serve. First to serve on the Board of Trustees were: Ada Mead, BN; Isabelle Nelson, DA; Gladys Titus, H; Floy Roper, DK; and Anna Loutzenheiser, AW.

The board realized that overseeing the operation of this retirement home would require broad skills. They needed to keep the interest of Nebraska P.E.O.s at a high level, thus assuring both financial and caring support; they also needed to develop practical skills beyond their personal home-managing experiences: the bedrooms must be kept warm enough for elderly residents on a 24-hour basis; much plumbing must be kept in good repair; and seemingly endless maintenance and renovations must be initiated. Each annual report since 1939 has noted work on the building as these vigilant trustees solved homeowners' problems of maintaining the building, in addition to hiring and evaluating staff, recruiting residents, and serving as public relations personnel in spreading the good news about the Home. The first board set a standard of never-ending commitment and enthusiastic leadership that has characterized succeeding boards.

Only months after the Home began to function as the board had envisioned, the United States entered World War II. The extraordinary problems of the complete wartime mobilization meant that vital items were rationed, including meat and sugar. Other goods were scarce, and one wartime report noted the need to make certain of a farm contact for a source of fresh eggs and chickens. Good help was difficult to keep as many women joined the men in factory work and took other jobs that supported the war effort. Travel during the war was difficult and the number of Home residents increased very gradually. Only when the peace returned in 1945 were the activities of the Home and the number of residents to increase.

Developing a "Home family" relationship among the residents was a priority from the beginning. Nebraska P.E.O.s made certain that the first residents were aware of the chapters' feelings of care and concern, and a tradition of chapters giving gifts developed. Popular gifts are: jams and jellies, hams and turkeys, flowers and personal items, as well as money. When the war ended, the rooms were soon filled and furnished and the board began to think in terms of waiting lists and expansion. In 1949, two large bedrooms were partitioned into four smaller ones and the practice of giving each resident a private room came into being.

In the postwar period came the first superintendent who would remain for more than a decade and become a part of the change and expansion that was to come. Nettie Brown, DX, Lincoln, came in 1947, replacing a number of interim superintendents who had kept the Home open during the war years. She was enthusiastic and hard-working, quickly loved by the residents and chapters alike. After thirteen years, she retired in 1960 to become a resident in this Home where she had served so well in previous years.

P.E.O. Home formal entry area

In 1950, P.E.O. Home Board chairman Gladys Titus, H, Holdrege, presented an amendment to the Convention stating that a Building Fund would be added to the financial structure of the Home. This Building Fund would be used for an infirmary as well as for more adequate housing for Home residents. The amendment was passed and a Building Committee was formed to promote interest and enthusiasm among the chapters statewide, encouraging both individual and chapter gifts to this new fund. The committee represented all sections of the state: Mary Lee Denney, AO, Fairbury, chairman; Florence Knight, AH, Alliance; Dorothy Johnson, E, Omaha; and Norma Carpenter, DN, Lincoln.

Each reciprocity group in the state was represented by one member, called a Home Builder. Her duties were to help acquaint chapters with the expansion needs and to promote enthusiasm for the solicitation of funds. In 1953, board chairman Helen Riddell, A, York, reported that the total cost of the project would be $75,000, including renovation of the kitchen and dining room. A new wing would be built to include seven bedrooms and four baths on the first floor; two bedrooms and a four-bed infirmary on the second floor; plus the nurses' station, baths, utility room and kitchenette.

In the late forties, Amber Hartquest, AC, Aurora, had bequeathed $25,000 to the Home, a sum that was now used as a nest egg for this new fund. The booming economy of the fifties aided the commitment of the committee in achieving the goal set. Other major bequests arrived. Those from Anna Leonard, Chapter K, and Rose Owens, BN, were among the first. Dorothy Mahn, BW, Orleans, never moved to the Home as planned, but in 1952 bequeathed to the Home 160 acres of land in Phillips County, Kansas. This land brought varying amounts of income to the Home for thirty years before it was sold in 1984 for $60,000.

Chairman Helen Riddell noted in 1953 that eighteen applications were on file from P.E.O.s desiring to live at the Home and that over $60,000 had been received for the Building Fund so that plans could proceed for ground-breaking in the coming months. The contract with Beall Construction Company was accepted in February 1954, and on February 27th the Home Board braved inclement weather to witness a brief ceremony and to turn the first spade of dirt.

That spring, Alice Dobson, BY, Lincoln, presented to the state convention a copper box made by Walton Ferris to be placed in the cornerstone; and on June 12th a cornerstone ceremony was held in the First Presbyterian Church in Beatrice. Building Chairman Mary Lee Denney organized the event and Home Chairman Lucy Livingston presided. Participating were Ruth Gellatly, Nebraska State Chapter president; Rose Owens and Nettie Brown, representing Nebraska P.E.O.s; and speakers Ada Mead, Anna Loutzenheiser, and Bertha Clarke Hughes.

Residents of the Home, — and of course the staff — lived with the confusion of a major building project during the following year. The outline of the new structure could be quickly seen so that great excitement overshadowed any inconvenience or interrupted naps due to noisy activity.

The 1955 convention heard retiring board member Anna Loutzenheiser speak of the changes during her seventeen-year tenure. She gave the final figures for the cost of the project, a sum of $94,893.08. This far exceeded the estimate, but the delegates rose in a standing ovation of thanks following Anna's report, knowing that Nebraska chapters would gather the needed funds. (And they were correct.) When convention closed, P.E.O.s joined Supreme Chapter Third Vice President Margaret Emily Stoner in Beatrice for a service of dedication.

Ada Mead spoke at the simple ceremony. Her topic was "Faith Made Perfect."

The keys for the new structure were presented by Martin Aitken, architect, to Nebraska State Chapter President Dorothy Smithberger; P.E.O. Home Board of Trustees Chairman Lucy Livingston; and Home Superintendent Nettie Brown.

The Home family soon increased, filling the extra rooms provided. Beds in the infirmary were utilized for those needing special care. However, the addition of an infirmary did not change the status of the Home to that of a nursing home.

The Home would not become a licensed nursing home until 2013. Up to that time, it was a retirement residence, though it did care for those suffering the frailties of advanced years. The Home is classified as non-profit under the Internal Revenue Service Code 501-C3 and contributions to the Home are tax-deductible. Articles of Incorporation were completed in 1962.

The P.E.O. Home of the mid-1950's reflected change, both because of increased size and because of thoughtful evaluation by the Board of Trustees. A food supervisor began to work full-time, relieving Mrs. Brown of some duties. The Notifier-Alarm system was installed to ensure safety of all residents and staff. The open stairway was closed at the direction of the Fire Marshall. Much repair and many renovations were underway as the Home reached twenty years of age. In addition, appliances—including air conditioners, dehumidifiers, a clothes dryer, a portable TV, and hair dryer with shampoo chair in the beauty shop—were added as funds became available. An alert Home Board oversaw repairs and improvements so that the building was kept in the best possible condition.

Bertha Clark Hughes entered the Home as a resident in 1963 and remained until her death in 1967. In 1968, the board announced plans for a room to be built in memory of Bertha, esteemed member of Chapter M, Omaha, who had worked in Nebraska State Chapter and also in Supreme Chapter for over 60 years. She served as president of both state and Supreme Chapter and also as the Nebraska State Chapter Historian. Nebraska P.E.O.s again responded enthusiastically with gifts for this commemorative family room, built at the front of the house to the left of the living room. Chapter M gave a large framed portrait of Bertha in honor of their distinguished member, and it remains the center of interest in this homey, comfortable room.

The years from 1964 to 1980 are sometimes known as the "Helen Wallace years." Helen came to the job of Home superintendent with good business skills and served the Home efficiently, working always in the most practical and economical way. Her energies were boundless; her day began early and continued late. She was an avid gardener, famous for her work in the rose garden, officially named in her honor. She became most widely known for her ability to gather and use books of trading stamps. It was not unusual for an annual report to show that with 143 books of S&H Green Stamps, she had bought pillows, sheets, pillow cases, nine blankets, a steam iron, a lamp, and a night stand. Often called "the jewel of the Home," Helen was a member of Chapter DX, Lincoln, and a past president of the Lincoln Reciprocity Roundtable. Helen became a resident of the Home in 1980; she died on October 31, 1995.

Communication with the chapters was a priority from the beginning and continued through the years on a regular basis. Nettie Brown began writing letters to chapters, and the board later took up this task, changing first to quarterly newsletters written by one member and then to "Home Happenings," and now to the monthly online posts found on the Nebraska State Chapter website, www.nebraskapeo.org.

P.E.O. Home parlor grand piano

The maintenance of the beautiful decor and appointments in the Home has been possible because of the number of major donors from among the members of Nebraska State Chapter. Jane Robertson Layman's gifts and bequests have amounted to over one million dollars, all given in memory of her mother Elizabeth Robertson, chairman of the first building committee and original contact person with the Elliotts. Both Jane and her mother were members of Chapter Z, Beatrice. Clarice Goodall, CL, Ogallala, provided funds to completely redecorate the foyer, living room, and dining room, including a Strass crystal chandelier. Amber Hartquest's gift, used for the construction of the building addition, has been previously noted. Rose Owens, BN, Lila Leonard, K, and Ivan Fletcher were early donors and many Home residents and their families are among those who have helped the vision become reality.

A substantial addition to the lovely building is the enlarged and stately dining room, added in 1983-1984. The earlier dining room was inadequate since the building addition naturally increased the number of residents. Some funds were available as interest rates on savings and investments had risen in the late 1970's. However, the Home Board of Trustees again turned to the Nebraska State Chapter membership for support. They declared 1984 "The Year of the Home" to serve as a focus on the special project and as a reminder of the need for extra funds. Each chapter was sent a red paper sock and encouraged to fill it with a gift to be used for the new dining room. The economy of the 1980's had brought higher interest rates, but also resulted in inflated prices, so costs were much greater than costs for the earlier projects. The total costs went over $127,000, but this included a completely new kitchen. Chapters HH, York, and CJ, Burwell, were honored for chapter gifts of $1,400 and $1,000 respectively. All who attended the grand opening celebration agreed that the elegant dining room is a fitting addition to the beautiful building.

That project is another indication of the high standard of excellence to which the P.E.O. Home Board of Trustees has adhered since it began work in the 1930's. Members who have agreed to serve have been vigilant and keenly aware of the necessity of maintaining the integrity of the original building and of providing a quality living facility. Nebraska State Chapter has been blessed in the ability and commitment of these women and has benefitted by the length of tenure of many board members.

Heading the list of dedicated leaders is Ada Mead, BN, Omaha, who served from the time of the inception of the idea of a Home in 1933 until 1971, a total of thirty-eight years. Many of those years, Ada served as chairman. The Ada Mead Suite honors her work and provides a pleasant meeting room for the trustees and a place for visiting chapters to hold meetings. Anna Loutzenheiser, AW, Gothenburg, served for seventeen years; and later her daughter, Carolyn Hedstrom, GK, Hastings, served where her mother had worked in earlier years. Carolyn gave fifteen years of leadership, sometimes assisted by her BIL Elton when the "work of the day" involved redecorating. Isabelle Nelson, DA, Hastings, and Gladys Titus, H, Holdrege, were two early members who served over a decade in leadership roles. Other trustees who have served ten years or more are: Dorothy Yeager, E, Omaha; Ethelyn Hermanson, AI, Lincoln; Joan Donley, GP, Grand Island; Bernadine Wherry, AV, Pawnee City; Mary Mice Pumphrey, EP, Wisner; George Ann Ludlum, EE, Lincoln; and Beverley Karrer, FD, Omaha.

There is no way that these women may be adequately thanked for their work; however, each trustee has expressed the sense of fulfillment which has been her reward as she has seen the Home continue to provide a high level of care and concern. The board has done an important part of its work at state convention and area reciprocity meetings when trustees have presented workshops, displays, and talks to Nebraska chapter members to help them to be well-informed and up-to-date on the needs of the Home. Their energies have been put to use many times in both conversation and correspondence to interpret the Home to any member who may be seeking a retirement home that provides a high quality of care and a congenial and homelike atmosphere. Members from other state chapters are accepted when rooms are available.

A 2010 amendment which passed at Convention of Nebraska State Chapter allowed the Home to open its doors not only to P.E.O. sisters, but to the close female relatives of a P.E.O. The bylaws now state that residency is open to "active members of the P.E.O. Sisterhood, and the eligible mother, mother-in-law, aunt, niece, sister, daughter, grandmother or great-grandmother of an active member."

The P.E.O. Record featured a photograph of the P.E.O. Home in Beatrice on its cover in 1940, some months after the opening of the Home. Ada Mead wrote the accompanying article. Fifty years later, The Record again carried a story on the Home, by another Trustee and past state president, Mary Ruth Wilson, AU, Peru. Entitled "Buckeyes for Luck," the story tells of the buckeye tree which stood for many years near the southwest corner of the house and of Administrator Helen Wallace's enjoyment in placing a bowl of buckeyes by the front door. "Take a buckeye with you," she would say to visitors as they were leaving. "It will bring you good luck." Her article also tells of the fiftieth anniversary birthday party given by the Board of Trustees, including the following paragraph:

"September of 1988 marked 50 years of operation of 'The Home that Love Built,' as Nebraskans fondly call their P.E.O. Home. The Board of Trustees, the governing board composed of seven P.E.O.s from all over the state, designated the 1988-89 year, convention to convention, as a 50 Year Jubilee. On September 25, a birthday party was held at the Home to which all chapters in the state were invited. To celebrate the event, the family room was completely redecorated, and gorgeous floral arrangements were placed throughout the Home. Resident-guests gave tours of the Home to callers, and members of the Board of Trustees served as gracious hostesses. Refreshments were served in a beautifully-appointed dining room, with soft lights reflected on the gleaming silver, set on tables covered with apricot satin and lace. Former Trustees presided at the punch bowl and coffee service, while background music came from the newly-renovated concert grand piano left in the Home by the Elliotts...Pianists were past state president Bernice Zajicek, BF, Wilber, and BIL Harold Larmon (husband of past state president Marion Larmon, X, McCook). It was quite a party."

The 1990's found the Home humming along under Administrator Jeanne DeVore, FM, Beatrice. Jeanne, a former Home Board Trustee from CL, Ogallala, served through 2004—nearly nineteen years—as administrator, and the residents enjoyed her creativity and sparkle.

Many Nebraska members and BILs, in addition to the Board of Trustees, are enthusiastic boosters of the Home. Perhaps the need for members to have a "sense of place" is a motivating force, undergirding the strong support Nebraska chapters give to this project. Some might say that the buckeye did indeed bring the needed good luck, and others might credit the charm of the warm and cozy atmosphere of this extraordinary home. Maybe it is simply the Nebraska way of bringing to life the vow to "express a loving concern for each sister" that has given more than 200 members the opportunity to live in this very special place, "The House That Love Built."

A letter from a family member of one of the residents during the 90's gives expression of her personal experience regarding her mother's care:

"I never cease to marvel at your staff and the really warm care they gave her. I think they had more patience with her than I might have been able to maintain. I could tell when I visited that the pleasant interactions she had with the staff were an everyday occurrence; she wasn't in a condition to fake anything."

P.E.O. love is a way of life at the P.E.O. Home.

In 1991, a change in the minimum wage law had a great impact on the Home, and of necessity the per member assessment increased to two dollars.

An endowment opportunity launched in the late 1990's culminated with 124 chapters accomplishing the remarkable commitment of contributing $1,000. Fifty-seven additional chapters nearly accomplished that same goal.

Chalice Harvey, who served on the Home Board for a multitude of years, said in her 2004 final report as board president,:

"I have said this so many times, and am saying it for one last time. 'A picture is worth a thousand words.' You have to visit the Home to

experience the love and care that abounds there. You have to visit to inhale the wonderful smells of freshly baked bread and ladies who wear lavender. You have to visit to hear the stimulating conversations from octogenarians. You have to visit to marvel at the lushness of the grounds and serenity of the sun porch. You have to visit."

In the spring of 2004, the Nebraska P.E.O. Home had the pleasure of being visited by the P.E.O. International Executive Board. Nebraska's own Joyce Goff, HJ, was serving as president of International Chapter. The visiting officers had the privilege of seeing firsthand the beautiful Home supported by the Nebraska State Chapter of the P.E.O. Sisterhood. Director Jeanne DeVore and the residents rolled out the red carpet and welcomed the visitors warmly. The International officers were most impressed with our beautiful Home.

Residents enjoy the lovely P.E.O. Home formal dining room

Later in 2004, the State of Nebraska notified the Board of Directors that the P.E.O. Home would no longer be grandfathered as an assisted living facility and would need to apply for licensure in the state of Nebraska. The Nebraska P.E.O. Home Board of Directors, under the leadership of Debra Hanlon, EY, began the process of applying for licensure. Other members of the board at this time were Kathryn Olson, EE, Judith Workman, EE, Lucille Wolvin, CL, LaVonne Rowe, AT, Sharon Hammar, HB, Robley Carrigan, HL, Nancy Meyer, BE, and Mary Kay Tuma, HJ.

It's true that most P.E.O.s could not resist a smug smile when the State discovered that in nearly every way, the Nebraska P.E.O. Home already exceeded the state's highest standards. Not only that, but it had achieved that condition by the mere diligence and devotion of its superb administrators, the dedicated Home Board, and the Sisterhood's commitment to its senior members who sought residence there.

Still, coming into compliance meant installing an enhanced sprinkler system; a complete overhaul of paperwork for staff, residents and the board; electrical and telephone updates; changes to the kitchen and nursing areas, and more. As the Home began to scale these new hurdles, there was one more major change they had to face. Administrator Jeanne DeVore announced her retirement.

Jeanne resigned as administrator of the P.E.O. Home in the spring of 2005. A reception thanking her for her service to the P.E.O. Home was held at state convention in Grand Island in June of 2005. Tracy Magill, AT, assumed the helm in 2005 and capably assisted the board in completing the necessary requirements for licensure. In October of 2006, the Nebraska P.E.O. Home was granted licensure as a Nebraska assisted living facility. The board and Tracy are to be commended for their hard work and tenacity in completing the lengthy process for licensure.

But it had been no simple feat. To apply for a license to become an assisted living facility, the Home had first to pass Nebraska Fire Code and Food Code requirements. Once that was accomplished, the Home also met assisted-living requirements by Nebraska Health and Human Services. Some requirements meant a different way of doing things, with the Home's historic commitment ever in mind: *Take care of our sisters in a loving, caring environment.*

Amid all the construction and turmoil, that's just what Tracy Magill and her staff did. With their competent and kind care, the residents weathered the changes with dignity and grace intact.

The sprinkler system was the most costly piece of the licensure process, requiring an investment of over $100,000. A less costly alternative was considered, until the board discovered that it meant in an emergency the residents would have to be evacuated without benefit of electricity (in other words, without elevators) in less than thirteen seconds. With the 13R sprinkler system in place, the residents could stay in their rooms. All closets, bathrooms and storage rooms were retrofitted with sprinklers. Getting the water to the Home from several blocks away and with the right size of pipe cost nearly $19,000. Three sets of fire doors costing approximately $6,000 were needed, as well. When at last all was installed, the Home's talented maintenance/gardener/wallpaper and paint person Deloris had to repair the areas torn up during the installation.

Once reconciled to the costs which amounted to more than $150,000, the Home faced yet another rude awakening. The on-going costs of licensure would be higher than they had been led to believe. For example, thermometers were needed for each refrigerator and freezer, and daily charting and recording of the information is mandatory. The kitchen staff can no longer use cloth dish towels and cloth hand towels. Only expensive, disposable paper products can now be utilized.

Undaunted by these and many more unexpected budgetary blips, the fundraising began, and Nebraska P.E.O.s answered the need. Home Board members wore umbrella pins throughout convention that year, to remind delegates of the need to "Sprinkle" the Home with dollars.

In 2006, Board President Debra Hanlon reported that the licensure process was not quite complete. Though much had been accomplished, there remained some paperwork and inspections. But late in the year, the work was at last completed and the inspections made. As board president, Debra Hanlon stated in her 2006 report, Nebraska P.E.O.s did not seek this licensure, which dramatically impacted the finances of the residents. But because by law the Home must be licensed, Home residents who cannot afford the costs for their appropriate level of care now had other state and federal resources available to them to meet the financial need. In addition, some long-term health care policies now covered living at the Nebraska P.E.O. Home.

The formal ambiance of a high ceiling and marbel fireplace and hearth grace the Home's elegant liviing room.

In 2009, Past State President Anne Baumhover became president of the Home Board. At the time, her mother was a resident at the Home. In her 2011 Report to Convention, Anne said:

> "Quoting my mother, who is a resident there, 'This place just takes too good care of me. I should have met my Maker a long time ago.' Mother is 95 and has lived at the Home for five years. When she first came to the Home, we all believed that because of her health, she would be at the Home only a short time. Yes, this is a Home that Love has built."

In 2013, the Nebraska P.E.O. Home celebrated 75 years of providing the kind of retirement life that only a loving sister might envision.

A 2014 report from the Home Board summed it up this way:

> "The Nebraska P.E.O. Home continues to provide quality assisted living in a gracious home atmosphere to our residents. Our ladies enjoy musical presentations from local artists, trips to surrounding shopping venues and area attractions in addition to regular visits from nearby P.E.O. chapters. From homemade bread to the TLC administered by the staff, our Home continues to be "The Home that love built."

What refreshing, recurring themes we hear about our Home—tender care, sisterly love, commitment to providing a gracious home environment, and so much more. Maybe you, too, should visit and "inhale the wonderful smells of freshly baked bread and ladies who wear lavender." Then you, too, will know that it is indeed true. Yes, it cannot be denied. 413 North Fifth Street in Beatrice will forever be "The Home that Love Built."

> Sources used for compiling this report were *The Saga of Nebraska P.E.O.*, 1975, section by Ada Mead; *The History of the P.E.O. Home* by Clarice Hicks, DN, Lincoln; *Spirit of the Prairie* edited by Robley Garrigan; historical articles by Julie McDougal; *It's in the Blood - The Story of the Kilpatrick Brothers* by Millspaugh and Swarthing; and Annual Reports written by recent chairmen of the Nebraska P.E.O. Home Board.

P.E.O. HOME BOARD MEMBER AND PAST STATE PRESIDENT PAM KREGG

Nebraska P.E.O. Home Administrator Tracy Magill, AT, Tecumseh at right with Director of Nursing Barb Freese, FM, Beatrice, at left

P.E.O. Home recreation room

This portrait of Bertha Clark Hughes in her golden years is admired by all who enter the Nebraska P.E.O. Home

Administrators of the P.E.O. Home

Gertrude Brown, CM Crete	1938-1941
Nora Killian, AS, Kearney	1942-1943, interim
Edith Williams, CC, Seward	1943-1944, interim
Beatrice Craig, K, Lincoln	1945-1946
Cordelia Brown, AN, Lexington	1946-1947
Nettie Brown, Z, Beatrice	1947-1960
Alta Stark, AO, Fairbury	1960-1962
Mary Hobbs	1962-1964
Helen Wallace, DX, Lincoln	1964-1980
Katherine Little, AT, Tecumseh	1980-1981
Mavis Booth, T, Clay Center	1982-1984
Jeanne DeVore, CL, Ogallala & FM, Beatrice	1984-2005
Tracy Magill, AT, Tecumseh	2005-present

Members of the P.E.O. Home Board
* indicates President

Corinne Adams, AU, Peru	1988-1993
Anne Baumhover, HK, Fremont *	2006-2015
Carol Bohling, CT, North Bend	2009-present
Patsy Bridge, FO, Hay Springs	1999-2000
June Brunmeier, FB, Lincoln	1993-1997
Barbara Brunzell, EH, Grand Island	2002-2004
Dori Bush, II, Grand Island	1988-1993
Doris Cunningham, CS, Lincoln	1977-1982
Gertrude Dafoe, AT, Tecumseh (Committee)	1933-1937
Josephine Davis, FV, Nebraska City *	1974-1976
Shirley Deyke, CH, Columbus	1988-1994
Alice Dobson, BY, Lincoln	1953-1956
Joan Donley, GP, Grand Island	1970-1980
Jeanne DeVore, CL, Ogallala	1982-1985
Joanie Evans, IH, Elkhorn	2000-2005
Sue Fisher, FI, Omaha *	1987-1999
Delight Fox, GG, Kearney	1981-1987
Robley Garrigan, HL, Blair	1997-2006
Pat Gloor, AG, Fullerton	1993-2004
Georgia Griess, K, Lincoln	1944-1948
Sharon Hammar, HB, Kearney	2005-2014
Debra J. Hanlon, EY, Omaha *	1998-2007
Bonnie Harrington, HI, Ogallala	1999-2003
Chalice Harvey, CT, North Bend *	1994-2004
Carolyn Hedstrom, GK, Hastings *	1973-1988
Ethelyn Hermanson, AI, Lincoln	1958-1967
Chelys Hester, BY, Lincoln	1983-1992
Barbara Hinze, EH, Grand Island	2004-2005
Carol Ann Huckfeldt, EB, North Platte	1996-1999
Grace Julian, G, Hastings (Committee)	1933-1936

Cindy Kadavy, (CR) CR-DZ, Omaha	2007-present
Dorothy Kain, AN, Lexington	1956
Beverley Karrer, FD, Omaha	1975-1986
Katheryn S. Killenger, AE, Hebron *	1960-1967
Nina King, G, Hastings (Committee)	1936-1938
Pam Kregg, GM, Omaha	2009-present
Carolyn Dinsmore Lee, IG, Imperial	1998-2001
Rebecca Lee, AJ, Fremont	1949-1958
Lucy Livingston, AO, Fairbury *	1955-1959
Anna Loutzenheiser, AW, Gothenburg	1938-1955
George Ann Ludlum, EE, Lincoln	1968-1981
Karlyn (Susie) Mann, CI, Chappell	2014-present
Carmen Maurer, EE, Lincoln	1997-2000
Jane Dudgeon McCoy, DL, Lincoln	1974-1979
Catherine Mattoon, BO, Sidney	2011-2014
Ada Mead, BN, Omaha * (Committee)	1933-1976
Nancy Meyer, BE, Pierce	2004-2007
Thelma Millen, DJ, Albion	1966-1970
Isabelle Nelson, DA, Hastings	1938-1950
Kay Norden, S, Broken Bow	2007-2012
Marylin Nunn, GW, Lincoln	2012-present
Kathryn Olson, EE, Lincoln	2000-2009
Wyladee (Billy) Pecka, CM, Crete	2007-present
Mary Alice Pumphrey, EP, Wisner	1959-1972
Helen Riddell, A, York *	1949-1954
Patricia Robertson, BX, Omaha	2001-2002
Floy Roper, DK, Lincoln (Committee)	1933-1943
Lavonne Rowe, AT, Tecumseh	2004-2013
Marcia Schlegelmilch, A, York	2014-present
Lenore Schwentker, CL, Ogallala,	1962-1965
Dorothy Simmons, ET, Scottsbluff	1996-1998
Jane Smith, HB, Kearney	1993-2000
Dorothy Smithberger, DF, Stanton	1978-1982
Marie Sorum, GC, Alliance	1992-1996
Barbara Spencer, CL, Ogallala	1985-1992
June Steggs, S, Broken Bow *	1988-1993
Eunice Stuart, IP, Fairbury	2013-present
Gladys Titus, H, Holdrege *	1938-1952
Mary Kay Tuma, HJ, Grand Island	2005-2006
Barbara Vondras, AN, Lexington	1995-1996
Bernadine Wherry, AV, Pawnee City	1978-1988
Mary Ruth Wilson, AU, Peru	1982-1988
Lucille Wolvin, CL, Ogallala	2003-2011
Judith Workman, EE, Lincoln	2000-2009
Dorothy Yeager, E, Omaha *	1965-1974

P.E.O. Home Burials In P.E.O. Plots
At Evergreen Cemetery, Beatrice, Nebraska

The following information was found in *The History of the Nebraska P.E.O. Home–1933-1970* by Clarice G. Hicks, Chapter N, and *The Spirit of the Prairie*. *The Spirit of the Prairie* lists the date of death of P.E.O. Home residents, but makes no mention of burial location. The pages referenced are from *The History of the Nebraska P.E.O. Home–1933-1970*.

Page 11—She (Carolyn Miller of Chapter H, Holdrege) passed away January 27, 1944, and was buried in Lot 43 of the recently purchased P.E.O. plot in the Beatrice cemetery—the first one to be interred there.

Page 12—The Board, too, took note that a number of the original cemetery lots had been used and voted to purchase the next plot of eight lots for $200. (January 5, 1943)

Page 34—The Home owns three plots of eight graves each. To date there are seven sisters buried there. (The context appears to be November 1963-April 1964)

The following are interred in the P.E.O. plots at the Beatrice Cemetery.
Noted are date of death, name with chapter and city from *The Spirit of the Prairie*, and discrepancies found.

1-27-1944	Carolyn Miller (Stone states Carrie E. Miller), Chapter H, Holdrege
3-18-1946	Jesse Zachary (Stone states Jessie A. Zachary), Chapter E, Omaha. *Spirit of the Prairie* states date of death 3-19-1946
6-20-1946	Nellie N. McKay (Stone states Nellie A. McKay), Chapter AG, Fullerton
2-19-1949	Grace E. Clark, Chapter U, Rogers, Arkansas. *Spirit of the Prairie* states date of death 2-18-1949.
9-5-1955	Blanche Deary (Stone states Blanche Waldo Deary), Chapter P, Bloomington. *Spirit of the Prairie* states name as Blanch.
7-5-1958	Grace E. Oldham, Chapter I, Wahoo. *Spirit of the Prairie* states year of death 1955.
11-19-1963	Mae Street Morgan, Chapter F, Plattsmouth. *Spirit of the Prairie* states name Clara Mae Morgan.
10-28-1970	Helena W. Render, Chapter CU, Norfolk
9-8-1971	Nellie Baker Scott, Chapter CR, Omaha
9-27-1971	Edna Fulton Kissell, Chapter AC, Minnesota and Chapter K, Lincoln
1-26-1975	Fay W. Towl, Chapter CR, Omaha
8-14-1976	Mary E. Ogg Delzell, Chapter DA, Hastings
2-20-1994	Edith C. Giesler, Chapter FM, Beatrice
10-31-1995	Helen D. Wallace, Chapter FM, Beatrice. Helen served as superintendent of the P.E.O. Home from August 1,1964-1980, Chapter DX, Lincoln. She became a resident of the Home 9-1-1981.

It is noted that Helen N. Birch, Chapter Y, Red Cloud, date of death 3-3-1967, is interred in the Evergreen Cemetery. There is no grave marker on the P.E.O. plots.

5/30/2012

Alphabetical Listing of Chapters

Code	Chapter	Code	Chapter	Code	Chapter	Code	Chapter
A	York	BO	Sidney	EB	North Platte	GN	Kimball
B*	Fairfield	BP	Omaha	EC	Omaha	GO	North Platte
C*	Norfolk	BQ	David City	ED	Omaha	GP	Grand Island
D*	Superior	BR	Lincoln	EE	Lincoln	GQ	Lincoln
E	Omaha	BS	Omaha	EF	Omaha	GR	Lexington
F	Plattsmouth	BT	Weeping Water	EG	Kearney	GS	Norfolk
G	Hastings	BU	Atkinson	EH	Grand Island	GT	O'Neill
H	Holdrege	BV	Beaver City	EI	Bayard	GU	Omaha
I	Wahoo	BW	Orleans	EJ	Creighton	GV	Lincoln
J	Nelson	BX	Omaha	EK	Omaha	GW	Lincoln
K	Lincoln	BY	Lincoln	EL	Oakland	GX	So. Sioux City
L*	Harvard	BZ	Gordon	EM	Bloomfield	GY*	McCook
M*	Omaha	CA	Valentine	EN	Pender	GZ	Hastings
N	Minden	CB	Ravenna	EO	West Point	HA	Columbus
O	Geneva	CC	Seward	EP	Wisner	HB	Kearney
P	Bloomington	CD	Scottsbluff	EQ	Blair	HC	Bellevue
Q	Wymore	CE	Arapahoe	ER*	Benkelman	HD	Lincoln
R*	Crete	CF	Nebraska City	ES	Lincoln	HE	Lincoln
S	Broken Bow	CG	Curtis	ET	Scottsbluff	HF	Omaha
T	Clay Center	CH	Columbus	EU	Mitchell	HG	Schuyler
U*	Butte	CI	Chappell	EV	Gering	HH	York
V	Lincoln	CJ	Burwell	EW	Genoa	HI	Ogallala
W	Blue Hill	CK	Grand Island	EX	Fremont	HJ	Grand Island
X	McCook	CL	Ogallala	EY	Omaha	HK	Fremont
Y	Red Cloud	CM	Crete	EZ	Grand Island	HL	Blair
Z	Beatrice	CN	Osceola	FA	McCook	HM	Holdrege
AA	Edgar	CO	Cozad	FB	Lincoln	HN	Scottsbluff
AB	Central City	CP	Omaha	FC	Scottsbluff	HO	North Platte
AC	Aurora	CQ	Neligh	FD	Omaha	HP	Omaha
AD*	Seward	CR	(CR-DZ)*	FE	Plainview	HQ	North Platte
AE	Hebron	CR-DZ*	Omaha	FF	(FF-IA)	HR	Gibbon
AF*	Oxford	CS	Lincoln	FF-IA	Lincoln	HS	Alliance
AG	Fullerton	CT	North Bend	FG	Lincoln	HT	Hastings
AH	Alliance	CU	Norfolk	FH	Hastings	HU	Norfolk
AI	Lincoln	CV	Omaha	FI	(FI-IK)	HV	Lexington
AJ	Fremont	CW	Sargent	FI-IK	Omaha	HW	Lincoln
AK	North Platte	CX	Lyons	FJ	Columbus	HX	Omaha
AL	Madison	CY	Falls City	FK	Omaha	HY	Omaha
AM	Fairmont	CZ	Wakefield	FL	Omaha	HZ	Hartington
AN	Lexington	DA	Hastings	FM	Beatrice	IA	(FF-IA)
AO	Fairbury	DB*	Auburn	FN	Kearney	IB	Cozad
AP	Saint Paul	DC	Tekamah	FO	Hays Springs	IC	So. Sioux City
AQ	Loup City	DD*	Omaha	FP	Chadron	ID	Wayne
AR	Stromsburg	DE	So. Sioux City	FQ	Lincoln	IE	Omaha
AS	Kearney	DF	Stanton	FR	Sidney	IF*	Blair
AT	Tecumseh	DG	Ponca	FS	Lexington	IG	Imperial
AU	Peru	DH*	Omaha	FT	Omaha	IH	Elkhorn
AV	Pawnee City	DI	Humboldt	FU	Grant	II	Grand Island
AW	Gothenburg	DJ	Albion	FV	Nebraska City	IJ	Papillon
AX	Crawford	DK	Lincoln	FW	Lincoln	IK	(FI-IK)
AY*	Auburn	DL	Lincoln	FX	Lincoln	IL	Lincoln
AZ	Wayne	DM	Lincoln	FY	Omaha	IM	Omaha
BA*	Sidney	DN	Lincoln	FZ	Omaha	IN	Plattsmouth
BB	Ord	DO*	Newman Grove	GA	Scottsbluff	IO	York
BC	Cambridge	DP	Bridgeport	GB	Omaha	IP	Fairbury
BD	Ashland	DQ	Friend	GC	Alliance	IQ	Hebron
BE	Pierce	DR*	Omaha	GD*	Lincoln	IR	Bellevue
BF	Wilber	DS	Superior	GE	Omaha	IS	Hemingford
BG	Franklin	DT	Kimball	GF	Omaha	IT	Bellevue
BH	Sutton	DU	Omaha	GG	Kearney	IU	Waverly
BI	Shelton	DV	Saint Edward	GH	Fremont	IV	Hickman
BJ	Alma	DW	Rushville	GI	Gering	IW	Lincoln
BK	Omaha	DX	Lincoln	GJ	Lincoln	IX	Kearney
BL	Chadron	DY	Omaha	GK	Hastings	IY	Lincoln
BM	Ainsworth	DZ	(CR-DZ)*	GL	Omaha		
BN	Omaha	EA	Randolph	GM	Omaha		* disbanded

ALPHABETICAL LISTING OF TOWNS WITH CHAPTERS

Town	Chapters	Town	Chapters	Town	Chapters
AINSWORTH	BM	GORDON	BZ	ORLEANS	BW
ALBION	DJ	GOTHENBURG	AW	OSCEOLA	CN
ALLIANCE	AH, GC, HS	GRAND ISLAND	CK, EH, EZ, GP, HJ, II	PAPILLION	IJ
ALMA	BJ			PAWNEE CITY	AV
ARAPAHOE	CE	GRANT	FU	PENDER	EN
ASHLAND	BD	HARTINGTON	HZ	PERU	AU
ATKINSON	BU	HASTINGS	G, DA, FH, GK, GZ, HT	PIERCE	BE
AURORA	AC	HAY SPRINGS	FO	PLAINVIEW	FE
BAYARD	EI	HEBRON	AE, IQ	PLATTSMOUTH	F, IN
BEATRICE	Z, FM	HEMINGFORD	IS	PONCA	DG
BEAVER CITY	BV	HICKMAN	IV	RANDOLPH	EA
BELLEVUE	HC, IR, IT	HOLDREGE	H, HM	RAVENNA	CB
BLAIR	EQ, HL	HUMBOLDT	DI	RED CLOUD	Y
BLOOMFIELD	EM	IMPERIAL	IG	RUSHVILLE	DW
BLOOMINGTON	P	KEARNEY	AS, EG, FN, GG, HB, IX	SARGENT	CW
BLUE HILL	W	KIMBALL	DT, GN	SCHUYLER	HG
BRIDGEPORT	DP	LEXINGTON	AN, FS, GR, HV	SCOTTSBLUFF	CD, ET, FC, GA, HN
BROKEN BOW	S	LINCOLN	K, V, AI, BR, BY, CS, DK, DL, DM, DN, DX, EE, ES, FB, FF-IA, FG, FQ, FW, FX, GJ, GQ, GV, GW, HD, HE, HW, IL, IW, IY	SEWARD	CC
BURWELL	CJ			SHELTON	BI
CAMBRIDGE	BC			SIDNEY	BO, FR
CENTRAL CITY	AB			SOUTH SIOUX CITY	DE, GX, IC
CHADRON	BL, FP			SAINT EDWARD	DV
CHAPPELL	CI	LOUP CITY	AQ	SAINT PAUL	AP
CLAY CENTER	T	LYONS	CX	STANTON	DF
COLUMBUS	CH, FJ, HA	MADISON	AL	STROMSBURG	AR
COZAD	CO, IB	McCOOK	X, FA	SUPERIOR	DS
CRAWFORD	AX	MINDEN	N	SUTTON	BH
CREIGHTON	EJ	MITCHELL	EU	TECUMSEH	AT
CRETE	CM	NEBRASKA CITY	CF, FV	TEKAMAH	DC
CURTIS	CG	NELIGH	CQ	VALENTINE	CA
DAVID CITY	BQ	NELSON	J	WAHOO	I
EDGAR	AA	NORFOLK	CU, GS, HU	WAKEFIELD	CZ
ELKHORN	IH	NORTH BEND	CT	WAVERLY	IU
FAIRBURY	AO, IP	NORTH PLATTE	AK, EB, GO, HO, HQ	WAYNE	AZ, ID
FAIRMONT	AM			WEEPING WATER	BT
FALLS CITY	CY	O'NEILL	GT	WEST POINT	EO
FRANKLIN	BG	OAKLAND	EL	WILBER	BF
FREMONT	AJ, EX, GH, HK	OGALLALA	CL, HI	WISNER	EP
FRIEND	DQ	OMAHA	E, BK, BN, BP, BS, BX, CP, CV, DU, DY, EC, ED, EF, EK, EY, FD, FI-IK, FK, FL, FT, FY, FZ, GB, GE, GF, GL, GM, GU, HF, HP, HX, HY, IE, IM	WYMORE	Q
FULLERTON	AG			YORK	A, HH, IO
GENEVA	O				
GENOA	EW				
GERING	EV, GI				
GIBBON	HR	ORD	BB		

For all that has been
...*thanks*

For all that will be
...*yes!*

~Dag Hammarskjold

Afterword
"It's okay to talk about P.E.O."

BY JOAN FINK, AT, PAST STATE PRESIDENT
AND LEAD EDITOR, LEGACY OF NEBRASKA P.E.O.

    P.E.O. women in Nebraska have carried the banner for the P.E.O. Sisterhood since that first secret chapter was organized in 1874, just seven years after Nebraska achieved statehood. Past President of Supreme Chapter Bertha Clark Hughes, Chapter M, Omaha; Past State President Bernice Tillett, Chapter AH, Alliance; Past President of Supreme Chapter Irene S. Van Brunt, Chapter DD, Omaha, and Past State President Dorothy Smithberger, Chapter DF, Stanton, were pioneers in collecting early history. They were instrumental in preserving the early history of Nebraska P.E.O. We honor these women with our deep gratitude.

    Legacy of Nebraska P.E.O. is the third history published by Nebraska State Chapter. The first history, *Saga of Nebraska P.E.O.,* was published in 1975 and Past State President Dorothy Smithberger was the historian; the second history, *Spirit of the Prairie,* was published in 1995 and Past State President Robley Garrigan was the editor. These books contain fascinating stories of a group of women who wanted to make the world a better place for other women. In Nebraska we have proudly told these stories to each generation for the past forty years, so that each generation will not forget the incredible impact P.E.O. has had on the lives of women in our state. It is our hope that these stories will inspire the women who read them, not only in this generation, but in future generations. Our history offers insights into the things that have shaped our society. When reading *Legacy,* we hope Nebraska P.E.O.s will appreciate how we still uphold the reasons why we were founded.

    Friendship and loving concern for each other are still guideposts for P.E.O., and we continue to share these virtues with other women. Our goals encourage a strong Sisterhood that continues to grow.

    P.E.O. is built upon strong women—women who value education and build friendships and character. Friendship and a loving concern are the glue which has held Nebraska P.E.O. together for one hundred forty-one years. These attributes never change. Our lives may change with the social and economic factors that influence them, but our core values remain the same. P.E.O. builds leaders, shapes lives, and makes history. Our P.E.O. philanthropies leave a pattern of helping women to achieve their potential through education. There is no other organization for women that meets the standards defined by our Star.

We are going to depend on the young women in our Sisterhood to lead us into a new generation of P.E.O. We encourage these wonderful women to read our histories. Go ahead and chuckle at how outdated some of the language and customs seem in the early history. Laugh at some of the funny things that happened as these pioneers worked to make P.E.O. grow and make an impact on the lives of women. Read between the lines. One constant throughout the years is the loving concern for each other. It is still the core value of P.E.O.

Pass it on.

JOAN FINK, PAST STATE PRESIDENT
LEAD EDITOR *Legacy of Nebraska P.E.O.*

"...Let it (the star) shed over our hearts and lives a golden splendor and point us ever to God who guides us with his love. Our lives should be affected by our emblem in that we are pure minded, truthful, faithful and loving in character, wearing upon our hearts the zeal of our Master's love."

-FOUNDER ELLA STEWART

www.ingramcontent.com/pod-product-compliance
Lightning Source LLC
Chambersburg PA
CBHW070721240426
43673CB00003B/96